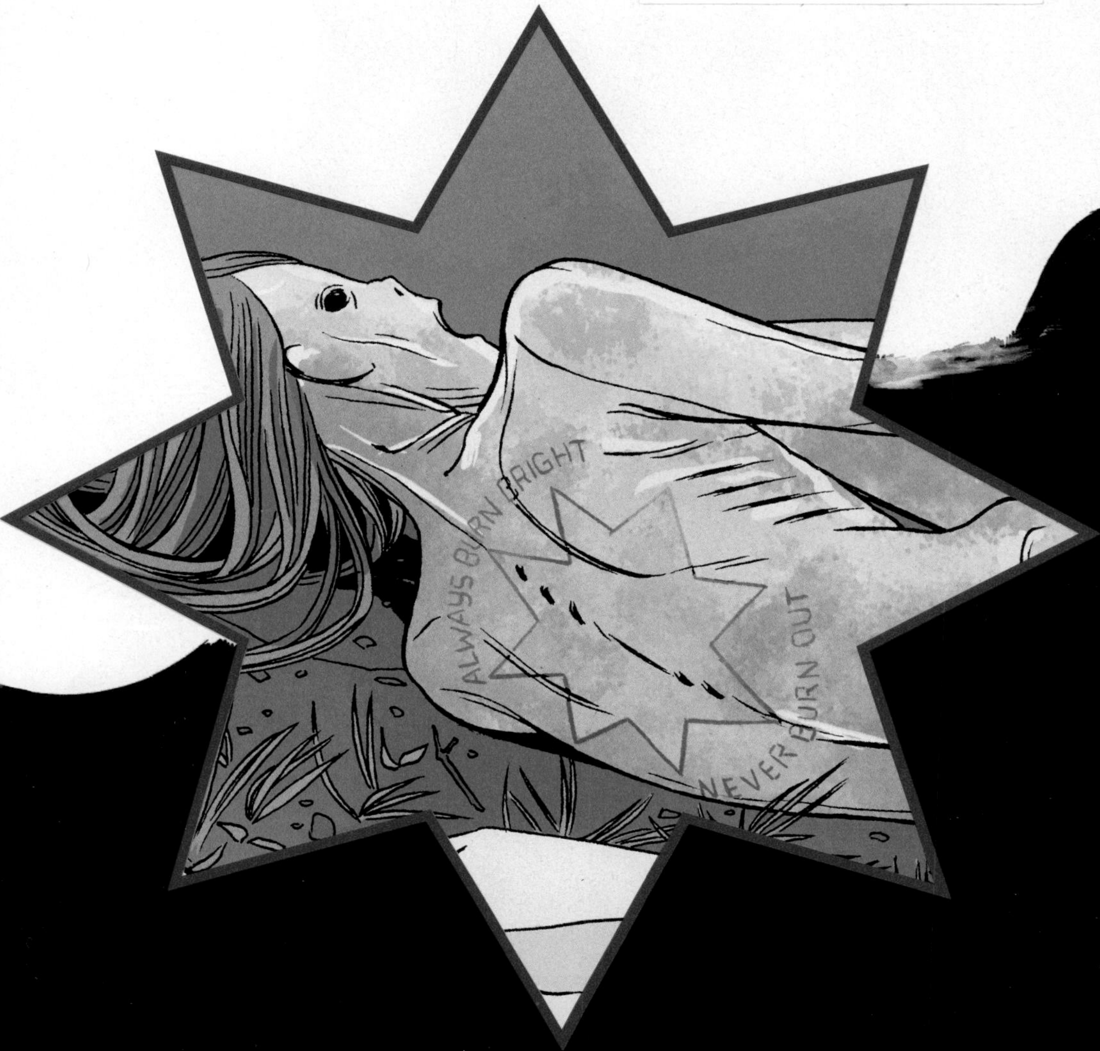
ALWAYS BURN BRIGHT
NEVER BURN OUT

EFFIGY

IDLE WORSHIP

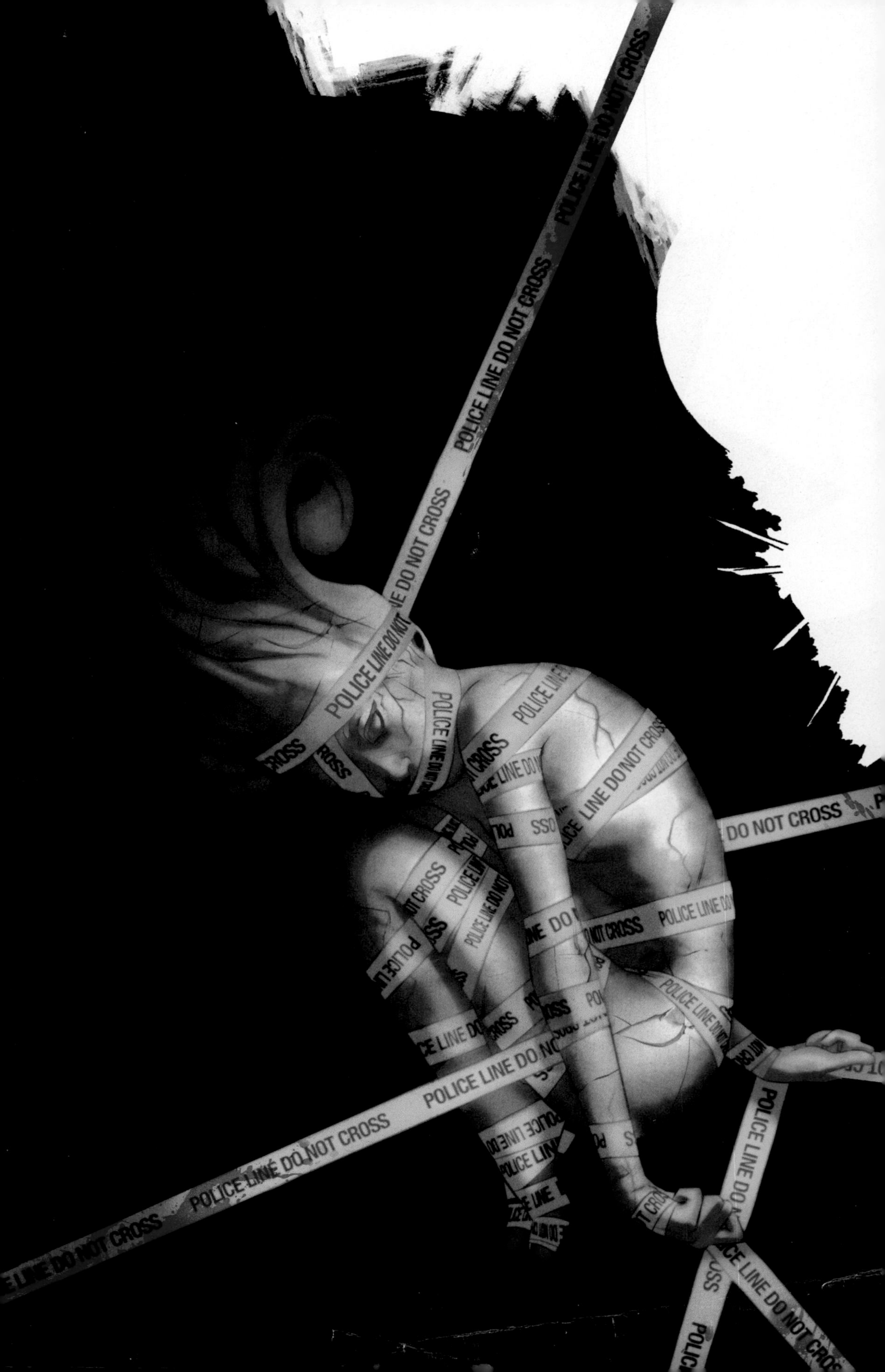
POLICE LINE DO NOT CROSS
POLICE LINE DO NOT CROSS
POLICE LINE DO NOT CROSS
DO NOT CROSS
POLICE LINE DO NOT CROSS
POLICE LINE DO NOT CROSS
POLICE LINE DO NOT CROSS

EFFIGY

IDLE WORSHIP

POLICE LINE DO NOT CROSS

written by
TIM SEELEY

art by
MARLEY ZARCONE
JESSE HAMM **JEN VAUGHAN** **MIKE NORTON**

color by
RYAN HILL

letters by
JARED K. FLETCHER

cover art and
original series covers by
W. SCOTT FORBES

EFFIGY created by
TIM SEELEY and **MARLEY ZARCONE**

SHELLY BOND JAMIE S. RICH Editors – Original Series
ROWENA YOW Associate Editor – Original Series
MOLLY MAHAN Assistant Editor – Original Series
JEB WOODARD Group Editor – Collected Editions
SCOTT NYBAKKEN Editor – Collected Edition
SARABETH KETT Publication Design

SHELLY BOND VP & Executive Editor – Vertigo

DIANE NELSON President
DAN DIDIO and JIM LEE Co-Publishers
GEOFF JOHNS Chief Creative Officer
AMIT DESAI Senior VP – Marketing & Global Franchise Management
NAIRI GARDINER Senior VP – Finance
SAM ADES VP – Digital Marketing
BOBBIE CHASE VP – Talent Development
MARK CHIARELLO Senior VP – Art, Design & Collected Editions
JOHN CUNNINGHAM VP – Content Strategy
ANNE DEPIES VP – Strategy Planning & Reporting
DON FALLETTI VP – Manufacturing Operations
LAWRENCE GANEM VP – Editorial Administration & Talent Relations
ALISON GILL Senior VP – Manufacturing & Operations
HANK KANALZ Senior VP – Editorial Strategy & Administration
JAY KOGAN VP – Legal Affairs
DEREK MADDALENA Senior VP – Sales & Business Development
DAN MIRON VP – Sales Planning & Trade Development
NICK NAPOLITANO VP – Manufacturing Administration
CAROL ROEDER VP – Marketing
EDDIE SCANNELL VP – Mass Account & Digital Sales
SUSAN SHEPPARD VP – Business Affairs
COURTNEY SIMMONS Senior VP – Publicity & Communications
JIM (SKI) SOKOLOWSKI VP – Comic Book Specialty & Newsstand Sales

Logo design by STEVE COOK.

EFFIGY: IDLE WORSHIP

DC Comics, 4000 Warner Blvd., Burbank, CA 91522
A Warner Bros. Entertainment Company.
Printed in the USA. First Printing.
ISBN: 978-1-4012-5685-2.

Library of Congress Cataloging-in-Publication Data

Seeley, Tim, author.
Effigy. Volume 1, Idle Worship / Tim Seeley, writer ; Marley Zarcone, artist.
pages cm
ISBN 978-1-4012-5685-2 (paperback)
1. Graphic novels. I. Zarcone, Marley, illustrator. II. Title. III. Title: Idle Worship
PN6727.S438E37 2015
741.5'973—dc23
2015011781

SUSTAINABLE FORESTRY INITIATIVE
Certified Chain of Custody
20% Certified Forest Content,
80% Certified Sourcing
www.sfiprogram.org
SFI-01042
APPLIES TO TEXT STOCK ONLY

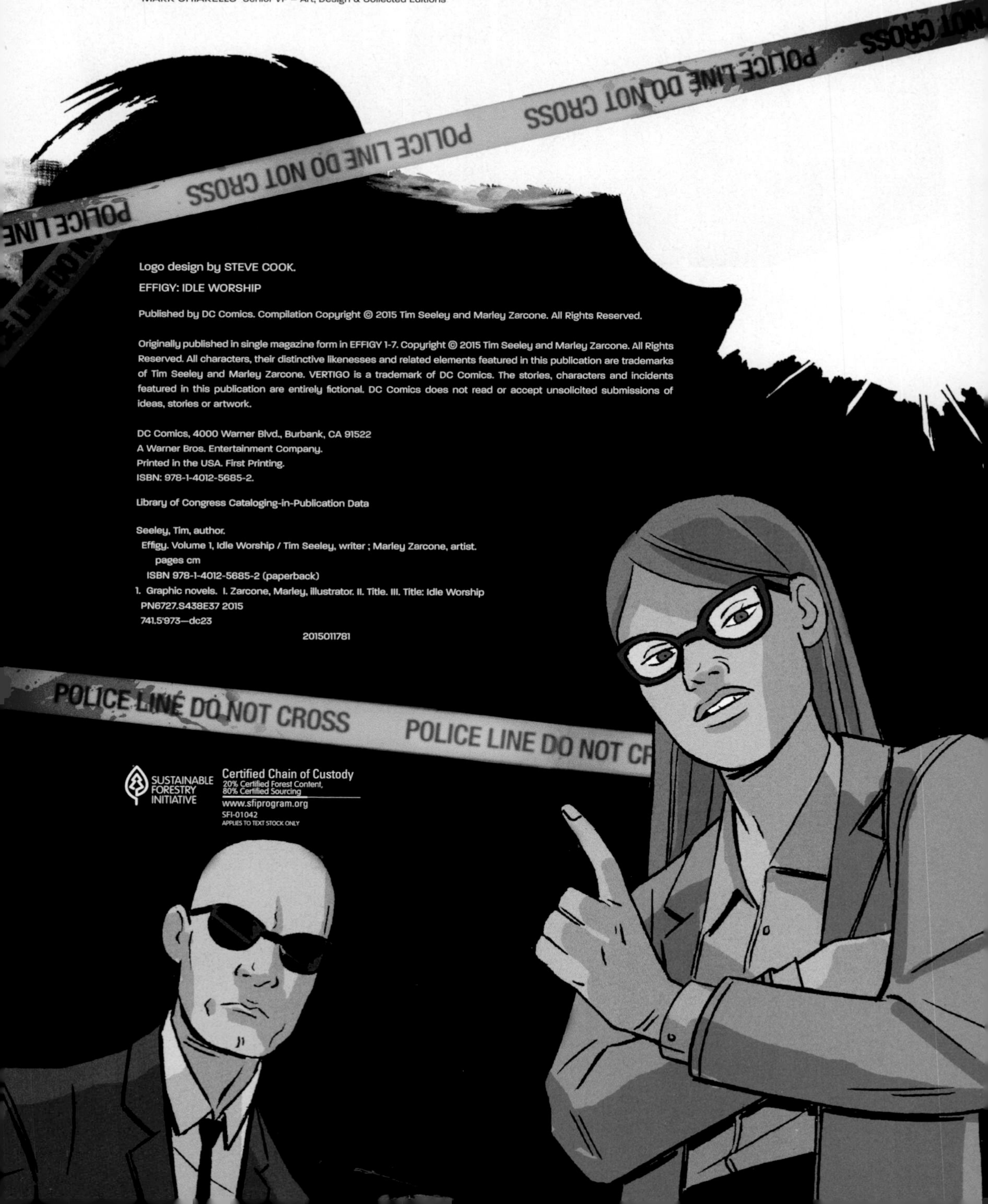

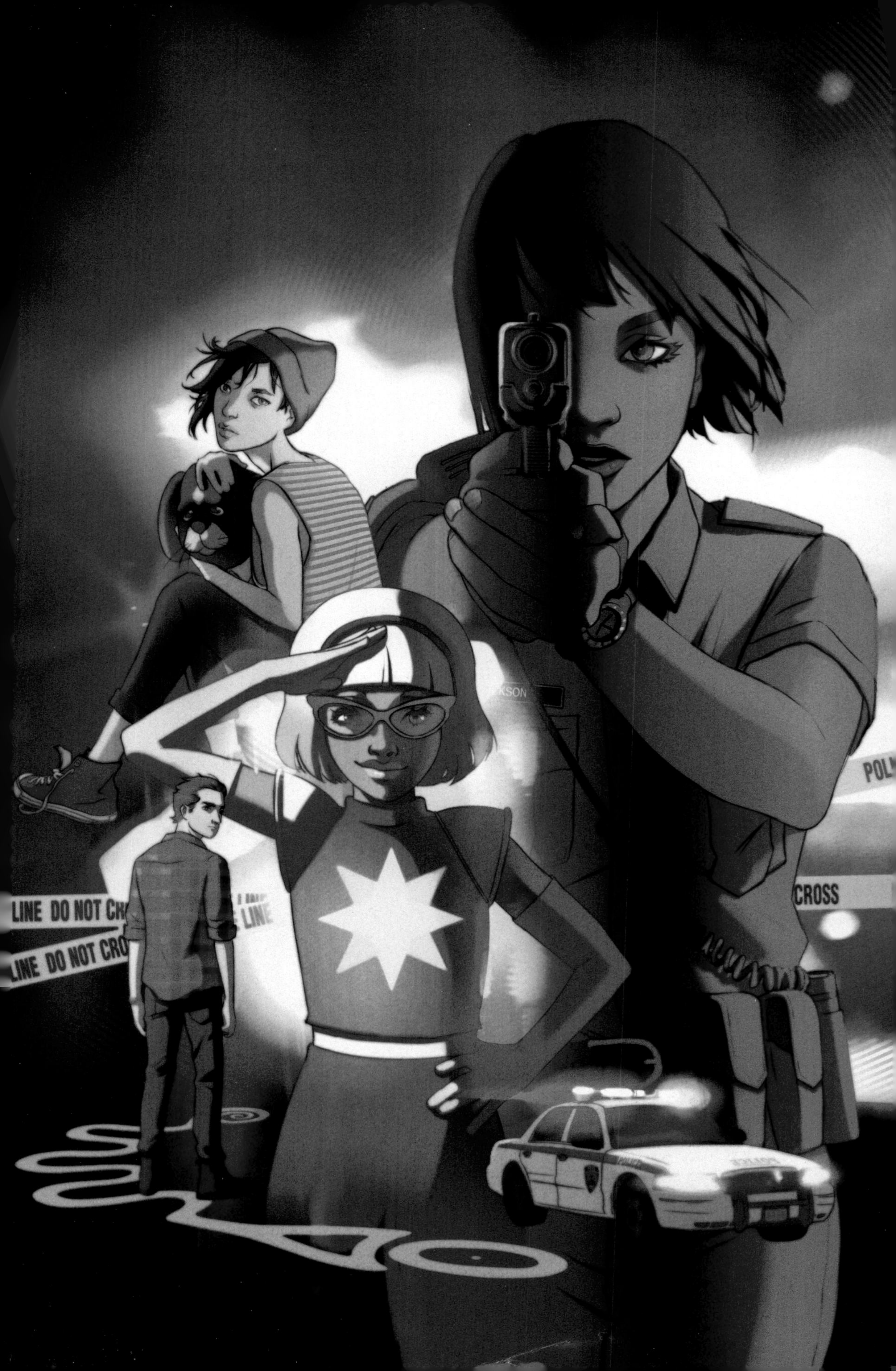
KSON
POL
LINE DO NOT CR
LINE DO NOT CRO
LINE
CROSS

variant cover art for issue #1 by
ANDREW ROBINSON

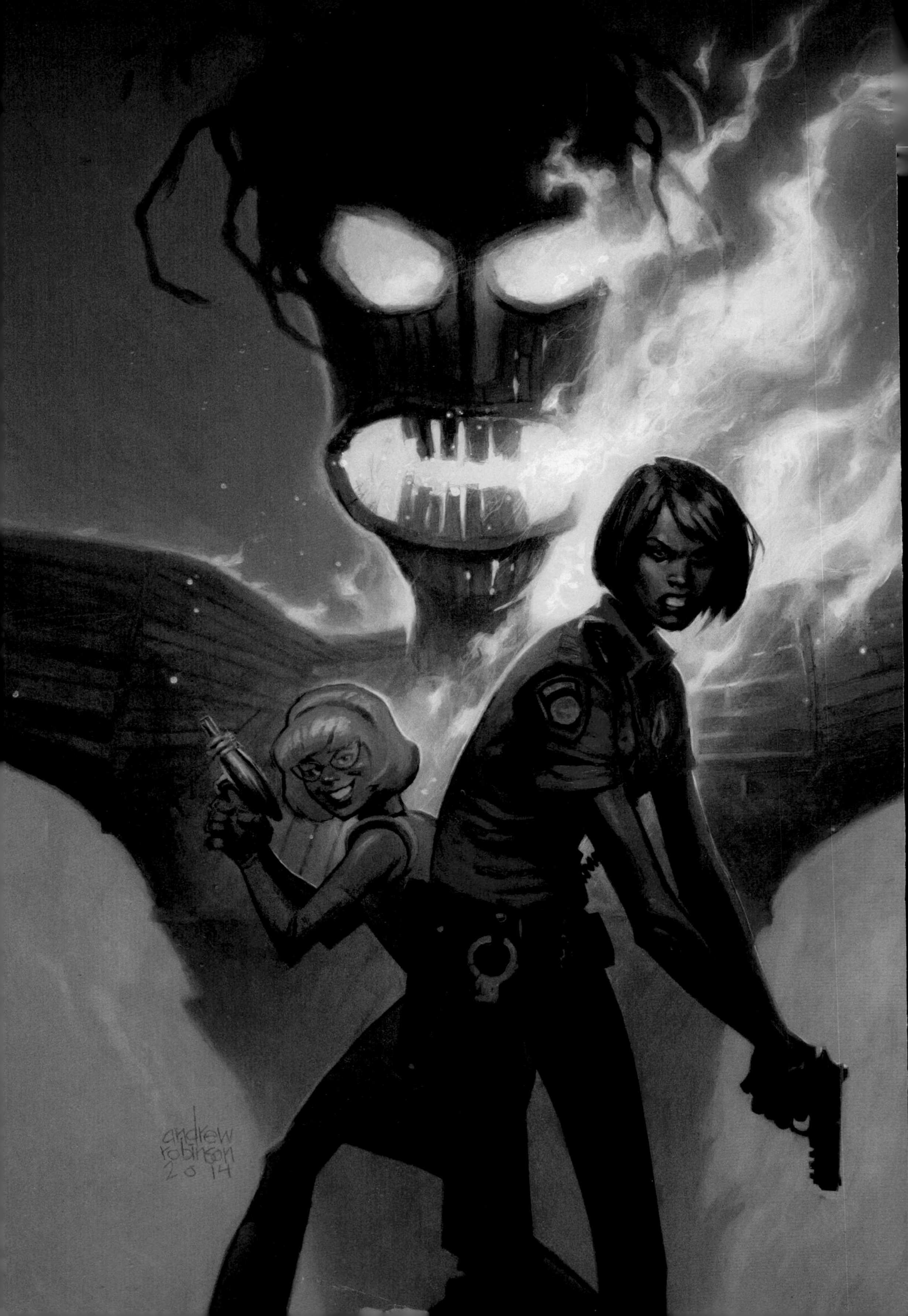
andrew
robinson
2014

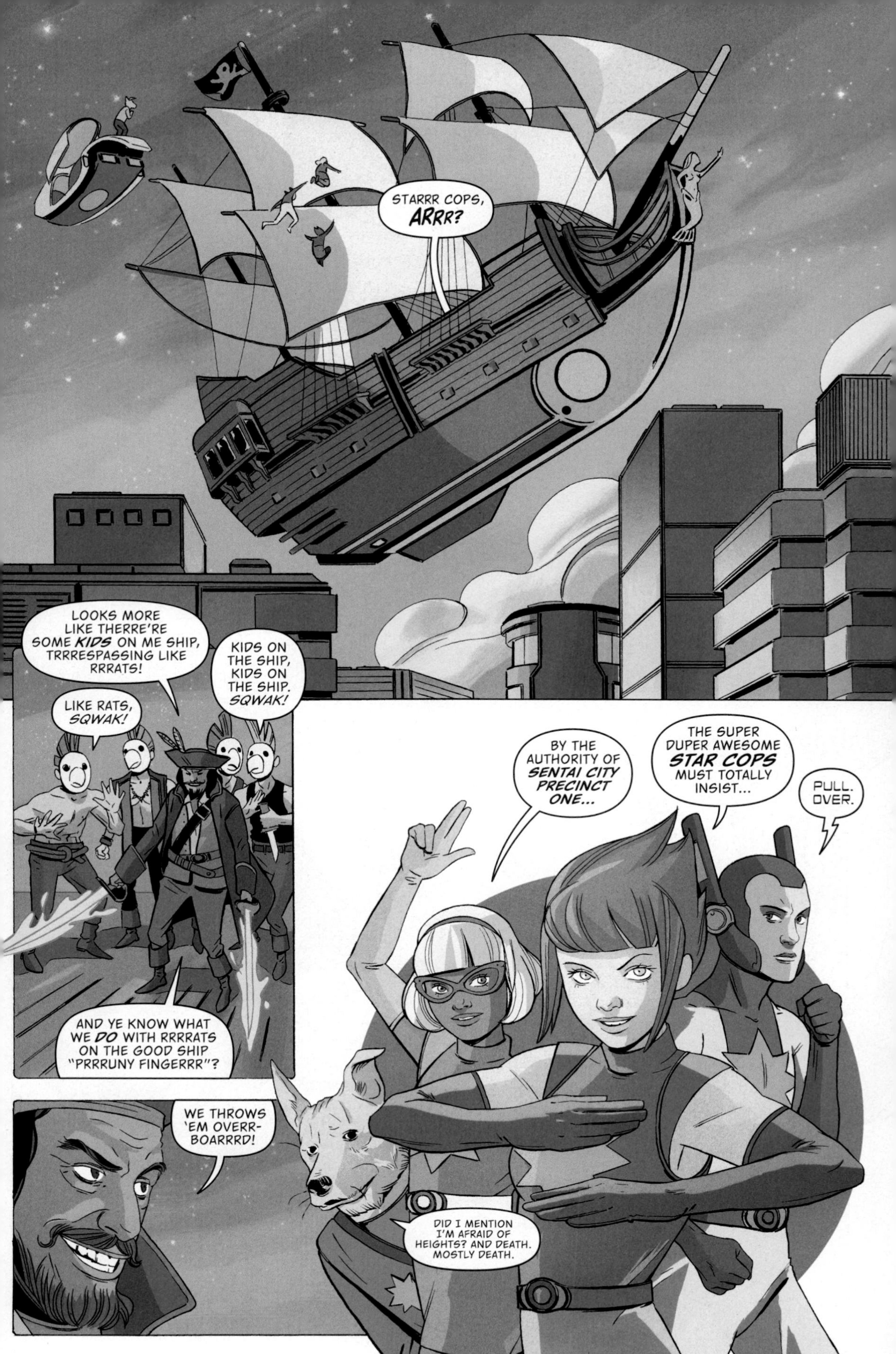
STARRR COPS, ARRR?
LOOKS MORE LIKE THERRE'RE SOME KIDS ON ME SHIP, TRRRESPASSING LIKE RRRATS!
KIDS ON THE SHIP, KIDS ON THE SHIP. SQWAK!
LIKE RATS, SQWAK!
AND YE KNOW WHAT WE DO WITH RRRRATS ON THE GOOD SHIP "PRRRUNY FINGERRR"?
WE THROWS 'EM OVERR-BOARRRD!
BY THE AUTHORITY OF SENTAI CITY PRECINCT ONE...
THE SUPER DUPER AWESOME STAR COPS MUST TOTALLY INSIST...
PULL. OVER.
DID I MENTION I'M AFRAID OF HEIGHTS? AND DEATH. MOSTLY DEATH.

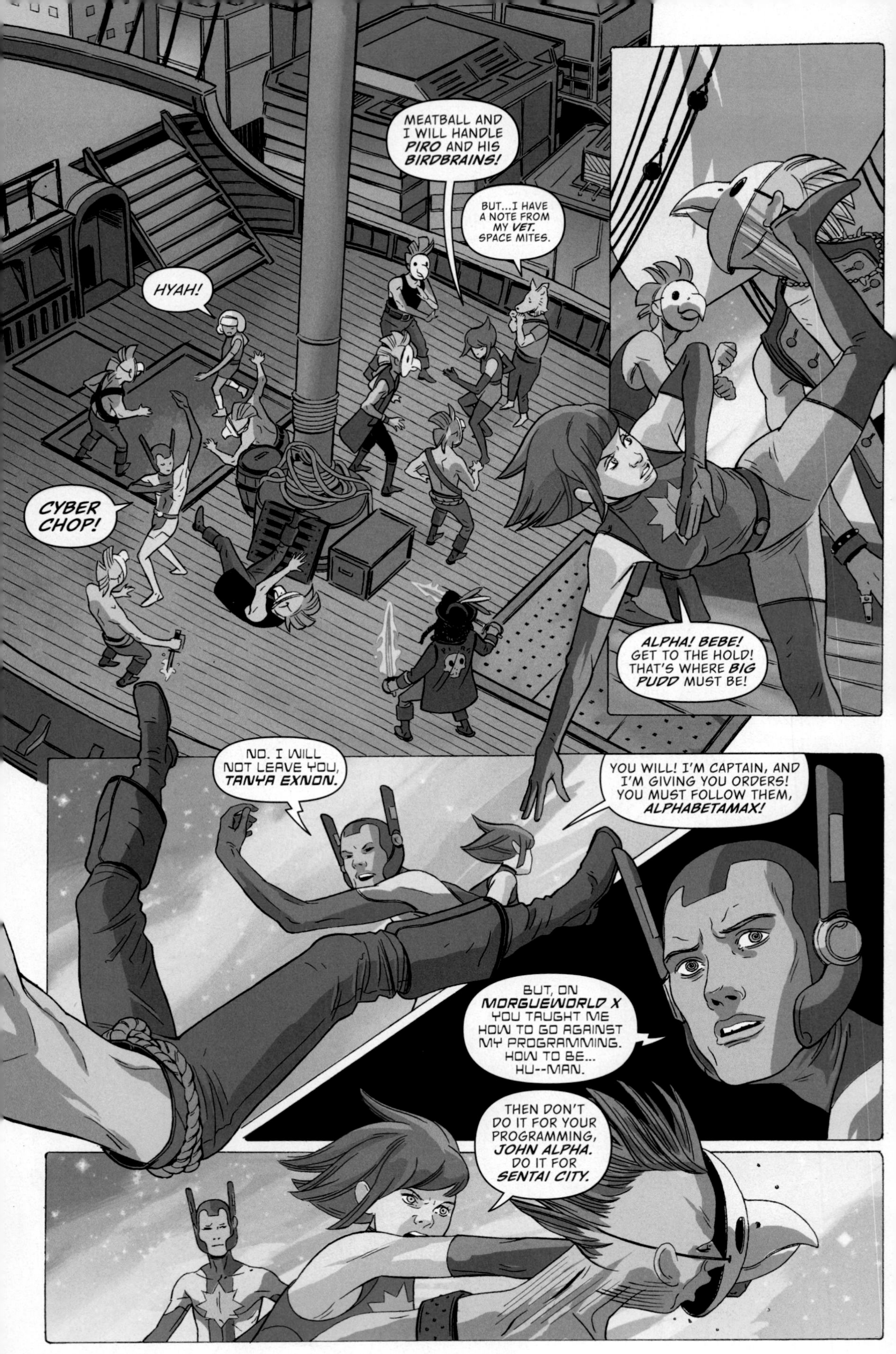

MEATBALL AND I WILL HANDLE PIRO AND HIS BIRDBRAINS!
BUT...I HAVE A NOTE FROM MY VET. SPACE MITES.
HYAH!
CYBER CHOP!
ALPHA! BEBE! GET TO THE HOLD! THAT'S WHERE BIG PUDD MUST BE!
NO. I WILL NOT LEAVE YOU, TANYA EXNON.
YOU WILL! I'M CAPTAIN, AND I'M GIVING YOU ORDERS! YOU MUST FOLLOW THEM, ALPHABETAMAX!
BUT, ON MORGUEWORLD X YOU TAUGHT ME HOW TO GO AGAINST MY PROGRAMMING. HOW TO BE... HU--MAN.
THEN DON'T DO IT FOR YOUR PROGRAMMING, JOHN ALPHA. DO IT FOR SENTAI CITY.

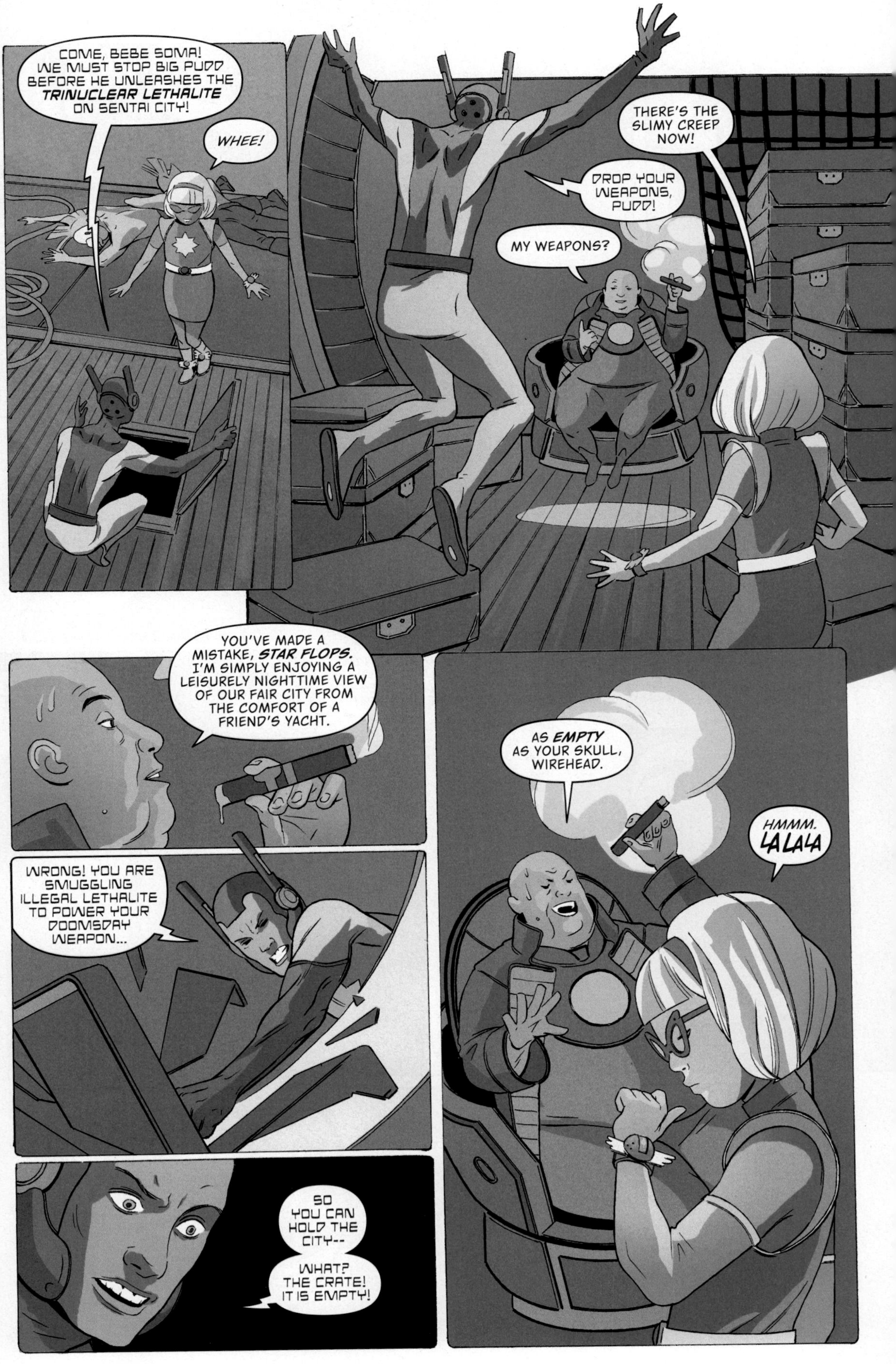

COME, BEBE SOMA! WE MUST STOP BIG PUDD BEFORE HE UNLEASHES THE TRINUCLEAR LETHALITE ON SENTAI CITY!
WHEE!
THERE'S THE SLIMY CREEP NOW!
DROP YOUR WEAPONS, PUDD!
MY WEAPONS?
YOU'VE MADE A MISTAKE, STAR FLOPS. I'M SIMPLY ENJOYING A LEISURELY NIGHTTIME VIEW OF OUR FAIR CITY FROM THE COMFORT OF A FRIEND'S YACHT.
WRONG! YOU ARE SMUGGLING ILLEGAL LETHALITE TO POWER YOUR DOOMSDAY WEAPON...
SO YOU CAN HOLD THE CITY--
WHAT? THE CRATE! IT IS EMPTY!
AS EMPTY AS YOUR SKULL, WIREHEAD.
HMMM. LALALA

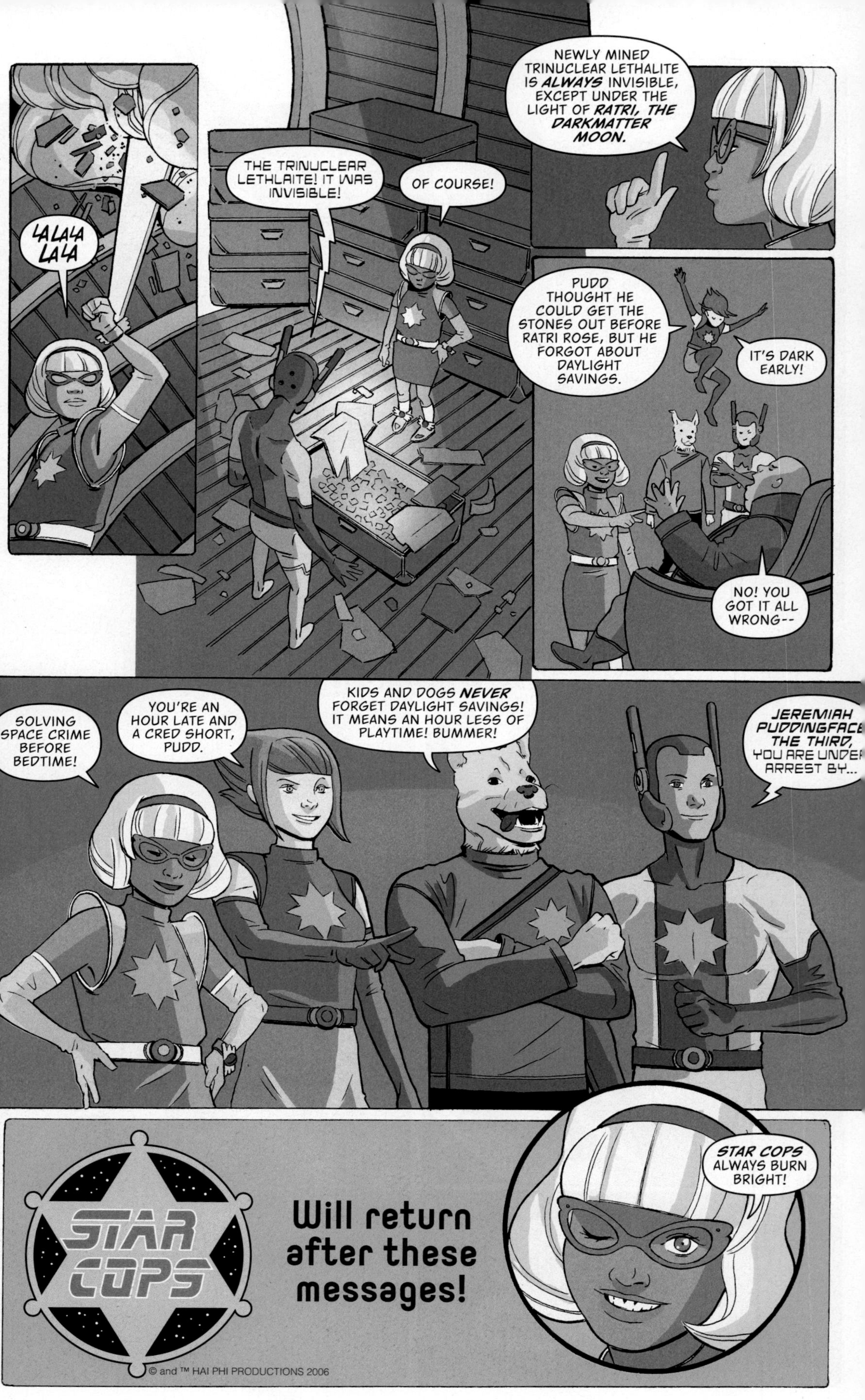

LALALA LALA
THE TRINUCLEAR LETHLAITE! IT WAS INVISIBLE!
OF COURSE!
NEWLY MINED TRINUCLEAR LETHALITE IS ALWAYS INVISIBLE, EXCEPT UNDER THE LIGHT OF RATRI, THE DARKMATTER MOON.
PUDD THOUGHT HE COULD GET THE STONES OUT BEFORE RATRI ROSE, BUT HE FORGOT ABOUT DAYLIGHT SAVINGS.
IT'S DARK EARLY!
NO! YOU GOT IT ALL WRONG--
SOLVING SPACE CRIME BEFORE BEDTIME!
YOU'RE AN HOUR LATE AND A CRED SHORT, PUDD.
KIDS AND DOGS NEVER FORGET DAYLIGHT SAVINGS! IT MEANS AN HOUR LESS OF PLAYTIME! BUMMER!
JEREMIAH PUDDINGFACE THE THIRD, YOU ARE UNDER ARREST BY...
STAR COPS
Will return after these messages!
STAR COPS ALWAYS BURN BRIGHT!

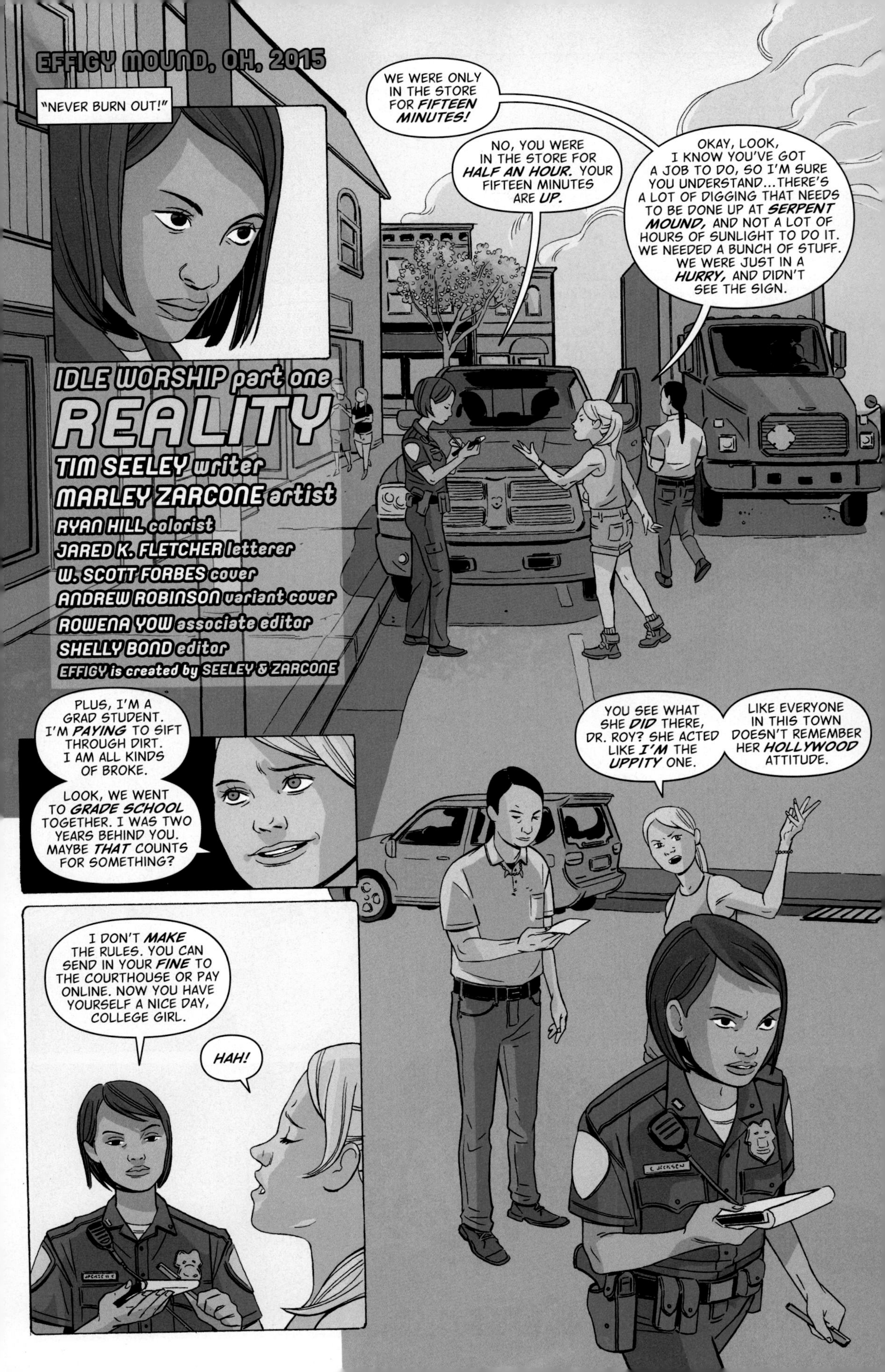

EFFIGY MOUND, OH, 2015
"NEVER BURN OUT!"
IDLE WORSHIP part one
REALITY
TIM SEELEY writer
MARLEY ZARCONE artist
RYAN HILL colorist
JARED K. FLETCHER letterer
W. SCOTT FORBES cover
ANDREW ROBINSON variant cover
ROWENA YOW associate editor
SHELLY BOND editor
EFFIGY is created by SEELEY & ZARCONE
WE WERE ONLY IN THE STORE FOR FIFTEEN MINUTES!
NO, YOU WERE IN THE STORE FOR HALF AN HOUR. YOUR FIFTEEN MINUTES ARE UP.
OKAY, LOOK, I KNOW YOU'VE GOT A JOB TO DO, SO I'M SURE YOU UNDERSTAND...THERE'S A LOT OF DIGGING THAT NEEDS TO BE DONE UP AT SERPENT MOUND, AND NOT A LOT OF HOURS OF SUNLIGHT TO DO IT. WE NEEDED A BUNCH OF STUFF. WE WERE JUST IN A HURRY, AND DIDN'T SEE THE SIGN.
PLUS, I'M A GRAD STUDENT. I'M PAYING TO SIFT THROUGH DIRT. I AM ALL KINDS OF BROKE.
LOOK, WE WENT TO GRADE SCHOOL TOGETHER. I WAS TWO YEARS BEHIND YOU. MAYBE THAT COUNTS FOR SOMETHING?
I DON'T MAKE THE RULES. YOU CAN SEND IN YOUR FINE TO THE COURTHOUSE OR PAY ONLINE. NOW YOU HAVE YOURSELF A NICE DAY, COLLEGE GIRL.
HAH!
YOU SEE WHAT SHE DID THERE, DR. ROY? SHE ACTED LIKE I'M THE UPPITY ONE.
LIKE EVERYONE IN THIS TOWN DOESN'T REMEMBER HER HOLLYWOOD ATTITUDE.

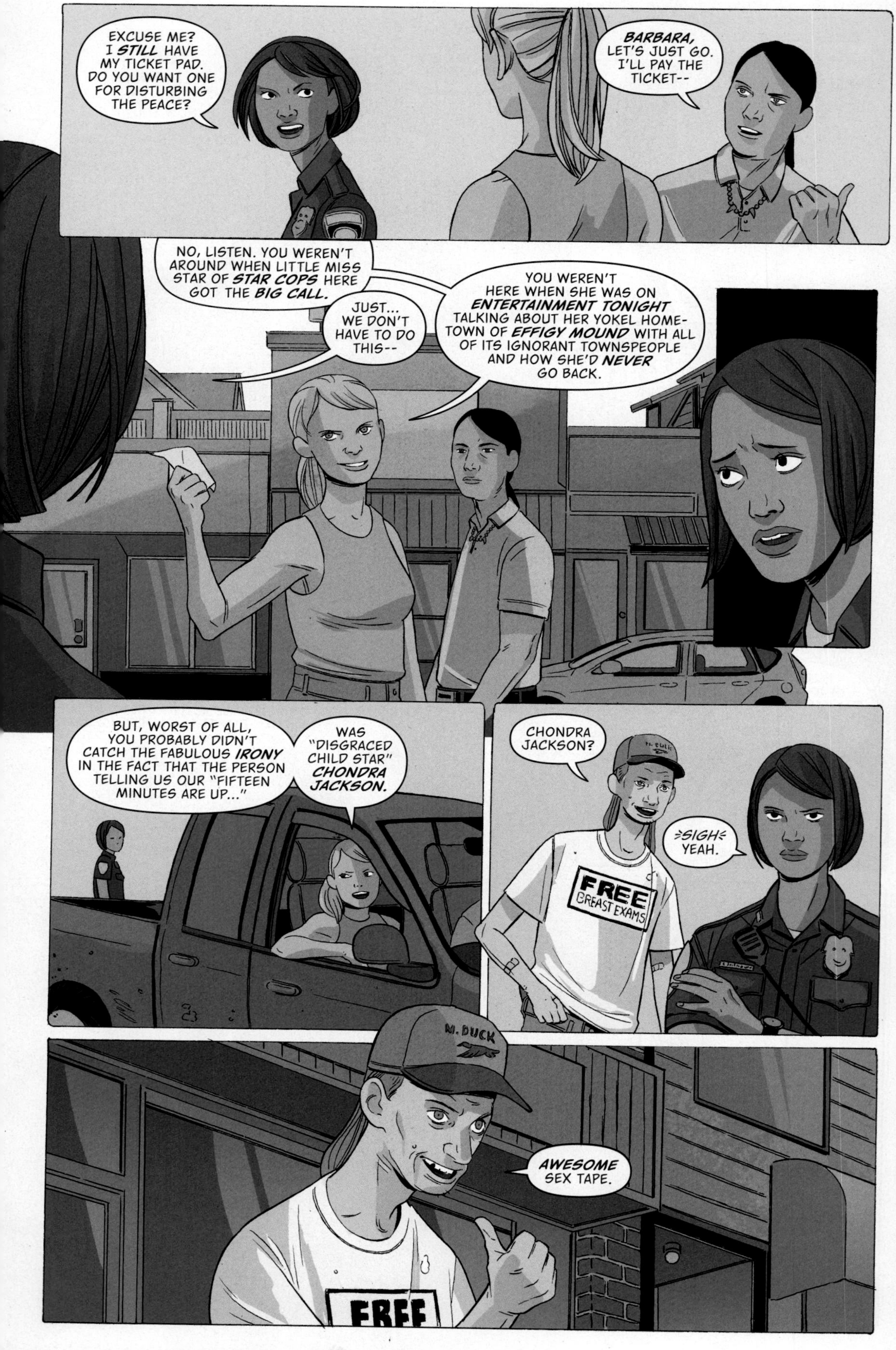
EXCUSE ME? I STILL HAVE MY TICKET PAD. DO YOU WANT ONE FOR DISTURBING THE PEACE?
BARBARA, LET'S JUST GO. I'LL PAY THE TICKET--
NO, LISTEN. YOU WEREN'T AROUND WHEN LITTLE MISS STAR OF STAR COPS HERE GOT THE BIG CALL.
JUST... WE DON'T HAVE TO DO THIS--
YOU WEREN'T HERE WHEN SHE WAS ON ENTERTAINMENT TONIGHT TALKING ABOUT HER YOKEL HOME-TOWN OF EFFIGY MOUND WITH ALL OF ITS IGNORANT TOWNSPEOPLE AND HOW SHE'D NEVER GO BACK.
BUT, WORST OF ALL, YOU PROBABLY DIDN'T CATCH THE FABULOUS IRONY IN THE FACT THAT THE PERSON TELLING US OUR "FIFTEEN MINUTES ARE UP..."
WAS "DISGRACED CHILD STAR" CHONDRA JACKSON.
CHONDRA JACKSON?
FREE BREAST EXAMS
SIGH YEAH.
M. DUCK
AWESOME SEX TAPE.
FREE

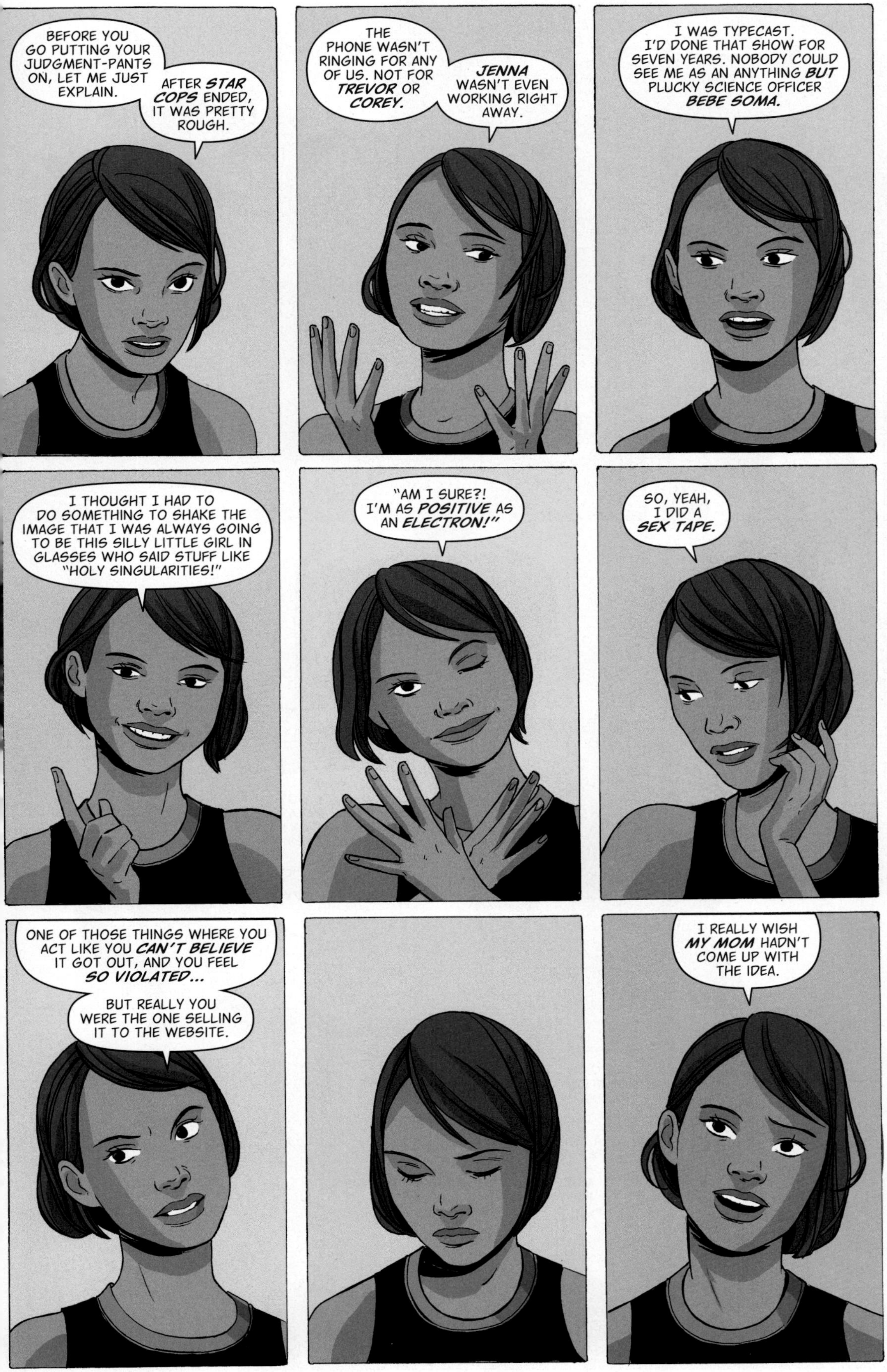
BEFORE YOU GO PUTTING YOUR JUDGMENT-PANTS ON, LET ME JUST EXPLAIN.
AFTER STAR COPS ENDED, IT WAS PRETTY ROUGH.
THE PHONE WASN'T RINGING FOR ANY OF US. NOT FOR TREVOR OR COREY.
JENNA WASN'T EVEN WORKING RIGHT AWAY.
I WAS TYPECAST. I'D DONE THAT SHOW FOR SEVEN YEARS. NOBODY COULD SEE ME AS AN ANYTHING BUT PLUCKY SCIENCE OFFICER BEBE SOMA.
I THOUGHT I HAD TO DO SOMETHING TO SHAKE THE IMAGE THAT I WAS ALWAYS GOING TO BE THIS SILLY LITTLE GIRL IN GLASSES WHO SAID STUFF LIKE "HOLY SINGULARITIES!"
"AM I SURE?! I'M AS POSITIVE AS AN ELECTRON!"
SO, YEAH, I DID A SEX TAPE.
ONE OF THOSE THINGS WHERE YOU ACT LIKE YOU CAN'T BELIEVE IT GOT OUT, AND YOU FEEL SO VIOLATED...
BUT REALLY YOU WERE THE ONE SELLING IT TO THE WEBSITE.
I REALLY WISH MY MOM HADN'T COME UP WITH THE IDEA.

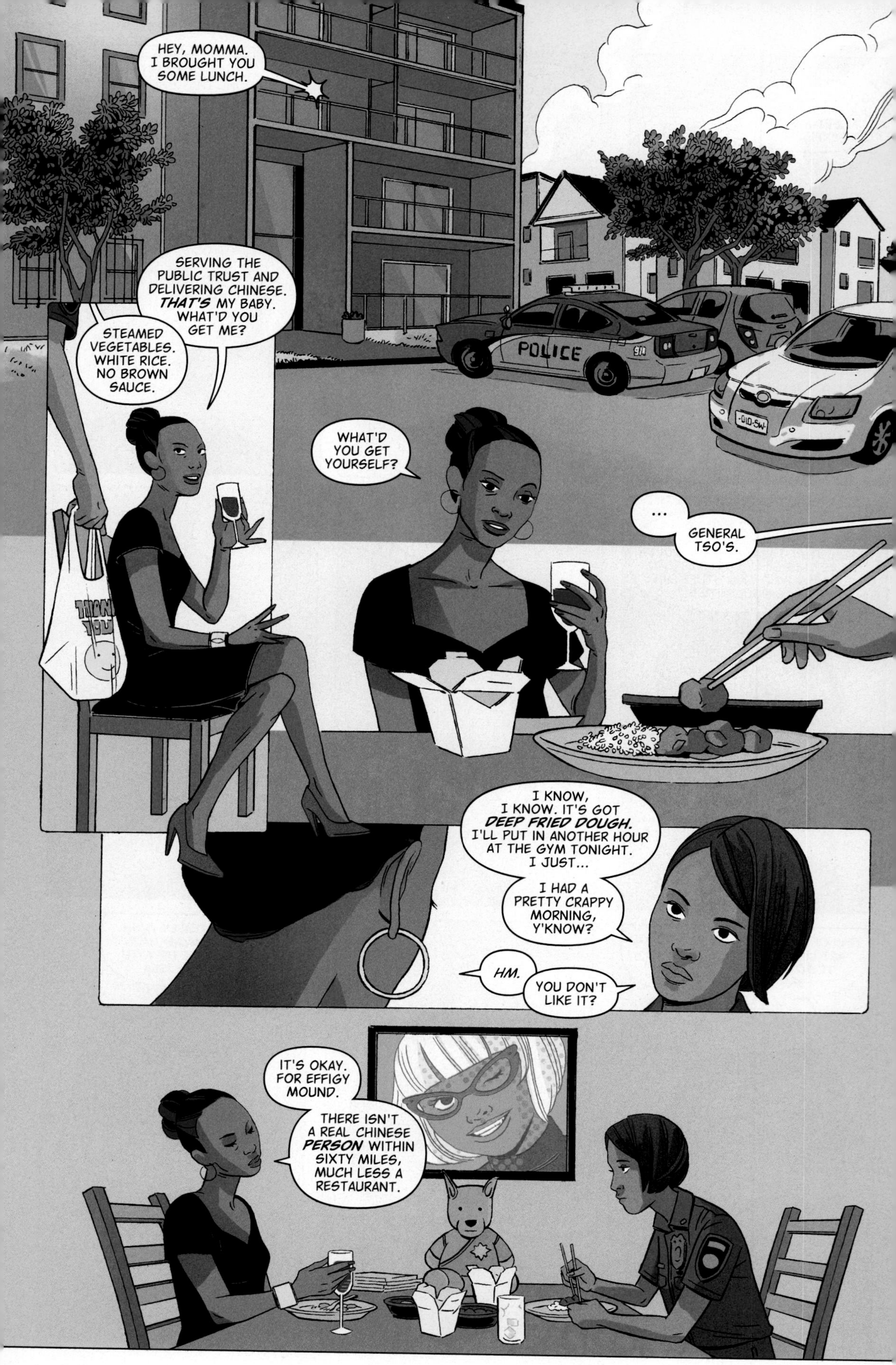
HEY, MOMMA. I BROUGHT YOU SOME LUNCH.
SERVING THE PUBLIC TRUST AND DELIVERING CHINESE. THAT'S MY BABY. WHAT'D YOU GET ME?
STEAMED VEGETABLES. WHITE RICE. NO BROWN SAUCE.
POLICE
WHAT'D YOU GET YOURSELF?
...
GENERAL TSO'S.
I KNOW, I KNOW. IT'S GOT DEEP FRIED DOUGH. I'LL PUT IN ANOTHER HOUR AT THE GYM TONIGHT. I JUST...
I HAD A PRETTY CRAPPY MORNING, Y'KNOW?
HM.
YOU DON'T LIKE IT?
IT'S OKAY. FOR EFFIGY MOUND.
THERE ISN'T A REAL CHINESE PERSON WITHIN SIXTY MILES, MUCH LESS A RESTAURANT.

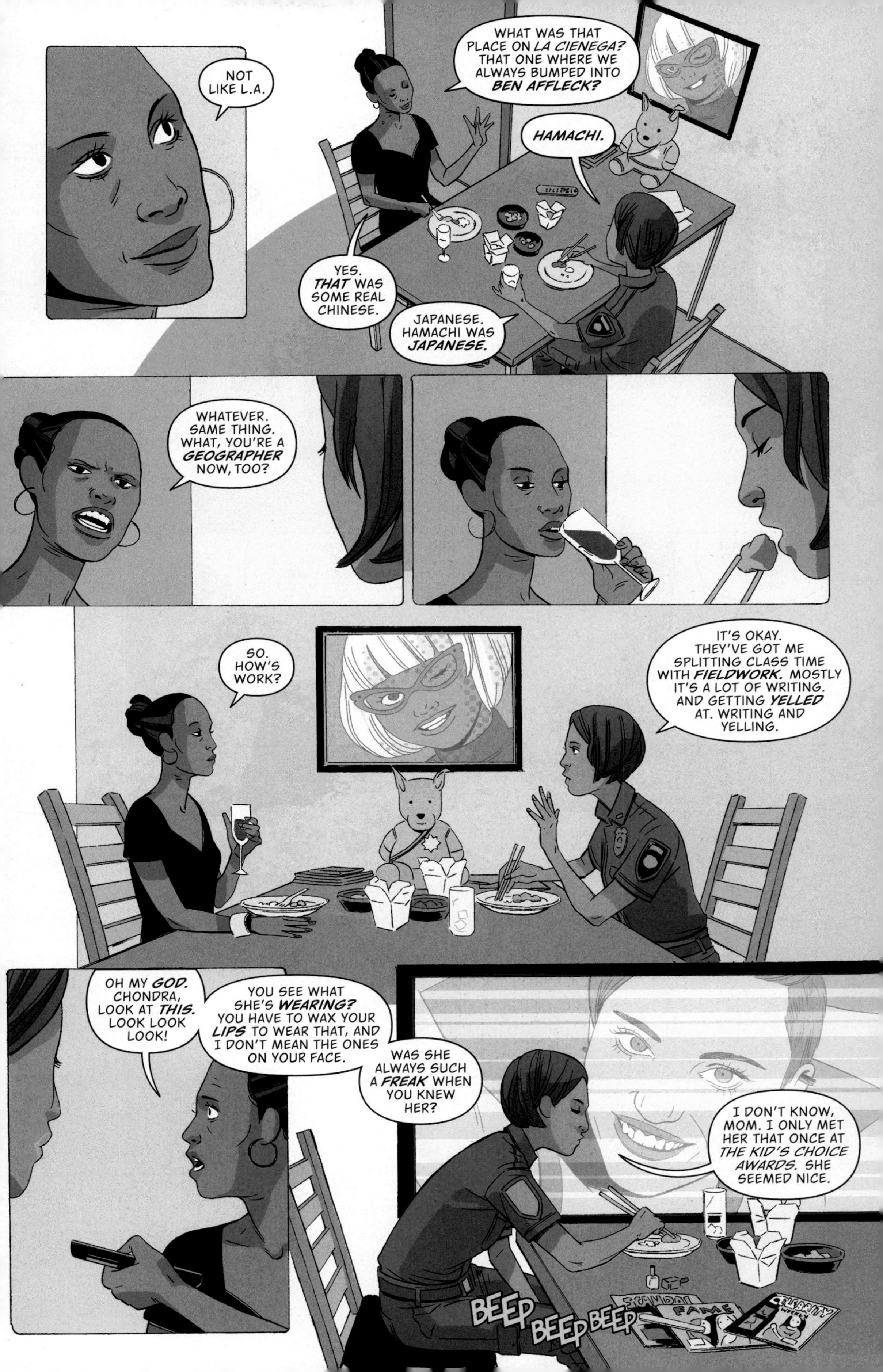
NOT LIKE L.A.
WHAT WAS THAT PLACE ON *LA CIENEGA?* THAT ONE WHERE WE ALWAYS BUMPED INTO **BEN AFFLECK?**
HAMACHI.
YES. **THAT** WAS SOME REAL CHINESE.
JAPANESE. HAMACHI WAS **JAPANESE.**
WHATEVER. SAME THING. WHAT, YOU'RE A **GEOGRAPHER** NOW, TOO?
SO. HOW'S WORK?
IT'S OKAY. THEY'VE GOT ME SPLITTING CLASS TIME WITH **FIELDWORK.** MOSTLY IT'S A LOT OF WRITING. AND GETTING **YELLED** AT. WRITING AND YELLING.
OH MY **GOD.** CHONDRA, LOOK AT **THIS.** LOOK LOOK LOOK!
YOU SEE WHAT SHE'S **WEARING?** YOU HAVE TO WAX YOUR **LIPS** TO WEAR THAT, AND I DON'T MEAN THE ONES ON YOUR FACE.
WAS SHE ALWAYS SUCH A **FREAK** WHEN YOU KNEW HER?
I DON'T KNOW, MOM. I ONLY MET HER THAT ONCE AT *THE KID'S CHOICE AWARDS.* SHE SEEMED NICE.
BEEP BEEP BEEP
SCANDAL
FAME
CELEBRITY WEEKLY

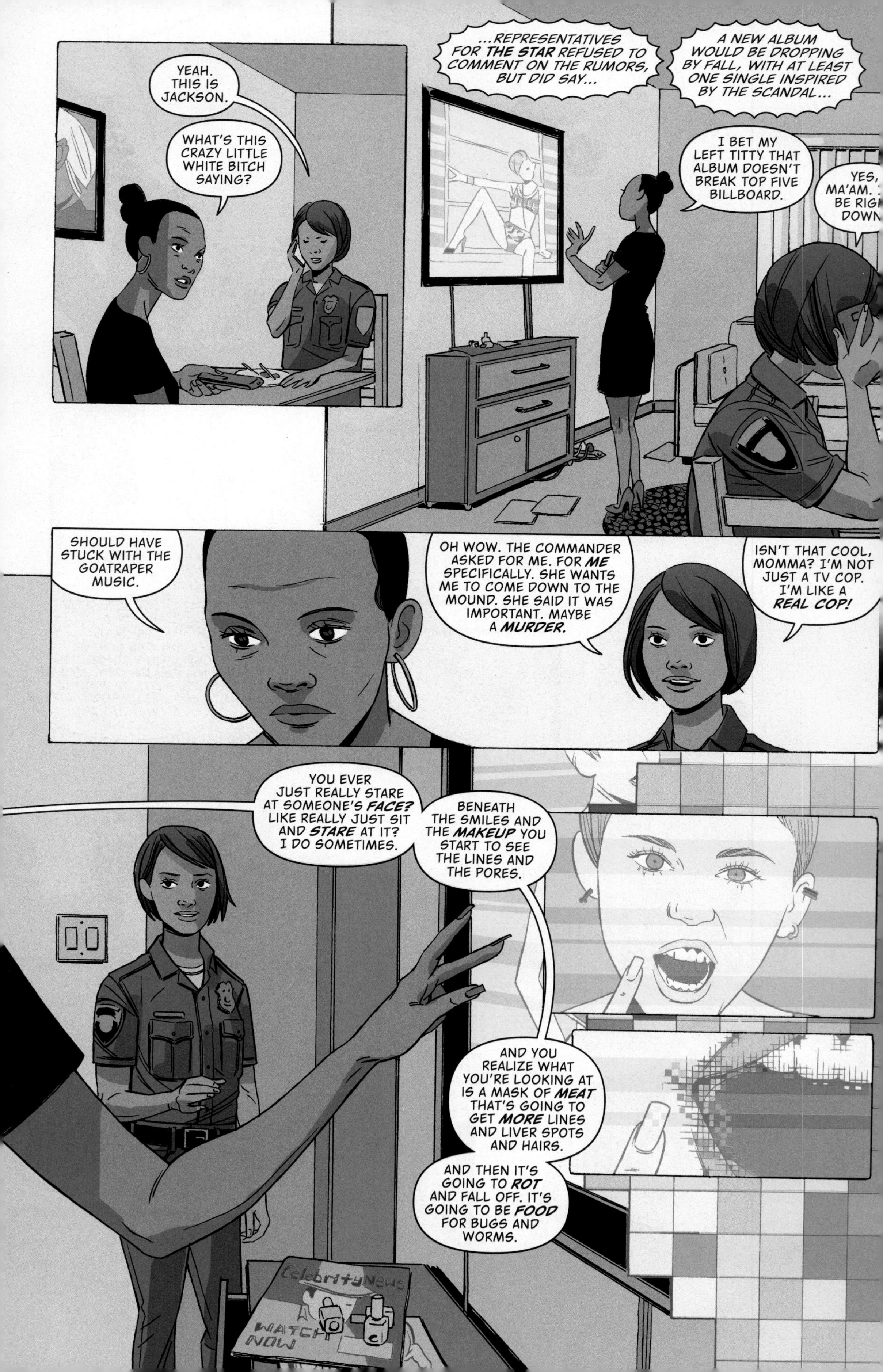
YEAH. THIS IS JACKSON.
WHAT'S THIS CRAZY LITTLE WHITE BITCH SAYING?
...REPRESENTATIVES FOR THE STAR REFUSED TO COMMENT ON THE RUMORS, BUT DID SAY...
A NEW ALBUM WOULD BE DROPPING BY FALL, WITH AT LEAST ONE SINGLE INSPIRED BY THE SCANDAL...
I BET MY LEFT TITTY THAT ALBUM DOESN'T BREAK TOP FIVE BILLBOARD.
YES, MA'AM.
SHOULD HAVE STUCK WITH THE GOATRAPER MUSIC.
OH WOW. THE COMMANDER ASKED FOR ME. FOR ME SPECIFICALLY. SHE WANTS ME TO COME DOWN TO THE MOUND. SHE SAID IT WAS IMPORTANT. MAYBE A MURDER.
ISN'T THAT COOL, MOMMA? I'M NOT JUST A TV COP. I'M LIKE A REAL COP!
YOU EVER JUST REALLY STARE AT SOMEONE'S FACE? LIKE REALLY JUST SIT AND STARE AT IT? I DO SOMETIMES.
BENEATH THE SMILES AND THE MAKEUP YOU START TO SEE THE LINES AND THE PORES.
AND YOU REALIZE WHAT YOU'RE LOOKING AT IS A MASK OF MEAT THAT'S GOING TO GET MORE LINES AND LIVER SPOTS AND HAIRS.
AND THEN IT'S GOING TO ROT AND FALL OFF. IT'S GOING TO BE FOOD FOR BUGS AND WORMS.
CelebrityNews
WATCH NOW

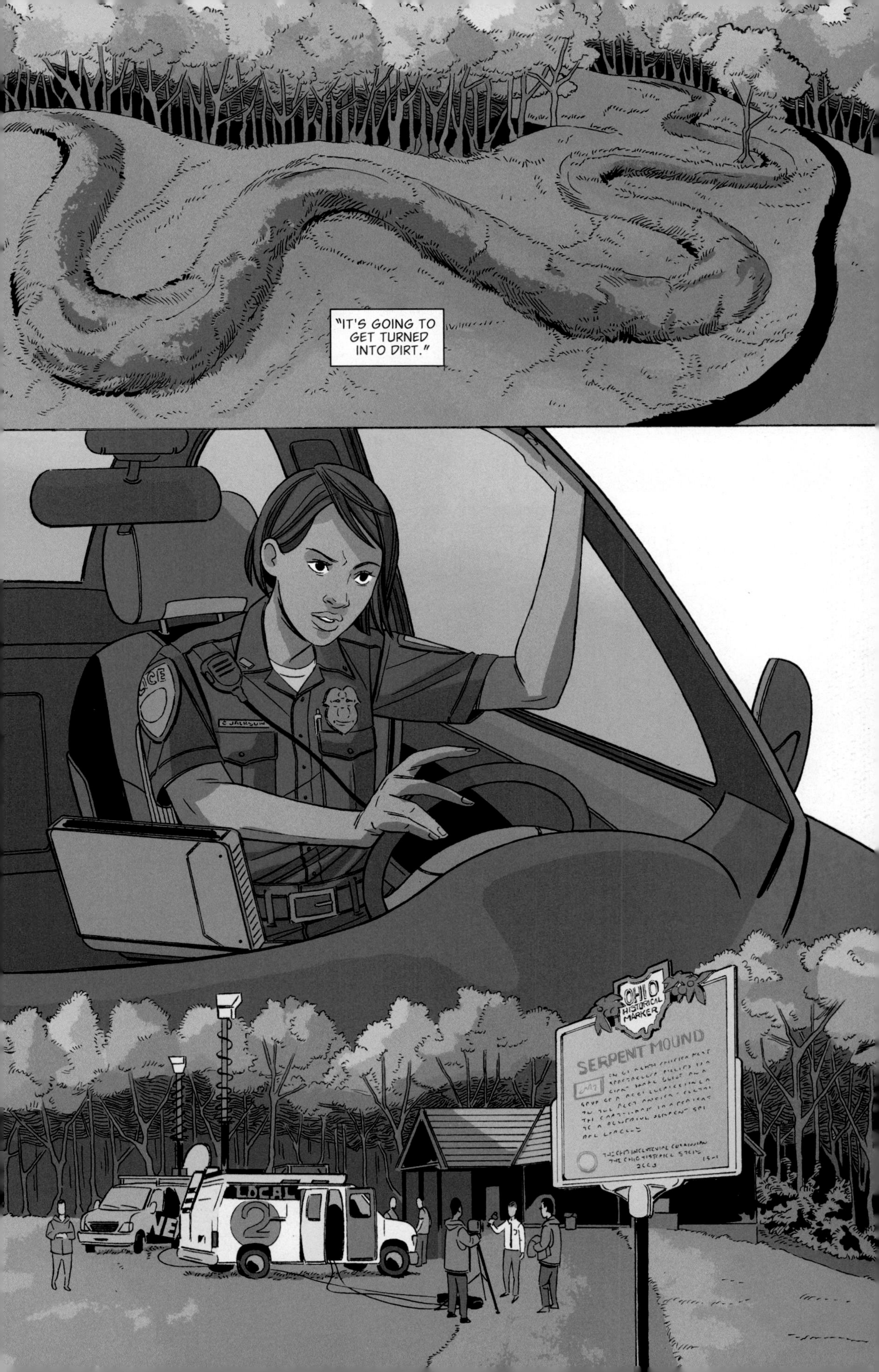
"IT'S GOING TO GET TURNED INTO DIRT."
OHIO HISTORICAL MARKER
SERPENT MOUND
LOCAL
2

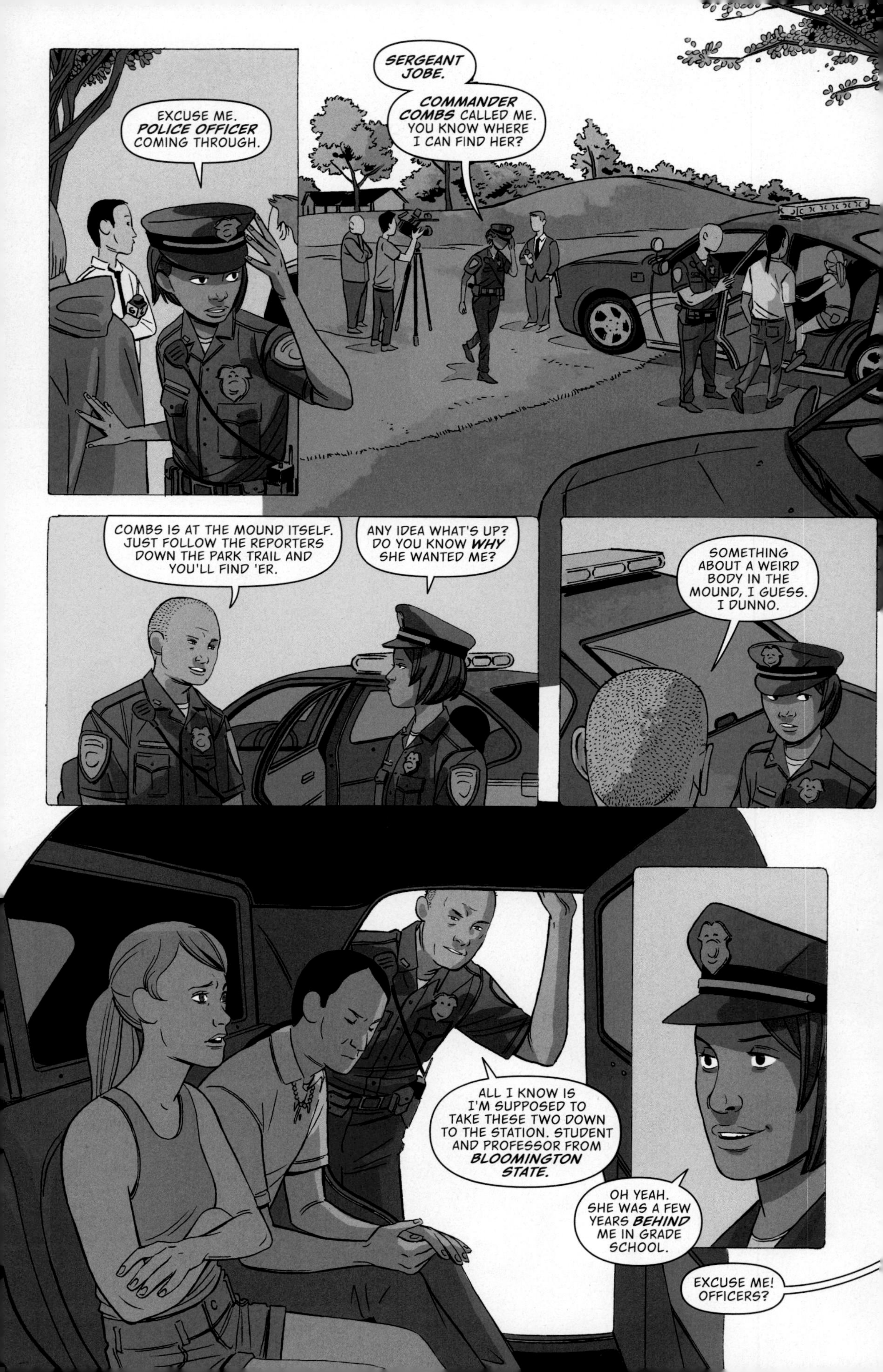
EXCUSE ME. POLICE OFFICER COMING THROUGH.
SERGEANT JOBE.
COMMANDER COMBS CALLED ME. YOU KNOW WHERE I CAN FIND HER?
COMBS IS AT THE MOUND ITSELF. JUST FOLLOW THE REPORTERS DOWN THE PARK TRAIL AND YOU'LL FIND 'ER.
ANY IDEA WHAT'S UP? DO YOU KNOW WHY SHE WANTED ME?
SOMETHING ABOUT A WEIRD BODY IN THE MOUND, I GUESS. I DUNNO.
ALL I KNOW IS I'M SUPPOSED TO TAKE THESE TWO DOWN TO THE STATION. STUDENT AND PROFESSOR FROM BLOOMINGTON STATE.
OH YEAH. SHE WAS A FEW YEARS BEHIND ME IN GRADE SCHOOL.
EXCUSE ME! OFFICERS?

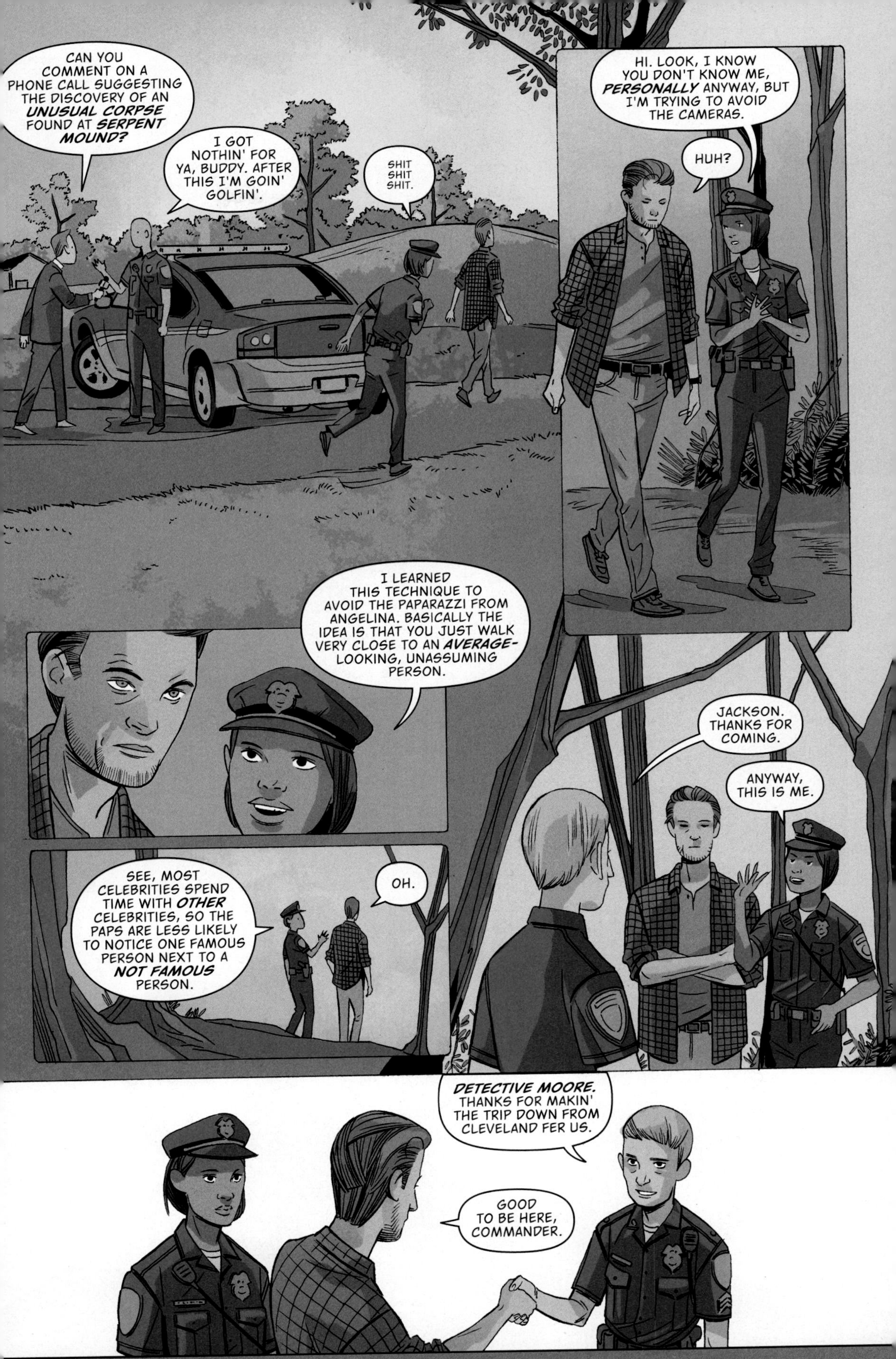
CAN YOU COMMENT ON A PHONE CALL SUGGESTING THE DISCOVERY OF AN UNUSUAL CORPSE FOUND AT SERPENT MOUND?
I GOT NOTHIN' FOR YA, BUDDY. AFTER THIS I'M GOIN' GOLFIN'.
SHIT SHIT SHIT.
HI. LOOK, I KNOW YOU DON'T KNOW ME, PERSONALLY ANYWAY, BUT I'M TRYING TO AVOID THE CAMERAS.
HUH?
I LEARNED THIS TECHNIQUE TO AVOID THE PAPARAZZI FROM ANGELINA. BASICALLY THE IDEA IS THAT YOU JUST WALK VERY CLOSE TO AN AVERAGE-LOOKING, UNASSUMING PERSON.
SEE, MOST CELEBRITIES SPEND TIME WITH OTHER CELEBRITIES, SO THE PAPS ARE LESS LIKELY TO NOTICE ONE FAMOUS PERSON NEXT TO A NOT FAMOUS PERSON.
OH.
JACKSON. THANKS FOR COMING.
ANYWAY, THIS IS ME.
DETECTIVE MOORE. THANKS FOR MAKIN' THE TRIP DOWN FROM CLEVELAND FER US.
GOOD TO BE HERE, COMMANDER.

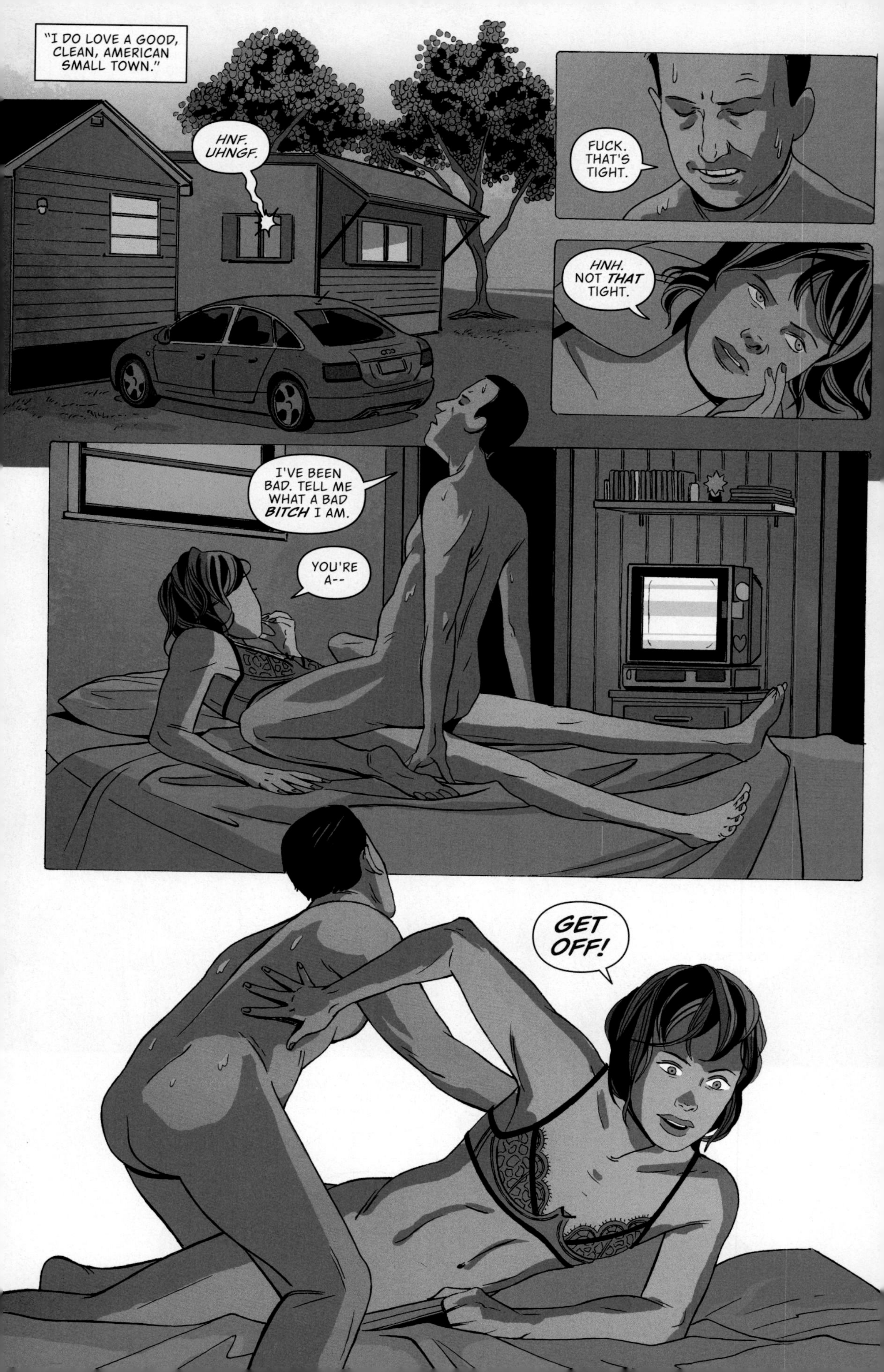
"I DO LOVE A GOOD, CLEAN, AMERICAN SMALL TOWN."
HNF. UHNGF.
FUCK. THAT'S TIGHT.
HNH. NOT *THAT* TIGHT.
I'VE BEEN BAD. TELL ME WHAT A BAD *BITCH* I AM.
YOU'RE A--
GET OFF!

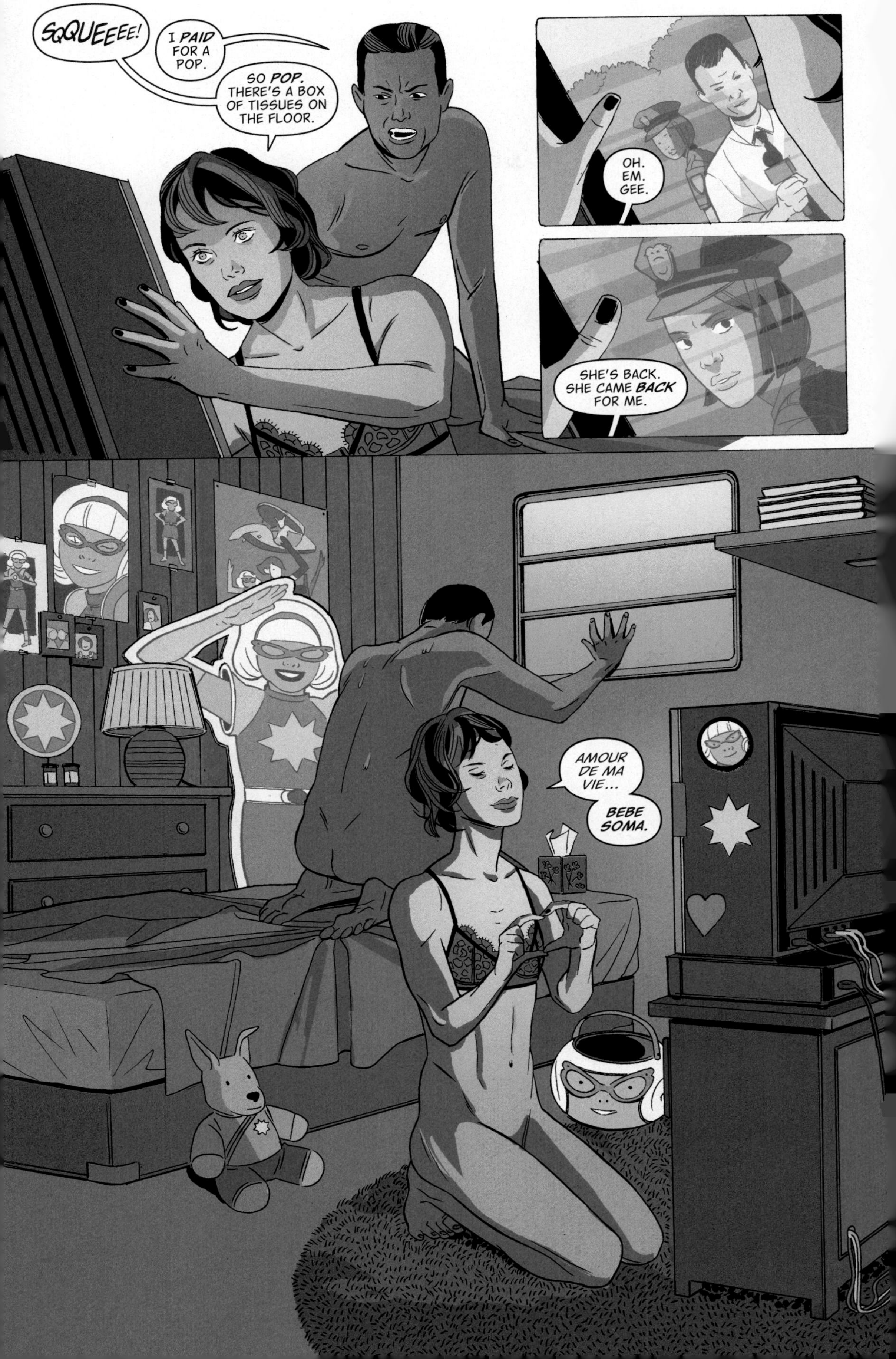
SQUEEEEE!
I PAID FOR A POP.
SO POP. THERE'S A BOX OF TISSUES ON THE FLOOR.
OH. EM. GEE.
SHE'S BACK. SHE CAME BACK FOR ME.
AMOUR DE MA VIE...
BEBE SOMA.

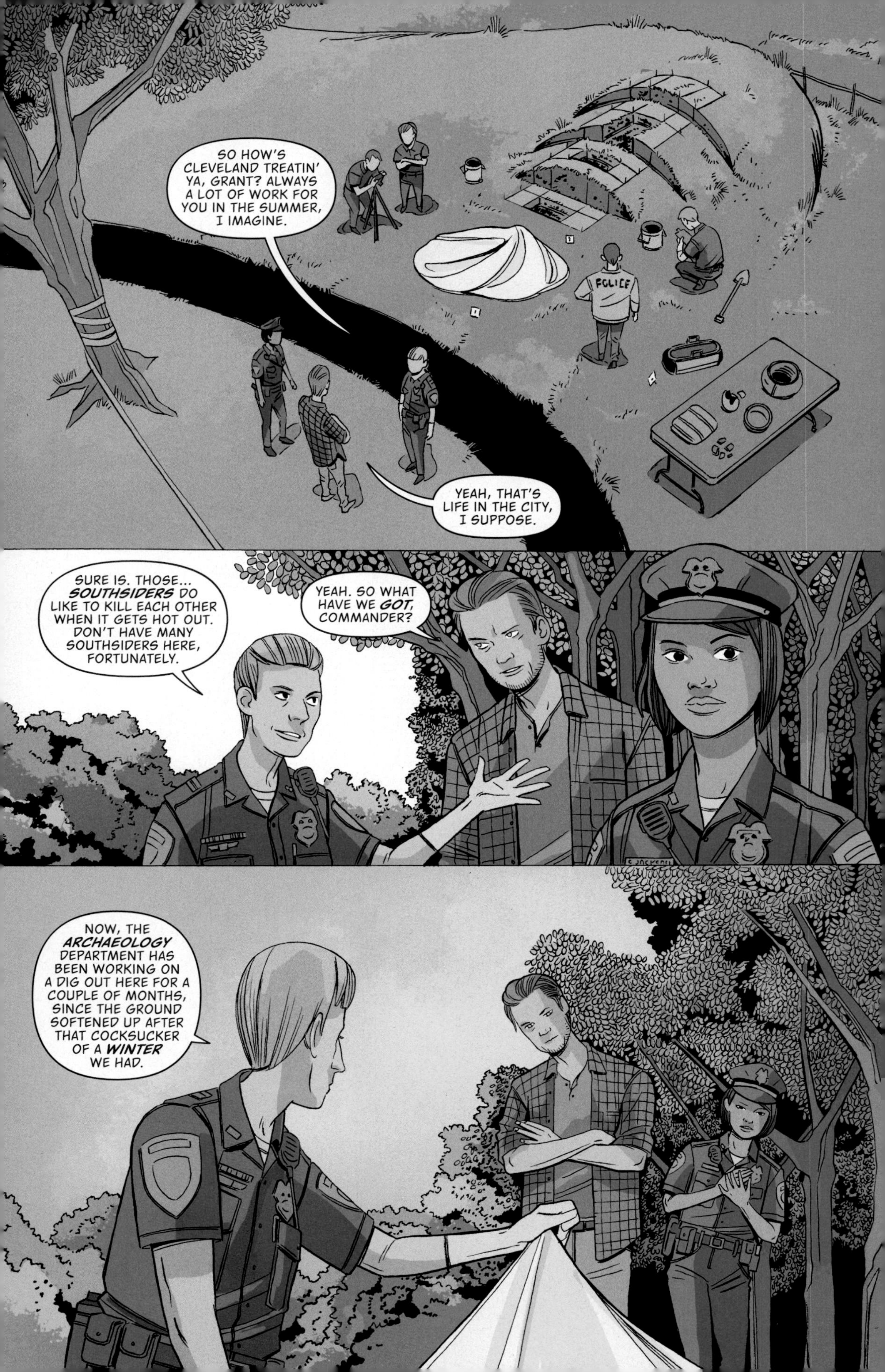
SO HOW'S CLEVELAND TREATIN' YA, GRANT? ALWAYS A LOT OF WORK FOR YOU IN THE SUMMER, I IMAGINE.
YEAH, THAT'S LIFE IN THE CITY, I SUPPOSE.
SURE IS. THOSE... SOUTHSIDERS DO LIKE TO KILL EACH OTHER WHEN IT GETS HOT OUT. DON'T HAVE MANY SOUTHSIDERS HERE, FORTUNATELY.
YEAH. SO WHAT HAVE WE GOT, COMMANDER?
NOW, THE ARCHAEOLOGY DEPARTMENT HAS BEEN WORKING ON A DIG OUT HERE FOR A COUPLE OF MONTHS, SINCE THE GROUND SOFTENED UP AFTER THAT COCKSUCKER OF A WINTER WE HAD.
POLICE

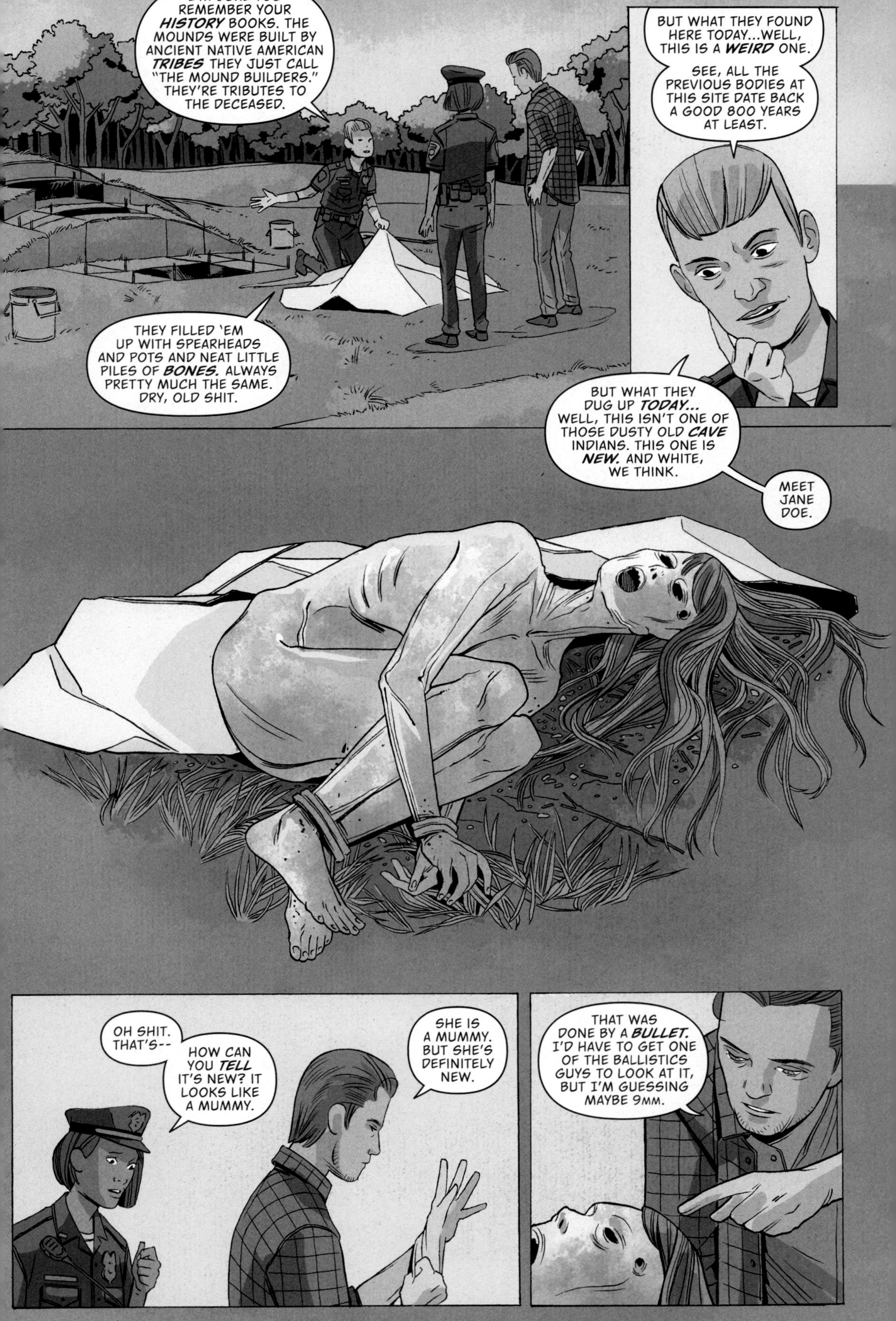
I'M SURE YOU REMEMBER YOUR HISTORY BOOKS. THE MOUNDS WERE BUILT BY ANCIENT NATIVE AMERICAN TRIBES THEY JUST CALL "THE MOUND BUILDERS." THEY'RE TRIBUTES TO THE DECEASED.
THEY FILLED 'EM UP WITH SPEARHEADS AND POTS AND NEAT LITTLE PILES OF BONES. ALWAYS PRETTY MUCH THE SAME. DRY, OLD SHIT.
BUT WHAT THEY FOUND HERE TODAY...WELL, THIS IS A WEIRD ONE.
SEE, ALL THE PREVIOUS BODIES AT THIS SITE DATE BACK A GOOD 800 YEARS AT LEAST.
BUT WHAT THEY DUG UP TODAY... WELL, THIS ISN'T ONE OF THOSE DUSTY OLD CAVE INDIANS. THIS ONE IS NEW. AND WHITE, WE THINK.
MEET JANE DOE.
OH SHIT. THAT'S--
HOW CAN YOU TELL IT'S NEW? IT LOOKS LIKE A MUMMY.
SHE IS A MUMMY. BUT SHE'S DEFINITELY NEW.
THAT WAS DONE BY A BULLET. I'D HAVE TO GET ONE OF THE BALLISTICS GUYS TO LOOK AT IT, BUT I'M GUESSING MAYBE 9MM.

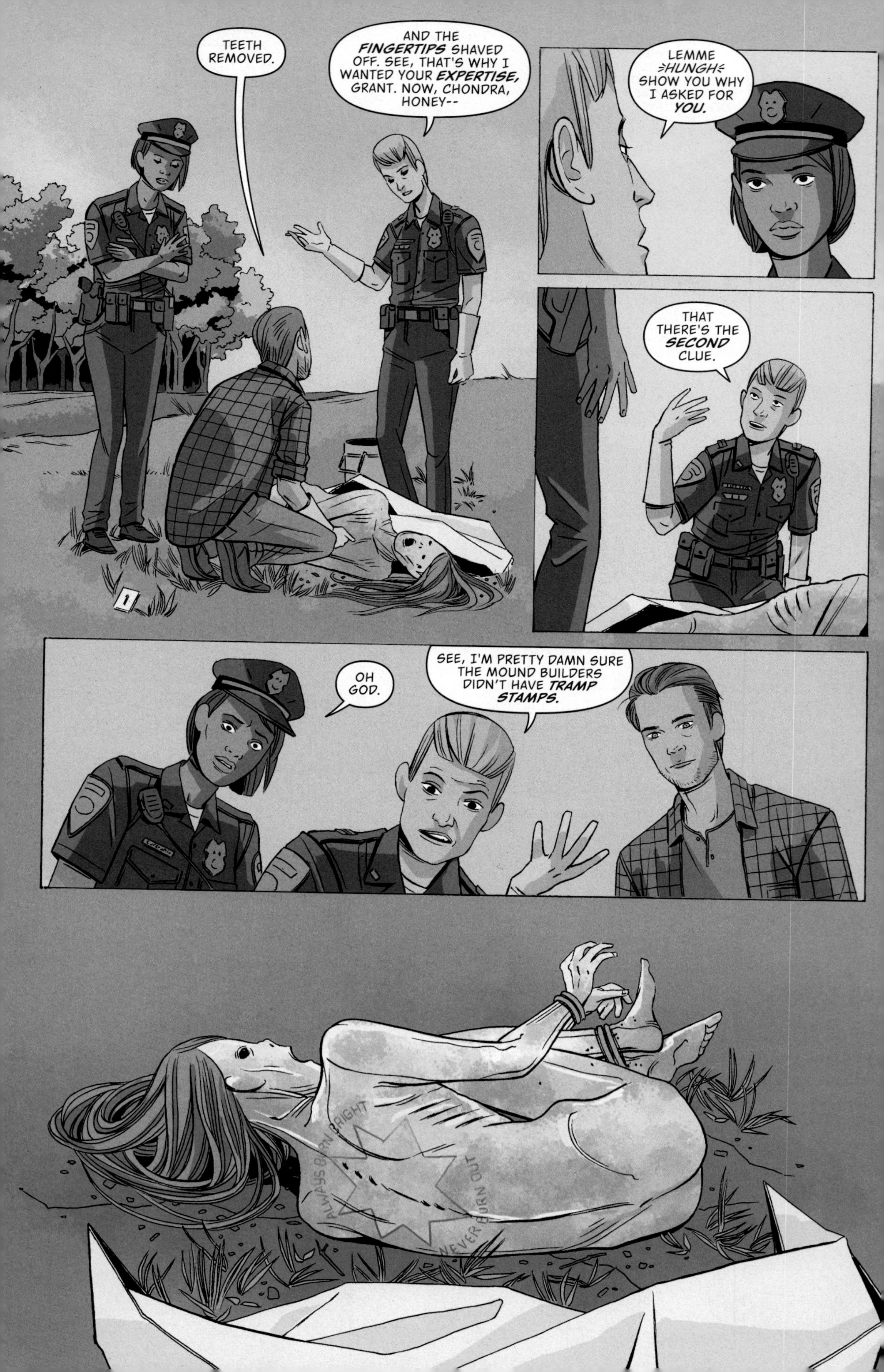
TEETH REMOVED.
AND THE FINGERTIPS SHAVED OFF. SEE, THAT'S WHY I WANTED YOUR EXPERTISE, GRANT. NOW, CHONDRA, HONEY--
LEMME ≥HUNGH≤ SHOW YOU WHY I ASKED FOR YOU.
THAT THERE'S THE SECOND CLUE.
OH GOD.
SEE, I'M PRETTY DAMN SURE THE MOUND BUILDERS DIDN'T HAVE TRAMP STAMPS.
ALWAYS BURN BRIGHT
NEVER BURN OUT

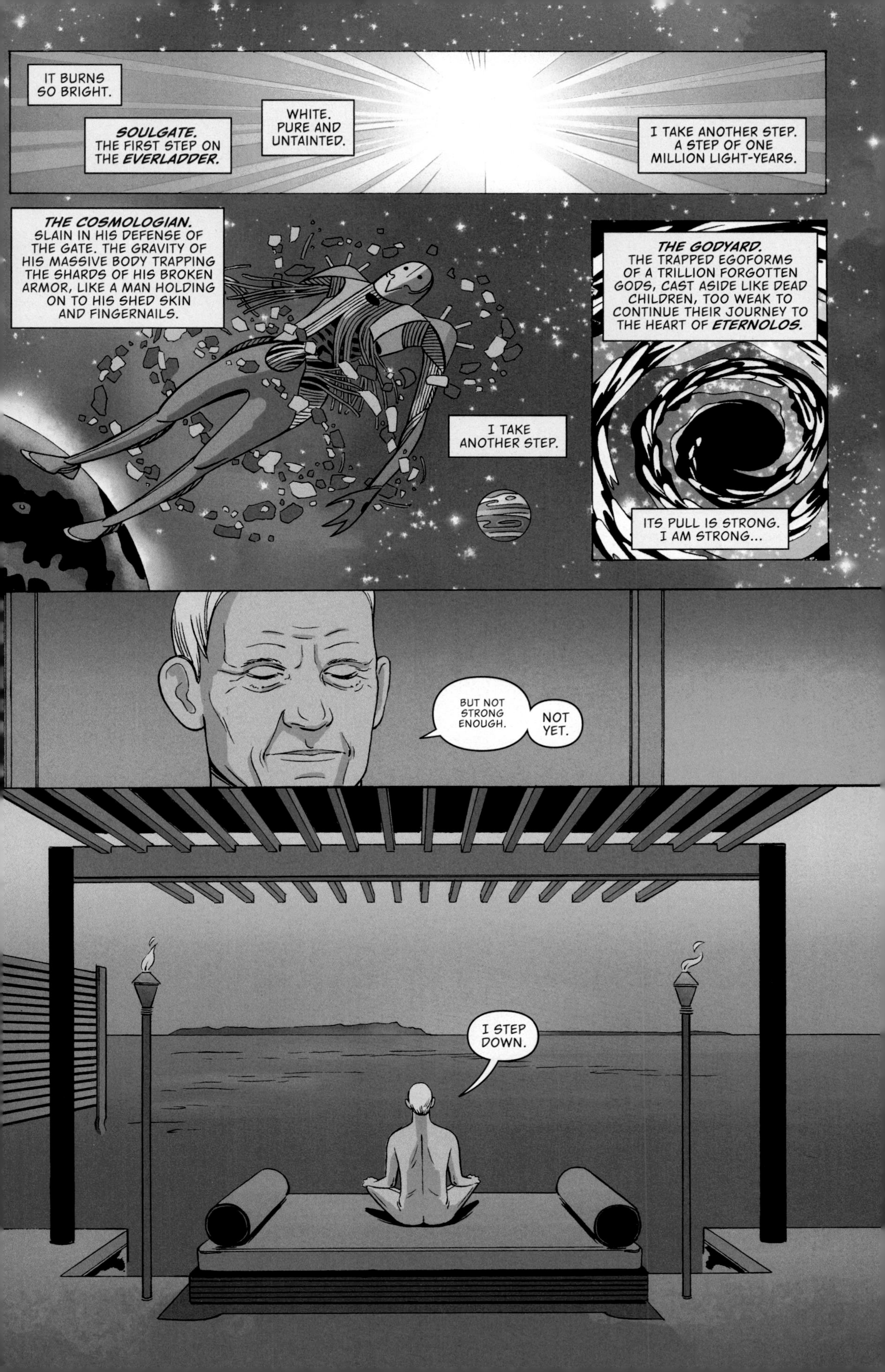
IT BURNS SO BRIGHT.
SOULGATE. THE FIRST STEP ON THE EVERLADDER.
WHITE. PURE AND UNTAINTED.
I TAKE ANOTHER STEP. A STEP OF ONE MILLION LIGHT-YEARS.
THE COSMOLOGIAN. SLAIN IN HIS DEFENSE OF THE GATE. THE GRAVITY OF HIS MASSIVE BODY TRAPPING THE SHARDS OF HIS BROKEN ARMOR, LIKE A MAN HOLDING ON TO HIS SHED SKIN AND FINGERNAILS.
I TAKE ANOTHER STEP.
THE GODYARD. THE TRAPPED EGOFORMS OF A TRILLION FORGOTTEN GODS, CAST ASIDE LIKE DEAD CHILDREN, TOO WEAK TO CONTINUE THEIR JOURNEY TO THE HEART OF ETERNOLOS.
ITS PULL IS STRONG. I AM STRONG...
BUT NOT STRONG ENOUGH.
NOT YET.
I STEP DOWN.

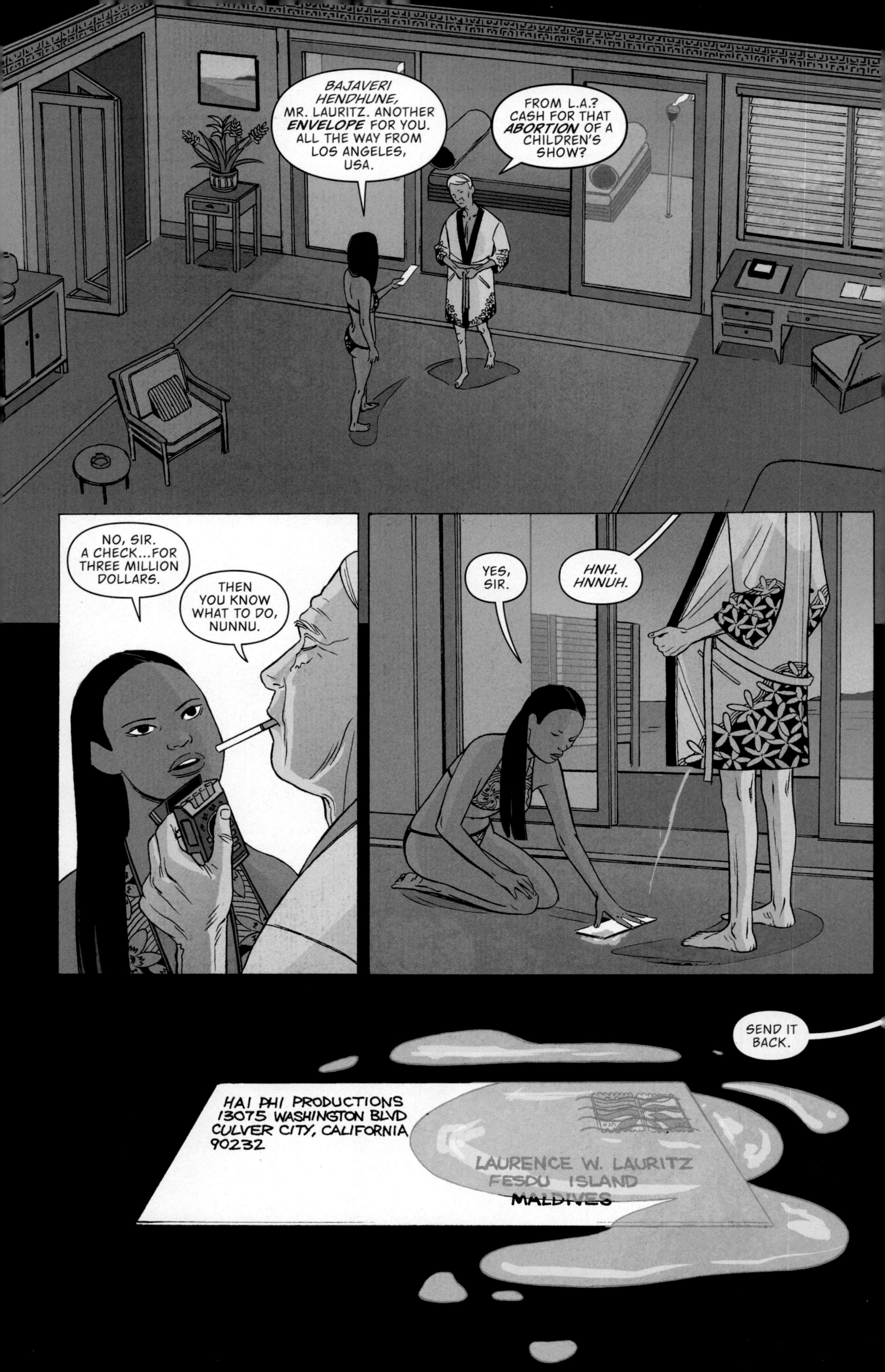
BAJAVERI HENDHUNE, MR. LAURITZ. ANOTHER ENVELOPE FOR YOU. ALL THE WAY FROM LOS ANGELES, USA.
FROM L.A.? CASH FOR THAT ABORTION OF A CHILDREN'S SHOW?
NO, SIR. A CHECK...FOR THREE MILLION DOLLARS.
THEN YOU KNOW WHAT TO DO, NUNNU.
YES, SIR.
HNH. HNNUH.
SEND IT BACK.
HAI PHI PRODUCTIONS
13075 WASHINGTON BLVD
CULVER CITY, CALIFORNIA
90232
LAURENCE W. LAURITZ
FESDU ISLAND
MALDIVES

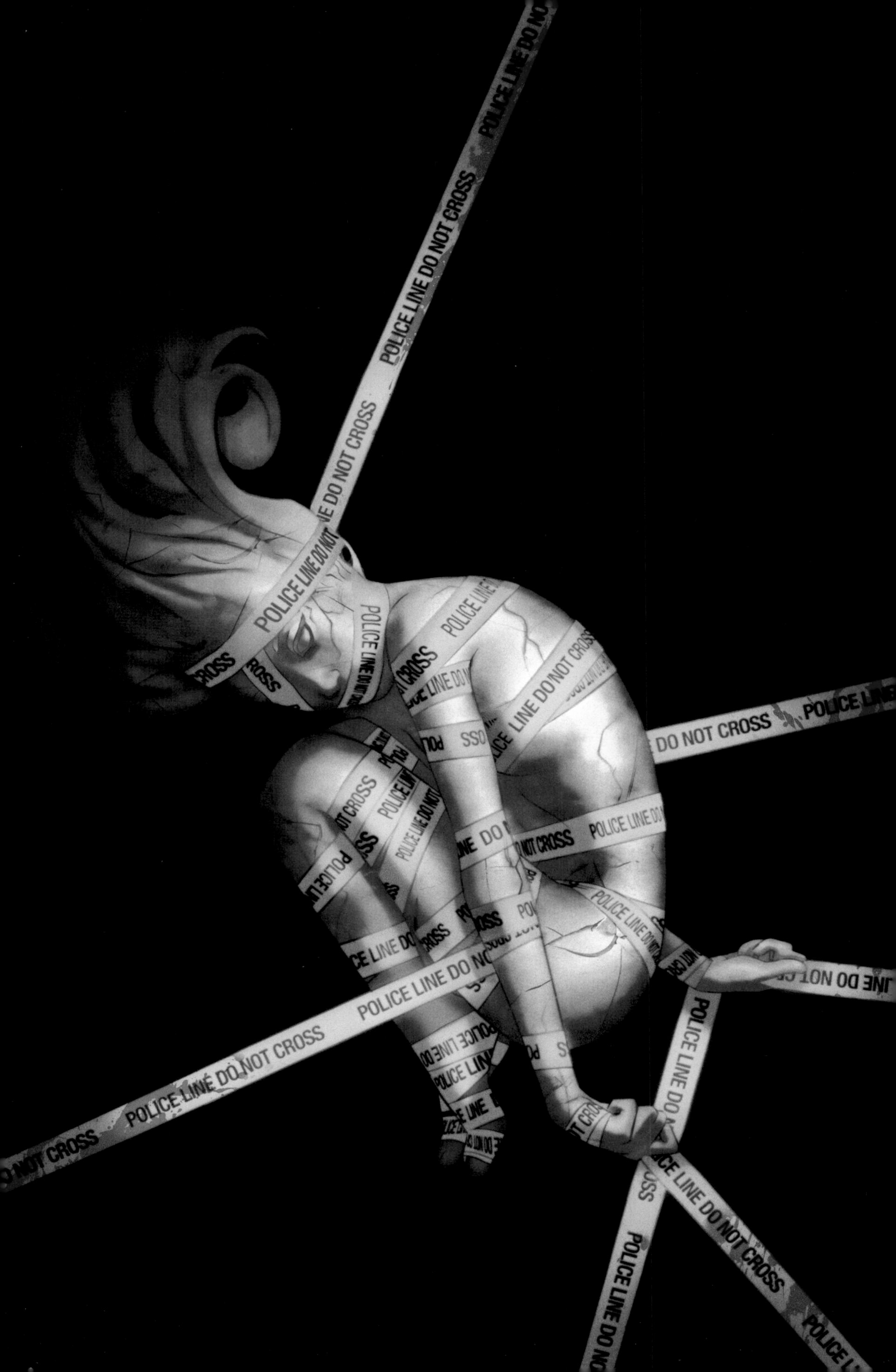
POLICE LINE DO NOT CROSS
POLICE LINE DO NOT CROSS
POLICE LINE DO NOT CROSS
DO NOT CROSS POLICE LINE
POLICE LINE DO NOT CROSS
POLICE LINE DO NOT CROSS
POLICE LINE DO NOT CROSS
POLICE LINE DO NOT CROSS

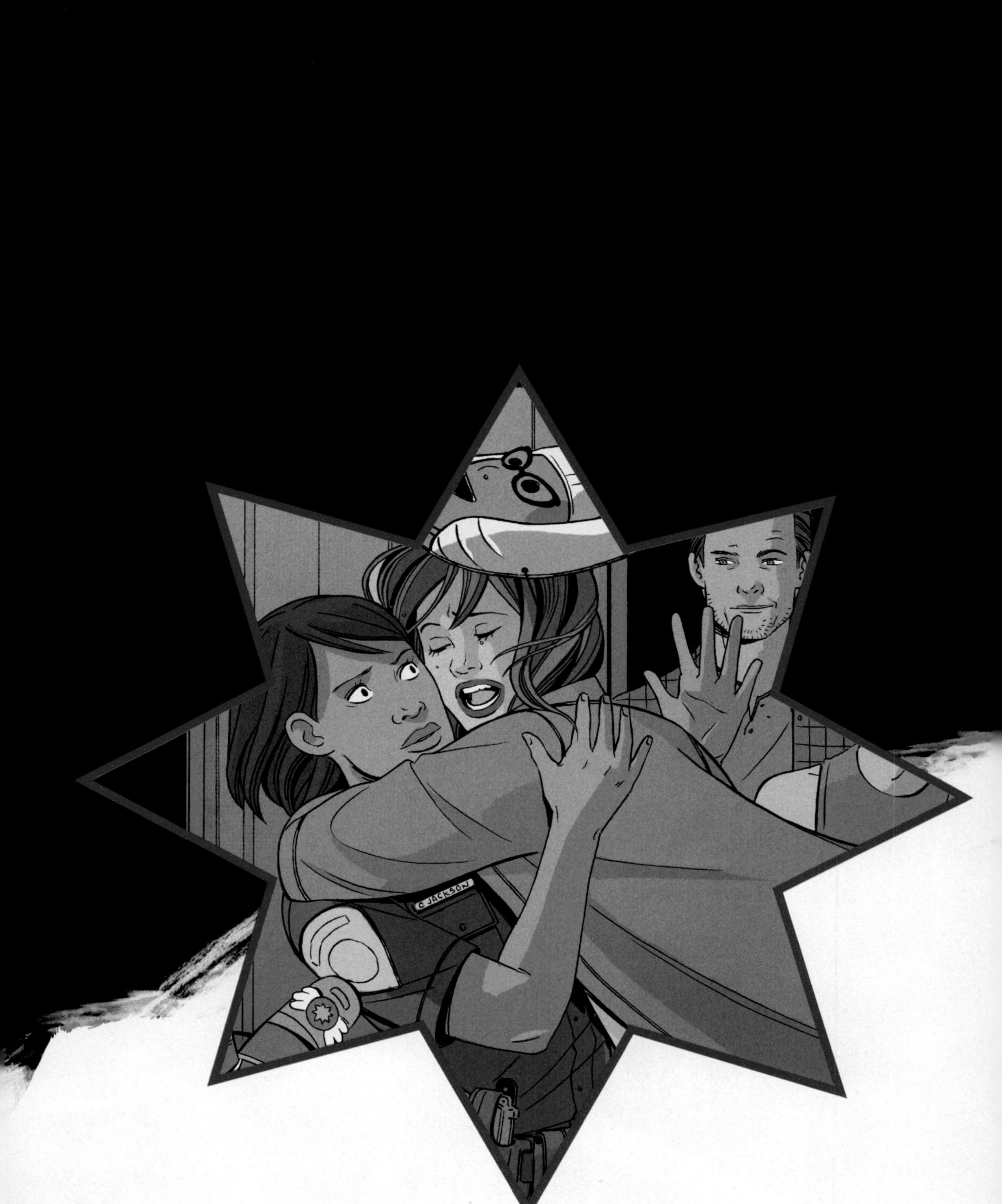
C JACKSON

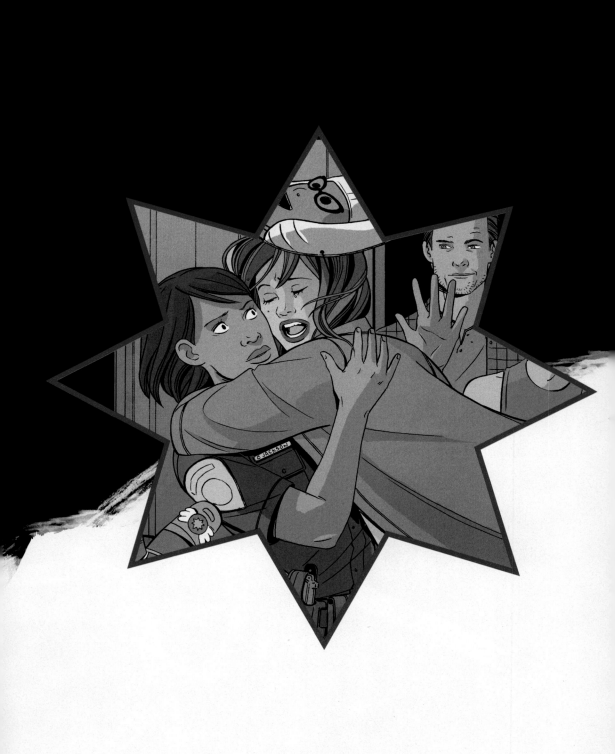

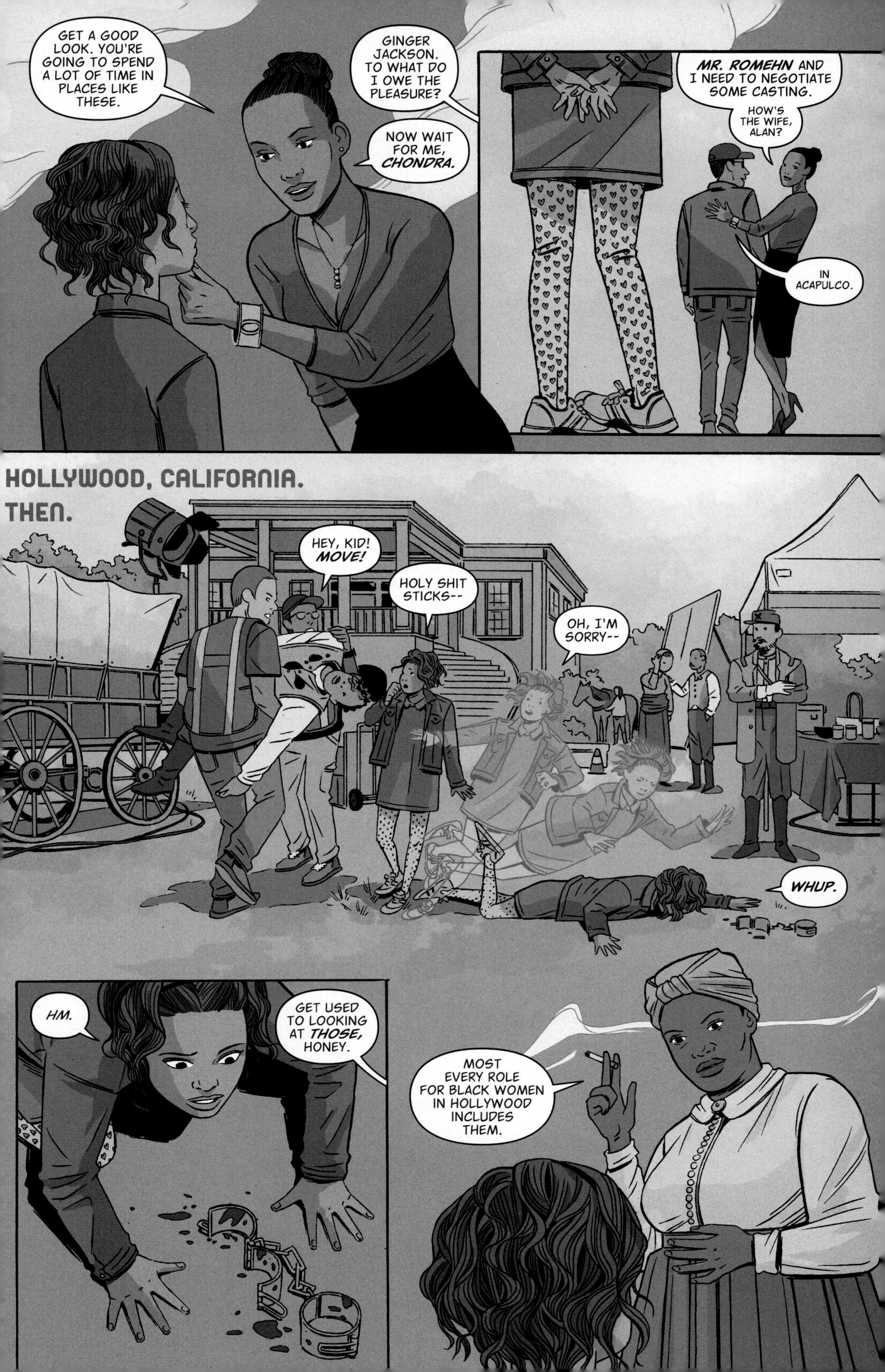
GET A GOOD LOOK. YOU'RE GOING TO SPEND A LOT OF TIME IN PLACES LIKE THESE.
GINGER JACKSON. TO WHAT DO I OWE THE PLEASURE?
NOW WAIT FOR ME, *CHONDRA.*
MR. ROMEHN AND I NEED TO NEGOTIATE SOME CASTING.
HOW'S THE WIFE, ALAN?
IN ACAPULCO.
HOLLYWOOD, CALIFORNIA.
THEN.
HEY, KID! *MOVE!*
HOLY SHIT STICKS--
OH, I'M SORRY--
WHUP.
HM.
GET USED TO LOOKING AT *THOSE,* HONEY.
MOST EVERY ROLE FOR BLACK WOMEN IN HOLLYWOOD INCLUDES THEM.

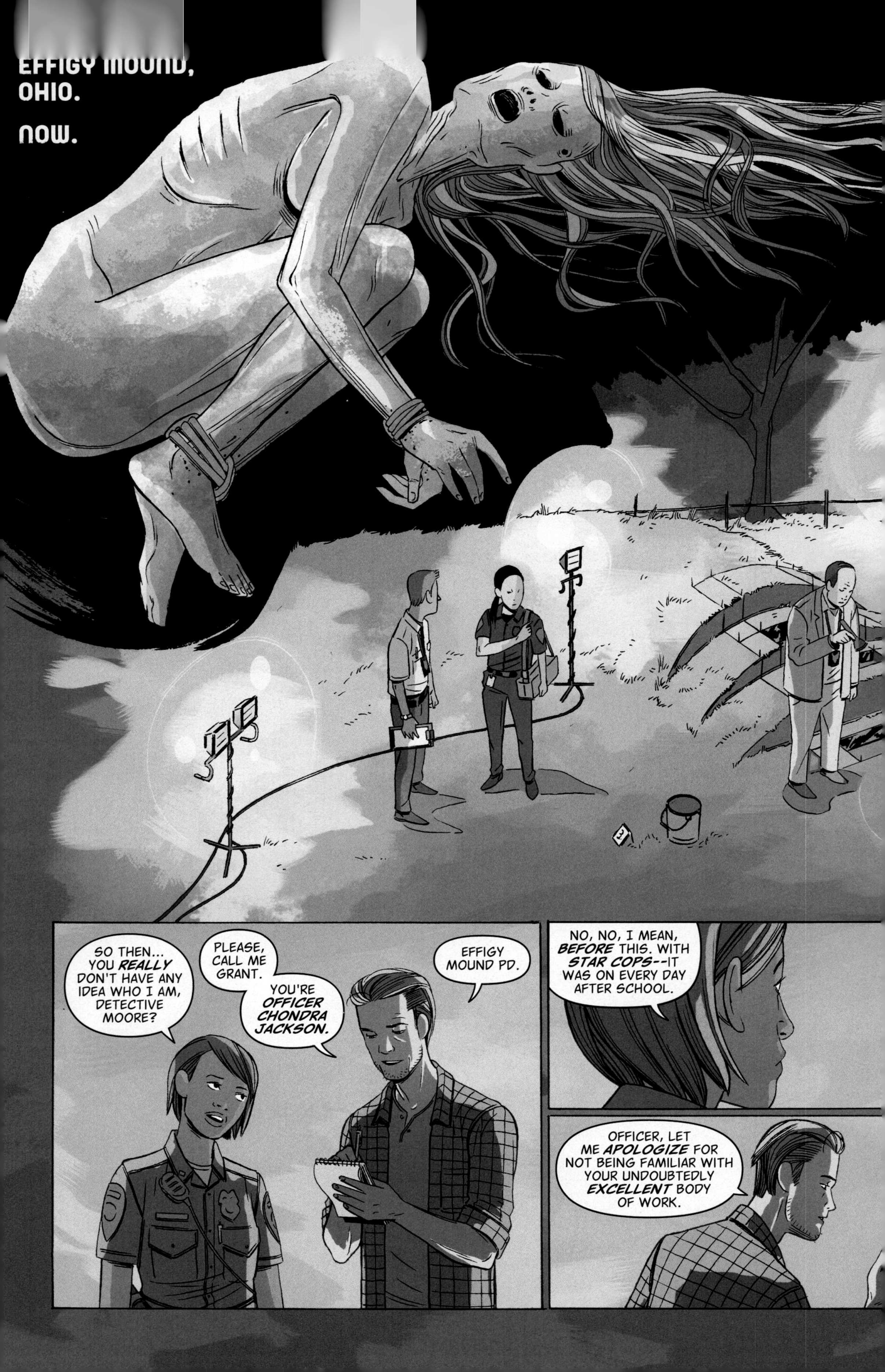
EFFIGY MOUND, OHIO.
NOW.
SO THEN... YOU REALLY DON'T HAVE ANY IDEA WHO I AM, DETECTIVE MOORE?
PLEASE, CALL ME GRANT.
YOU'RE OFFICER CHONDRA JACKSON.
EFFIGY MOUND PD.
NO, NO, I MEAN, BEFORE THIS. WITH STAR COPS--IT WAS ON EVERY DAY AFTER SCHOOL.
OFFICER, LET ME APOLOGIZE FOR NOT BEING FAMILIAR WITH YOUR UNDOUBTEDLY EXCELLENT BODY OF WORK.

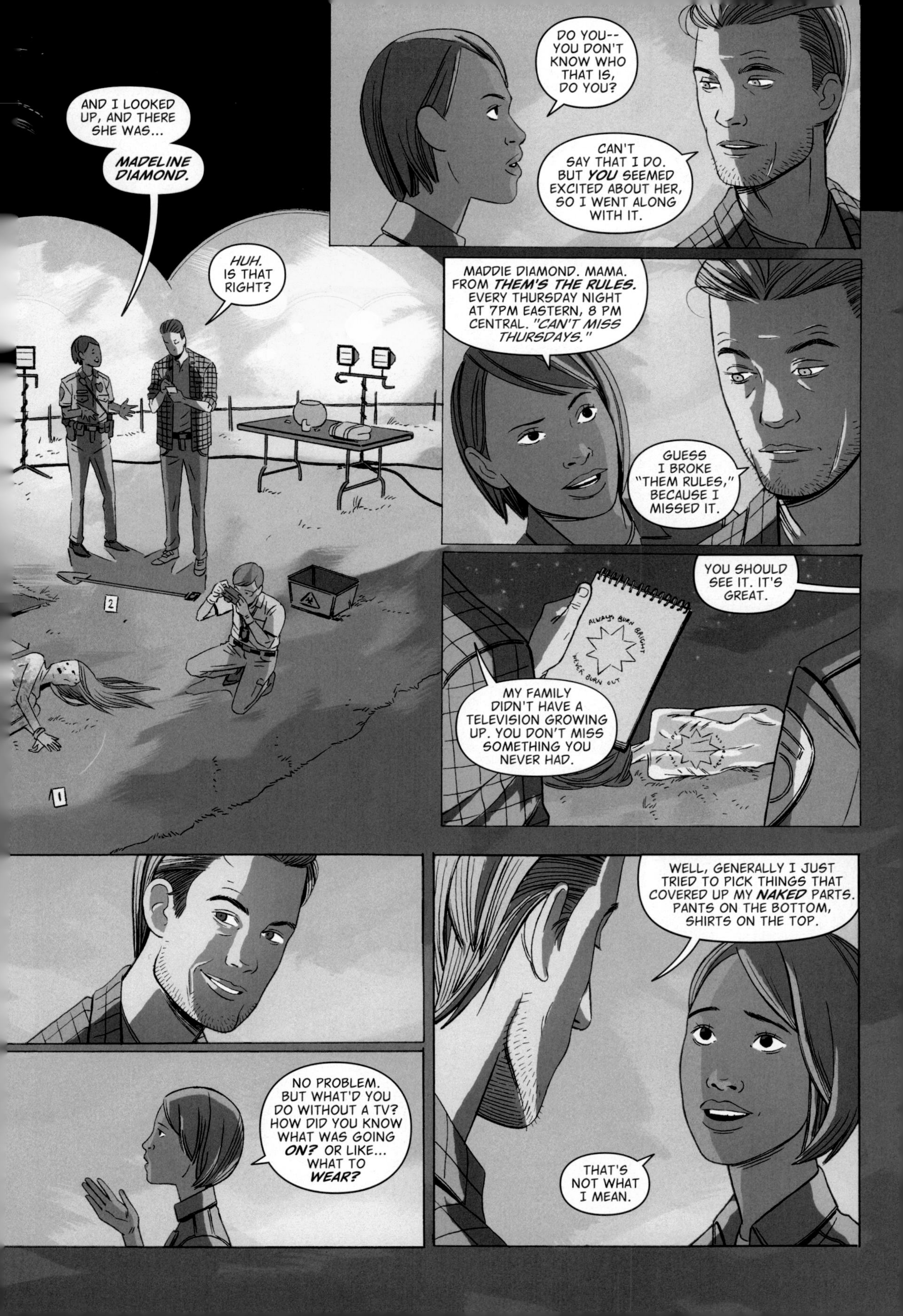
AND I LOOKED UP, AND THERE SHE WAS...
MADELINE DIAMOND.
HUH. IS THAT RIGHT?
DO YOU-- YOU DON'T KNOW WHO THAT IS, DO YOU?
CAN'T SAY THAT I DO. BUT *YOU* SEEMED EXCITED ABOUT HER, SO I WENT ALONG WITH IT.
MADDIE DIAMOND. MAMA. FROM *THEM'S THE RULES.* EVERY THURSDAY NIGHT AT 7PM EASTERN, 8 PM CENTRAL. *"CAN'T MISS THURSDAYS."*
GUESS I BROKE "THEM RULES," BECAUSE I MISSED IT.
YOU SHOULD SEE IT. IT'S GREAT.
ALWAYS BURN BRIGHT NEVER BURN OUT
MY FAMILY DIDN'T HAVE A TELEVISION GROWING UP. YOU DON'T MISS SOMETHING YOU NEVER HAD.
NO PROBLEM. BUT WHAT'D YOU DO WITHOUT A TV? HOW DID YOU KNOW WHAT WAS GOING *ON?* OR LIKE... WHAT TO *WEAR?*
WELL, GENERALLY I JUST TRIED TO PICK THINGS THAT COVERED UP MY *NAKED* PARTS. PANTS ON THE BOTTOM, SHIRTS ON THE TOP.
THAT'S NOT WHAT I MEAN.

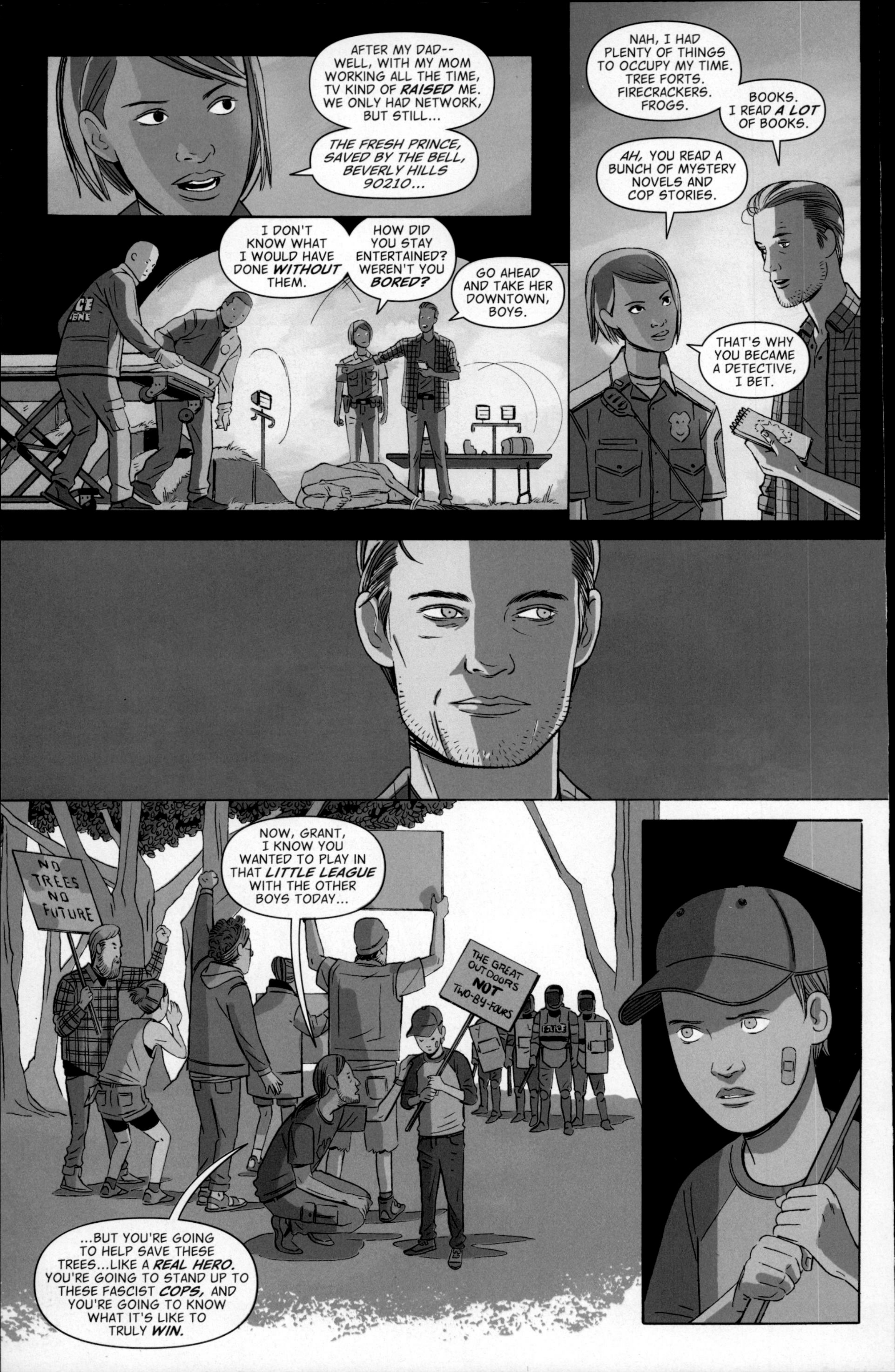
AFTER MY DAD-- WELL, WITH MY MOM WORKING ALL THE TIME, TV KIND OF *RAISED* ME. WE ONLY HAD NETWORK, BUT STILL...
THE FRESH PRINCE, SAVED BY THE BELL, BEVERLY HILLS 90210...
I DON'T KNOW WHAT I WOULD HAVE DONE *WITHOUT* THEM.
HOW DID YOU STAY ENTERTAINED? WEREN'T YOU *BORED?*
GO AHEAD AND TAKE HER DOWNTOWN, BOYS.
NAH, I HAD PLENTY OF THINGS TO OCCUPY MY TIME. TREE FORTS. FIRECRACKERS. FROGS.
BOOKS. I READ *A LOT* OF BOOKS.
AH, YOU READ A BUNCH OF MYSTERY NOVELS AND COP STORIES.
THAT'S WHY YOU BECAME A DETECTIVE, I BET.
NO TREES NO FUTURE
NOW, GRANT, I KNOW YOU WANTED TO PLAY IN THAT *LITTLE LEAGUE* WITH THE OTHER BOYS TODAY...
THE GREAT OUTDOORS *NOT* TWO-BY-FOURS
...BUT YOU'RE GOING TO HELP SAVE THESE TREES...LIKE A *REAL HERO.* YOU'RE GOING TO STAND UP TO THESE FASCIST *COPS,* AND YOU'RE GOING TO KNOW WHAT IT'S LIKE TO TRULY *WIN.*

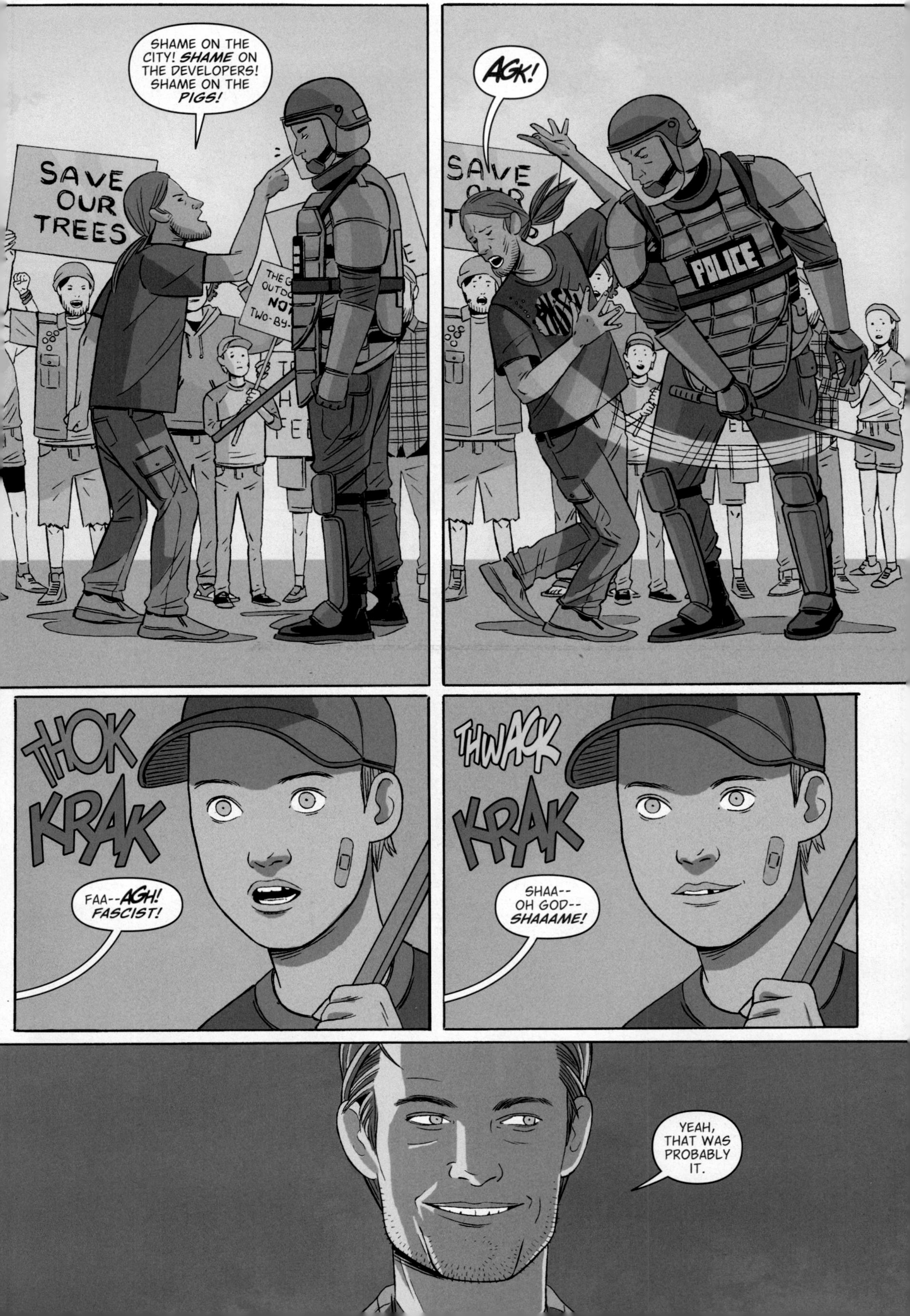
SHAME ON THE CITY! SHAME ON THE DEVELOPERS! SHAME ON THE PIGS!
SAVE OUR TREES
AGK!
POLICE
THOK
KRAK
FAA--AGH! FASCIST!
THWACK
KRAK
SHAA-- OH GOD-- SHAAAME!
YEAH, THAT WAS PROBABLY IT.

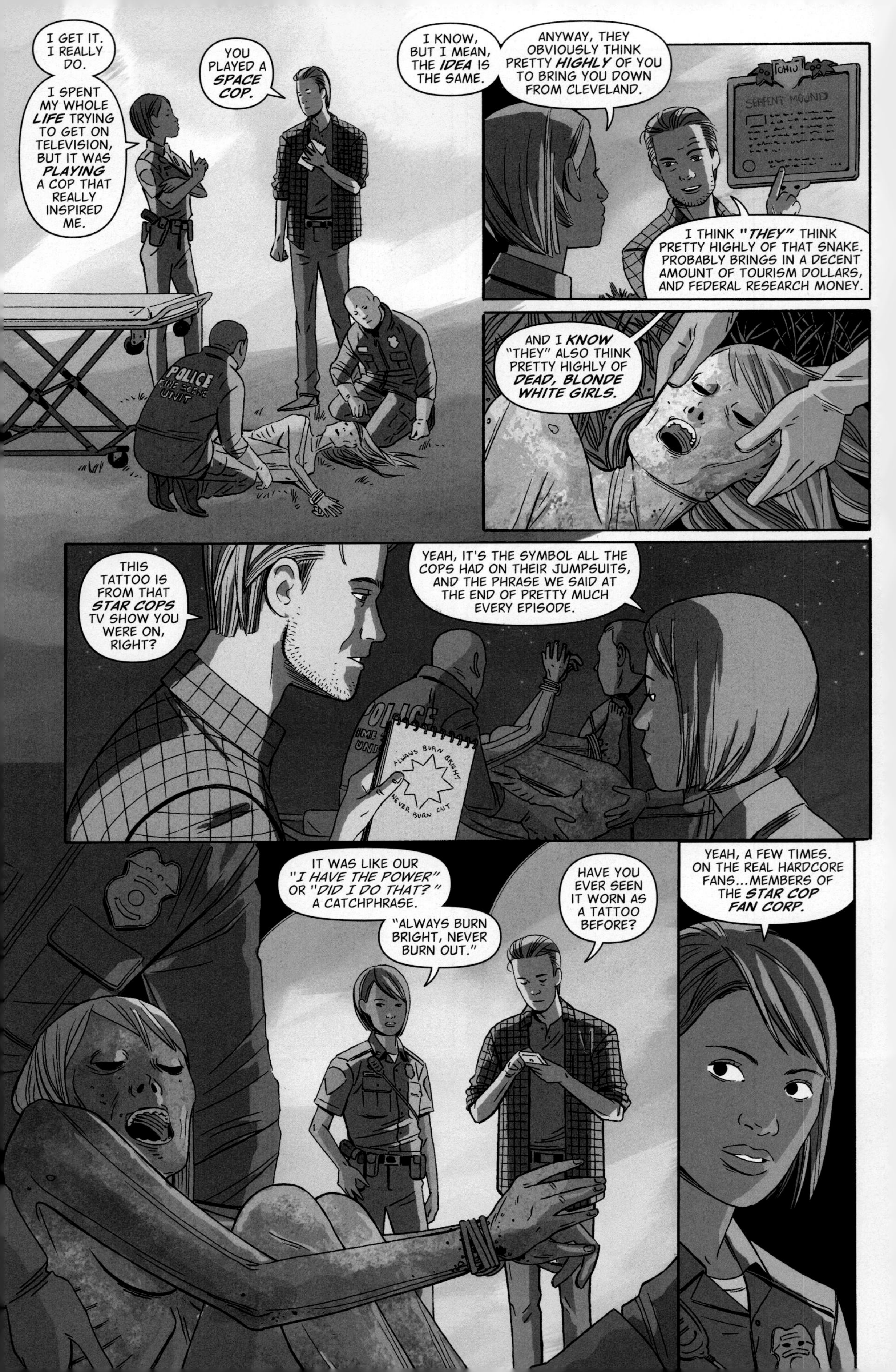

I GET IT. I REALLY DO.
I SPENT MY WHOLE LIFE TRYING TO GET ON TELEVISION, BUT IT WAS PLAYING A COP THAT REALLY INSPIRED ME.
YOU PLAYED A SPACE COP.
POLICE CRIME SCENE UNIT
I KNOW, BUT I MEAN, THE IDEA IS THE SAME.
ANYWAY, THEY OBVIOUSLY THINK PRETTY HIGHLY OF YOU TO BRING YOU DOWN FROM CLEVELAND.
OHIO
SERPENT MOUND
I THINK "THEY" THINK PRETTY HIGHLY OF THAT SNAKE. PROBABLY BRINGS IN A DECENT AMOUNT OF TOURISM DOLLARS, AND FEDERAL RESEARCH MONEY.
AND I KNOW "THEY" ALSO THINK PRETTY HIGHLY OF DEAD, BLONDE WHITE GIRLS.
THIS TATTOO IS FROM THAT STAR COPS TV SHOW YOU WERE ON, RIGHT?
YEAH, IT'S THE SYMBOL ALL THE COPS HAD ON THEIR JUMPSUITS, AND THE PHRASE WE SAID AT THE END OF PRETTY MUCH EVERY EPISODE.
ALWAYS BURN BRIGHT NEVER BURN OUT
IT WAS LIKE OUR "I HAVE THE POWER" OR "DID I DO THAT?" A CATCHPHRASE.
"ALWAYS BURN BRIGHT, NEVER BURN OUT."
HAVE YOU EVER SEEN IT WORN AS A TATTOO BEFORE?
YEAH, A FEW TIMES. ON THE REAL HARDCORE FANS...MEMBERS OF THE STAR COP FAN CORP.

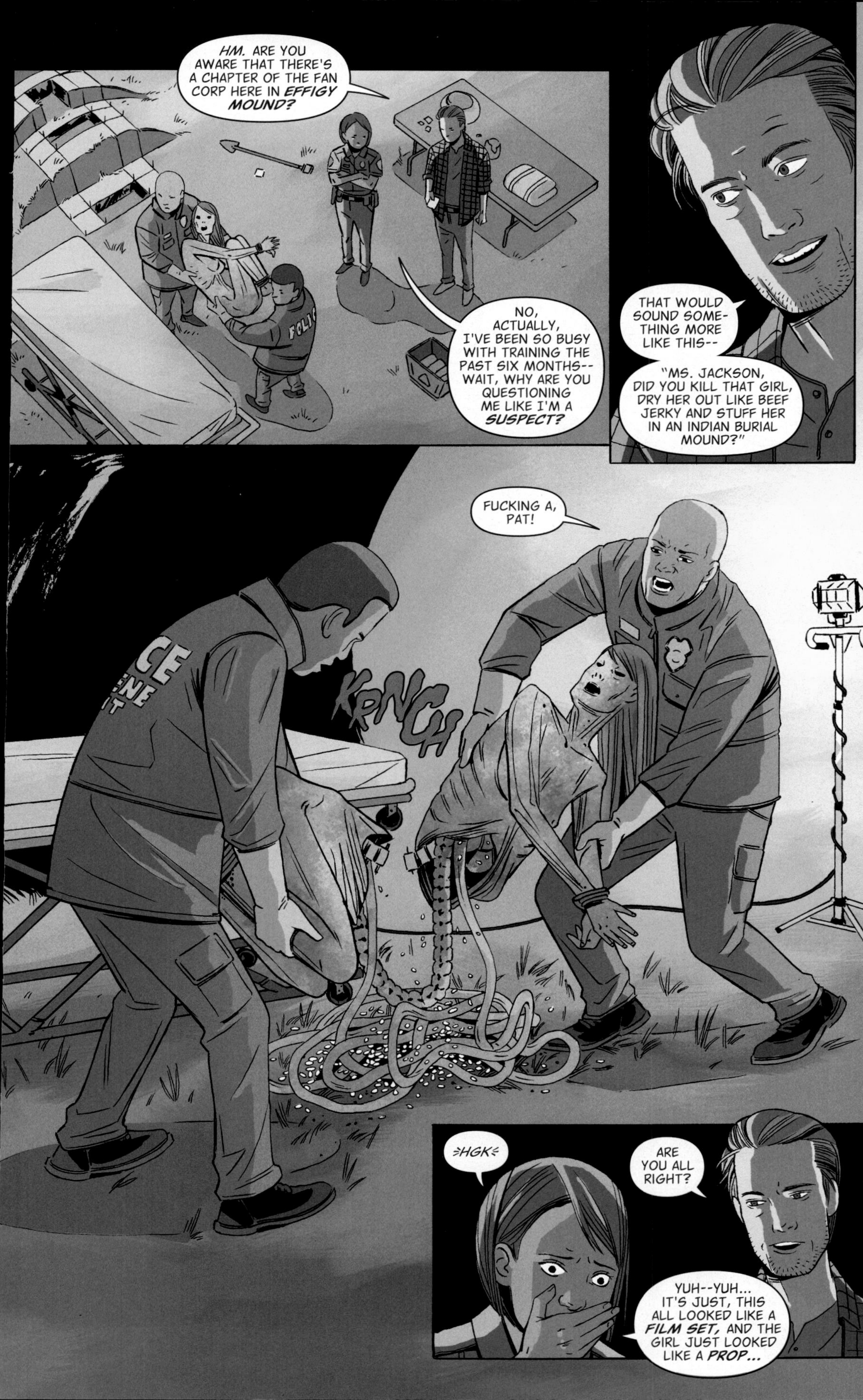
HM. ARE YOU AWARE THAT THERE'S A CHAPTER OF THE FAN CORP HERE IN EFFIGY MOUND?
NO, ACTUALLY, I'VE BEEN SO BUSY WITH TRAINING THE PAST SIX MONTHS-- WAIT, WHY ARE YOU QUESTIONING ME LIKE I'M A SUSPECT?
THAT WOULD SOUND SOMETHING MORE LIKE THIS--
"MS. JACKSON, DID YOU KILL THAT GIRL, DRY HER OUT LIKE BEEF JERKY AND STUFF HER IN AN INDIAN BURIAL MOUND?"
FUCKING A, PAT!
KRNCH
HGK
ARE YOU ALL RIGHT?
YUH--YUH... IT'S JUST, THIS ALL LOOKED LIKE A FILM SET, AND THE GIRL JUST LOOKED LIKE A PROP...

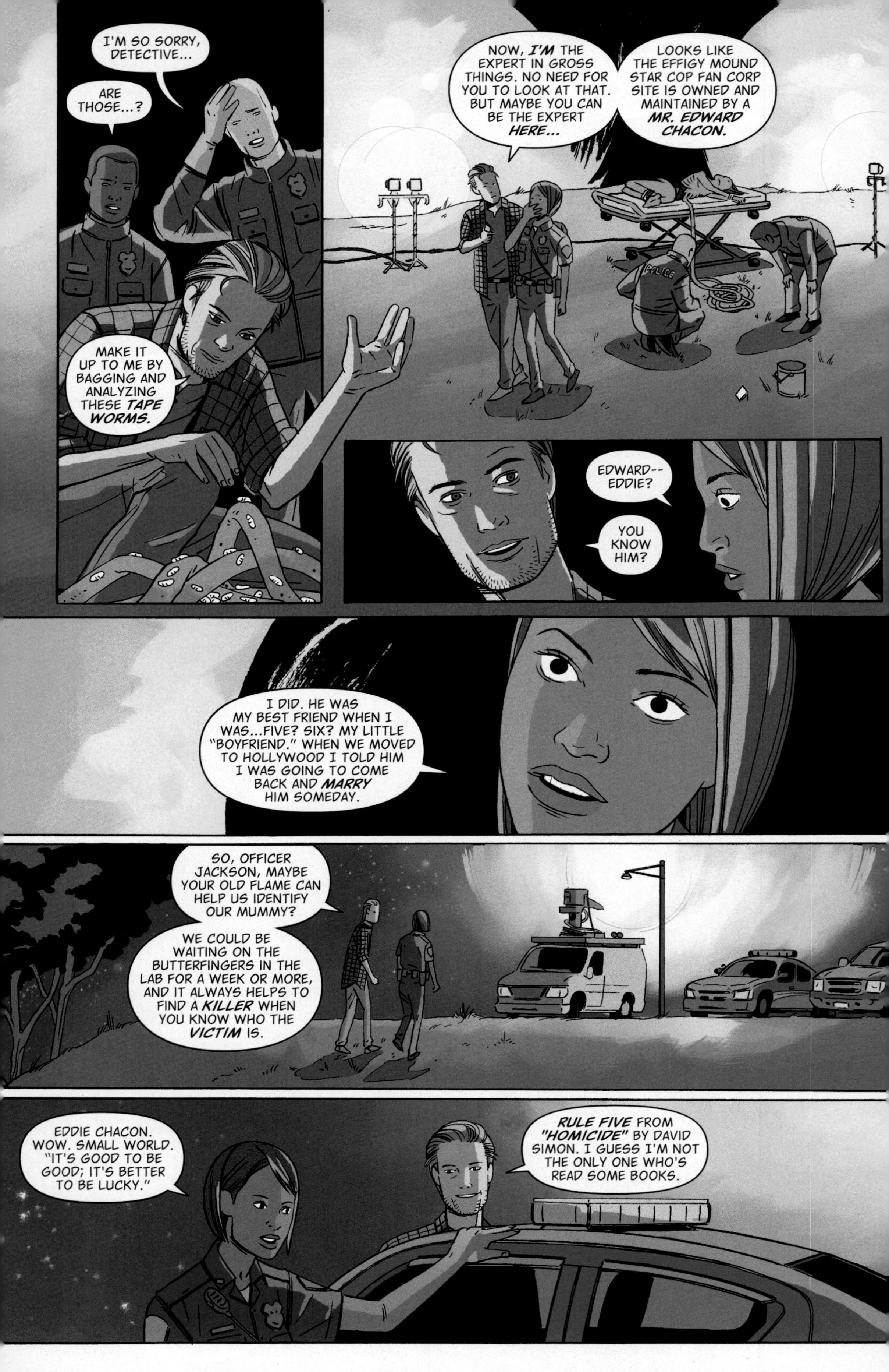
I'M SO SORRY, DETECTIVE...
ARE THOSE...?
MAKE IT UP TO ME BY BAGGING AND ANALYZING THESE TAPE WORMS.
NOW, I'M THE EXPERT IN GROSS THINGS. NO NEED FOR YOU TO LOOK AT THAT. BUT MAYBE YOU CAN BE THE EXPERT HERE...
LOOKS LIKE THE EFFIGY MOUND STAR COP FAN CORP SITE IS OWNED AND MAINTAINED BY A MR. EDWARD CHACON.
POLICE
EDWARD-- EDDIE?
YOU KNOW HIM?
I DID. HE WAS MY BEST FRIEND WHEN I WAS...FIVE? SIX? MY LITTLE "BOYFRIEND." WHEN WE MOVED TO HOLLYWOOD I TOLD HIM I WAS GOING TO COME BACK AND MARRY HIM SOMEDAY.
SO, OFFICER JACKSON, MAYBE YOUR OLD FLAME CAN HELP US IDENTIFY OUR MUMMY?
WE COULD BE WAITING ON THE BUTTERFINGERS IN THE LAB FOR A WEEK OR MORE, AND IT ALWAYS HELPS TO FIND A KILLER WHEN YOU KNOW WHO THE VICTIM IS.
EDDIE CHACON. WOW. SMALL WORLD. "IT'S GOOD TO BE GOOD; IT'S BETTER TO BE LUCKY."
RULE FIVE FROM "HOMICIDE" BY DAVID SIMON. I GUESS I'M NOT THE ONLY ONE WHO'S READ SOME BOOKS.

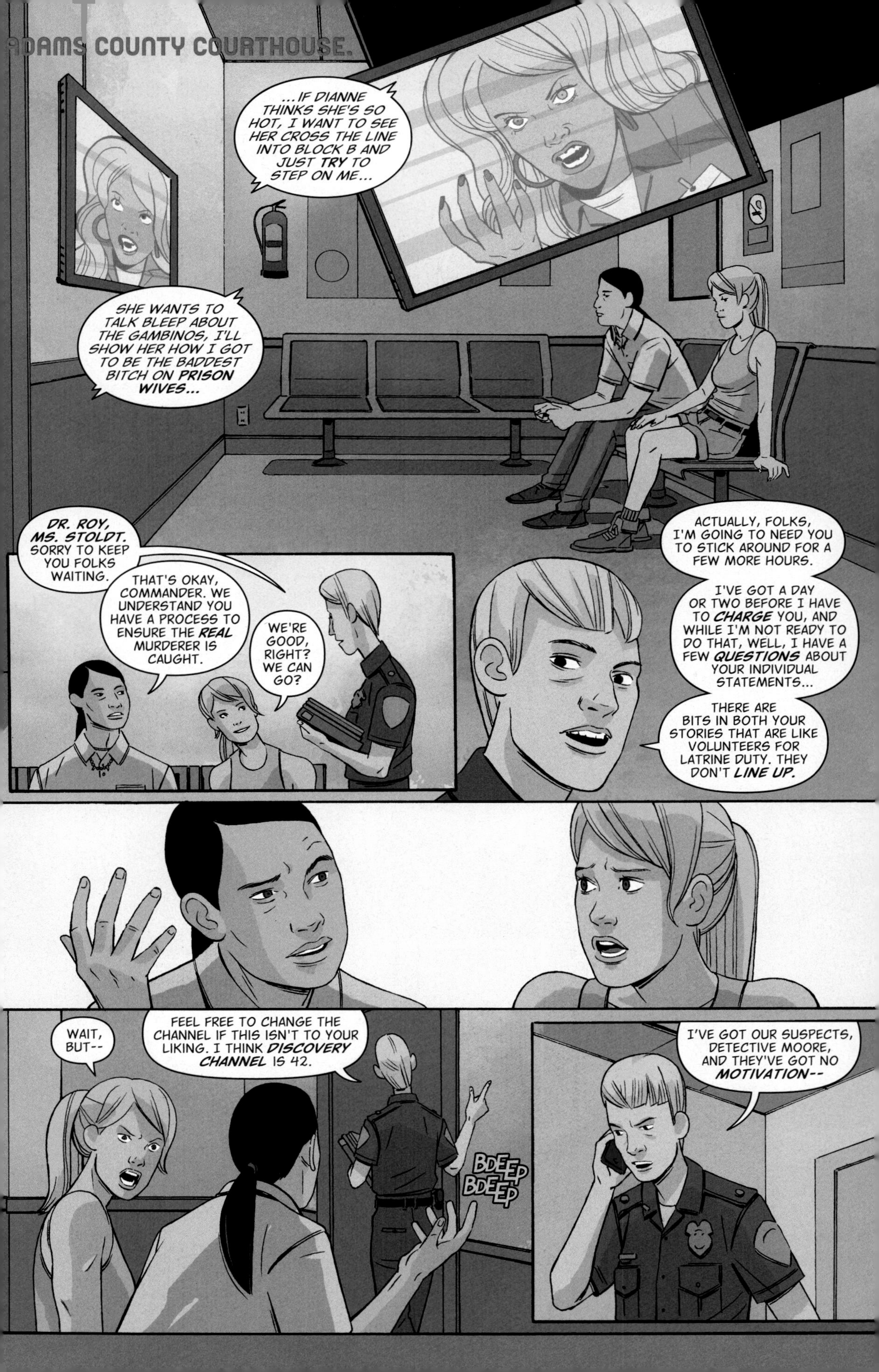
ADAMS COUNTY COURTHOUSE.
...IF DIANNE THINKS SHE'S SO HOT, I WANT TO SEE HER CROSS THE LINE INTO BLOCK B AND JUST TRY TO STEP ON ME...
SHE WANTS TO TALK BLEEP ABOUT THE GAMBINOS, I'LL SHOW HER HOW I GOT TO BE THE BADDEST BITCH ON PRISON WIVES...
DR. ROY, MS. STOLDT. SORRY TO KEEP YOU FOLKS WAITING.
THAT'S OKAY, COMMANDER. WE UNDERSTAND YOU HAVE A PROCESS TO ENSURE THE REAL MURDERER IS CAUGHT.
WE'RE GOOD, RIGHT? WE CAN GO?
ACTUALLY, FOLKS, I'M GOING TO NEED YOU TO STICK AROUND FOR A FEW MORE HOURS.
I'VE GOT A DAY OR TWO BEFORE I HAVE TO CHARGE YOU, AND WHILE I'M NOT READY TO DO THAT, WELL, I HAVE A FEW QUESTIONS ABOUT YOUR INDIVIDUAL STATEMENTS...
THERE ARE BITS IN BOTH YOUR STORIES THAT ARE LIKE VOLUNTEERS FOR LATRINE DUTY. THEY DON'T LINE UP.
WAIT, BUT--
FEEL FREE TO CHANGE THE CHANNEL IF THIS ISN'T TO YOUR LIKING. I THINK DISCOVERY CHANNEL IS 42.
BDEEP BDEEP
I'VE GOT OUR SUSPECTS, DETECTIVE MOORE, AND THEY'VE GOT NO MOTIVATION--

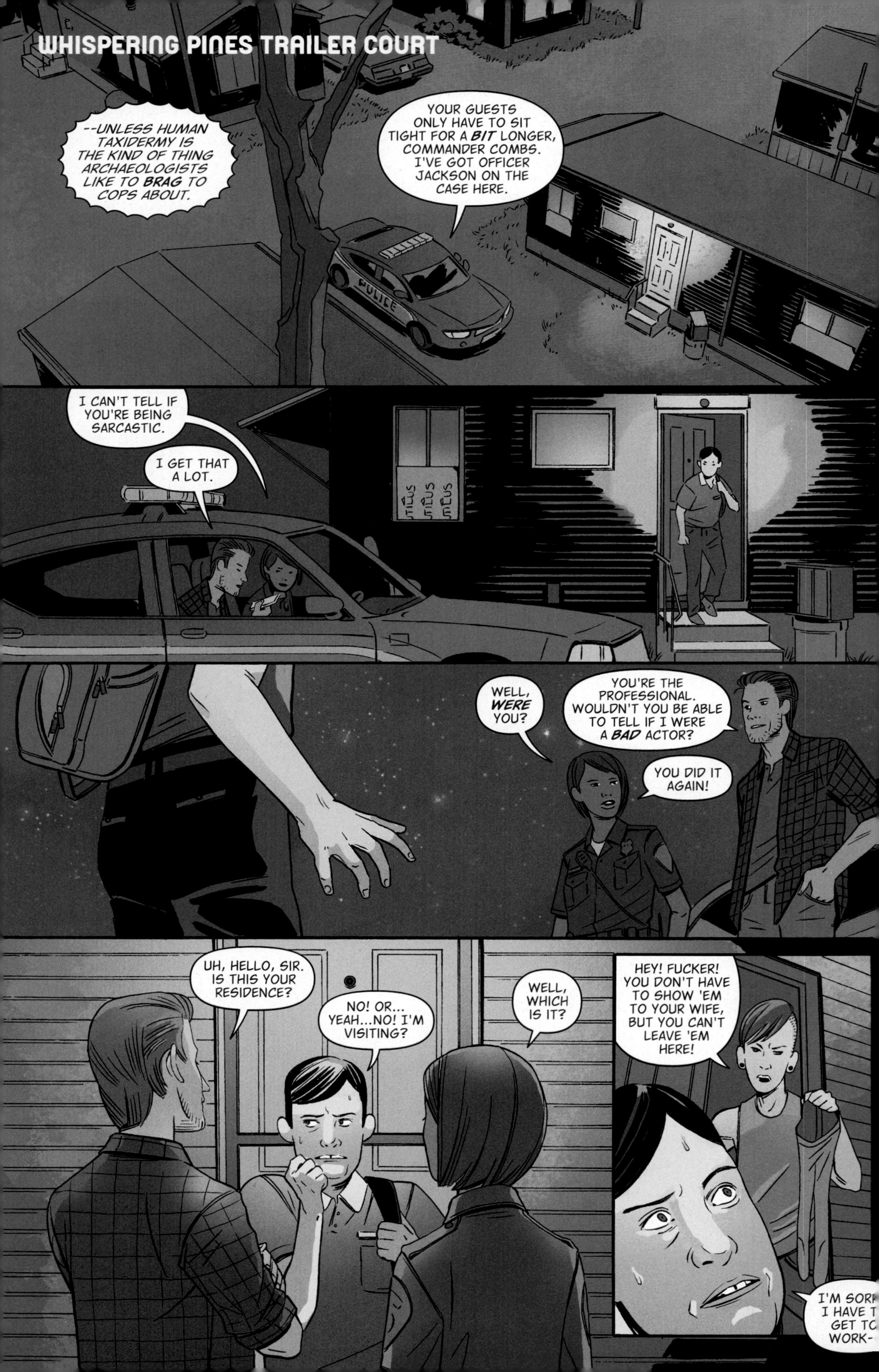
WHISPERING PINES TRAILER COURT
--UNLESS HUMAN TAXIDERMY IS THE KIND OF THING ARCHAEOLOGISTS LIKE TO BRAG TO COPS ABOUT.
YOUR GUESTS ONLY HAVE TO SIT TIGHT FOR A BIT LONGER, COMMANDER COMBS. I'VE GOT OFFICER JACKSON ON THE CASE HERE.
POLICE
I CAN'T TELL IF YOU'RE BEING SARCASTIC.
I GET THAT A LOT.
WELL, WERE YOU?
YOU'RE THE PROFESSIONAL. WOULDN'T YOU BE ABLE TO TELL IF I WERE A BAD ACTOR?
YOU DID IT AGAIN!
UH, HELLO, SIR. IS THIS YOUR RESIDENCE?
NO! OR... YEAH...NO! I'M VISITING?
WELL, WHICH IS IT?
HEY! FUCKER! YOU DON'T HAVE TO SHOW 'EM TO YOUR WIFE, BUT YOU CAN'T LEAVE 'EM HERE!
I'M SORR I HAVE T GET TO WORK-

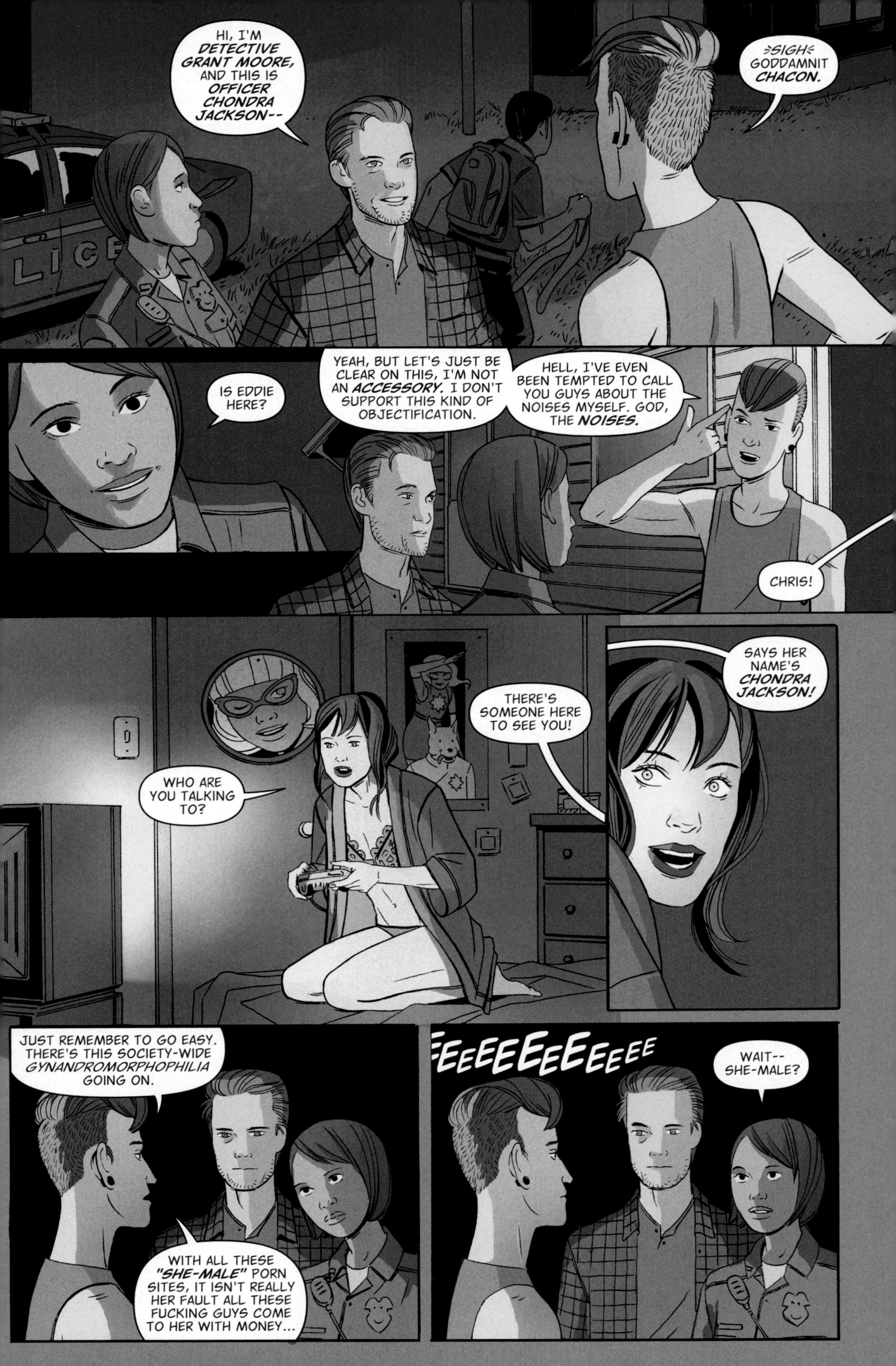
HI, I'M DETECTIVE GRANT MOORE, AND THIS IS OFFICER CHONDRA JACKSON--
SIGH GODDAMNIT CHACON.
POLICE
IS EDDIE HERE?
YEAH, BUT LET'S JUST BE CLEAR ON THIS, I'M NOT AN ACCESSORY. I DON'T SUPPORT THIS KIND OF OBJECTIFICATION.
HELL, I'VE EVEN BEEN TEMPTED TO CALL YOU GUYS ABOUT THE NOISES MYSELF. GOD, THE NOISES.
CHRIS!
WHO ARE YOU TALKING TO?
THERE'S SOMEONE HERE TO SEE YOU!
SAYS HER NAME'S CHONDRA JACKSON!
JUST REMEMBER TO GO EASY. THERE'S THIS SOCIETY-WIDE GYNANDROMORPHOPHILIA GOING ON.
WITH ALL THESE "SHE-MALE" PORN SITES, IT ISN'T REALLY HER FAULT ALL THESE FUCKING GUYS COME TO HER WITH MONEY...
EEEEEEEEEEEE
WAIT-- SHE-MALE?

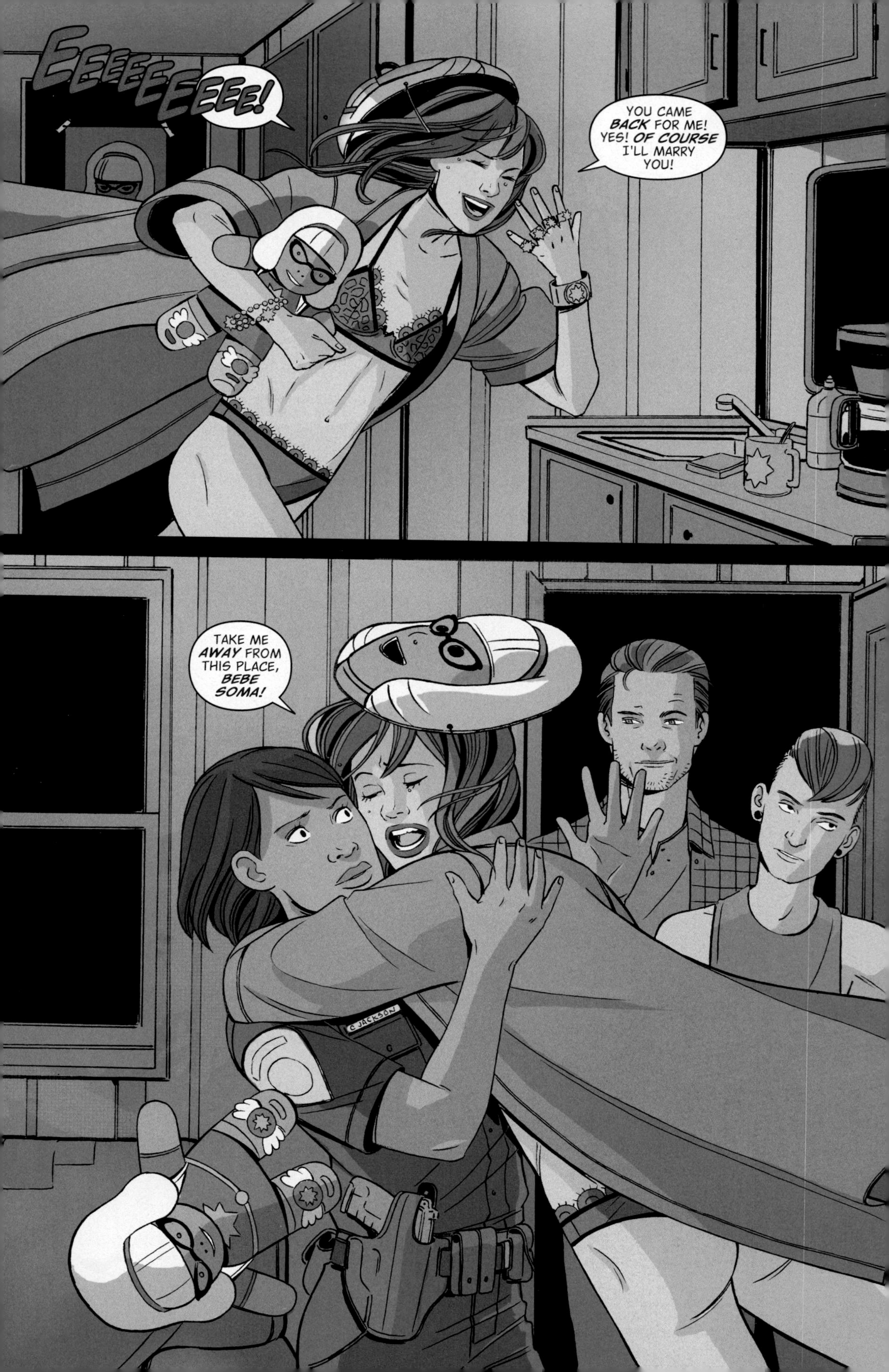
EEEEEEEEEEE!
YOU CAME BACK FOR ME! YES! OF COURSE I'LL MARRY YOU!
TAKE ME AWAY FROM THIS PLACE, BEBE SOMA!
C JACKSON

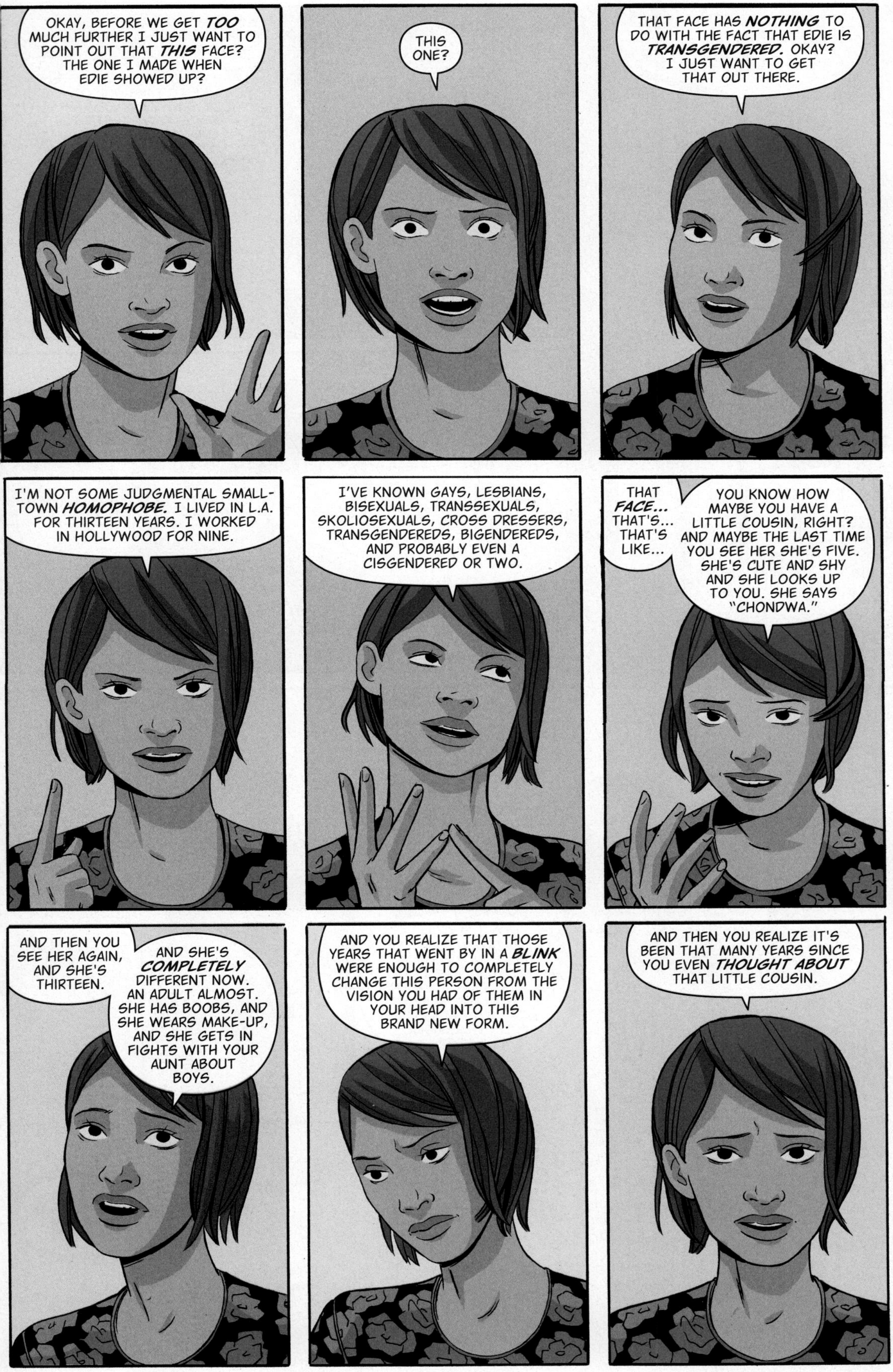
OKAY, BEFORE WE GET *TOO* MUCH FURTHER I JUST WANT TO POINT OUT THAT *THIS* FACE? THE ONE I MADE WHEN EDIE SHOWED UP?
THIS ONE?
THAT FACE HAS *NOTHING* TO DO WITH THE FACT THAT EDIE IS *TRANSGENDERED.* OKAY? I JUST WANT TO GET THAT OUT THERE.
I'M NOT SOME JUDGMENTAL SMALL-TOWN *HOMOPHOBE.* I LIVED IN L.A. FOR THIRTEEN YEARS. I WORKED IN HOLLYWOOD FOR NINE.
I'VE KNOWN GAYS, LESBIANS, BISEXUALS, TRANSSEXUALS, SKOLIOSEXUALS, CROSS DRESSERS, TRANSGENDEREDS, BIGENDEREDS, AND PROBABLY EVEN A CISGENDERED OR TWO.
THAT *FACE...* THAT'S... THAT'S LIKE...
YOU KNOW HOW MAYBE YOU HAVE A LITTLE COUSIN, RIGHT? AND MAYBE THE LAST TIME YOU SEE HER SHE'S FIVE. SHE'S CUTE AND SHY AND SHE LOOKS UP TO YOU. SHE SAYS "CHONDWA."
AND THEN YOU SEE HER AGAIN, AND SHE'S THIRTEEN.
AND SHE'S *COMPLETELY* DIFFERENT NOW. AN ADULT ALMOST. SHE HAS BOOBS, AND SHE WEARS MAKE-UP, AND SHE GETS IN FIGHTS WITH YOUR AUNT ABOUT BOYS.
AND YOU REALIZE THAT THOSE YEARS THAT WENT BY IN A *BLINK* WERE ENOUGH TO COMPLETELY CHANGE THIS PERSON FROM THE VISION YOU HAD OF THEM IN YOUR HEAD INTO THIS BRAND NEW FORM.
AND THEN YOU REALIZE IT'S BEEN THAT MANY YEARS SINCE YOU EVEN *THOUGHT ABOUT* THAT LITTLE COUSIN.

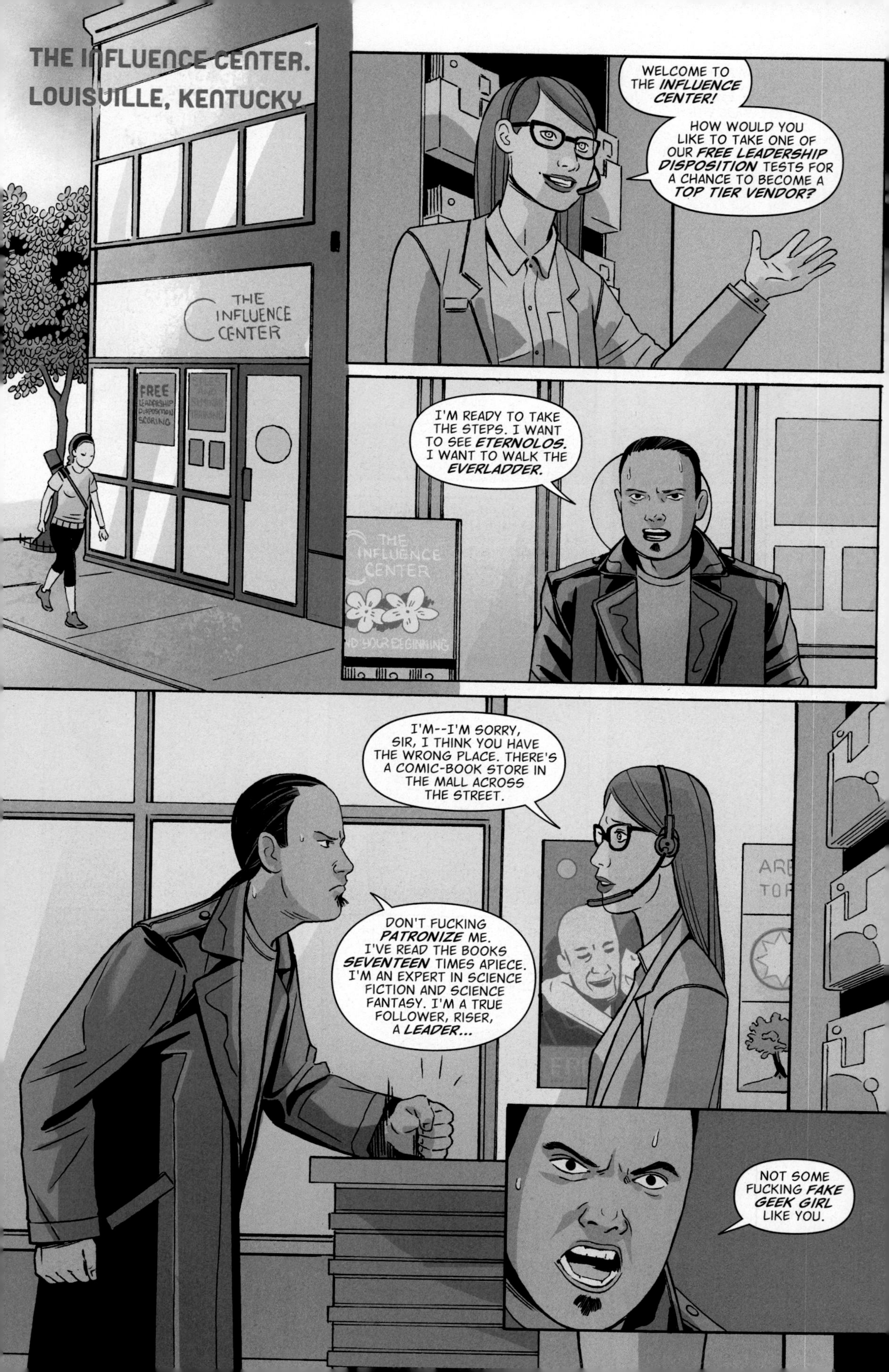
THE INFLUENCE CENTER.
LOUISVILLE, KENTUCKY.
THE INFLUENCE CENTER
FREE LEADERSHIP DISPOSITION SCORING
WELCOME TO THE INFLUENCE CENTER!
HOW WOULD YOU LIKE TO TAKE ONE OF OUR FREE LEADERSHIP DISPOSITION TESTS FOR A CHANCE TO BECOME A TOP TIER VENDOR?
I'M READY TO TAKE THE STEPS. I WANT TO SEE ETERNOLOS. I WANT TO WALK THE EVERLADDER.
THE INFLUENCE CENTER
I'M--I'M SORRY, SIR, I THINK YOU HAVE THE WRONG PLACE. THERE'S A COMIC-BOOK STORE IN THE MALL ACROSS THE STREET.
DON'T FUCKING PATRONIZE ME. I'VE READ THE BOOKS SEVENTEEN TIMES APIECE. I'M AN EXPERT IN SCIENCE FICTION AND SCIENCE FANTASY. I'M A TRUE FOLLOWER, RISER, A LEADER...
NOT SOME FUCKING FAKE GEEK GIRL LIKE YOU.

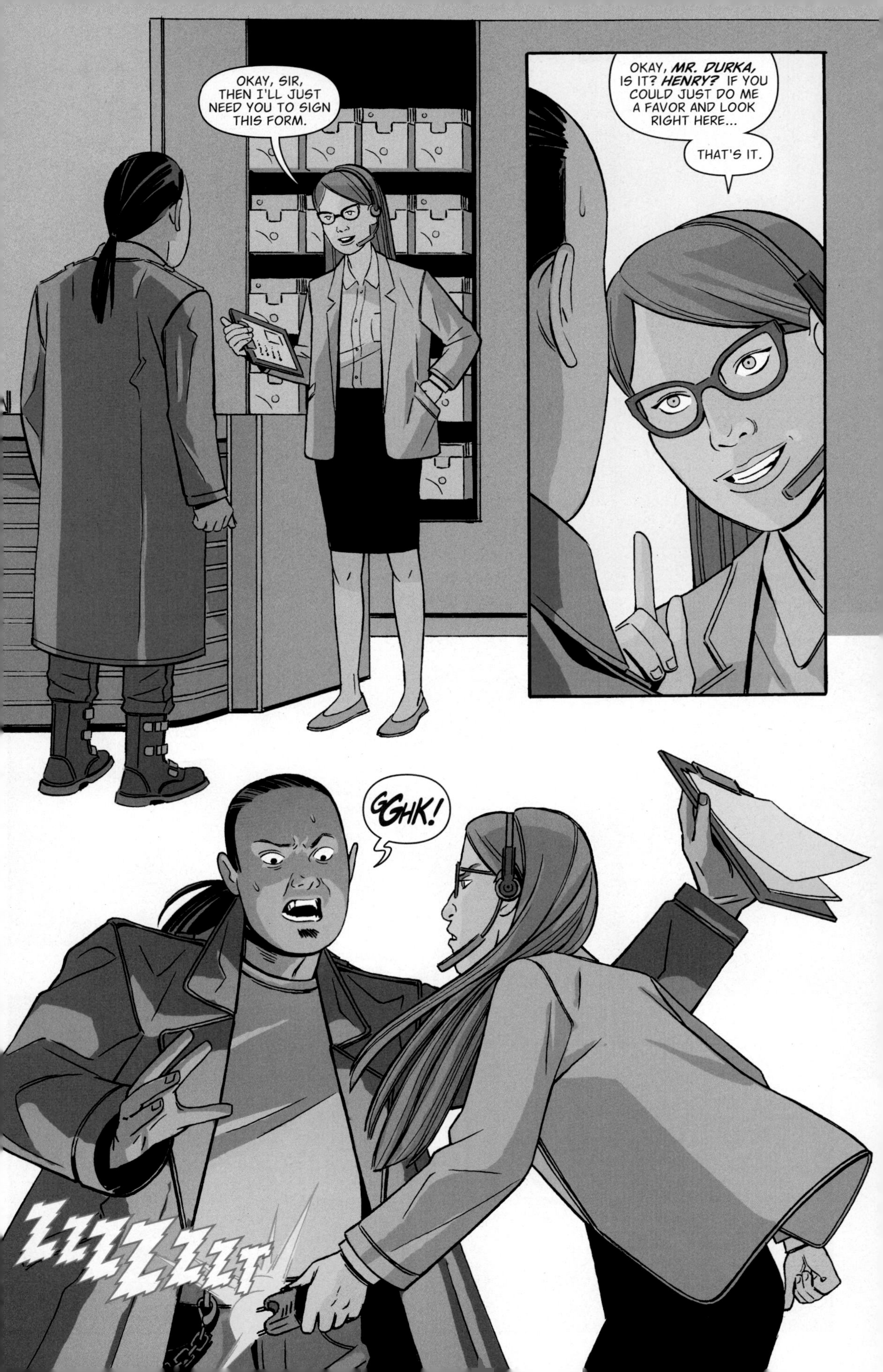
OKAY, SIR, THEN I'LL JUST NEED YOU TO SIGN THIS FORM.
OKAY, **MR. DURKA,** IS IT? **HENRY?** IF YOU COULD JUST DO ME A FAVOR AND LOOK RIGHT HERE...
THAT'S IT.
GGHK!
ZZZZZZZT

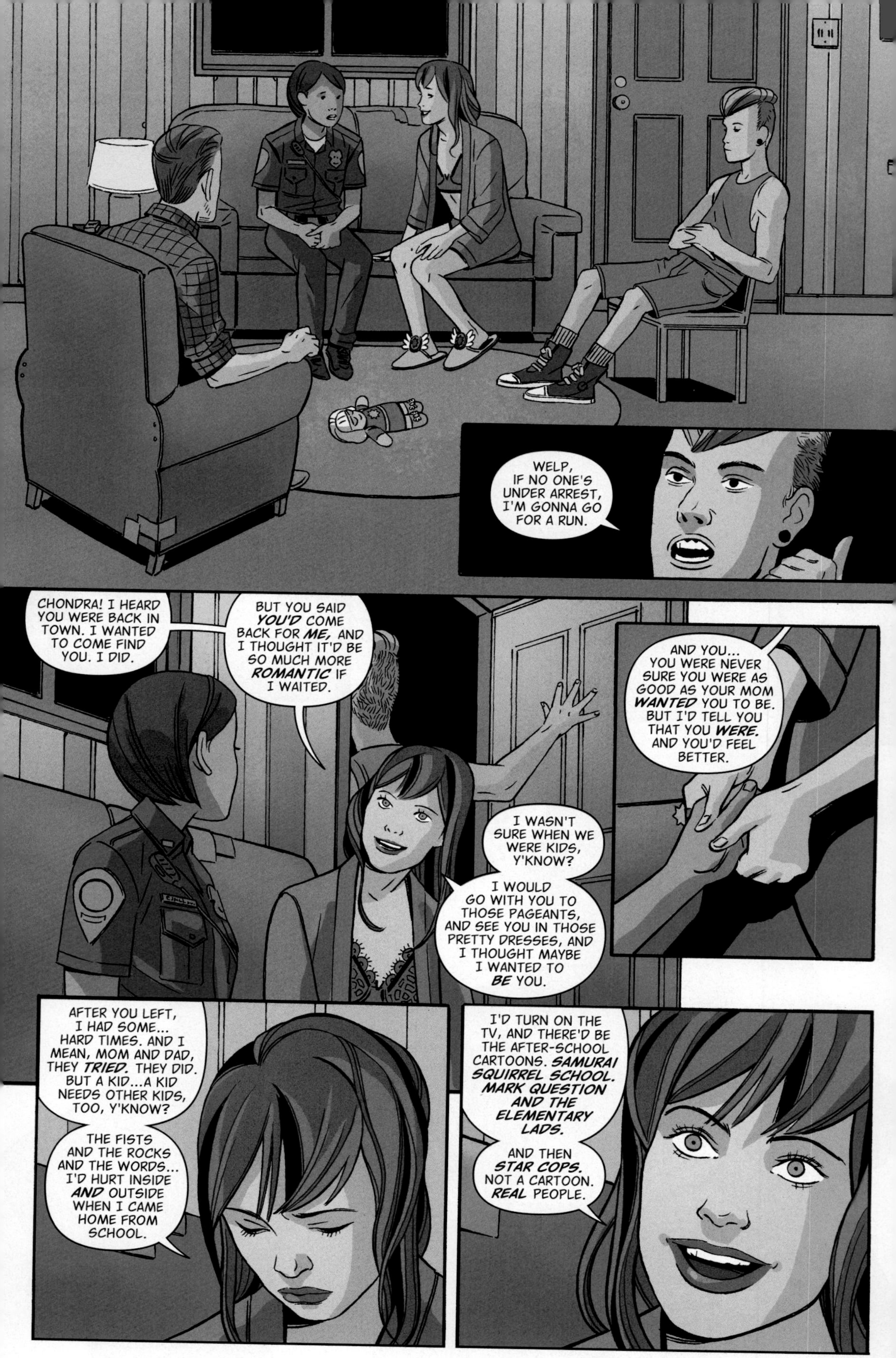
WELP, IF NO ONE'S UNDER ARREST, I'M GONNA GO FOR A RUN.
CHONDRA! I HEARD YOU WERE BACK IN TOWN. I WANTED TO COME FIND YOU. I DID.
BUT YOU SAID ***YOU'D*** COME BACK FOR ***ME,*** AND I THOUGHT IT'D BE SO MUCH MORE ***ROMANTIC*** IF I WAITED.
AND YOU... YOU WERE NEVER SURE YOU WERE AS GOOD AS YOUR MOM ***WANTED*** YOU TO BE. BUT I'D TELL YOU THAT YOU ***WERE.*** AND YOU'D FEEL BETTER.
I WASN'T SURE WHEN WE WERE KIDS, Y'KNOW?
I WOULD GO WITH YOU TO THOSE PAGEANTS, AND SEE YOU IN THOSE PRETTY DRESSES, AND I THOUGHT MAYBE I WANTED TO ***BE*** YOU.
AFTER YOU LEFT, I HAD SOME... HARD TIMES. AND I MEAN, MOM AND DAD, THEY ***TRIED.*** THEY DID. BUT A KID...A KID NEEDS OTHER KIDS, TOO, Y'KNOW?
THE FISTS AND THE ROCKS AND THE WORDS... I'D HURT INSIDE ***AND*** OUTSIDE WHEN I CAME HOME FROM SCHOOL.
I'D TURN ON THE TV, AND THERE'D BE THE AFTER-SCHOOL CARTOONS. ***SAMURAI SQUIRREL SCHOOL. MARK QUESTION AND THE ELEMENTARY LADS.***
AND THEN ***STAR COPS.*** NOT A CARTOON. ***REAL*** PEOPLE.

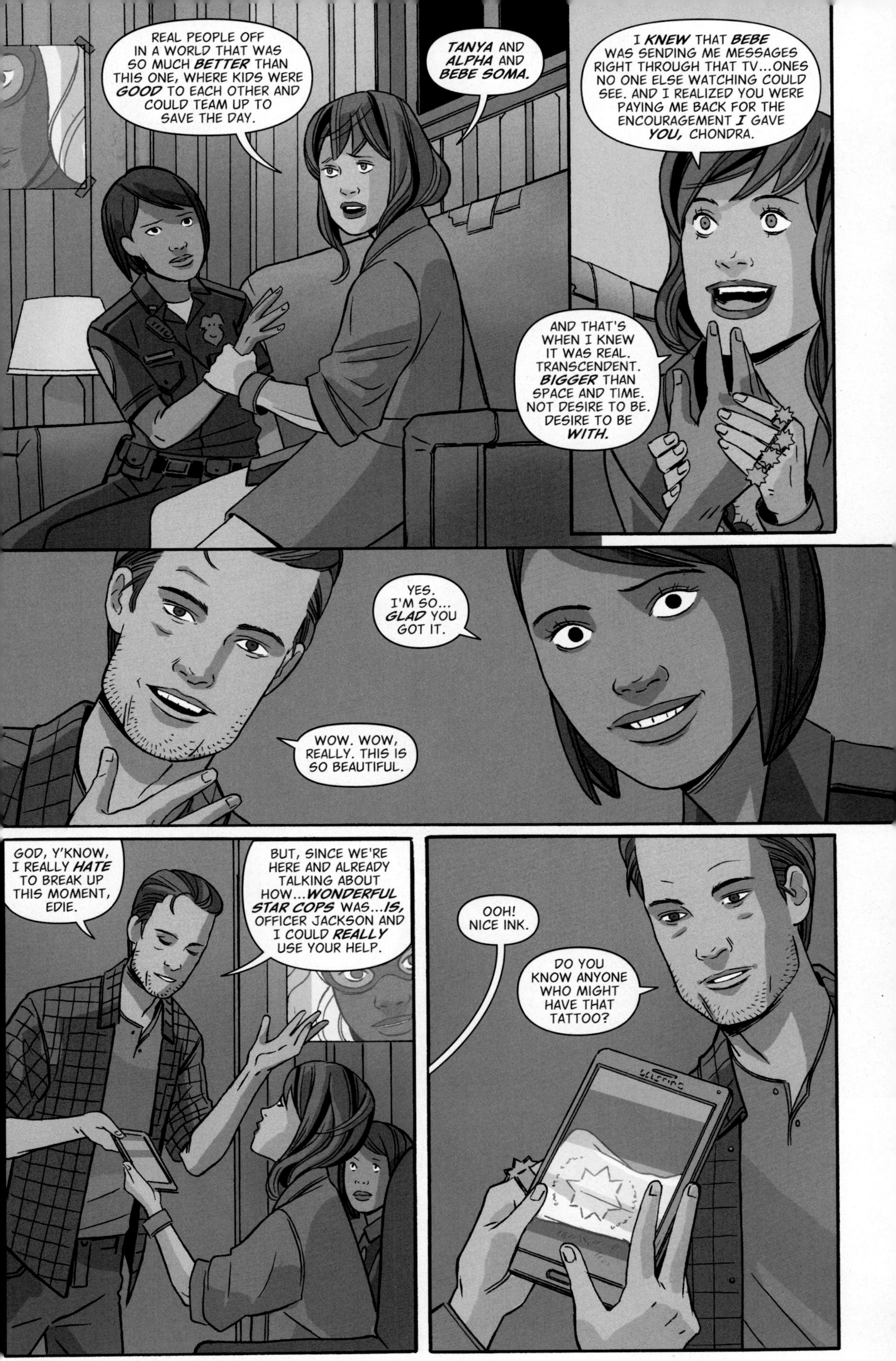
REAL PEOPLE OFF IN A WORLD THAT WAS SO MUCH **BETTER** THAN THIS ONE, WHERE KIDS WERE **GOOD** TO EACH OTHER AND COULD TEAM UP TO SAVE THE DAY.
TANYA AND **ALPHA** AND **BEBE SOMA.**
I **KNEW** THAT **BEBE** WAS SENDING ME MESSAGES RIGHT THROUGH THAT TV...ONES NO ONE ELSE WATCHING COULD SEE. AND I REALIZED YOU WERE PAYING ME BACK FOR THE ENCOURAGEMENT **I** GAVE **YOU,** CHONDRA.
AND THAT'S WHEN I KNEW IT WAS REAL. TRANSCENDENT. **BIGGER** THAN SPACE AND TIME. NOT DESIRE TO BE. DESIRE TO BE **WITH.**
WOW. WOW, REALLY. THIS IS SO BEAUTIFUL.
YES. I'M SO... **GLAD** YOU GOT IT.
GOD, Y'KNOW, I REALLY **HATE** TO BREAK UP THIS MOMENT, EDIE.
BUT, SINCE WE'RE HERE AND ALREADY TALKING ABOUT HOW...**WONDERFUL STAR COPS** WAS...**IS,** OFFICER JACKSON AND I COULD **REALLY** USE YOUR HELP.
OOH! NICE INK.
DO YOU KNOW ANYONE WHO MIGHT HAVE THAT TATTOO?

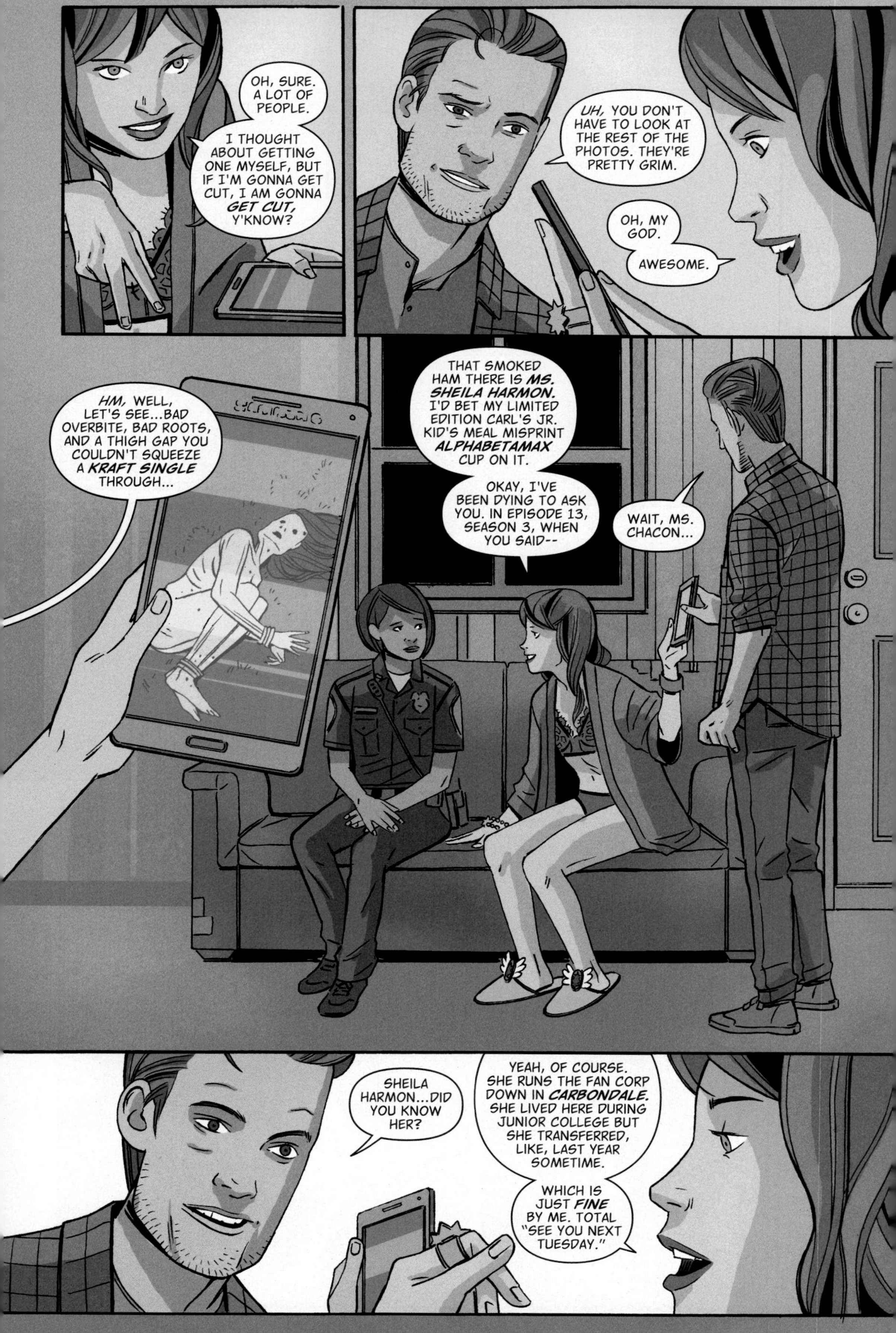
OH, SURE. A LOT OF PEOPLE.
I THOUGHT ABOUT GETTING ONE MYSELF, BUT IF I'M GONNA GET CUT, I AM GONNA GET CUT, Y'KNOW?
UH, YOU DON'T HAVE TO LOOK AT THE REST OF THE PHOTOS. THEY'RE PRETTY GRIM.
OH, MY GOD.
AWESOME.
HM, WELL, LET'S SEE...BAD OVERBITE, BAD ROOTS, AND A THIGH GAP YOU COULDN'T SQUEEZE A KRAFT SINGLE THROUGH...
THAT SMOKED HAM THERE IS MS. SHEILA HARMON. I'D BET MY LIMITED EDITION CARL'S JR. KID'S MEAL MISPRINT ALPHABETAMAX CUP ON IT.
OKAY, I'VE BEEN DYING TO ASK YOU. IN EPISODE 13, SEASON 3, WHEN YOU SAID--
WAIT, MS. CHACON...
SHEILA HARMON...DID YOU KNOW HER?
YEAH, OF COURSE. SHE RUNS THE FAN CORP DOWN IN CARBONDALE. SHE LIVED HERE DURING JUNIOR COLLEGE BUT SHE TRANSFERRED, LIKE, LAST YEAR SOMETIME.
WHICH IS JUST FINE BY ME. TOTAL "SEE YOU NEXT TUESDAY."

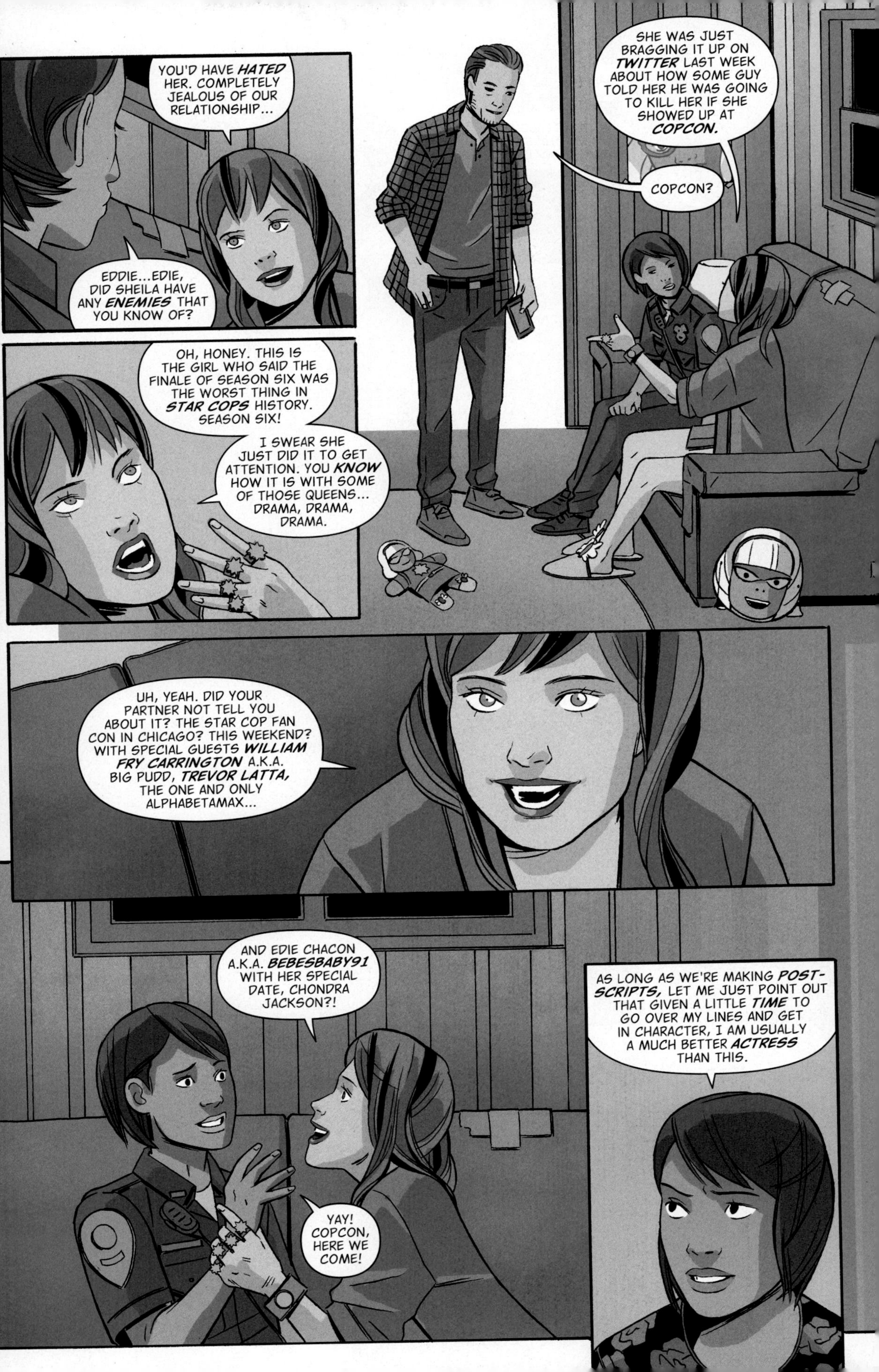
YOU'D HAVE HATED HER. COMPLETELY JEALOUS OF OUR RELATIONSHIP...
EDDIE...EDIE, DID SHEILA HAVE ANY ENEMIES THAT YOU KNOW OF?
SHE WAS JUST BRAGGING IT UP ON TWITTER LAST WEEK ABOUT HOW SOME GUY TOLD HER HE WAS GOING TO KILL HER IF SHE SHOWED UP AT COPCON.
COPCON?
OH, HONEY. THIS IS THE GIRL WHO SAID THE FINALE OF SEASON SIX WAS THE WORST THING IN STAR COPS HISTORY. SEASON SIX!
I SWEAR SHE JUST DID IT TO GET ATTENTION. YOU KNOW HOW IT IS WITH SOME OF THOSE QUEENS... DRAMA, DRAMA, DRAMA.
UH, YEAH. DID YOUR PARTNER NOT TELL YOU ABOUT IT? THE STAR COP FAN CON IN CHICAGO? THIS WEEKEND? WITH SPECIAL GUESTS WILLIAM FRY CARRINGTON A.K.A. BIG PUDD, TREVOR LATTA, THE ONE AND ONLY ALPHABETAMAX...
AND EDIE CHACON A.K.A. BEBESBABY91 WITH HER SPECIAL DATE, CHONDRA JACKSON?!
YAY! COPCON, HERE WE COME!
AS LONG AS WE'RE MAKING POST-SCRIPTS, LET ME JUST POINT OUT THAT GIVEN A LITTLE TIME TO GO OVER MY LINES AND GET IN CHARACTER, I AM USUALLY A MUCH BETTER ACTRESS THAN THIS.

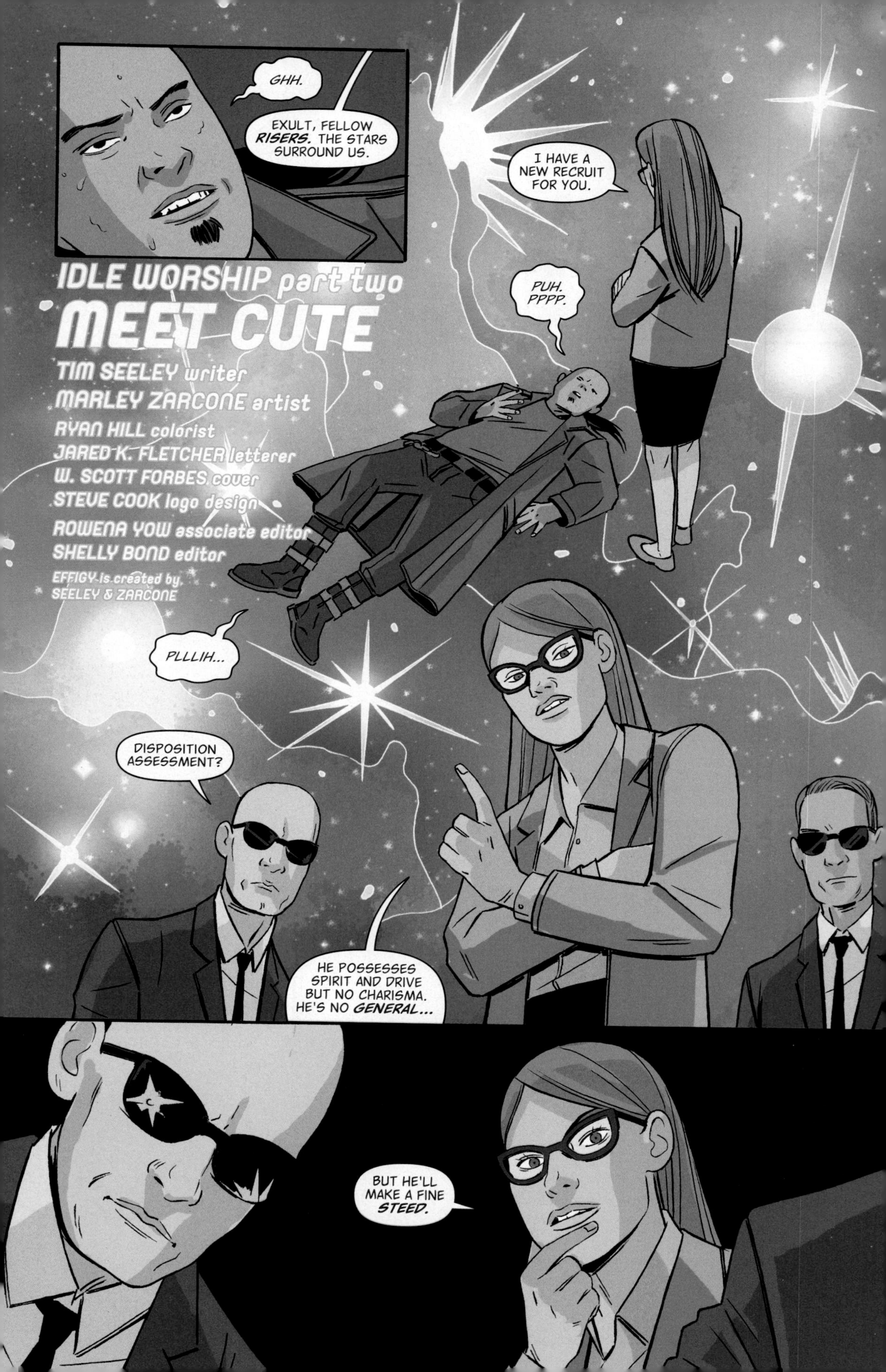
GHH.
EXULT, FELLOW RISERS. THE STARS SURROUND US.
I HAVE A NEW RECRUIT FOR YOU.
IDLE WORSHIP part two
MEET CUTE
TIM SEELEY writer
MARLEY ZARCONE artist
RYAN HILL colorist
JARED K. FLETCHER letterer
W. SCOTT FORBES cover
STEVE COOK logo design
ROWENA YOW associate editor
SHELLY BOND editor
EFFIGY is created by SEELEY & ZARCONE
PUH. PPPP.
PLLLIH...
DISPOSITION ASSESSMENT?
HE POSSESSES SPIRIT AND DRIVE BUT NO CHARISMA. HE'S NO GENERAL...
BUT HE'LL MAKE A FINE STEED.

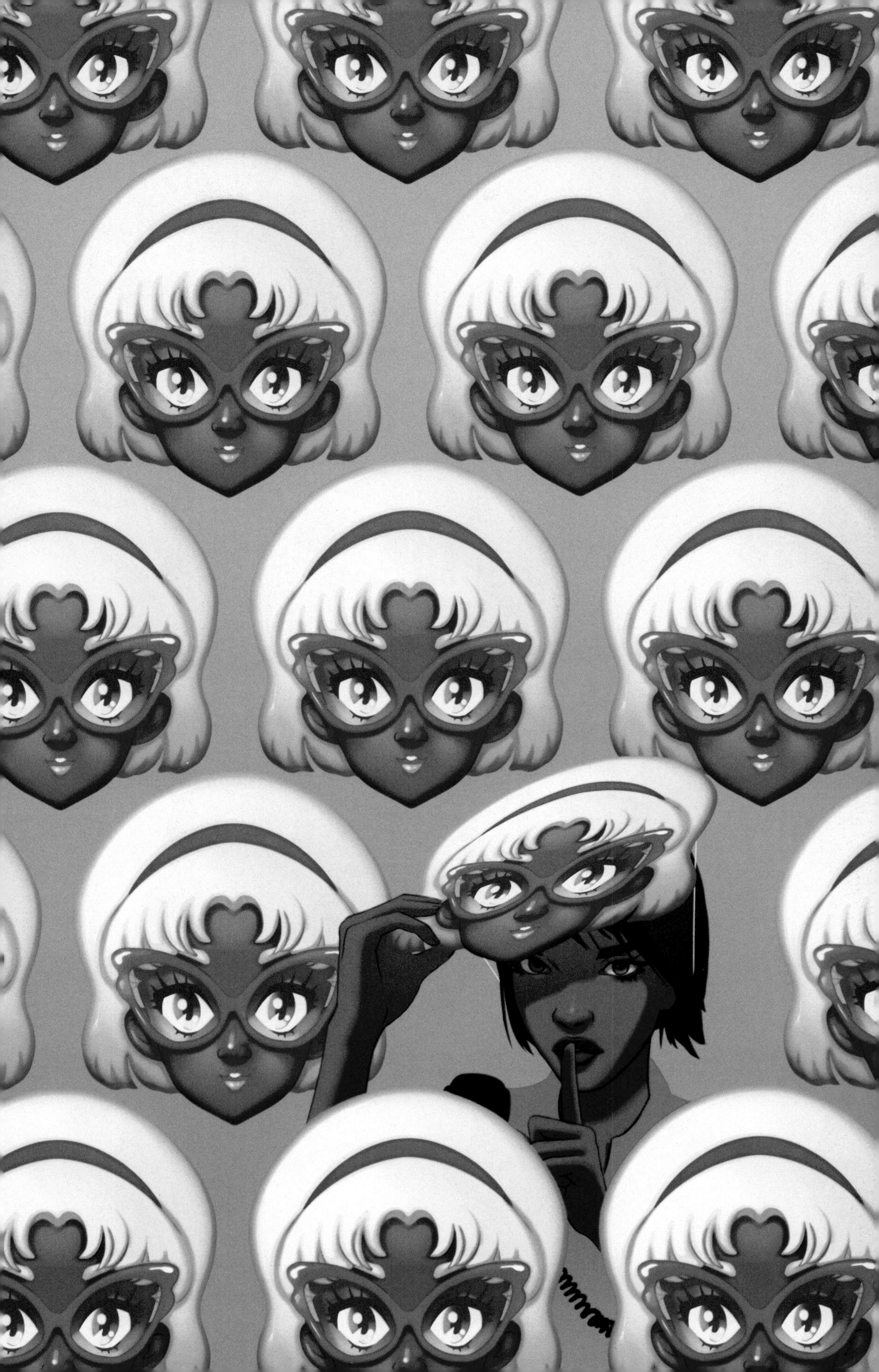

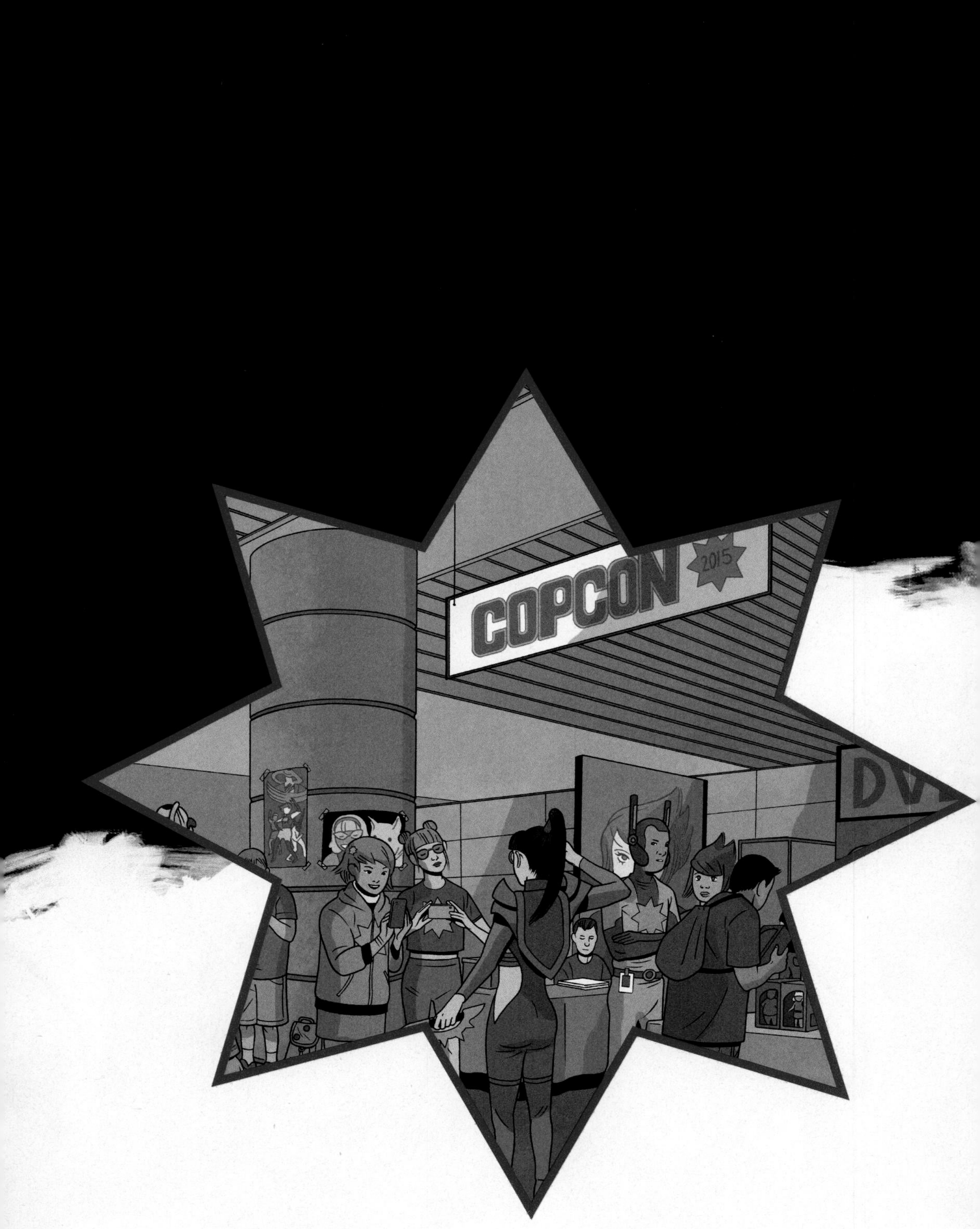
COPCON
2015

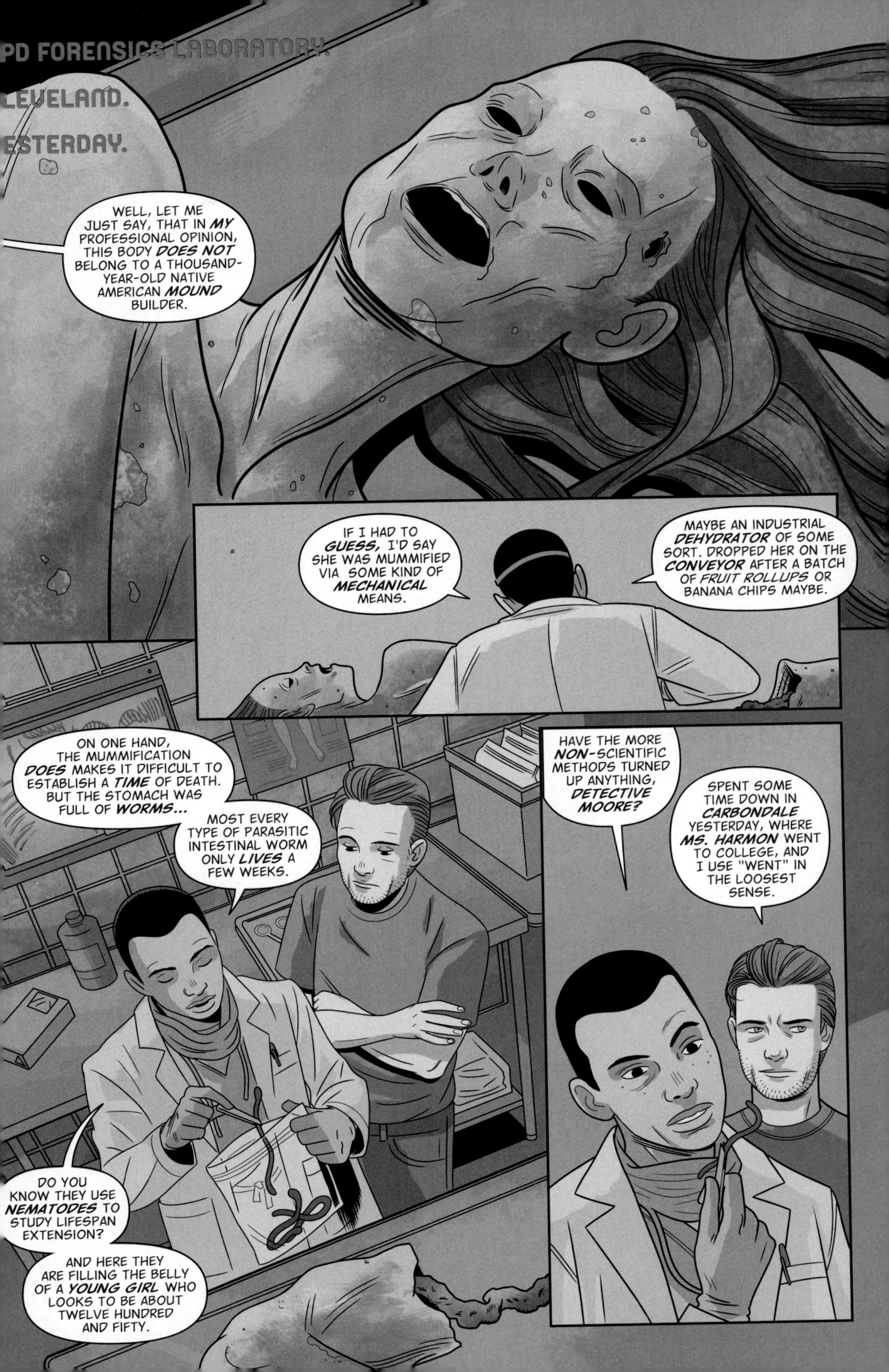
PD FORENSICS LABORATORY.
LEVELAND.
ESTERDAY.
WELL, LET ME JUST SAY, THAT IN MY PROFESSIONAL OPINION, THIS BODY DOES NOT BELONG TO A THOUSAND-YEAR-OLD NATIVE AMERICAN MOUND BUILDER.
IF I HAD TO GUESS, I'D SAY SHE WAS MUMMIFIED VIA SOME KIND OF MECHANICAL MEANS.
MAYBE AN INDUSTRIAL DEHYDRATOR OF SOME SORT. DROPPED HER ON THE CONVEYOR AFTER A BATCH OF FRUIT ROLLUPS OR BANANA CHIPS MAYBE.
ON ONE HAND, THE MUMMIFICATION DOES MAKES IT DIFFICULT TO ESTABLISH A TIME OF DEATH. BUT THE STOMACH WAS FULL OF WORMS...
MOST EVERY TYPE OF PARASITIC INTESTINAL WORM ONLY LIVES A FEW WEEKS.
DO YOU KNOW THEY USE NEMATODES TO STUDY LIFESPAN EXTENSION?
AND HERE THEY ARE FILLING THE BELLY OF A YOUNG GIRL WHO LOOKS TO BE ABOUT TWELVE HUNDRED AND FIFTY.
HAVE THE MORE NON-SCIENTIFIC METHODS TURNED UP ANYTHING, DETECTIVE MOORE?
SPENT SOME TIME DOWN IN CARBONDALE YESTERDAY, WHERE MS. HARMON WENT TO COLLEGE, AND I USE "WENT" IN THE LOOSEST SENSE.

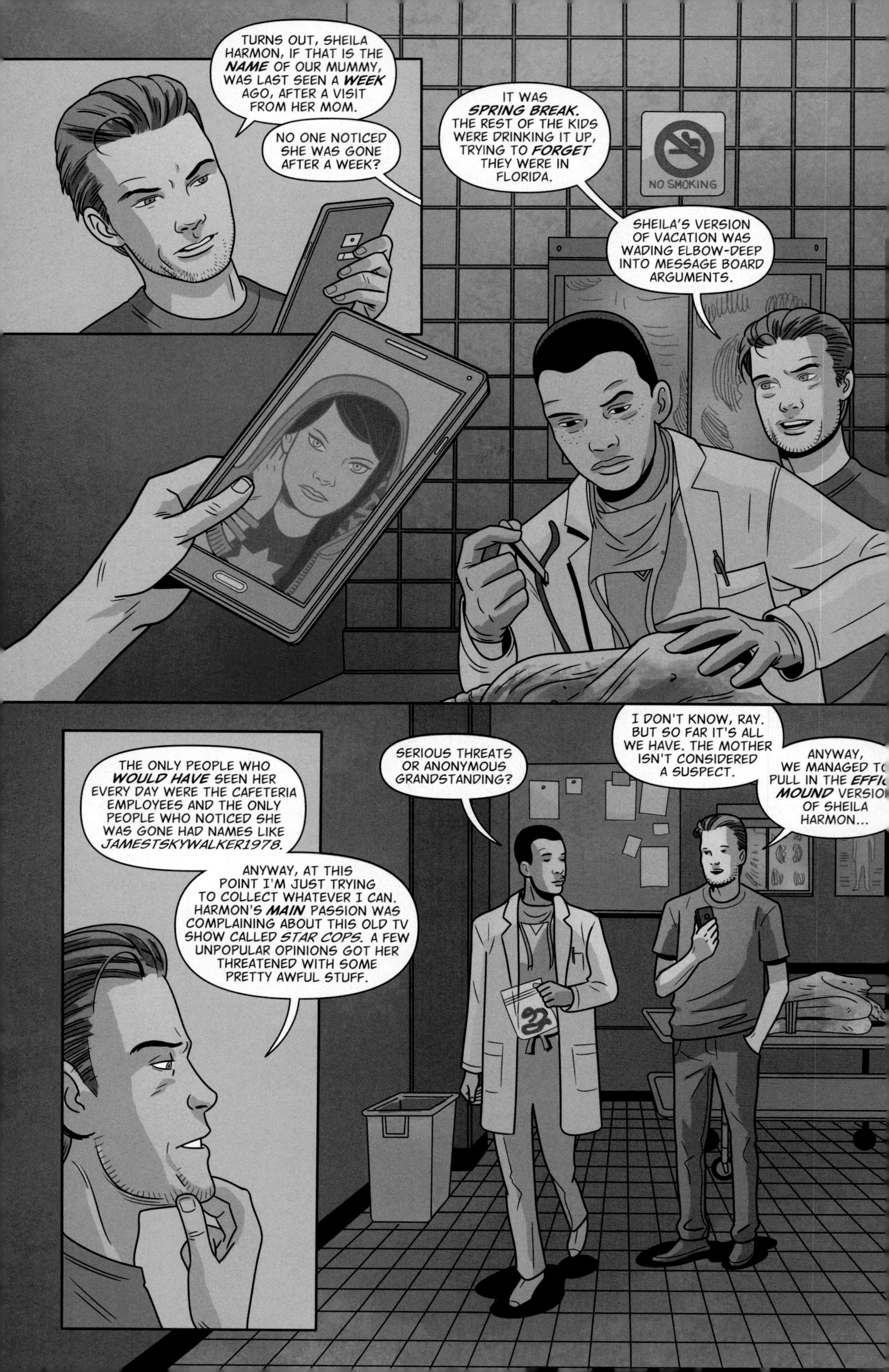
TURNS OUT, SHEILA HARMON, IF THAT IS THE NAME OF OUR MUMMY, WAS LAST SEEN A WEEK AGO, AFTER A VISIT FROM HER MOM.
NO ONE NOTICED SHE WAS GONE AFTER A WEEK?
IT WAS SPRING BREAK. THE REST OF THE KIDS WERE DRINKING IT UP, TRYING TO FORGET THEY WERE IN FLORIDA.
NO SMOKING
SHEILA'S VERSION OF VACATION WAS WADING ELBOW-DEEP INTO MESSAGE BOARD ARGUMENTS.
THE ONLY PEOPLE WHO WOULD HAVE SEEN HER EVERY DAY WERE THE CAFETERIA EMPLOYEES AND THE ONLY PEOPLE WHO NOTICED SHE WAS GONE HAD NAMES LIKE JAMESTSKYWALKER1978.
ANYWAY, AT THIS POINT I'M JUST TRYING TO COLLECT WHATEVER I CAN. HARMON'S MAIN PASSION WAS COMPLAINING ABOUT THIS OLD TV SHOW CALLED STAR COPS. A FEW UNPOPULAR OPINIONS GOT HER THREATENED WITH SOME PRETTY AWFUL STUFF.
SERIOUS THREATS OR ANONYMOUS GRANDSTANDING?
I DON'T KNOW, RAY. BUT SO FAR IT'S ALL WE HAVE. THE MOTHER ISN'T CONSIDERED A SUSPECT.
ANYWAY, WE MANAGED TO PULL IN THE EFFIC MOUND VERSIO OF SHEILA HARMON...

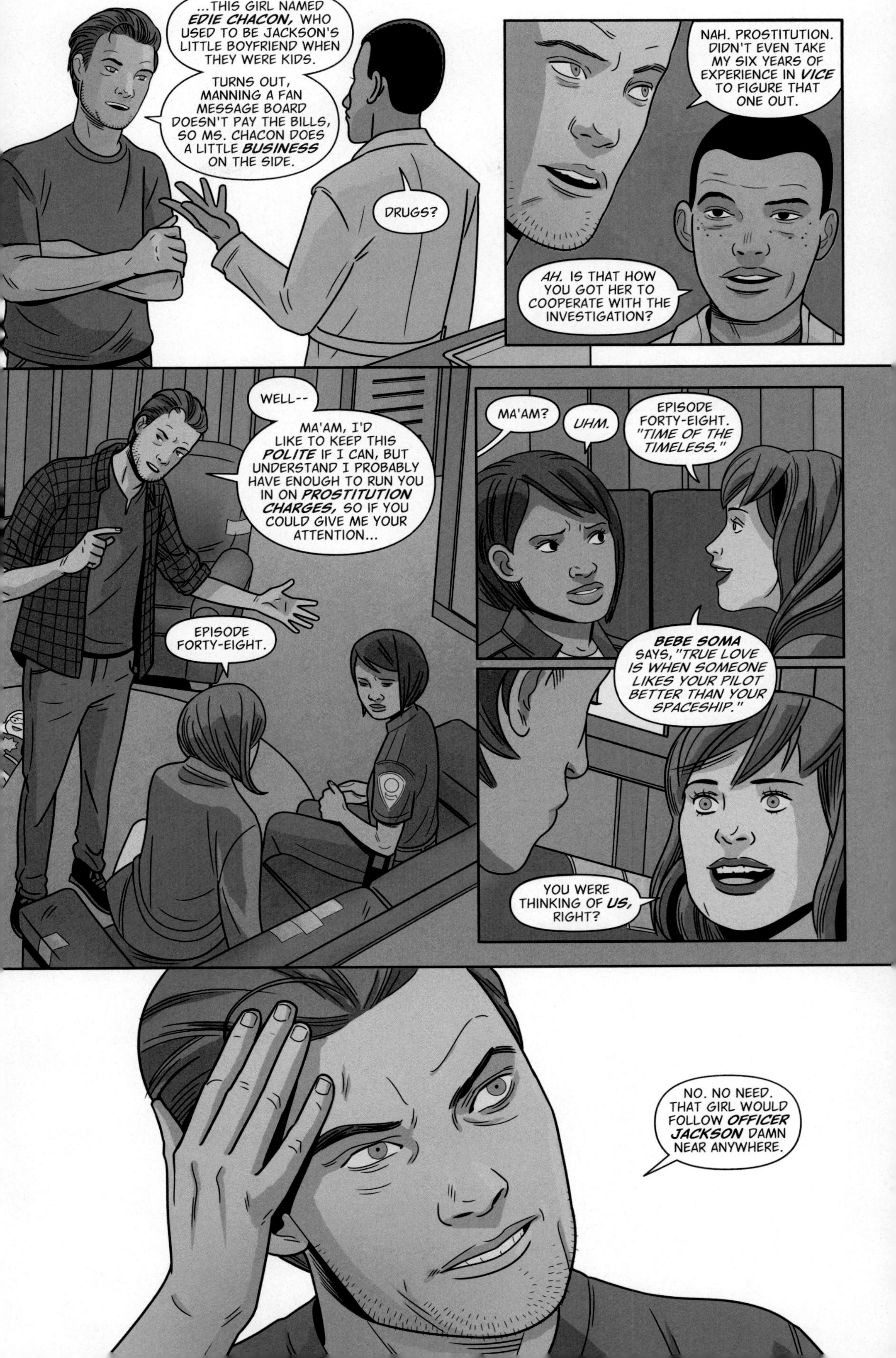
...THIS GIRL NAMED EDIE CHACON, WHO USED TO BE JACKSON'S LITTLE BOYFRIEND WHEN THEY WERE KIDS.
TURNS OUT, MANNING A FAN MESSAGE BOARD DOESN'T PAY THE BILLS, SO MS. CHACON DOES A LITTLE BUSINESS ON THE SIDE.
DRUGS?
NAH. PROSTITUTION. DIDN'T EVEN TAKE MY SIX YEARS OF EXPERIENCE IN VICE TO FIGURE THAT ONE OUT.
AH. IS THAT HOW YOU GOT HER TO COOPERATE WITH THE INVESTIGATION?
WELL--
MA'AM, I'D LIKE TO KEEP THIS POLITE IF I CAN, BUT UNDERSTAND I PROBABLY HAVE ENOUGH TO RUN YOU IN ON PROSTITUTION CHARGES, SO IF YOU COULD GIVE ME YOUR ATTENTION...
EPISODE FORTY-EIGHT.
MA'AM?
UHM.
EPISODE FORTY-EIGHT. "TIME OF THE TIMELESS."
BEBE SOMA SAYS, "TRUE LOVE IS WHEN SOMEONE LIKES YOUR PILOT BETTER THAN YOUR SPACESHIP."
YOU WERE THINKING OF US, RIGHT?
NO. NO NEED. THAT GIRL WOULD FOLLOW OFFICER JACKSON DAMN NEAR ANYWHERE.

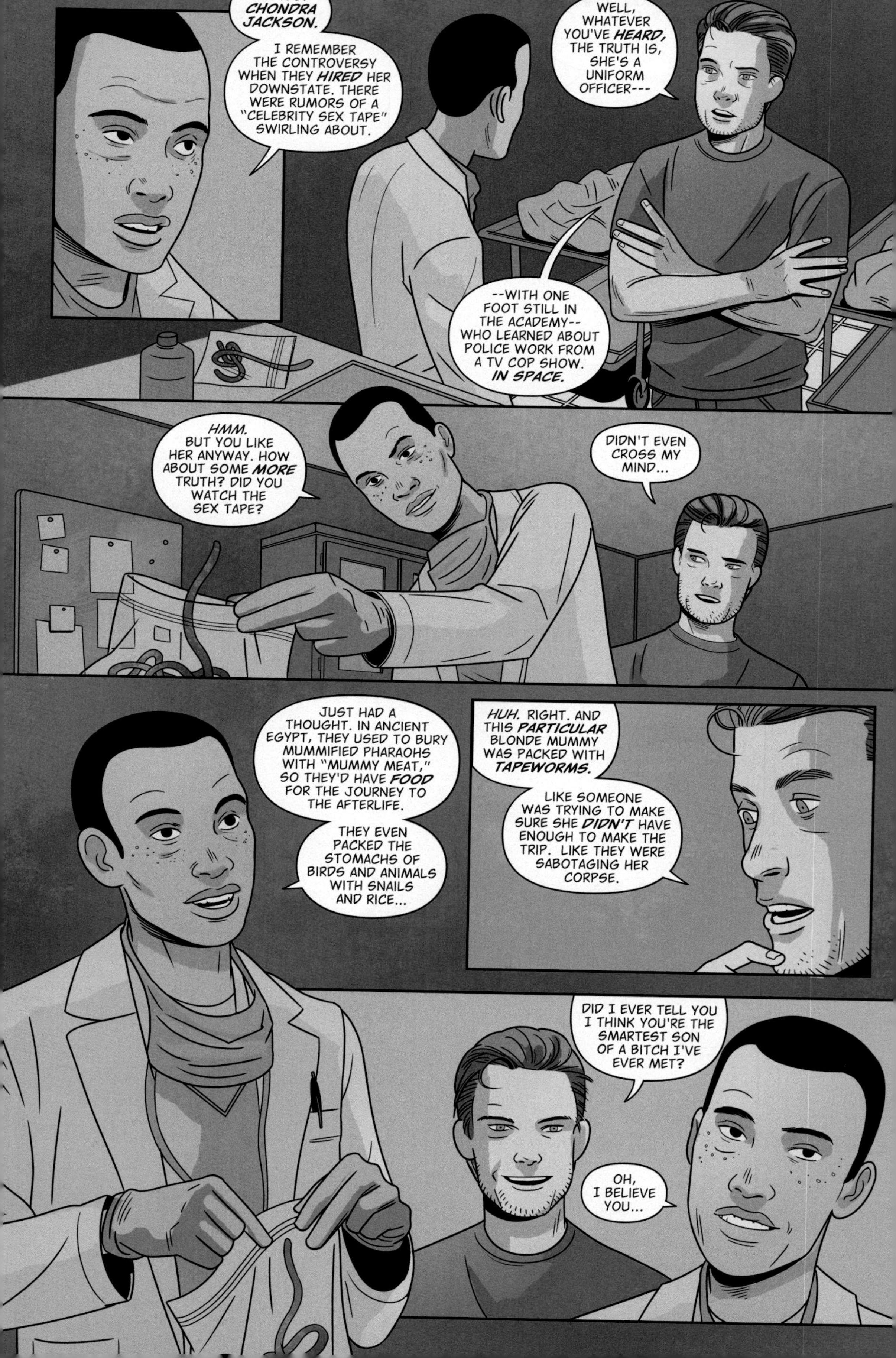
AH YES. CHONDRA JACKSON.
I REMEMBER THE CONTROVERSY WHEN THEY HIRED HER DOWNSTATE. THERE WERE RUMORS OF A "CELEBRITY SEX TAPE" SWIRLING ABOUT.
WELL, WHATEVER YOU'VE HEARD, THE TRUTH IS, SHE'S A UNIFORM OFFICER---
--WITH ONE FOOT STILL IN THE ACADEMY-- WHO LEARNED ABOUT POLICE WORK FROM A TV COP SHOW. IN SPACE.
HMM. BUT YOU LIKE HER ANYWAY. HOW ABOUT SOME MORE TRUTH? DID YOU WATCH THE SEX TAPE?
DIDN'T EVEN CROSS MY MIND...
JUST HAD A THOUGHT. IN ANCIENT EGYPT, THEY USED TO BURY MUMMIFIED PHARAOHS WITH "MUMMY MEAT," SO THEY'D HAVE FOOD FOR THE JOURNEY TO THE AFTERLIFE.
THEY EVEN PACKED THE STOMACHS OF BIRDS AND ANIMALS WITH SNAILS AND RICE...
HUH. RIGHT. AND THIS PARTICULAR BLONDE MUMMY WAS PACKED WITH TAPEWORMS.
LIKE SOMEONE WAS TRYING TO MAKE SURE SHE DIDN'T HAVE ENOUGH TO MAKE THE TRIP. LIKE THEY WERE SABOTAGING HER CORPSE.
DID I EVER TELL YOU I THINK YOU'RE THE SMARTEST SON OF A BITCH I'VE EVER MET?
OH, I BELIEVE YOU...

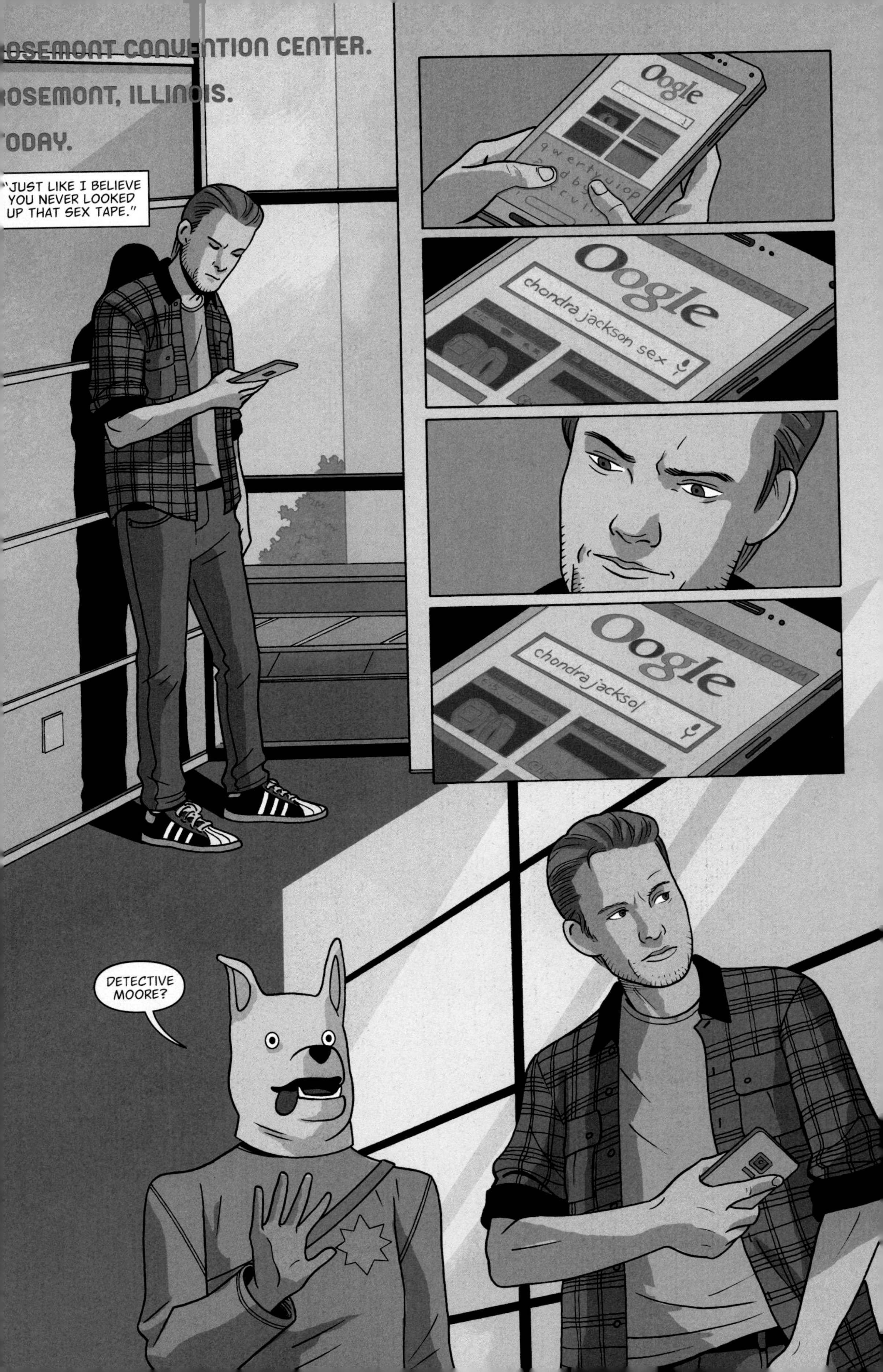
ROSEMONT CONVENTION CENTER.
ROSEMONT, ILLINOIS.
TODAY.
"JUST LIKE I BELIEVE YOU NEVER LOOKED UP THAT SEX TAPE."
Oogle
Oogle
chondra jackson sex
Oogle
chondra jacksol
DETECTIVE MOORE?

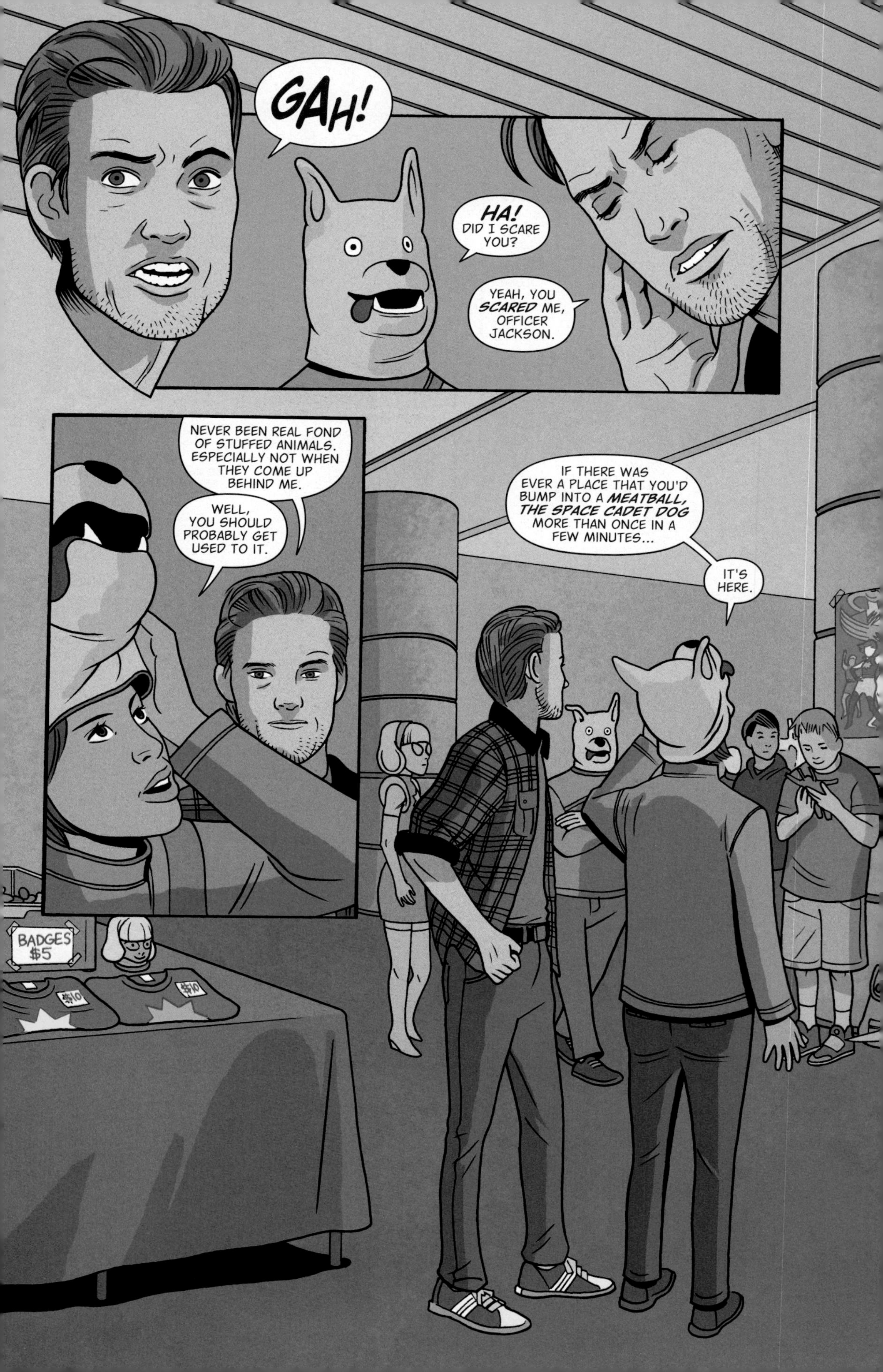
GAH!
HA! DID I SCARE YOU?
YEAH, YOU SCARED ME, OFFICER JACKSON.
NEVER BEEN REAL FOND OF STUFFED ANIMALS. ESPECIALLY NOT WHEN THEY COME UP BEHIND ME.
WELL, YOU SHOULD PROBABLY GET USED TO IT.
IF THERE WAS EVER A PLACE THAT YOU'D BUMP INTO A MEATBALL, THE SPACE CADET DOG MORE THAN ONCE IN A FEW MINUTES...
IT'S HERE.
BADGES $5
$10
$10

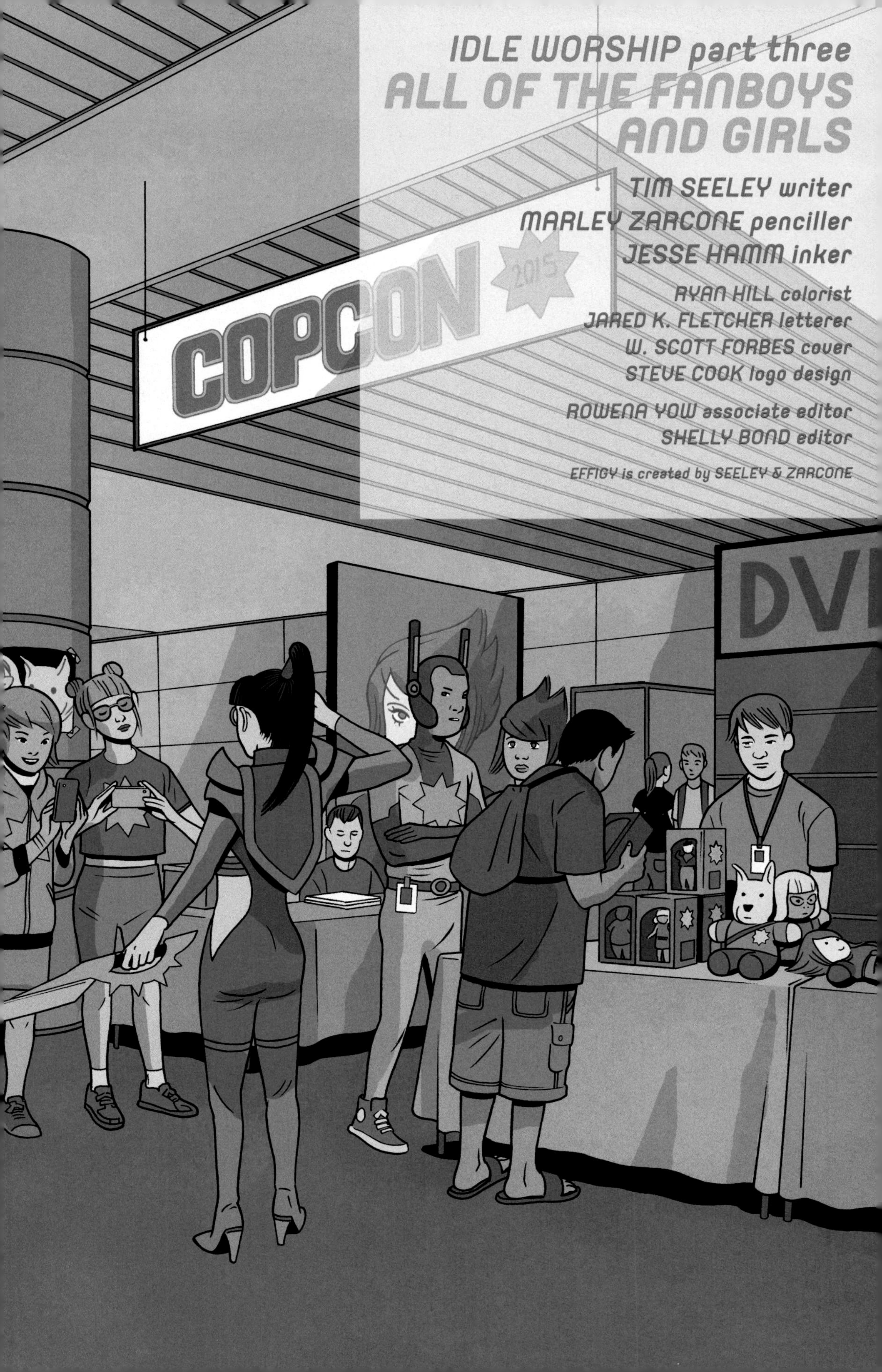
COPCON
2015
DV

IDLE WORSHIP part three
ALL OF THE FANBOYS AND GIRLS

TIM SEELEY writer
MARLEY ZARCONE penciller
JESSE HAMM inker
RYAN HILL colorist
JARED K. FLETCHER letterer
W. SCOTT FORBES cover
STEVE COOK logo design
ROWENA YOW associate editor
SHELLY BOND editor

EFFIGY is created by SEELEY & ZARCONE

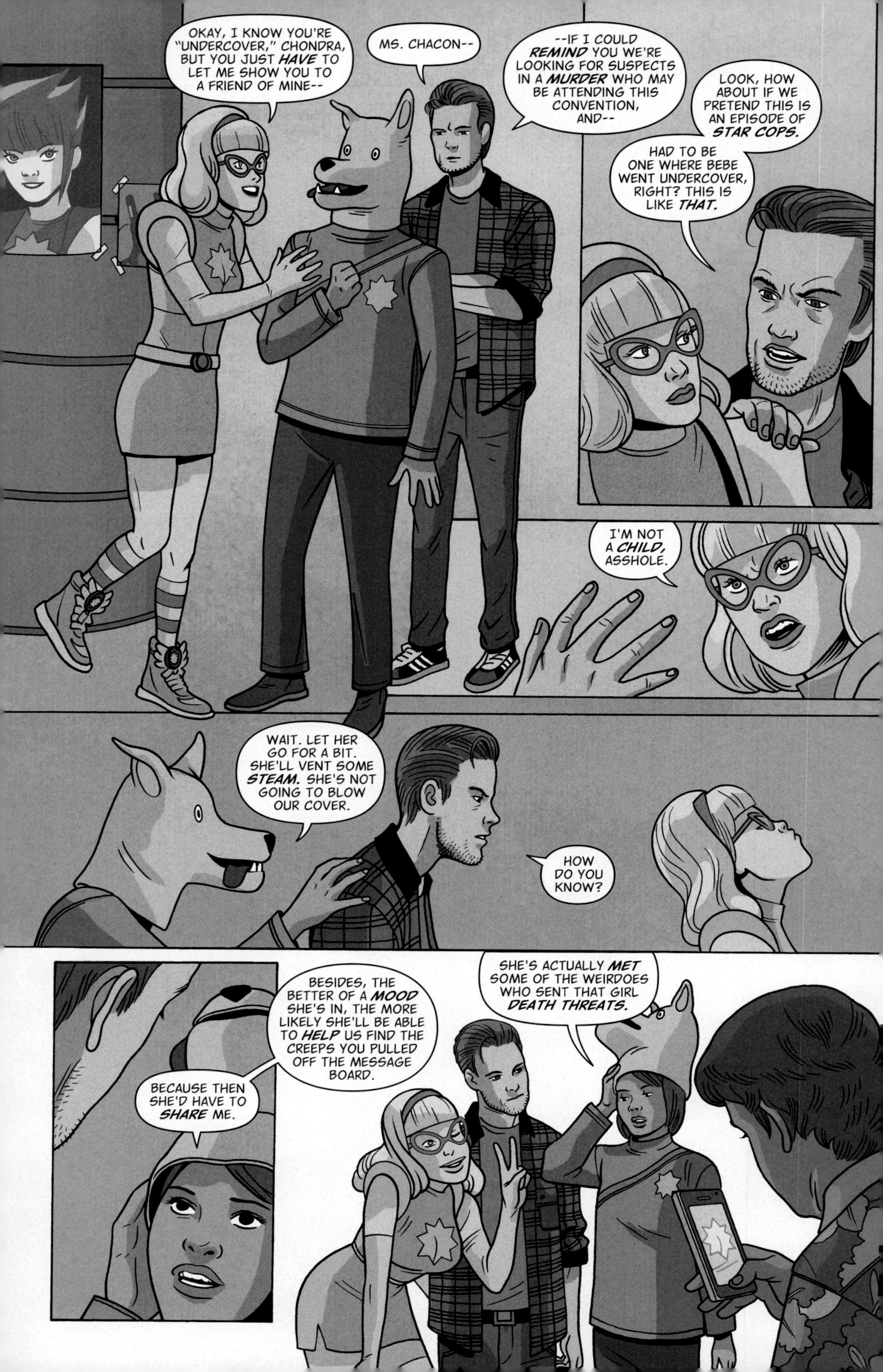

OKAY, I KNOW YOU'RE "UNDERCOVER," CHONDRA, BUT YOU JUST HAVE TO LET ME SHOW YOU TO A FRIEND OF MINE--
MS. CHACON--
--IF I COULD REMIND YOU WE'RE LOOKING FOR SUSPECTS IN A MURDER WHO MAY BE ATTENDING THIS CONVENTION, AND--
LOOK, HOW ABOUT IF WE PRETEND THIS IS AN EPISODE OF STAR COPS.
HAD TO BE ONE WHERE BEBE WENT UNDERCOVER, RIGHT? THIS IS LIKE THAT.
I'M NOT A CHILD, ASSHOLE.
WAIT. LET HER GO FOR A BIT. SHE'LL VENT SOME STEAM. SHE'S NOT GOING TO BLOW OUR COVER.
HOW DO YOU KNOW?
BESIDES, THE BETTER OF A MOOD SHE'S IN, THE MORE LIKELY SHE'LL BE ABLE TO HELP US FIND THE CREEPS YOU PULLED OFF THE MESSAGE BOARD.
BECAUSE THEN SHE'D HAVE TO SHARE ME.
SHE'S ACTUALLY MET SOME OF THE WEIRDOES WHO SENT THAT GIRL DEATH THREATS.

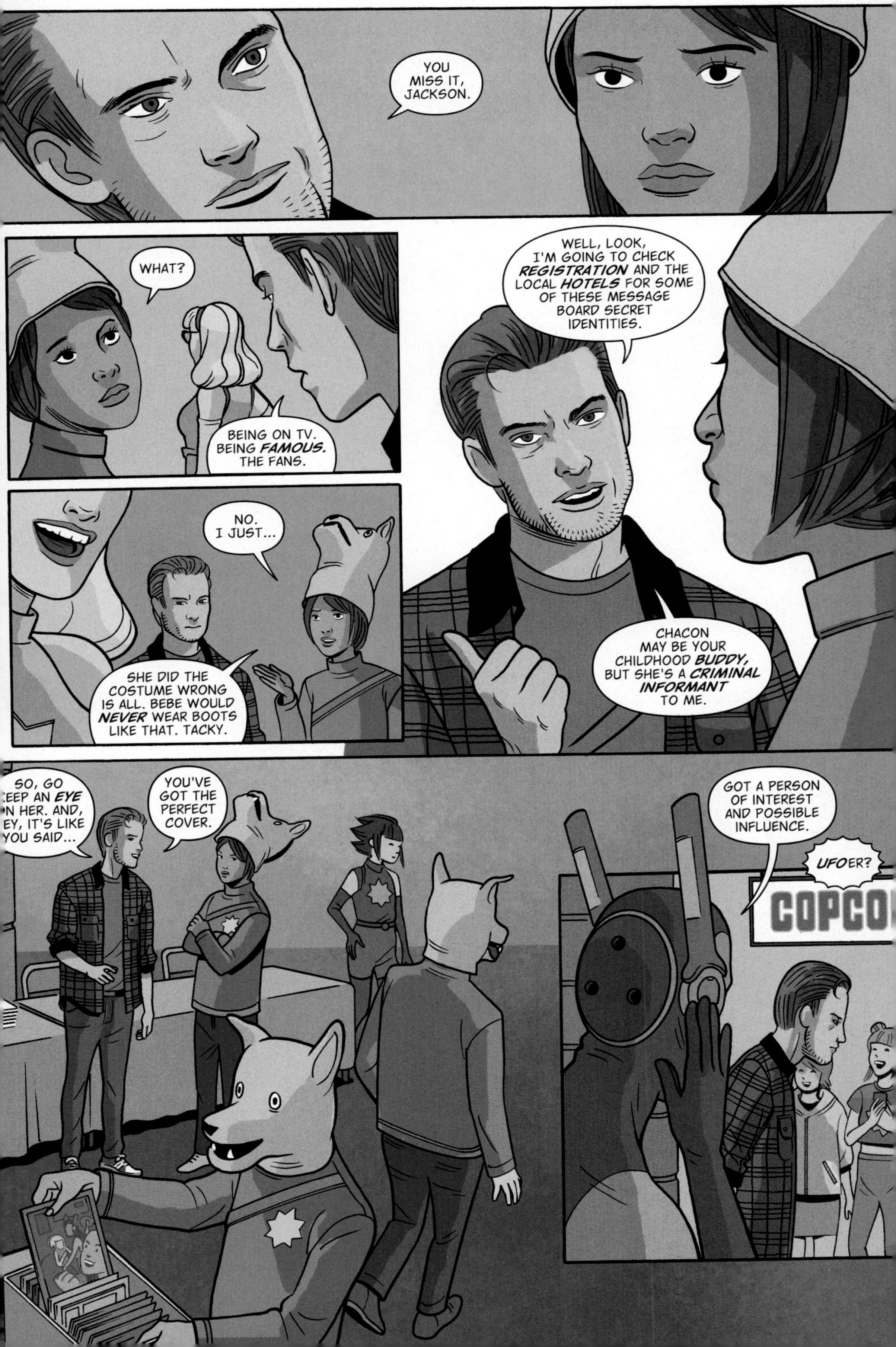
YOU MISS IT, JACKSON.
WHAT?
BEING ON TV. BEING FAMOUS. THE FANS.
NO. I JUST...
SHE DID THE COSTUME WRONG IS ALL. BEBE WOULD NEVER WEAR BOOTS LIKE THAT. TACKY.
WELL, LOOK, I'M GOING TO CHECK REGISTRATION AND THE LOCAL HOTELS FOR SOME OF THESE MESSAGE BOARD SECRET IDENTITIES.
CHACON MAY BE YOUR CHILDHOOD BUDDY, BUT SHE'S A CRIMINAL INFORMANT TO ME.
SO, GO KEEP AN EYE ON HER. AND, HEY, IT'S LIKE YOU SAID...
YOU'VE GOT THE PERFECT COVER.
GOT A PERSON OF INTEREST AND POSSIBLE INFLUENCE.
UFOER?
COPCO

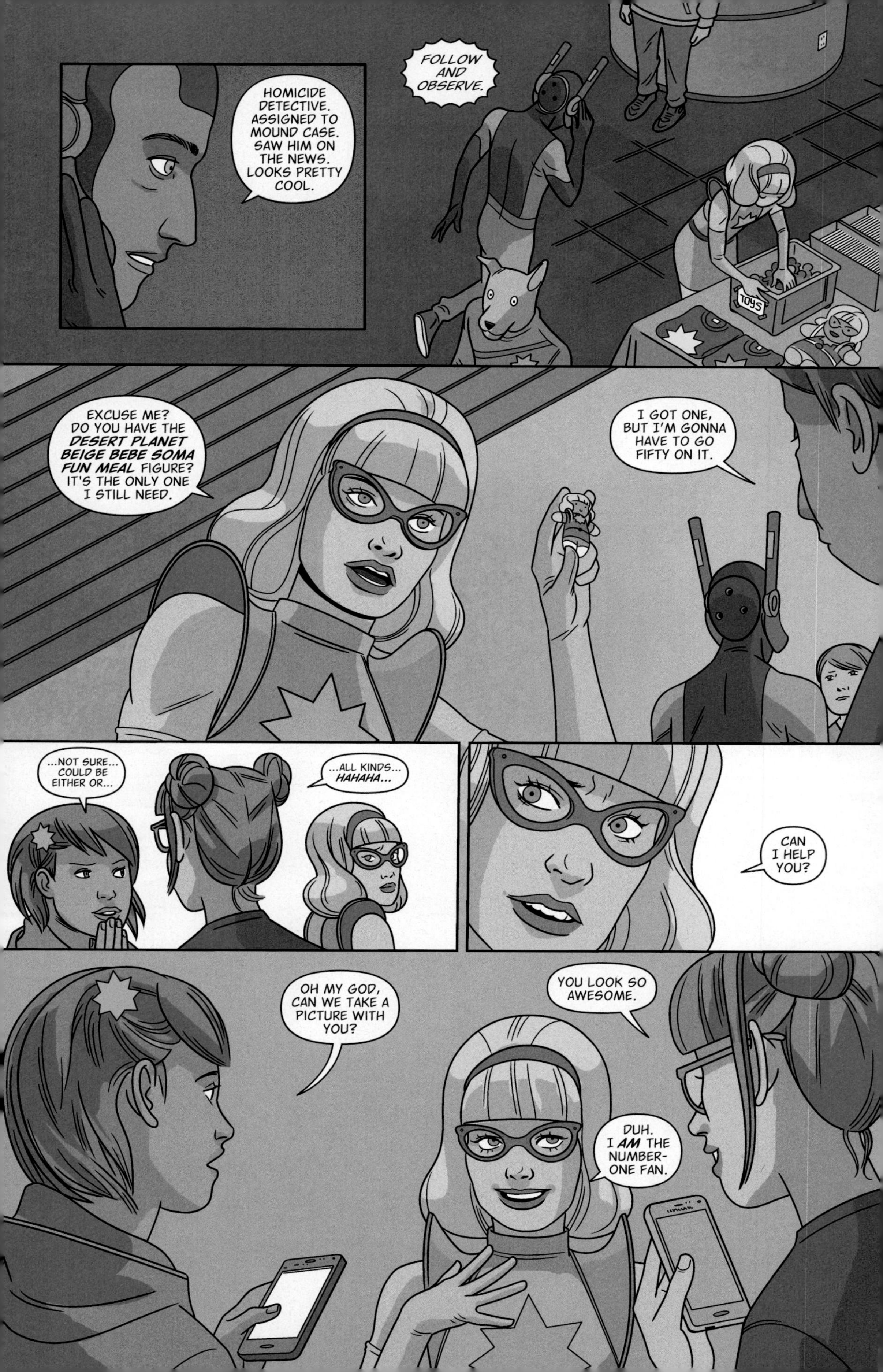
HOMICIDE DETECTIVE. ASSIGNED TO MOUND CASE. SAW HIM ON THE NEWS. LOOKS PRETTY COOL.
FOLLOW AND OBSERVE.
TOYS
EXCUSE ME? DO YOU HAVE THE *DESERT PLANET BEIGE BEBE SOMA FUN MEAL* FIGURE? IT'S THE ONLY ONE I STILL NEED.
I GOT ONE, BUT I'M GONNA HAVE TO GO FIFTY ON IT.
...NOT SURE... COULD BE EITHER OR...
...ALL KINDS... *HAHAHA...*
CAN I HELP YOU?
OH MY GOD, CAN WE TAKE A PICTURE WITH YOU?
YOU LOOK SO AWESOME.
DUH. I *AM* THE NUMBER-ONE FAN.

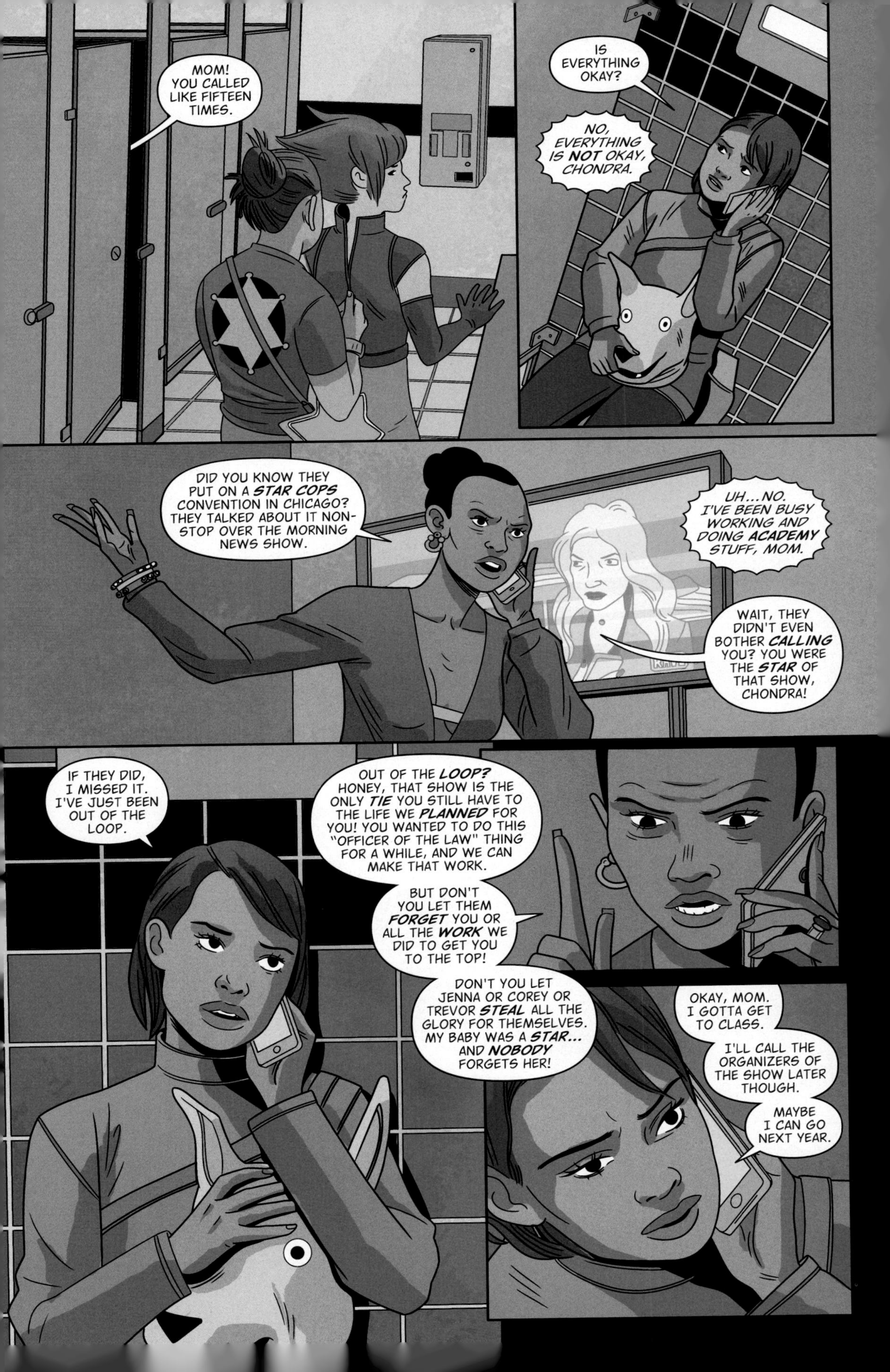
MOM! YOU CALLED LIKE FIFTEEN TIMES.
IS EVERYTHING OKAY?
NO, EVERYTHING IS **NOT** OKAY, CHONDRA.
DID YOU KNOW THEY PUT ON A ***STAR COPS*** CONVENTION IN CHICAGO? THEY TALKED ABOUT IT NON-STOP OVER THE MORNING NEWS SHOW.
UH...NO. I'VE BEEN BUSY WORKING AND DOING ***ACADEMY*** STUFF, MOM.
WAIT, THEY DIDN'T EVEN BOTHER ***CALLING*** YOU? YOU WERE THE ***STAR*** OF THAT SHOW, CHONDRA!
IF THEY DID, I MISSED IT. I'VE JUST BEEN OUT OF THE LOOP.
OUT OF THE ***LOOP?*** HONEY, THAT SHOW IS THE ONLY ***TIE*** YOU STILL HAVE TO THE LIFE WE ***PLANNED*** FOR YOU! YOU WANTED TO DO THIS "OFFICER OF THE LAW" THING FOR A WHILE, AND WE CAN MAKE THAT WORK.
BUT DON'T YOU LET THEM ***FORGET*** YOU OR ALL THE ***WORK*** WE DID TO GET YOU TO THE TOP!
DON'T YOU LET JENNA OR COREY OR TREVOR ***STEAL*** ALL THE GLORY FOR THEMSELVES. MY BABY WAS A ***STAR...*** AND ***NOBODY*** FORGETS HER!
OKAY, MOM. I GOTTA GET TO CLASS.
I'LL CALL THE ORGANIZERS OF THE SHOW LATER THOUGH.
MAYBE I CAN GO NEXT YEAR.

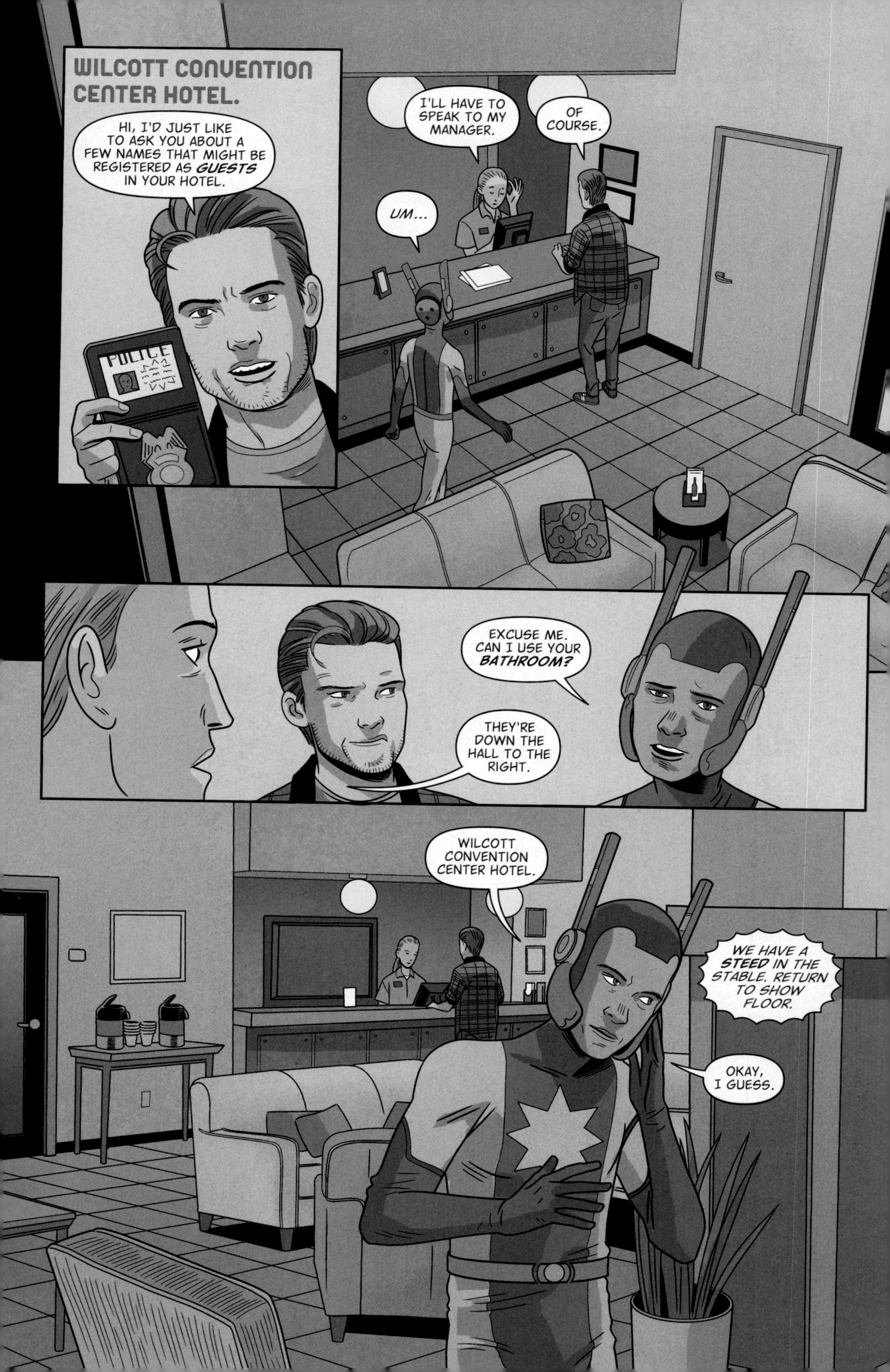
WILCOTT CONVENTION CENTER HOTEL.
HI, I'D JUST LIKE TO ASK YOU ABOUT A FEW NAMES THAT MIGHT BE REGISTERED AS *GUESTS* IN YOUR HOTEL.
POLICE
UM...
I'LL HAVE TO SPEAK TO MY MANAGER.
OF COURSE.
EXCUSE ME. CAN I USE YOUR *BATHROOM?*
THEY'RE DOWN THE HALL TO THE RIGHT.
WILCOTT CONVENTION CENTER HOTEL.
*WE HAVE A **STEED** IN THE STABLE. RETURN TO SHOW FLOOR.*
OKAY, I GUESS.

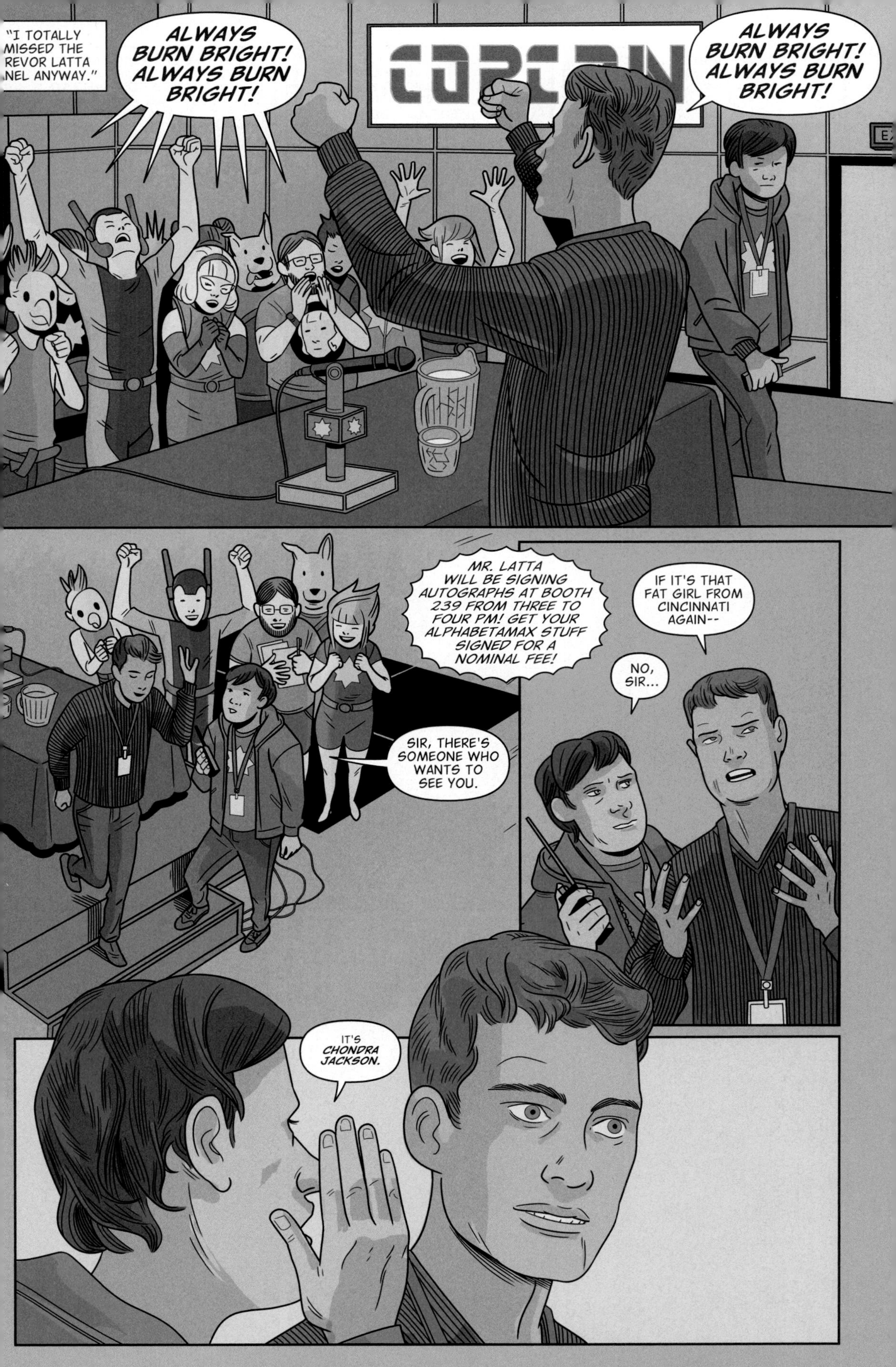

"I TOTALLY MISSED THE REVOR LATTA NEL ANYWAY."
ALWAYS BURN BRIGHT! ALWAYS BURN BRIGHT!
ALWAYS BURN BRIGHT! ALWAYS BURN BRIGHT!
MR. LATTA WILL BE SIGNING AUTOGRAPHS AT BOOTH 239 FROM THREE TO FOUR PM! GET YOUR ALPHABETAMAX STUFF SIGNED FOR A NOMINAL FEE!
SIR, THERE'S SOMEONE WHO WANTS TO SEE YOU.
IF IT'S THAT FAT GIRL FROM CINCINNATI AGAIN--
NO, SIR...
IT'S CHONDRA JACKSON.

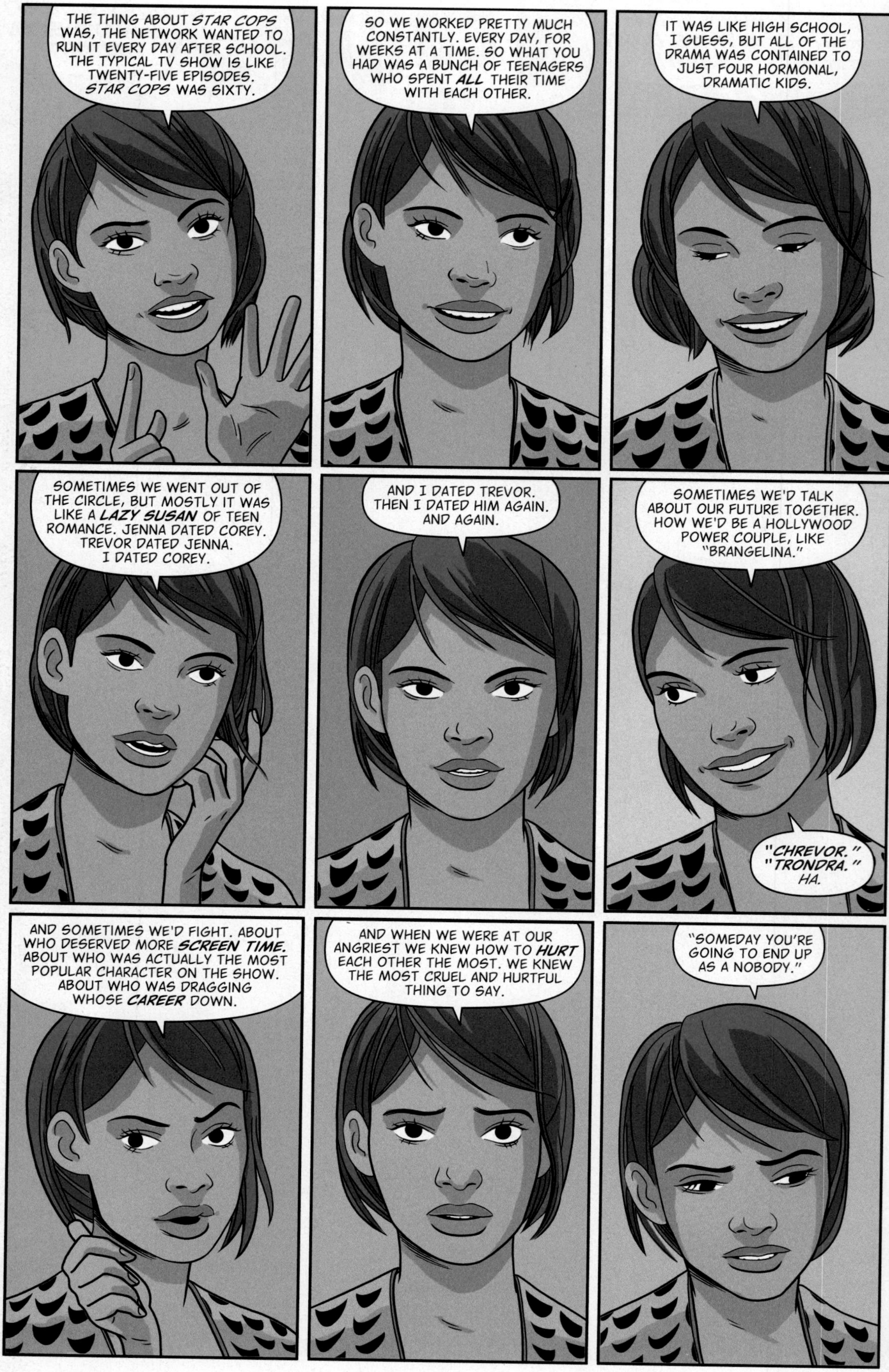
THE THING ABOUT *STAR COPS* WAS, THE NETWORK WANTED TO RUN IT EVERY DAY AFTER SCHOOL. THE TYPICAL TV SHOW IS LIKE TWENTY-FIVE EPISODES. *STAR COPS* WAS SIXTY.
SO WE WORKED PRETTY MUCH CONSTANTLY. EVERY DAY, FOR WEEKS AT A TIME. SO WHAT YOU HAD WAS A BUNCH OF TEENAGERS WHO SPENT ***ALL*** THEIR TIME WITH EACH OTHER.
IT WAS LIKE HIGH SCHOOL, I GUESS, BUT ALL OF THE DRAMA WAS CONTAINED TO JUST FOUR HORMONAL, DRAMATIC KIDS.
SOMETIMES WE WENT OUT OF THE CIRCLE, BUT MOSTLY IT WAS LIKE A ***LAZY SUSAN*** OF TEEN ROMANCE. JENNA DATED COREY. TREVOR DATED JENNA. I DATED COREY.
AND I DATED TREVOR. THEN I DATED HIM AGAIN. AND AGAIN.
SOMETIMES WE'D TALK ABOUT OUR FUTURE TOGETHER. HOW WE'D BE A HOLLYWOOD POWER COUPLE, LIKE "BRANGELINA."
"CHREVOR." "TRONDRA." *HA.*
AND SOMETIMES WE'D FIGHT. ABOUT WHO DESERVED MORE ***SCREEN TIME.*** ABOUT WHO WAS ACTUALLY THE MOST POPULAR CHARACTER ON THE SHOW. ABOUT WHO WAS DRAGGING WHOSE ***CAREER*** DOWN.
AND WHEN WE WERE AT OUR ANGRIEST WE KNEW HOW TO ***HURT*** EACH OTHER THE MOST. WE KNEW THE MOST CRUEL AND HURTFUL THING TO SAY.
"SOMEDAY YOU'RE GOING TO END UP AS A NOBODY."

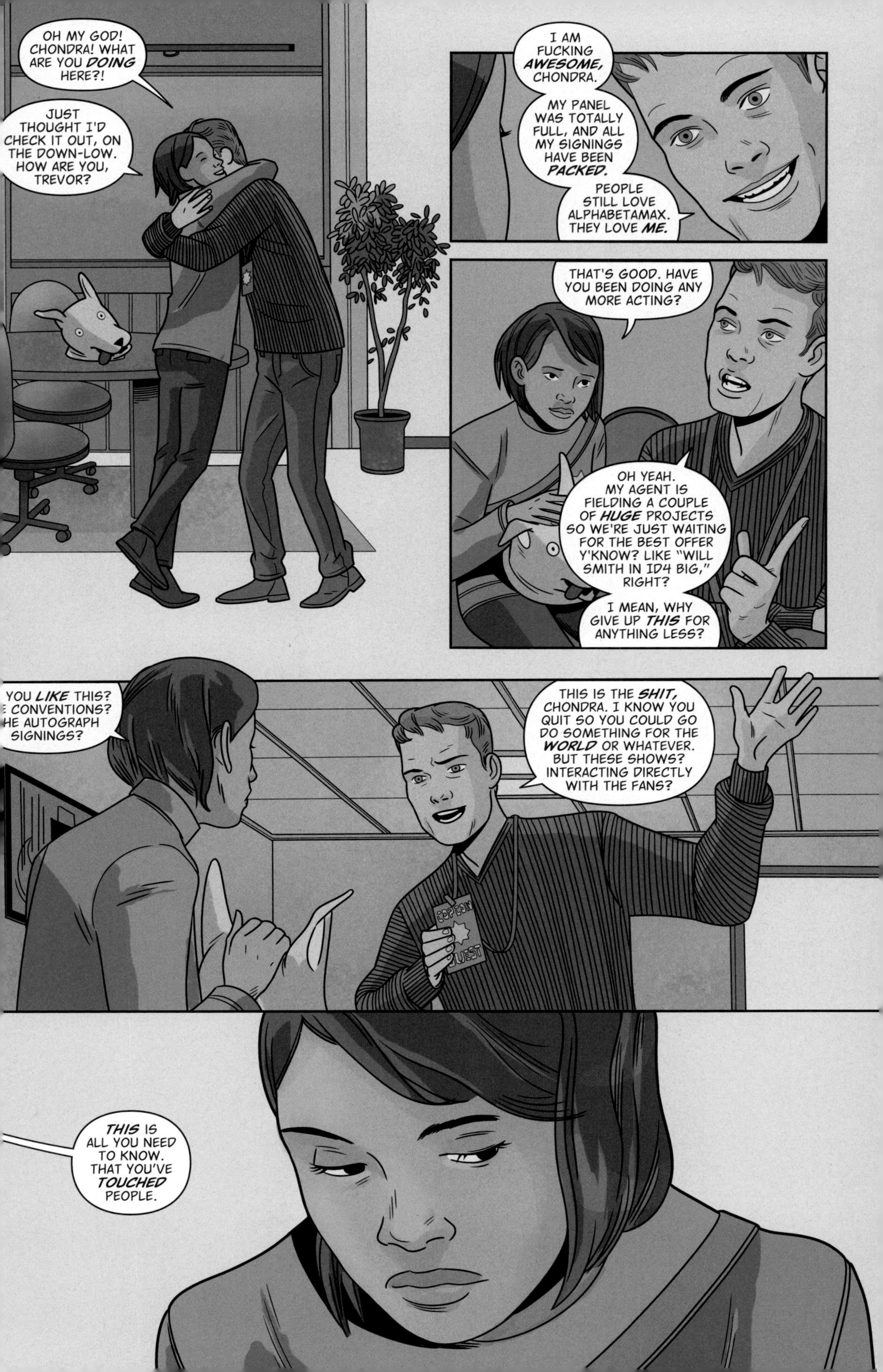
OH MY GOD! CHONDRA! WHAT ARE YOU DOING HERE?!
JUST THOUGHT I'D CHECK IT OUT, ON THE DOWN-LOW. HOW ARE YOU, TREVOR?
I AM FUCKING AWESOME, CHONDRA.
MY PANEL WAS TOTALLY FULL, AND ALL MY SIGNINGS HAVE BEEN PACKED.
PEOPLE STILL LOVE ALPHABETAMAX. THEY LOVE ME.
THAT'S GOOD. HAVE YOU BEEN DOING ANY MORE ACTING?
OH YEAH. MY AGENT IS FIELDING A COUPLE OF HUGE PROJECTS SO WE'RE JUST WAITING FOR THE BEST OFFER Y'KNOW? LIKE "WILL SMITH IN ID4 BIG," RIGHT?
I MEAN, WHY GIVE UP THIS FOR ANYTHING LESS?
YOU LIKE THIS? CONVENTIONS? AUTOGRAPH SIGNINGS?
THIS IS THE SHIT, CHONDRA. I KNOW YOU QUIT SO YOU COULD GO DO SOMETHING FOR THE WORLD OR WHATEVER. BUT THESE SHOWS? INTERACTING DIRECTLY WITH THE FANS?
THIS IS ALL YOU NEED TO KNOW. THAT YOU'VE TOUCHED PEOPLE.

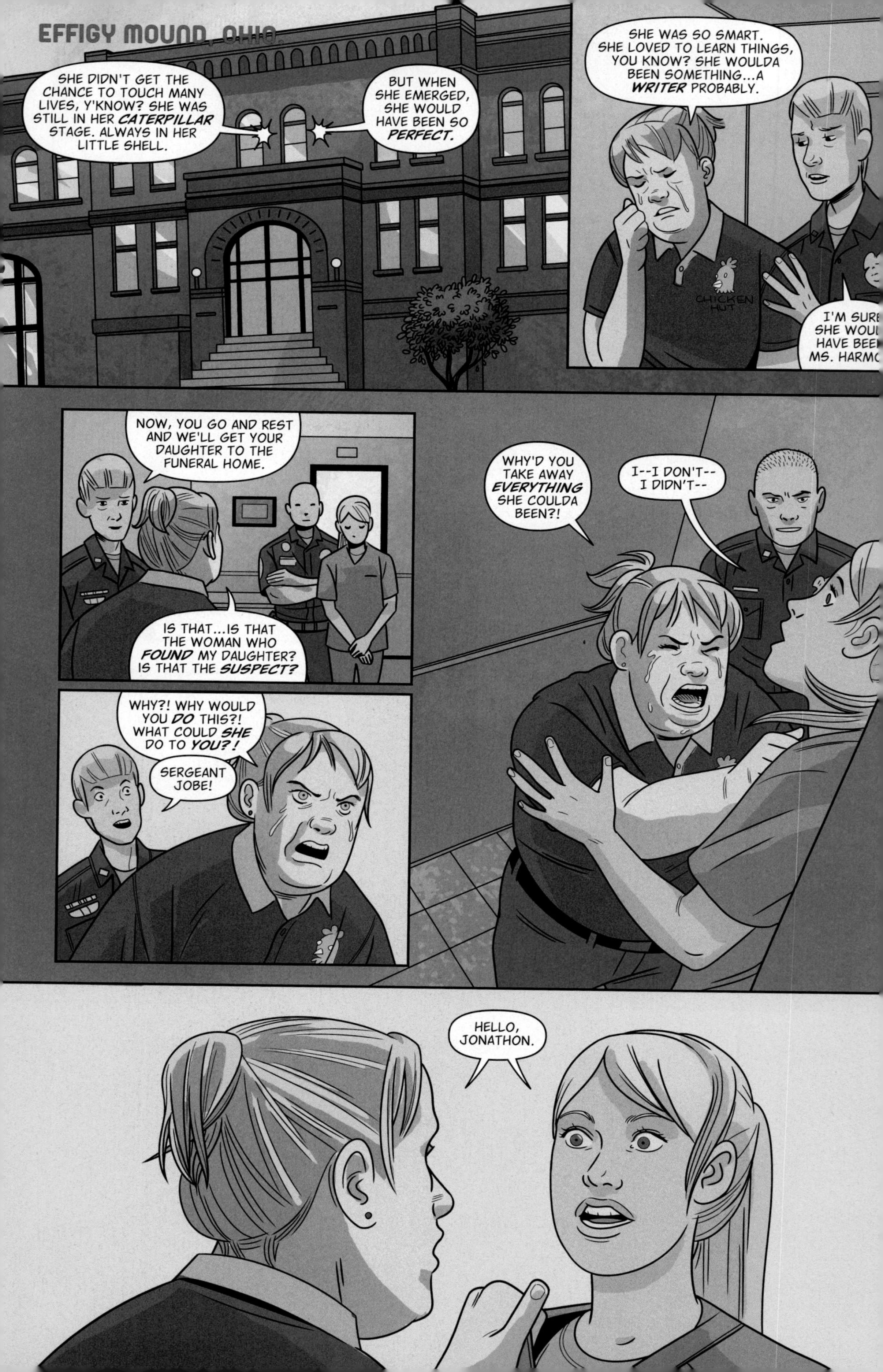
EFFIGY MOUND, OHIO.
SHE DIDN'T GET THE CHANCE TO TOUCH MANY LIVES, Y'KNOW? SHE WAS STILL IN HER *CATERPILLAR* STAGE. ALWAYS IN HER LITTLE SHELL.
BUT WHEN SHE EMERGED, SHE WOULD HAVE BEEN SO *PERFECT.*
SHE WAS SO SMART. SHE LOVED TO LEARN THINGS, YOU KNOW? SHE WOULDA BEEN SOMETHING...A *WRITER* PROBABLY.
CHICKEN HUT
I'M SURE SHE WOUL HAVE BEE MS. HARMO
NOW, YOU GO AND REST AND WE'LL GET YOUR DAUGHTER TO THE FUNERAL HOME.
IS THAT...IS THAT THE WOMAN WHO *FOUND* MY DAUGHTER? IS THAT THE *SUSPECT?*
WHY?! WHY WOULD YOU *DO* THIS?! WHAT COULD *SHE* DO TO *YOU?!*
SERGEANT JOBE!
WHY'D YOU TAKE AWAY *EVERYTHING* SHE COULDA BEEN?!
I--I DON'T-- I DIDN'T--
HELLO, JONATHON.

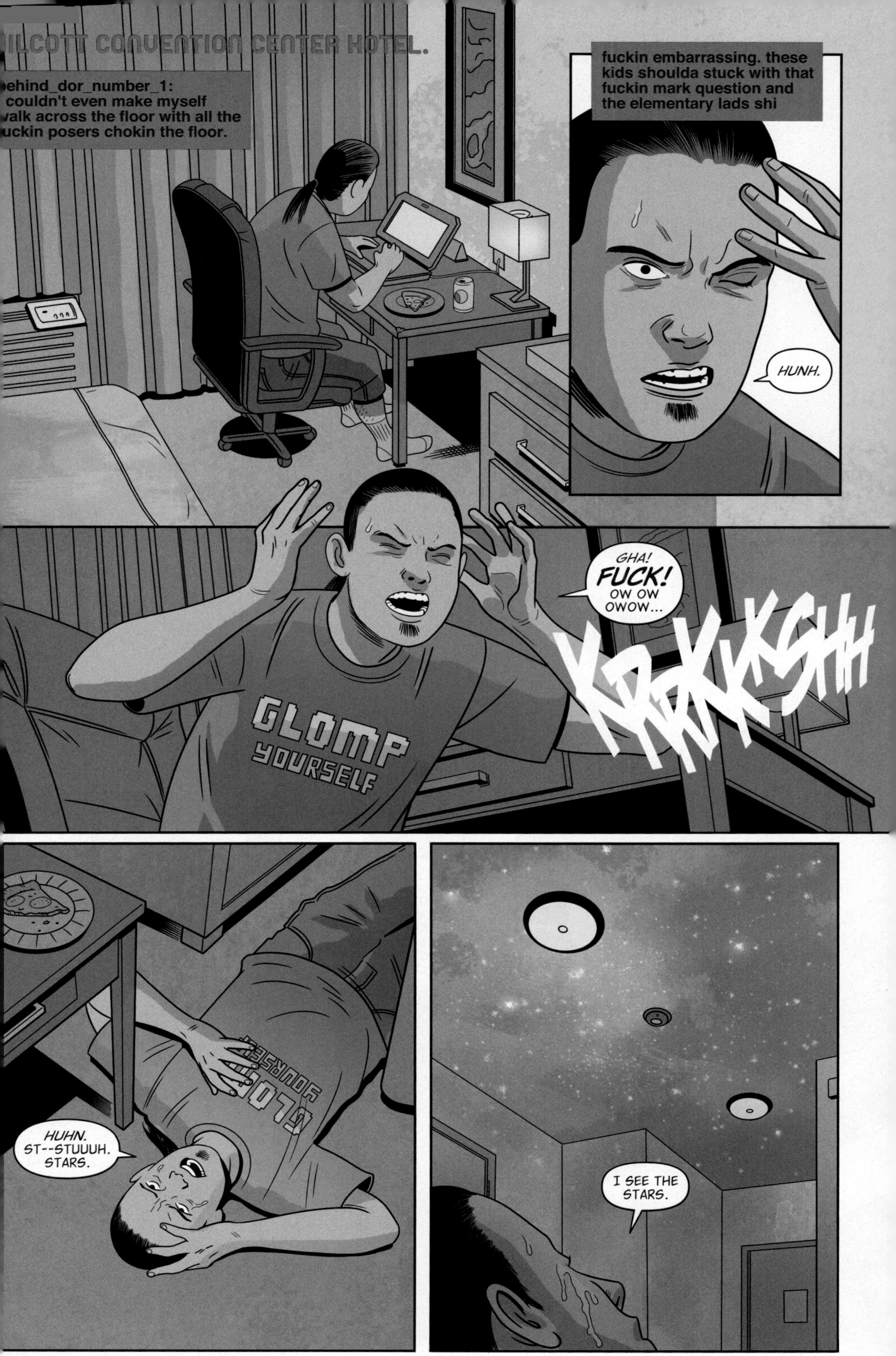
ILCOTT CONVENTION CENTER HOTEL.
ehind_dor_number_1:
couldn't even make myself
alk across the floor with all the
uckin posers chokin the floor.
fuckin embarrassing. these
kids shoulda stuck with that
fuckin mark question and
the elementary lads shi
HUNH.
GHA!
FUCK!
OW OW
OWOW...
KRKKKSHH
GLOMP
YOURSELF
HUHN.
ST--STUUUH.
STARS.
I SEE THE
STARS.

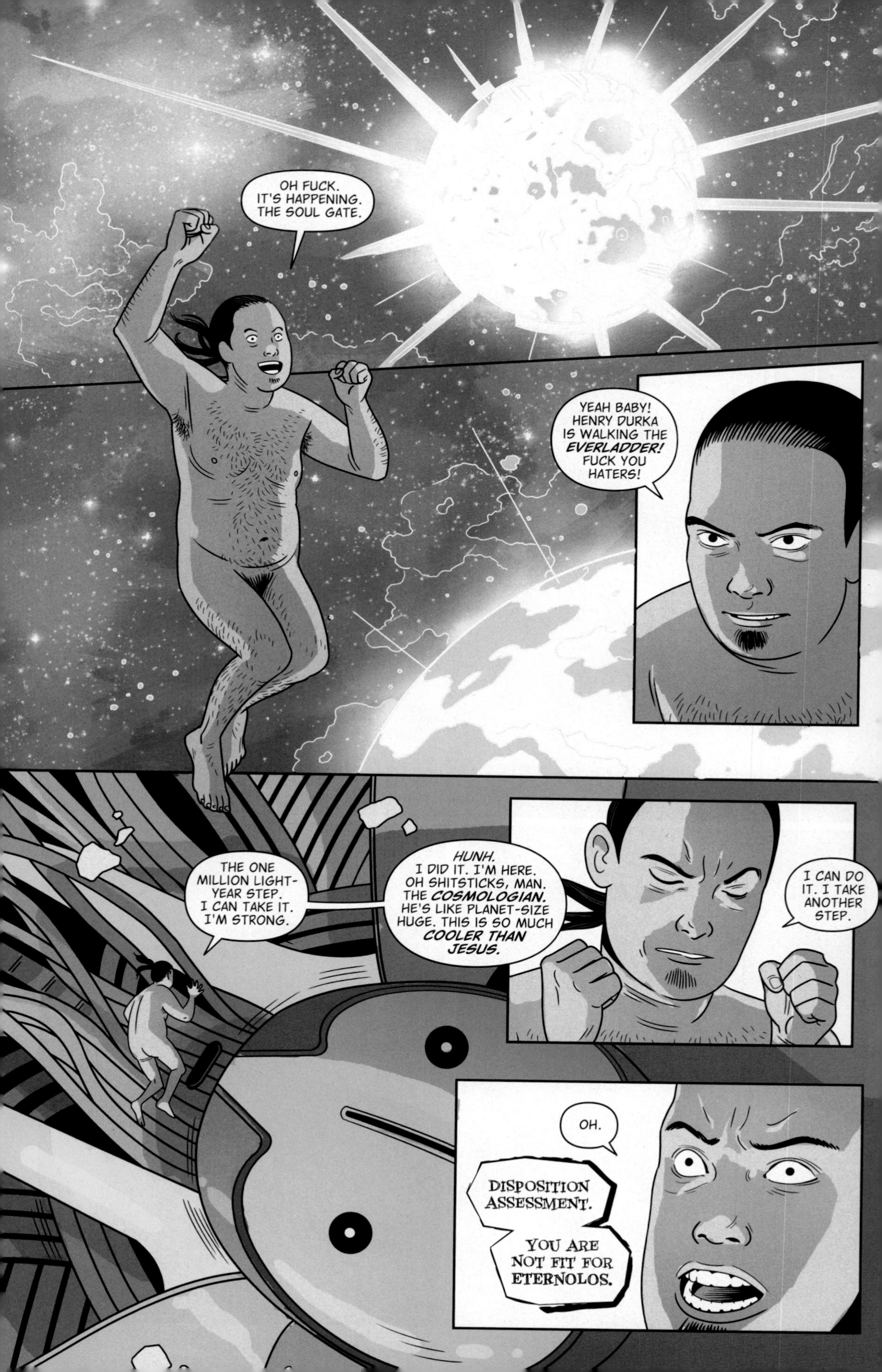
OH FUCK. IT'S HAPPENING. THE SOUL GATE.
YEAH BABY! HENRY DURKA IS WALKING THE *EVERLADDER!* FUCK YOU HATERS!
THE ONE MILLION LIGHT-YEAR STEP. I CAN TAKE IT. I'M STRONG.
HUNH. I DID IT. I'M HERE. OH SHITSTICKS, MAN. THE *COSMOLOGIAN.* HE'S LIKE PLANET-SIZE HUGE. THIS IS SO MUCH *COOLER THAN JESUS.*
I CAN DO IT. I TAKE ANOTHER STEP.
OH.
DISPOSITION ASSESSMENT.
YOU ARE NOT FIT FOR ETERNOLOS.

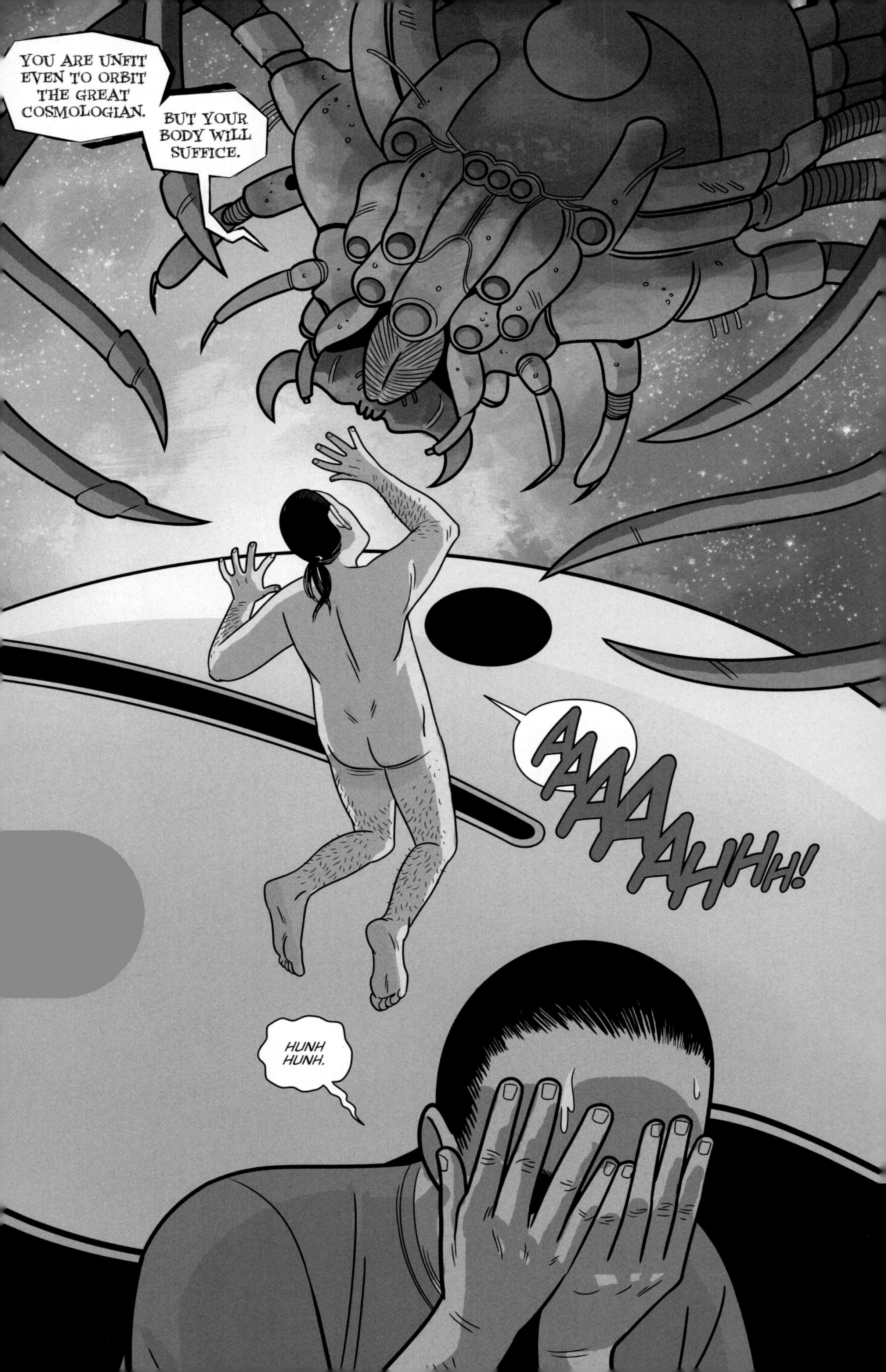
YOU ARE UNFIT EVEN TO ORBIT THE GREAT COSMOLOGIAN.
BUT YOUR BODY WILL SUFFICE.
AAAAAHHH!
HUNH HUNH.

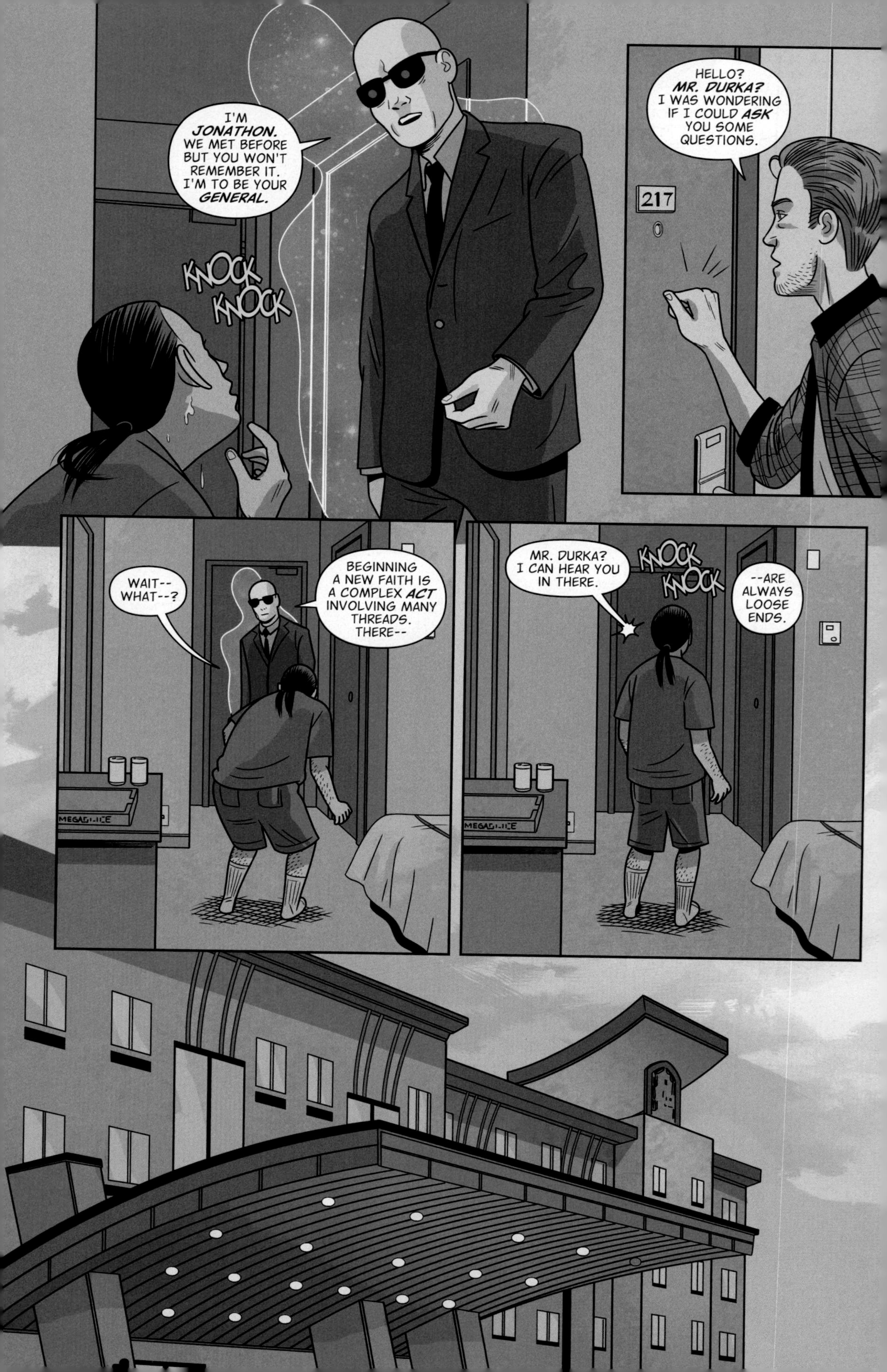
I'M JONATHON. WE MET BEFORE BUT YOU WON'T REMEMBER IT. I'M TO BE YOUR GENERAL.
KNOCK KNOCK
HELLO? MR. DURKA? I WAS WONDERING IF I COULD ASK YOU SOME QUESTIONS.
217
WAIT-- WHAT--?
BEGINNING A NEW FAITH IS A COMPLEX ACT INVOLVING MANY THREADS. THERE--
MEGASLICE
MR. DURKA? I CAN HEAR YOU IN THERE.
KNOCK KNOCK
--ARE ALWAYS LOOSE ENDS.
MEGASLICE

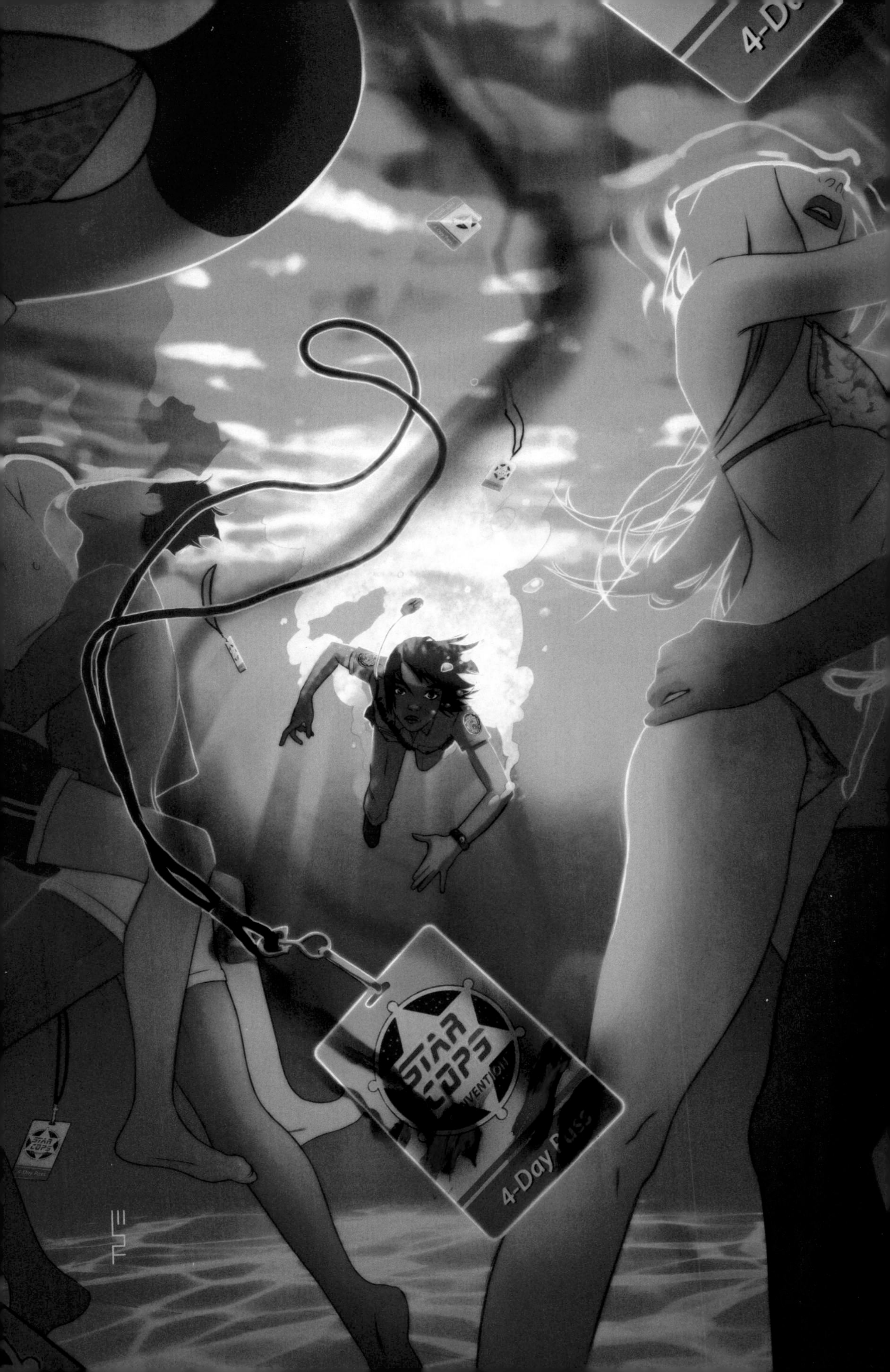
4-Day

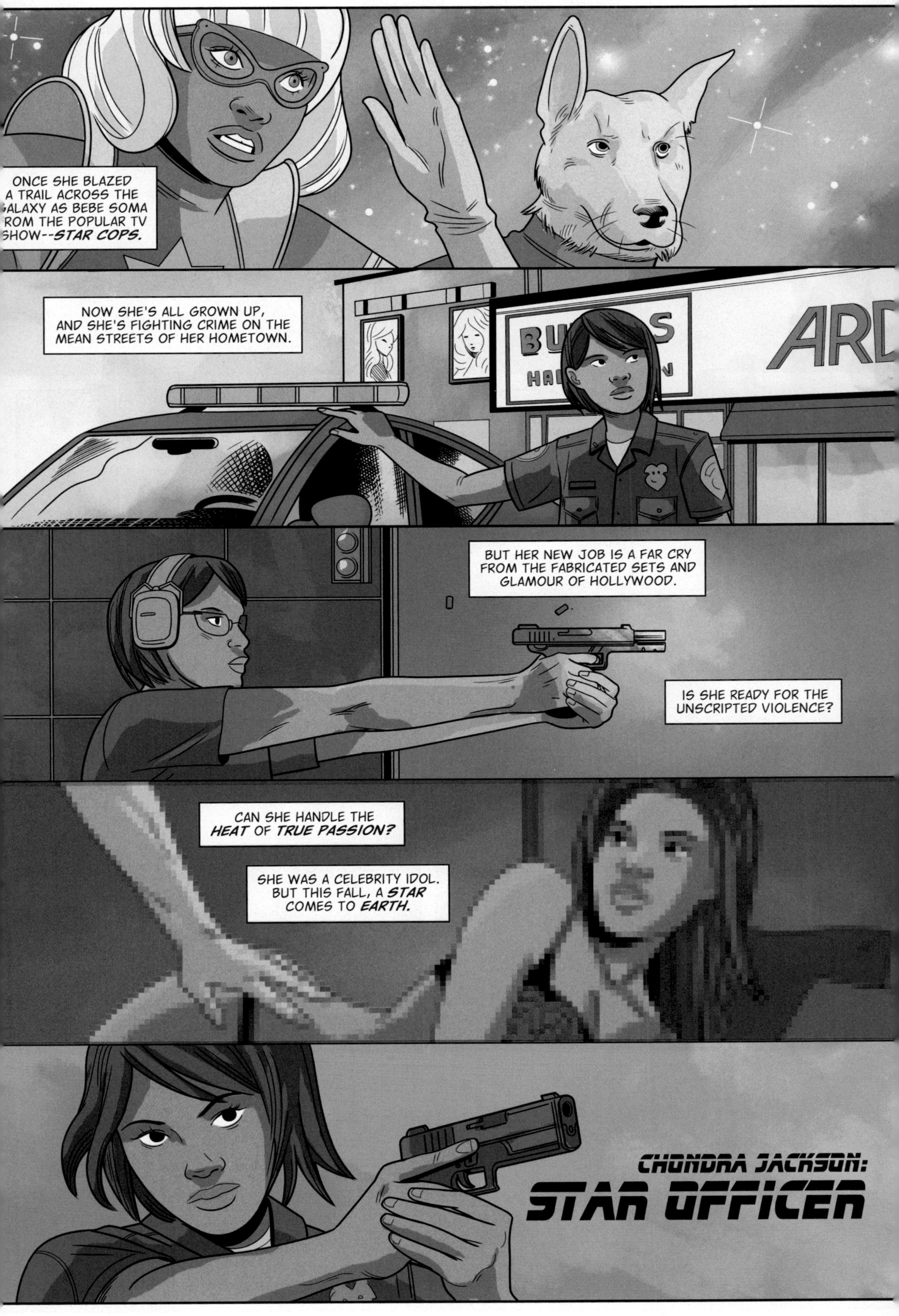
ONCE SHE BLAZED A TRAIL ACROSS THE GALAXY AS BEBE SOMA FROM THE POPULAR TV SHOW--STAR COPS.
NOW SHE'S ALL GROWN UP, AND SHE'S FIGHTING CRIME ON THE MEAN STREETS OF HER HOMETOWN.
ARD
BUT HER NEW JOB IS A FAR CRY FROM THE FABRICATED SETS AND GLAMOUR OF HOLLYWOOD.
IS SHE READY FOR THE UNSCRIPTED VIOLENCE?
CAN SHE HANDLE THE HEAT OF TRUE PASSION?
SHE WAS A CELEBRITY IDOL. BUT THIS FALL, A STAR COMES TO EARTH.
CHONDRA JACKSON:
STAR OFFICER

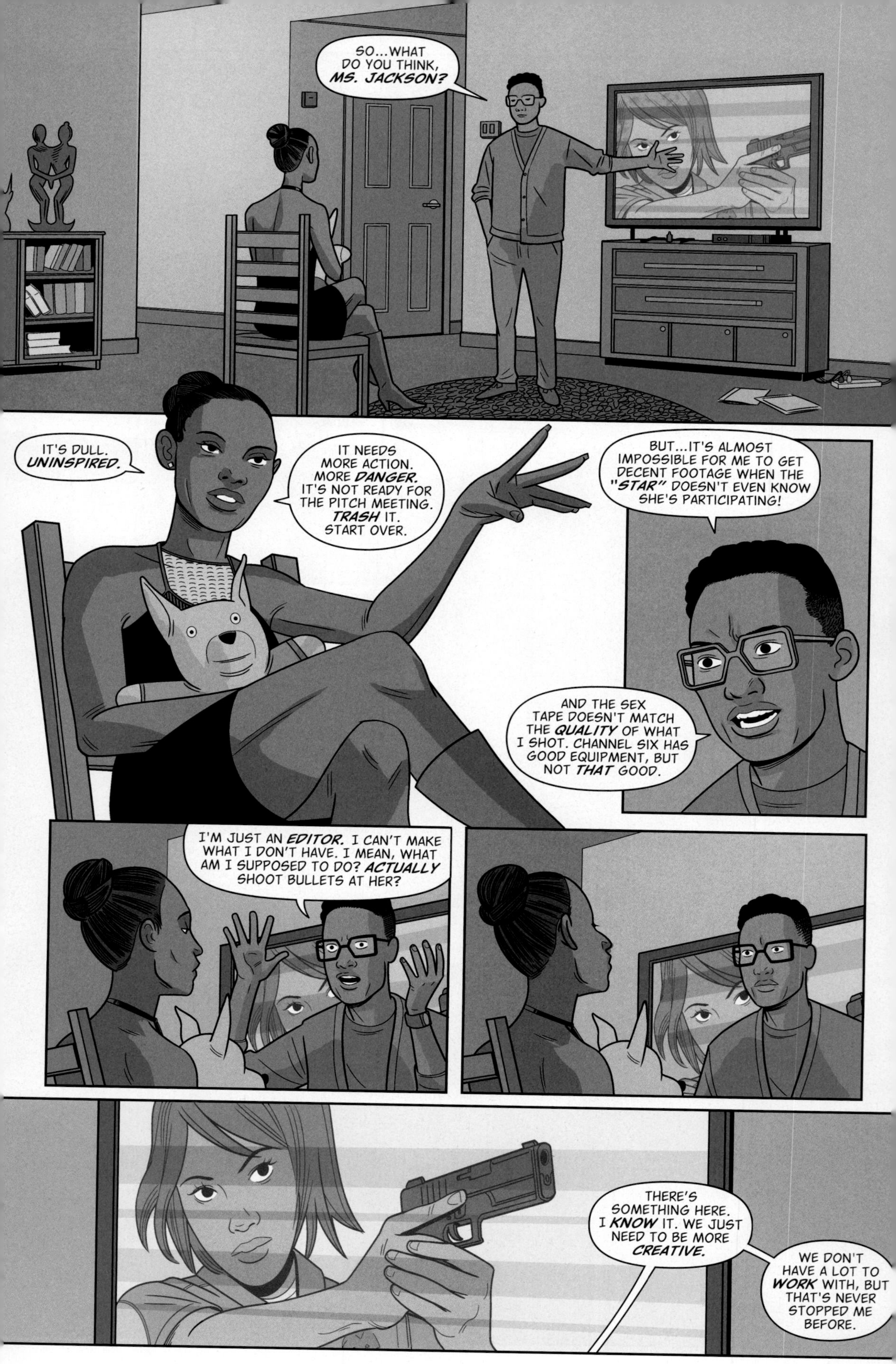
SO...WHAT DO YOU THINK, MS. JACKSON?
IT'S DULL. UNINSPIRED.
IT NEEDS MORE ACTION. MORE DANGER. IT'S NOT READY FOR THE PITCH MEETING. TRASH IT. START OVER.
BUT...IT'S ALMOST IMPOSSIBLE FOR ME TO GET DECENT FOOTAGE WHEN THE "STAR" DOESN'T EVEN KNOW SHE'S PARTICIPATING!
AND THE SEX TAPE DOESN'T MATCH THE QUALITY OF WHAT I SHOT. CHANNEL SIX HAS GOOD EQUIPMENT, BUT NOT THAT GOOD.
I'M JUST AN EDITOR. I CAN'T MAKE WHAT I DON'T HAVE. I MEAN, WHAT AM I SUPPOSED TO DO? ACTUALLY SHOOT BULLETS AT HER?
THERE'S SOMETHING HERE. I KNOW IT. WE JUST NEED TO BE MORE CREATIVE.
WE DON'T HAVE A LOT TO WORK WITH, BUT THAT'S NEVER STOPPED ME BEFORE.

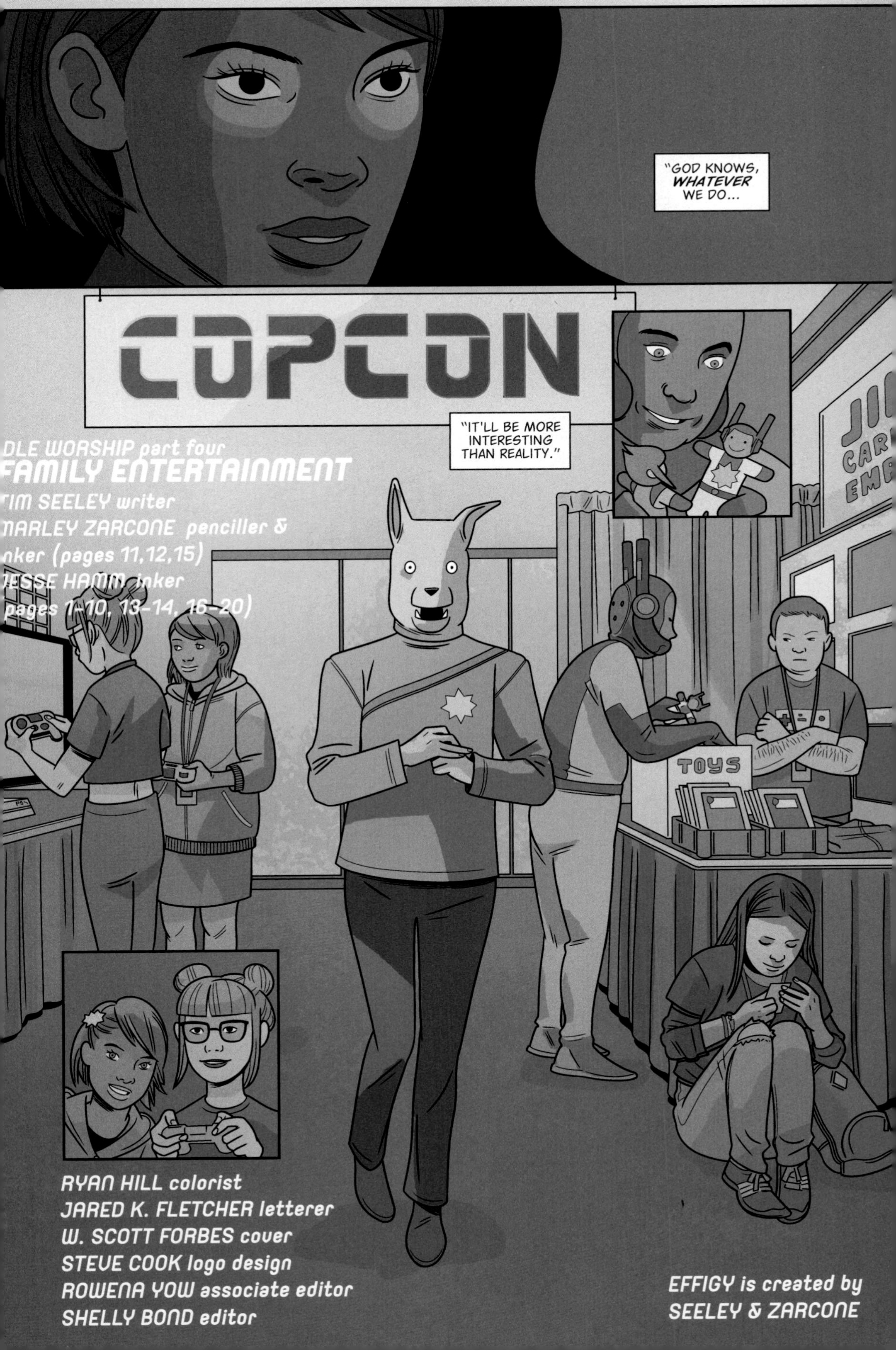

"GOD KNOWS, *WHATEVER* WE DO...
COPCON
"IT'LL BE MORE INTERESTING THAN REALITY."
DLE WORSHIP part four
FAMILY ENTERTAINMENT
TIM SEELEY writer
MARLEY ZARCONE penciller &
nker (pages 11,12,15)
JESSE HAMM inker
pages 1-10, 13-14, 16-20)
TOYS
RYAN HILL colorist
JARED K. FLETCHER letterer
W. SCOTT FORBES cover
STEVE COOK logo design
ROWENA YOW associate editor
SHELLY BOND editor
EFFIGY is created by
SEELEY & ZARCONE

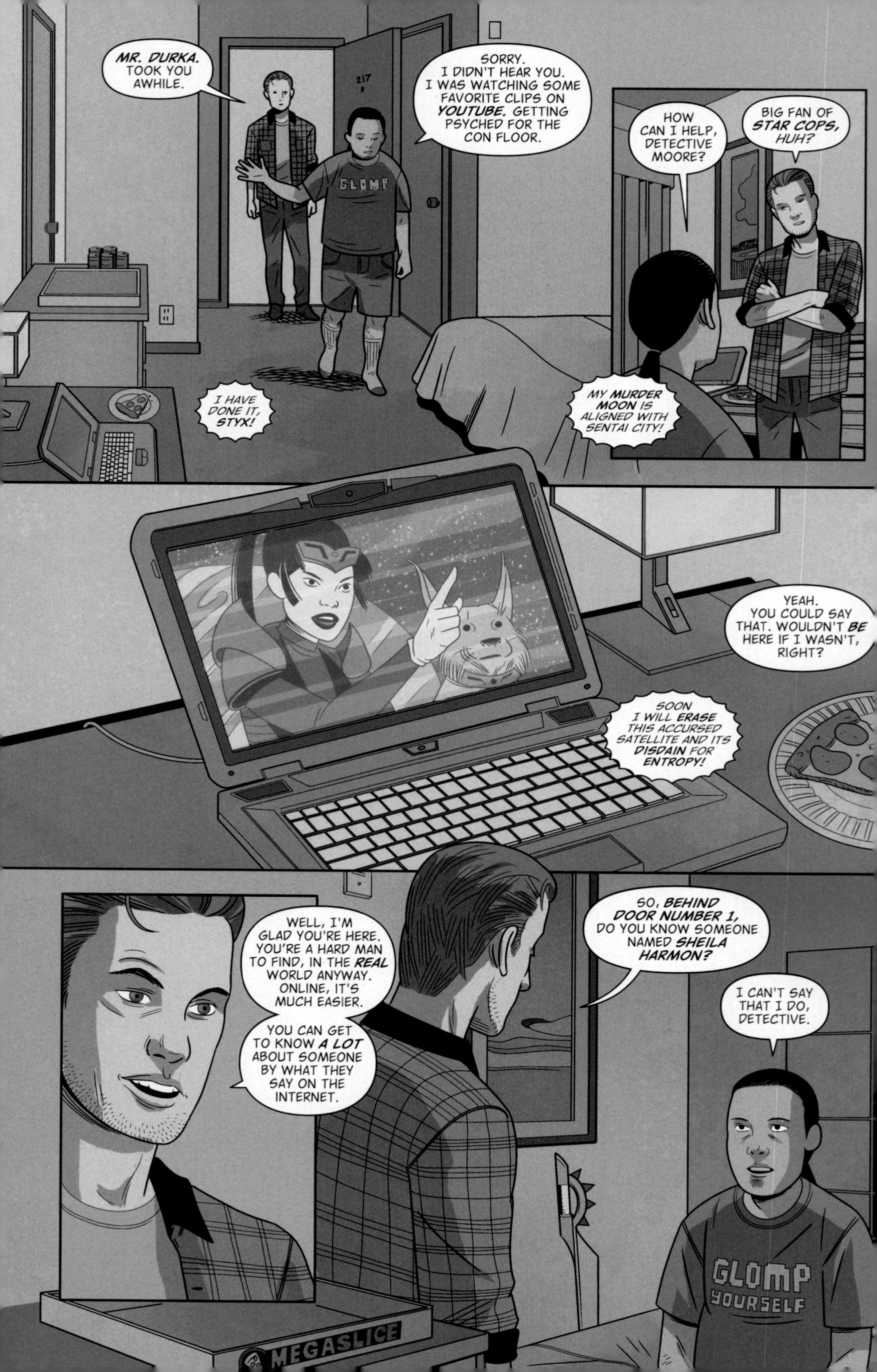
MR. DURKA. TOOK YOU AWHILE.
217
SORRY. I DIDN'T HEAR YOU. I WAS WATCHING SOME FAVORITE CLIPS ON YOUTUBE. GETTING PSYCHED FOR THE CON FLOOR.
GLOMP
HOW CAN I HELP, DETECTIVE MOORE?
BIG FAN OF STAR COPS, HUH?
I HAVE DONE IT, STYX!
MY MURDER MOON IS ALIGNED WITH SENTAI CITY!
YEAH. YOU COULD SAY THAT. WOULDN'T BE HERE IF I WASN'T, RIGHT?
SOON I WILL ERASE THIS ACCURSED SATELLITE AND ITS DISDAIN FOR ENTROPY!
WELL, I'M GLAD YOU'RE HERE. YOU'RE A HARD MAN TO FIND, IN THE REAL WORLD ANYWAY. ONLINE, IT'S MUCH EASIER.
YOU CAN GET TO KNOW A LOT ABOUT SOMEONE BY WHAT THEY SAY ON THE INTERNET.
SO, BEHIND DOOR NUMBER 1, DO YOU KNOW SOMEONE NAMED SHEILA HARMON?
I CAN'T SAY THAT I DO, DETECTIVE.
GLOMP YOURSELF
MEGASLICE

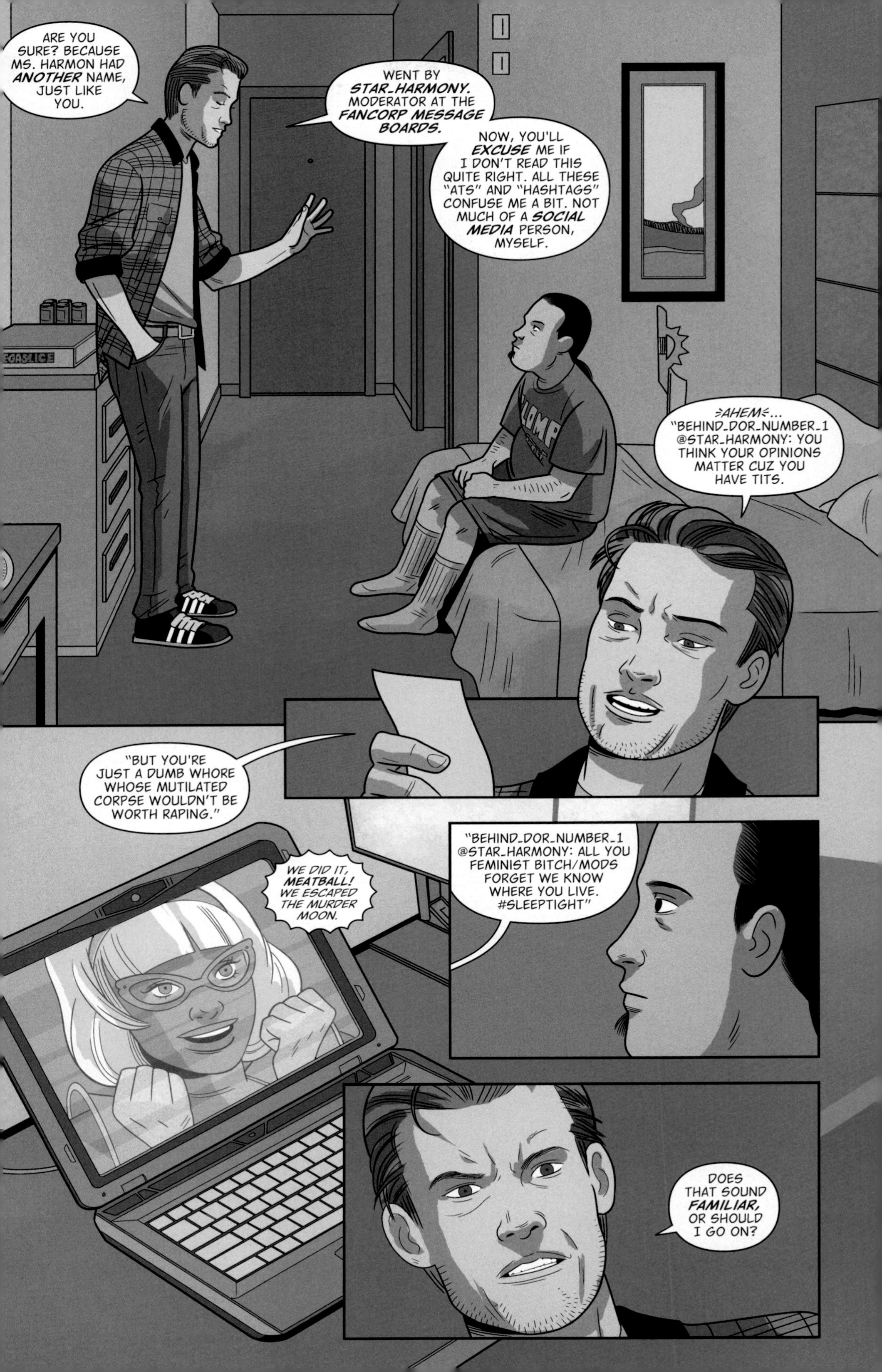
ARE YOU SURE? BECAUSE MS. HARMON HAD ANOTHER NAME, JUST LIKE YOU.
WENT BY STAR_HARMONY. MODERATOR AT THE FANCORP MESSAGE BOARDS.
NOW, YOU'LL EXCUSE ME IF I DON'T READ THIS QUITE RIGHT. ALL THESE "ATS" AND "HASHTAGS" CONFUSE ME A BIT. NOT MUCH OF A SOCIAL MEDIA PERSON, MYSELF.
≥AHEM≤... "BEHIND_DOR_NUMBER_1 @STAR_HARMONY: YOU THINK YOUR OPINIONS MATTER CUZ YOU HAVE TITS.
"BUT YOU'RE JUST A DUMB WHORE WHOSE MUTILATED CORPSE WOULDN'T BE WORTH RAPING."
WE DID IT, MEATBALL! WE ESCAPED THE MURDER MOON.
"BEHIND_DOR_NUMBER_1 @STAR_HARMONY: ALL YOU FEMINIST BITCH/MODS FORGET WE KNOW WHERE YOU LIVE. #SLEEPTIGHT"
DOES THAT SOUND FAMILIAR, OR SHOULD I GO ON?

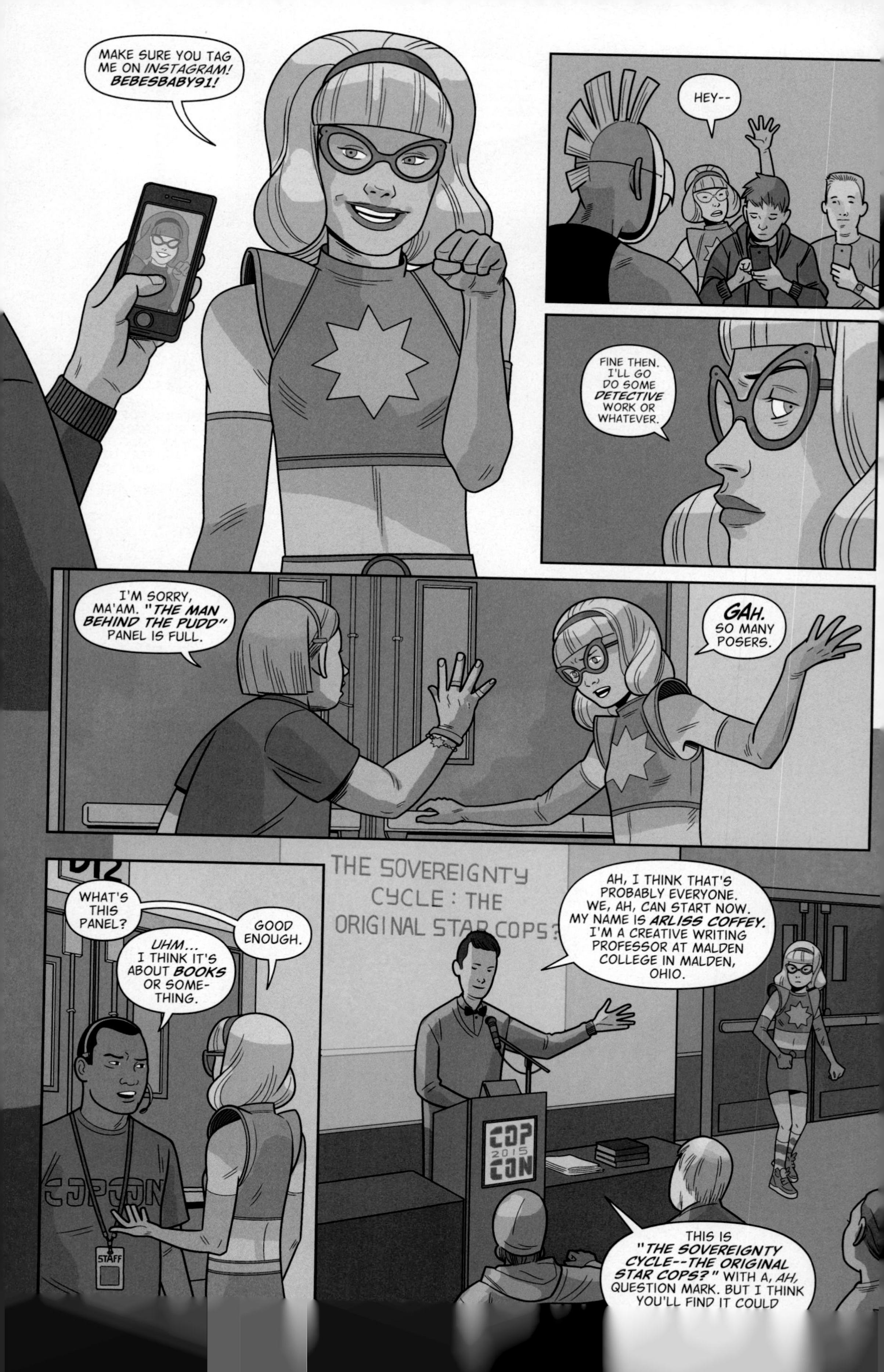
MAKE SURE YOU TAG ME ON *INSTAGRAM!* ***BEBESBABY91!***
HEY--
FINE THEN. I'LL GO DO SOME ***DETECTIVE*** WORK OR WHATEVER.
I'M SORRY, MA'AM. ***"THE MAN BEHIND THE PUDD"*** PANEL IS FULL.
GAH. SO MANY POSERS.
THE SOVEREIGNTY CYCLE : THE ORIGINAL STAR COPS?
WHAT'S THIS PANEL?
UHM... I THINK IT'S ABOUT ***BOOKS*** OR SOME-THING.
GOOD ENOUGH.
AH, I THINK THAT'S PROBABLY EVERYONE. WE, AH, CAN START NOW. MY NAME IS ***ARLISS COFFEY.*** I'M A CREATIVE WRITING PROFESSOR AT MALDEN COLLEGE IN MALDEN, OHIO.
COP CON 2015
STAFF
THIS IS ***"THE SOVEREIGNTY CYCLE--THE ORIGINAL STAR COPS?"*** WITH A, *AH,* QUESTION MARK. BUT I THINK YOU'LL FIND IT COULD

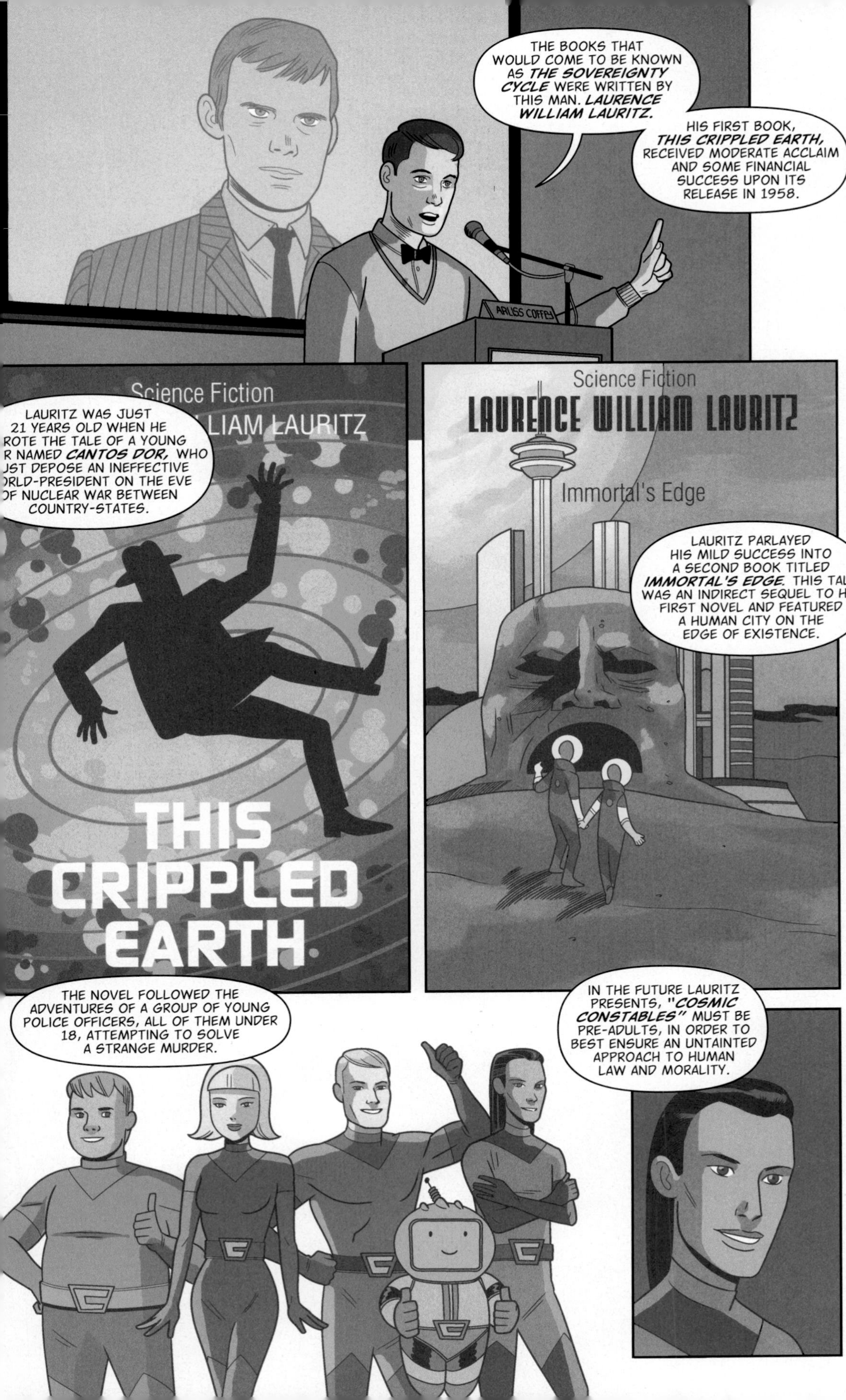
THE BOOKS THAT WOULD COME TO BE KNOWN AS THE SOVEREIGNTY CYCLE WERE WRITTEN BY THIS MAN. LAURENCE WILLIAM LAURITZ.
HIS FIRST BOOK, THIS CRIPPLED EARTH, RECEIVED MODERATE ACCLAIM AND SOME FINANCIAL SUCCESS UPON ITS RELEASE IN 1958.
ARLISS COFFEY
Science Fiction
LLIAM LAURITZ
LAURITZ WAS JUST 21 YEARS OLD WHEN HE ROTE THE TALE OF A YOUNG R NAMED CANTOS DOR, WHO JST DEPOSE AN INEFFECTIVE ORLD-PRESIDENT ON THE EVE OF NUCLEAR WAR BETWEEN COUNTRY-STATES.
THIS CRIPPLED EARTH
Science Fiction
LAURENCE WILLIAM LAURITZ
Immortal's Edge
LAURITZ PARLAYED HIS MILD SUCCESS INTO A SECOND BOOK TITLED IMMORTAL'S EDGE. THIS TALE WAS AN INDIRECT SEQUEL TO HIS FIRST NOVEL AND FEATURED A HUMAN CITY ON THE EDGE OF EXISTENCE.
THE NOVEL FOLLOWED THE ADVENTURES OF A GROUP OF YOUNG POLICE OFFICERS, ALL OF THEM UNDER 18, ATTEMPTING TO SOLVE A STRANGE MURDER.
IN THE FUTURE LAURITZ PRESENTS, "COSMIC CONSTABLES" MUST BE PRE-ADULTS, IN ORDER TO BEST ENSURE AN UNTAINTED APPROACH TO HUMAN LAW AND MORALITY.

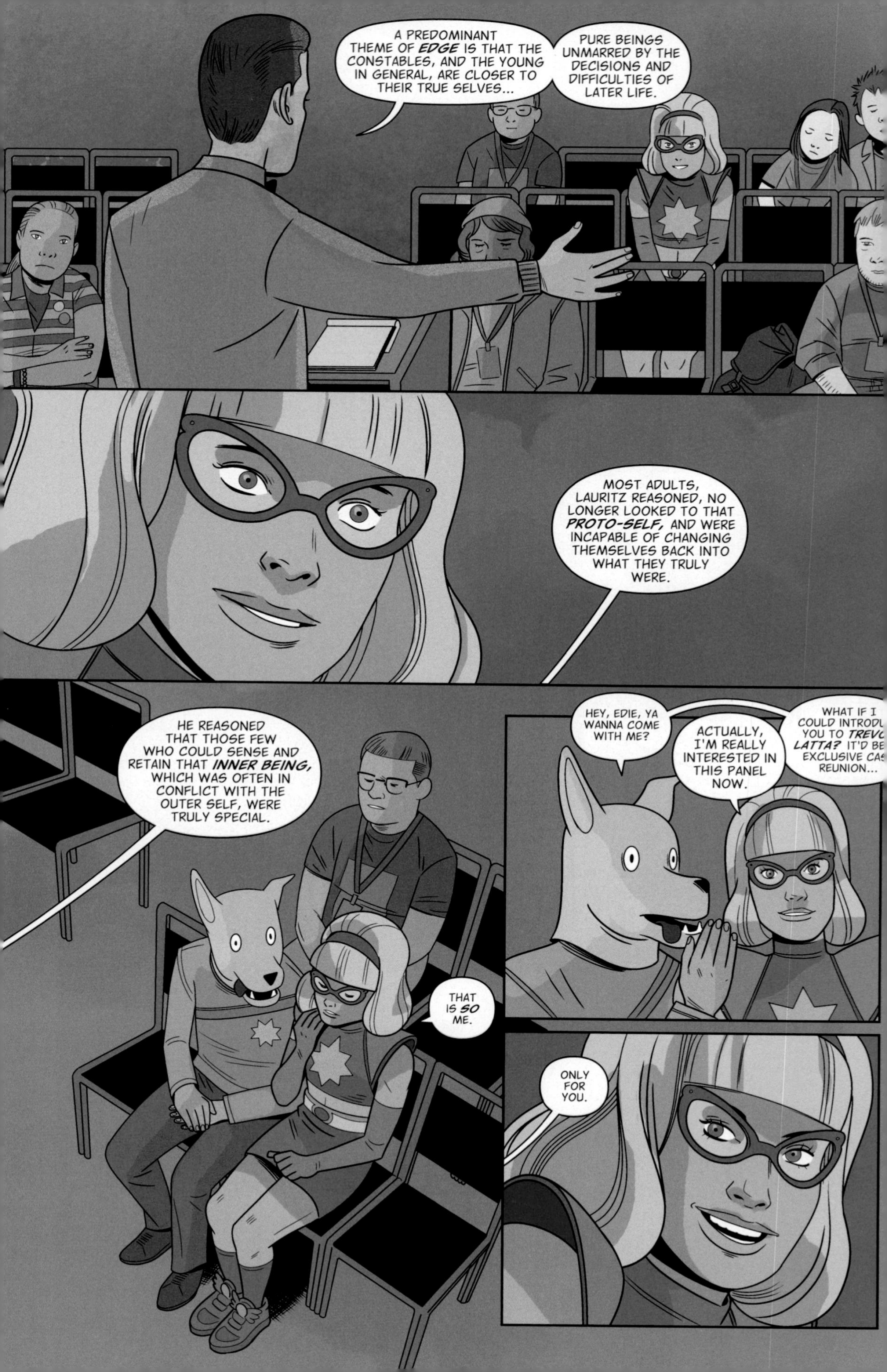
A PREDOMINANT THEME OF EDGE IS THAT THE CONSTABLES, AND THE YOUNG IN GENERAL, ARE CLOSER TO THEIR TRUE SELVES...
PURE BEINGS UNMARRED BY THE DECISIONS AND DIFFICULTIES OF LATER LIFE.
MOST ADULTS, LAURITZ REASONED, NO LONGER LOOKED TO THAT PROTO-SELF, AND WERE INCAPABLE OF CHANGING THEMSELVES BACK INTO WHAT THEY TRULY WERE.
HE REASONED THAT THOSE FEW WHO COULD SENSE AND RETAIN THAT INNER BEING, WHICH WAS OFTEN IN CONFLICT WITH THE OUTER SELF, WERE TRULY SPECIAL.
THAT IS SO ME.
HEY, EDIE, YA WANNA COME WITH ME?
WHAT IF I COULD INTRODU YOU TO TREVO LATTA? IT'D BE EXCLUSIVE CAS REUNION...
ACTUALLY, I'M REALLY INTERESTED IN THIS PANEL NOW.
ONLY FOR YOU.

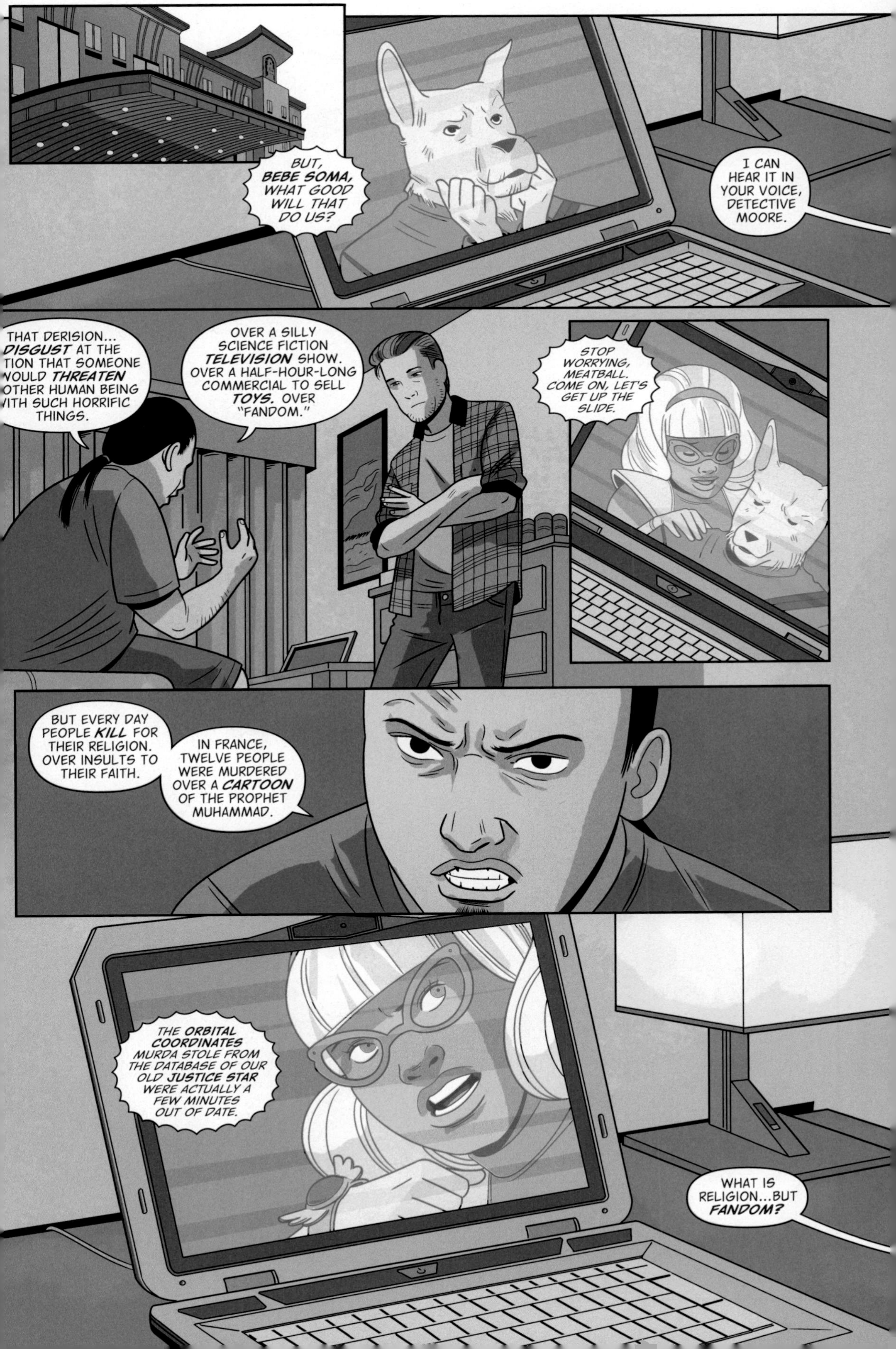
BUT, BEBE SOMA, WHAT GOOD WILL THAT DO US?
I CAN HEAR IT IN YOUR VOICE, DETECTIVE MOORE.
THAT DERISION... DISGUST AT THE TION THAT SOMEONE WOULD THREATEN OTHER HUMAN BEING WITH SUCH HORRIFIC THINGS.
OVER A SILLY SCIENCE FICTION TELEVISION SHOW. OVER A HALF-HOUR-LONG COMMERCIAL TO SELL TOYS. OVER "FANDOM."
STOP WORRYING, MEATBALL. COME ON, LET'S GET UP THE SLIDE.
BUT EVERY DAY PEOPLE KILL FOR THEIR RELIGION. OVER INSULTS TO THEIR FAITH.
IN FRANCE, TWELVE PEOPLE WERE MURDERED OVER A CARTOON OF THE PROPHET MUHAMMAD.
THE ORBITAL COORDINATES MURDA STOLE FROM THE DATABASE OF OUR OLD JUSTICE STAR WERE ACTUALLY A FEW MINUTES OUT OF DATE.
WHAT IS RELIGION...BUT FANDOM?

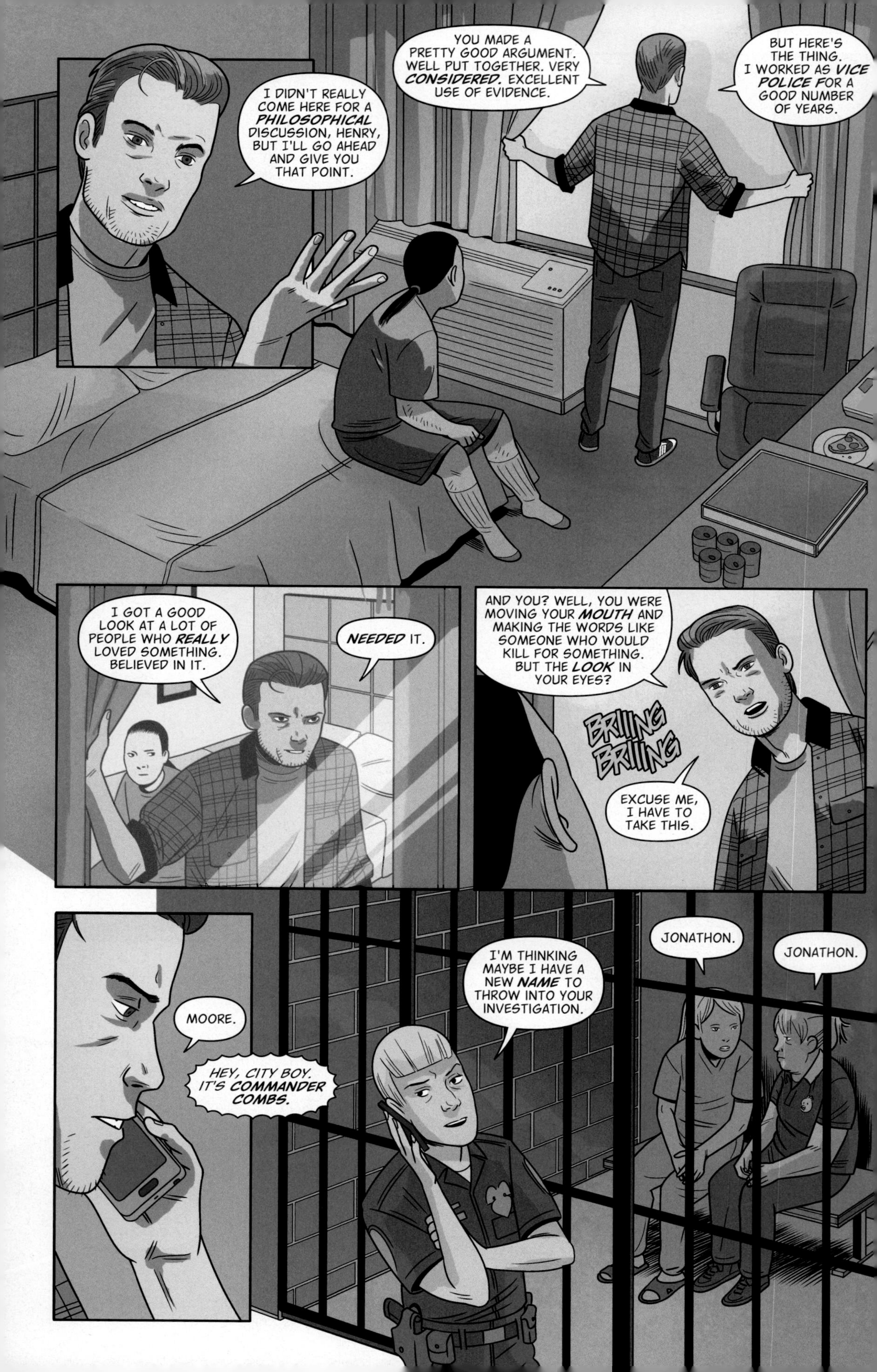
I DIDN'T REALLY COME HERE FOR A PHILOSOPHICAL DISCUSSION, HENRY, BUT I'LL GO AHEAD AND GIVE YOU THAT POINT.
YOU MADE A PRETTY GOOD ARGUMENT. WELL PUT TOGETHER. VERY CONSIDERED. EXCELLENT USE OF EVIDENCE.
BUT HERE'S THE THING. I WORKED AS VICE POLICE FOR A GOOD NUMBER OF YEARS.
I GOT A GOOD LOOK AT A LOT OF PEOPLE WHO REALLY LOVED SOMETHING. BELIEVED IN IT.
NEEDED IT.
AND YOU? WELL, YOU WERE MOVING YOUR MOUTH AND MAKING THE WORDS LIKE SOMEONE WHO WOULD KILL FOR SOMETHING. BUT THE LOOK IN YOUR EYES?
BRIIING BRIIING
EXCUSE ME, I HAVE TO TAKE THIS.
MOORE.
HEY, CITY BOY. IT'S COMMANDER COMBS.
I'M THINKING MAYBE I HAVE A NEW NAME TO THROW INTO YOUR INVESTIGATION.
JONATHON.
JONATHON.

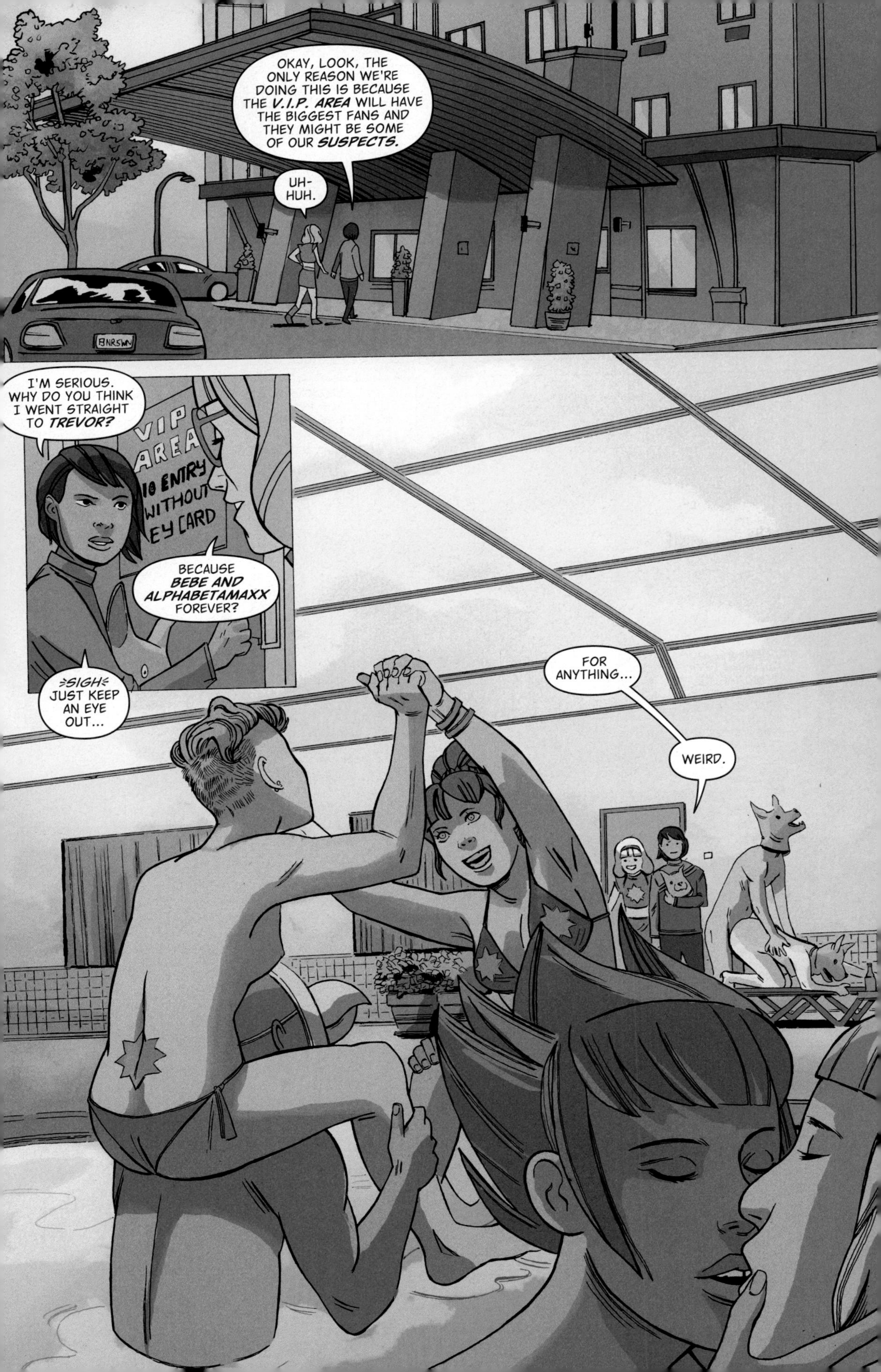

OKAY, LOOK, THE ONLY REASON WE'RE DOING THIS IS BECAUSE THE V.I.P. AREA WILL HAVE THE BIGGEST FANS AND THEY MIGHT BE SOME OF OUR SUSPECTS.
UH-HUH.
I'M SERIOUS. WHY DO YOU THINK I WENT STRAIGHT TO TREVOR?
VIP AREA
NO ENTRY WITHOUT KEY CARD
BECAUSE BEBE AND ALPHABETAMAXX FOREVER?
SIGH JUST KEEP AN EYE OUT...
FOR ANYTHING...
WEIRD.

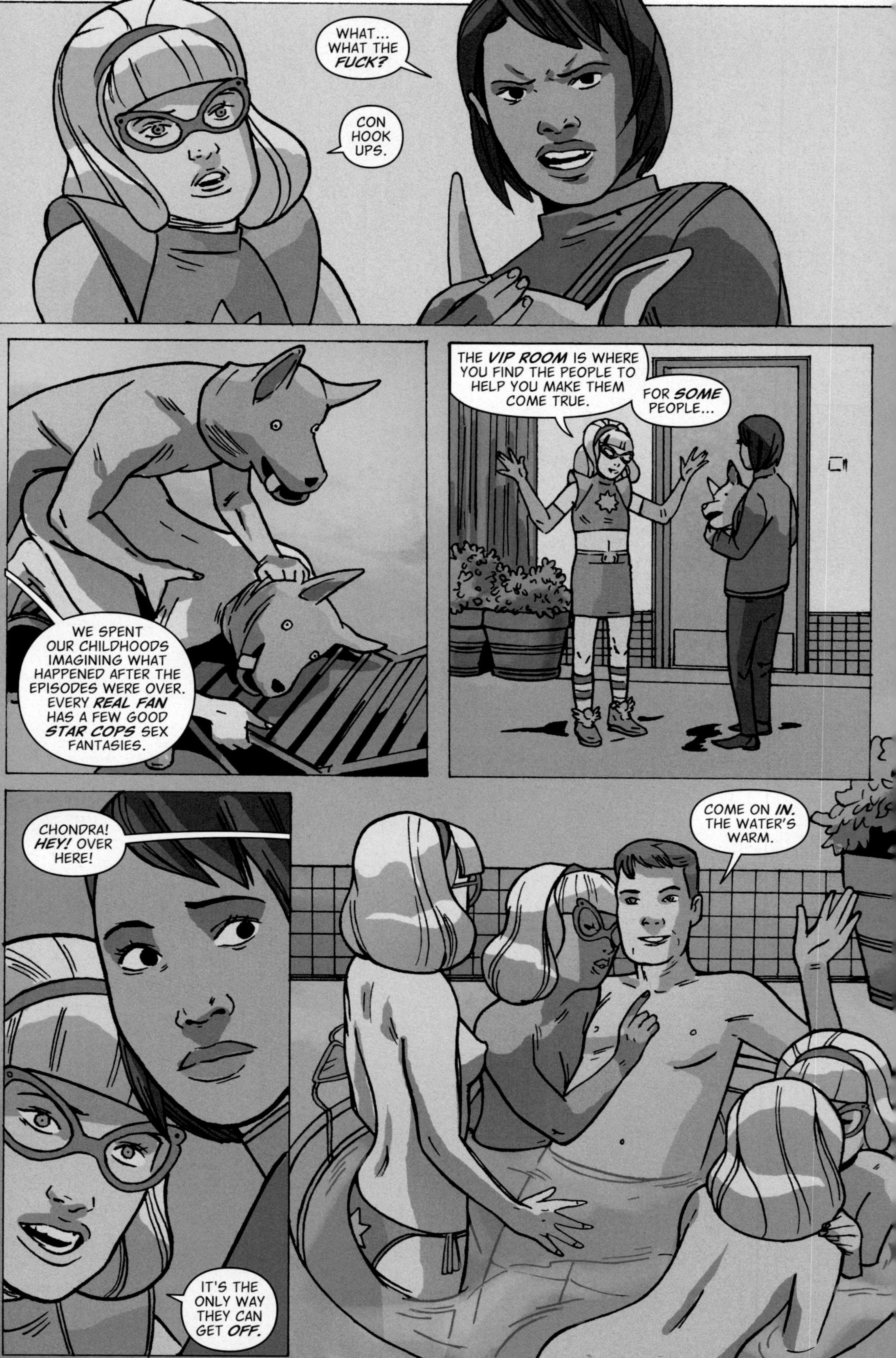
WHAT... WHAT THE FUCK?
CON HOOK UPS.
WE SPENT OUR CHILDHOODS IMAGINING WHAT HAPPENED AFTER THE EPISODES WERE OVER. EVERY REAL FAN HAS A FEW GOOD STAR COPS SEX FANTASIES.
THE VIP ROOM IS WHERE YOU FIND THE PEOPLE TO HELP YOU MAKE THEM COME TRUE.
FOR SOME PEOPLE...
CHONDRA! HEY! OVER HERE!
COME ON IN. THE WATER'S WARM.
IT'S THE ONLY WAY THEY CAN GET OFF.

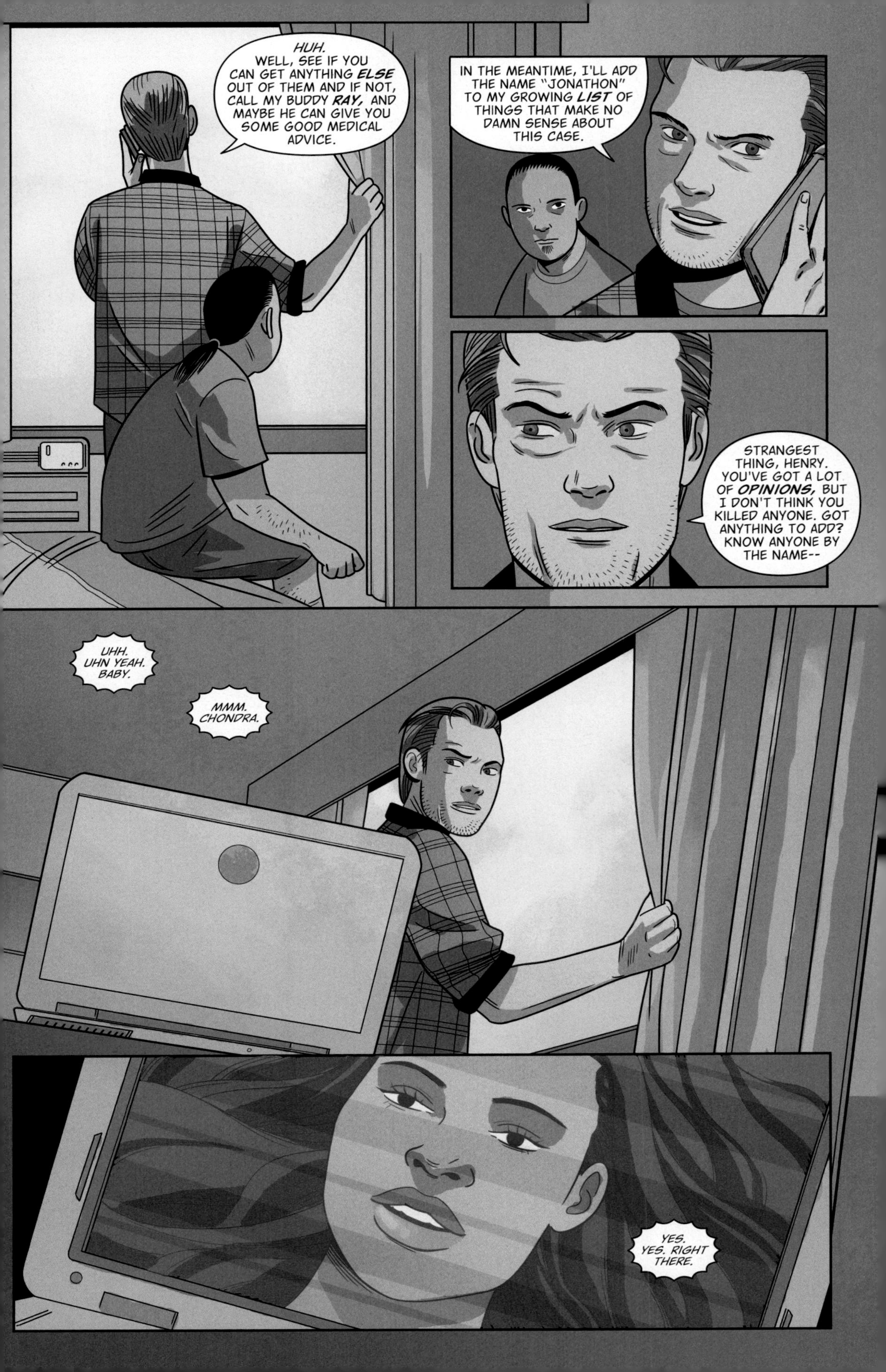
HUH. WELL, SEE IF YOU CAN GET ANYTHING ELSE OUT OF THEM AND IF NOT, CALL MY BUDDY RAY, AND MAYBE HE CAN GIVE YOU SOME GOOD MEDICAL ADVICE.
IN THE MEANTIME, I'LL ADD THE NAME "JONATHON" TO MY GROWING LIST OF THINGS THAT MAKE NO DAMN SENSE ABOUT THIS CASE.
STRANGEST THING, HENRY. YOU'VE GOT A LOT OF OPINIONS, BUT I DON'T THINK YOU KILLED ANYONE. GOT ANYTHING TO ADD? KNOW ANYONE BY THE NAME--
UHH. UHN YEAH. BABY.
MMM. CHONDRA.
YES. YES. RIGHT THERE.

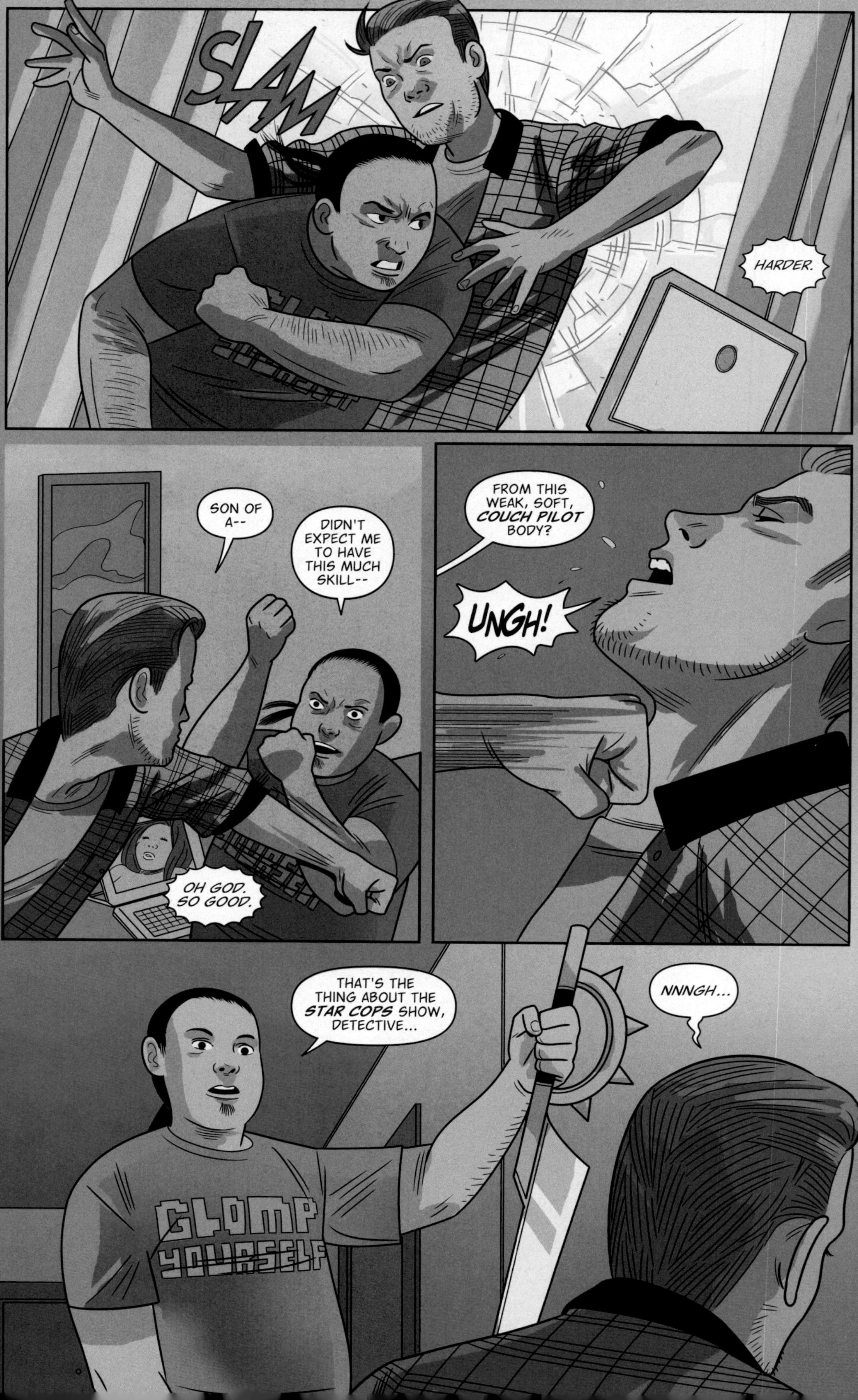
SLAM
HARDER.
SON OF A--
DIDN'T EXPECT ME TO HAVE THIS MUCH SKILL--
OH GOD. SO GOOD.
FROM THIS WEAK, SOFT, COUCH PILOT BODY?
UNGH!
THAT'S THE THING ABOUT THE STAR COPS SHOW, DETECTIVE...
NNNGH...
GLOMP YOURSELF

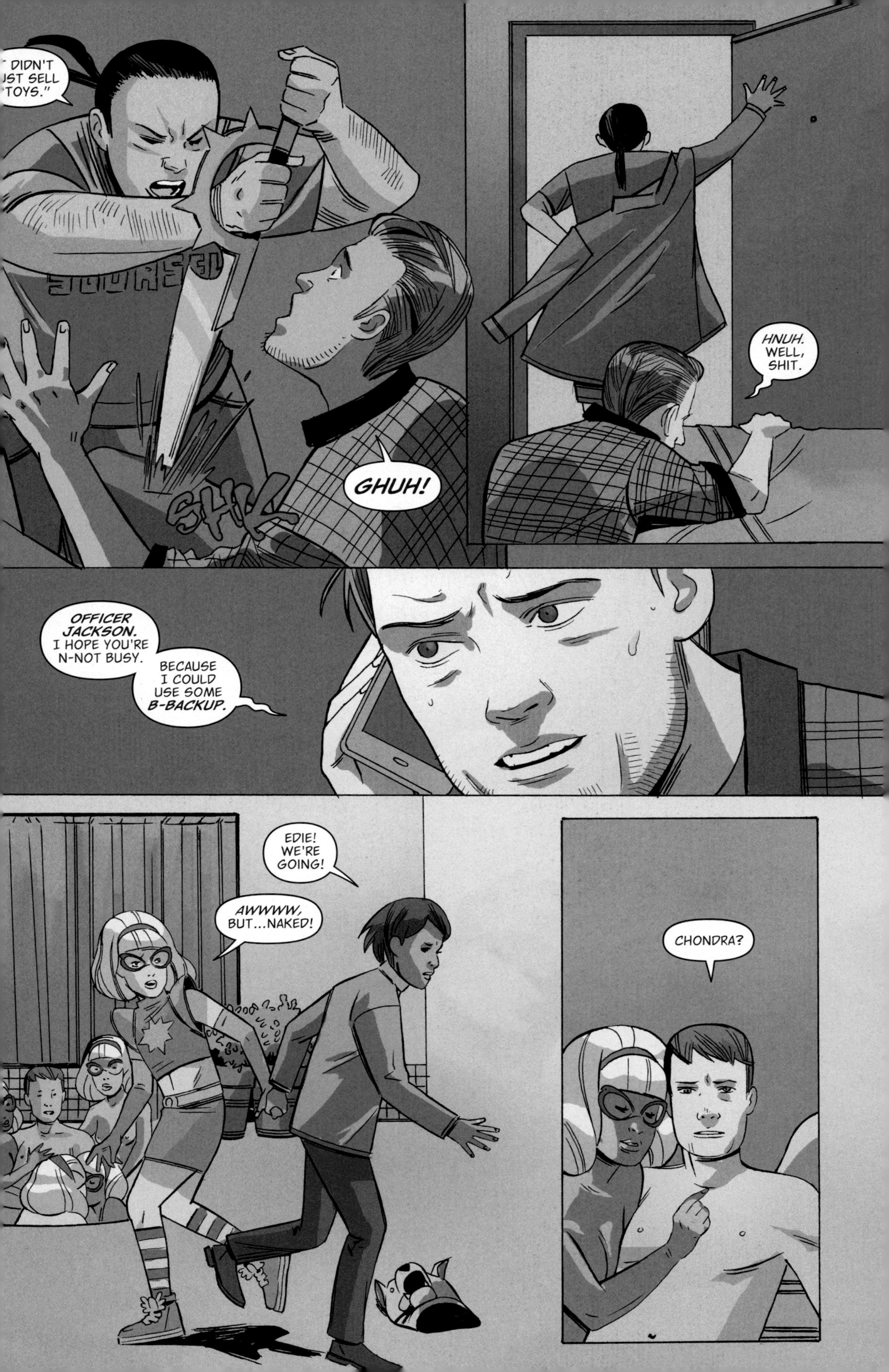

T DIDN'T
JST SELL
TOYS."
SHK
GHUH!
HNUH. WELL, SHIT.
OFFICER JACKSON. I HOPE YOU'RE N-NOT BUSY.
BECAUSE I COULD USE SOME B-BACKUP.
EDIE! WE'RE GOING!
AWWWW, BUT...NAKED!
CHONDRA?

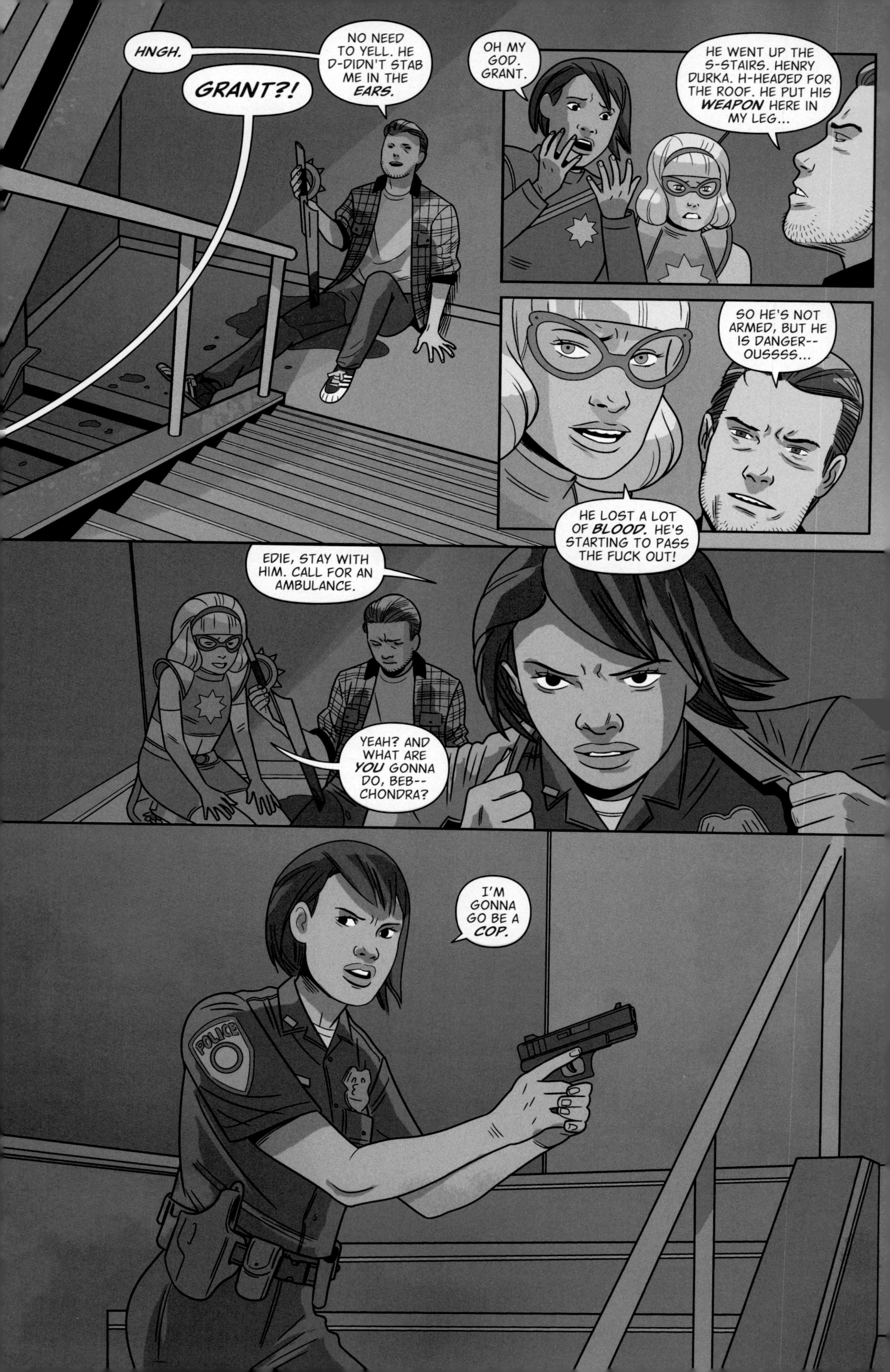
HNGH.
GRANT?!
NO NEED TO YELL. HE D-DIDN'T STAB ME IN THE EARS.
OH MY GOD. GRANT.
HE WENT UP THE S-STAIRS. HENRY DURKA. H-HEADED FOR THE ROOF. HE PUT HIS WEAPON HERE IN MY LEG...
SO HE'S NOT ARMED, BUT HE IS DANGER--OUSSSS...
HE LOST A LOT OF BLOOD. HE'S STARTING TO PASS THE FUCK OUT!
EDIE, STAY WITH HIM. CALL FOR AN AMBULANCE.
YEAH? AND WHAT ARE YOU GONNA DO, BEB--CHONDRA?
I'M GONNA GO BE A COP.
POLICE

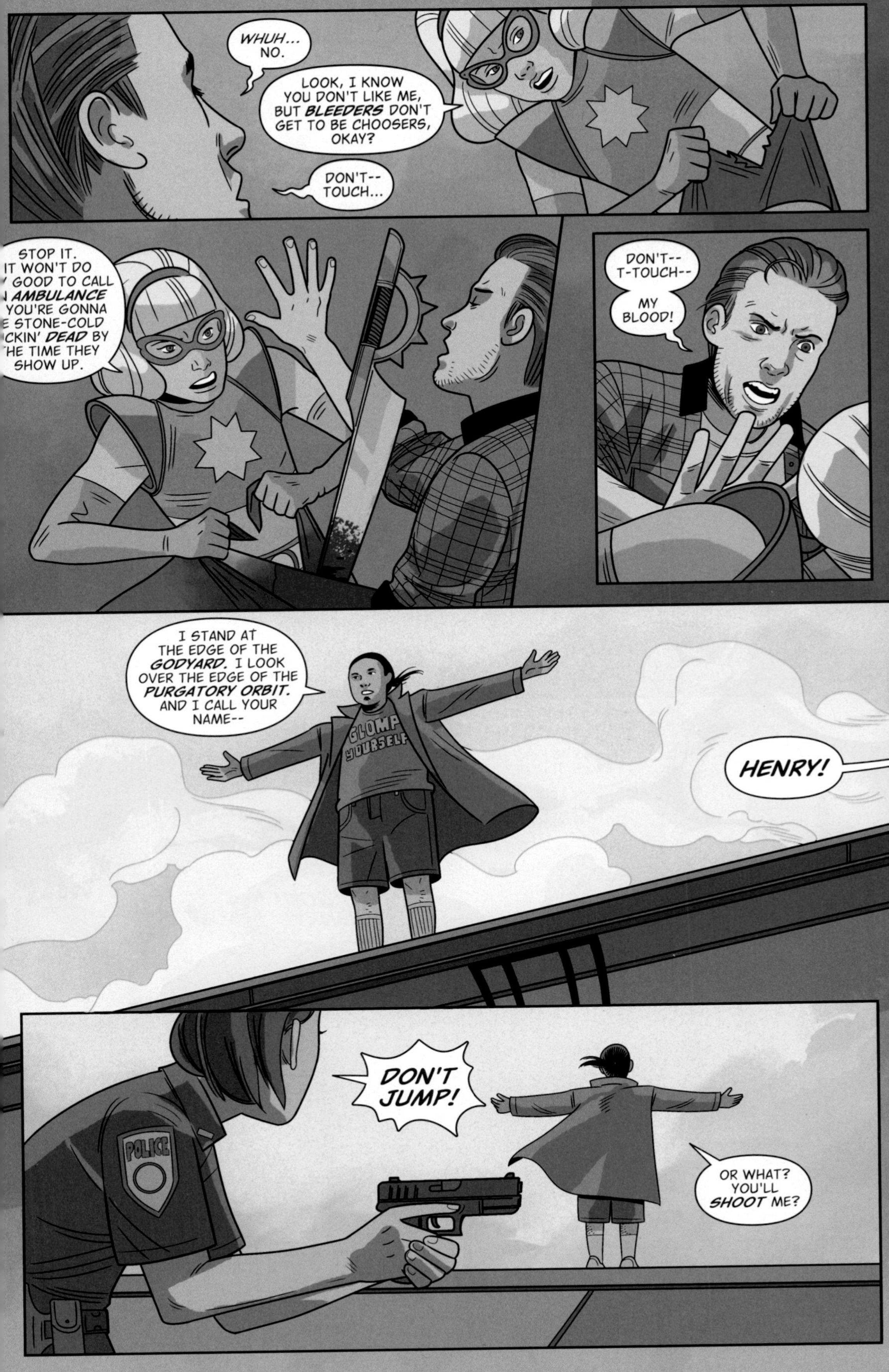
WHUH... NO.
LOOK, I KNOW YOU DON'T LIKE ME, BUT BLEEDERS DON'T GET TO BE CHOOSERS, OKAY?
DON'T-- TOUCH...
STOP IT. IT WON'T DO GOOD TO CALL AMBULANCE YOU'RE GONNA STONE-COLD DEAD BY THE TIME THEY SHOW UP.
DON'T-- T-TOUCH--
MY BLOOD!
I STAND AT THE EDGE OF THE GODYARD. I LOOK OVER THE EDGE OF THE PURGATORY ORBIT. AND I CALL YOUR NAME--
GLOMP YOURSELF
HENRY!
DON'T JUMP!
POLICE
OR WHAT? YOU'LL SHOOT ME?

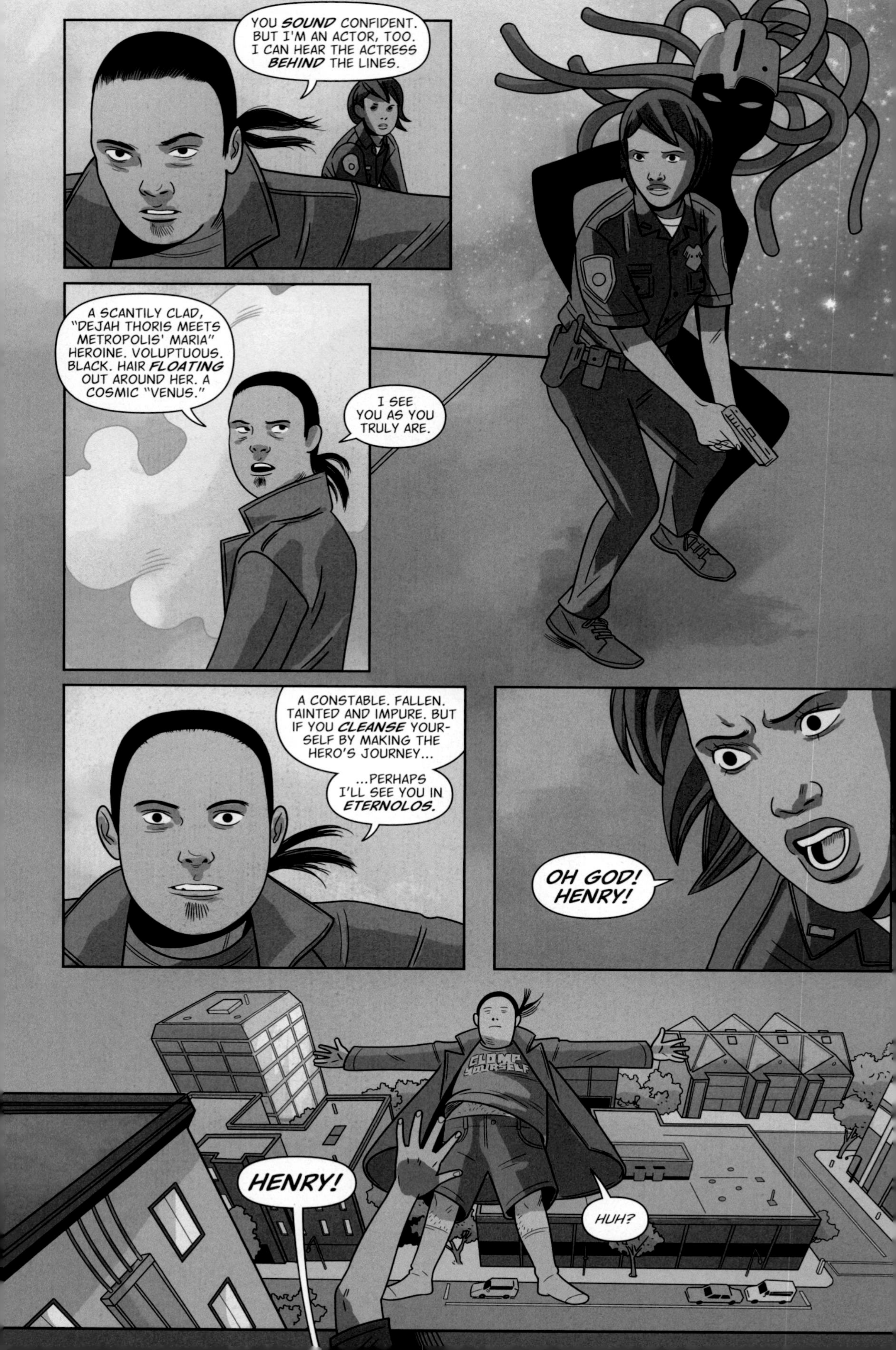
YOU SOUND CONFIDENT. BUT I'M AN ACTOR, TOO. I CAN HEAR THE ACTRESS BEHIND THE LINES.
A SCANTILY CLAD, "DEJAH THORIS MEETS METROPOLIS' MARIA" HEROINE. VOLUPTUOUS. BLACK. HAIR FLOATING OUT AROUND HER. A COSMIC "VENUS."
I SEE YOU AS YOU TRULY ARE.
A CONSTABLE. FALLEN. TAINTED AND IMPURE. BUT IF YOU CLEANSE YOURSELF BY MAKING THE HERO'S JOURNEY...
...PERHAPS I'LL SEE YOU IN ETERNOLOS.
OH GOD! HENRY!
GLOMP YOURSELF
HENRY!
HUH?

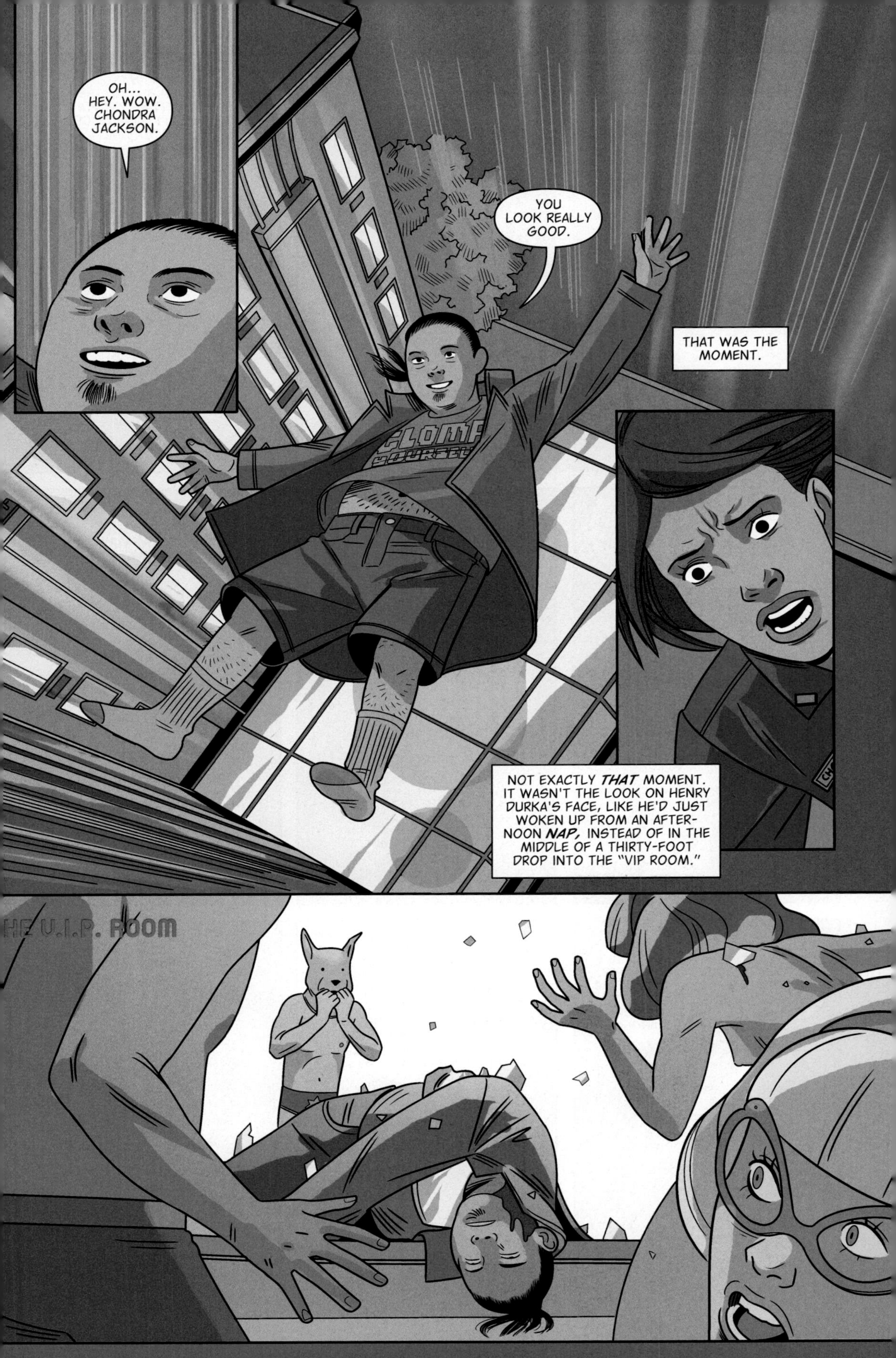
OH... HEY. WOW. CHONDRA JACKSON.
YOU LOOK REALLY GOOD.
THAT WAS THE MOMENT.
NOT EXACTLY THAT MOMENT. IT WASN'T THE LOOK ON HENRY DURKA'S FACE, LIKE HE'D JUST WOKEN UP FROM AN AFTER-NOON NAP, INSTEAD OF IN THE MIDDLE OF A THIRTY-FOOT DROP INTO THE "VIP ROOM."
HE V.I.P. ROOM

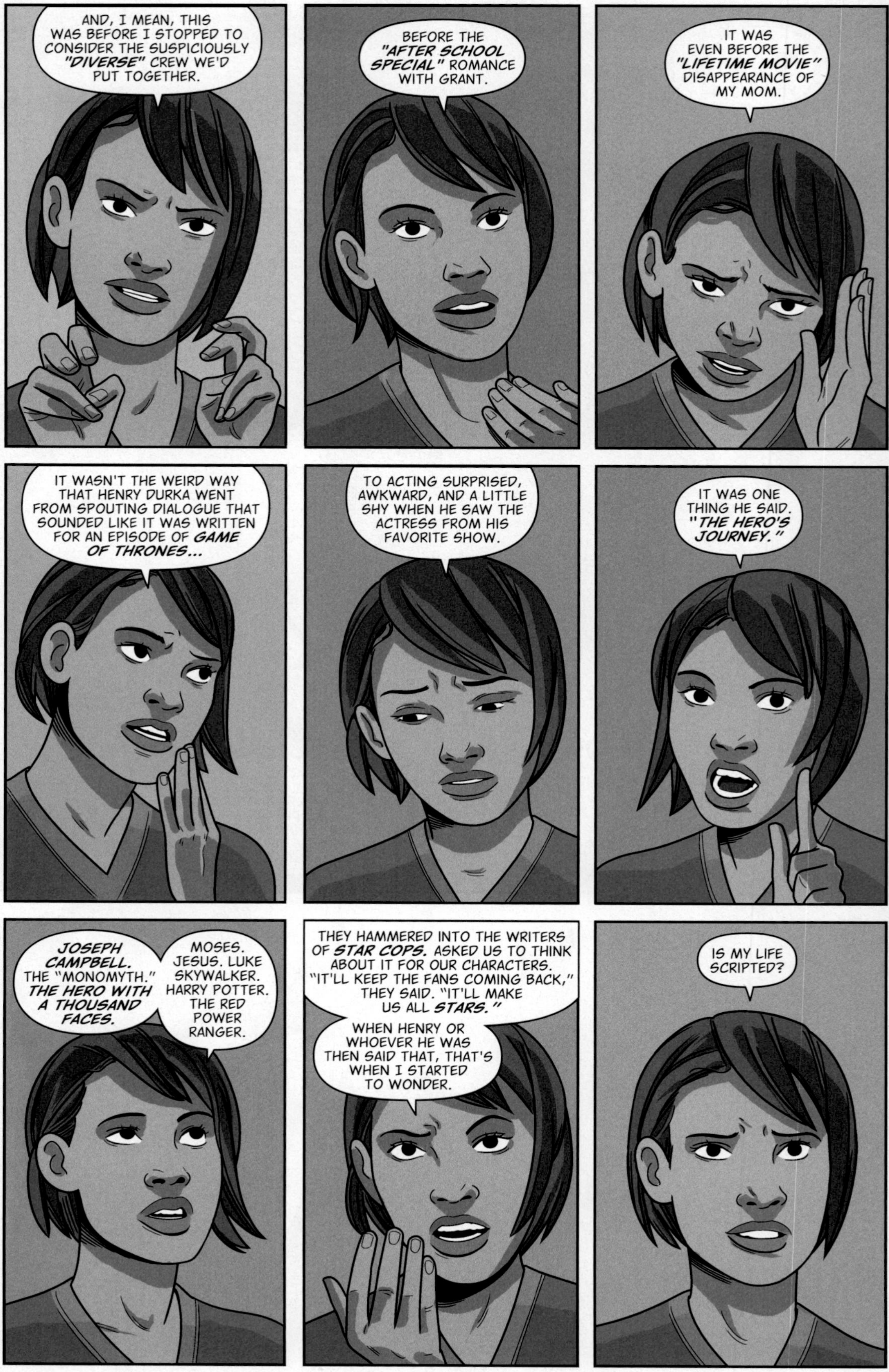
AND, I MEAN, THIS WAS BEFORE I STOPPED TO CONSIDER THE SUSPICIOUSLY "DIVERSE" CREW WE'D PUT TOGETHER.
BEFORE THE "AFTER SCHOOL SPECIAL" ROMANCE WITH GRANT.
IT WAS EVEN BEFORE THE "LIFETIME MOVIE" DISAPPEARANCE OF MY MOM.
IT WASN'T THE WEIRD WAY THAT HENRY DURKA WENT FROM SPOUTING DIALOGUE THAT SOUNDED LIKE IT WAS WRITTEN FOR AN EPISODE OF GAME OF THRONES...
TO ACTING SURPRISED, AWKWARD, AND A LITTLE SHY WHEN HE SAW THE ACTRESS FROM HIS FAVORITE SHOW.
IT WAS ONE THING HE SAID. "THE HERO'S JOURNEY."
JOSEPH CAMPBELL. THE "MONOMYTH." THE HERO WITH A THOUSAND FACES.
MOSES. JESUS. LUKE SKYWALKER. HARRY POTTER. THE RED POWER RANGER.
THEY HAMMERED INTO THE WRITERS OF STAR COPS. ASKED US TO THINK ABOUT IT FOR OUR CHARACTERS. "IT'LL KEEP THE FANS COMING BACK," THEY SAID. "IT'LL MAKE US ALL STARS."
WHEN HENRY OR WHOEVER HE WAS THEN SAID THAT, THAT'S WHEN I STARTED TO WONDER.
IS MY LIFE SCRIPTED?

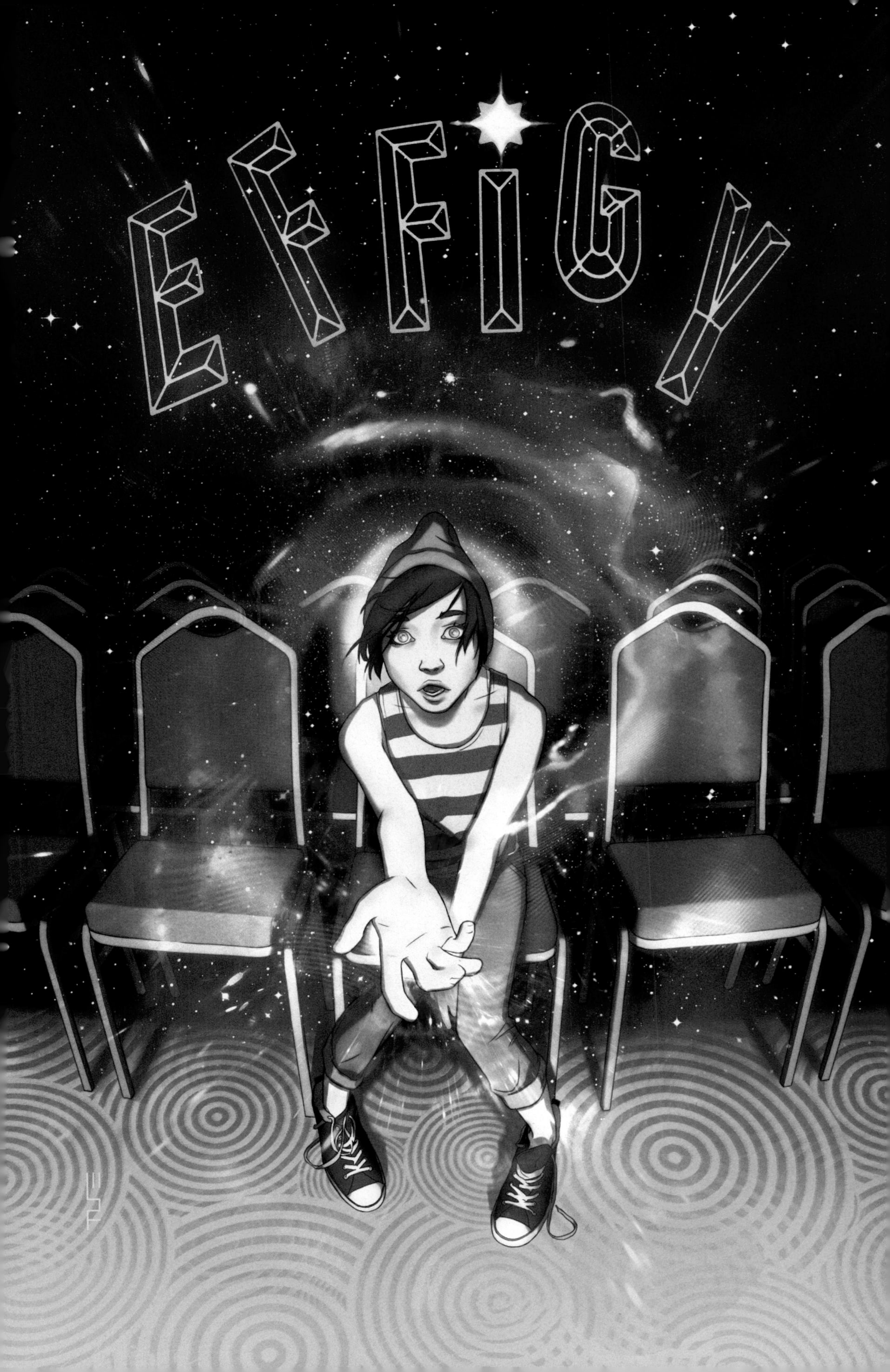
EFFIGY

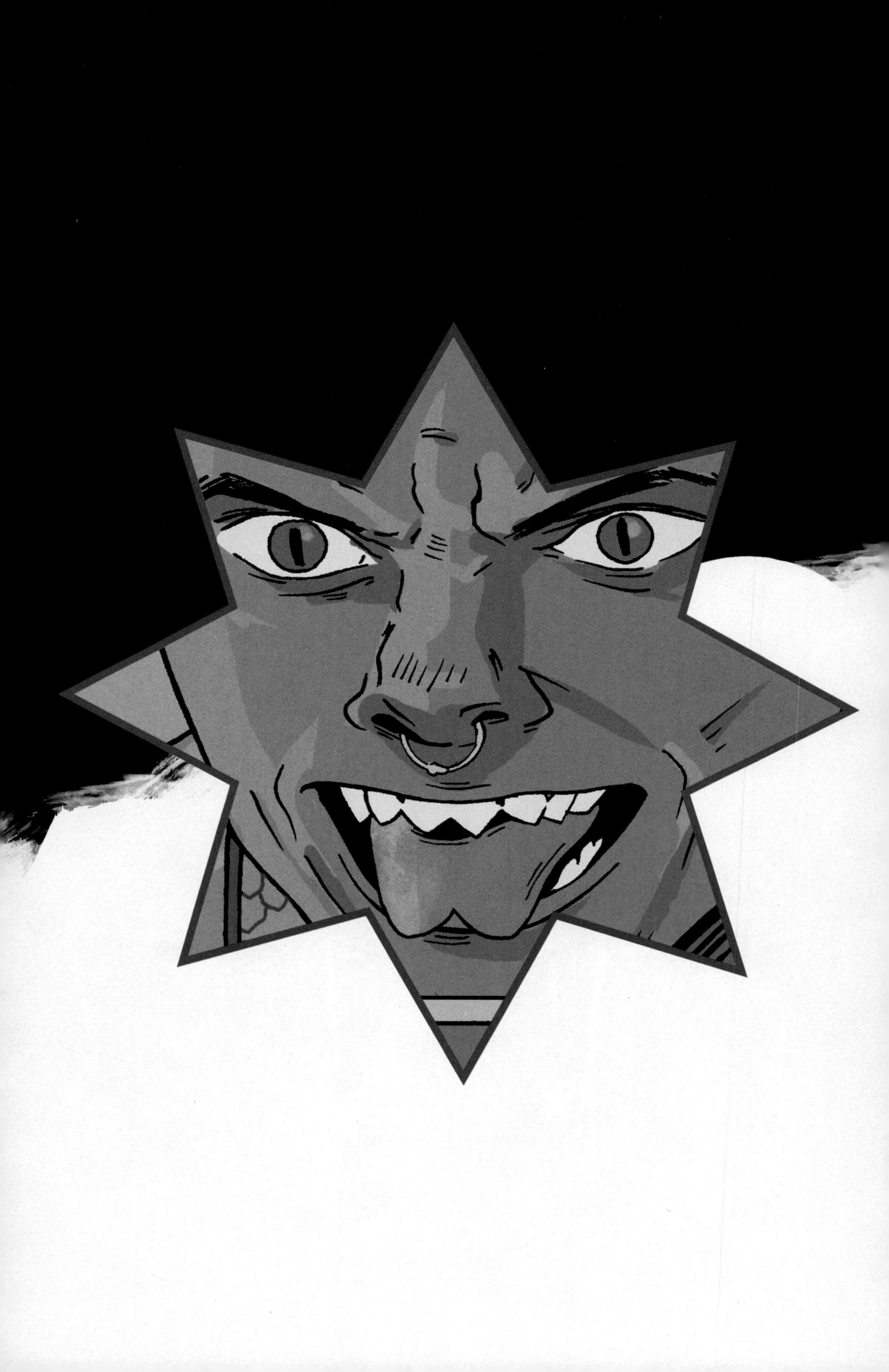

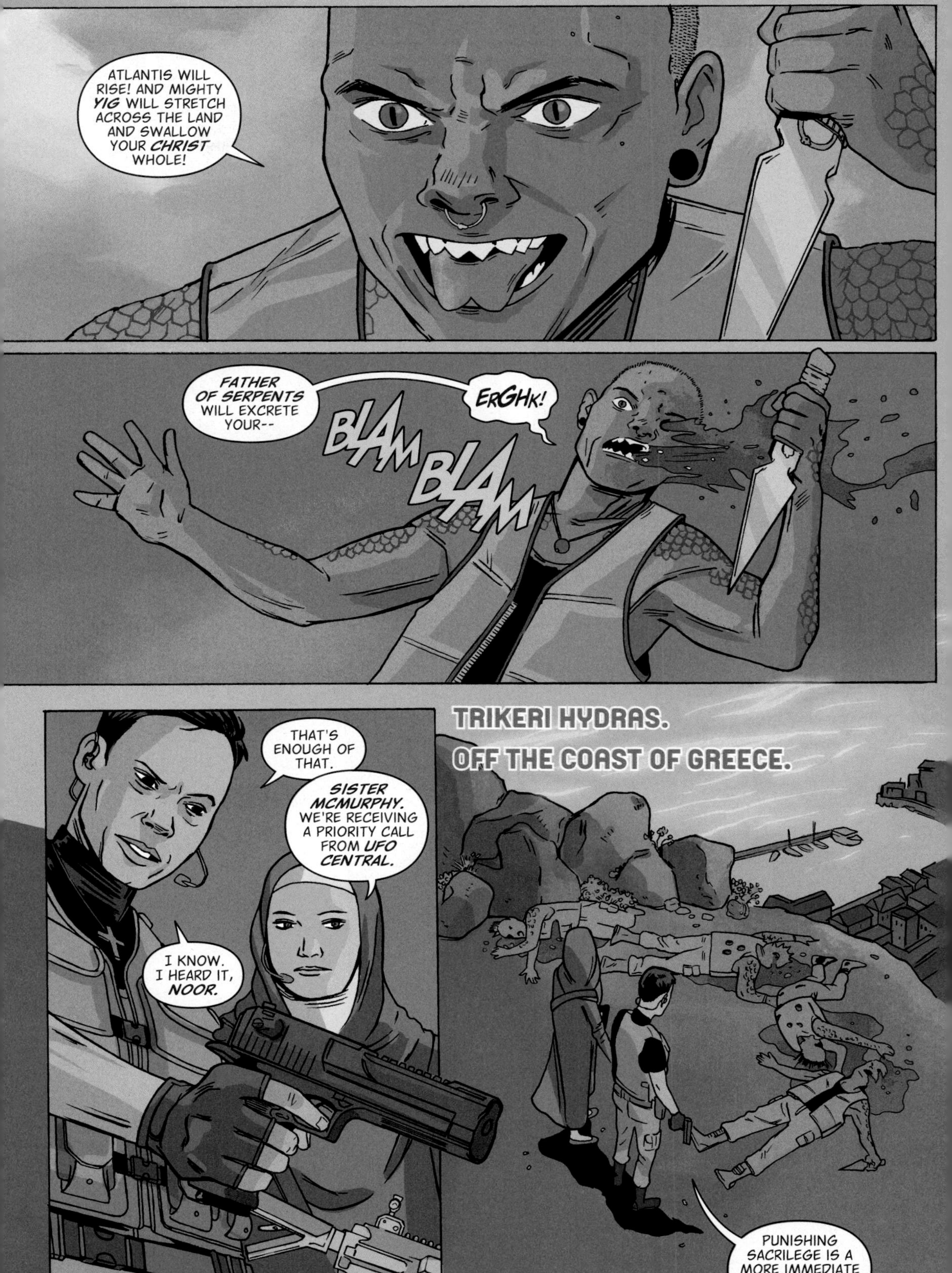

ATLANTIS WILL RISE! AND MIGHTY YIG WILL STRETCH ACROSS THE LAND AND SWALLOW YOUR CHRIST WHOLE!
FATHER OF SERPENTS WILL EXCRETE YOUR--
BLAM
BLAM
ERGHK!
TRIKERI HYDRAS.
OFF THE COAST OF GREECE.
THAT'S ENOUGH OF THAT.
SISTER MCMURPHY. WE'RE RECEIVING A PRIORITY CALL FROM UFO CENTRAL.
I KNOW. I HEARD IT, NOOR.
PUNISHING SACRILEGE IS A MORE IMMEDIATE PRIORITY. PATCH 'EM IN.

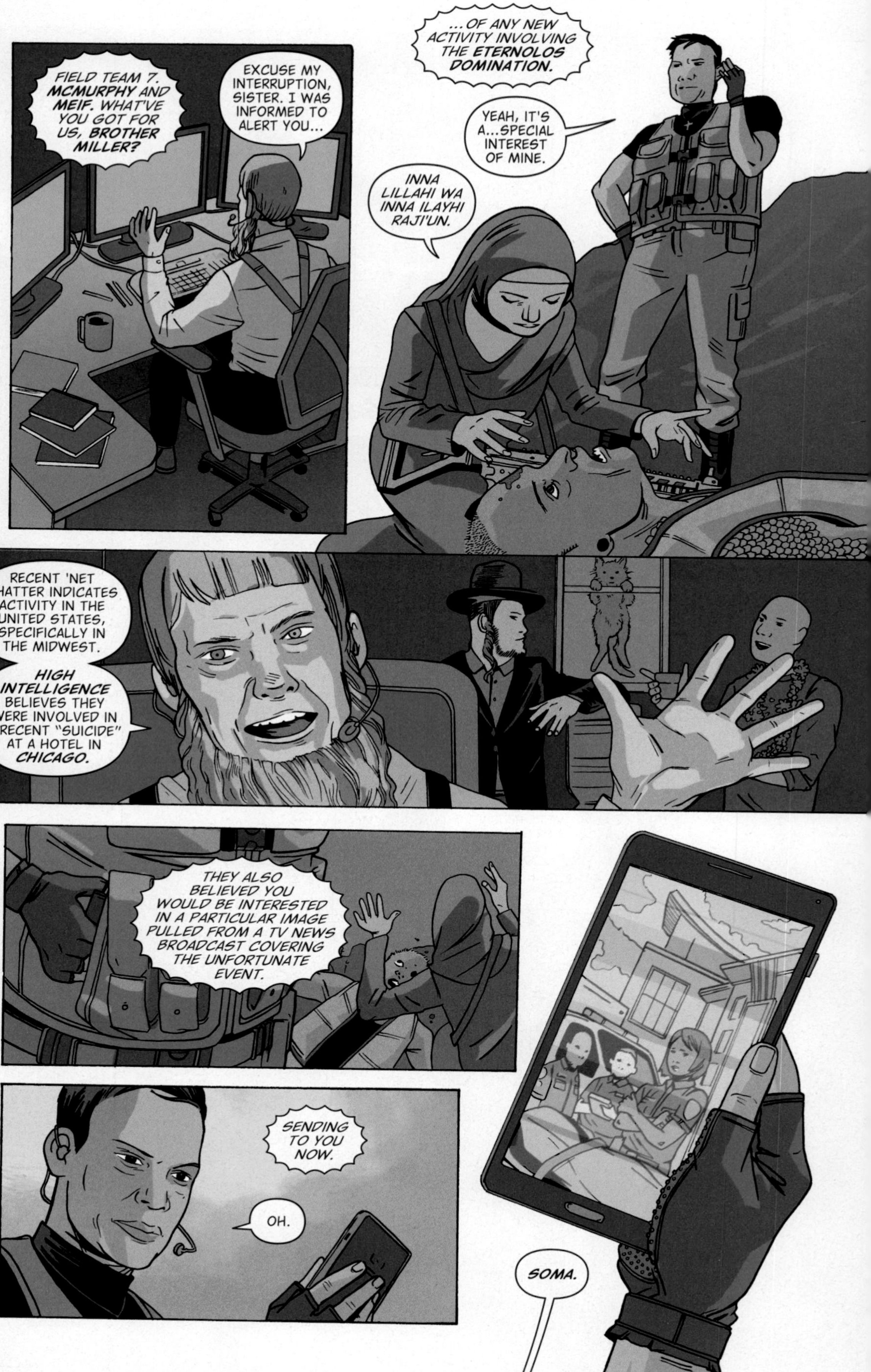
FIELD TEAM 7. MCMURPHY AND MEIF. WHAT'VE YOU GOT FOR US, BROTHER MILLER?
EXCUSE MY INTERRUPTION, SISTER. I WAS INFORMED TO ALERT YOU...
...OF ANY NEW ACTIVITY INVOLVING THE ETERNOLOS DOMINATION.
YEAH, IT'S A...SPECIAL INTEREST OF MINE.
INNA LILLAHI WA INNA ILAYHI RAJI'UN.
RECENT 'NET CHATTER INDICATES ACTIVITY IN THE UNITED STATES, SPECIFICALLY IN THE MIDWEST.
HIGH INTELLIGENCE BELIEVES THEY WERE INVOLVED IN A RECENT "SUICIDE" AT A HOTEL IN CHICAGO.
THEY ALSO BELIEVED YOU WOULD BE INTERESTED IN A PARTICULAR IMAGE PULLED FROM A TV NEWS BROADCAST COVERING THE UNFORTUNATE EVENT.
SENDING TO YOU NOW.
OH.
SOMA.

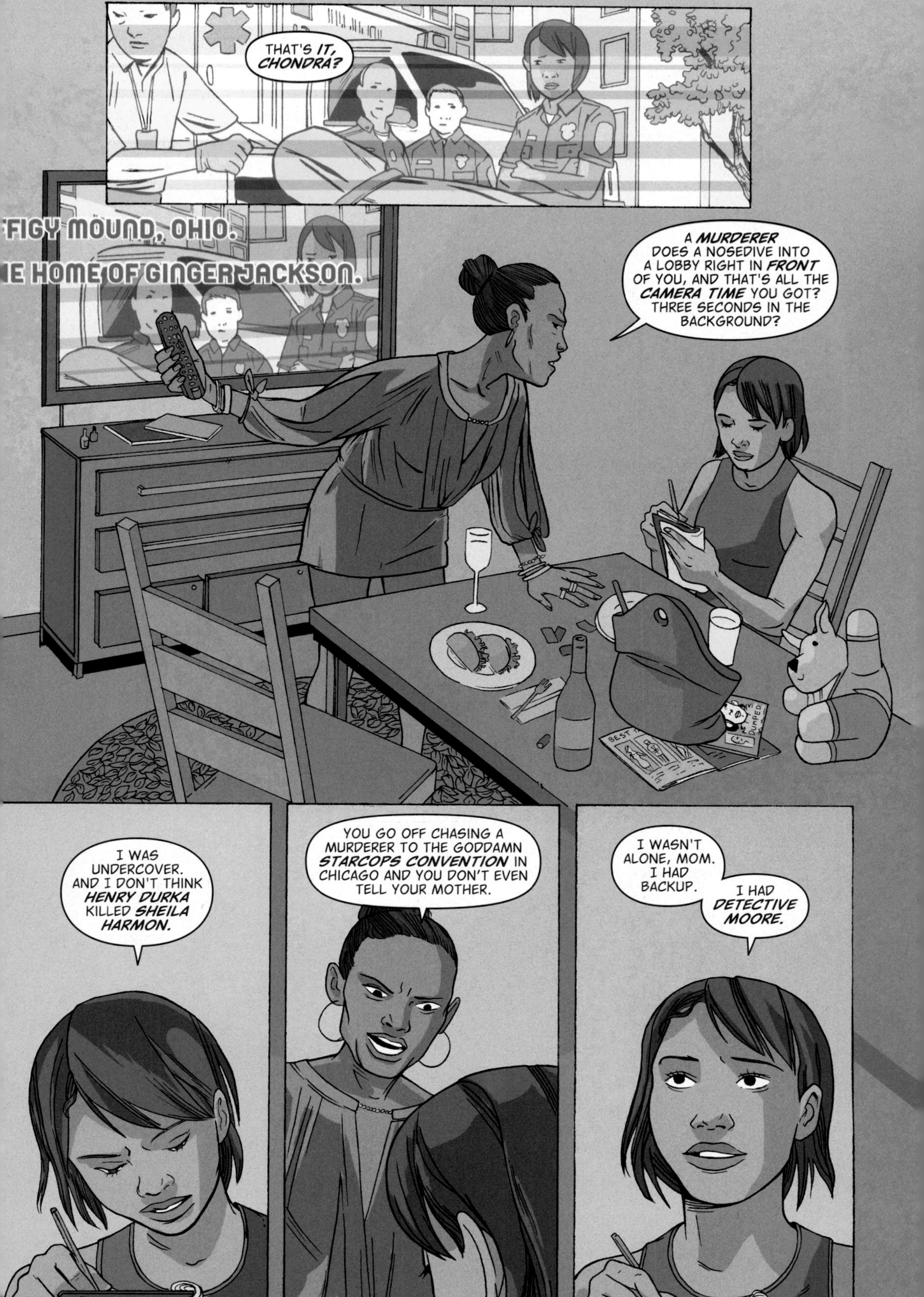
THAT'S IT, CHONDRA?
FIGY MOUND, OHIO.
E HOME OF GINGER JACKSON.
A MURDERER DOES A NOSEDIVE INTO A LOBBY RIGHT IN FRONT OF YOU, AND THAT'S ALL THE CAMERA TIME YOU GOT? THREE SECONDS IN THE BACKGROUND?
BEST
DUMPED
I WAS UNDERCOVER. AND I DON'T THINK HENRY DURKA KILLED SHEILA HARMON.
YOU GO OFF CHASING A MURDERER TO THE GODDAMN STARCOPS CONVENTION IN CHICAGO AND YOU DON'T EVEN TELL YOUR MOTHER.
I WASN'T ALONE, MOM. I HAD BACKUP.
I HAD DETECTIVE MOORE.

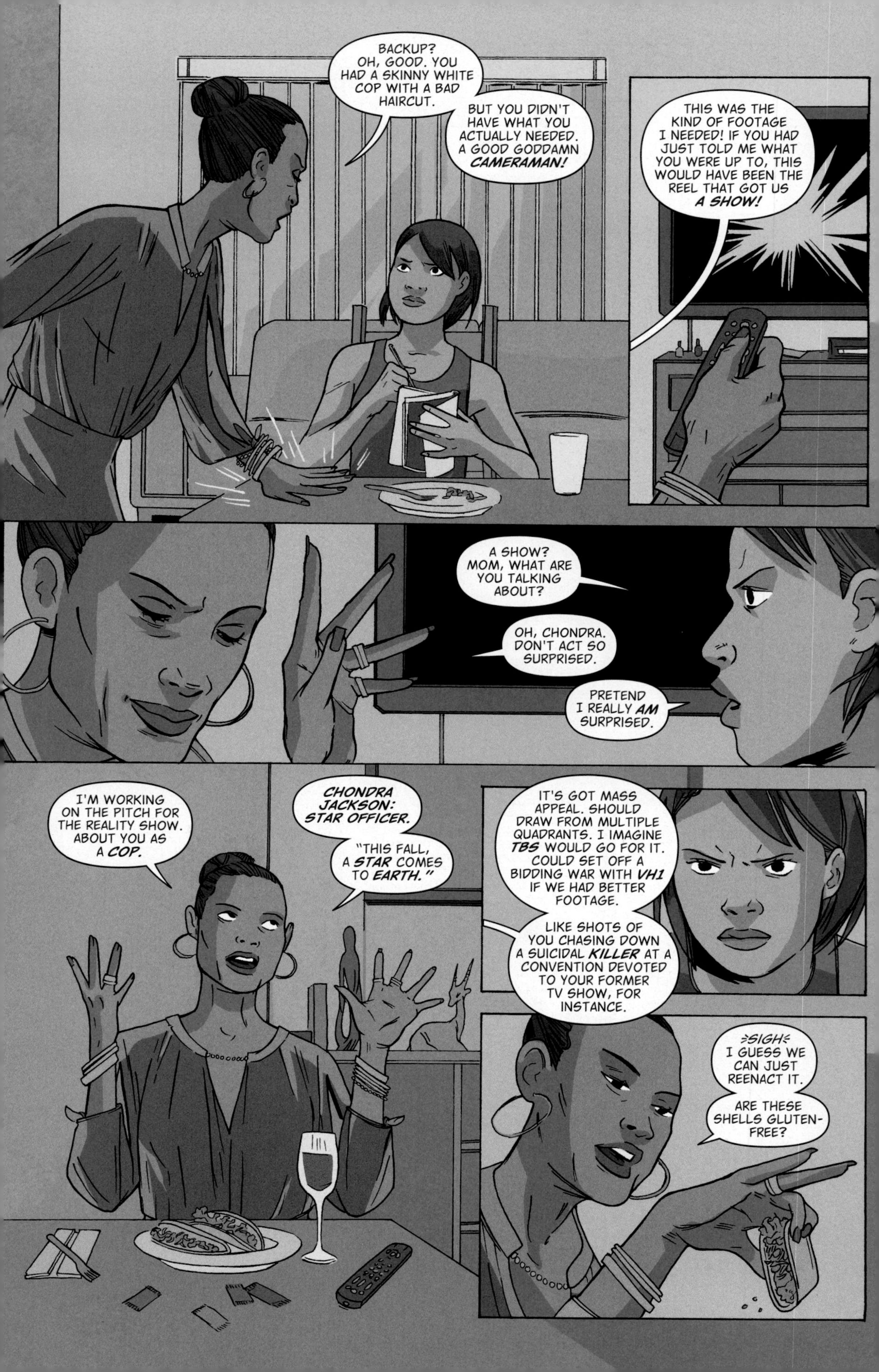
BACKUP? OH, GOOD. YOU HAD A SKINNY WHITE COP WITH A BAD HAIRCUT.
BUT YOU DIDN'T HAVE WHAT YOU ACTUALLY NEEDED. A GOOD GODDAMN CAMERAMAN!
THIS WAS THE KIND OF FOOTAGE I NEEDED! IF YOU HAD JUST TOLD ME WHAT YOU WERE UP TO, THIS WOULD HAVE BEEN THE REEL THAT GOT US A SHOW!
A SHOW? MOM, WHAT ARE YOU TALKING ABOUT?
OH, CHONDRA. DON'T ACT SO SURPRISED.
PRETEND I REALLY AM SURPRISED.
I'M WORKING ON THE PITCH FOR THE REALITY SHOW. ABOUT YOU AS A COP.
CHONDRA JACKSON: STAR OFFICER.
"THIS FALL, A STAR COMES TO EARTH."
IT'S GOT MASS APPEAL. SHOULD DRAW FROM MULTIPLE QUADRANTS. I IMAGINE TBS WOULD GO FOR IT. COULD SET OFF A BIDDING WAR WITH VH1 IF WE HAD BETTER FOOTAGE.
LIKE SHOTS OF YOU CHASING DOWN A SUICIDAL KILLER AT A CONVENTION DEVOTED TO YOUR FORMER TV SHOW, FOR INSTANCE.
SIGH
I GUESS WE CAN JUST REENACT IT.
ARE THESE SHELLS GLUTEN-FREE?

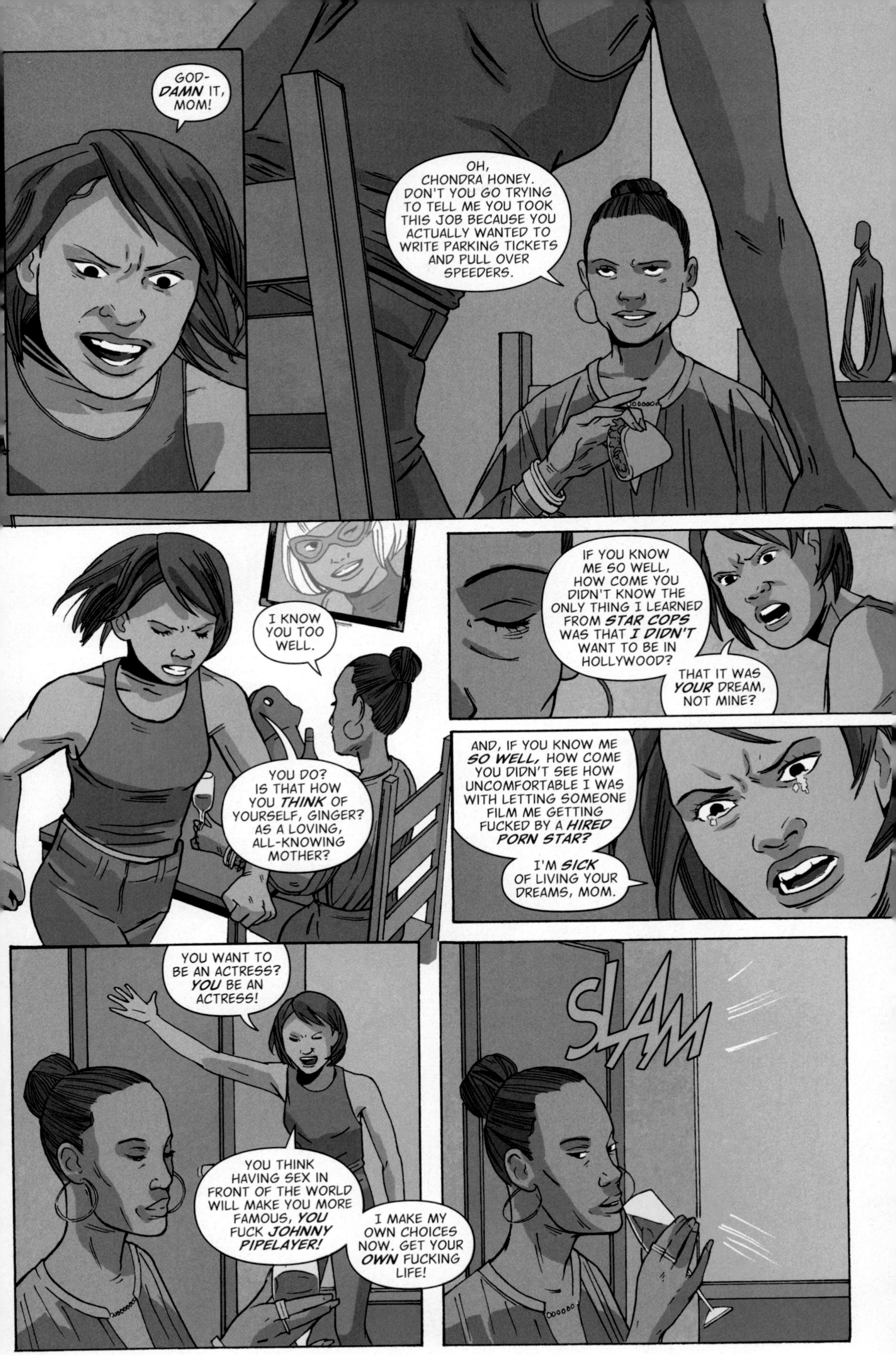
GOD-DAMN IT, MOM!
OH, CHONDRA HONEY. DON'T YOU GO TRYING TO TELL ME YOU TOOK THIS JOB BECAUSE YOU ACTUALLY WANTED TO WRITE PARKING TICKETS AND PULL OVER SPEEDERS.
I KNOW YOU TOO WELL.
YOU DO? IS THAT HOW YOU THINK OF YOURSELF, GINGER? AS A LOVING, ALL-KNOWING MOTHER?
IF YOU KNOW ME SO WELL, HOW COME YOU DIDN'T KNOW THE ONLY THING I LEARNED FROM STAR COPS WAS THAT I DIDN'T WANT TO BE IN HOLLYWOOD?
THAT IT WAS YOUR DREAM, NOT MINE?
AND, IF YOU KNOW ME SO WELL, HOW COME YOU DIDN'T SEE HOW UNCOMFORTABLE I WAS WITH LETTING SOMEONE FILM ME GETTING FUCKED BY A HIRED PORN STAR?
I'M SICK OF LIVING YOUR DREAMS, MOM.
YOU WANT TO BE AN ACTRESS? YOU BE AN ACTRESS!
YOU THINK HAVING SEX IN FRONT OF THE WORLD WILL MAKE YOU MORE FAMOUS, YOU FUCK JOHNNY PIPELAYER!
I MAKE MY OWN CHOICES NOW. GET YOUR OWN FUCKING LIFE!
SLAM

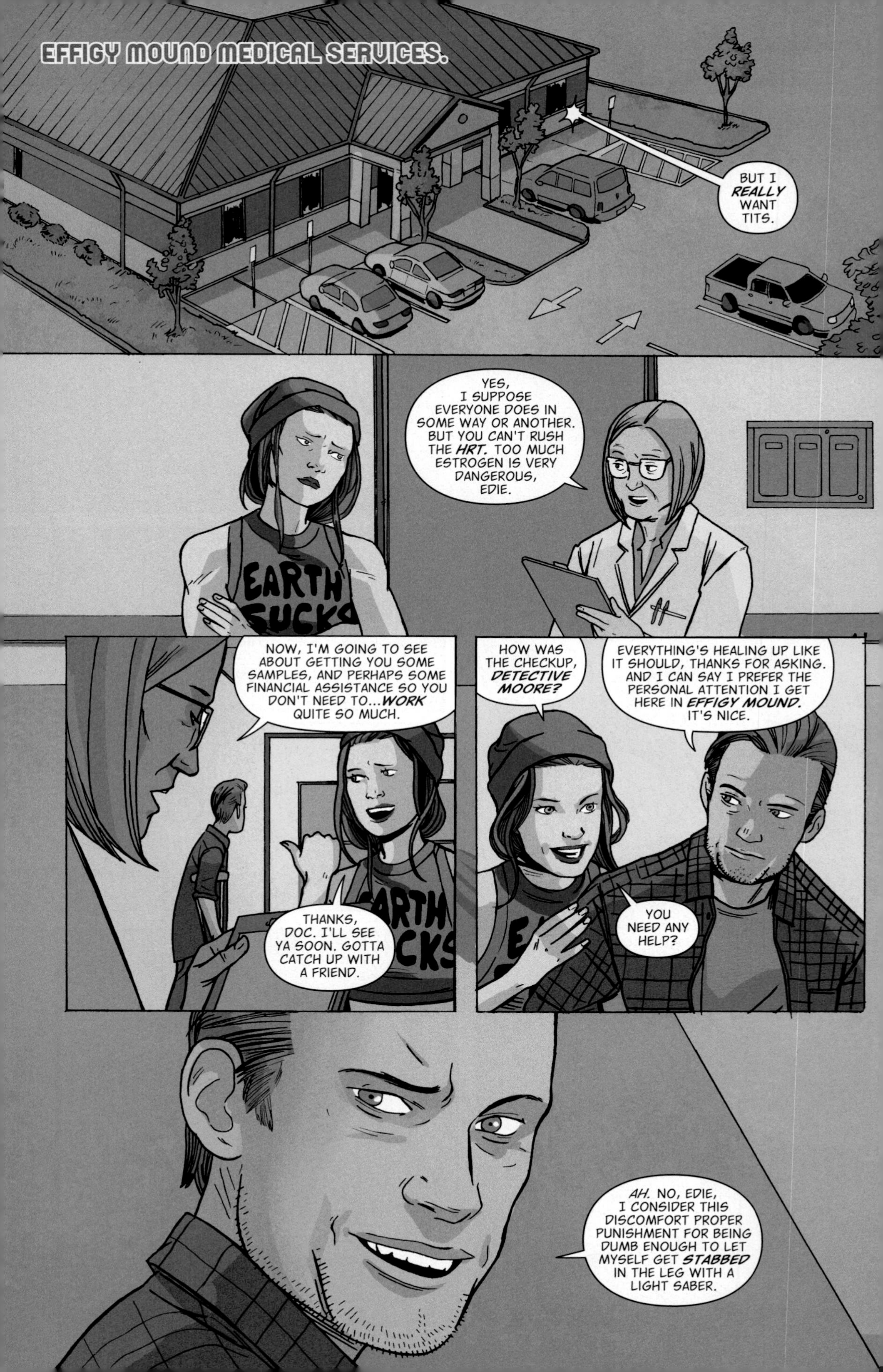
EFFIGY MOUND MEDICAL SERVICES.
BUT I REALLY WANT TITS.
YES, I SUPPOSE EVERYONE DOES IN SOME WAY OR ANOTHER. BUT YOU CAN'T RUSH THE HRT. TOO MUCH ESTROGEN IS VERY DANGEROUS, EDIE.
EARTH SUCKS
NOW, I'M GOING TO SEE ABOUT GETTING YOU SOME SAMPLES, AND PERHAPS SOME FINANCIAL ASSISTANCE SO YOU DON'T NEED TO...WORK QUITE SO MUCH.
THANKS, DOC. I'LL SEE YA SOON. GOTTA CATCH UP WITH A FRIEND.
HOW WAS THE CHECKUP, DETECTIVE MOORE?
EVERYTHING'S HEALING UP LIKE IT SHOULD, THANKS FOR ASKING. AND I CAN SAY I PREFER THE PERSONAL ATTENTION I GET HERE IN EFFIGY MOUND. IT'S NICE.
YOU NEED ANY HELP?
AH. NO, EDIE, I CONSIDER THIS DISCOMFORT PROPER PUNISHMENT FOR BEING DUMB ENOUGH TO LET MYSELF GET STABBED IN THE LEG WITH A LIGHT SABER.

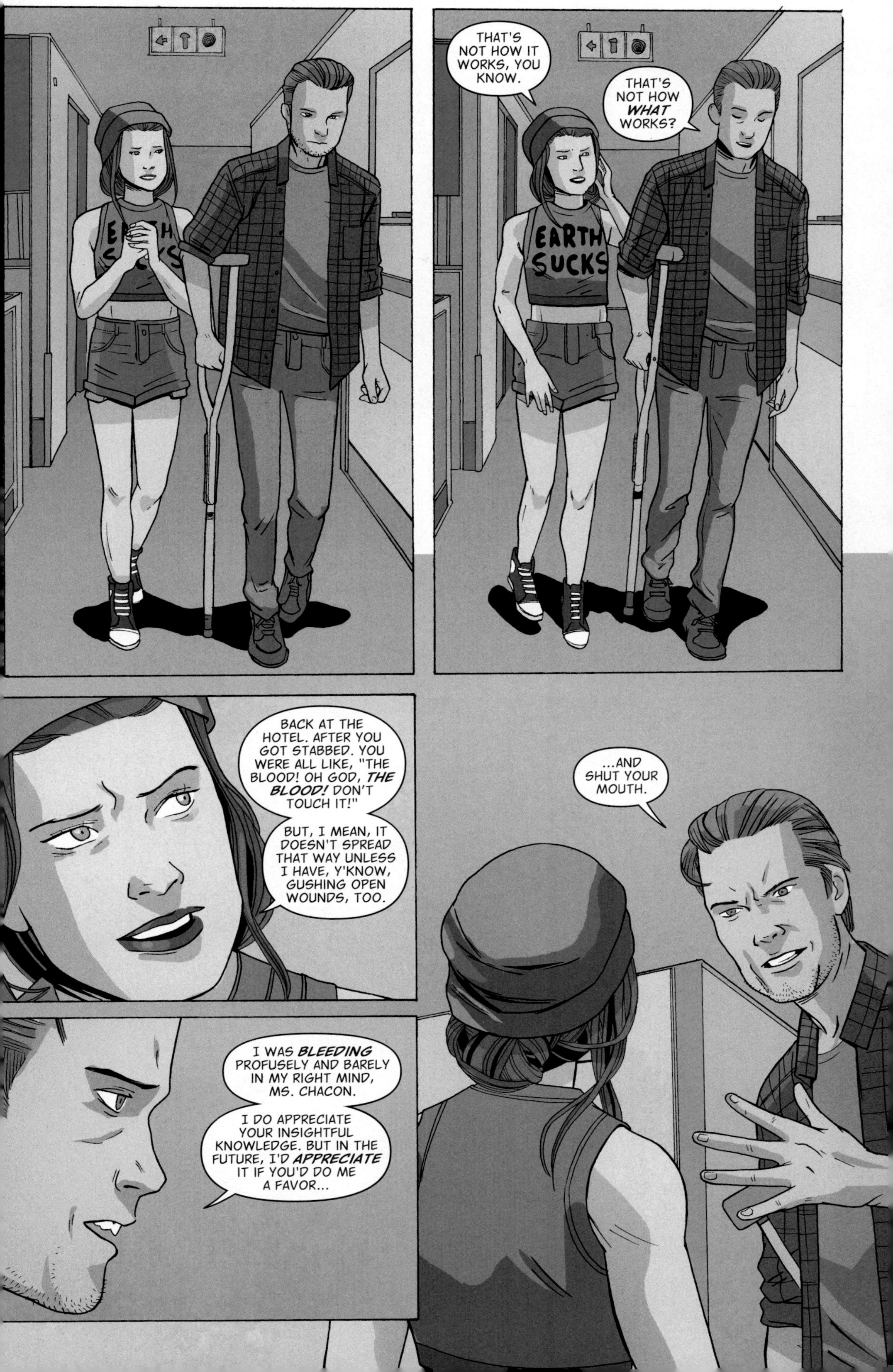

EARTH SUCKS
THAT'S NOT HOW IT WORKS, YOU KNOW.
THAT'S NOT HOW WHAT WORKS?
EARTH SUCKS
BACK AT THE HOTEL. AFTER YOU GOT STABBED. YOU WERE ALL LIKE, "THE BLOOD! OH GOD, THE BLOOD! DON'T TOUCH IT!"
BUT, I MEAN, IT DOESN'T SPREAD THAT WAY UNLESS I HAVE, Y'KNOW, GUSHING OPEN WOUNDS, TOO.
I WAS BLEEDING PROFUSELY AND BARELY IN MY RIGHT MIND, MS. CHACON.
I DO APPRECIATE YOUR INSIGHTFUL KNOWLEDGE. BUT IN THE FUTURE, I'D APPRECIATE IT IF YOU'D DO ME A FAVOR...
...AND SHUT YOUR MOUTH.

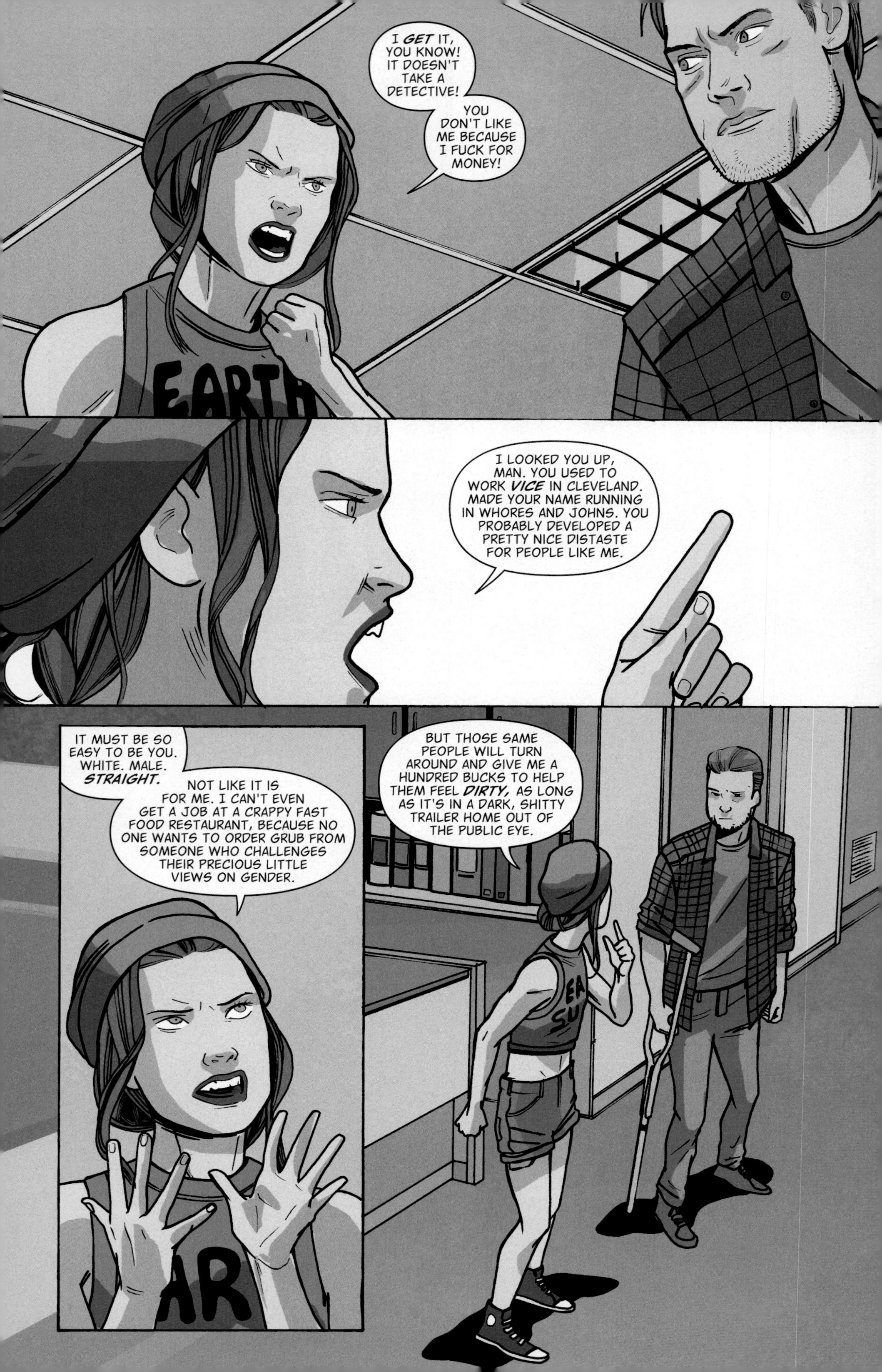
I GET IT, YOU KNOW! IT DOESN'T TAKE A DETECTIVE!
YOU DON'T LIKE ME BECAUSE I FUCK FOR MONEY!
EARTH
I LOOKED YOU UP, MAN. YOU USED TO WORK VICE IN CLEVELAND. MADE YOUR NAME RUNNING IN WHORES AND JOHNS. YOU PROBABLY DEVELOPED A PRETTY NICE DISTASTE FOR PEOPLE LIKE ME.
IT MUST BE SO EASY TO BE YOU. WHITE. MALE. STRAIGHT.
NOT LIKE IT IS FOR ME. I CAN'T EVEN GET A JOB AT A CRAPPY FAST FOOD RESTAURANT, BECAUSE NO ONE WANTS TO ORDER GRUB FROM SOMEONE WHO CHALLENGES THEIR PRECIOUS LITTLE VIEWS ON GENDER.
BUT THOSE SAME PEOPLE WILL TURN AROUND AND GIVE ME A HUNDRED BUCKS TO HELP THEM FEEL DIRTY, AS LONG AS IT'S IN A DARK, SHITTY TRAILER HOME OUT OF THE PUBLIC EYE.

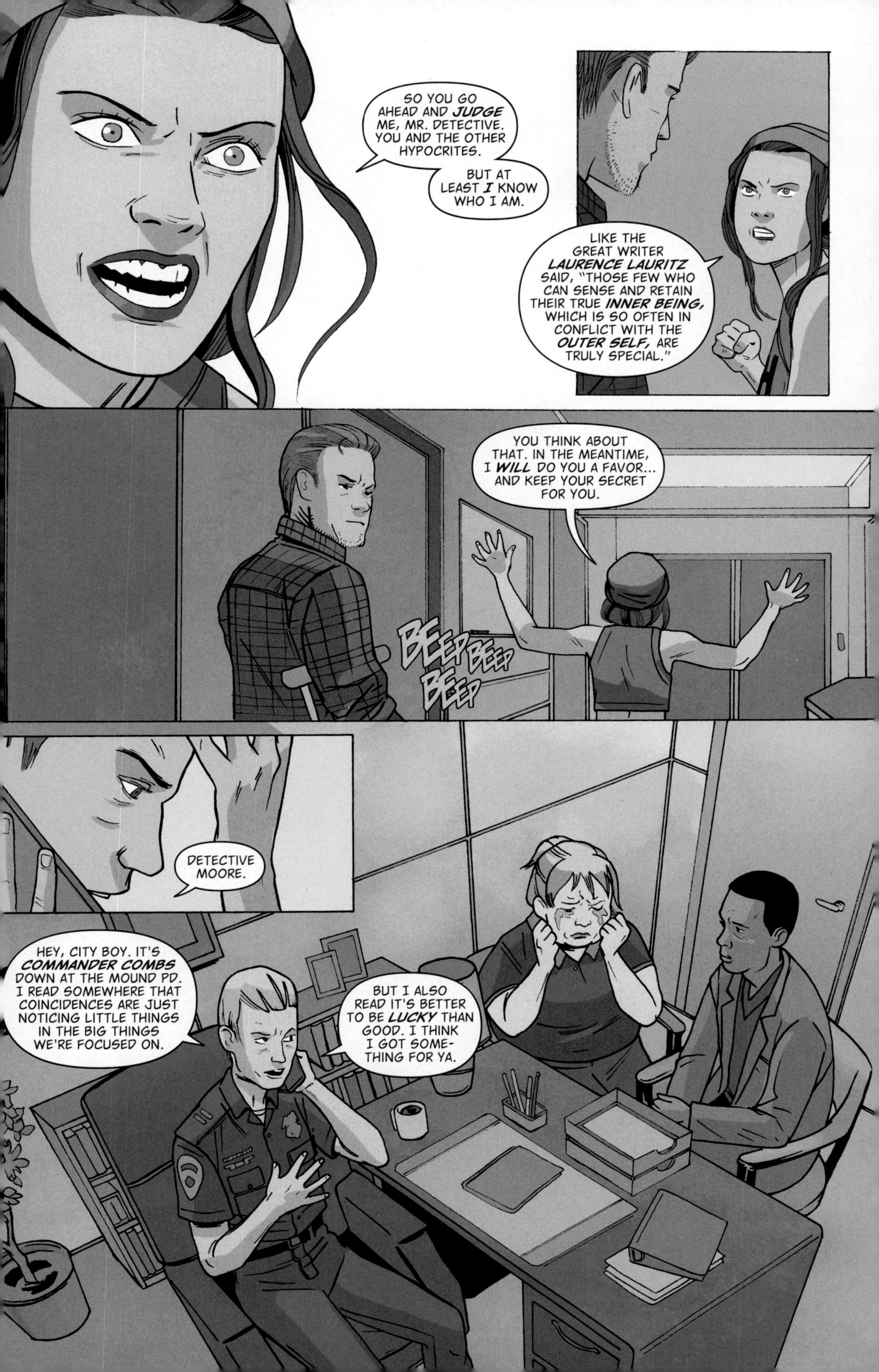
SO YOU GO AHEAD AND *JUDGE* ME, MR. DETECTIVE. YOU AND THE OTHER HYPOCRITES.
BUT AT LEAST *I* KNOW WHO I AM.
LIKE THE GREAT WRITER *LAURENCE LAURITZ* SAID, "THOSE FEW WHO CAN SENSE AND RETAIN THEIR TRUE *INNER BEING,* WHICH IS SO OFTEN IN CONFLICT WITH THE *OUTER SELF,* ARE TRULY SPECIAL."
YOU THINK ABOUT THAT. IN THE MEANTIME, I *WILL* DO YOU A FAVOR... AND KEEP YOUR SECRET FOR YOU.
BEEP BEEP BEEP
DETECTIVE MOORE.
HEY, CITY BOY. IT'S *COMMANDER COMBS* DOWN AT THE MOUND PD. I READ SOMEWHERE THAT COINCIDENCES ARE JUST NOTICING LITTLE THINGS IN THE BIG THINGS WE'RE FOCUSED ON.
BUT I ALSO READ IT'S BETTER TO BE *LUCKY* THAN GOOD. I THINK I GOT SOME-THING FOR YA.

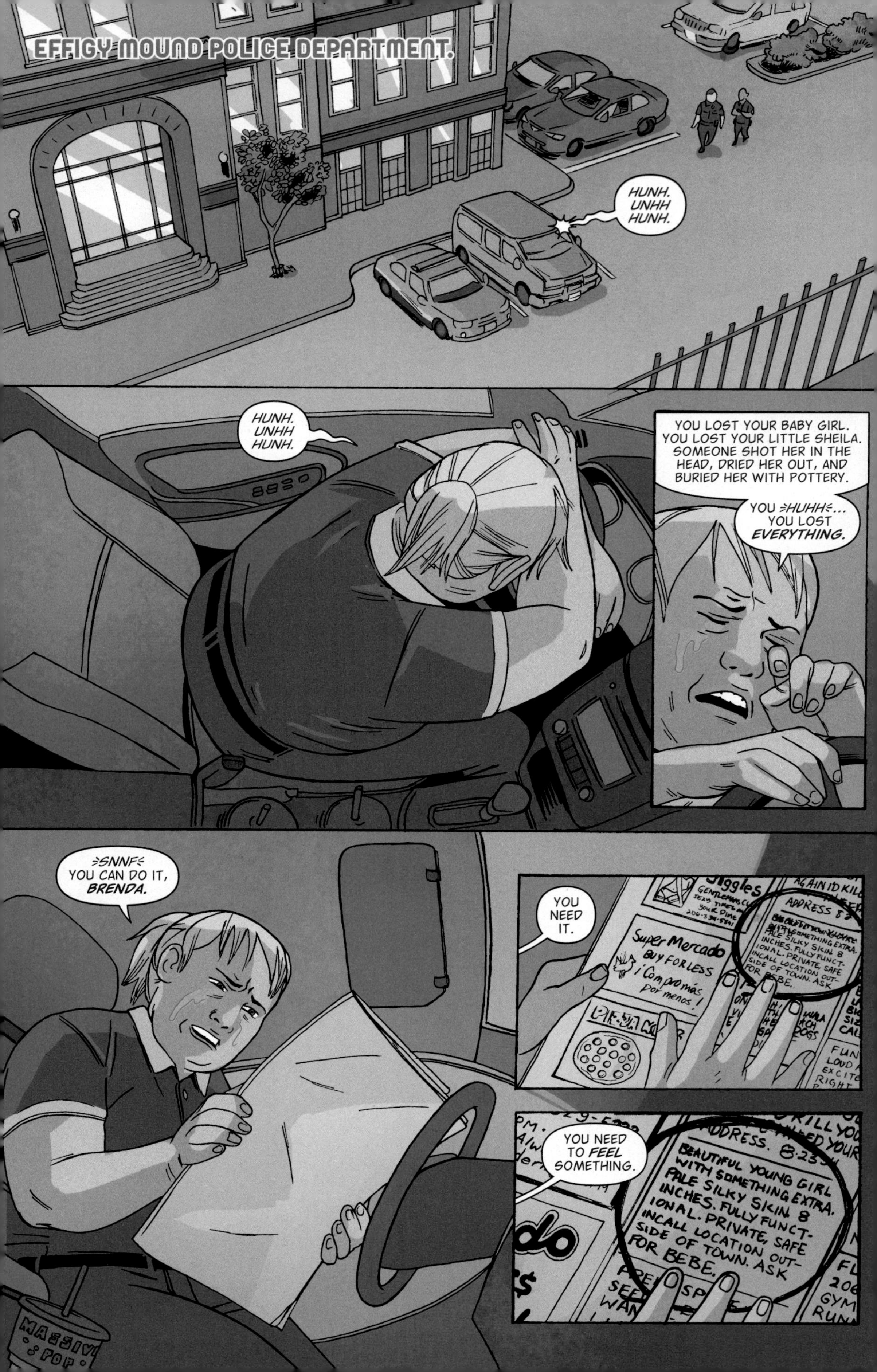

EFFIGY MOUND POLICE DEPARTMENT.
HUNH. UNHH HUNH.
HUNH. UNHH HUNH.
YOU LOST YOUR BABY GIRL. YOU LOST YOUR LITTLE SHEILA. SOMEONE SHOT HER IN THE HEAD, DRIED HER OUT, AND BURIED HER WITH POTTERY.
YOU ≥HUHH≤... YOU LOST EVERYTHING.
≥SNNF≤ YOU CAN DO IT, BRENDA.
YOU NEED IT.
Jiggles
Super Mercado
BUY FOR LESS
¡Compra más por menos!
YOU NEED TO FEEL SOMETHING.
BEAUTIFUL YOUNG GIRL WITH SOMETHING EXTRA. PALE SILKY SKIN 8 INCHES. FULLY FUNCT-IONAL. PRIVATE, SAFE INCALL LOCATION OUT-SIDE OF TOWN. ASK FOR BEBE.

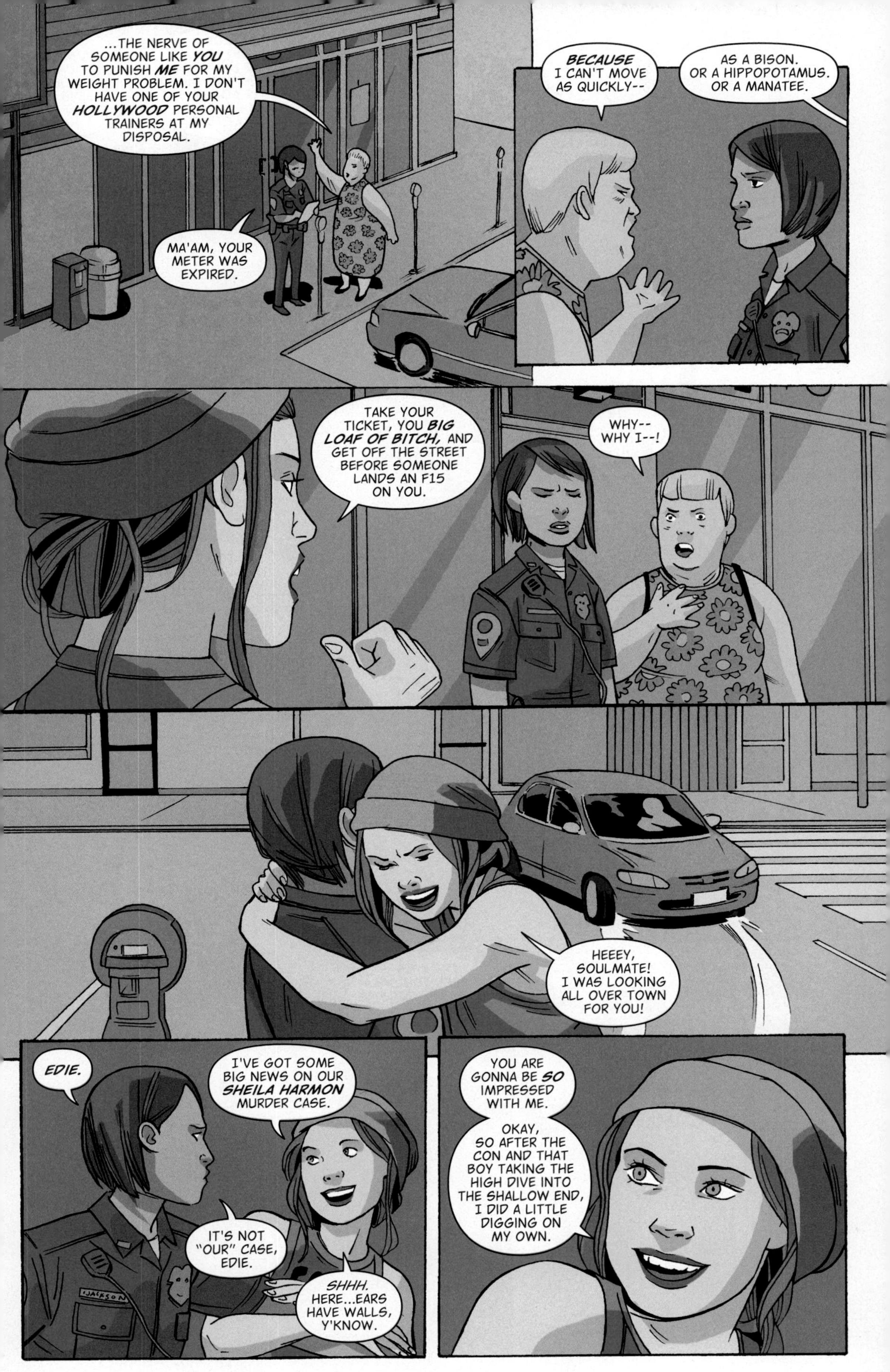
...THE NERVE OF SOMEONE LIKE YOU TO PUNISH ME FOR MY WEIGHT PROBLEM. I DON'T HAVE ONE OF YOUR HOLLYWOOD PERSONAL TRAINERS AT MY DISPOSAL.
MA'AM, YOUR METER WAS EXPIRED.
BECAUSE I CAN'T MOVE AS QUICKLY--
AS A BISON. OR A HIPPOPOTAMUS. OR A MANATEE.
TAKE YOUR TICKET, YOU BIG LOAF OF BITCH, AND GET OFF THE STREET BEFORE SOMEONE LANDS AN F15 ON YOU.
WHY-- WHY I--!
HEEEY, SOULMATE! I WAS LOOKING ALL OVER TOWN FOR YOU!
EDIE.
I'VE GOT SOME BIG NEWS ON OUR SHEILA HARMON MURDER CASE.
IT'S NOT "OUR" CASE, EDIE.
SHHH. HERE...EARS HAVE WALLS, Y'KNOW.
JACKSON
YOU ARE GONNA BE SO IMPRESSED WITH ME.
OKAY, SO AFTER THE CON AND THAT BOY TAKING THE HIGH DIVE INTO THE SHALLOW END, I DID A LITTLE DIGGING ON MY OWN.

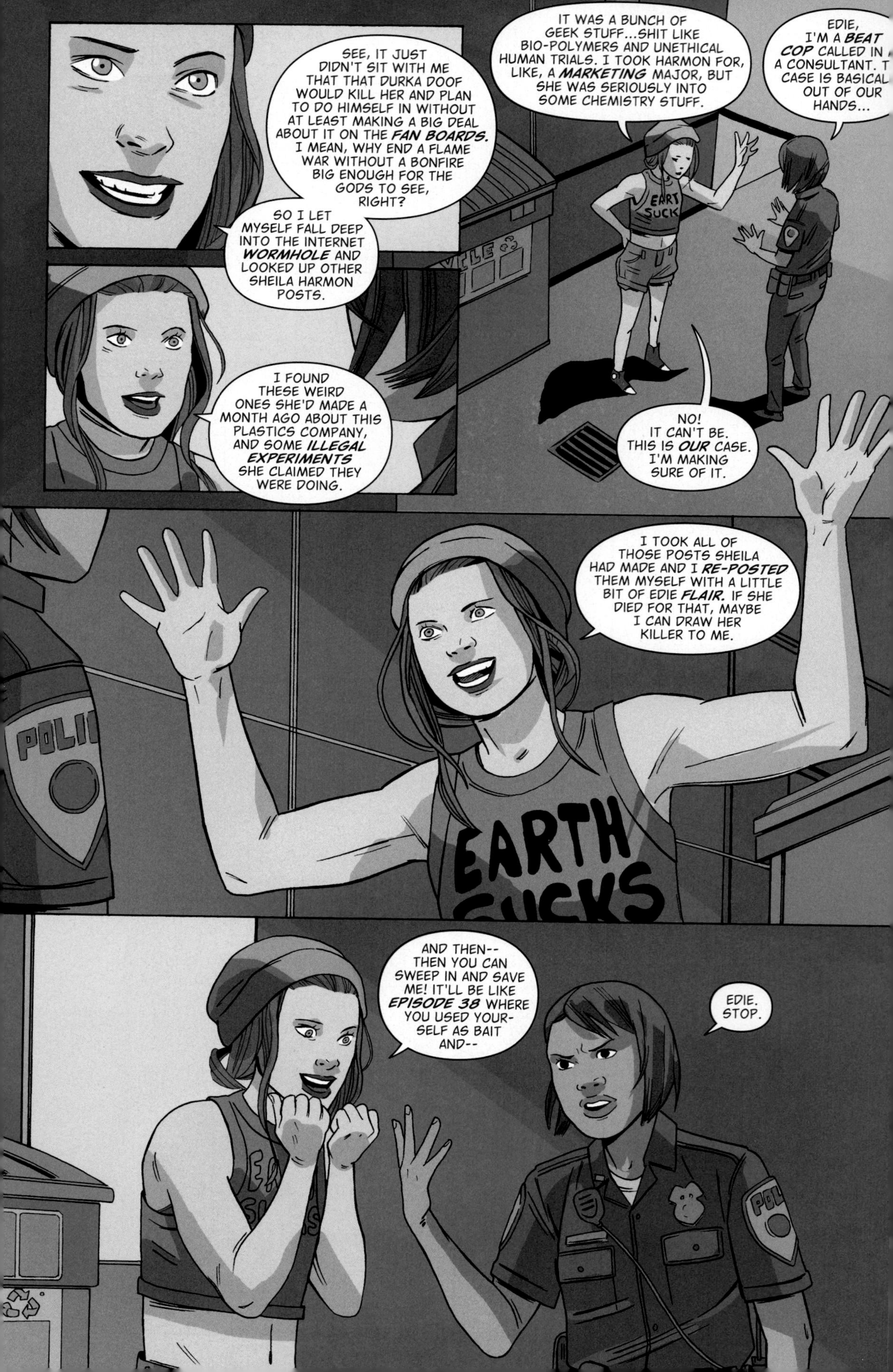
SEE, IT JUST DIDN'T SIT WITH ME THAT THAT DURKA DOOF WOULD KILL HER AND PLAN TO DO HIMSELF IN WITHOUT AT LEAST MAKING A BIG DEAL ABOUT IT ON THE FAN BOARDS. I MEAN, WHY END A FLAME WAR WITHOUT A BONFIRE BIG ENOUGH FOR THE GODS TO SEE, RIGHT?
SO I LET MYSELF FALL DEEP INTO THE INTERNET WORMHOLE AND LOOKED UP OTHER SHEILA HARMON POSTS.
I FOUND THESE WEIRD ONES SHE'D MADE A MONTH AGO ABOUT THIS PLASTICS COMPANY, AND SOME ILLEGAL EXPERIMENTS SHE CLAIMED THEY WERE DOING.
IT WAS A BUNCH OF GEEK STUFF...SHIT LIKE BIO-POLYMERS AND UNETHICAL HUMAN TRIALS. I TOOK HARMON FOR, LIKE, A MARKETING MAJOR, BUT SHE WAS SERIOUSLY INTO SOME CHEMISTRY STUFF.
EDIE, I'M A BEAT COP CALLED IN A CONSULTANT. T CASE IS BASICAL OUT OF OUR HANDS...
NO! IT CAN'T BE. THIS IS OUR CASE. I'M MAKING SURE OF IT.
I TOOK ALL OF THOSE POSTS SHEILA HAD MADE AND I RE-POSTED THEM MYSELF WITH A LITTLE BIT OF EDIE FLAIR. IF SHE DIED FOR THAT, MAYBE I CAN DRAW HER KILLER TO ME.
EARTH SUCKS
POLI
AND THEN-- THEN YOU CAN SWEEP IN AND SAVE ME! IT'LL BE LIKE EPISODE 38 WHERE YOU USED YOUR-SELF AS BAIT AND--
EDIE. STOP.

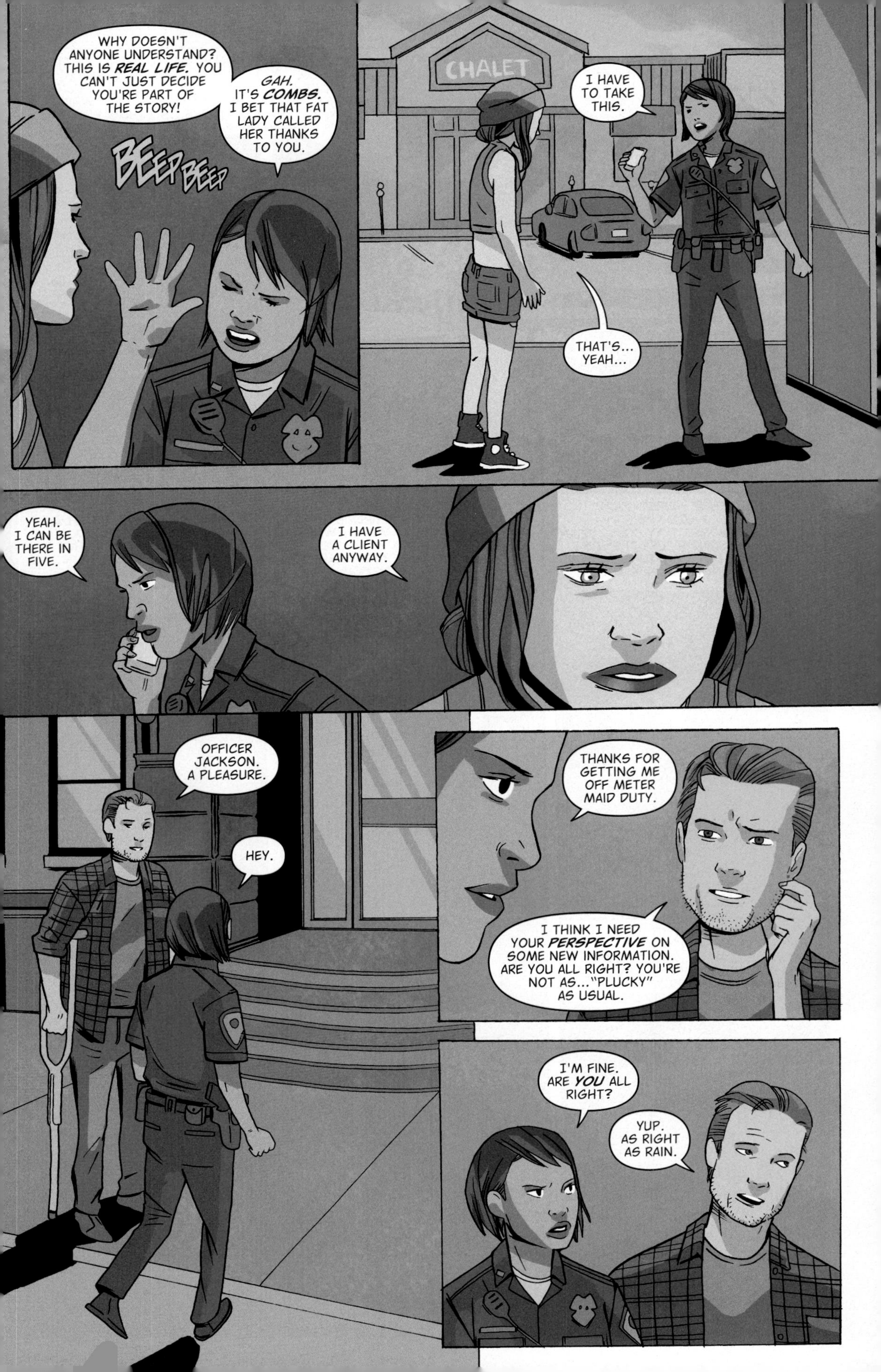
WHY DOESN'T ANYONE UNDERSTAND? THIS IS *REAL LIFE.* YOU CAN'T JUST DECIDE YOU'RE PART OF THE STORY!
BEEP BEEP
GAH. IT'S ***COMBS.*** I BET THAT FAT LADY CALLED HER THANKS TO YOU.
CHALET
I HAVE TO TAKE THIS.
THAT'S... YEAH...
YEAH. I CAN BE THERE IN FIVE.
I HAVE A CLIENT ANYWAY.
OFFICER JACKSON. A PLEASURE.
HEY.
THANKS FOR GETTING ME OFF METER MAID DUTY.
I THINK I NEED YOUR ***PERSPECTIVE*** ON SOME NEW INFORMATION. ARE YOU ALL RIGHT? YOU'RE NOT AS..."PLUCKY" AS USUAL.
I'M FINE. ARE ***YOU*** ALL RIGHT?
YUP. AS RIGHT AS RAIN.

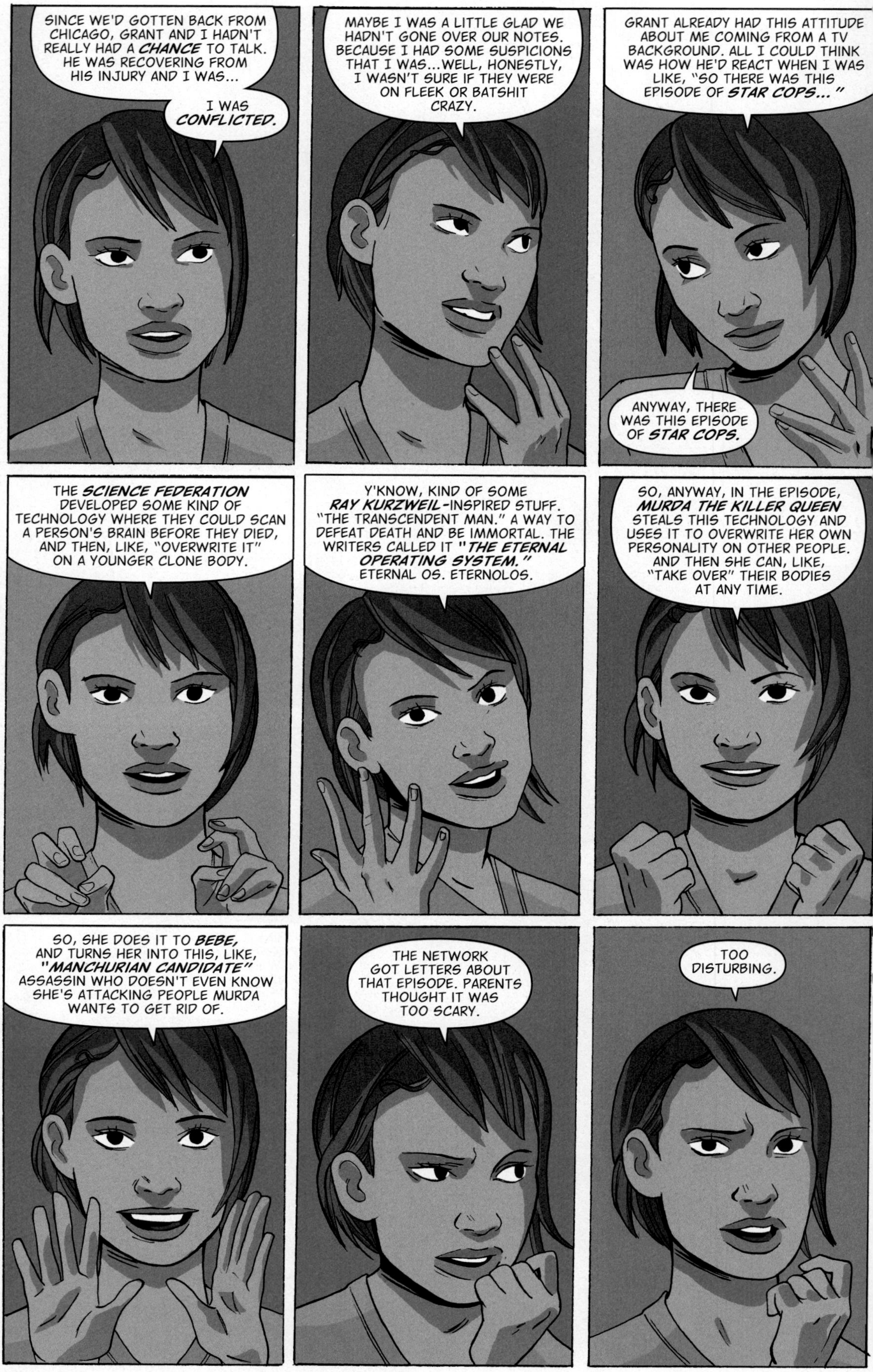
SINCE WE'D GOTTEN BACK FROM CHICAGO, GRANT AND I HADN'T REALLY HAD A CHANCE TO TALK. HE WAS RECOVERING FROM HIS INJURY AND I WAS...
I WAS CONFLICTED.
MAYBE I WAS A LITTLE GLAD WE HADN'T GONE OVER OUR NOTES. BECAUSE I HAD SOME SUSPICIONS THAT I WAS...WELL, HONESTLY, I WASN'T SURE IF THEY WERE ON FLEEK OR BATSHIT CRAZY.
GRANT ALREADY HAD THIS ATTITUDE ABOUT ME COMING FROM A TV BACKGROUND. ALL I COULD THINK WAS HOW HE'D REACT WHEN I WAS LIKE, "SO THERE WAS THIS EPISODE OF STAR COPS..."
ANYWAY, THERE WAS THIS EPISODE OF STAR COPS.
THE SCIENCE FEDERATION DEVELOPED SOME KIND OF TECHNOLOGY WHERE THEY COULD SCAN A PERSON'S BRAIN BEFORE THEY DIED, AND THEN, LIKE, "OVERWRITE IT" ON A YOUNGER CLONE BODY.
Y'KNOW, KIND OF SOME RAY KURZWEIL-INSPIRED STUFF. "THE TRANSCENDENT MAN." A WAY TO DEFEAT DEATH AND BE IMMORTAL. THE WRITERS CALLED IT "THE ETERNAL OPERATING SYSTEM." ETERNAL OS. ETERNOLOS.
SO, ANYWAY, IN THE EPISODE, MURDA THE KILLER QUEEN STEALS THIS TECHNOLOGY AND USES IT TO OVERWRITE HER OWN PERSONALITY ON OTHER PEOPLE. AND THEN SHE CAN, LIKE, "TAKE OVER" THEIR BODIES AT ANY TIME.
SO, SHE DOES IT TO BEBE, AND TURNS HER INTO THIS, LIKE, "MANCHURIAN CANDIDATE" ASSASSIN WHO DOESN'T EVEN KNOW SHE'S ATTACKING PEOPLE MURDA WANTS TO GET RID OF.
THE NETWORK GOT LETTERS ABOUT THAT EPISODE. PARENTS THOUGHT IT WAS TOO SCARY.
TOO DISTURBING.

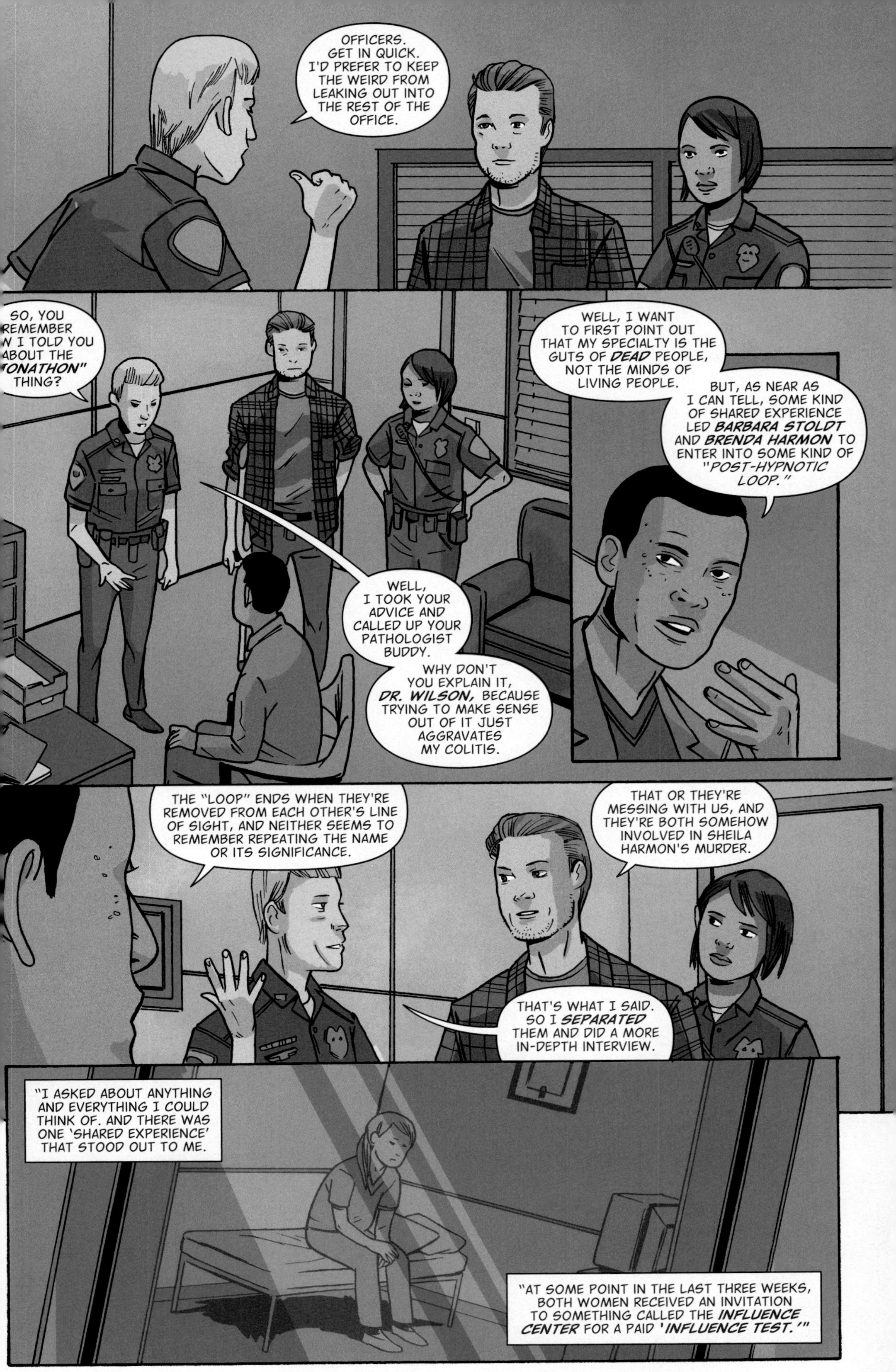
OFFICERS. GET IN QUICK. I'D PREFER TO KEEP THE WEIRD FROM LEAKING OUT INTO THE REST OF THE OFFICE.
SO, YOU REMEMBER ...W I TOLD YOU ABOUT THE ...ONATHON" THING?
WELL, I TOOK YOUR ADVICE AND CALLED UP YOUR PATHOLOGIST BUDDY.
WHY DON'T YOU EXPLAIN IT, DR. WILSON, BECAUSE TRYING TO MAKE SENSE OUT OF IT JUST AGGRAVATES MY COLITIS.
WELL, I WANT TO FIRST POINT OUT THAT MY SPECIALTY IS THE GUTS OF DEAD PEOPLE, NOT THE MINDS OF LIVING PEOPLE.
BUT, AS NEAR AS I CAN TELL, SOME KIND OF SHARED EXPERIENCE LED BARBARA STOLDT AND BRENDA HARMON TO ENTER INTO SOME KIND OF "POST-HYPNOTIC LOOP."
THE "LOOP" ENDS WHEN THEY'RE REMOVED FROM EACH OTHER'S LINE OF SIGHT, AND NEITHER SEEMS TO REMEMBER REPEATING THE NAME OR ITS SIGNIFICANCE.
THAT OR THEY'RE MESSING WITH US, AND THEY'RE BOTH SOMEHOW INVOLVED IN SHEILA HARMON'S MURDER.
THAT'S WHAT I SAID. SO I SEPARATED THEM AND DID A MORE IN-DEPTH INTERVIEW.
"I ASKED ABOUT ANYTHING AND EVERYTHING I COULD THINK OF. AND THERE WAS ONE 'SHARED EXPERIENCE' THAT STOOD OUT TO ME.
"AT SOME POINT IN THE LAST THREE WEEKS, BOTH WOMEN RECEIVED AN INVITATION TO SOMETHING CALLED THE INFLUENCE CENTER FOR A PAID 'INFLUENCE TEST.'"

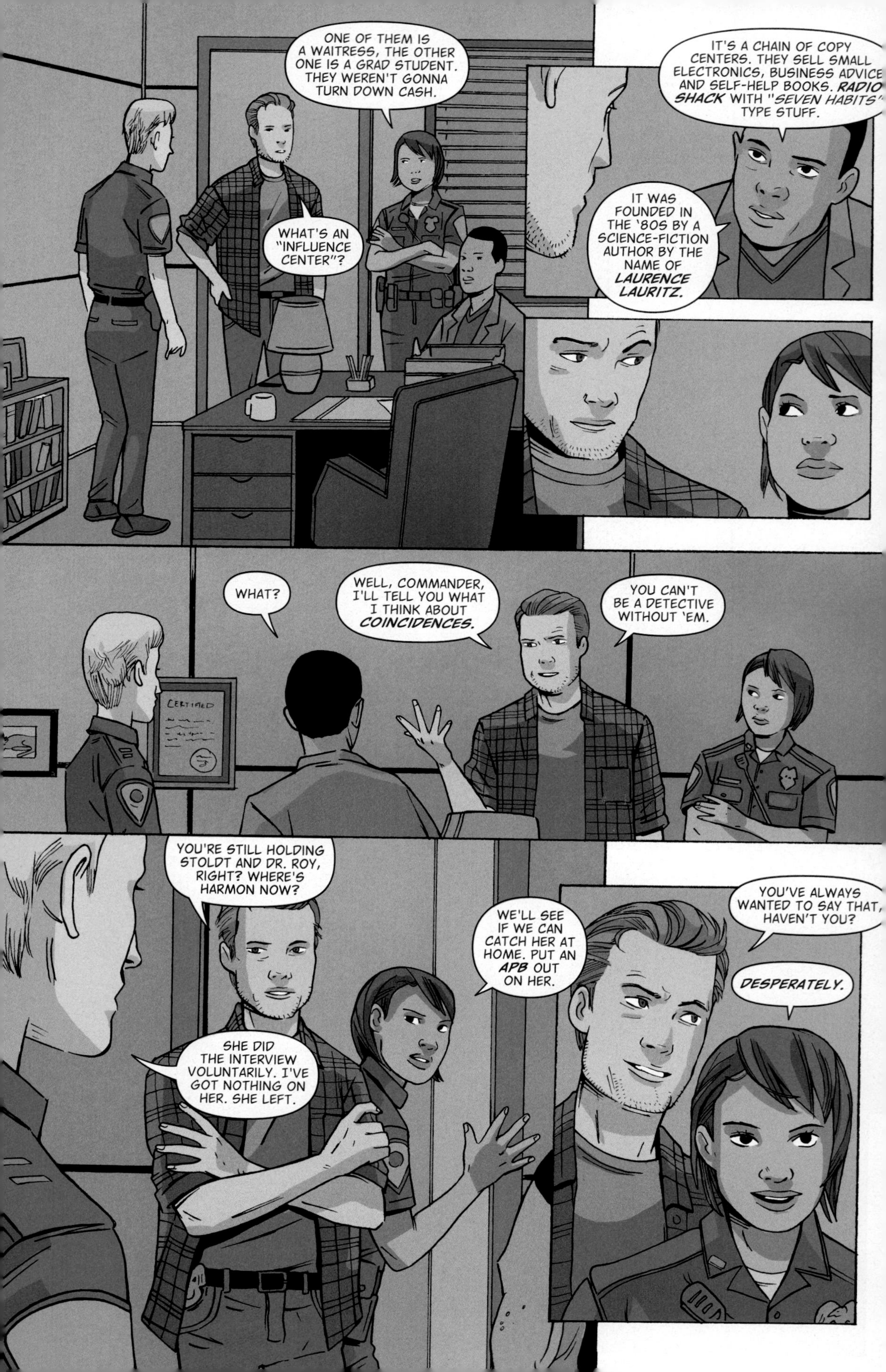
ONE OF THEM IS A WAITRESS, THE OTHER ONE IS A GRAD STUDENT. THEY WEREN'T GONNA TURN DOWN CASH.
WHAT'S AN "INFLUENCE CENTER"?
IT'S A CHAIN OF COPY CENTERS. THEY SELL SMALL ELECTRONICS, BUSINESS ADVICE AND SELF-HELP BOOKS. RADIO SHACK WITH "SEVEN HABITS" TYPE STUFF.
IT WAS FOUNDED IN THE '80S BY A SCIENCE-FICTION AUTHOR BY THE NAME OF LAURENCE LAURITZ.
WHAT?
WELL, COMMANDER, I'LL TELL YOU WHAT I THINK ABOUT COINCIDENCES.
YOU CAN'T BE A DETECTIVE WITHOUT 'EM.
CERTIFIED
YOU'RE STILL HOLDING STOLDT AND DR. ROY, RIGHT? WHERE'S HARMON NOW?
SHE DID THE INTERVIEW VOLUNTARILY. I'VE GOT NOTHING ON HER. SHE LEFT.
WE'LL SEE IF WE CAN CATCH HER AT HOME. PUT AN APB OUT ON HER.
YOU'VE ALWAYS WANTED TO SAY THAT, HAVEN'T YOU?
DESPERATELY.

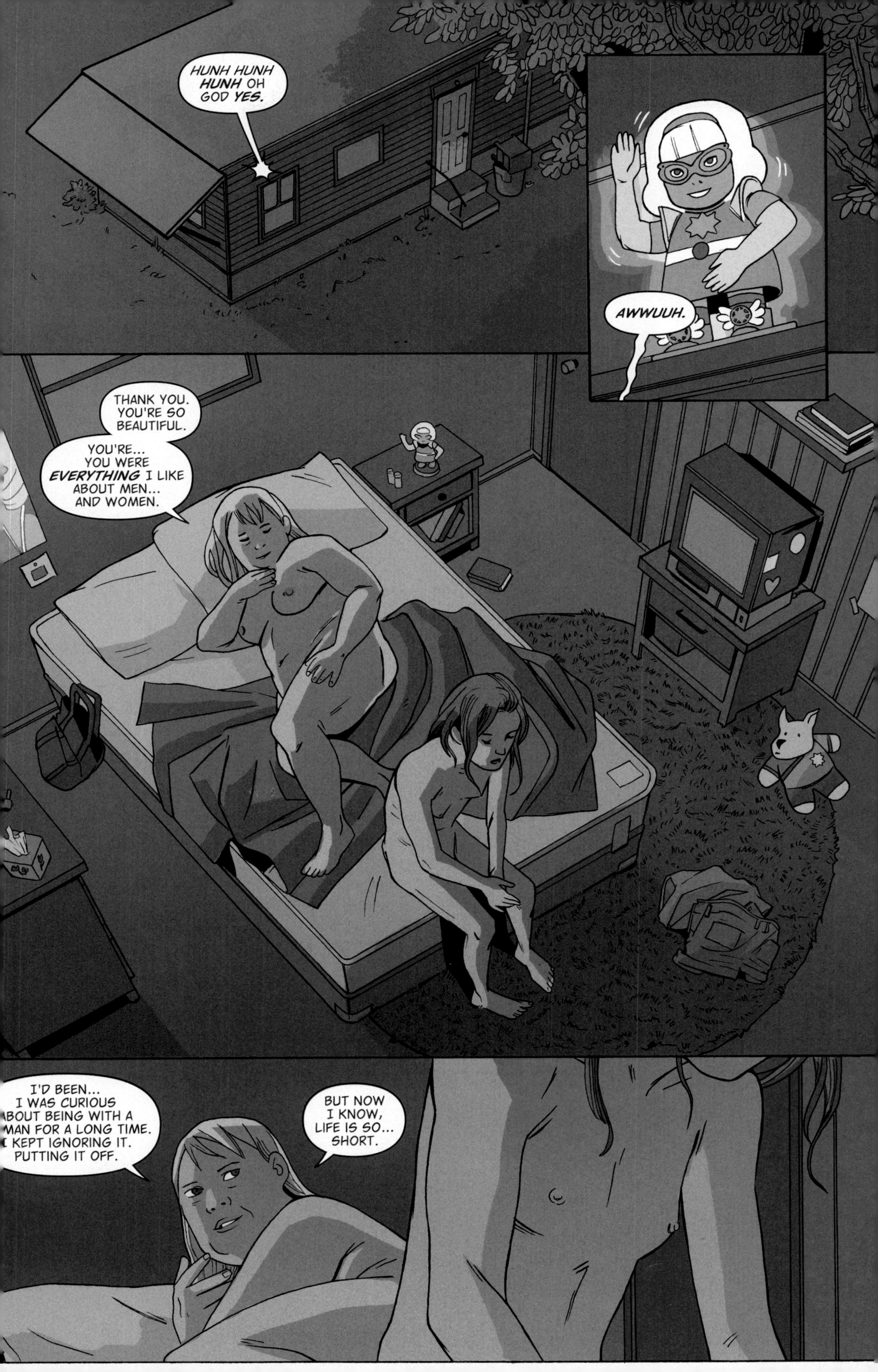
HUNH HUNH HUNH OH GOD YES.
AWWUUH.
THANK YOU. YOU'RE SO BEAUTIFUL.
YOU'RE... YOU WERE EVERYTHING I LIKE ABOUT MEN... AND WOMEN.
I'D BEEN... I WAS CURIOUS BOUT BEING WITH A MAN FOR A LONG TIME. KEPT IGNORING IT. PUTTING IT OFF.
BUT NOW I KNOW, LIFE IS SO... SHORT.

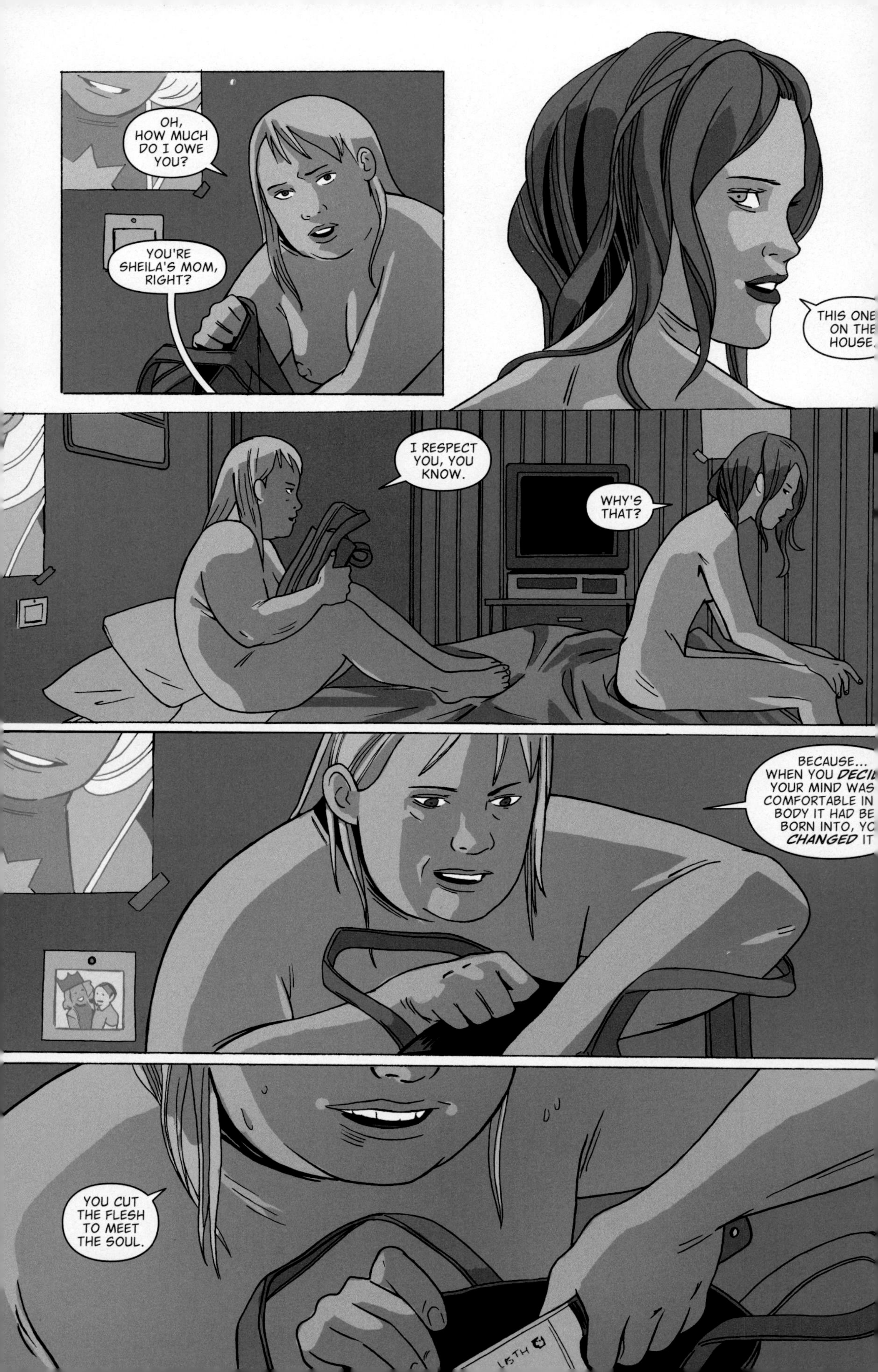
OH, HOW MUCH DO I OWE YOU?
YOU'RE SHEILA'S MOM, RIGHT?
THIS ONE ON THE HOUSE.
I RESPECT YOU, YOU KNOW.
WHY'S THAT?
BECAUSE... WHEN YOU DECI YOUR MIND WAS COMFORTABLE IN BODY IT HAD BE BORN INTO, YO CHANGED IT
YOU CUT THE FLESH TO MEET THE SOUL.

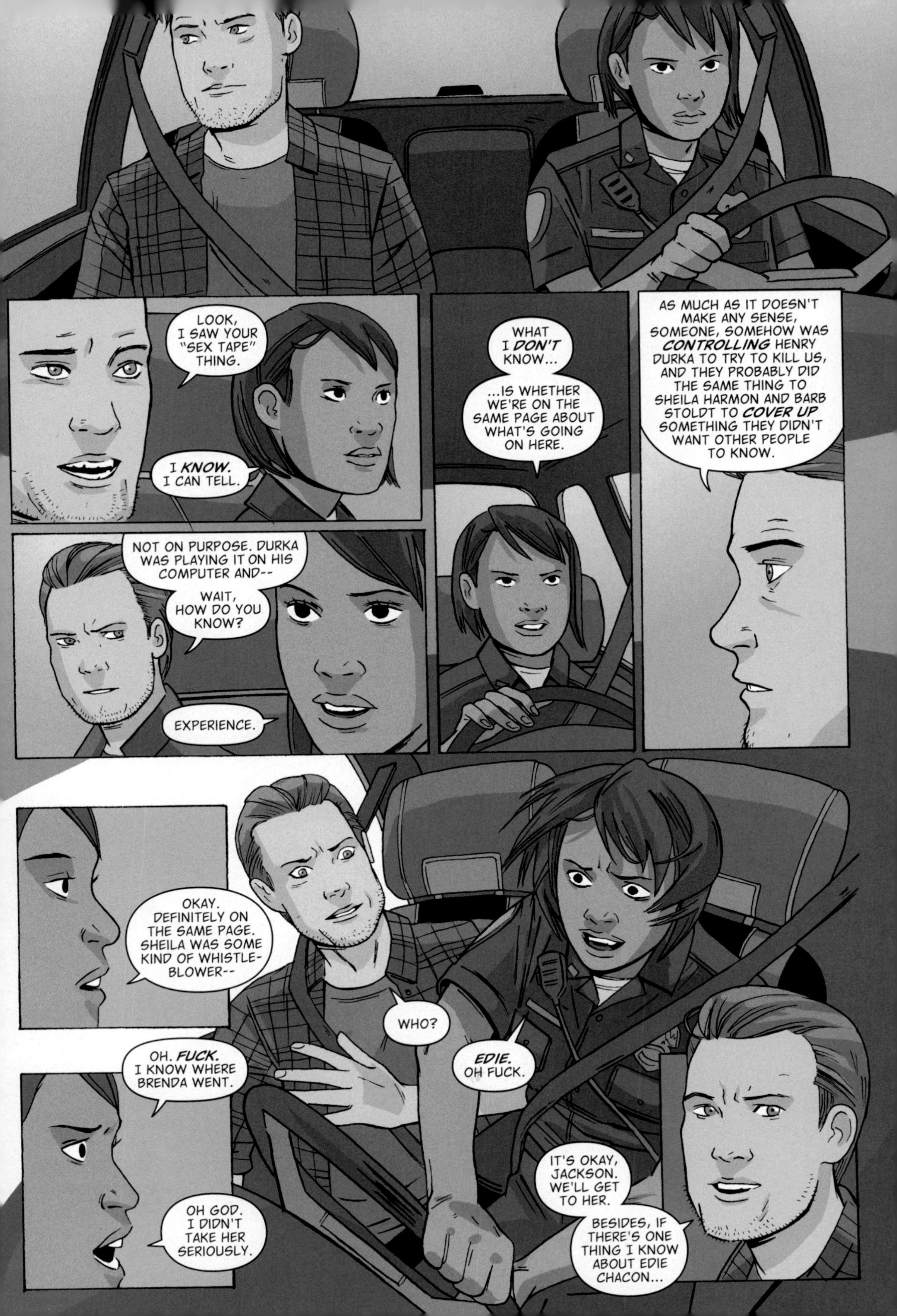

LOOK, I SAW YOUR "SEX TAPE" THING.
I *KNOW.* I CAN TELL.
NOT ON PURPOSE. DURKA WAS PLAYING IT ON HIS COMPUTER AND--
WAIT, HOW DO YOU KNOW?
EXPERIENCE.
WHAT I *DON'T* KNOW...
...IS WHETHER WE'RE ON THE SAME PAGE ABOUT WHAT'S GOING ON HERE.
AS MUCH AS IT DOESN'T MAKE ANY SENSE, SOMEONE, SOMEHOW WAS *CONTROLLING* HENRY DURKA TO TRY TO KILL US, AND THEY PROBABLY DID THE SAME THING TO SHEILA HARMON AND BARB STOLDT TO *COVER UP* SOMETHING THEY DIDN'T WANT OTHER PEOPLE TO KNOW.
OKAY. DEFINITELY ON THE SAME PAGE. SHEILA WAS SOME KIND OF WHISTLE-BLOWER--
WHO?
EDIE. OH FUCK.
OH. *FUCK.* I KNOW WHERE BRENDA WENT.
OH GOD. I DIDN'T TAKE HER SERIOUSLY.
IT'S OKAY, JACKSON. WE'LL GET TO HER.
BESIDES, IF THERE'S ONE THING I KNOW ABOUT EDIE CHACON...

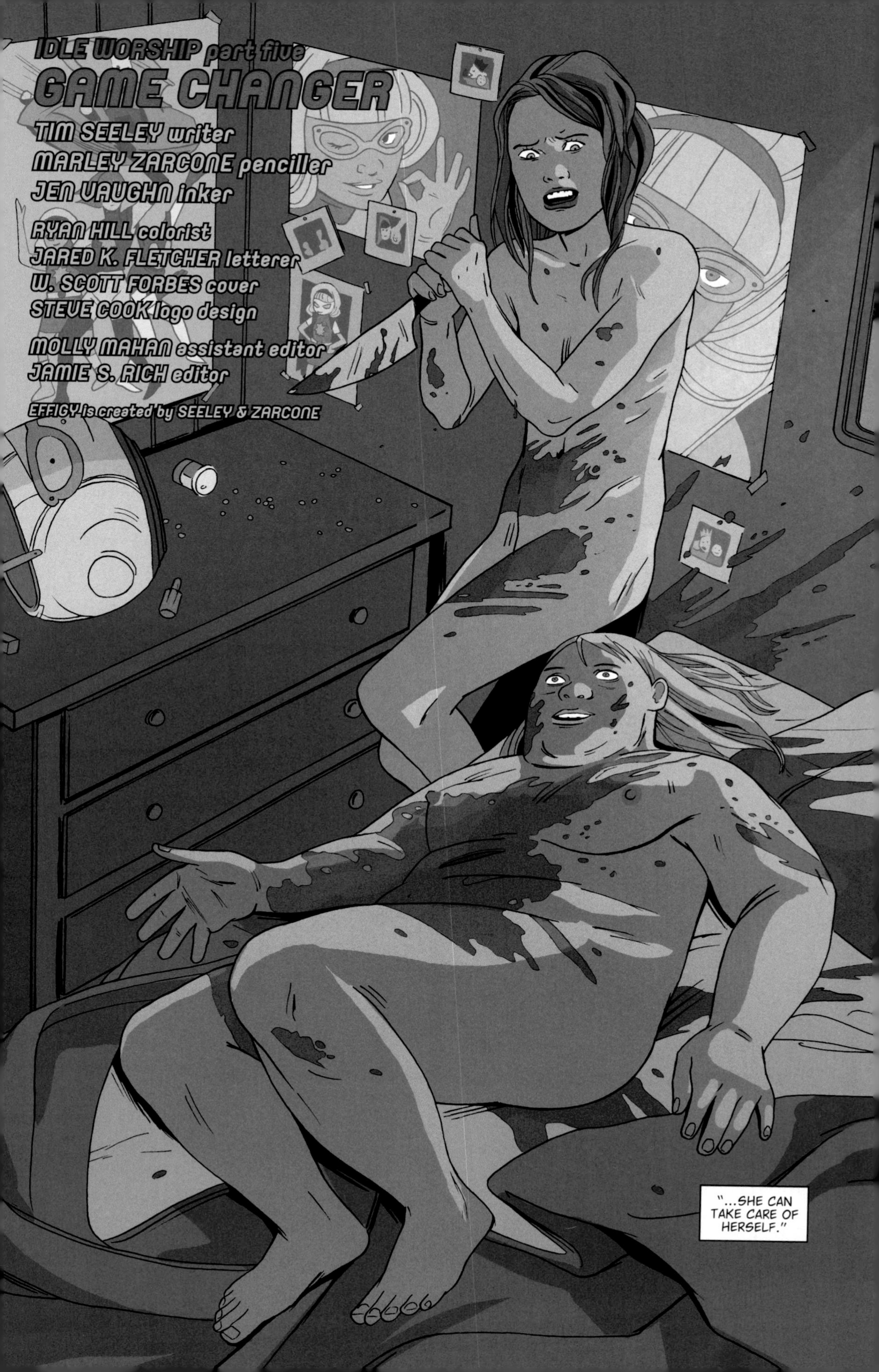
IDLE WORSHIP part five
GAME CHANGER
TIM SEELEY writer
MARLEY ZARCONE penciller
JEN VAUGHN inker
RYAN HILL colorist
JARED K. FLETCHER letterer
W. SCOTT FORBES cover
STEVE COOK logo design
MOLLY MAHAN assistant editor
JAMIE S. RICH editor
EFFIGY is created by SEELEY & ZARCONE
"...SHE CAN TAKE CARE OF HERSELF."

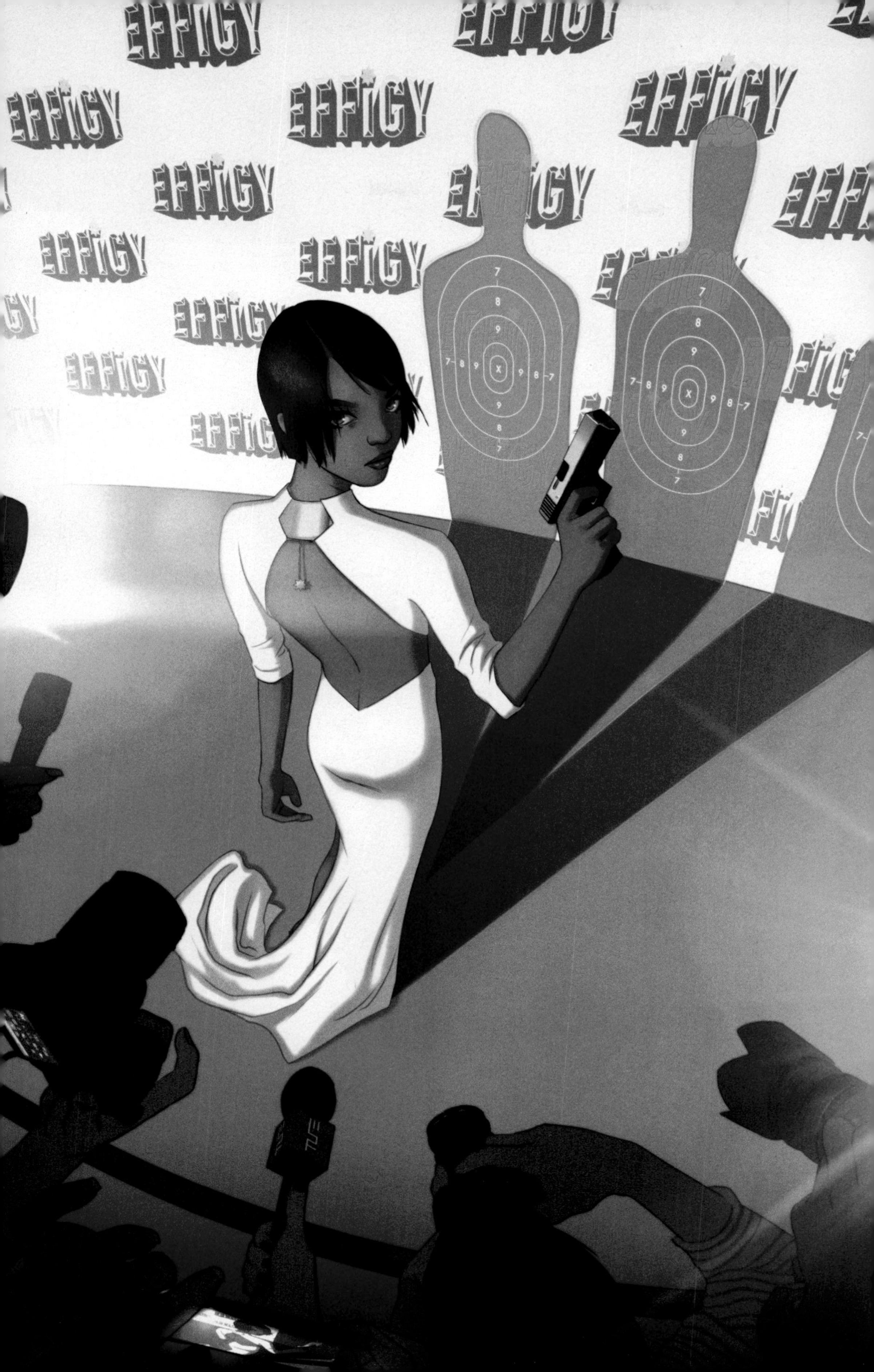
EFFIGY

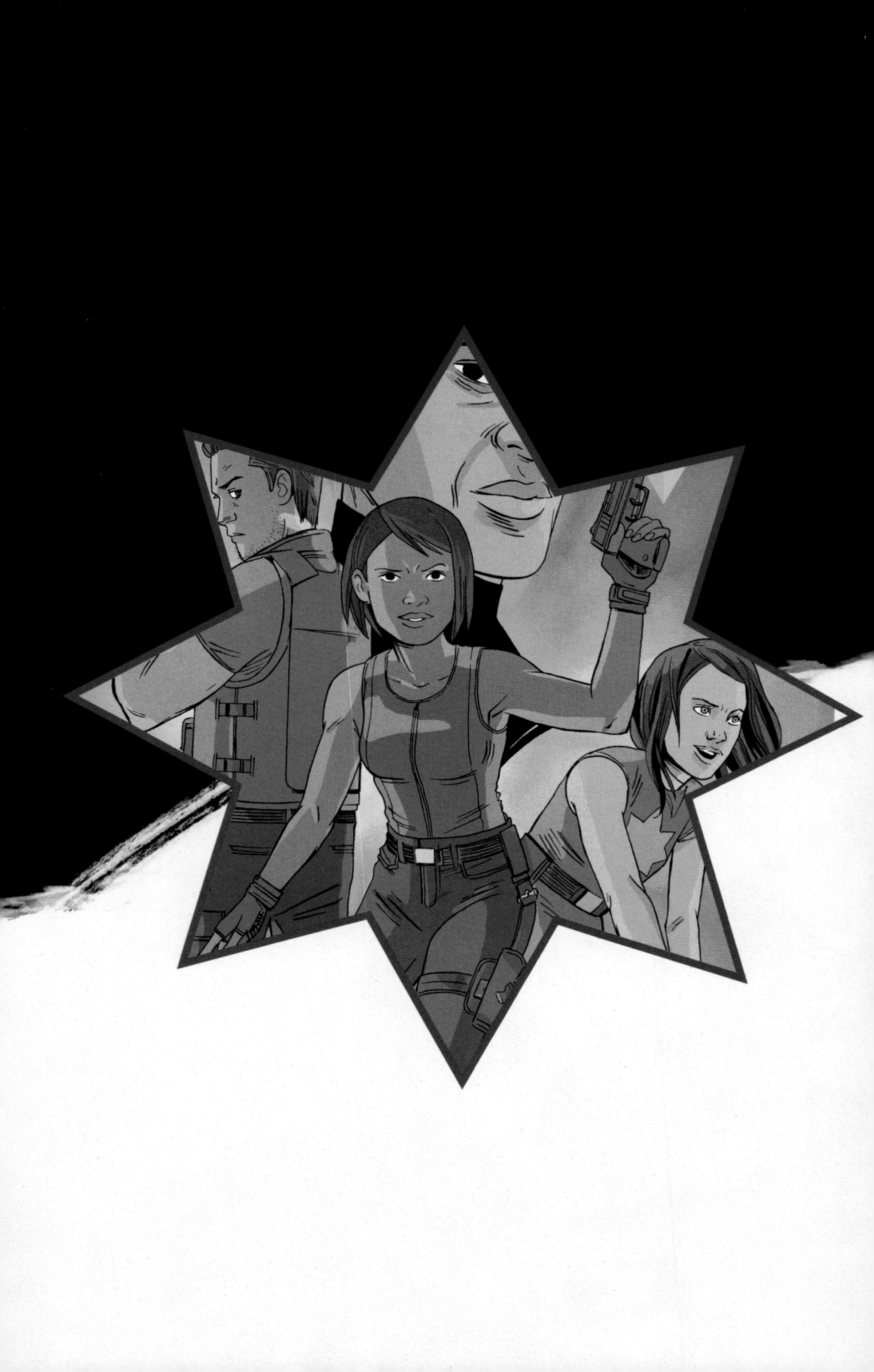

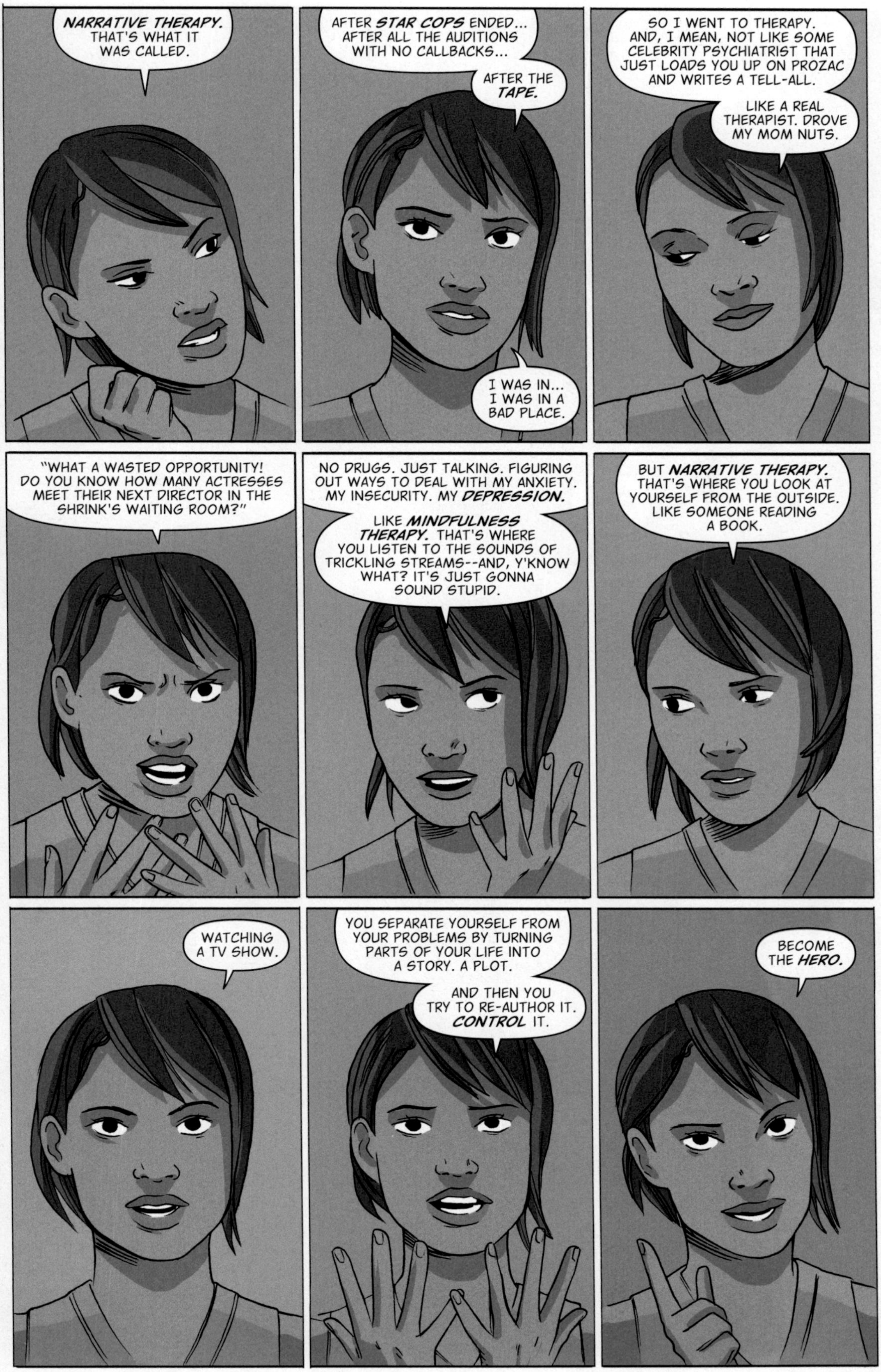
NARRATIVE THERAPY. THAT'S WHAT IT WAS CALLED.
AFTER STAR COPS ENDED... AFTER ALL THE AUDITIONS WITH NO CALLBACKS...
AFTER THE TAPE.
I WAS IN... I WAS IN A BAD PLACE.
SO I WENT TO THERAPY. AND, I MEAN, NOT LIKE SOME CELEBRITY PSYCHIATRIST THAT JUST LOADS YOU UP ON PROZAC AND WRITES A TELL-ALL.
LIKE A REAL THERAPIST. DROVE MY MOM NUTS.
"WHAT A WASTED OPPORTUNITY! DO YOU KNOW HOW MANY ACTRESSES MEET THEIR NEXT DIRECTOR IN THE SHRINK'S WAITING ROOM?"
NO DRUGS. JUST TALKING. FIGURING OUT WAYS TO DEAL WITH MY ANXIETY. MY INSECURITY. MY DEPRESSION.
LIKE MINDFULNESS THERAPY. THAT'S WHERE YOU LISTEN TO THE SOUNDS OF TRICKLING STREAMS--AND, Y'KNOW WHAT? IT'S JUST GONNA SOUND STUPID.
BUT NARRATIVE THERAPY. THAT'S WHERE YOU LOOK AT YOURSELF FROM THE OUTSIDE. LIKE SOMEONE READING A BOOK.
WATCHING A TV SHOW.
YOU SEPARATE YOURSELF FROM YOUR PROBLEMS BY TURNING PARTS OF YOUR LIFE INTO A STORY. A PLOT.
AND THEN YOU TRY TO RE-AUTHOR IT. CONTROL IT.
BECOME THE HERO.

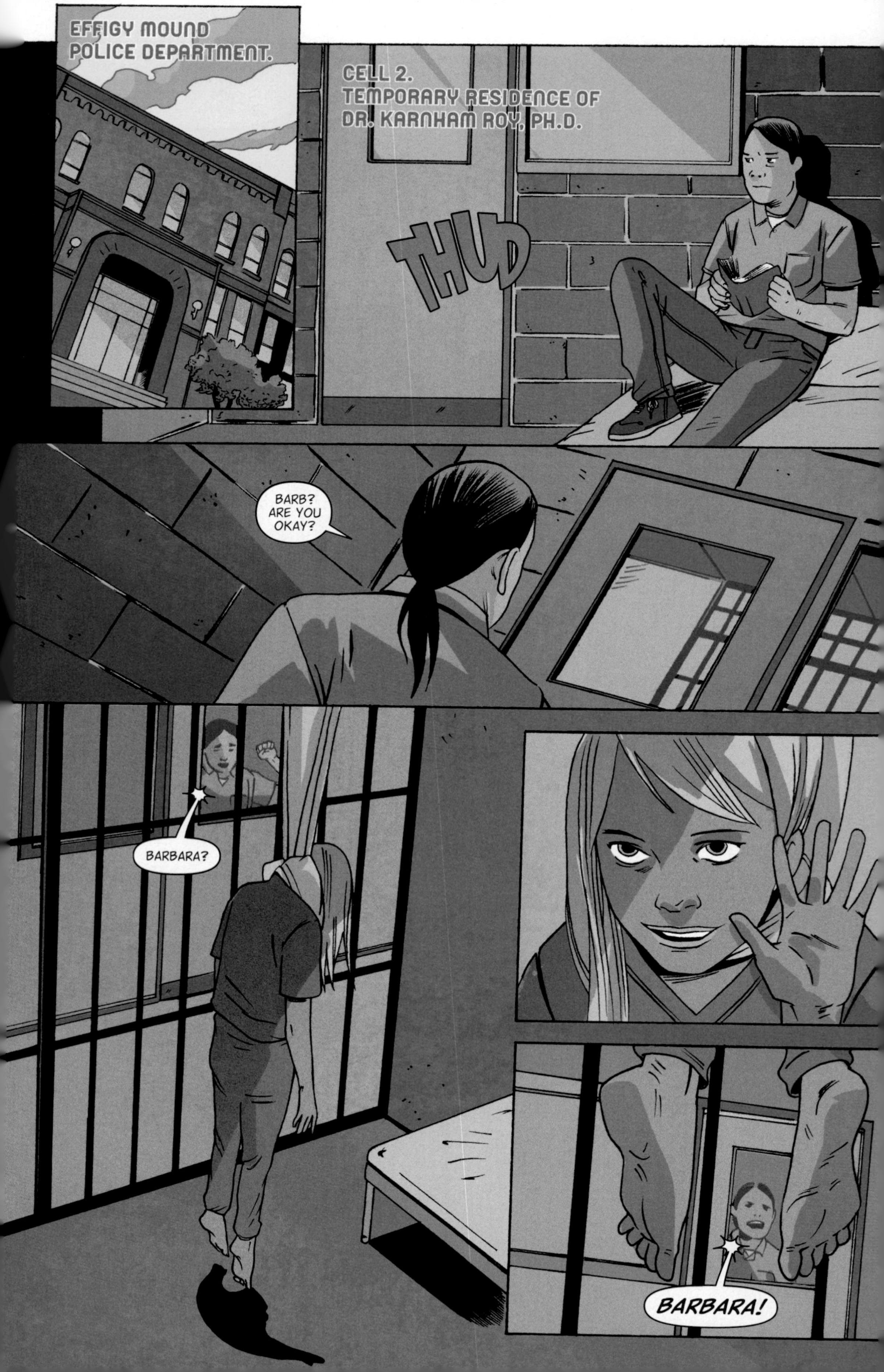
EFFIGY MOUND POLICE DEPARTMENT.
CELL 2. TEMPORARY RESIDENCE OF DR. KARNHAM ROY, PH.D.
THUD
BARB? ARE YOU OKAY?
BARBARA?
BARBARA!

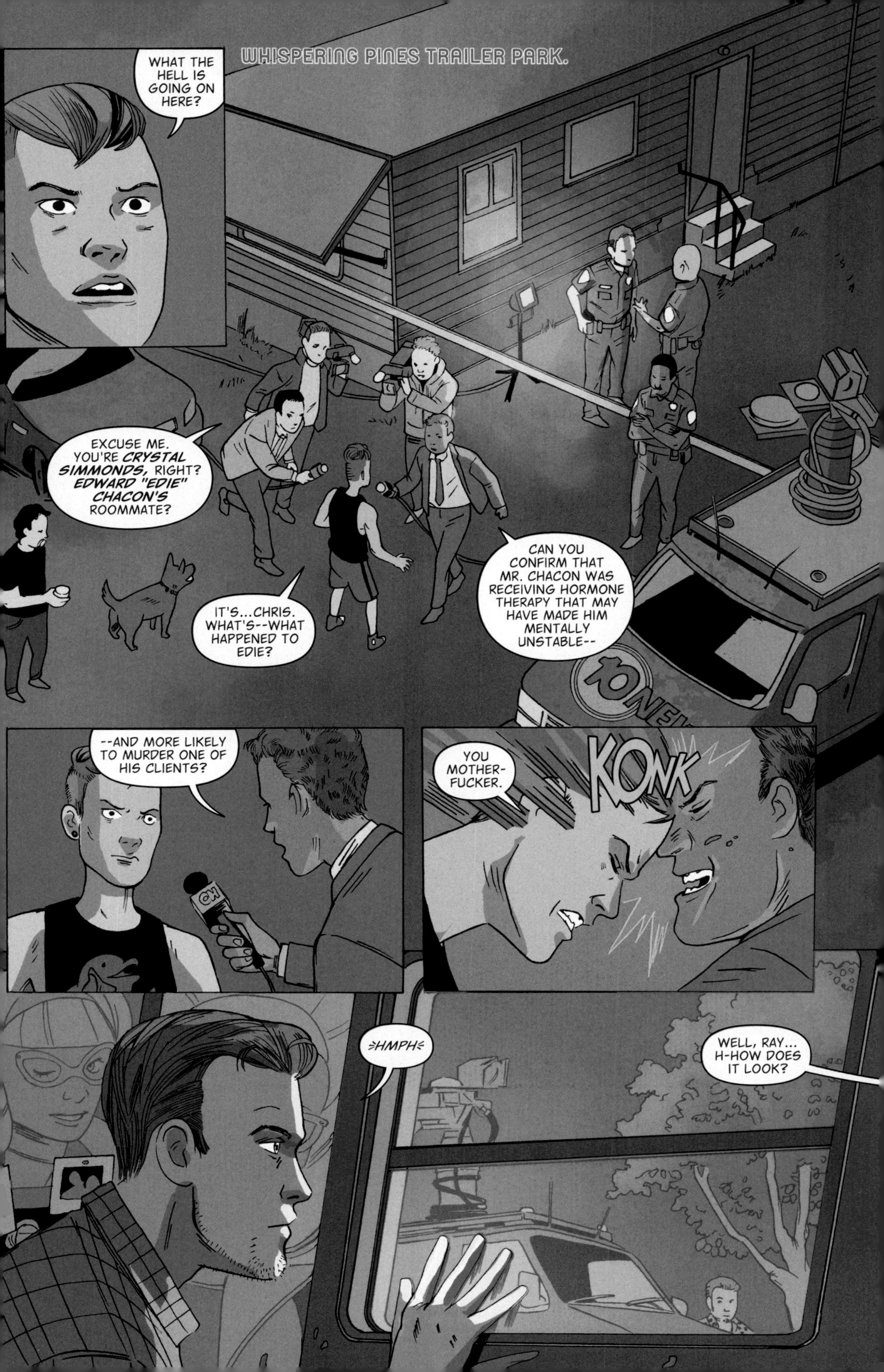
WHISPERING PINES TRAILER PARK.
WHAT THE HELL IS GOING ON HERE?
EXCUSE ME. YOU'RE CRYSTAL SIMMONDS, RIGHT? EDWARD "EDIE" CHACON'S ROOMMATE?
IT'S...CHRIS. WHAT'S--WHAT HAPPENED TO EDIE?
CAN YOU CONFIRM THAT MR. CHACON WAS RECEIVING HORMONE THERAPY THAT MAY HAVE MADE HIM MENTALLY UNSTABLE--
--AND MORE LIKELY TO MURDER ONE OF HIS CLIENTS?
YOU MOTHER-FUCKER.
KONK
HMPH
WELL, RAY... H-HOW DOES IT LOOK?

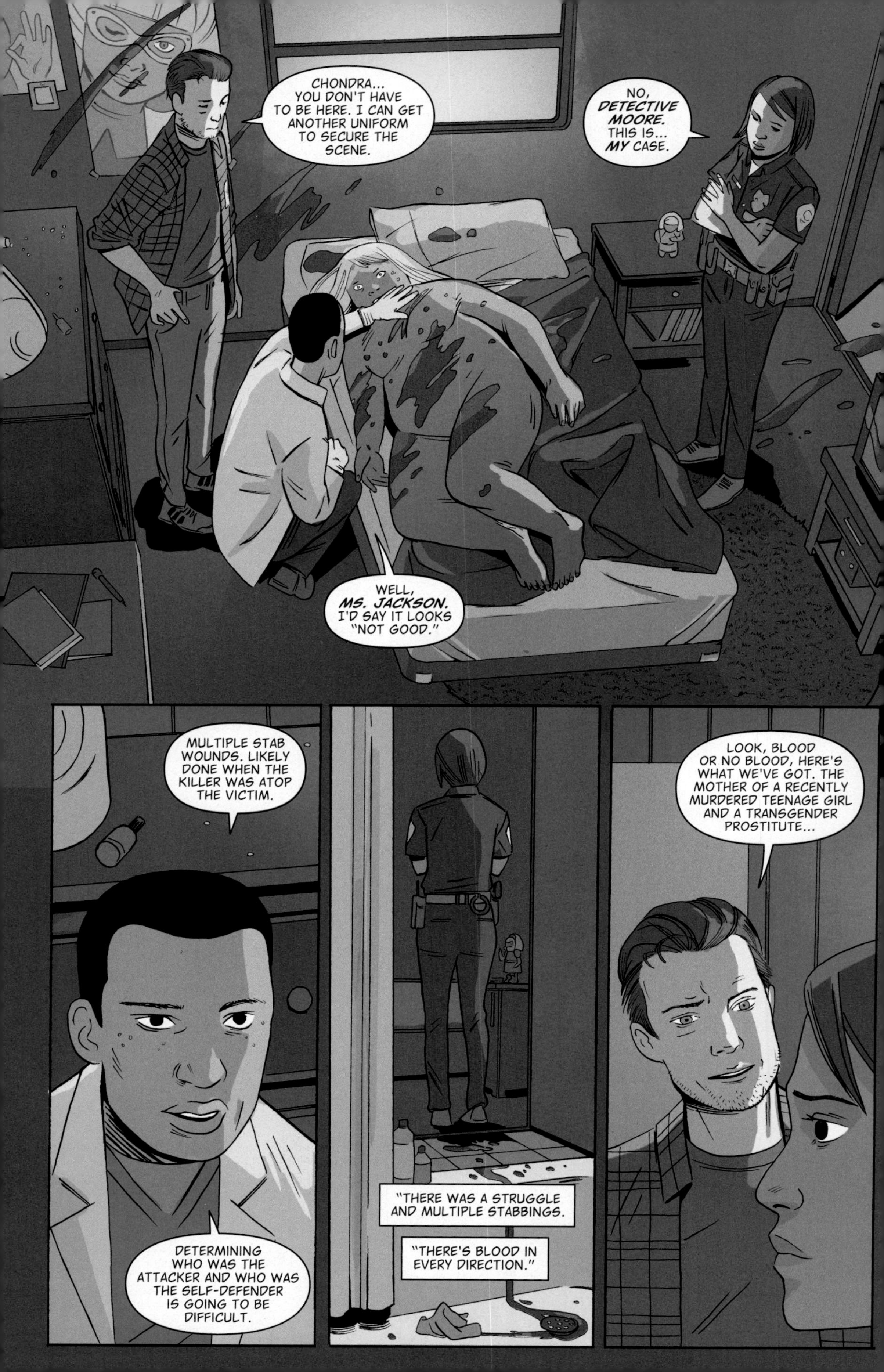
CHONDRA... YOU DON'T HAVE TO BE HERE. I CAN GET ANOTHER UNIFORM TO SECURE THE SCENE.
NO, DETECTIVE MOORE. THIS IS... MY CASE.
WELL, MS. JACKSON. I'D SAY IT LOOKS "NOT GOOD."
MULTIPLE STAB WOUNDS. LIKELY DONE WHEN THE KILLER WAS ATOP THE VICTIM.
DETERMINING WHO WAS THE ATTACKER AND WHO WAS THE SELF-DEFENDER IS GOING TO BE DIFFICULT.
"THERE WAS A STRUGGLE AND MULTIPLE STABBINGS.
"THERE'S BLOOD IN EVERY DIRECTION."
LOOK, BLOOD OR NO BLOOD, HERE'S WHAT WE'VE GOT. THE MOTHER OF A RECENTLY MURDERED TEENAGE GIRL AND A TRANSGENDER PROSTITUTE...

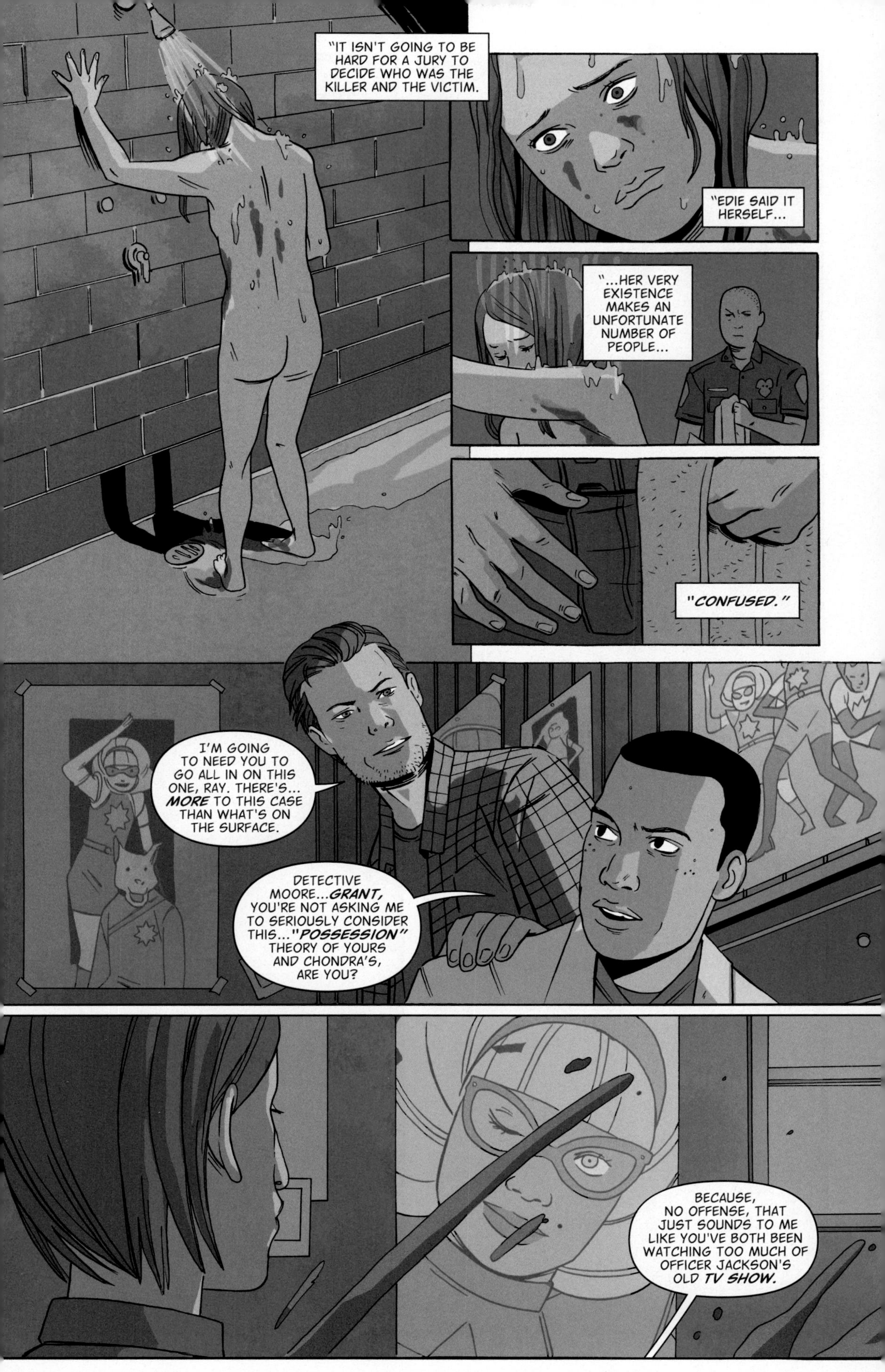
"IT ISN'T GOING TO BE HARD FOR A JURY TO DECIDE WHO WAS THE KILLER AND THE VICTIM.
"EDIE SAID IT HERSELF...
"...HER VERY EXISTENCE MAKES AN UNFORTUNATE NUMBER OF PEOPLE...
"CONFUSED."
I'M GOING TO NEED YOU TO GO ALL IN ON THIS ONE, RAY. THERE'S... MORE TO THIS CASE THAN WHAT'S ON THE SURFACE.
DETECTIVE MOORE...GRANT, YOU'RE NOT ASKING ME TO SERIOUSLY CONSIDER THIS..."POSSESSION" THEORY OF YOURS AND CHONDRA'S, ARE YOU?
BECAUSE, NO OFFENSE, THAT JUST SOUNDS TO ME LIKE YOU'VE BOTH BEEN WATCHING TOO MUCH OF OFFICER JACKSON'S OLD TV SHOW.

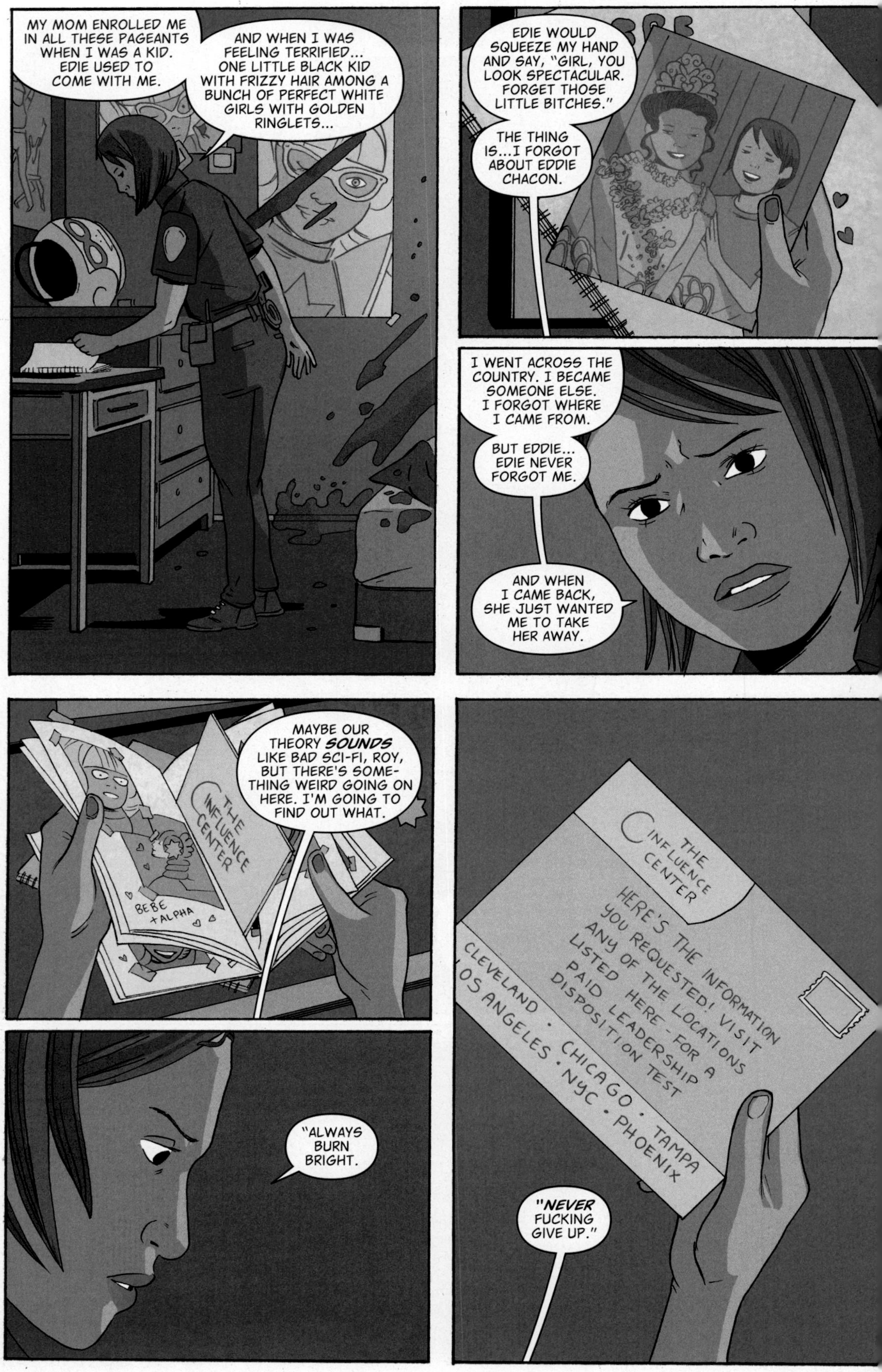
MY MOM ENROLLED ME IN ALL THESE PAGEANTS WHEN I WAS A KID. EDIE USED TO COME WITH ME.
AND WHEN I WAS FEELING TERRIFIED... ONE LITTLE BLACK KID WITH FRIZZY HAIR AMONG A BUNCH OF PERFECT WHITE GIRLS WITH GOLDEN RINGLETS...
EDIE WOULD SQUEEZE MY HAND AND SAY, "GIRL, YOU LOOK SPECTACULAR. FORGET THOSE LITTLE BITCHES."
THE THING IS...I FORGOT ABOUT EDDIE CHACON.
I WENT ACROSS THE COUNTRY. I BECAME SOMEONE ELSE. I FORGOT WHERE I CAME FROM.
BUT EDDIE... EDIE NEVER FORGOT ME.
AND WHEN I CAME BACK, SHE JUST WANTED ME TO TAKE HER AWAY.
THE INFLUENCE CENTER
BEBE + ALPHA
MAYBE OUR THEORY **SOUNDS** LIKE BAD SCI-FI, ROY, BUT THERE'S SOMETHING WEIRD GOING ON HERE. I'M GOING TO FIND OUT WHAT.
"ALWAYS BURN BRIGHT.
THE INFLUENCE CENTER
HERE'S THE INFORMATION YOU REQUESTED! VISIT ANY OF THE LOCATIONS LISTED HERE - FOR A PAID LEADERSHIP DISPOSITION TEST
CLEVELAND · CHICAGO · TAMPA
LOS ANGELES · NYC · PHOENIX
"**NEVER** FUCKING GIVE UP."

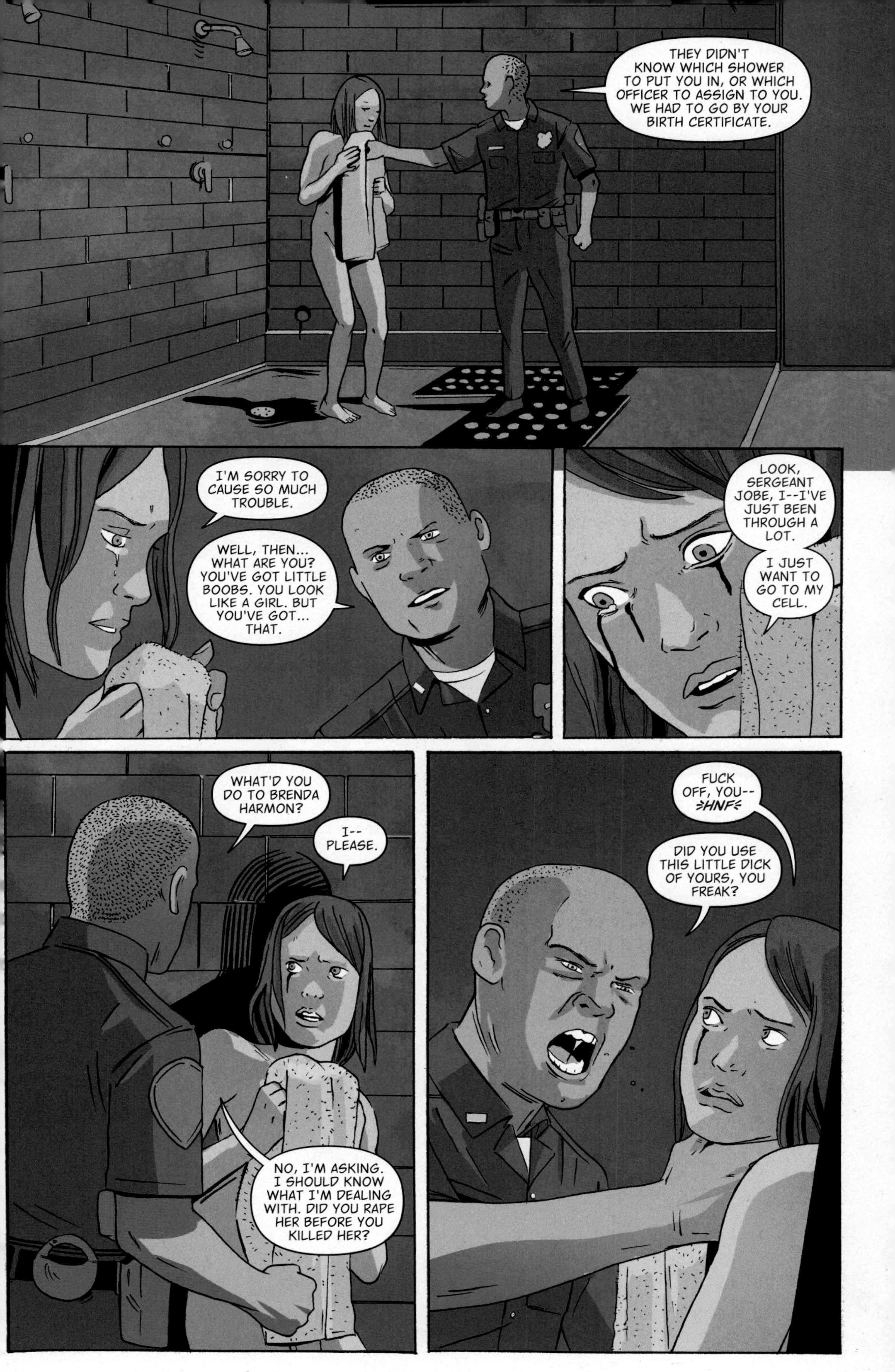
THEY DIDN'T KNOW WHICH SHOWER TO PUT YOU IN, OR WHICH OFFICER TO ASSIGN TO YOU. WE HAD TO GO BY YOUR BIRTH CERTIFICATE.
I'M SORRY TO CAUSE SO MUCH TROUBLE.
WELL, THEN... WHAT ARE YOU? YOU'VE GOT LITTLE BOOBS. YOU LOOK LIKE A GIRL. BUT YOU'VE GOT... THAT.
LOOK, SERGEANT JOBE, I--I'VE JUST BEEN THROUGH A LOT.
I JUST WANT TO GO TO MY CELL.
WHAT'D YOU DO TO BRENDA HARMON?
I-- PLEASE.
NO, I'M ASKING. I SHOULD KNOW WHAT I'M DEALING WITH. DID YOU RAPE HER BEFORE YOU KILLED HER?
FUCK OFF, YOU-- HNF
DID YOU USE THIS LITTLE DICK OF YOURS, YOU FREAK?

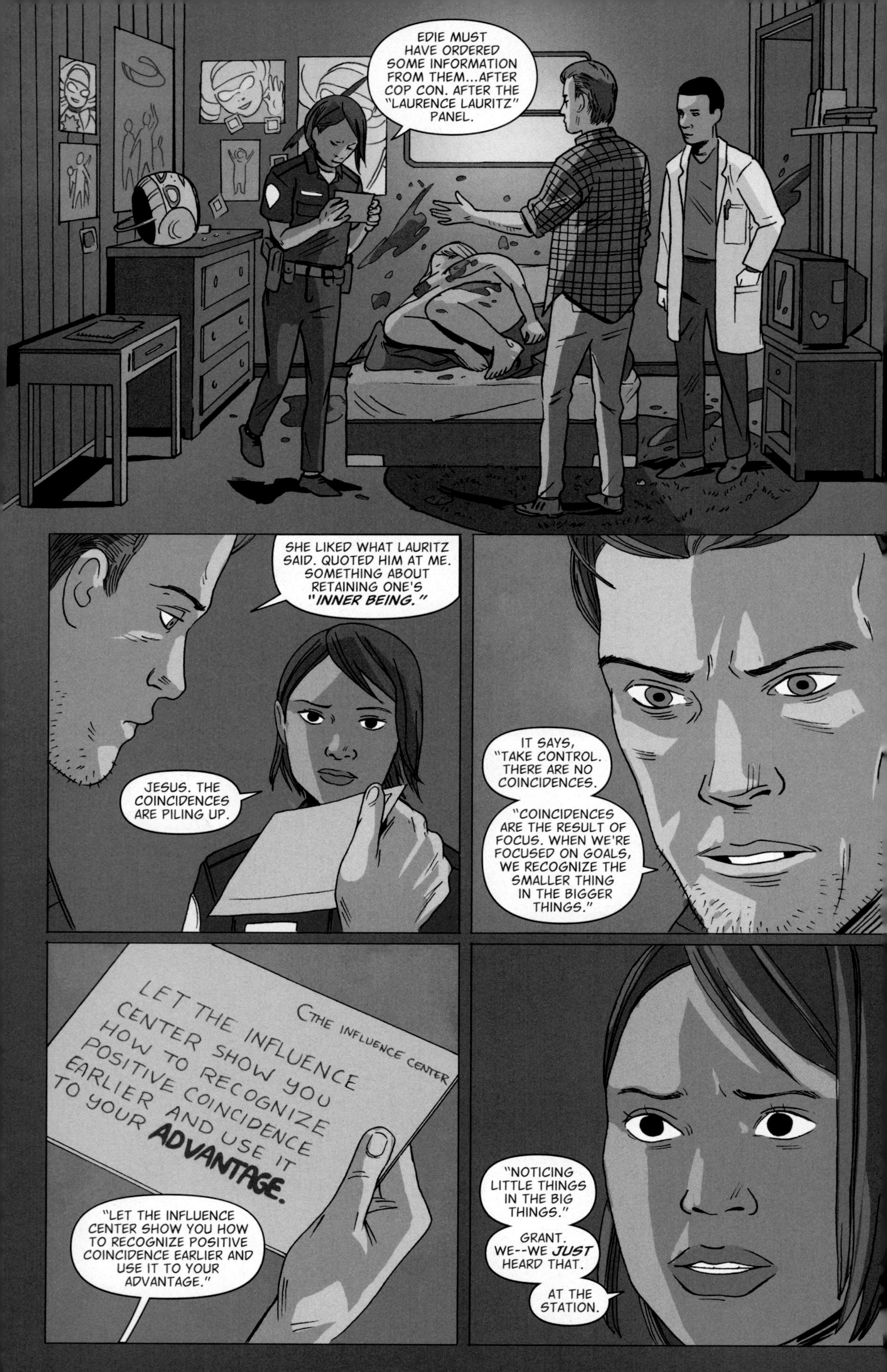
EDIE MUST HAVE ORDERED SOME INFORMATION FROM THEM...AFTER COP CON. AFTER THE "LAURENCE LAURITZ" PANEL.
SHE LIKED WHAT LAURITZ SAID. QUOTED HIM AT ME. SOMETHING ABOUT RETAINING ONE'S *"INNER BEING."*
JESUS. THE COINCIDENCES ARE PILING UP.
IT SAYS, "TAKE CONTROL. THERE ARE NO COINCIDENCES.
"COINCIDENCES ARE THE RESULT OF FOCUS. WHEN WE'RE FOCUSED ON GOALS, WE RECOGNIZE THE SMALLER THING IN THE BIGGER THINGS."
CTHE INFLUENCE CENTER
LET THE INFLUENCE CENTER SHOW YOU HOW TO RECOGNIZE POSITIVE COINCIDENCE EARLIER AND USE IT TO YOUR ADVANTAGE.
"LET THE INFLUENCE CENTER SHOW YOU HOW TO RECOGNIZE POSITIVE COINCIDENCE EARLIER AND USE IT TO YOUR ADVANTAGE."
"NOTICING LITTLE THINGS IN THE BIG THINGS."
GRANT. WE--WE *JUST* HEARD THAT.
AT THE STATION.

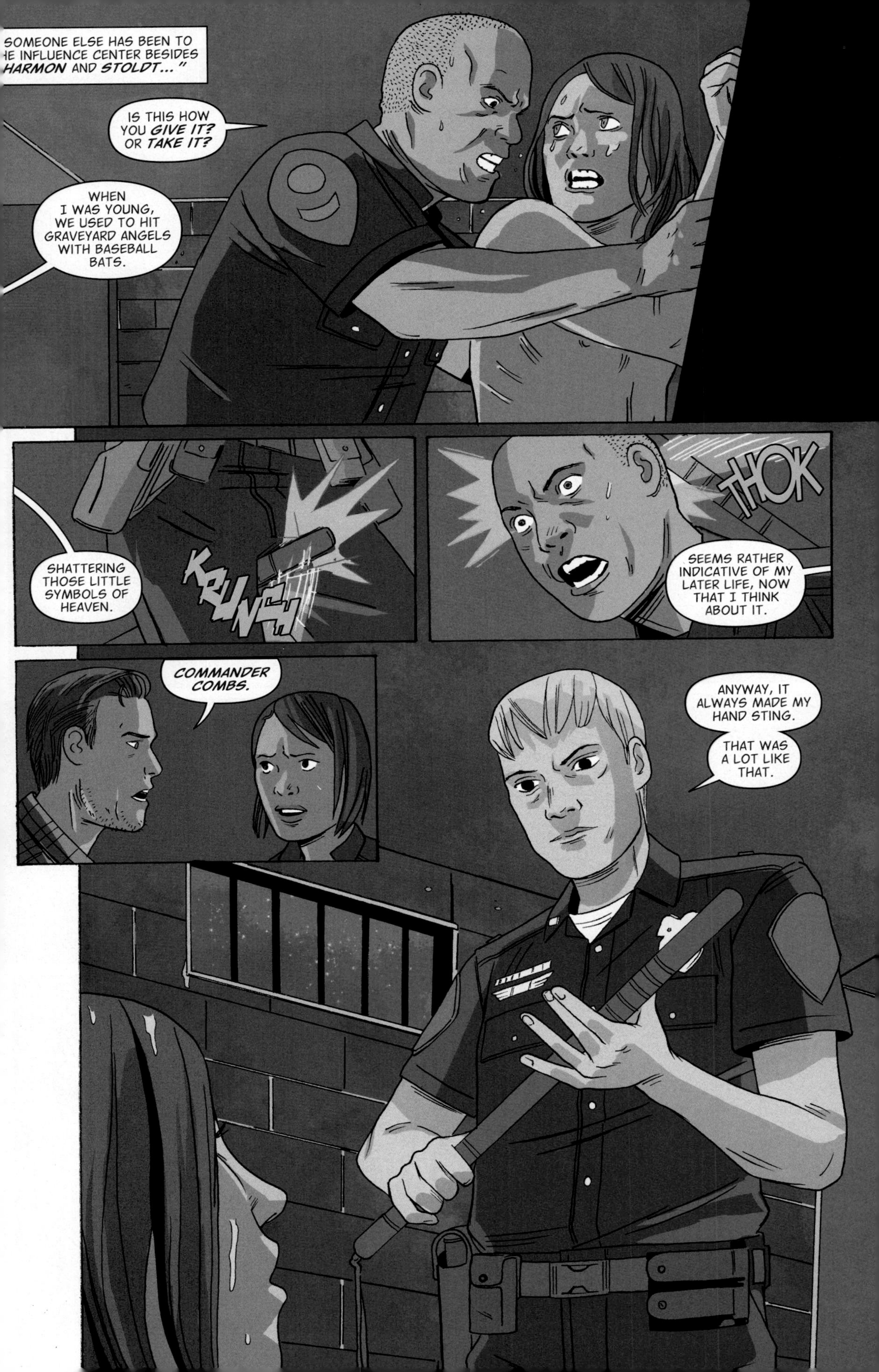
SOMEONE ELSE HAS BEEN TO
HE INFLUENCE CENTER BESIDES
HARMON AND STOLDT..."
IS THIS HOW YOU GIVE IT? OR TAKE IT?
WHEN I WAS YOUNG, WE USED TO HIT GRAVEYARD ANGELS WITH BASEBALL BATS.
SHATTERING THOSE LITTLE SYMBOLS OF HEAVEN.
KRUNCH
THOK
SEEMS RATHER INDICATIVE OF MY LATER LIFE, NOW THAT I THINK ABOUT IT.
COMMANDER COMBS.
ANYWAY, IT ALWAYS MADE MY HAND STING.
THAT WAS A LOT LIKE THAT.

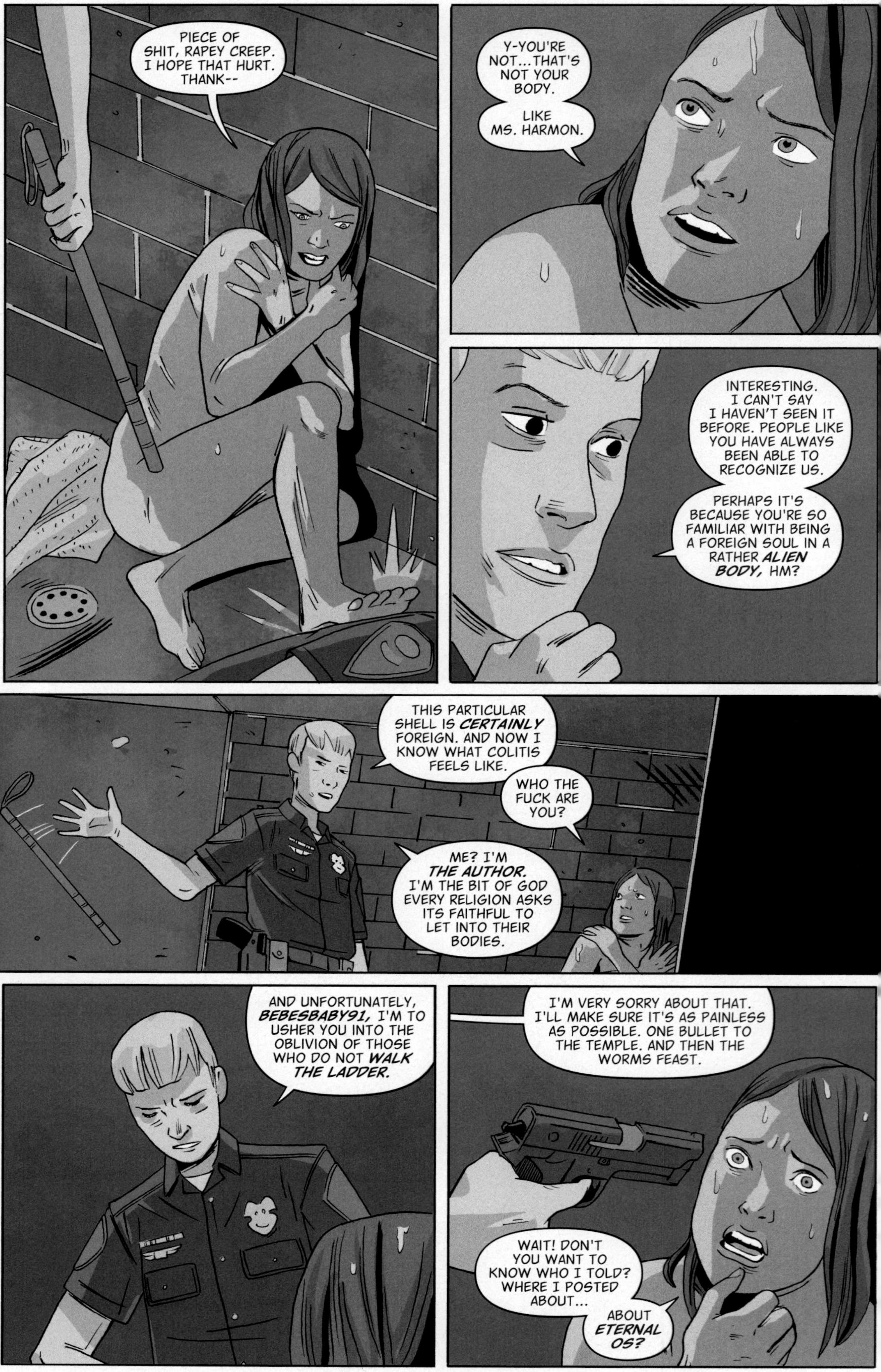
PIECE OF SHIT, RAPEY CREEP. I HOPE THAT HURT. THANK--
Y-YOU'RE NOT...THAT'S NOT YOUR BODY.
LIKE MS. HARMON.
INTERESTING. I CAN'T SAY I HAVEN'T SEEN IT BEFORE. PEOPLE LIKE YOU HAVE ALWAYS BEEN ABLE TO RECOGNIZE US.
PERHAPS IT'S BECAUSE YOU'RE SO FAMILIAR WITH BEING A FOREIGN SOUL IN A RATHER ALIEN BODY, HM?
THIS PARTICULAR SHELL IS CERTAINLY FOREIGN. AND NOW I KNOW WHAT COLITIS FEELS LIKE.
WHO THE FUCK ARE YOU?
ME? I'M THE AUTHOR. I'M THE BIT OF GOD EVERY RELIGION ASKS ITS FAITHFUL TO LET INTO THEIR BODIES.
AND UNFORTUNATELY, BEBESBABY91, I'M TO USHER YOU INTO THE OBLIVION OF THOSE WHO DO NOT WALK THE LADDER.
I'M VERY SORRY ABOUT THAT. I'LL MAKE SURE IT'S AS PAINLESS AS POSSIBLE. ONE BULLET TO THE TEMPLE. AND THEN THE WORMS FEAST.
WAIT! DON'T YOU WANT TO KNOW WHO I TOLD? WHERE I POSTED ABOUT...
ABOUT ETERNAL OS?

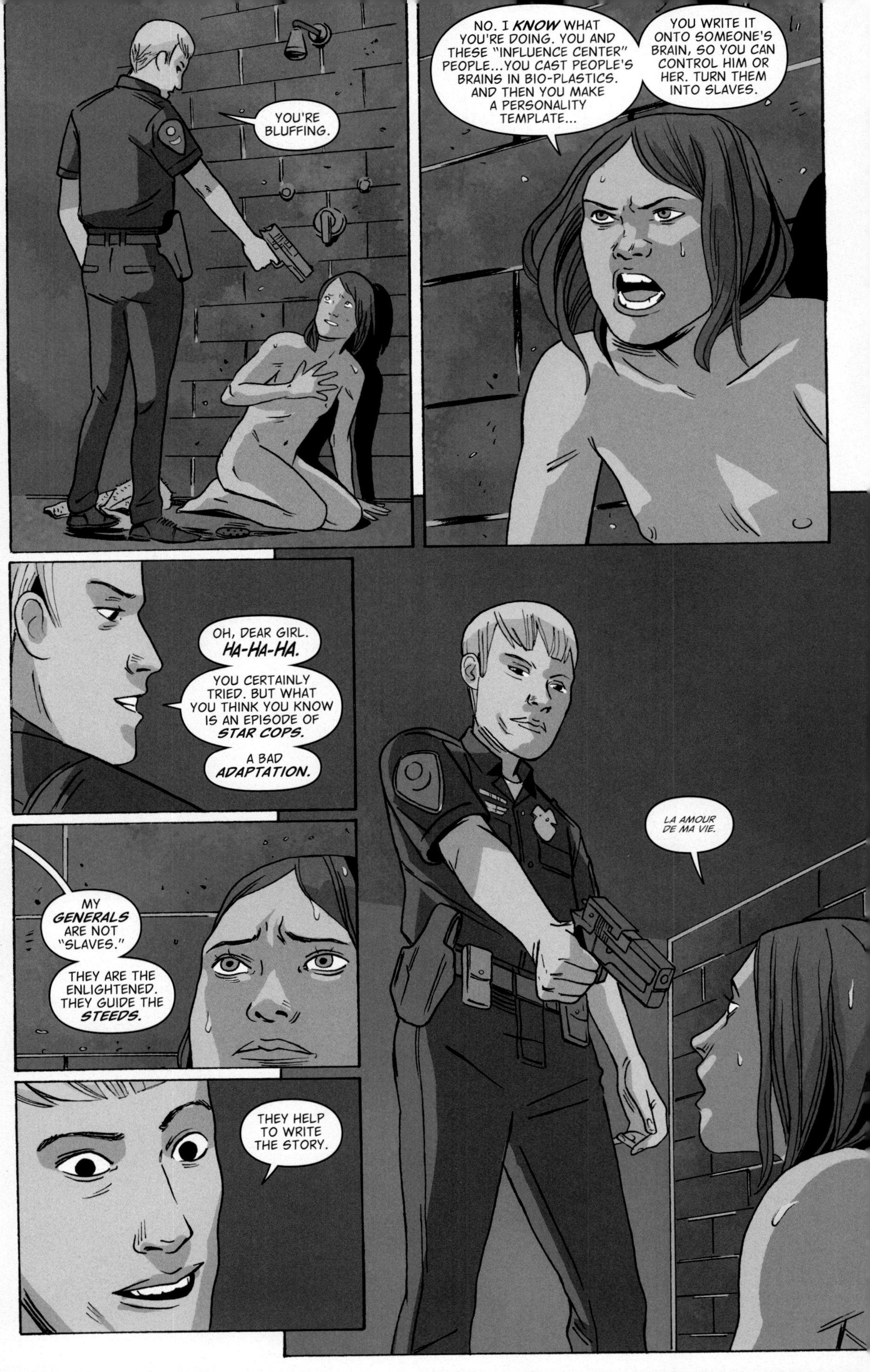

YOU'RE BLUFFING.
NO. I KNOW WHAT YOU'RE DOING. YOU AND THESE "INFLUENCE CENTER" PEOPLE...YOU CAST PEOPLE'S BRAINS IN BIO-PLASTICS. AND THEN YOU MAKE A PERSONALITY TEMPLATE...
YOU WRITE IT ONTO SOMEONE'S BRAIN, SO YOU CAN CONTROL HIM OR HER. TURN THEM INTO SLAVES.
OH, DEAR GIRL. HA-HA-HA.
YOU CERTAINLY TRIED. BUT WHAT YOU THINK YOU KNOW IS AN EPISODE OF STAR COPS.
A BAD ADAPTATION.
MY GENERALS ARE NOT "SLAVES."
THEY ARE THE ENLIGHTENED. THEY GUIDE THE STEEDS.
THEY HELP TO WRITE THE STORY.
LA AMOUR DE MA VIE.

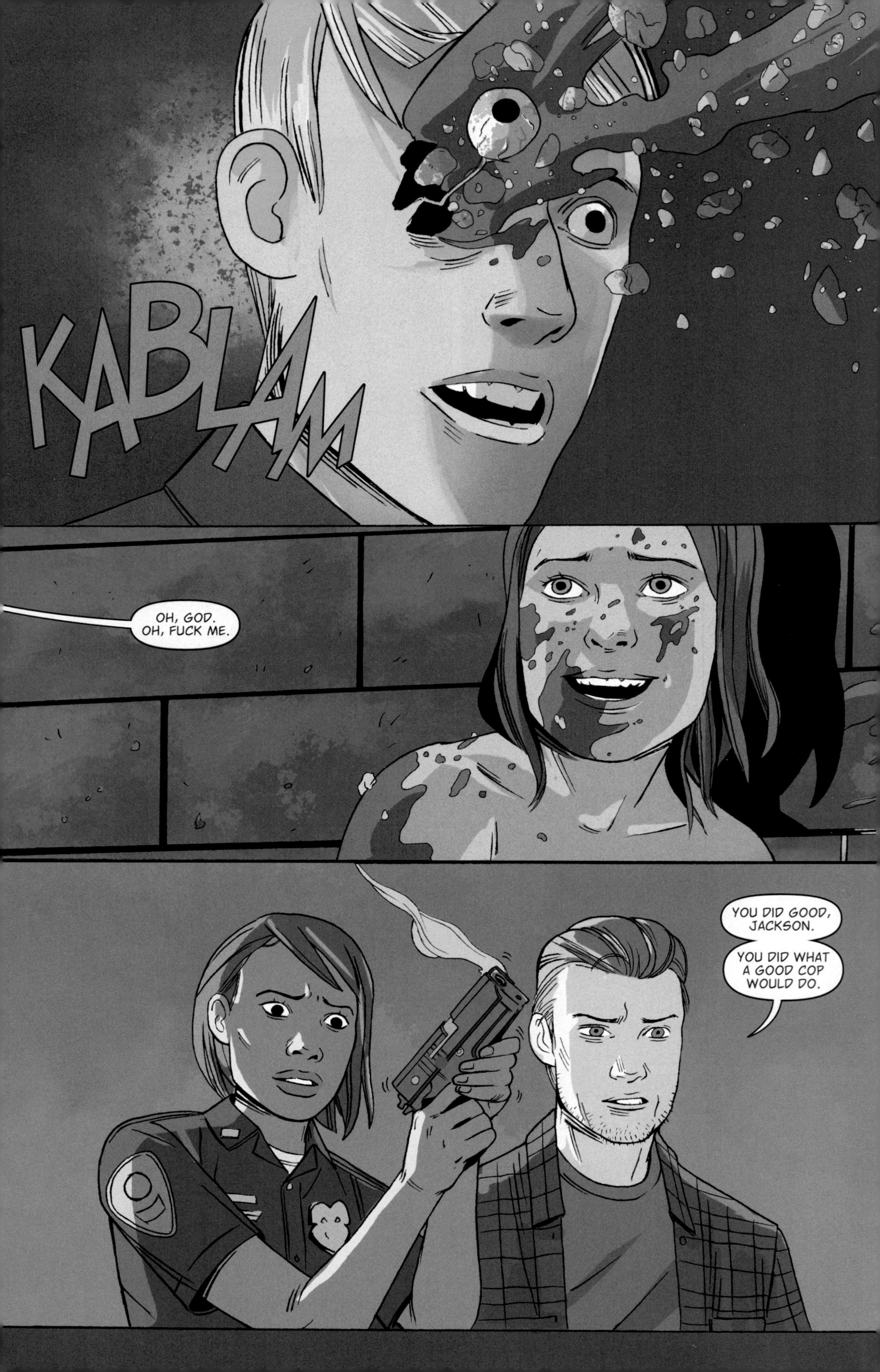
KABLAM
OH, GOD. OH, FUCK ME.
YOU DID GOOD, JACKSON.
YOU DID WHAT A GOOD COP WOULD DO.

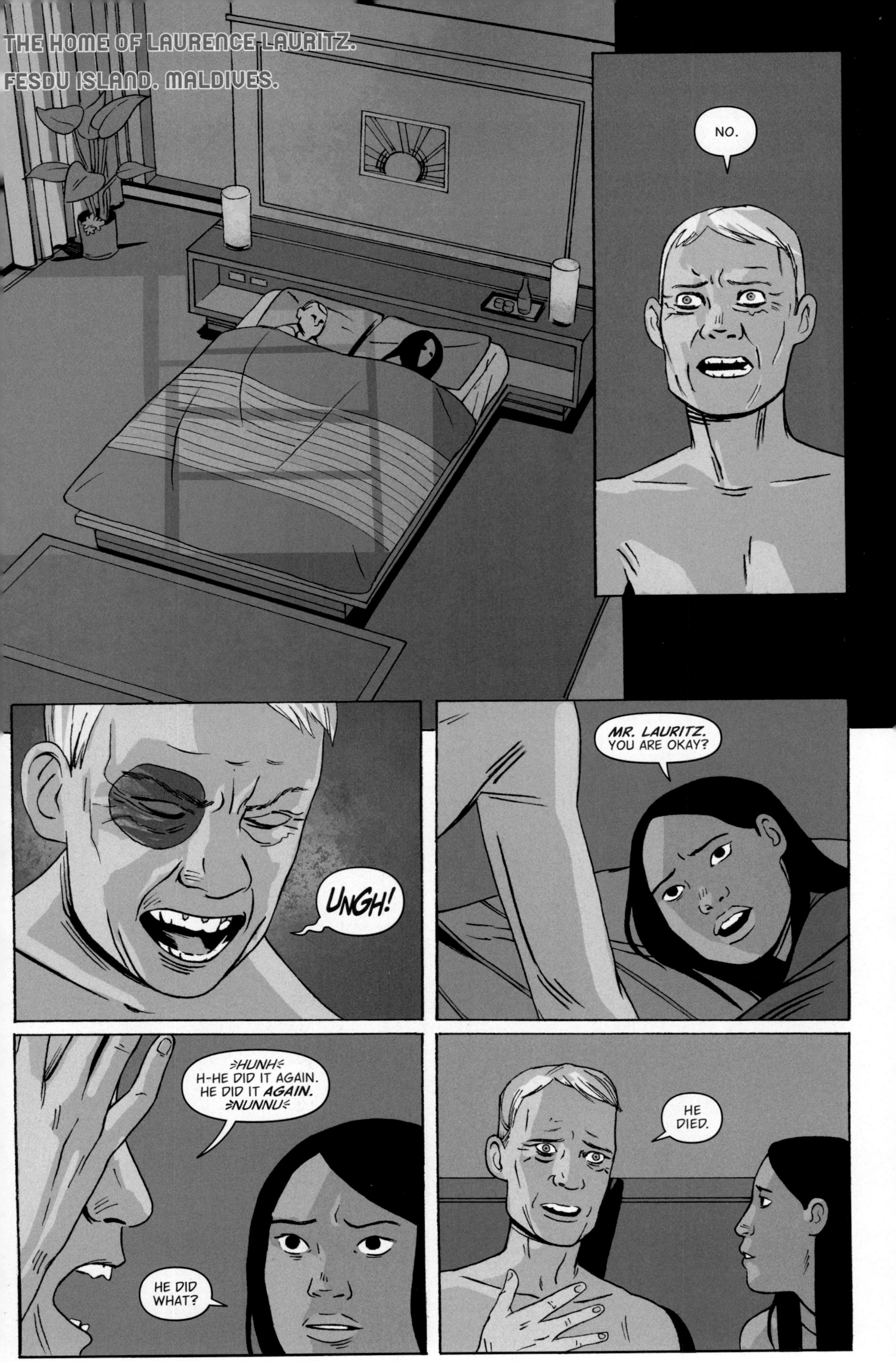
THE HOME OF LAURENCE LAURITZ.
FESDU ISLAND. MALDIVES.
NO.
UNGH!
MR. LAURITZ. YOU ARE OKAY?
HUNH H-HE DID IT AGAIN. HE DID IT AGAIN. NUNNU
HE DID WHAT?
HE DIED.

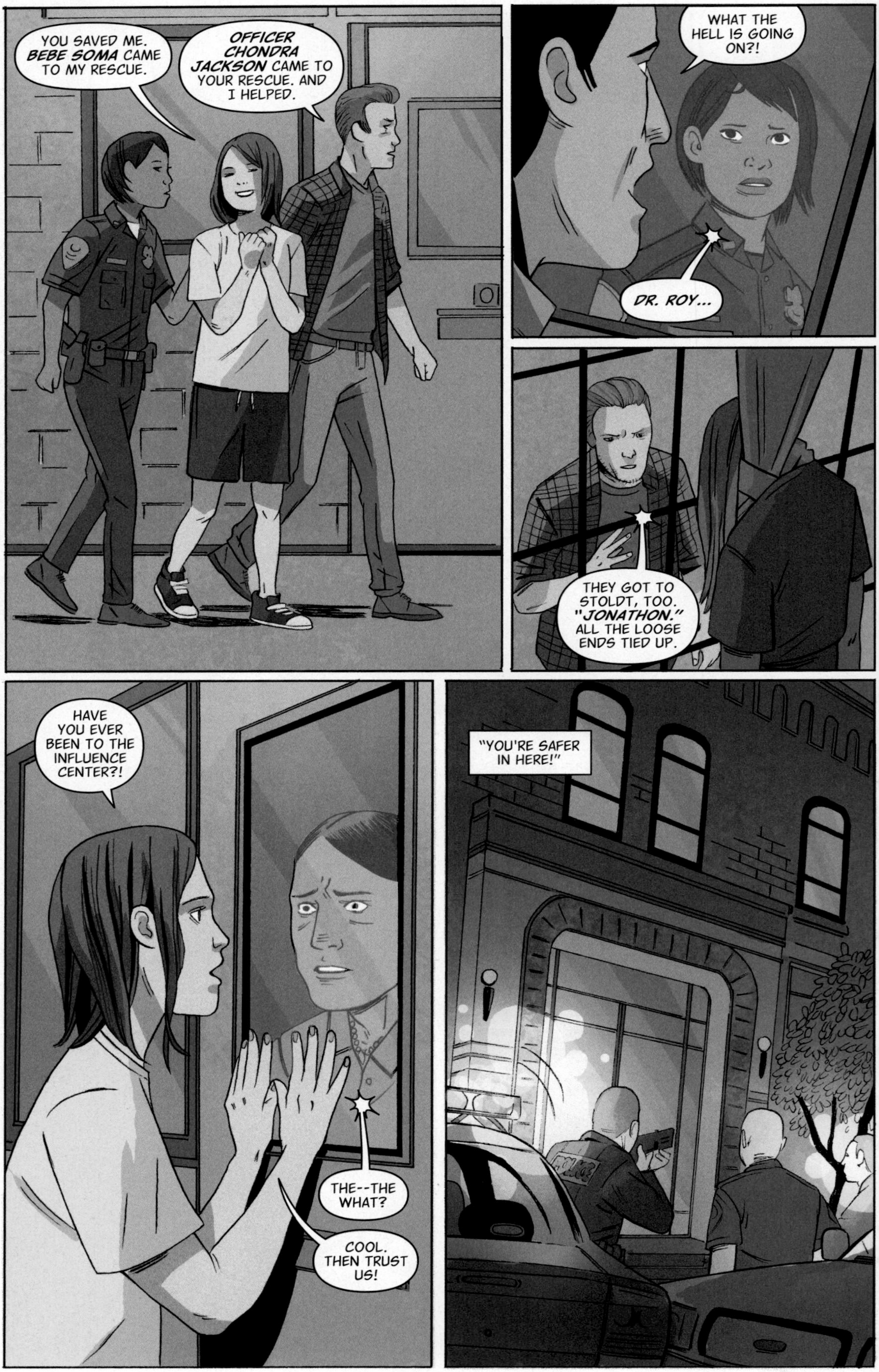
YOU SAVED ME. BEBE SOMA CAME TO MY RESCUE.
OFFICER CHONDRA JACKSON CAME TO YOUR RESCUE. AND I HELPED.
WHAT THE HELL IS GOING ON?!
DR. ROY...
THEY GOT TO STOLDT, TOO. "JONATHON." ALL THE LOOSE ENDS TIED UP.
HAVE YOU EVER BEEN TO THE INFLUENCE CENTER?!
THE--THE WHAT?
COOL. THEN TRUST US!
"YOU'RE SAFER IN HERE!"
POLICE

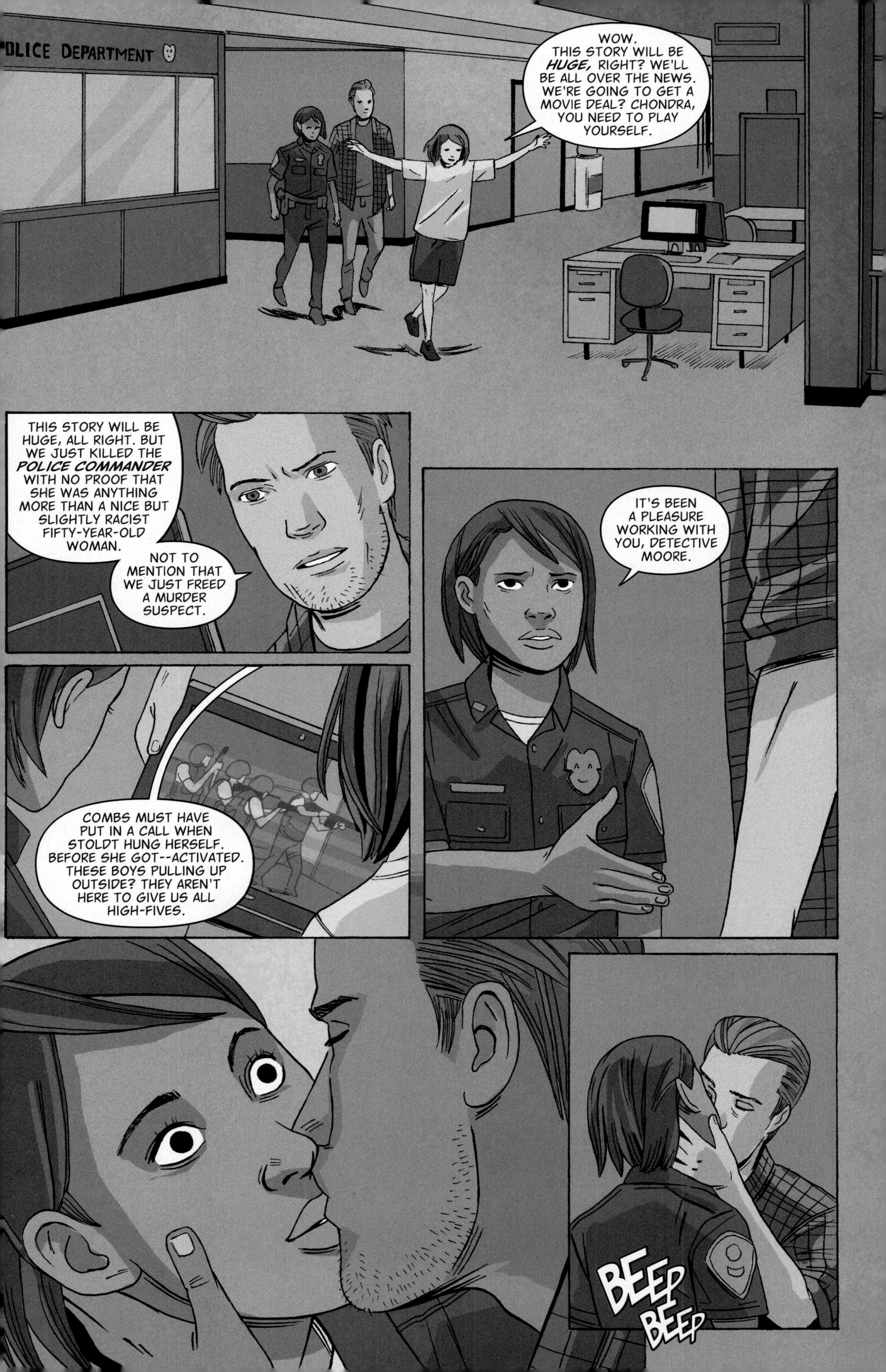

POLICE DEPARTMENT
WOW. THIS STORY WILL BE HUGE, RIGHT? WE'LL BE ALL OVER THE NEWS. WE'RE GOING TO GET A MOVIE DEAL? CHONDRA, YOU NEED TO PLAY YOURSELF.
THIS STORY WILL BE HUGE, ALL RIGHT. BUT WE JUST KILLED THE POLICE COMMANDER WITH NO PROOF THAT SHE WAS ANYTHING MORE THAN A NICE BUT SLIGHTLY RACIST FIFTY-YEAR-OLD WOMAN.
NOT TO MENTION THAT WE JUST FREED A MURDER SUSPECT.
COMBS MUST HAVE PUT IN A CALL WHEN STOLDT HUNG HERSELF. BEFORE SHE GOT--ACTIVATED. THESE BOYS PULLING UP OUTSIDE? THEY AREN'T HERE TO GIVE US ALL HIGH-FIVES.
IT'S BEEN A PLEASURE WORKING WITH YOU, DETECTIVE MOORE.
BEEP BEEP

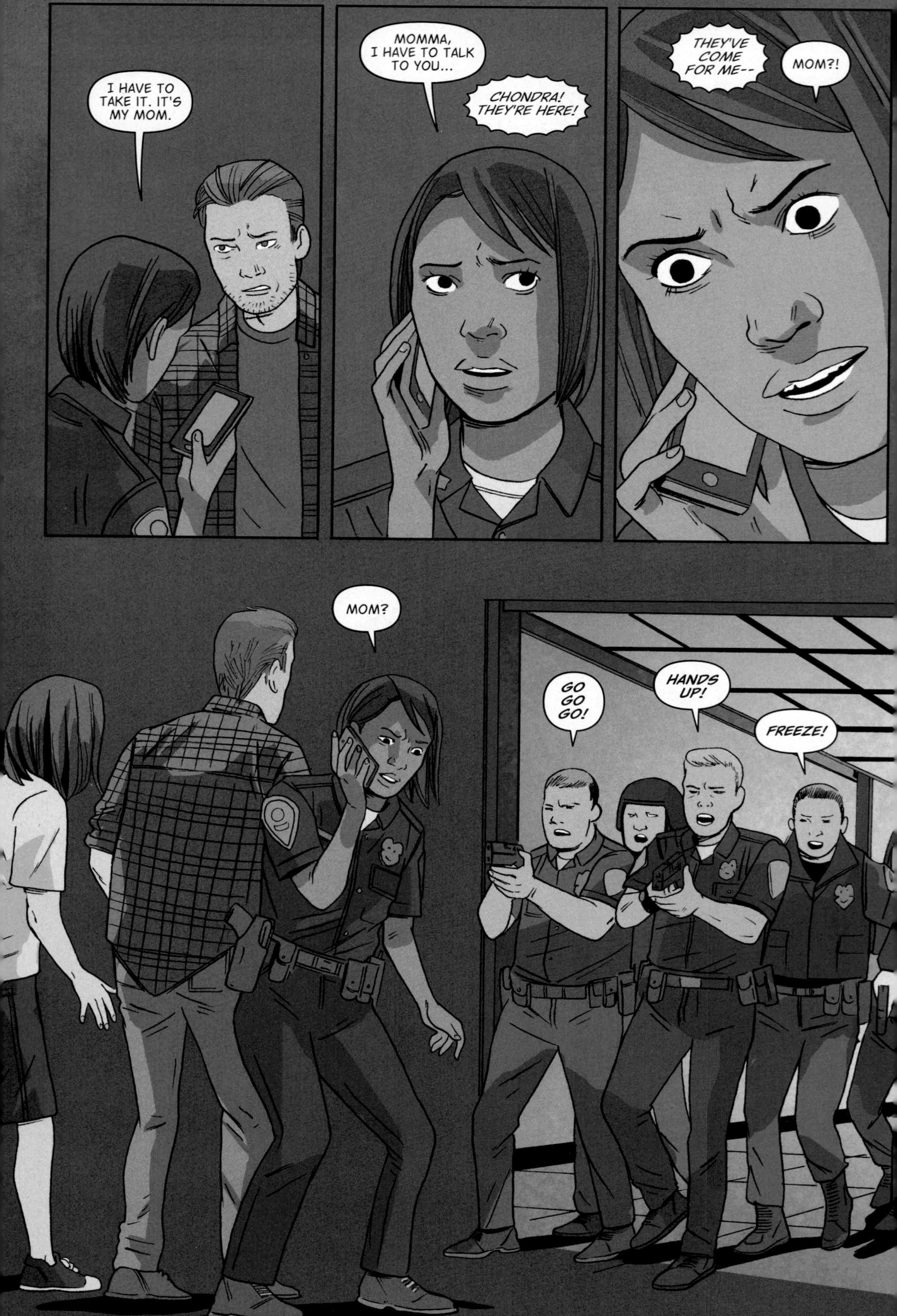
I HAVE TO TAKE IT. IT'S MY MOM.
MOMMA, I HAVE TO TALK TO YOU...
CHONDRA! THEY'RE HERE!
THEY'VE COME FOR ME--
MOM?!
MOM?
GO GO GO!
HANDS UP!
FREEZE!

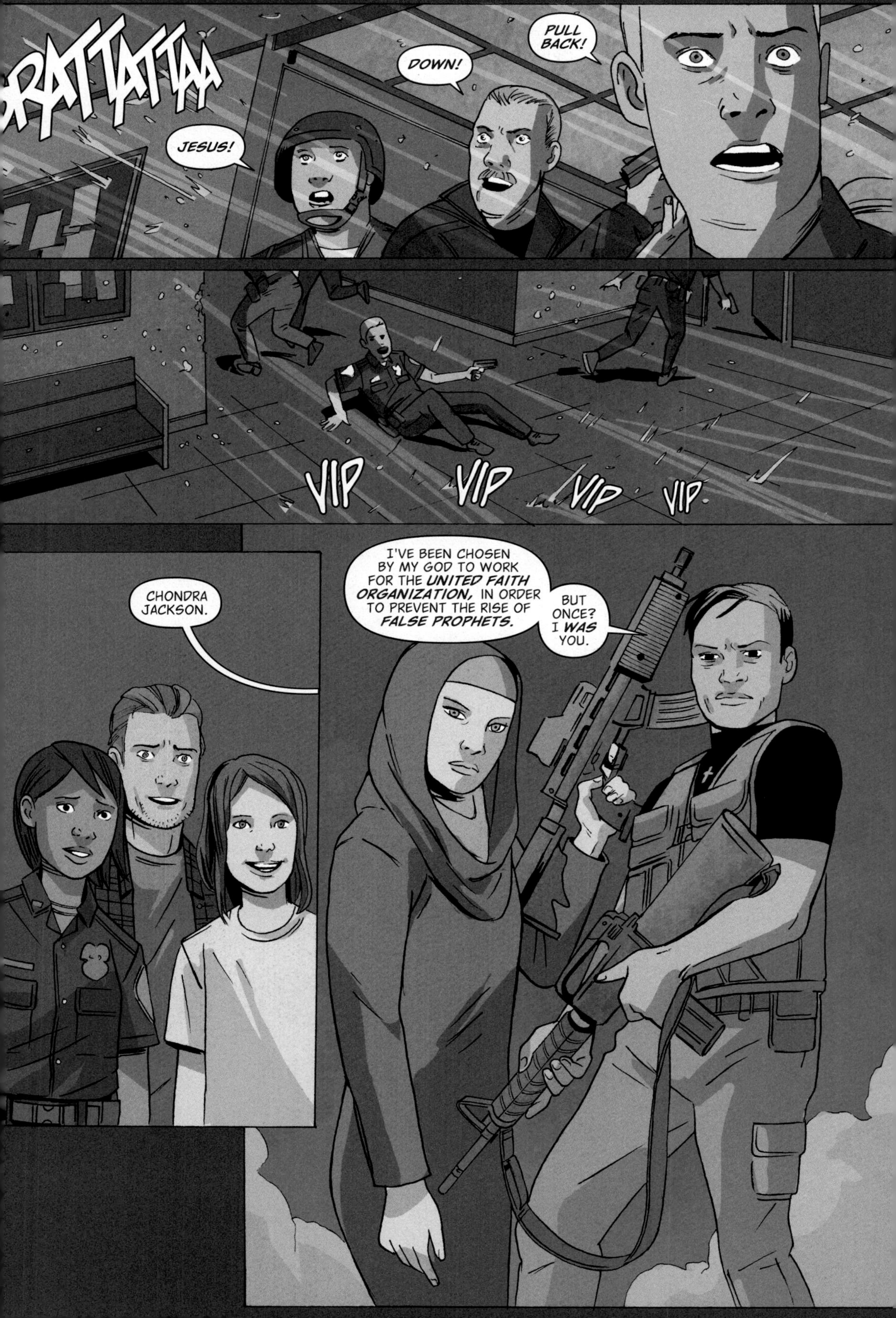
RATTATTAA
JESUS!
DOWN!
PULL BACK!
VIP VIP VIP VIP
CHONDRA JACKSON.
I'VE BEEN CHOSEN BY MY GOD TO WORK FOR THE UNITED FAITH ORGANIZATION, IN ORDER TO PREVENT THE RISE OF FALSE PROPHETS.
BUT ONCE? I WAS YOU.

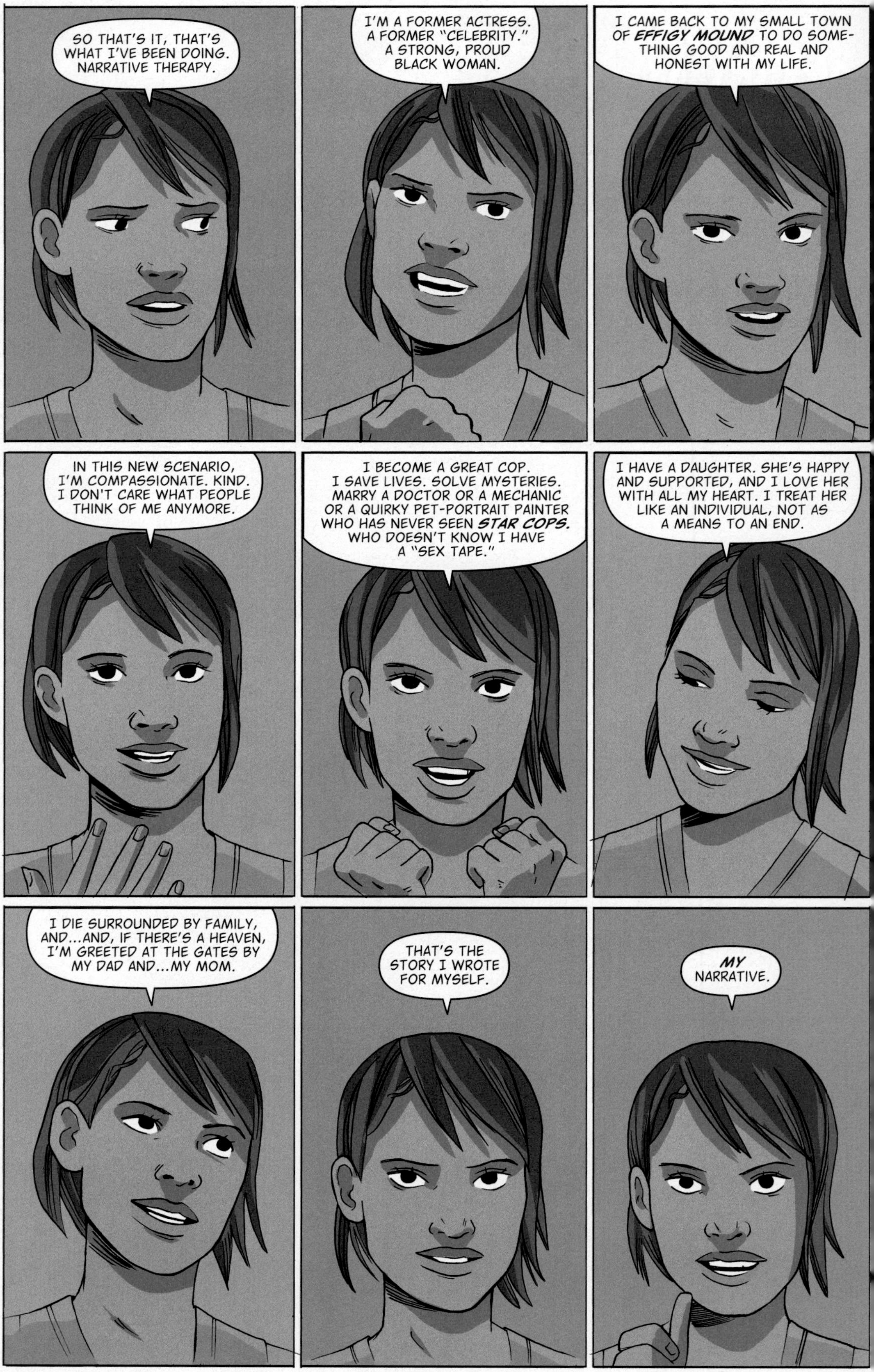
SO THAT'S IT, THAT'S WHAT I'VE BEEN DOING. NARRATIVE THERAPY.
I'M A FORMER ACTRESS. A FORMER "CELEBRITY." A STRONG, PROUD BLACK WOMAN.
I CAME BACK TO MY SMALL TOWN OF *EFFIGY MOUND* TO DO SOMETHING GOOD AND REAL AND HONEST WITH MY LIFE.
IN THIS NEW SCENARIO, I'M COMPASSIONATE. KIND. I DON'T CARE WHAT PEOPLE THINK OF ME ANYMORE.
I BECOME A GREAT COP. I SAVE LIVES. SOLVE MYSTERIES. MARRY A DOCTOR OR A MECHANIC OR A QUIRKY PET-PORTRAIT PAINTER WHO HAS NEVER SEEN *STAR COPS.* WHO DOESN'T KNOW I HAVE A "SEX TAPE."
I HAVE A DAUGHTER. SHE'S HAPPY AND SUPPORTED, AND I LOVE HER WITH ALL MY HEART. I TREAT HER LIKE AN INDIVIDUAL, NOT AS A MEANS TO AN END.
I DIE SURROUNDED BY FAMILY, AND...AND, IF THERE'S A HEAVEN, I'M GREETED AT THE GATES BY MY DAD AND...MY MOM.
THAT'S THE STORY I WROTE FOR MYSELF.
MY NARRATIVE.

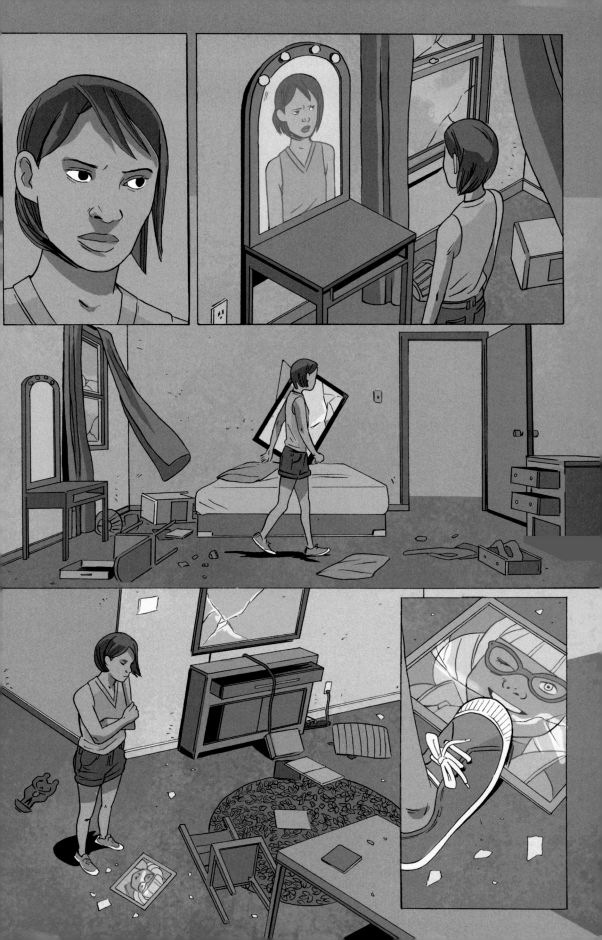

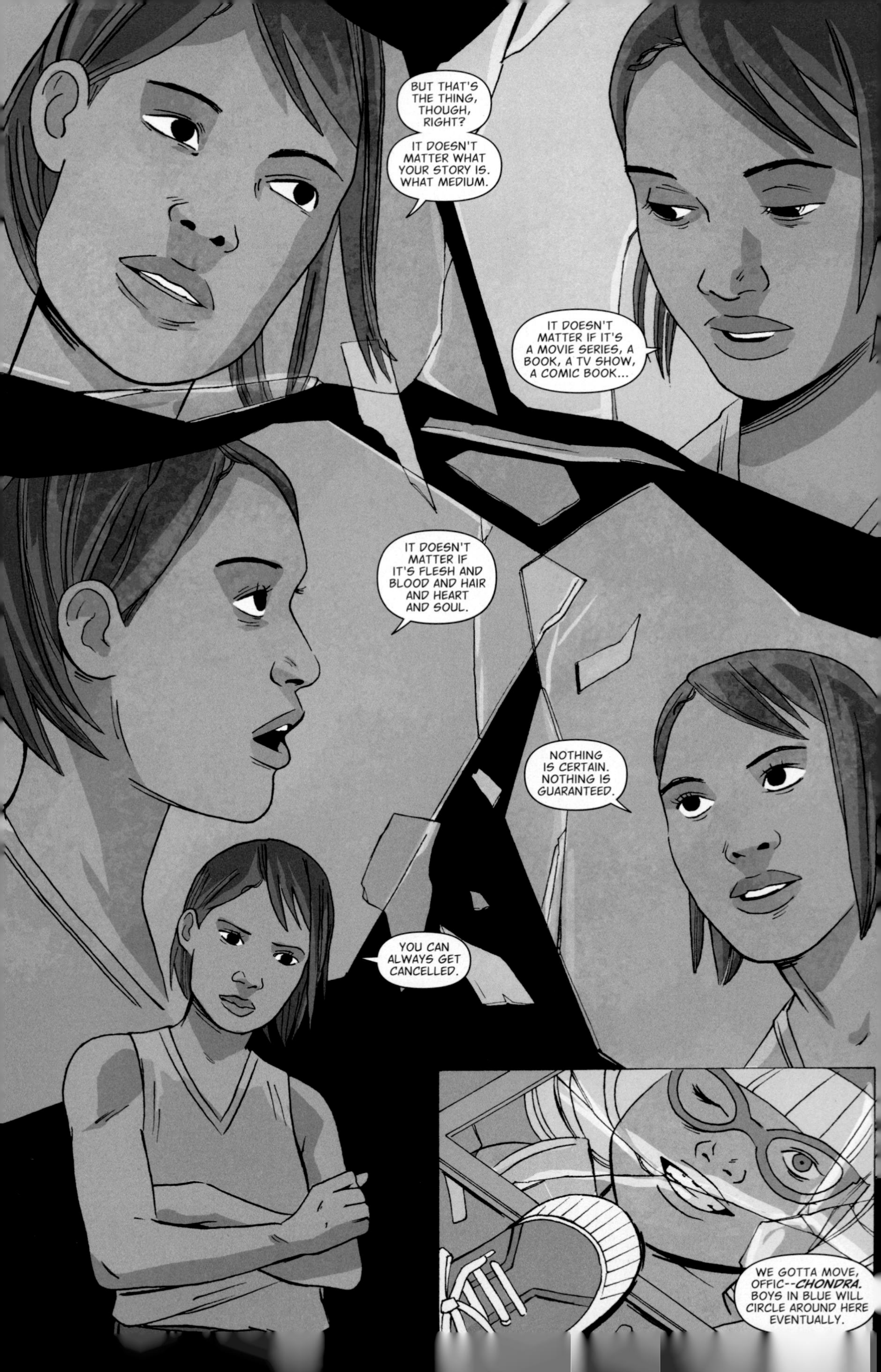
BUT THAT'S THE THING, THOUGH, RIGHT?
IT DOESN'T MATTER WHAT YOUR STORY IS. WHAT MEDIUM.
IT DOESN'T MATTER IF IT'S A MOVIE SERIES, A BOOK, A TV SHOW, A COMIC BOOK...
IT DOESN'T MATTER IF IT'S FLESH AND BLOOD AND HAIR AND HEART AND SOUL.
NOTHING IS CERTAIN. NOTHING IS GUARANTEED.
YOU CAN ALWAYS GET CANCELLED.
WE GOTTA MOVE, OFFIC--*CHONDRA.* BOYS IN BLUE WILL CIRCLE AROUND HERE EVENTUALLY.

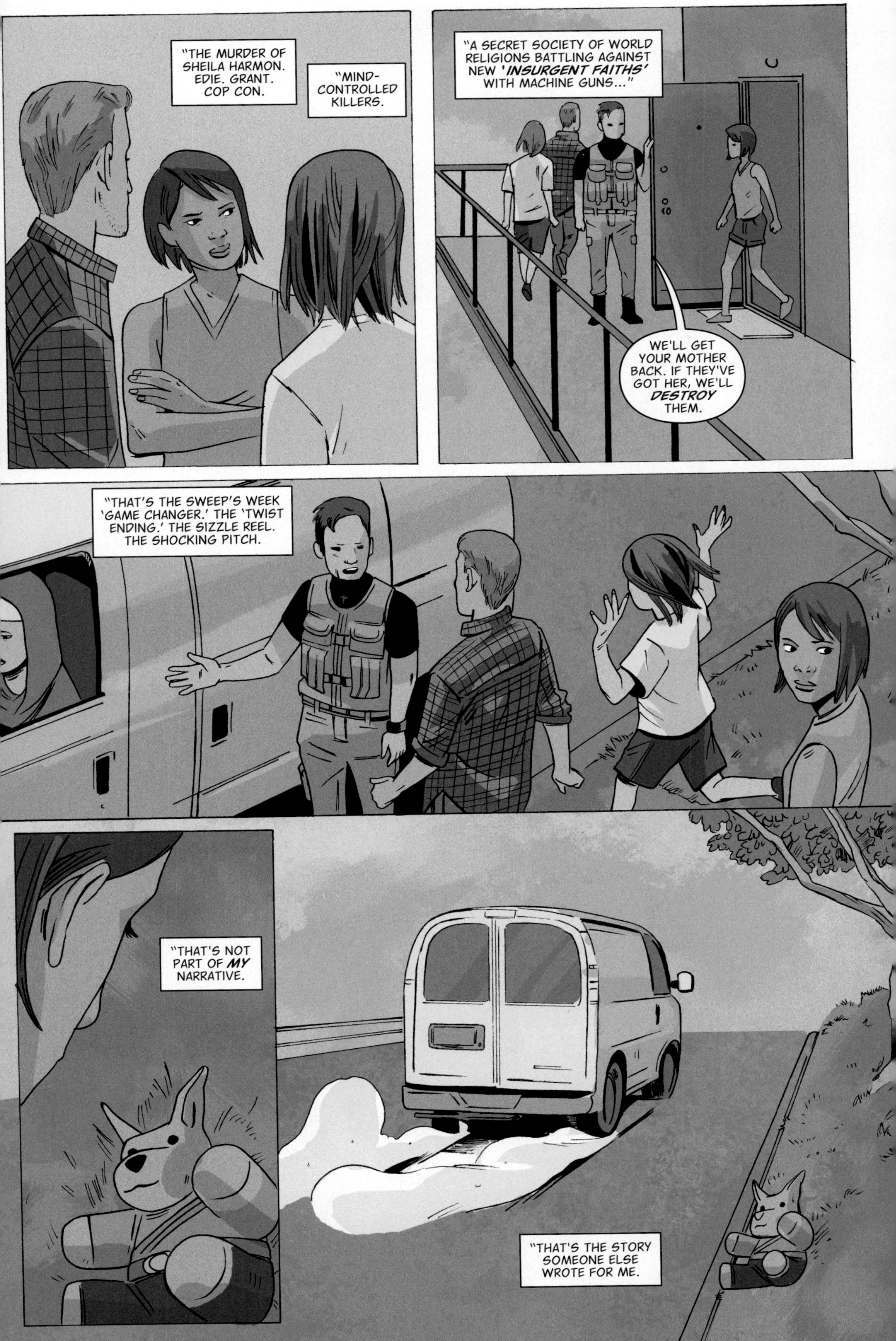
"THE MURDER OF SHEILA HARMON. EDIE. GRANT. COP CON.
"MIND-CONTROLLED KILLERS.
"A SECRET SOCIETY OF WORLD RELIGIONS BATTLING AGAINST NEW '*INSURGENT FAITHS*' WITH MACHINE GUNS..."
WE'LL GET YOUR MOTHER BACK. IF THEY'VE GOT HER, WE'LL *DESTROY* THEM.
"THAT'S THE SWEEP'S WEEK 'GAME CHANGER.' THE 'TWIST ENDING.' THE SIZZLE REEL. THE SHOCKING PITCH.
"THAT'S NOT PART OF *MY* NARRATIVE.
"THAT'S THE STORY SOMEONE ELSE WROTE FOR ME.

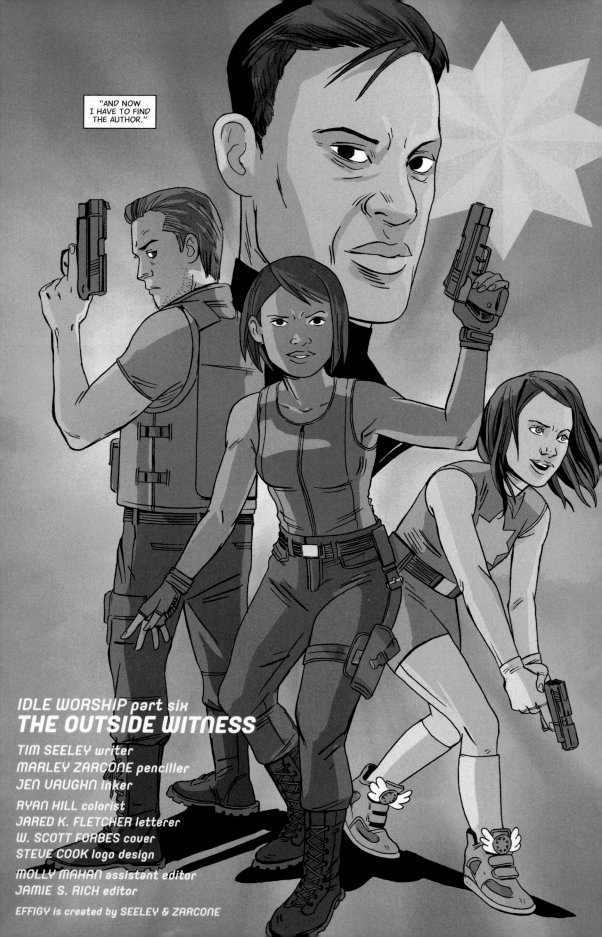

"AND NOW I HAVE TO FIND THE AUTHOR."

IDLE WORSHIP part six
THE OUTSIDE WITNESS

TIM SEELEY writer
MARLEY ZARCONE penciller
JEN VAUGHN inker

RYAN HILL colorist
JARED K. FLETCHER letterer
W. SCOTT FORBES cover
STEVE COOK logo design

MOLLY MAHAN assistant editor
JAMIE S. RICH editor

EFFIGY is created by SEELEY & ZARCONE

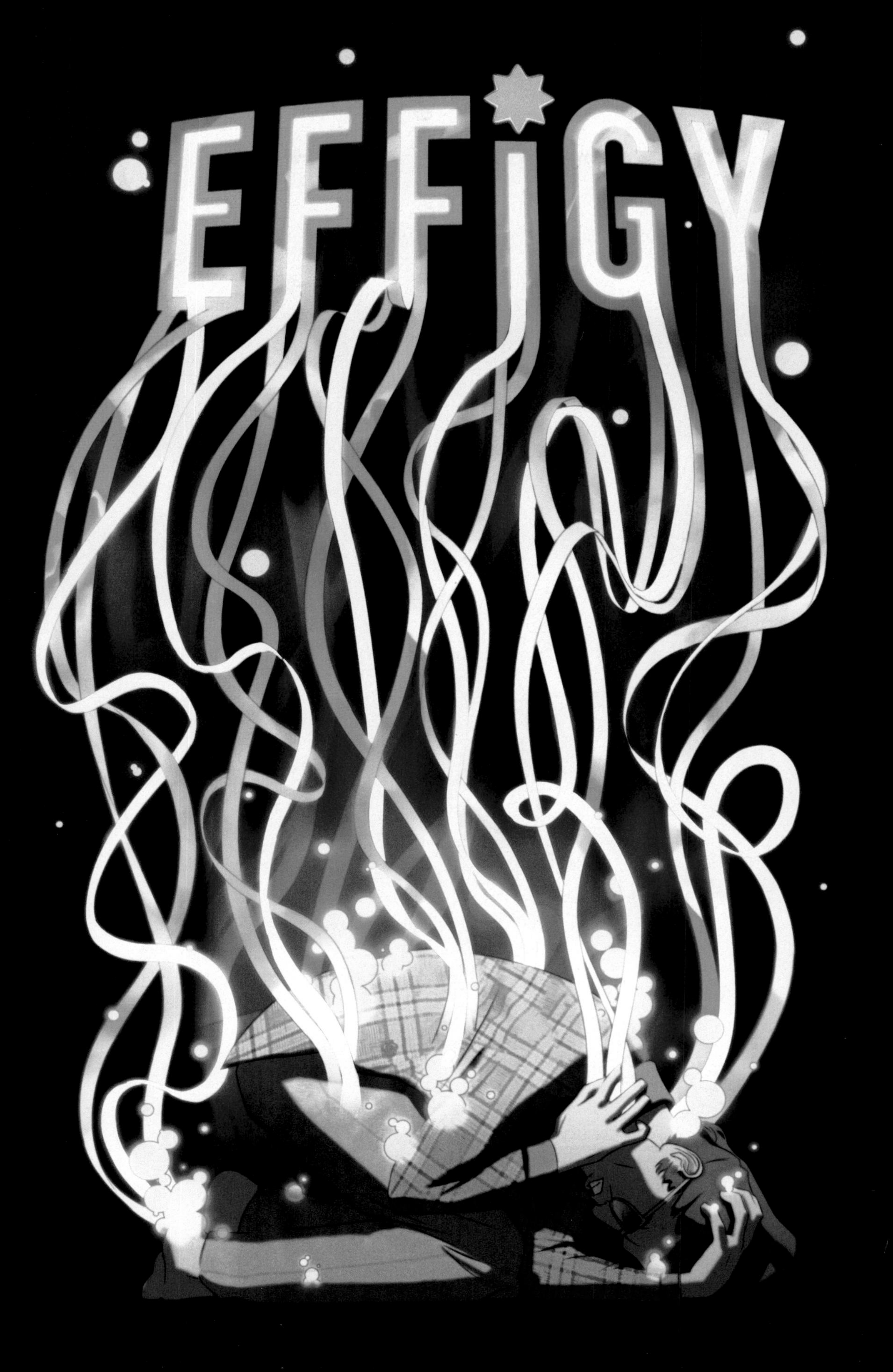
EFFIGY

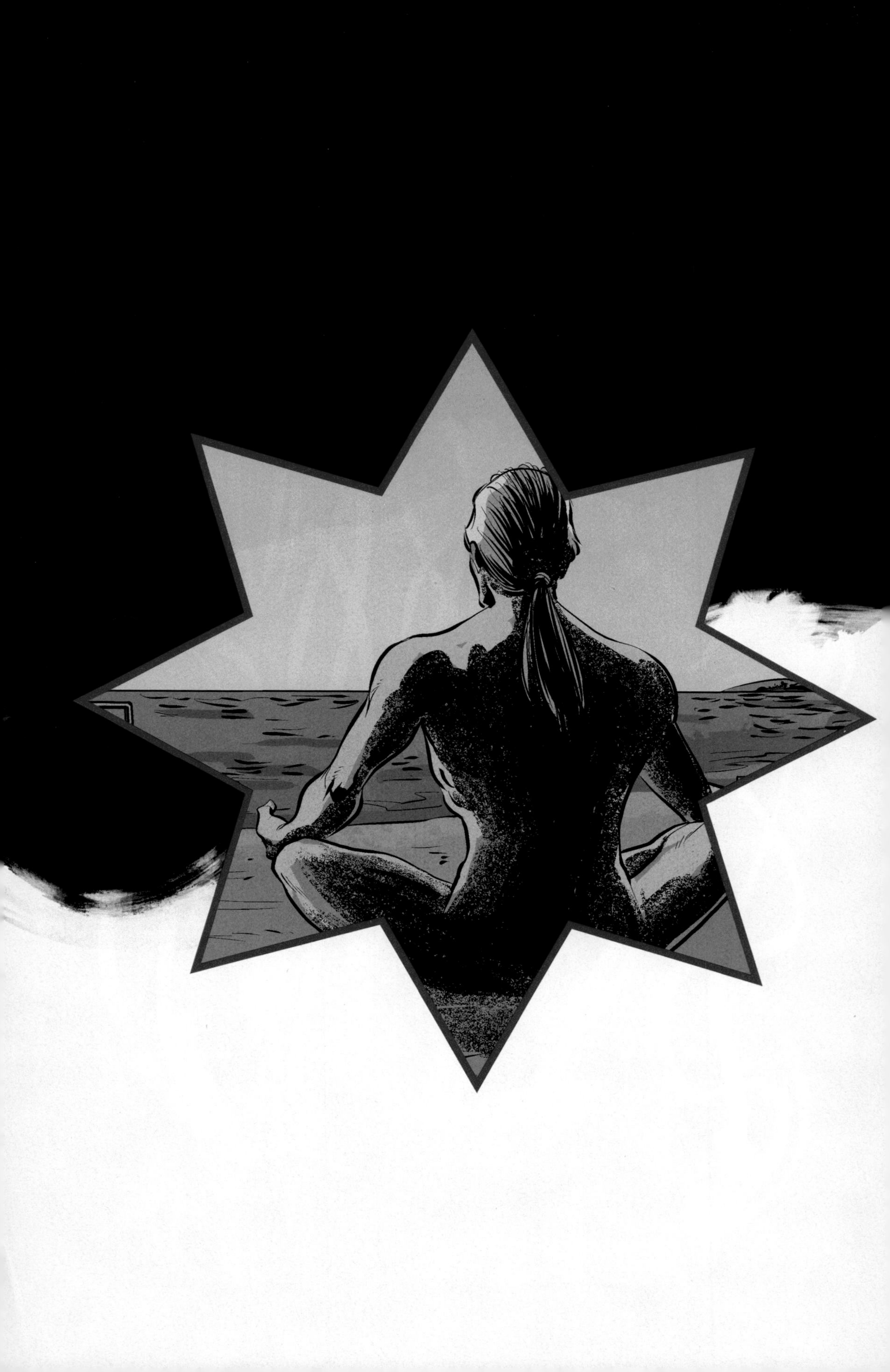

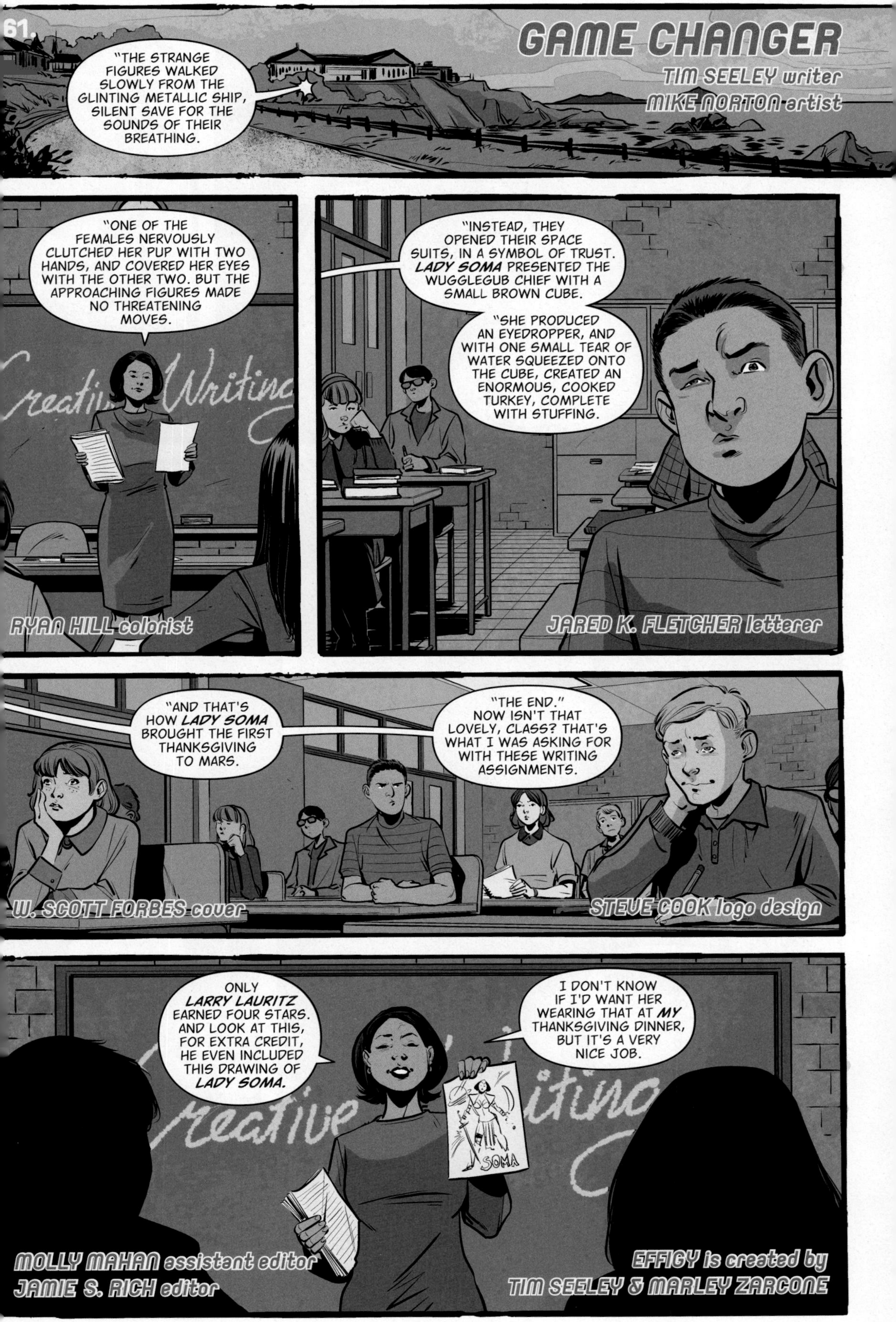
61.
GAME CHANGER
TIM SEELEY writer
MIKE NORTON artist
"THE STRANGE FIGURES WALKED SLOWLY FROM THE GLINTING METALLIC SHIP, SILENT SAVE FOR THE SOUNDS OF THEIR BREATHING.
"ONE OF THE FEMALES NERVOUSLY CLUTCHED HER PUP WITH TWO HANDS, AND COVERED HER EYES WITH THE OTHER TWO. BUT THE APPROACHING FIGURES MADE NO THREATENING MOVES.
RYAN HILL colorist
"INSTEAD, THEY OPENED THEIR SPACE SUITS, IN A SYMBOL OF TRUST. LADY SOMA PRESENTED THE WUGGLEGUB CHIEF WITH A SMALL BROWN CUBE.
"SHE PRODUCED AN EYEDROPPER, AND WITH ONE SMALL TEAR OF WATER SQUEEZED ONTO THE CUBE, CREATED AN ENORMOUS, COOKED TURKEY, COMPLETE WITH STUFFING.
JARED K. FLETCHER letterer
"AND THAT'S HOW LADY SOMA BROUGHT THE FIRST THANKSGIVING TO MARS.
"THE END." NOW ISN'T THAT LOVELY, CLASS? THAT'S WHAT I WAS ASKING FOR WITH THESE WRITING ASSIGNMENTS.
W. SCOTT FORBES cover
STEVE COOK logo design
ONLY LARRY LAURITZ EARNED FOUR STARS. AND LOOK AT THIS, FOR EXTRA CREDIT, HE EVEN INCLUDED THIS DRAWING OF LADY SOMA.
I DON'T KNOW IF I'D WANT HER WEARING THAT AT MY THANKSGIVING DINNER, BUT IT'S A VERY NICE JOB.
SOMA
MOLLY MAHAN assistant editor
JAMIE S. RICH editor
EFFIGY is created by
TIM SEELEY & MARLEY ZARCONE

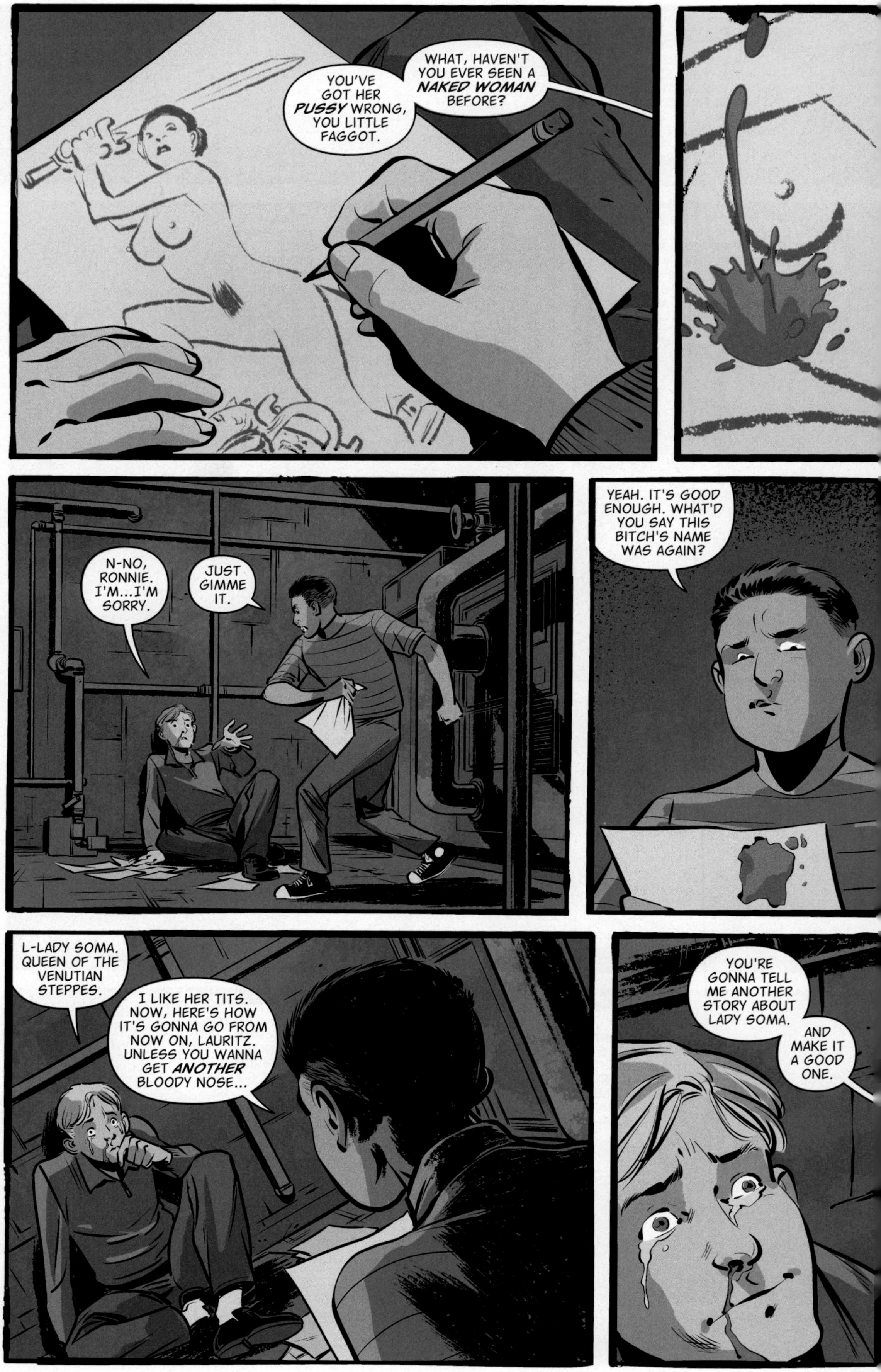
YOU'VE GOT HER PUSSY WRONG, YOU LITTLE FAGGOT.
WHAT, HAVEN'T YOU EVER SEEN A NAKED WOMAN BEFORE?
N-NO, RONNIE. I'M...I'M SORRY.
JUST GIMME IT.
YEAH. IT'S GOOD ENOUGH. WHAT'D YOU SAY THIS BITCH'S NAME WAS AGAIN?
L-LADY SOMA. QUEEN OF THE VENUTIAN STEPPES.
I LIKE HER TITS. NOW, HERE'S HOW IT'S GONNA GO FROM NOW ON, LAURITZ. UNLESS YOU WANNA GET ANOTHER BLOODY NOSE...
YOU'RE GONNA TELL ME ANOTHER STORY ABOUT LADY SOMA.
AND MAKE IT A GOOD ONE.

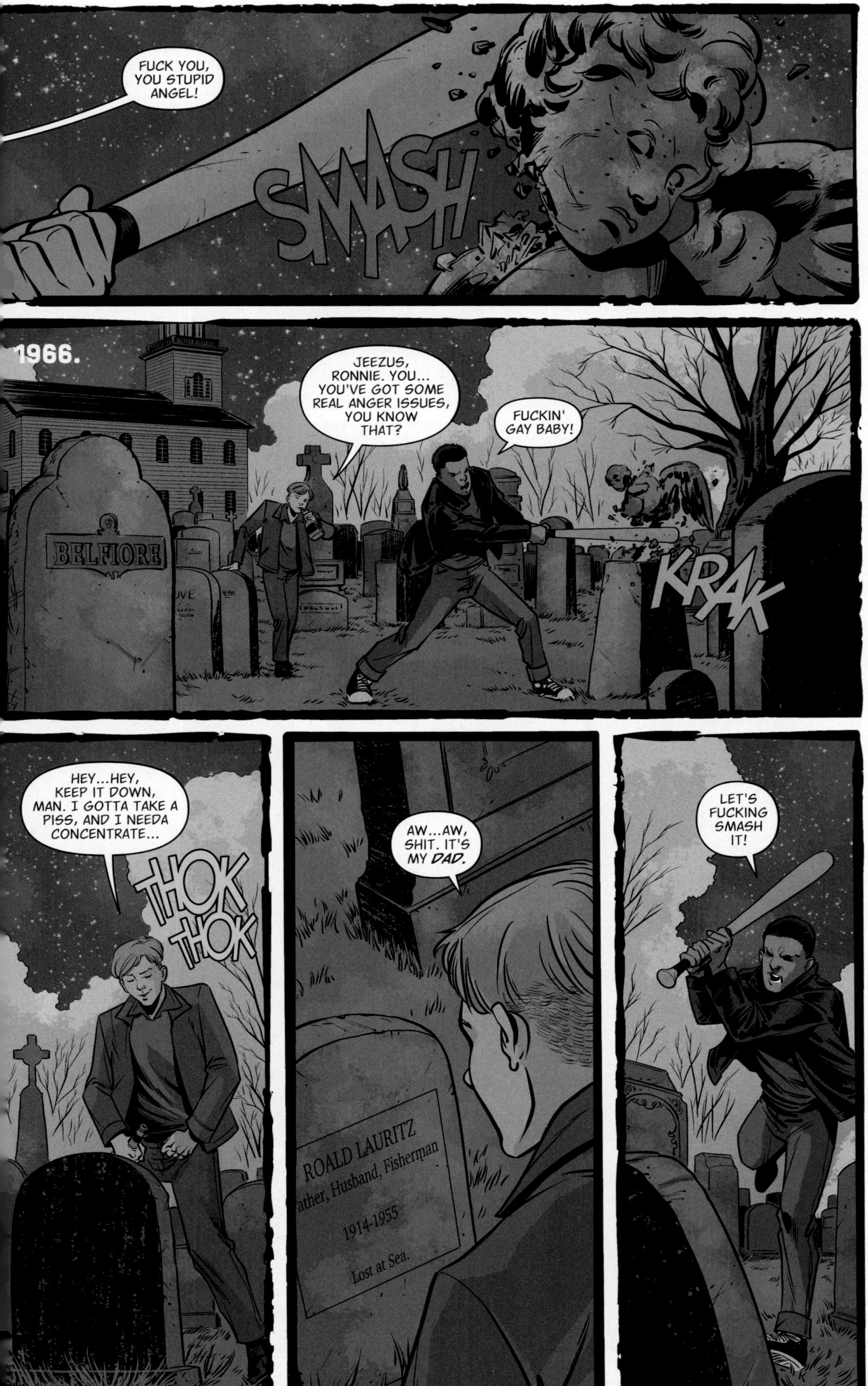
FUCK YOU, YOU STUPID ANGEL!
SMASH
1966.
JEEZUS, RONNIE. YOU... YOU'VE GOT SOME REAL ANGER ISSUES, YOU KNOW THAT?
FUCKIN' GAY BABY!
BELFIORE
KRAK
HEY...HEY, KEEP IT DOWN, MAN. I GOTTA TAKE A PISS, AND I NEEDA CONCENTRATE...
THOK THOK
AW...AW, SHIT. IT'S MY *DAD*.
ROALD LAURITZ
ather, Husband, Fisherman
1914-1955
Lost at Sea.
LET'S FUCKING SMASH IT!

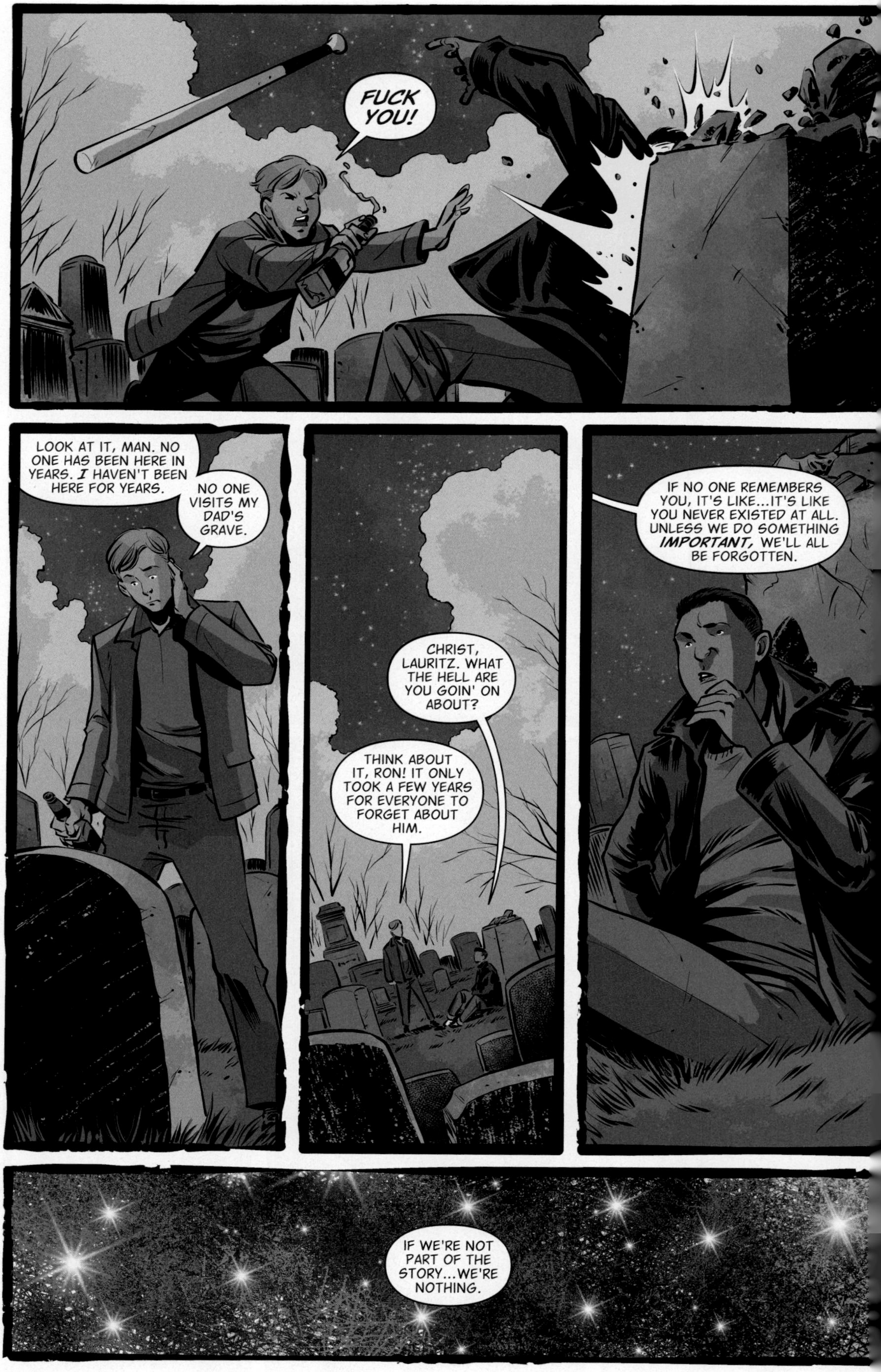
FUCK YOU!
LOOK AT IT, MAN. NO ONE HAS BEEN HERE IN YEARS. *I* HAVEN'T BEEN HERE FOR YEARS.
NO ONE VISITS MY DAD'S GRAVE.
CHRIST, LAURITZ. WHAT THE HELL ARE YOU GOIN' ON ABOUT?
THINK ABOUT IT, RON! IT ONLY TOOK A FEW YEARS FOR EVERYONE TO FORGET ABOUT HIM.
IF NO ONE REMEMBERS YOU, IT'S LIKE...IT'S LIKE YOU NEVER EXISTED AT ALL. UNLESS WE DO SOMETHING ***IMPORTANT,*** WE'LL ALL BE FORGOTTEN.
IF WE'RE NOT PART OF THE STORY...WE'RE NOTHING.

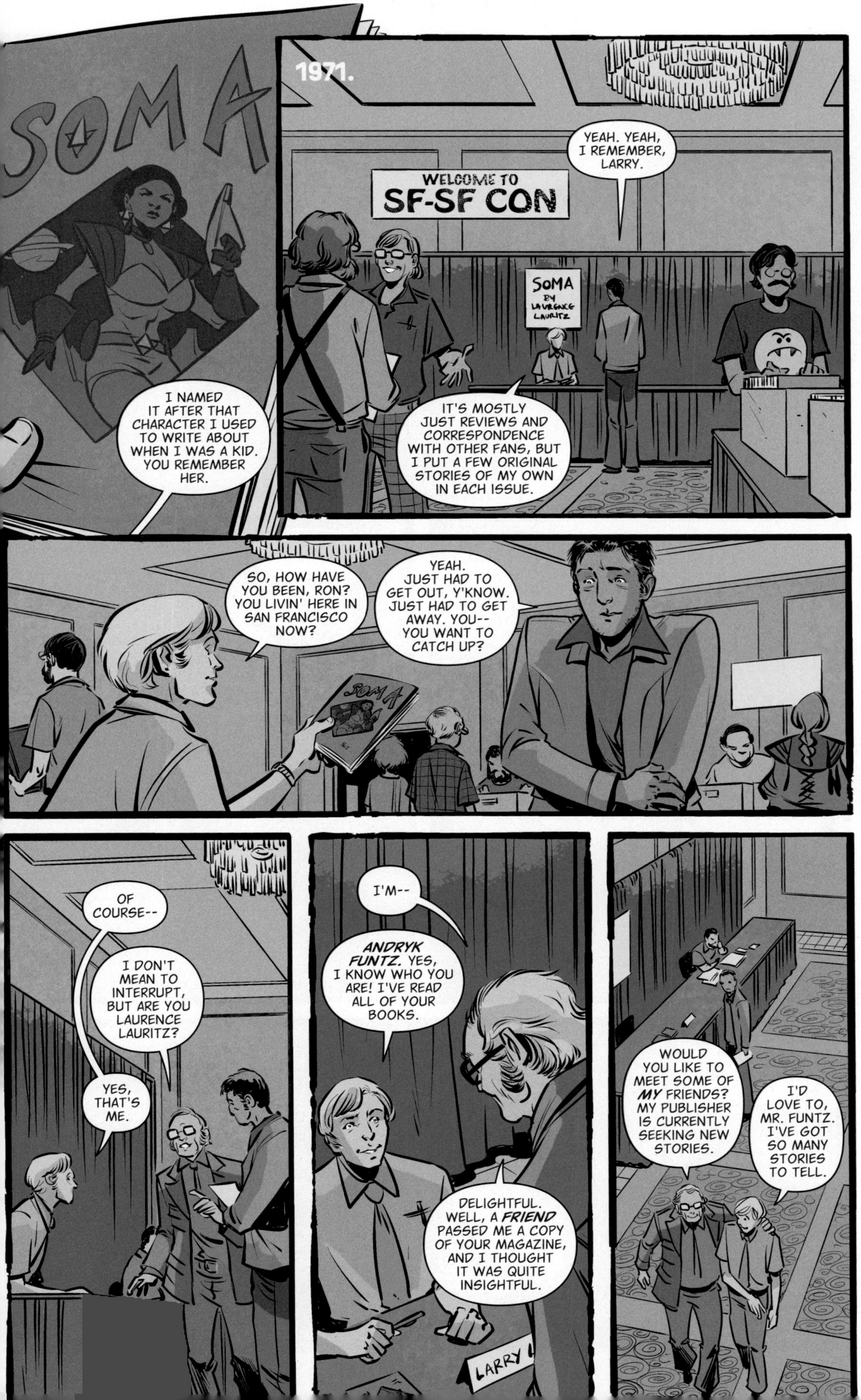
SOMA
1971.
WELCOME TO SF-SF CON
SOMA BY LAURENCE LAURITZ
I NAMED IT AFTER THAT CHARACTER I USED TO WRITE ABOUT WHEN I WAS A KID. YOU REMEMBER HER.
YEAH. YEAH, I REMEMBER, LARRY.
IT'S MOSTLY JUST REVIEWS AND CORRESPONDENCE WITH OTHER FANS, BUT I PUT A FEW ORIGINAL STORIES OF MY OWN IN EACH ISSUE.
SO, HOW HAVE YOU BEEN, RON? YOU LIVIN' HERE IN SAN FRANCISCO NOW?
YEAH. JUST HAD TO GET OUT, Y'KNOW. JUST HAD TO GET AWAY. YOU-- YOU WANT TO CATCH UP?
SOMA
OF COURSE--
I DON'T MEAN TO INTERRUPT, BUT ARE YOU LAURENCE LAURITZ?
YES, THAT'S ME.
I'M--
ANDRYK FUNTZ. YES, I KNOW WHO YOU ARE! I'VE READ ALL OF YOUR BOOKS.
DELIGHTFUL. WELL, A *FRIEND* PASSED ME A COPY OF YOUR MAGAZINE, AND I THOUGHT IT WAS QUITE INSIGHTFUL.
LARRY L
WOULD YOU LIKE TO MEET SOME OF *MY* FRIENDS? MY PUBLISHER IS CURRENTLY SEEKING NEW STORIES.
I'D LOVE TO, MR. FUNTZ. I'VE GOT SO MANY STORIES TO TELL.

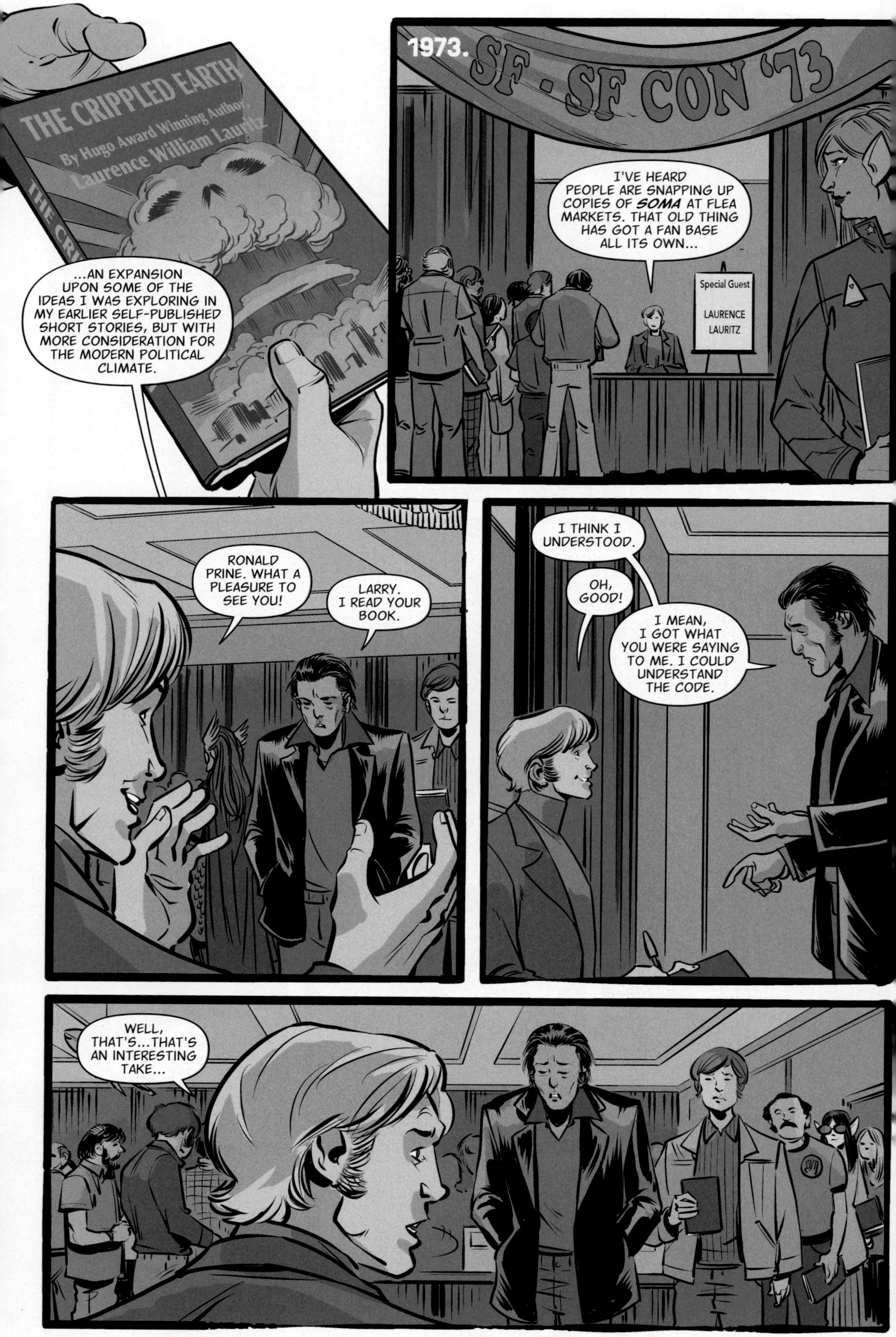
THE CRIPPLED EARTH
By Hugo Award Winning Author,
Laurence William Lauritz
...AN EXPANSION UPON SOME OF THE IDEAS I WAS EXPLORING IN MY EARLIER SELF-PUBLISHED SHORT STORIES, BUT WITH MORE CONSIDERATION FOR THE MODERN POLITICAL CLIMATE.
1973.
SF - SF CON '73
I'VE HEARD PEOPLE ARE SNAPPING UP COPIES OF *SOMA* AT FLEA MARKETS. THAT OLD THING HAS GOT A FAN BASE ALL ITS OWN...
Special Guest
LAURENCE LAURITZ
RONALD PRINE. WHAT A PLEASURE TO SEE YOU!
LARRY. I READ YOUR BOOK.
I THINK I UNDERSTOOD.
OH, GOOD!
I MEAN, I GOT WHAT YOU WERE SAYING TO ME. I COULD UNDERSTAND THE CODE.
WELL, THAT'S...THAT'S AN INTERESTING TAKE...

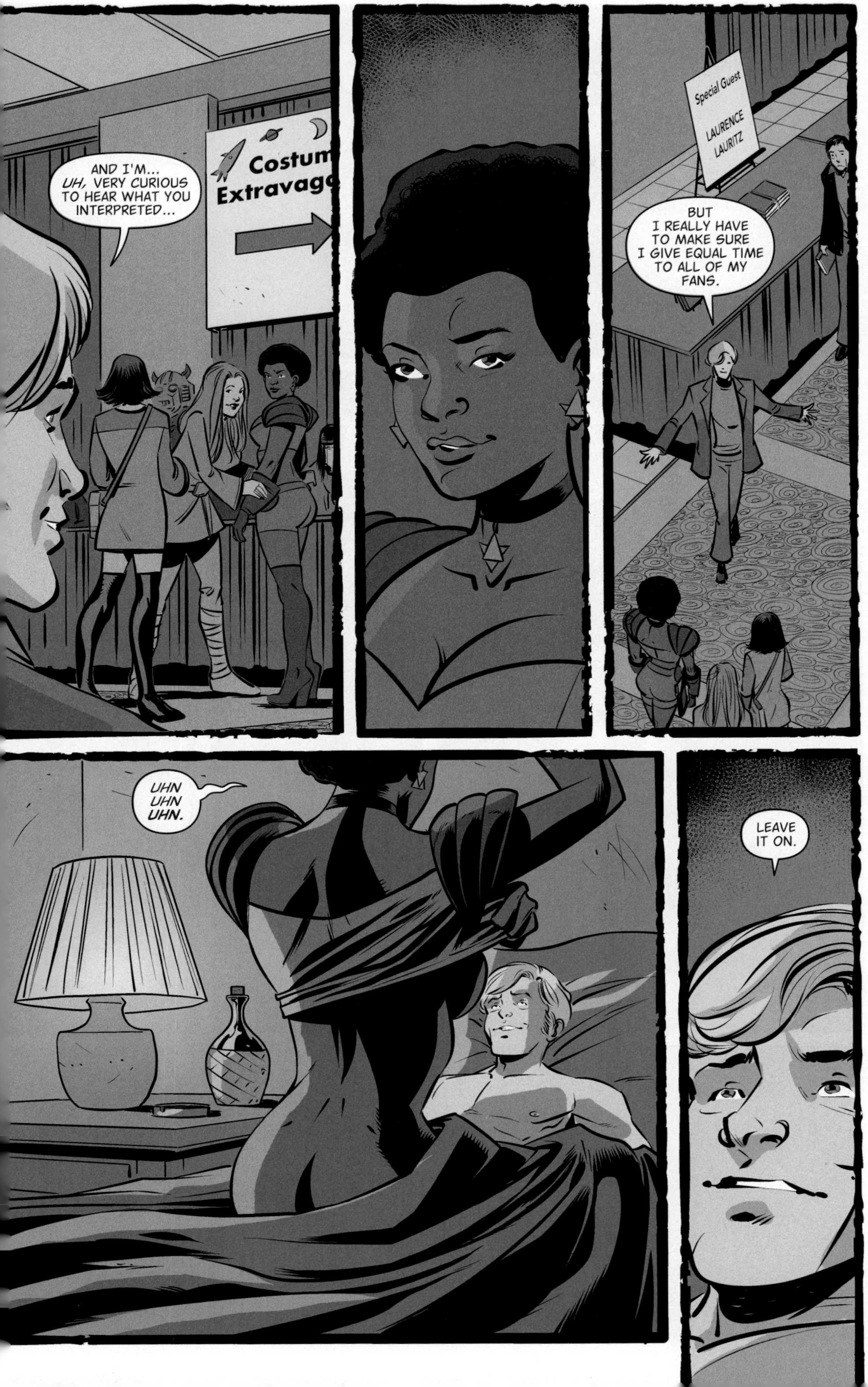
AND I'M... UH, VERY CURIOUS TO HEAR WHAT YOU INTERPRETED...
Costum
Extravag
Special Guest
LAURENCE LAURITZ
BUT I REALLY HAVE TO MAKE SURE I GIVE EQUAL TIME TO ALL OF MY FANS.
UHN UHN UHN.
LEAVE IT ON.

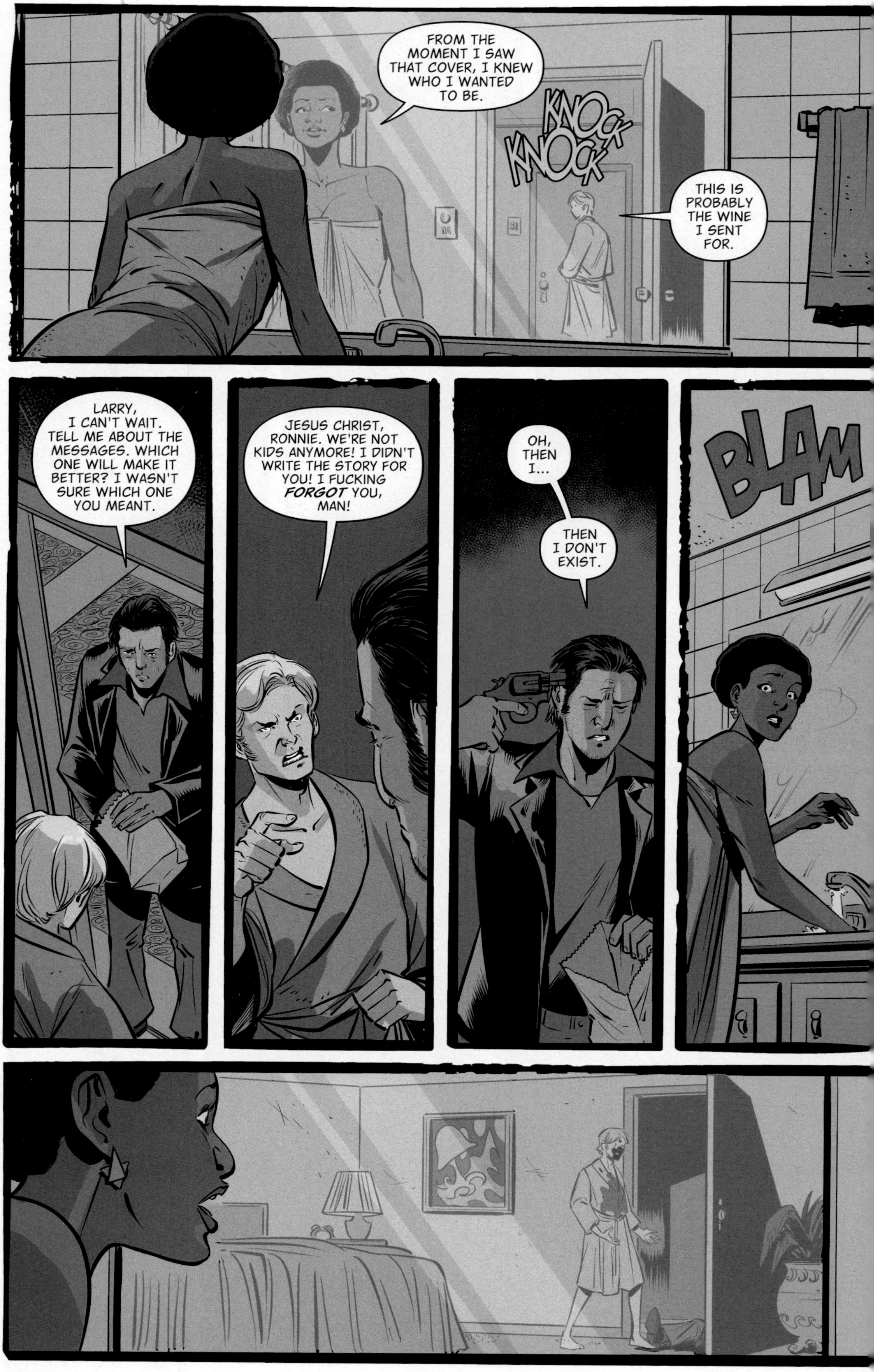
FROM THE MOMENT I SAW THAT COVER, I KNEW WHO I WANTED TO BE.
KNOCK KNOCK
THIS IS PROBABLY THE WINE I SENT FOR.
LARRY, I CAN'T WAIT. TELL ME ABOUT THE MESSAGES. WHICH ONE WILL MAKE IT BETTER? I WASN'T SURE WHICH ONE YOU MEANT.
JESUS CHRIST, RONNIE. WE'RE NOT KIDS ANYMORE! I DIDN'T WRITE THE STORY FOR YOU! I FUCKING FORGOT YOU, MAN!
OH, THEN I...
THEN I DON'T EXIST.
BLAM

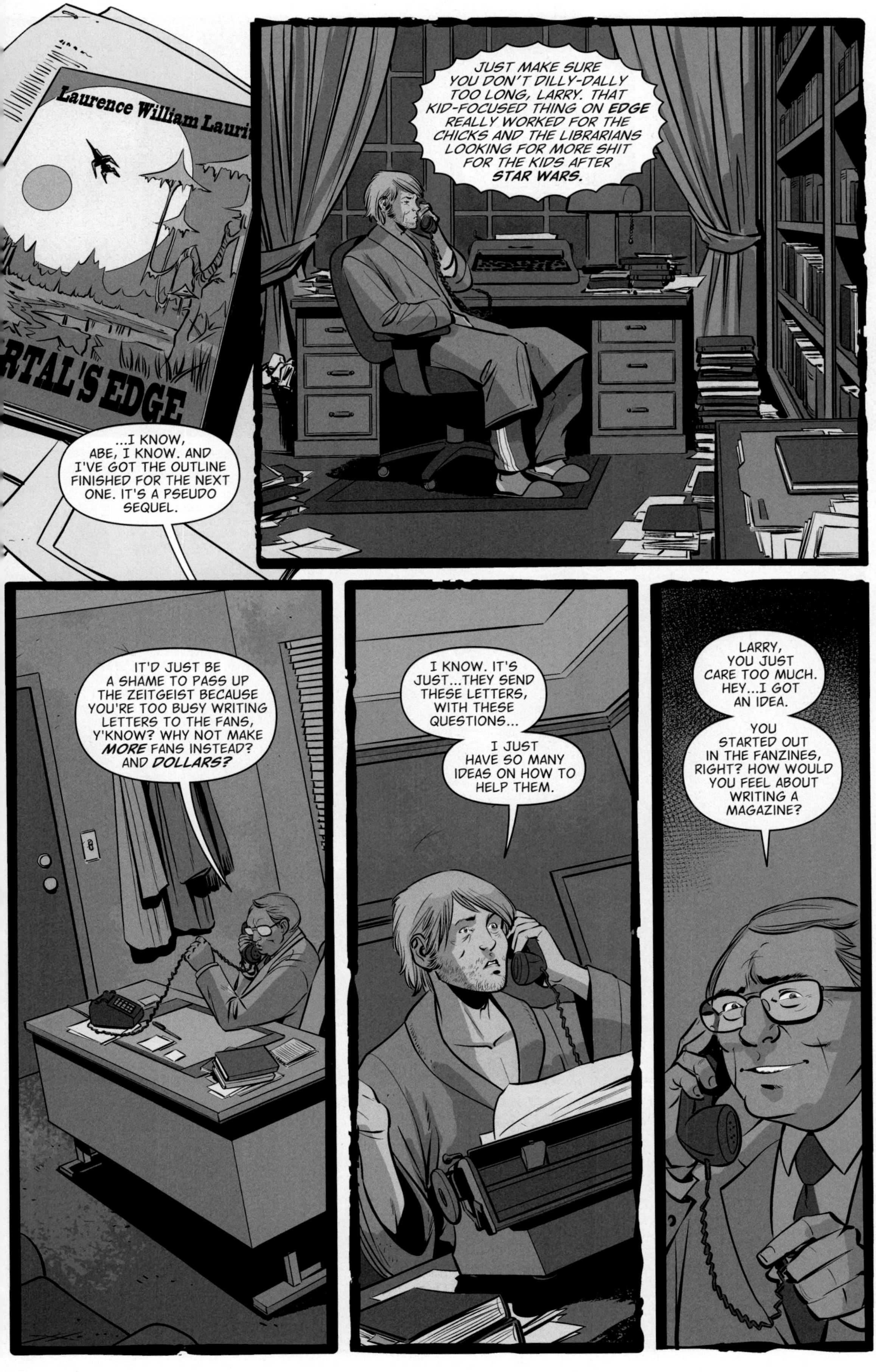
Laurence William Lauri
RTAL'S EDGE
JUST MAKE SURE YOU DON'T DILLY-DALLY TOO LONG, LARRY. THAT KID-FOCUSED THING ON EDGE REALLY WORKED FOR THE CHICKS AND THE LIBRARIANS LOOKING FOR MORE SHIT FOR THE KIDS AFTER STAR WARS.
...I KNOW, ABE, I KNOW. AND I'VE GOT THE OUTLINE FINISHED FOR THE NEXT ONE. IT'S A PSEUDO SEQUEL.
IT'D JUST BE A SHAME TO PASS UP THE ZEITGEIST BECAUSE YOU'RE TOO BUSY WRITING LETTERS TO THE FANS, Y'KNOW? WHY NOT MAKE MORE FANS INSTEAD? AND DOLLARS?
I KNOW. IT'S JUST...THEY SEND THESE LETTERS, WITH THESE QUESTIONS...
I JUST HAVE SO MANY IDEAS ON HOW TO HELP THEM.
LARRY, YOU JUST CARE TOO MUCH. HEY...I GOT AN IDEA.
YOU STARTED OUT IN THE FANZINES, RIGHT? HOW WOULD YOU FEEL ABOUT WRITING A MAGAZINE?

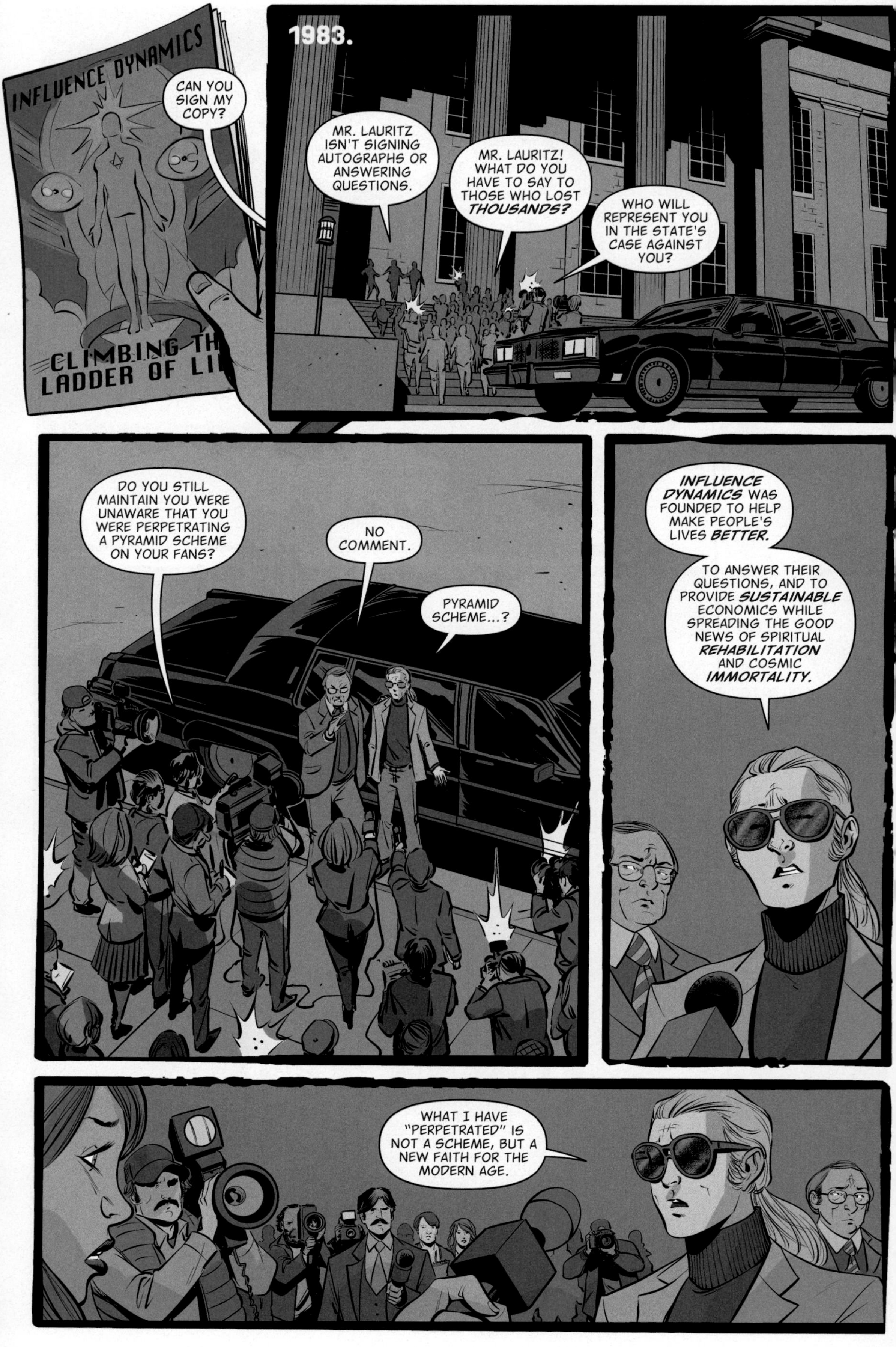
INFLUENCE DYNAMICS
CLIMBING TH
LADDER OF LI
CAN YOU SIGN MY COPY?
1983.
MR. LAURITZ ISN'T SIGNING AUTOGRAPHS OR ANSWERING QUESTIONS.
MR. LAURITZ! WHAT DO YOU HAVE TO SAY TO THOSE WHO LOST *THOUSANDS?*
WHO WILL REPRESENT YOU IN THE STATE'S CASE AGAINST YOU?
DO YOU STILL MAINTAIN YOU WERE UNAWARE THAT YOU WERE PERPETRATING A PYRAMID SCHEME ON YOUR FANS?
NO COMMENT.
PYRAMID SCHEME...?
INFLUENCE DYNAMICS WAS FOUNDED TO HELP MAKE PEOPLE'S LIVES *BETTER.*
TO ANSWER THEIR QUESTIONS, AND TO PROVIDE *SUSTAINABLE* ECONOMICS WHILE SPREADING THE GOOD NEWS OF SPIRITUAL *REHABILITATION* AND COSMIC *IMMORTALITY.*
WHAT I HAVE "PERPETRATED" IS NOT A SCHEME, BUT A NEW FAITH FOR THE MODERN AGE.

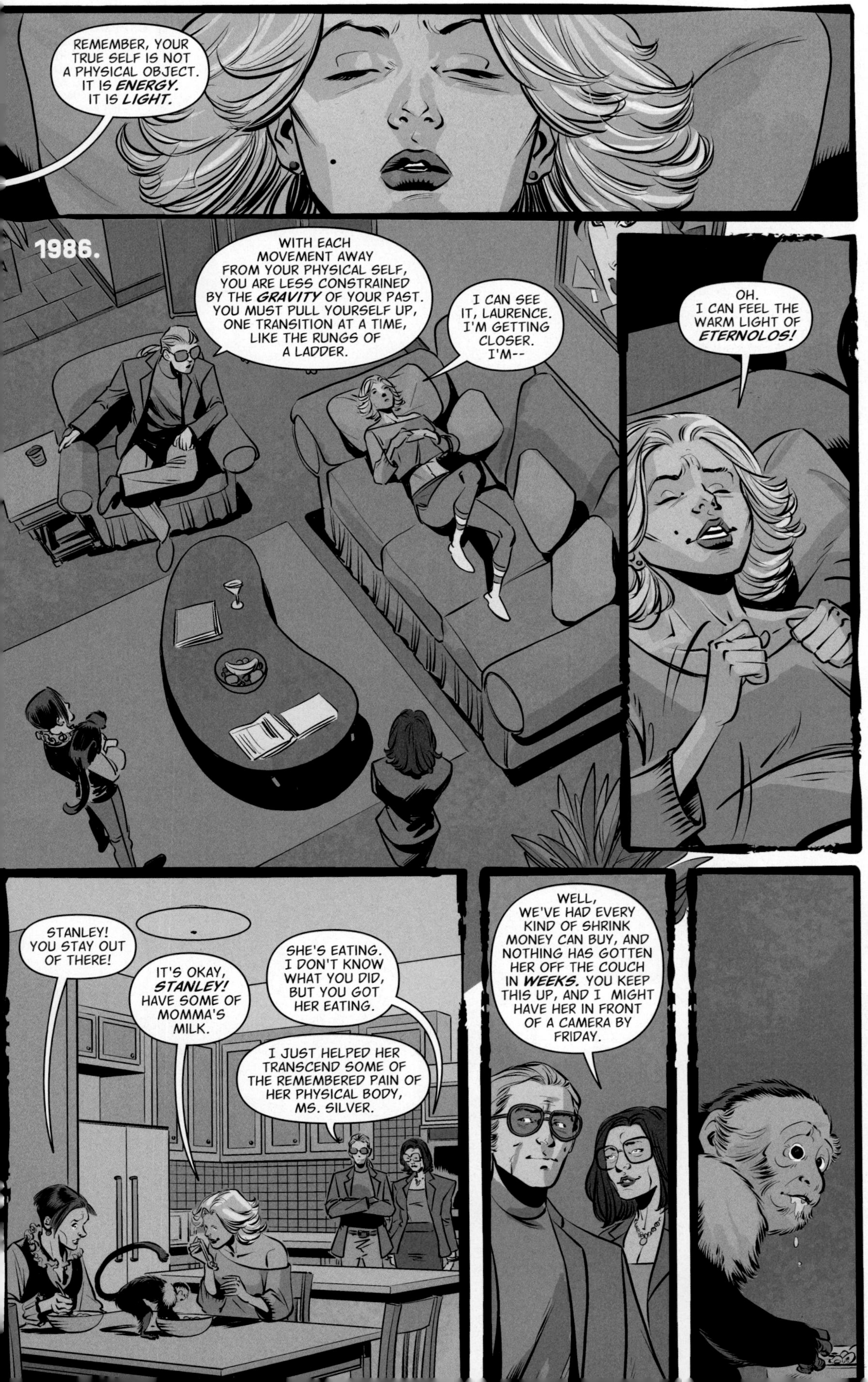
REMEMBER, YOUR TRUE SELF IS NOT A PHYSICAL OBJECT. IT IS ENERGY. IT IS LIGHT.
1986.
WITH EACH MOVEMENT AWAY FROM YOUR PHYSICAL SELF, YOU ARE LESS CONSTRAINED BY THE GRAVITY OF YOUR PAST. YOU MUST PULL YOURSELF UP, ONE TRANSITION AT A TIME, LIKE THE RUNGS OF A LADDER.
I CAN SEE IT, LAURENCE. I'M GETTING CLOSER. I'M--
OH. I CAN FEEL THE WARM LIGHT OF ETERNOLOS!
STANLEY! YOU STAY OUT OF THERE!
IT'S OKAY, STANLEY! HAVE SOME OF MOMMA'S MILK.
SHE'S EATING. I DON'T KNOW WHAT YOU DID, BUT YOU GOT HER EATING.
I JUST HELPED HER TRANSCEND SOME OF THE REMEMBERED PAIN OF HER PHYSICAL BODY, MS. SILVER.
WELL, WE'VE HAD EVERY KIND OF SHRINK MONEY CAN BUY, AND NOTHING HAS GOTTEN HER OFF THE COUCH IN WEEKS. YOU KEEP THIS UP, AND I MIGHT HAVE HER IN FRONT OF A CAMERA BY FRIDAY.

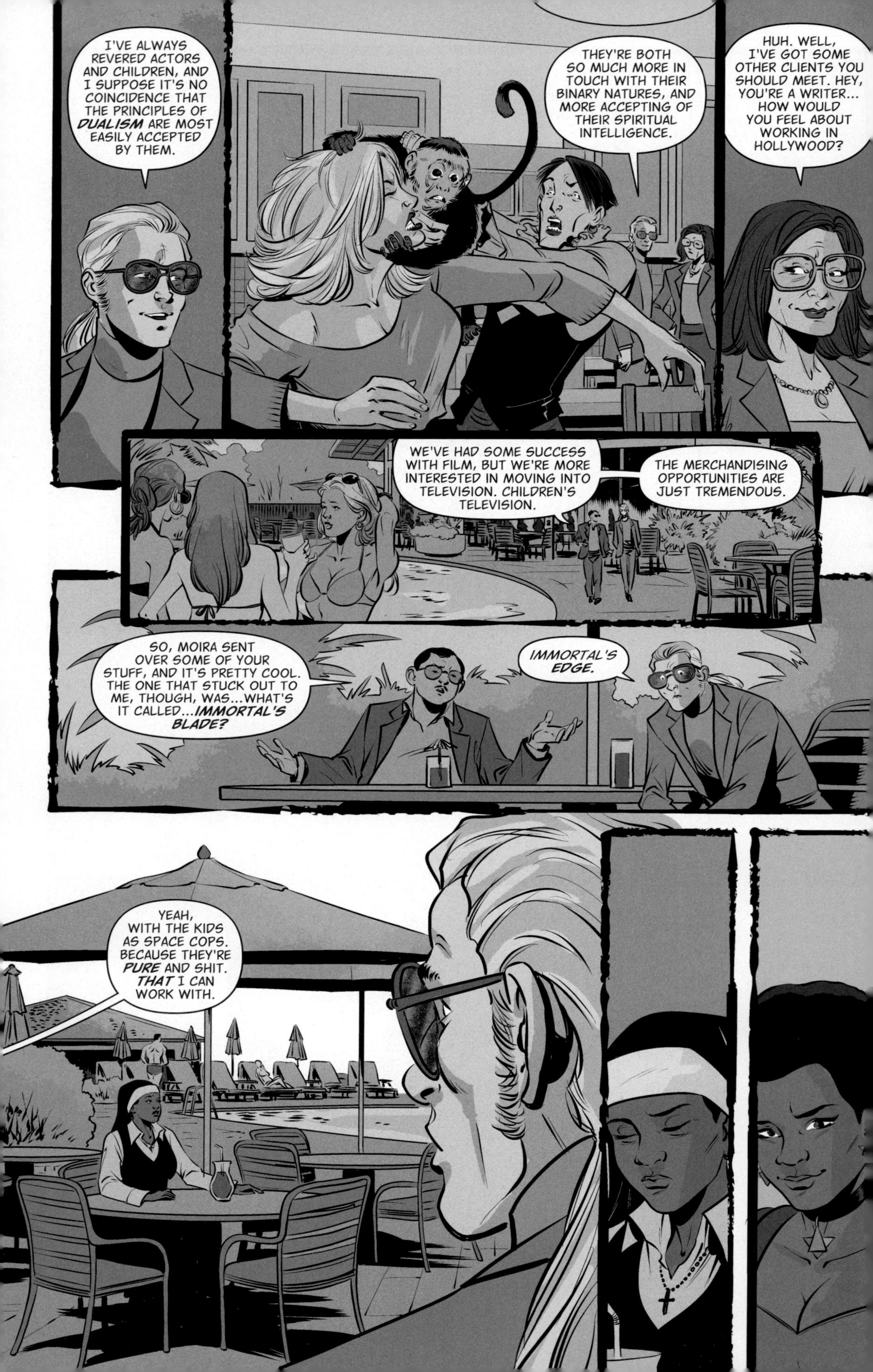

I'VE ALWAYS REVERED ACTORS AND CHILDREN, AND I SUPPOSE IT'S NO COINCIDENCE THAT THE PRINCIPLES OF *DUALISM* ARE MOST EASILY ACCEPTED BY THEM.
THEY'RE BOTH SO MUCH MORE IN TOUCH WITH THEIR BINARY NATURES, AND MORE ACCEPTING OF THEIR SPIRITUAL INTELLIGENCE.
HUH. WELL, I'VE GOT SOME OTHER CLIENTS YOU SHOULD MEET. HEY, YOU'RE A WRITER... HOW WOULD YOU FEEL ABOUT WORKING IN HOLLYWOOD?
WE'VE HAD SOME SUCCESS WITH FILM, BUT WE'RE MORE INTERESTED IN MOVING INTO TELEVISION. CHILDREN'S TELEVISION.
THE MERCHANDISING OPPORTUNITIES ARE JUST TREMENDOUS.
SO, MOIRA SENT OVER SOME OF YOUR STUFF, AND IT'S PRETTY COOL. THE ONE THAT STUCK OUT TO ME, THOUGH, WAS...WHAT'S IT CALLED...*IMMORTAL'S BLADE?*
IMMORTAL'S EDGE.
YEAH, WITH THE KIDS AS SPACE COPS. BECAUSE THEY'RE *PURE* AND SHIT. *THAT* I CAN WORK WITH.

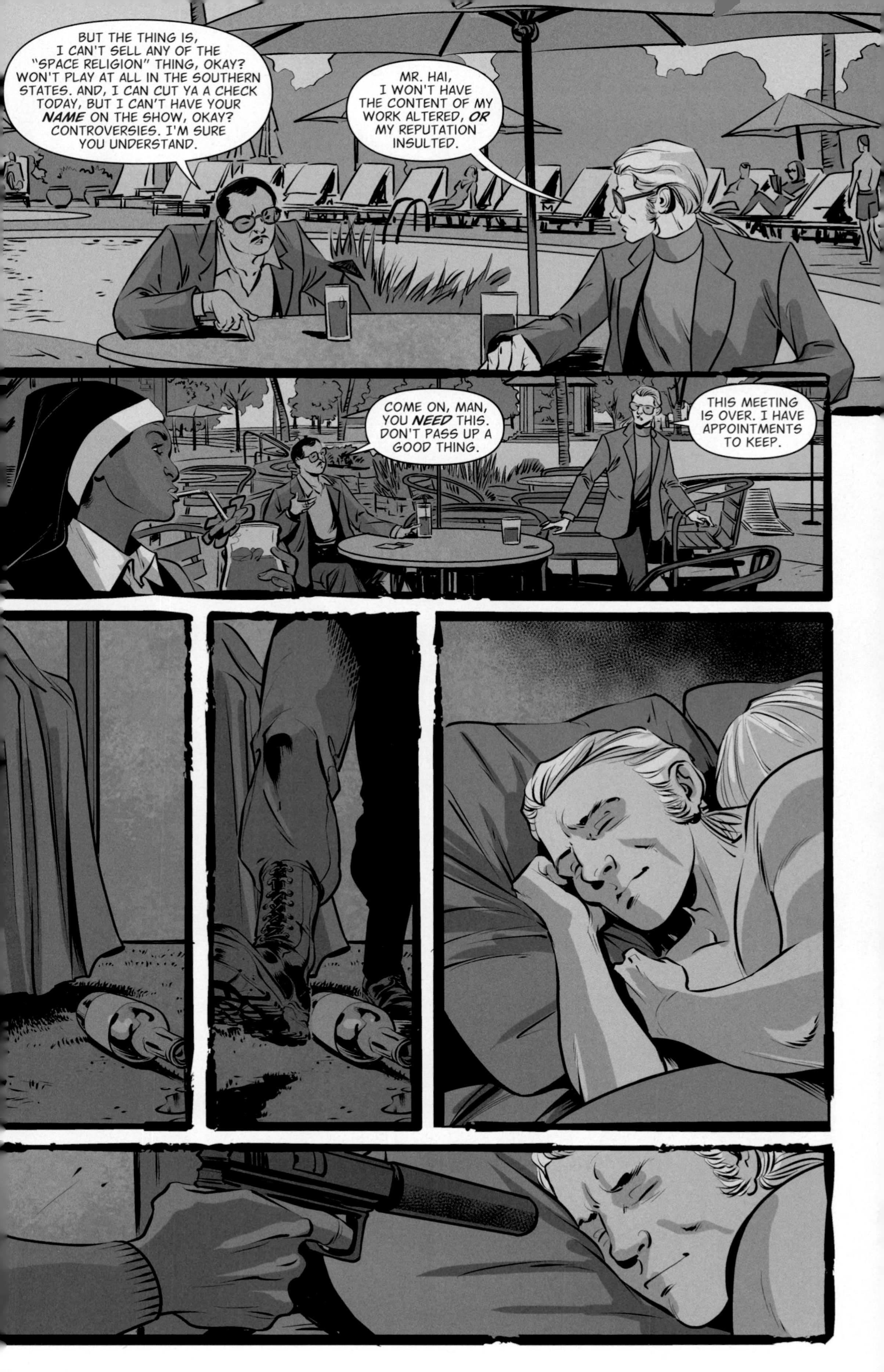
BUT THE THING IS, I CAN'T SELL ANY OF THE "SPACE RELIGION" THING, OKAY? WON'T PLAY AT ALL IN THE SOUTHERN STATES. AND, I CAN CUT YA A CHECK TODAY, BUT I CAN'T HAVE YOUR *NAME* ON THE SHOW, OKAY? CONTROVERSIES. I'M SURE YOU UNDERSTAND.
MR. HAI, I WON'T HAVE THE CONTENT OF MY WORK ALTERED, *OR* MY REPUTATION INSULTED.
COME ON, MAN, YOU *NEED* THIS. DON'T PASS UP A GOOD THING.
THIS MEETING IS OVER. I HAVE APPOINTMENTS TO KEEP.

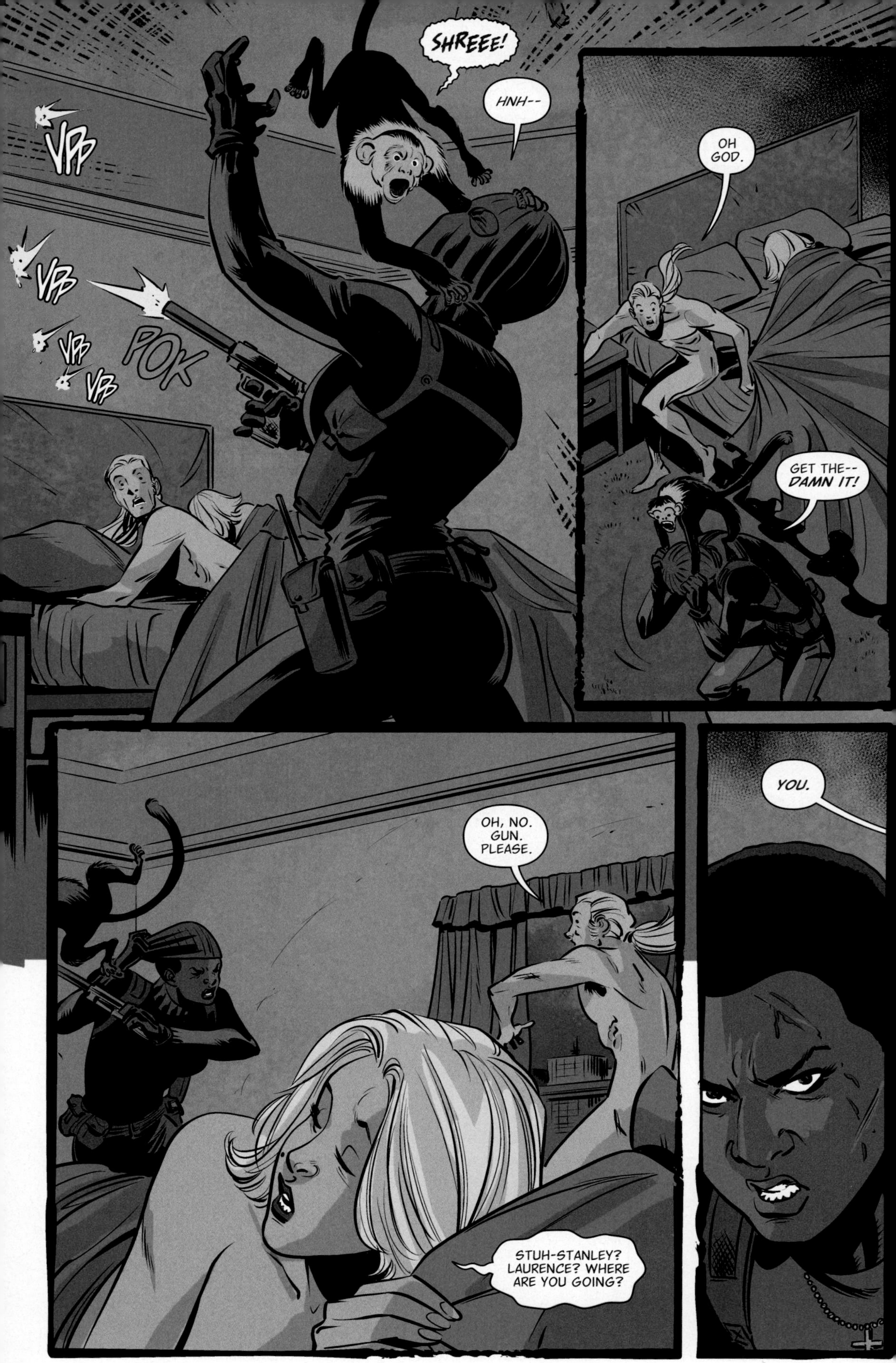
SHREEE!
HNH--
VPB
VPB
VPB
VPB
POK
OH GOD.
GET THE-- DAMN IT!
OH, NO. GUN. PLEASE.
STUH-STANLEY? LAURENCE? WHERE ARE YOU GOING?
YOU.

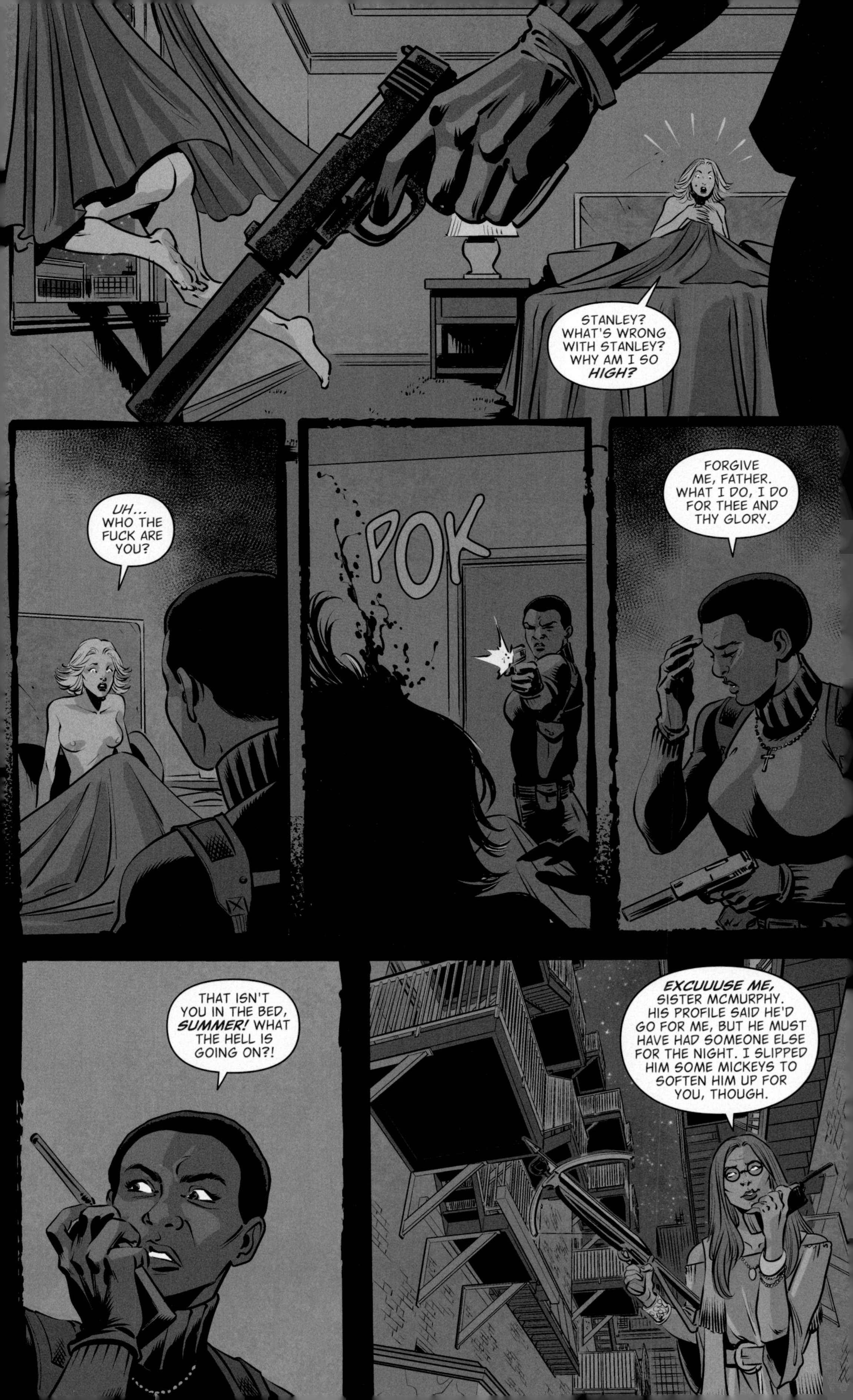
STANLEY? WHAT'S WRONG WITH STANLEY? WHY AM I SO *HIGH?*
UH... WHO THE FUCK ARE YOU?
POK
FORGIVE ME, FATHER. WHAT I DO, I DO FOR THEE AND THY GLORY.
THAT ISN'T YOU IN THE BED, *SUMMER!* WHAT THE HELL IS GOING ON?!
EXCUUUSE ME, SISTER MCMURPHY. HIS PROFILE SAID HE'D GO FOR ME, BUT HE MUST HAVE HAD SOMEONE ELSE FOR THE NIGHT. I SLIPPED HIM SOME MICKEYS TO SOFTEN HIM UP FOR YOU, THOUGH.

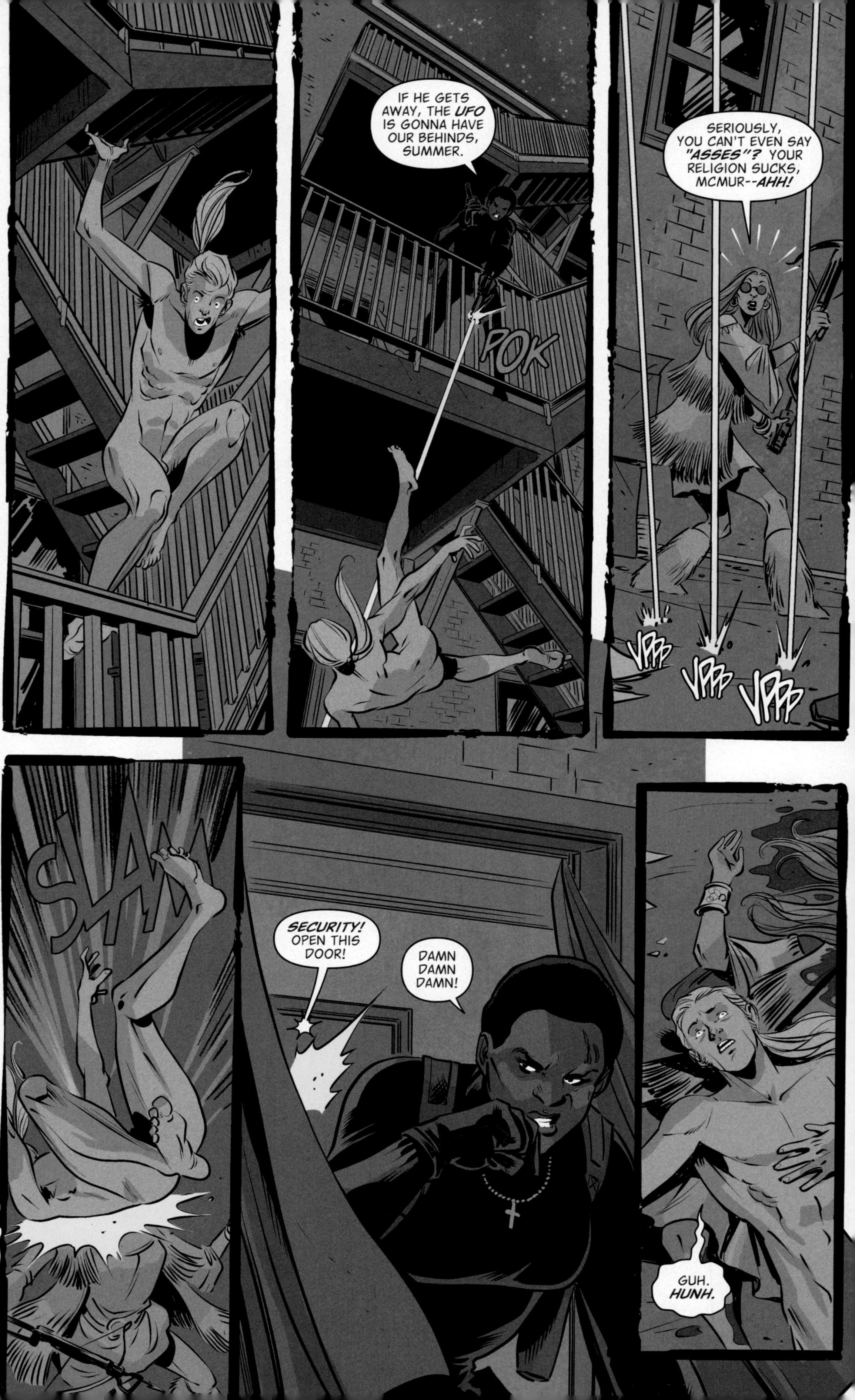
IF HE GETS AWAY, THE UFO IS GONNA HAVE OUR BEHINDS, SUMMER.
POK
SERIOUSLY, YOU CAN'T EVEN SAY "ASSES"? YOUR RELIGION SUCKS, MCMUR--AHH!
VPPP
VPPP
VPPP
SLAM
SECURITY! OPEN THIS DOOR!
DAMN DAMN DAMN!
GUH. HUNH.

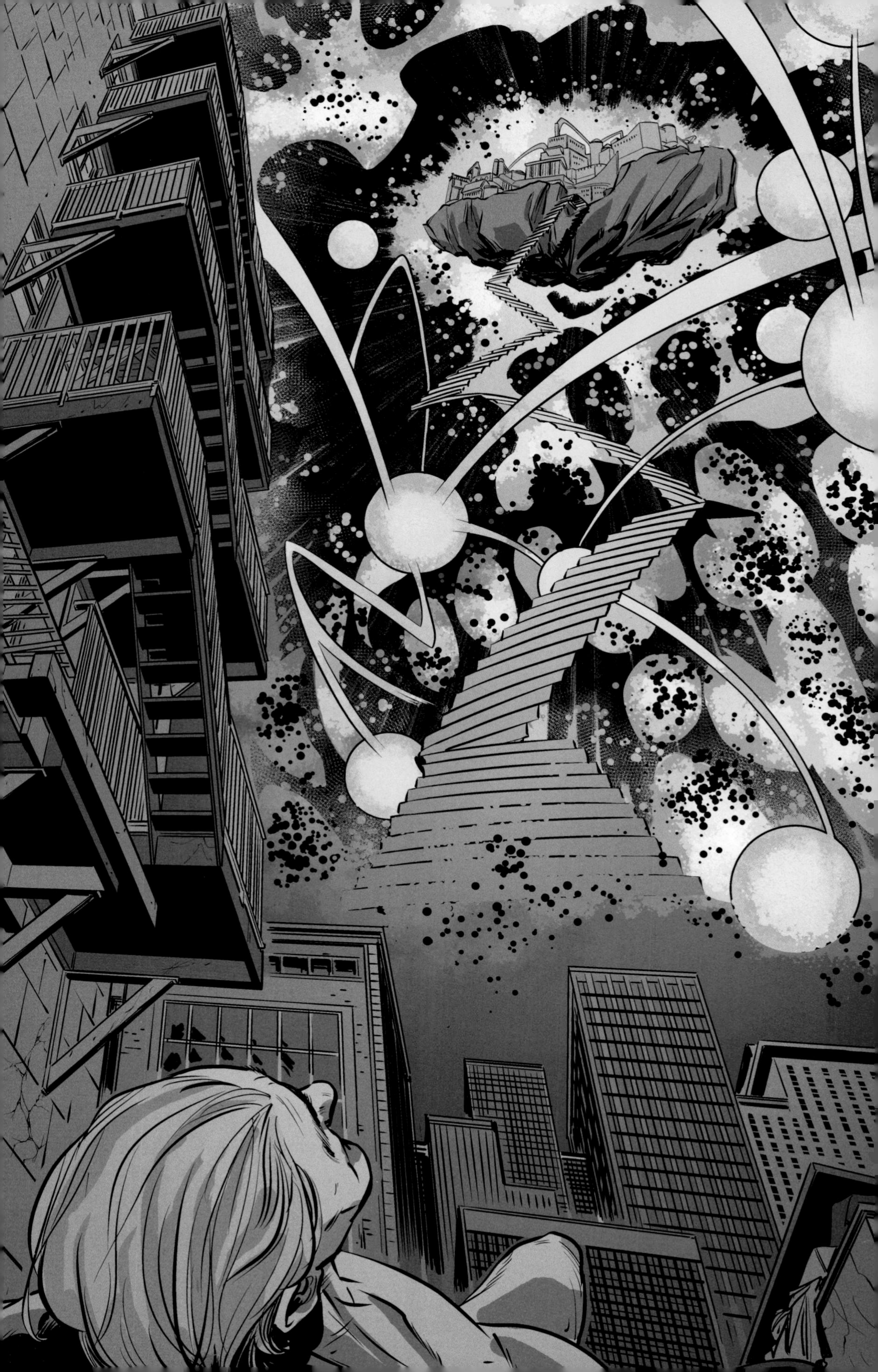

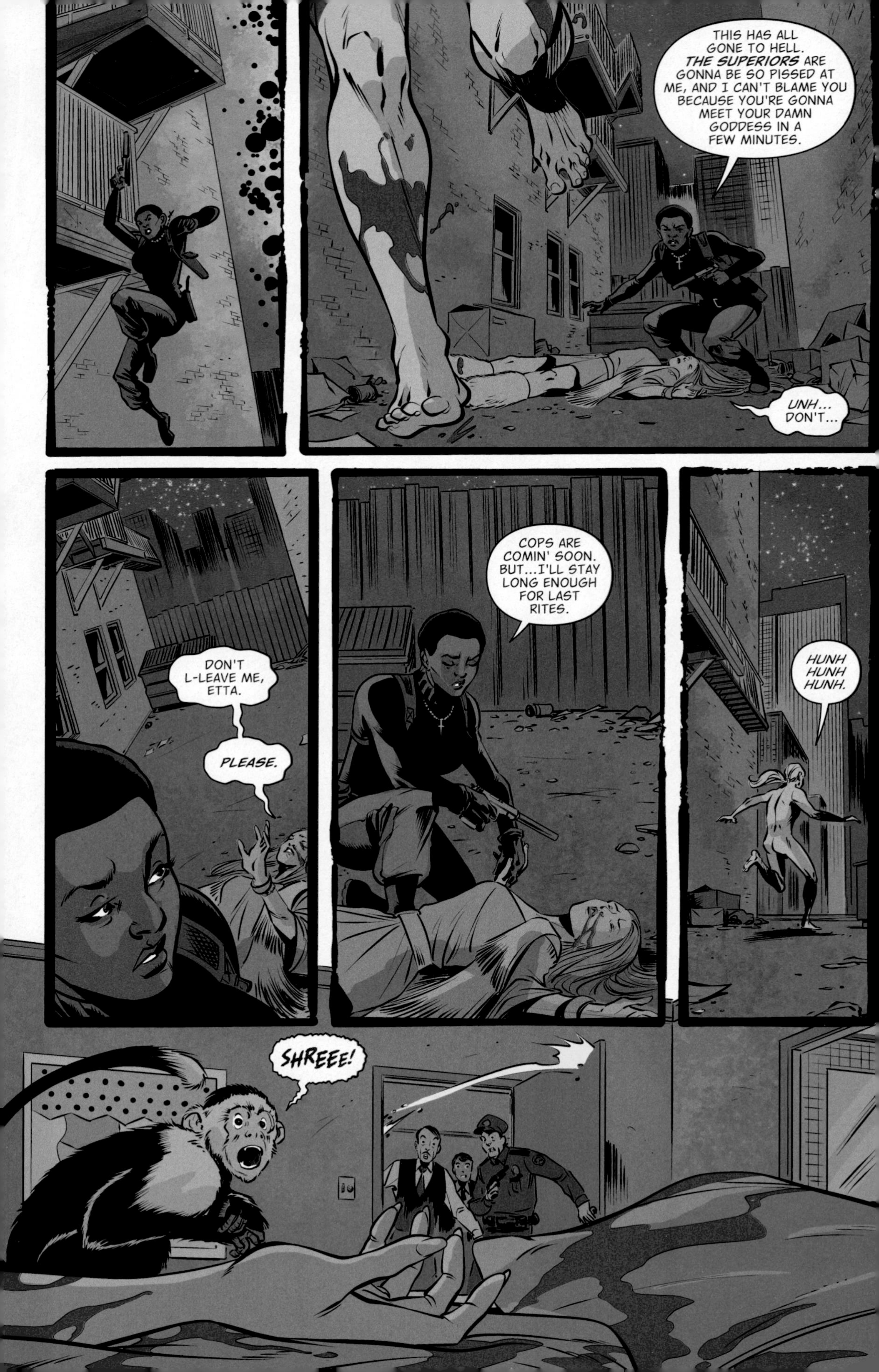
THIS HAS ALL GONE TO HELL. THE SUPERIORS ARE GONNA BE SO PISSED AT ME, AND I CAN'T BLAME YOU BECAUSE YOU'RE GONNA MEET YOUR DAMN GODDESS IN A FEW MINUTES.
UNH... DON'T...
DON'T L-LEAVE ME, ETTA.
PLEASE.
COPS ARE COMIN' SOON. BUT...I'LL STAY LONG ENOUGH FOR LAST RITES.
HUNH HUNH HUNH.
SHREEE!

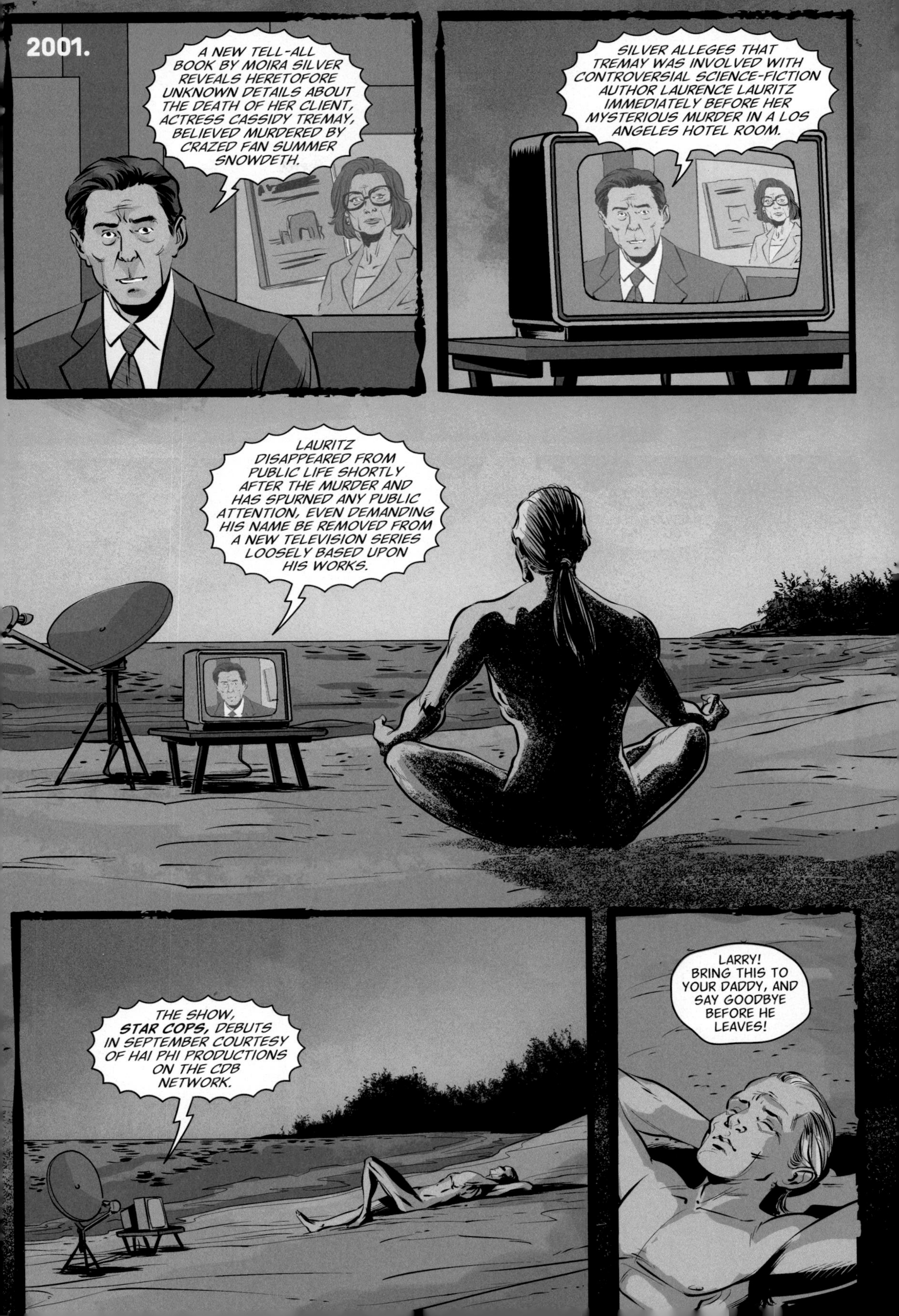
2001.
A NEW TELL-ALL BOOK BY MOIRA SILVER REVEALS HERETOFORE UNKNOWN DETAILS ABOUT THE DEATH OF HER CLIENT, ACTRESS CASSIDY TREMAY, BELIEVED MURDERED BY CRAZED FAN SUMMER SNOWDETH.
SILVER ALLEGES THAT TREMAY WAS INVOLVED WITH CONTROVERSIAL SCIENCE-FICTION AUTHOR LAURENCE LAURITZ IMMEDIATELY BEFORE HER MYSTERIOUS MURDER IN A LOS ANGELES HOTEL ROOM.
LAURITZ DISAPPEARED FROM PUBLIC LIFE SHORTLY AFTER THE MURDER AND HAS SPURNED ANY PUBLIC ATTENTION, EVEN DEMANDING HIS NAME BE REMOVED FROM A NEW TELEVISION SERIES LOOSELY BASED UPON HIS WORKS.
THE SHOW, STAR COPS, DEBUTS IN SEPTEMBER COURTESY OF HAI PHI PRODUCTIONS ON THE CDB NETWORK.
LARRY! BRING THIS TO YOUR DADDY, AND SAY GOODBYE BEFORE HE LEAVES!

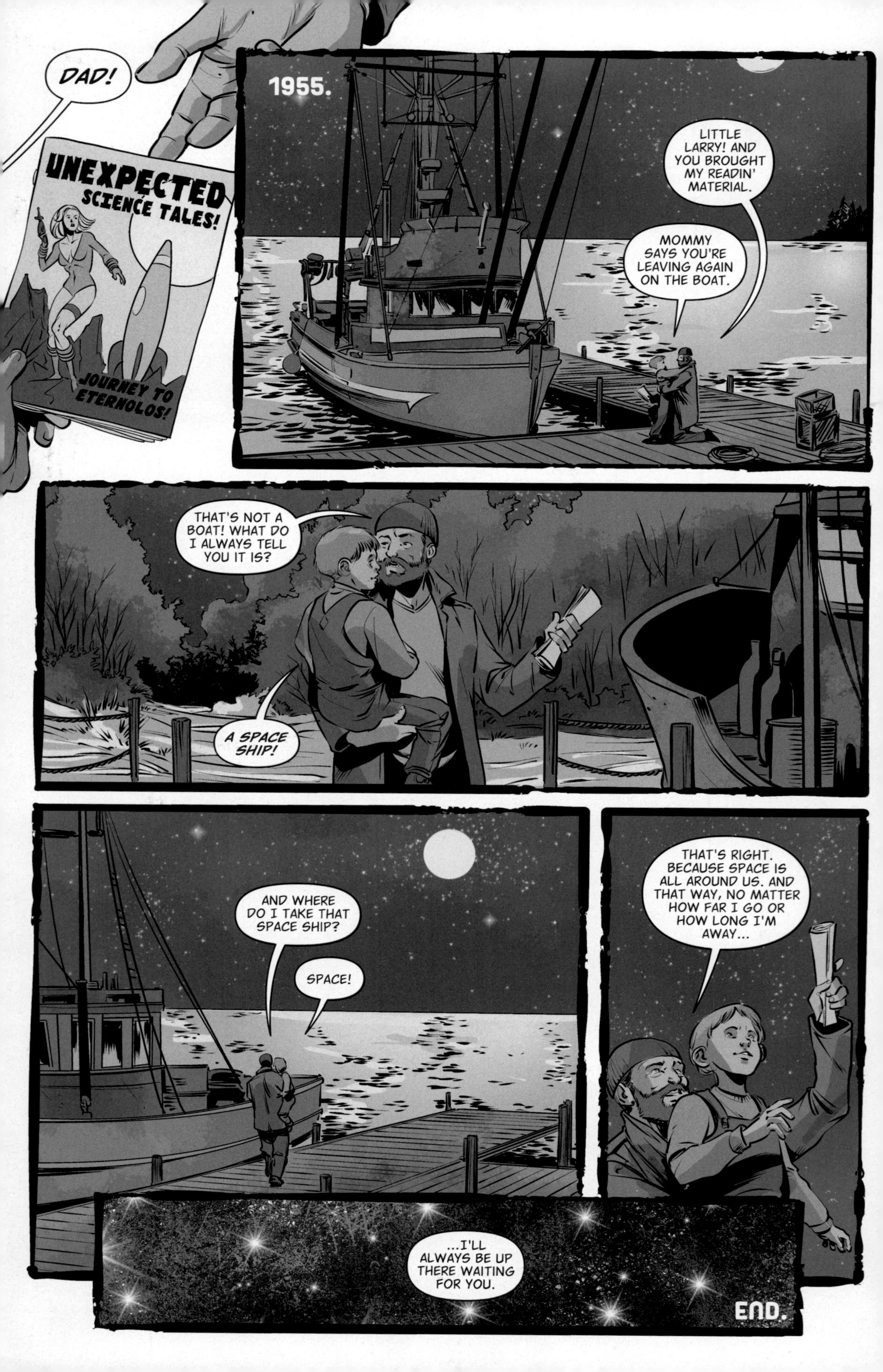
DAD!
UNEXPECTED SCIENCE TALES!
JOURNEY TO ETERNOLOS!
1955.
LITTLE LARRY! AND YOU BROUGHT MY READIN' MATERIAL.
MOMMY SAYS YOU'RE LEAVING AGAIN ON THE BOAT.
THAT'S NOT A BOAT! WHAT DO I ALWAYS TELL YOU IT IS?
A SPACE SHIP!
AND WHERE DO I TAKE THAT SPACE SHIP?
SPACE!
THAT'S RIGHT. BECAUSE SPACE IS ALL AROUND US. AND THAT WAY, NO MATTER HOW FAR I GO OR HOW LONG I'M AWAY...
...I'LL ALWAYS BE UP THERE WAITING FOR YOU.
END.

FACT. FICTION. FAITH. FANDOM.
REALITY IS ABOUT
TO GET F****D UP.

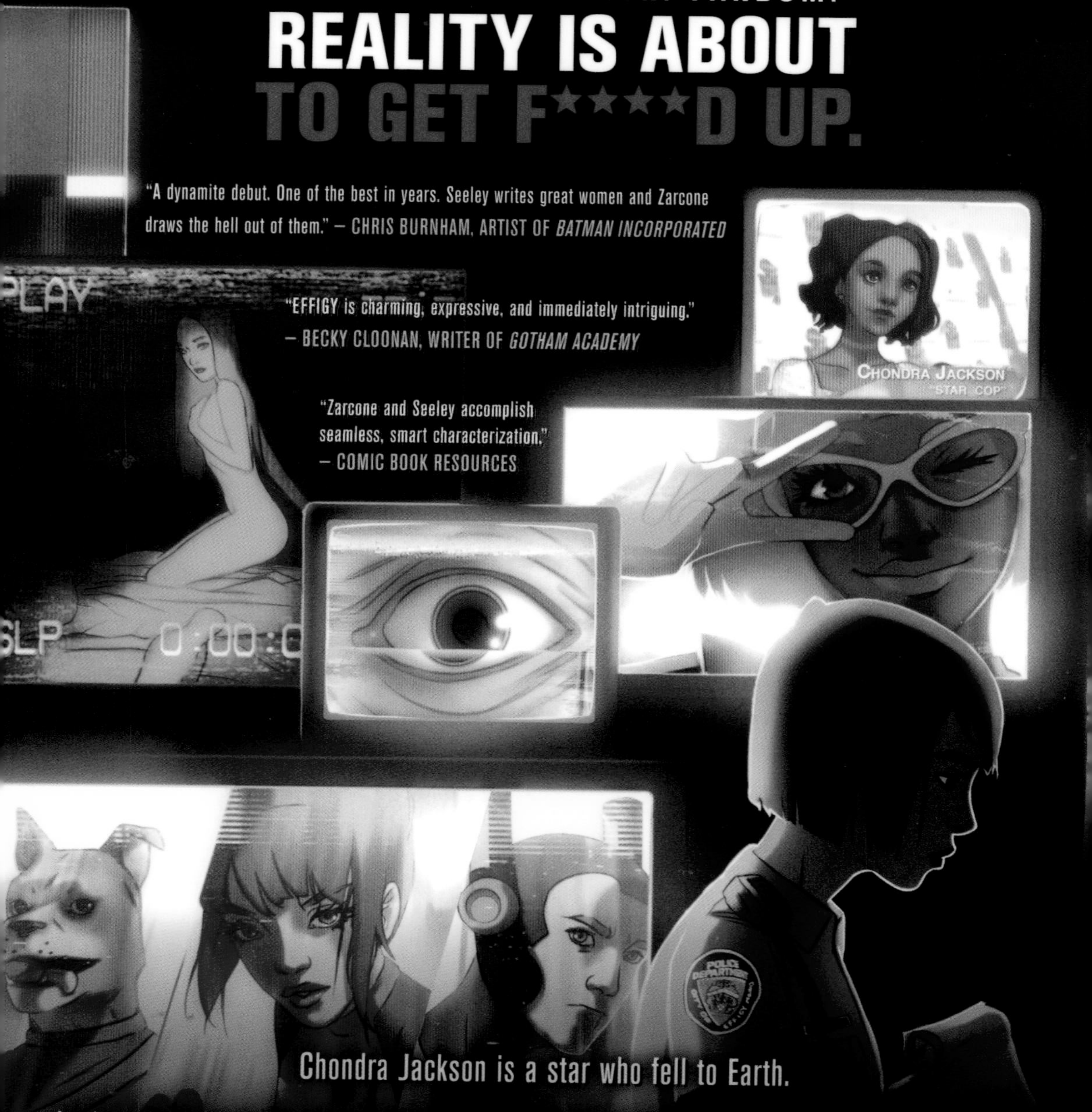

"A dynamite debut. One of the best in years. Seeley writes great women and Zarcone draws the hell out of them." – CHRIS BURNHAM, ARTIST OF *BATMAN INCORPORATED*

"*EFFIGY* is charming, expressive, and immediately intriguing." – BECKY CLOONAN, WRITER OF *GOTHAM ACADEMY*

"Zarcone and Seeley accomplish seamless, smart characterization." – COMIC BOOK RESOURCES

CHONDRA JACKSON "STAR COP"

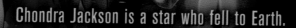

Chondra Jackson is a star who fell to Earth.

A preteen actress who was an idol to millions, she solved space crimes before dinnertime playing Bebe Soma on the smash-hit kids' TV show *Star Cops*. But all stars fade, and after Chondra aged out of the spotlight, the sex tape she made in an attempt to extend her 15 minutes wound up destroying her career.

Now she works as a beat cop in her hometown of Effigy Mound, Ohio, where she's about to catch a case as crazy as anything the Star Cops ever faced.

Chondra's fans, it turns out, are still obsessively dedicated to her, having built a close-knit community through message boards, conventions and cosplay. And someone is killing them, one by one. Someone who knows the strange truth behind *Star Cops*' fiction and the reclusive writer who created it. Someone who knows that fandom is the new true religion. Someone who knows that God is an alien life form, and that real stars shine on forever...

Co-creators **TIM SEELEY** and **MARLEY ZARCONE** put the "cult" back in "pop culture" with **EFFIGY: IDLE WORSHIP** — a small-town supernova of sex, sci-fi and celebrity!

$14.99 USA $17.99 CAN   ISBN: 978-1-4012-5685-2

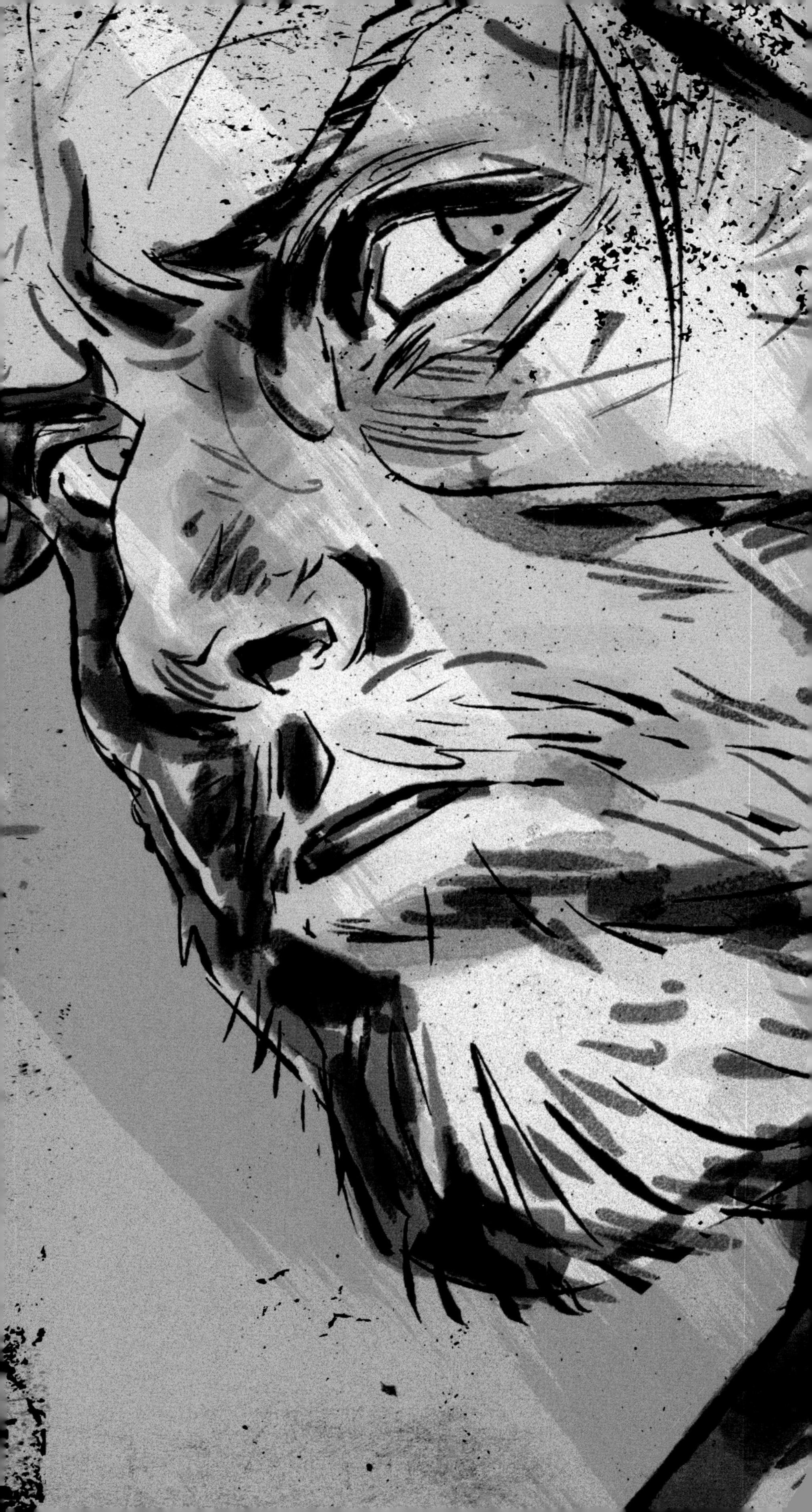

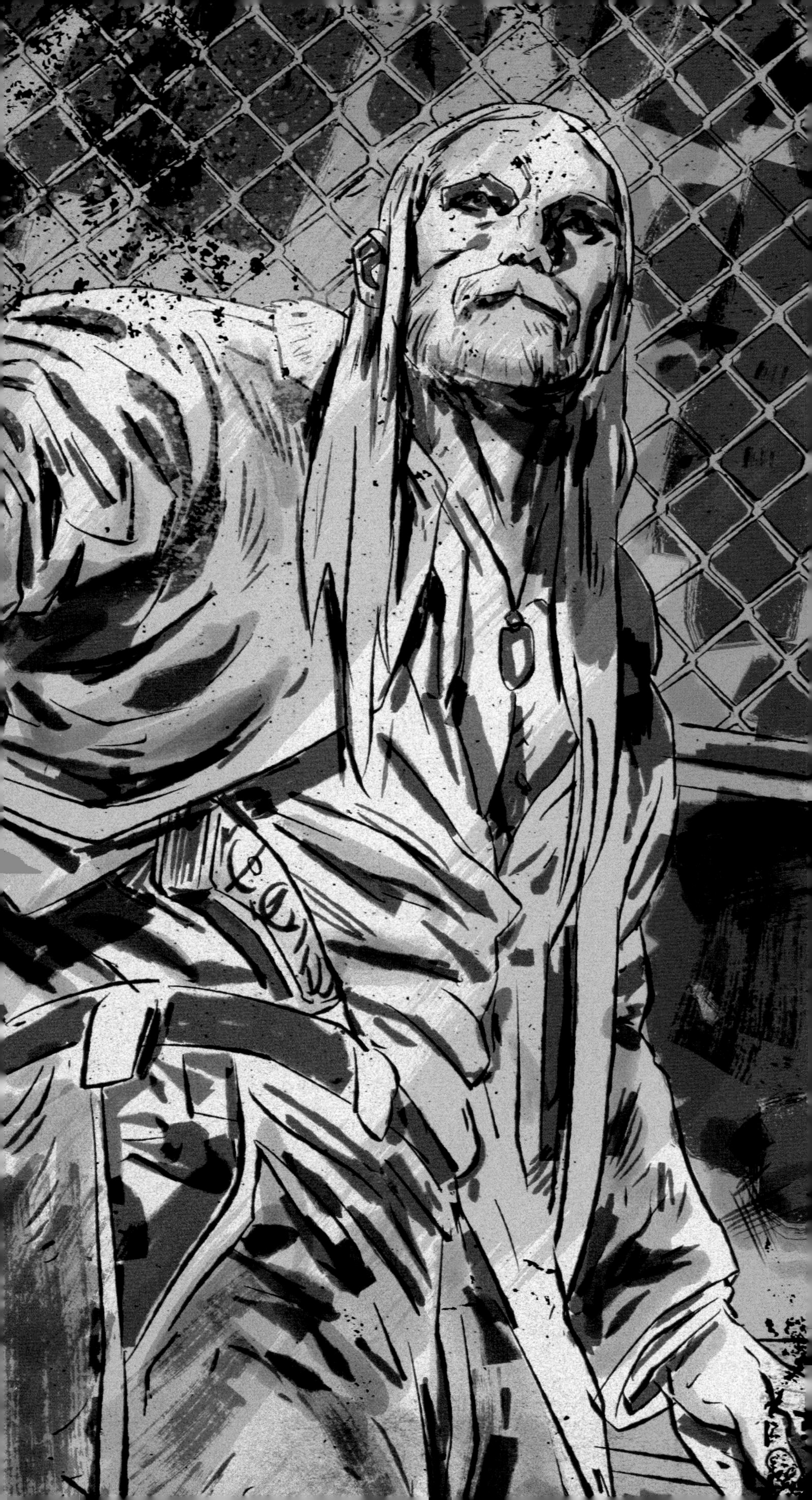

WRITTEN BY
**KURT SUTTER
& CAITLIN KITTREDGE**

ILLUSTRATED BY
JESÚS HERVÁS
CHAPTER THREE PAGES 17-22 BY RODRIGO LORENZO

COLORED BY
ALEX GUIMARÃES

LETTERED BY
JIM CAMPBELL

COVER BY
ADAM GORHAM
COLORS BY MICHAEL SPICER

SERIES DESIGNER
MARIE KRUPINA

COLLECTION DESIGNER
KARA LEOPARD

EDITORS
**CHRIS ROSA
DAFNA PLEBAN
MATT GAGNON**

LUCAS STAND ™

INNER DEMONS

CREATED BY
KURT SUTTER

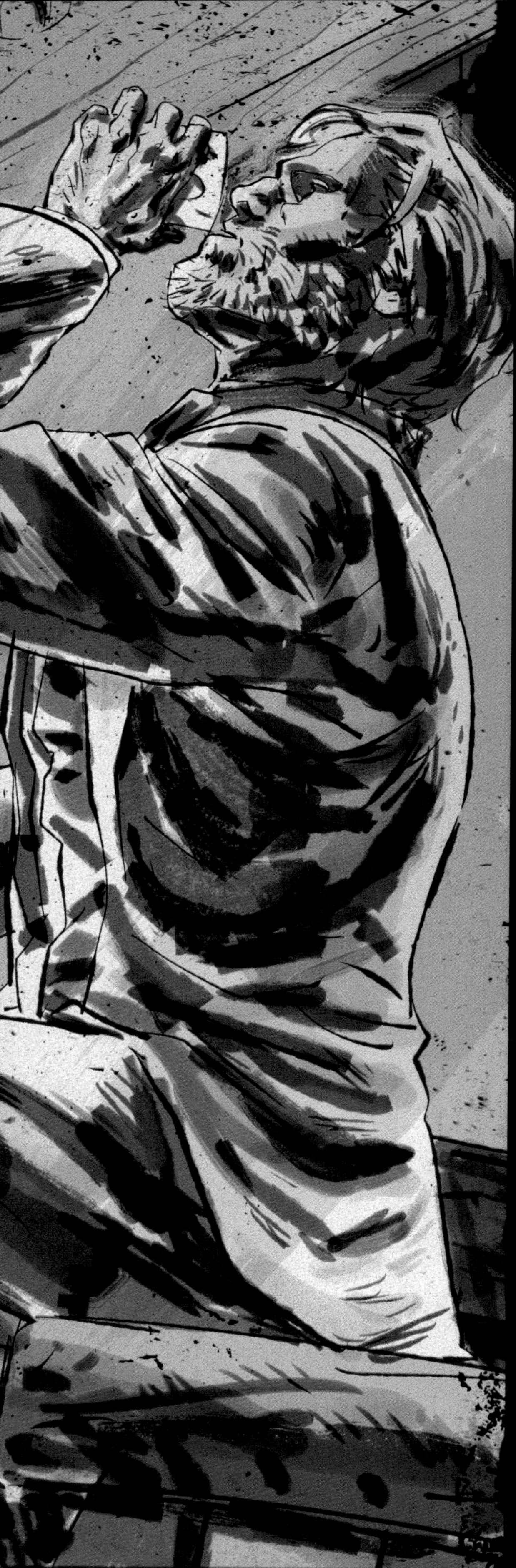

ONE

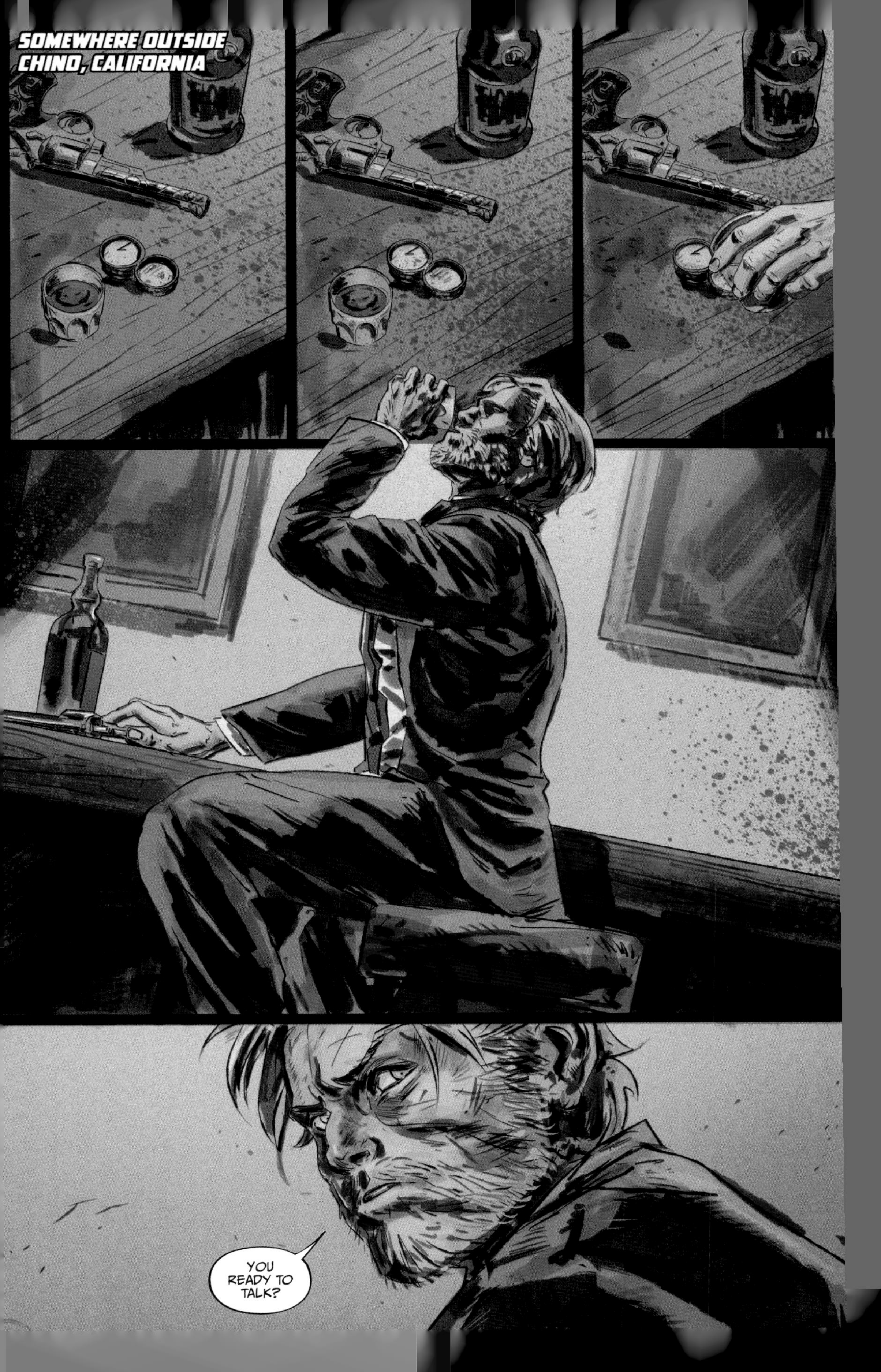
SOMEWHERE OUTSIDE CHINO, CALIFORNIA
YOU READY TO TALK?

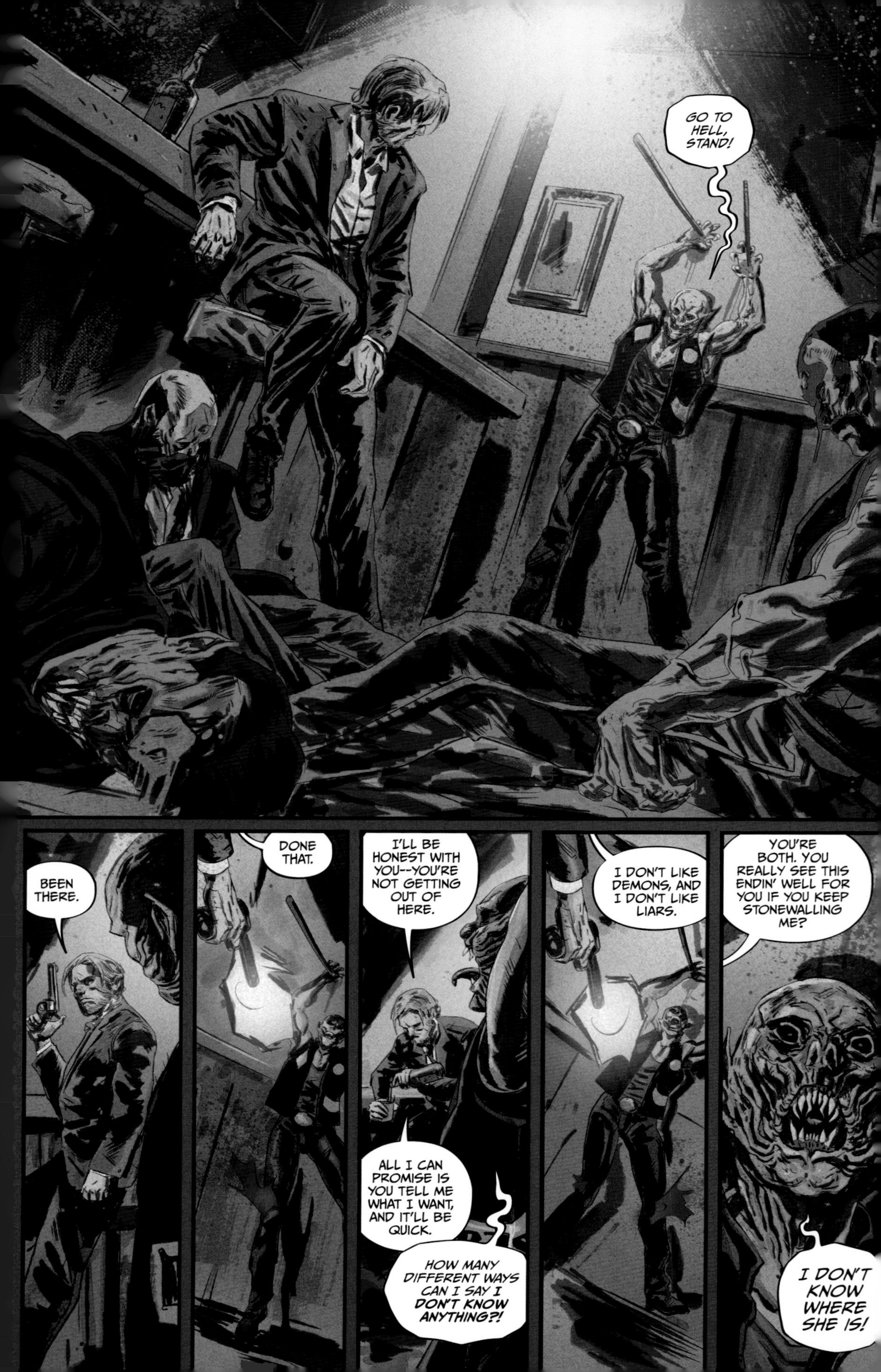
GO TO HELL, STAND!
BEEN THERE.
DONE THAT.
I'LL BE HONEST WITH YOU--YOU'RE NOT GETTING OUT OF HERE.
ALL I CAN PROMISE IS YOU TELL ME WHAT I WANT, AND IT'LL BE QUICK.
HOW MANY DIFFERENT WAYS CAN I SAY I **DON'T KNOW ANYTHING?!**
I DON'T LIKE DEMONS, AND I DON'T LIKE LIARS.
YOU'RE BOTH. YOU REALLY SEE THIS ENDIN' WELL FOR YOU IF YOU KEEP STONEWALLING ME?
I DON'T KNOW WHERE SHE IS!

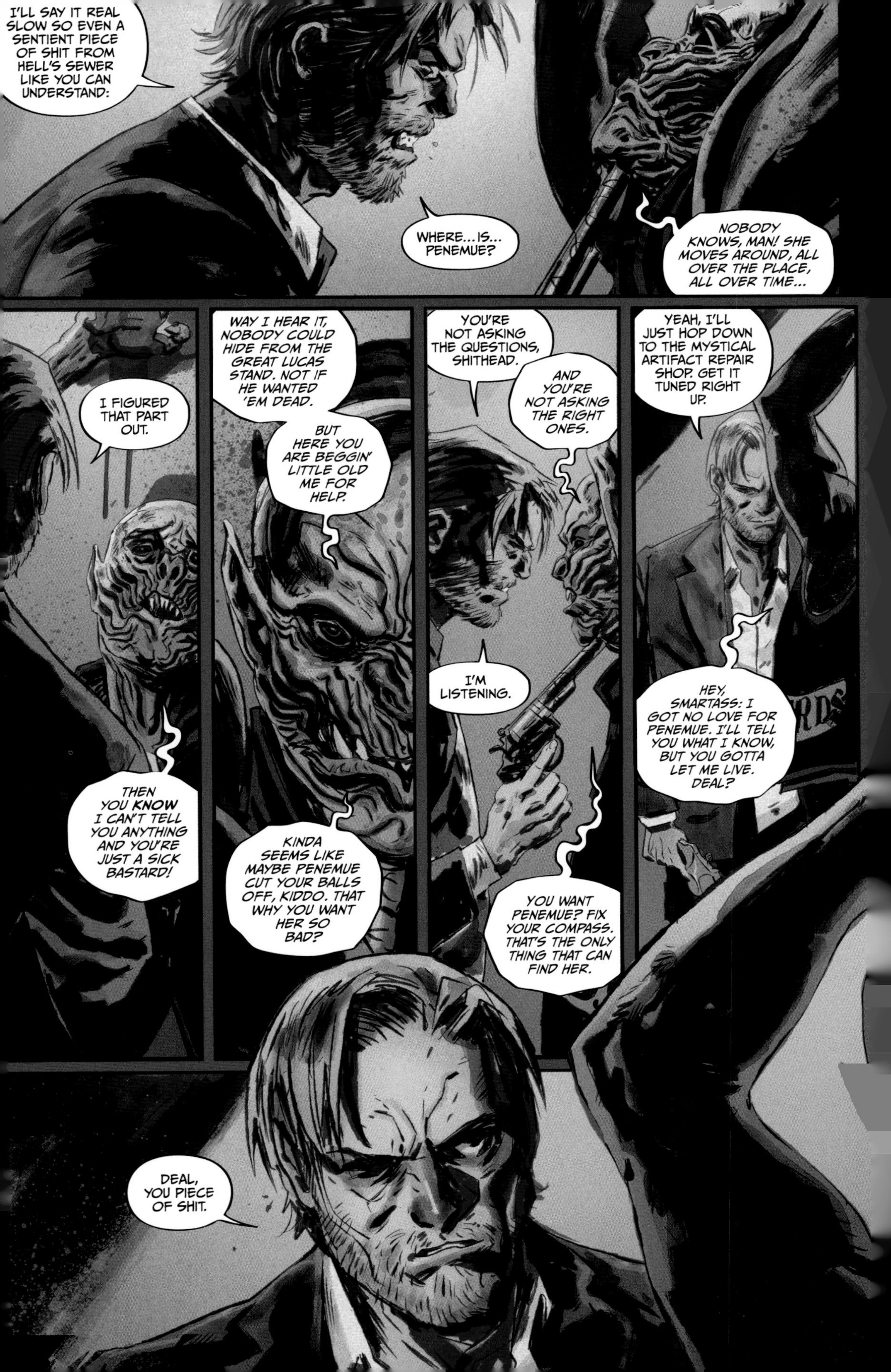
I'LL SAY IT REAL SLOW SO EVEN A SENTIENT PIECE OF SHIT FROM HELL'S SEWER LIKE YOU CAN UNDERSTAND:
WHERE... IS... PENEMUE?
NOBODY KNOWS, MAN! SHE MOVES AROUND, ALL OVER THE PLACE, ALL OVER TIME...
I FIGURED THAT PART OUT.
THEN YOU KNOW I CAN'T TELL YOU ANYTHING AND YOU'RE JUST A SICK BASTARD!
WAY I HEAR IT, NOBODY COULD HIDE FROM THE GREAT LUCAS STAND. NOT IF HE WANTED 'EM DEAD.
BUT HERE YOU ARE BEGGIN' LITTLE OLD ME FOR HELP.
KINDA SEEMS LIKE MAYBE PENEMUE CUT YOUR BALLS OFF, KIDDO. THAT WHY YOU WANT HER SO BAD?
YOU'RE NOT ASKING THE QUESTIONS, SHITHEAD.
AND YOU'RE NOT ASKING THE RIGHT ONES.
I'M LISTENING.
YOU WANT PENEMUE? FIX YOUR COMPASS. THAT'S THE ONLY THING THAT CAN FIND HER.
YEAH, I'LL JUST HOP DOWN TO THE MYSTICAL ARTIFACT REPAIR SHOP. GET IT TUNED RIGHT UP.
HEY, SMARTASS: I GOT NO LOVE FOR PENEMUE. I'LL TELL YOU WHAT I KNOW, BUT YOU GOTTA LET ME LIVE. DEAL?
DEAL, YOU PIECE OF SHIT.

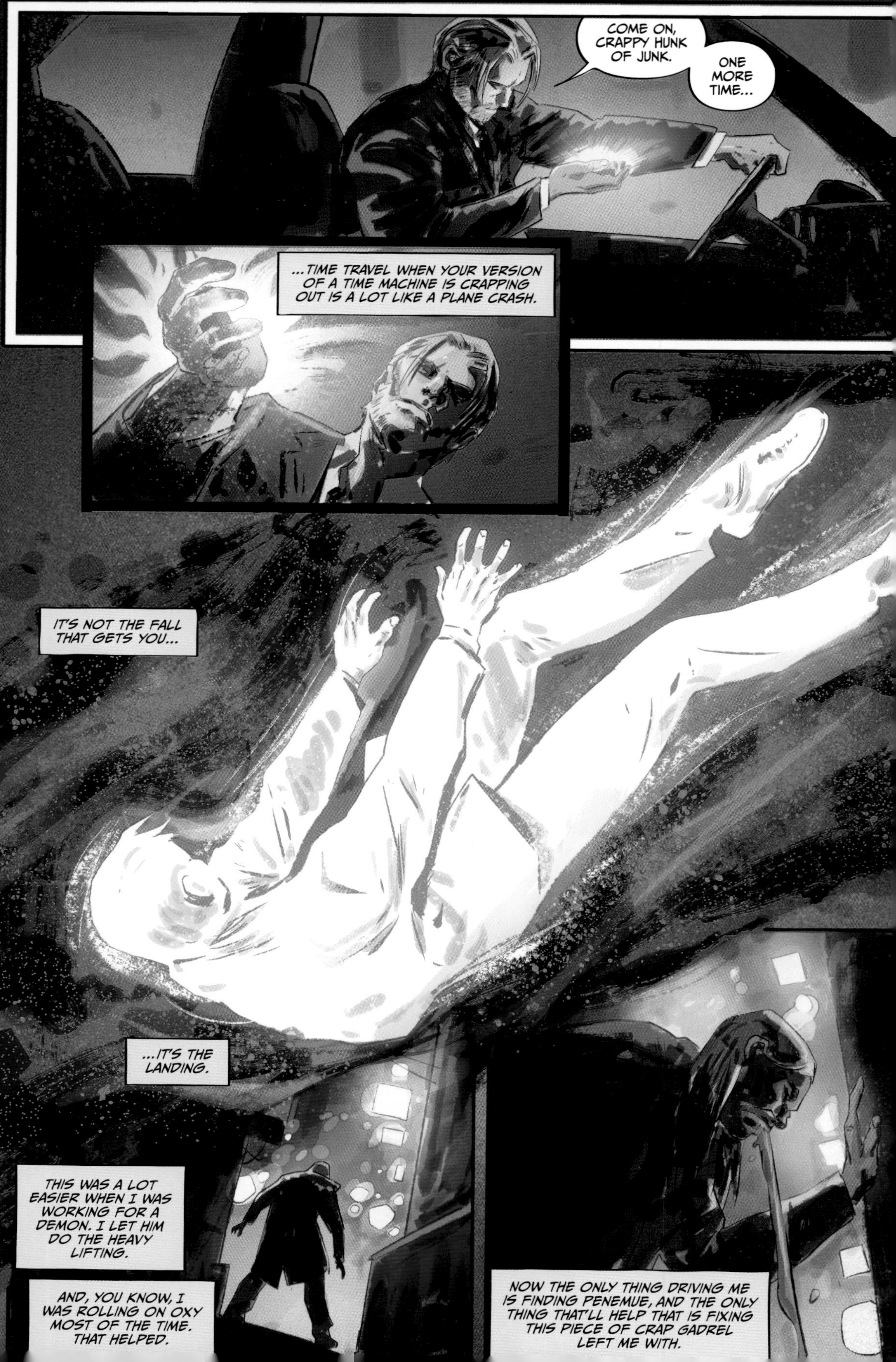
COME ON, CRAPPY HUNK OF JUNK.
ONE MORE TIME...
...TIME TRAVEL WHEN YOUR VERSION OF A TIME MACHINE IS CRAPPING OUT IS A LOT LIKE A PLANE CRASH.
IT'S NOT THE FALL THAT GETS YOU...
...IT'S THE LANDING.
THIS WAS A LOT EASIER WHEN I WAS WORKING FOR A DEMON. I LET HIM DO THE HEAVY LIFTING.
AND, YOU KNOW, I WAS ROLLING ON OXY MOST OF THE TIME. THAT HELPED.
NOW THE ONLY THING DRIVING ME IS FINDING PENEMUE, AND THE ONLY THING THAT'LL HELP THAT IS FIXING THIS PIECE OF CRAP GADREL LEFT ME WITH.

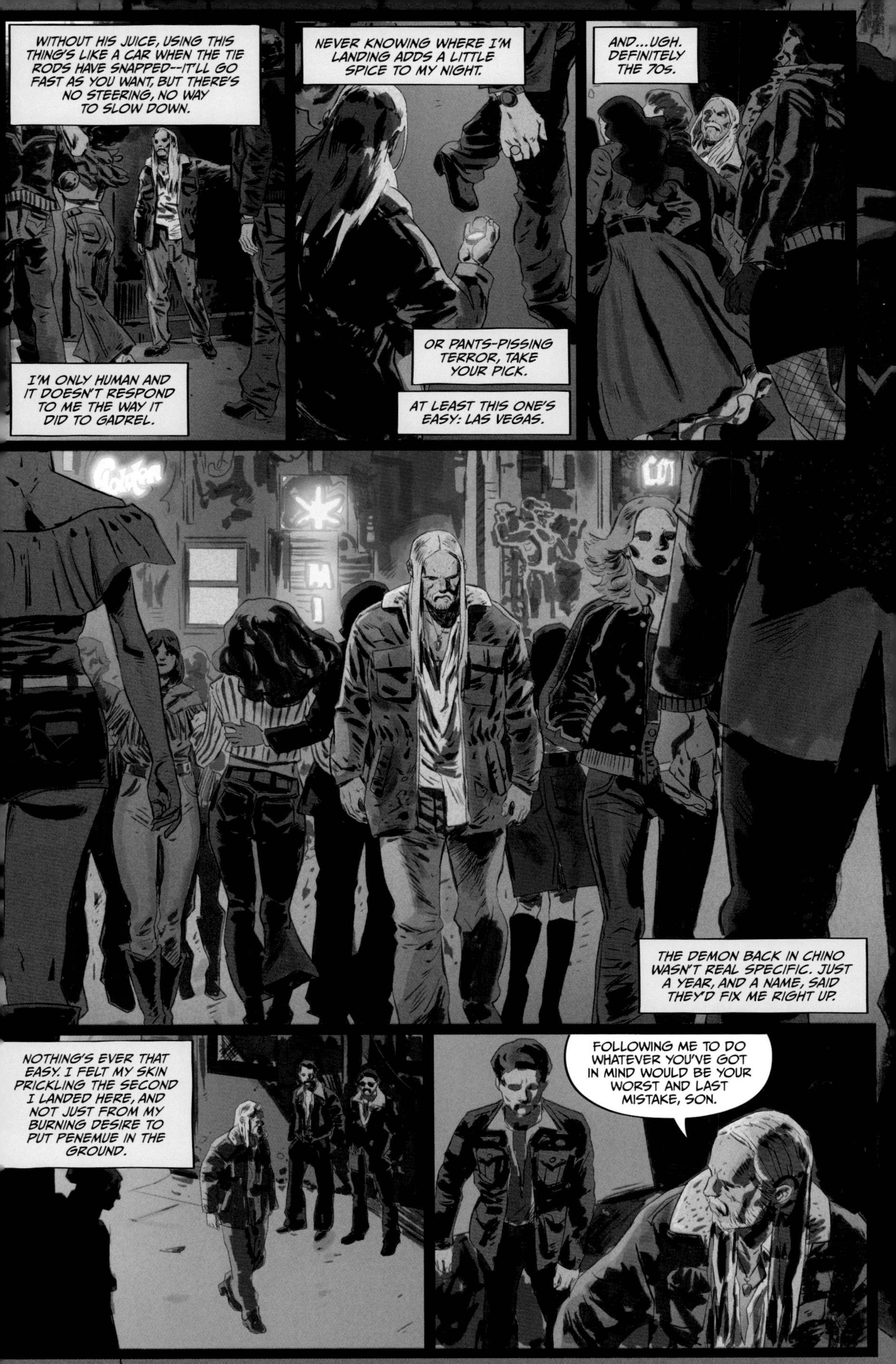
WITHOUT HIS JUICE, USING THIS THING'S LIKE A CAR WHEN THE TIE RODS HAVE SNAPPED--IT'LL GO FAST AS YOU WANT, BUT THERE'S NO STEERING, NO WAY TO SLOW DOWN.
I'M ONLY HUMAN AND IT DOESN'T RESPOND TO ME THE WAY IT DID TO GADREL.
NEVER KNOWING WHERE I'M LANDING ADDS A LITTLE SPICE TO MY NIGHT.
OR PANTS-PISSING TERROR, TAKE YOUR PICK.
AT LEAST THIS ONE'S EASY: LAS VEGAS.
AND...UGH. DEFINITELY THE 70s.
THE DEMON BACK IN CHINO WASN'T REAL SPECIFIC. JUST A YEAR, AND A NAME, SAID THEY'D FIX ME RIGHT UP.
NOTHING'S EVER THAT EASY. I FELT MY SKIN PRICKLING THE SECOND I LANDED HERE, AND NOT JUST FROM MY BURNING DESIRE TO PUT PENEMUE IN THE GROUND.
FOLLOWING ME TO DO WHATEVER YOU'VE GOT IN MIND WOULD BE YOUR WORST AND LAST MISTAKE, SON.

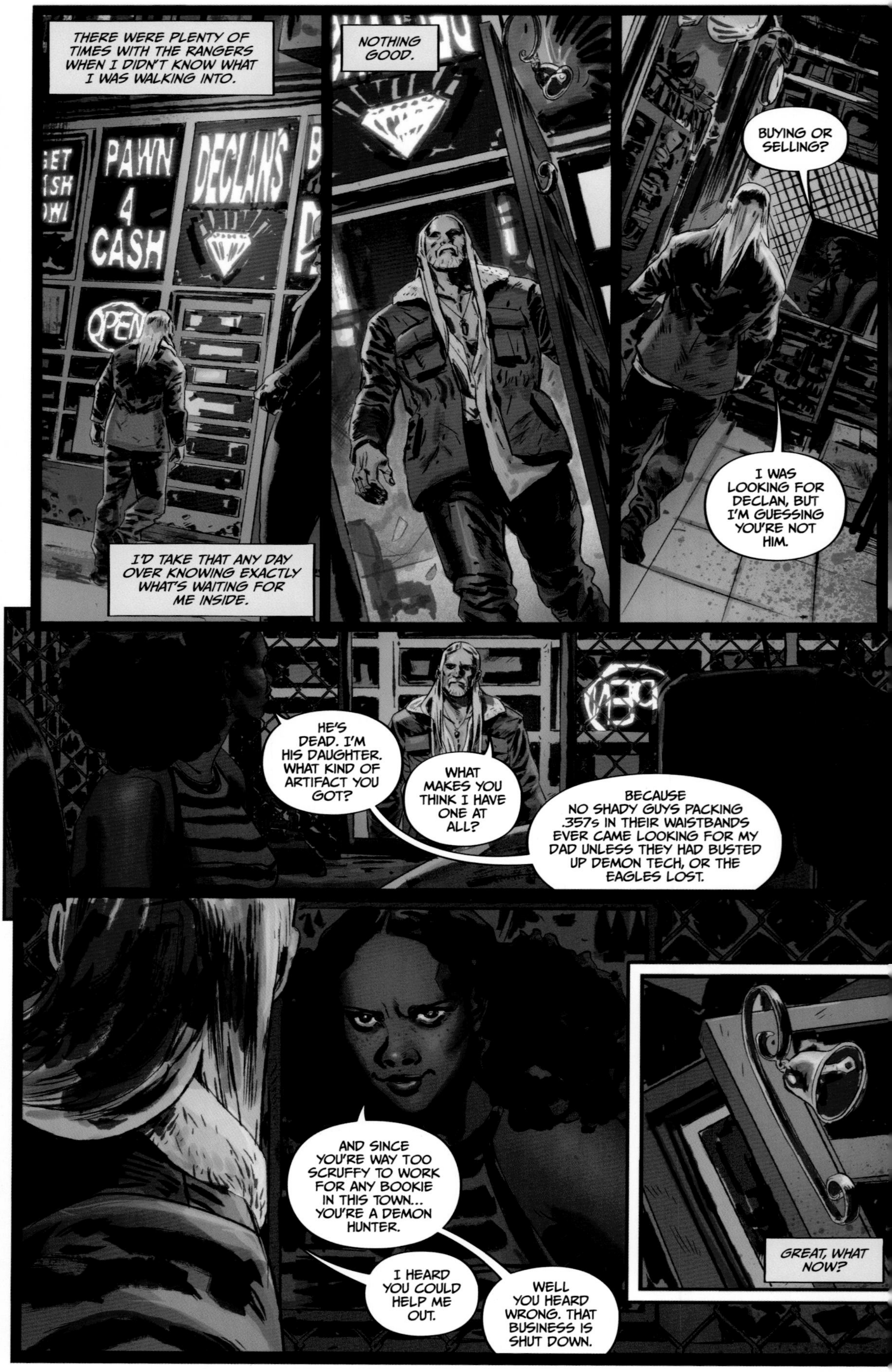

THERE WERE PLENTY OF TIMES WITH THE RANGERS WHEN I DIDN'T KNOW WHAT I WAS WALKING INTO.
PAWN 4 CASH
DECLAN'S
OPEN
I'D TAKE THAT ANY DAY OVER KNOWING EXACTLY WHAT'S WAITING FOR ME INSIDE.
NOTHING GOOD.
BUYING OR SELLING?
I WAS LOOKING FOR DECLAN, BUT I'M GUESSING YOU'RE NOT HIM.
HE'S DEAD. I'M HIS DAUGHTER. WHAT KIND OF ARTIFACT YOU GOT?
WHAT MAKES YOU THINK I HAVE ONE AT ALL?
BECAUSE NO SHADY GUYS PACKING .357s IN THEIR WAISTBANDS EVER CAME LOOKING FOR MY DAD UNLESS THEY HAD BUSTED UP DEMON TECH, OR THE EAGLES LOST.
AND SINCE YOU'RE WAY TOO SCRUFFY TO WORK FOR ANY BOOKIE IN THIS TOWN... YOU'RE A DEMON HUNTER.
I HEARD YOU COULD HELP ME OUT.
WELL YOU HEARD WRONG. THAT BUSINESS IS SHUT DOWN.
GREAT, WHAT NOW?

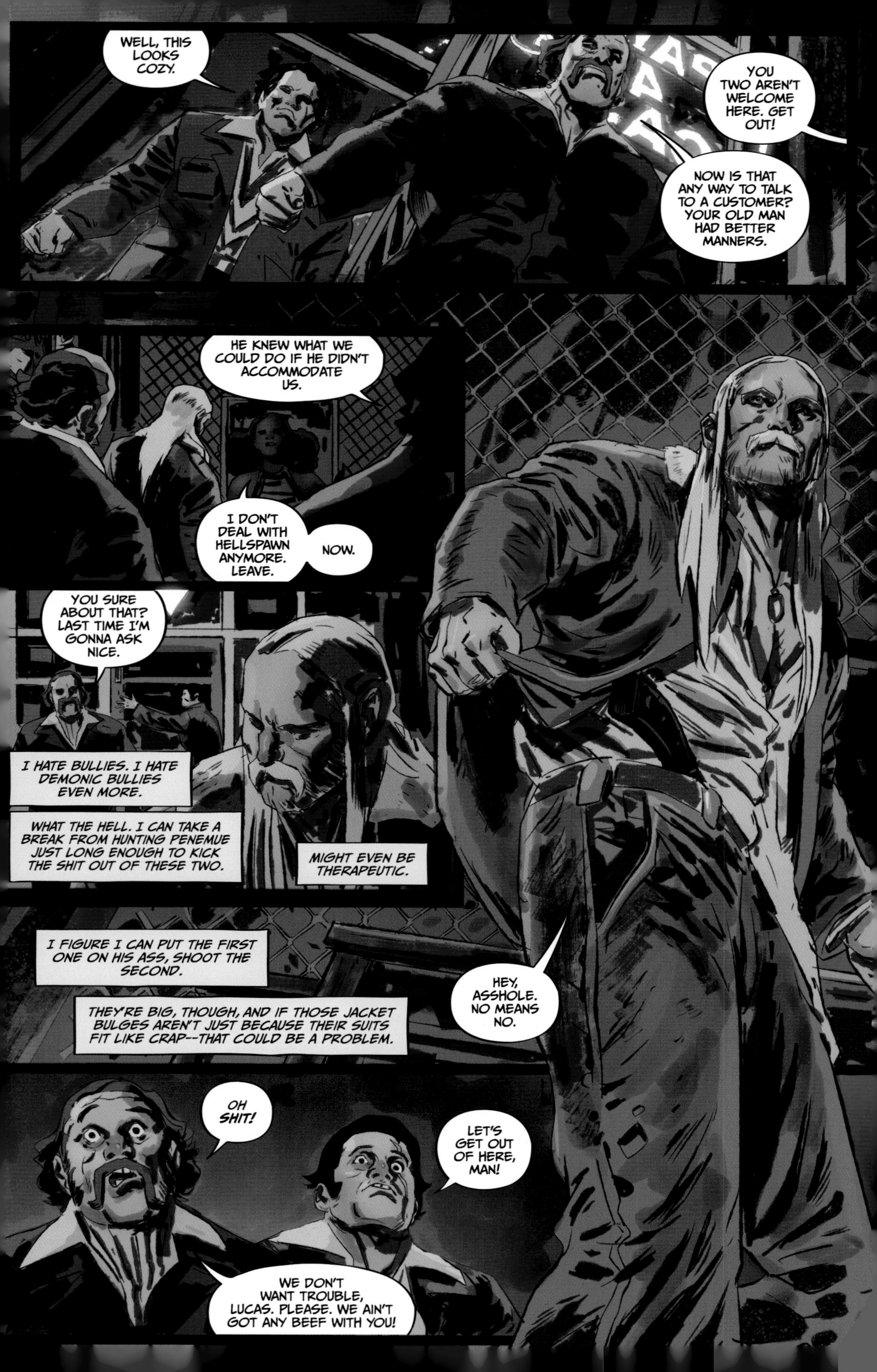
WELL, THIS LOOKS COZY.
YOU TWO AREN'T WELCOME HERE. GET OUT!
NOW IS THAT ANY WAY TO TALK TO A CUSTOMER? YOUR OLD MAN HAD BETTER MANNERS.
HE KNEW WHAT WE COULD DO IF HE DIDN'T ACCOMMODATE US.
I DON'T DEAL WITH HELLSPAWN ANYMORE. LEAVE.
NOW.
YOU SURE ABOUT THAT? LAST TIME I'M GONNA ASK NICE.
I HATE BULLIES. I HATE DEMONIC BULLIES EVEN MORE.
WHAT THE HELL. I CAN TAKE A BREAK FROM HUNTING PENEMUE JUST LONG ENOUGH TO KICK THE SHIT OUT OF THESE TWO.
MIGHT EVEN BE THERAPEUTIC.
I FIGURE I CAN PUT THE FIRST ONE ON HIS ASS, SHOOT THE SECOND.
THEY'RE BIG, THOUGH, AND IF THOSE JACKET BULGES AREN'T JUST BECAUSE THEIR SUITS FIT LIKE CRAP--THAT COULD BE A PROBLEM.
HEY, ASSHOLE. NO MEANS NO.
OH SHIT!
LET'S GET OUT OF HERE, MAN!
WE DON'T WANT TROUBLE, LUCAS. PLEASE. WE AIN'T GOT ANY BEEF WITH YOU!

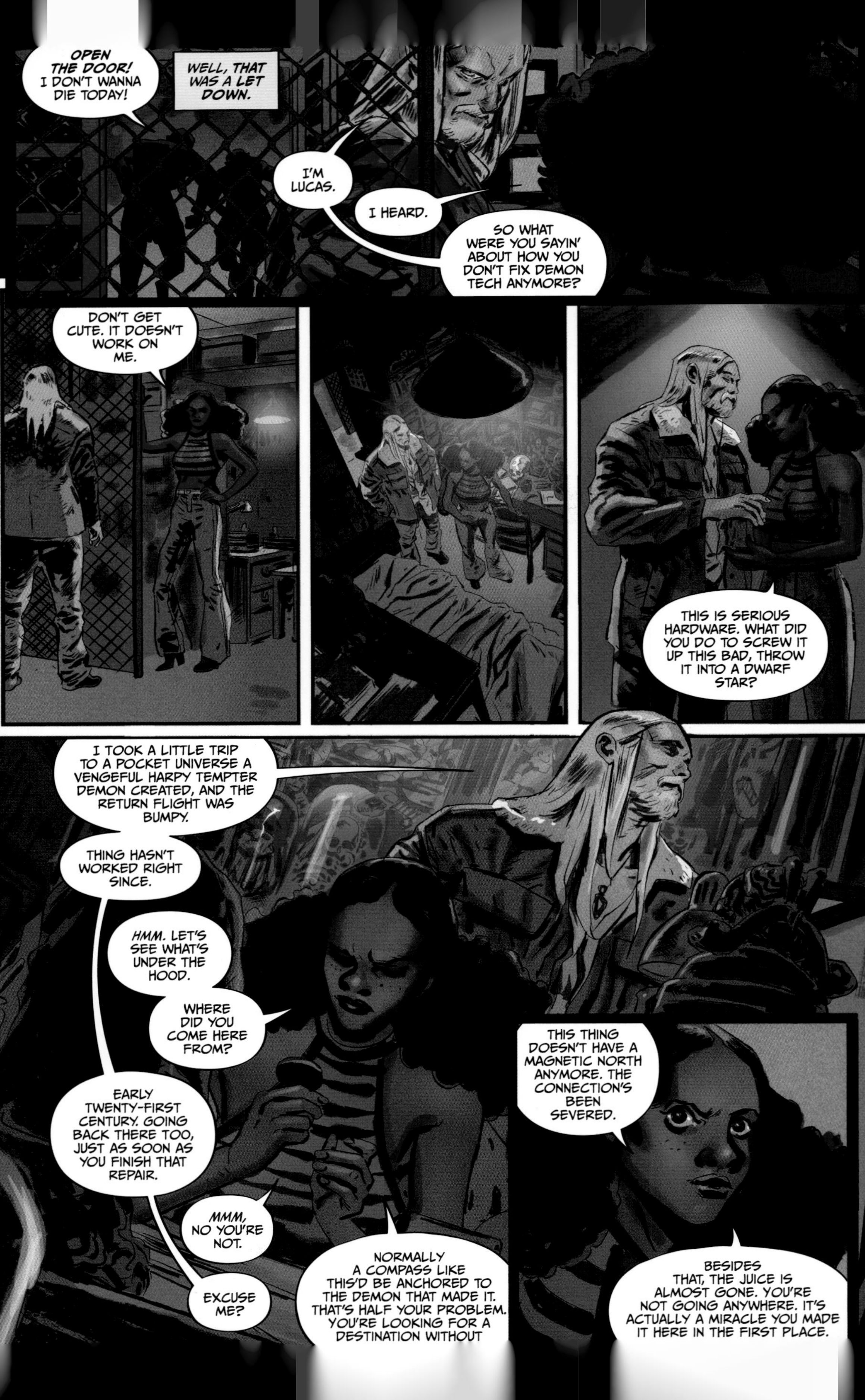
OPEN THE DOOR! I DON'T WANNA DIE TODAY!
WELL, THAT WAS A LET DOWN.
I'M LUCAS.
I HEARD.
SO WHAT WERE YOU SAYIN' ABOUT HOW YOU DON'T FIX DEMON TECH ANYMORE?
DON'T GET CUTE. IT DOESN'T WORK ON ME.
THIS IS SERIOUS HARDWARE. WHAT DID YOU DO TO SCREW IT UP THIS BAD, THROW IT INTO A DWARF STAR?
I TOOK A LITTLE TRIP TO A POCKET UNIVERSE A VENGEFUL HARPY TEMPTER DEMON CREATED, AND THE RETURN FLIGHT WAS BUMPY.
THING HASN'T WORKED RIGHT SINCE.
HMM. LET'S SEE WHAT'S UNDER THE HOOD.
WHERE DID YOU COME HERE FROM?
EARLY TWENTY-FIRST CENTURY. GOING BACK THERE TOO, JUST AS SOON AS YOU FINISH THAT REPAIR.
MMM, NO YOU'RE NOT.
EXCUSE ME?
NORMALLY A COMPASS LIKE THIS'D BE ANCHORED TO THE DEMON THAT MADE IT. THAT'S HALF YOUR PROBLEM. YOU'RE LOOKING FOR A DESTINATION WITHOUT
THIS THING DOESN'T HAVE A MAGNETIC NORTH ANYMORE. THE CONNECTION'S BEEN SEVERED.
BESIDES THAT, THE JUICE IS ALMOST GONE. YOU'RE NOT GOING ANYWHERE. IT'S ACTUALLY A MIRACLE YOU MADE IT HERE IN THE FIRST PLACE.

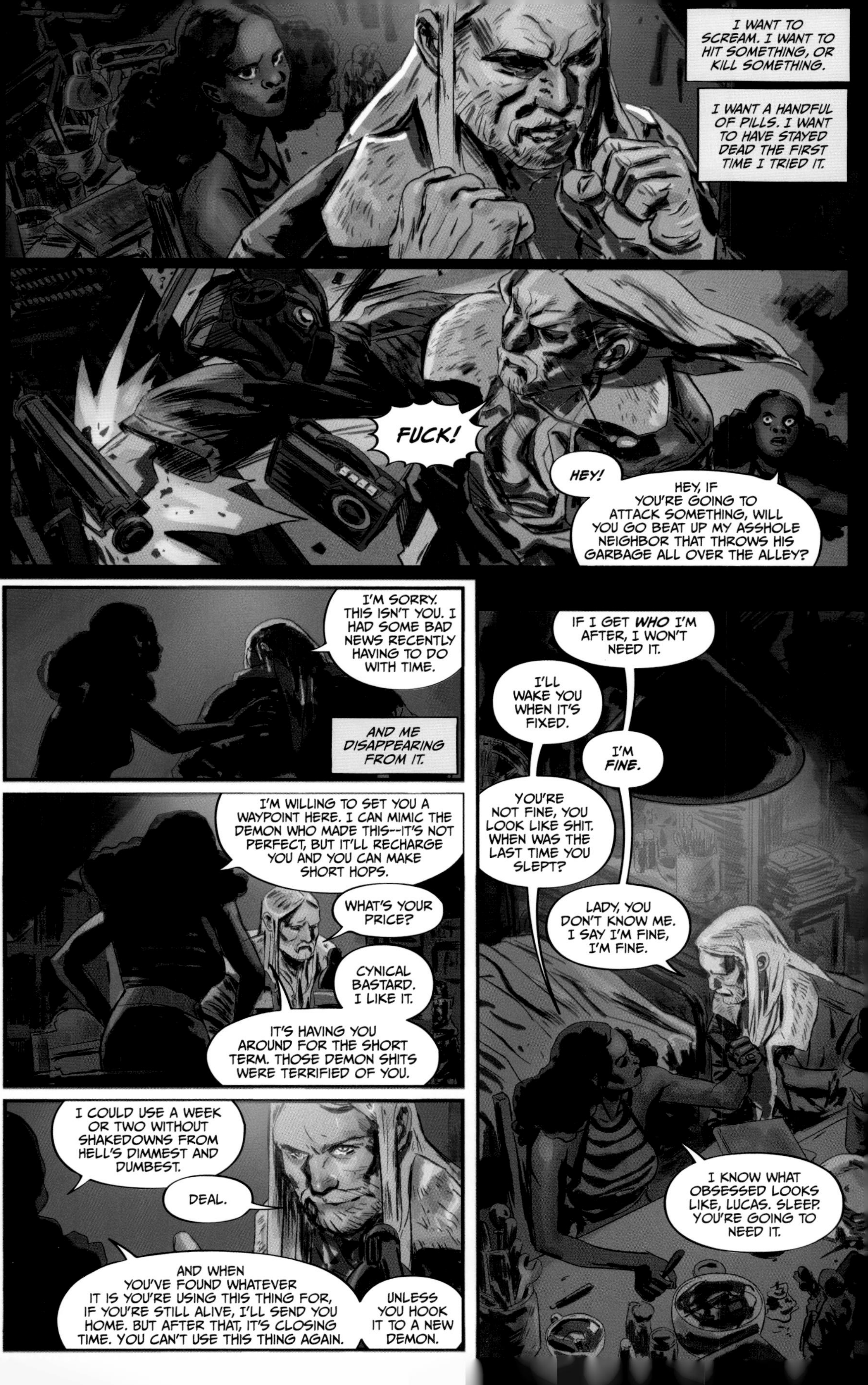
I WANT TO SCREAM. I WANT TO HIT SOMETHING, OR KILL SOMETHING.
I WANT A HANDFUL OF PILLS. I WANT TO HAVE STAYED DEAD THE FIRST TIME I TRIED IT.
FUCK!
HEY!
HEY, IF YOU'RE GOING TO ATTACK SOMETHING, WILL YOU GO BEAT UP MY ASSHOLE NEIGHBOR THAT THROWS HIS GARBAGE ALL OVER THE ALLEY?
I'M SORRY. THIS ISN'T YOU. I HAD SOME BAD NEWS RECENTLY HAVING TO DO WITH TIME.
AND ME DISAPPEARING FROM IT.
I'M WILLING TO SET YOU A WAYPOINT HERE. I CAN MIMIC THE DEMON WHO MADE THIS--IT'S NOT PERFECT, BUT IT'LL RECHARGE YOU AND YOU CAN MAKE SHORT HOPS.
WHAT'S YOUR PRICE?
CYNICAL BASTARD. I LIKE IT.
IT'S HAVING YOU AROUND FOR THE SHORT TERM. THOSE DEMON SHITS WERE TERRIFIED OF YOU.
I COULD USE A WEEK OR TWO WITHOUT SHAKEDOWNS FROM HELL'S DIMMEST AND DUMBEST.
DEAL.
AND WHEN YOU'VE FOUND WHATEVER IT IS YOU'RE USING THIS THING FOR, IF YOU'RE STILL ALIVE, I'LL SEND YOU HOME. BUT AFTER THAT, IT'S CLOSING TIME. YOU CAN'T USE THIS THING AGAIN.
UNLESS YOU HOOK IT TO A NEW DEMON.
IF I GET WHO I'M AFTER, I WON'T NEED IT.
I'LL WAKE YOU WHEN IT'S FIXED.
I'M FINE.
YOU'RE NOT FINE, YOU LOOK LIKE SHIT. WHEN WAS THE LAST TIME YOU SLEPT?
LADY, YOU DON'T KNOW ME. I SAY I'M FINE, I'M FINE.
I KNOW WHAT OBSESSED LOOKS LIKE, LUCAS. SLEEP. YOU'RE GOING TO NEED IT.

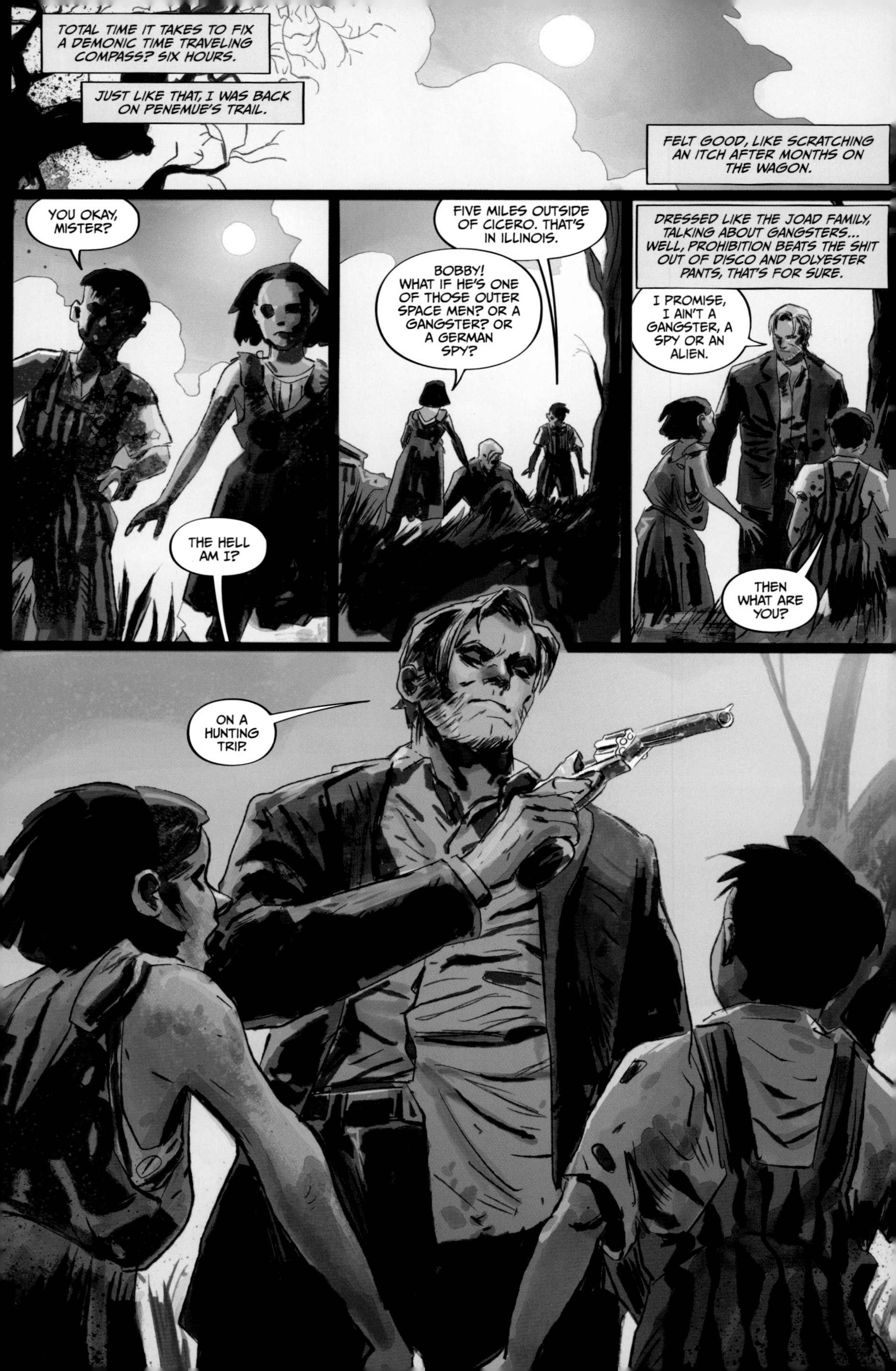
TOTAL TIME IT TAKES TO FIX A DEMONIC TIME TRAVELING COMPASS? SIX HOURS.
JUST LIKE THAT, I WAS BACK ON PENEMUE'S TRAIL.
FELT GOOD, LIKE SCRATCHING AN ITCH AFTER MONTHS ON THE WAGON.
YOU OKAY, MISTER?
THE HELL AM I?
FIVE MILES OUTSIDE OF CICERO. THAT'S IN ILLINOIS.
BOBBY! WHAT IF HE'S ONE OF THOSE OUTER SPACE MEN? OR A GANGSTER? OR A GERMAN SPY?
DRESSED LIKE THE JOAD FAMILY, TALKING ABOUT GANGSTERS... WELL, PROHIBITION BEATS THE SHIT OUT OF DISCO AND POLYESTER PANTS, THAT'S FOR SURE.
I PROMISE, I AIN'T A GANGSTER, A SPY OR AN ALIEN.
THEN WHAT ARE YOU?
ON A HUNTING TRIP.

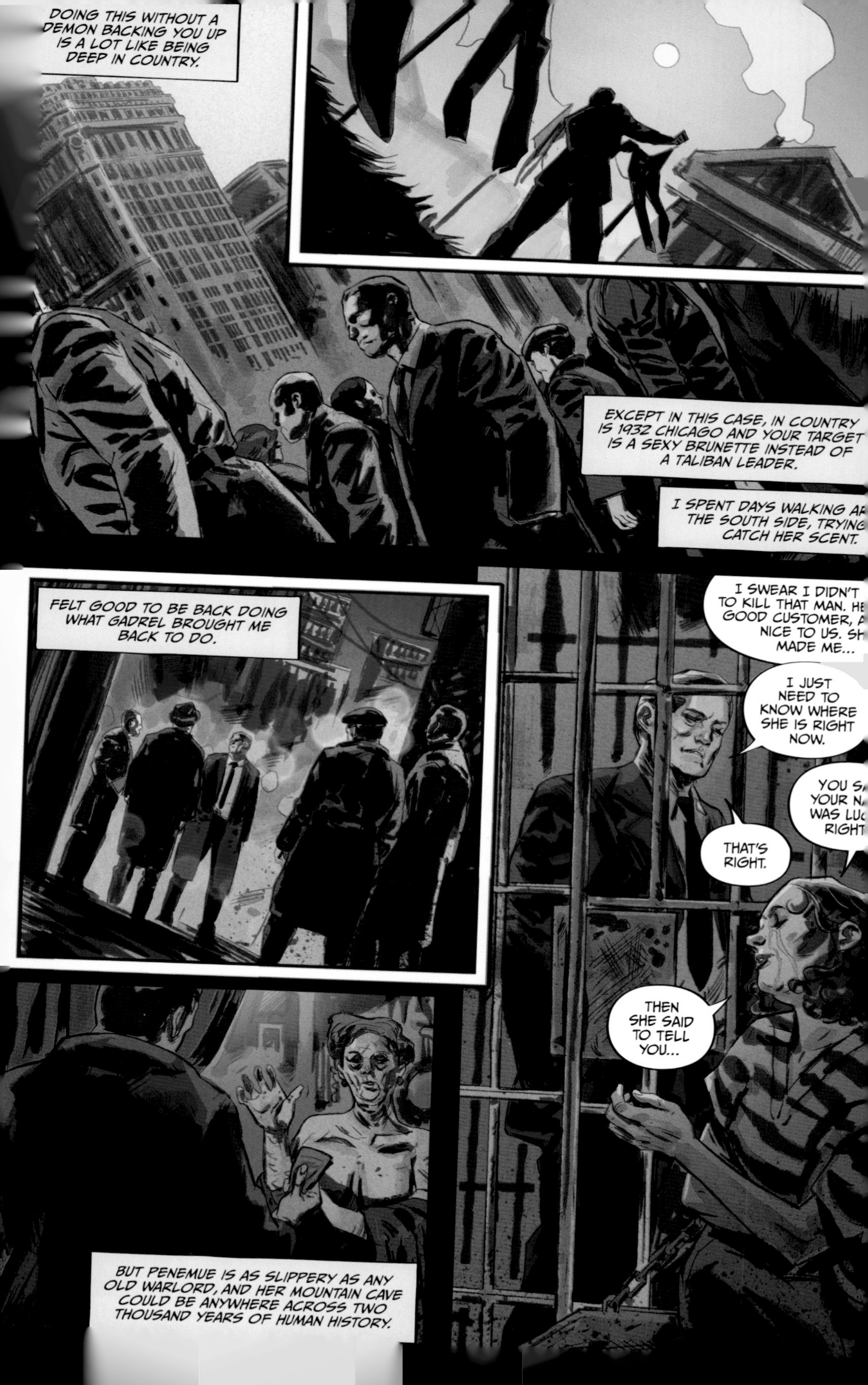
DOING THIS WITHOUT A DEMON BACKING YOU UP IS A LOT LIKE BEING DEEP IN COUNTRY.
EXCEPT IN THIS CASE, IN COUNTRY IS 1932 CHICAGO AND YOUR TARGET IS A SEXY BRUNETTE INSTEAD OF A TALIBAN LEADER.
I SPENT DAYS WALKING A THE SOUTH SIDE, TRYING CATCH HER SCENT.
FELT GOOD TO BE BACK DOING WHAT GADREL BROUGHT ME BACK TO DO.
BUT PENEMUE IS AS SLIPPERY AS ANY OLD WARLORD, AND HER MOUNTAIN CAVE COULD BE ANYWHERE ACROSS TWO THOUSAND YEARS OF HUMAN HISTORY.
I SWEAR I DIDN'T TO KILL THAT MAN. H GOOD CUSTOMER, NICE TO US. S MADE ME...
I JUST NEED TO KNOW WHERE SHE IS RIGHT NOW.
YOU S YOUR N WAS LU RIGHT
THAT'S RIGHT.
THEN SHE SAID TO TELL YOU...

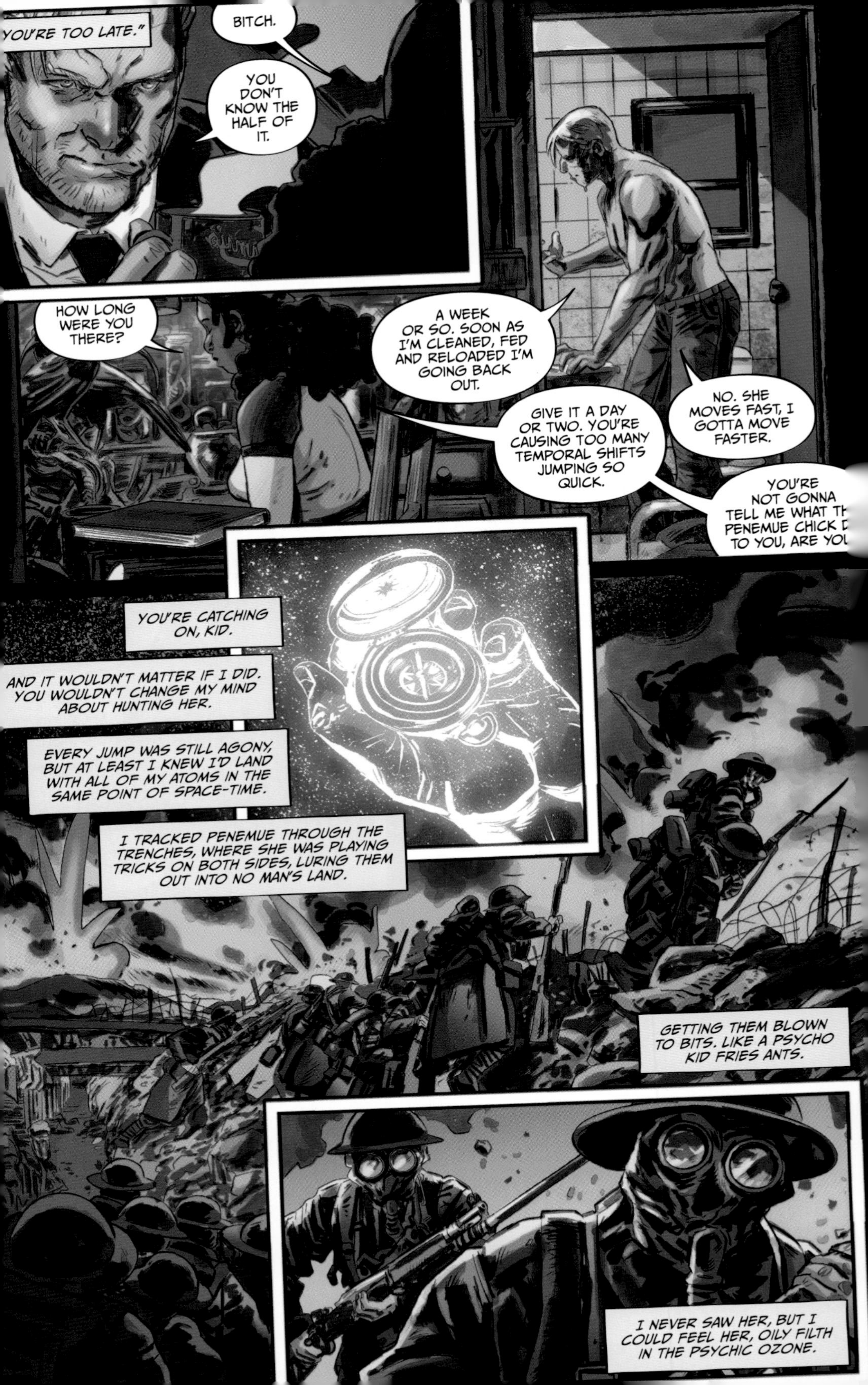
YOU'RE TOO LATE."
BITCH.
YOU DON'T KNOW THE HALF OF IT.
HOW LONG WERE YOU THERE?
A WEEK OR SO. SOON AS I'M CLEANED, FED AND RELOADED I'M GOING BACK OUT.
GIVE IT A DAY OR TWO. YOU'RE CAUSING TOO MANY TEMPORAL SHIFTS JUMPING SO QUICK.
NO. SHE MOVES FAST, I GOTTA MOVE FASTER.
YOU'RE NOT GONNA TELL ME WHAT TH PENEMUE CHICK D TO YOU, ARE YOU
YOU'RE CATCHING ON, KID.
AND IT WOULDN'T MATTER IF I DID. YOU WOULDN'T CHANGE MY MIND ABOUT HUNTING HER.
EVERY JUMP WAS STILL AGONY, BUT AT LEAST I KNEW I'D LAND WITH ALL OF MY ATOMS IN THE SAME POINT OF SPACE-TIME.
I TRACKED PENEMUE THROUGH THE TRENCHES, WHERE SHE WAS PLAYING TRICKS ON BOTH SIDES, LURING THEM OUT INTO NO MAN'S LAND.
GETTING THEM BLOWN TO BITS. LIKE A PSYCHO KID FRIES ANTS.
I NEVER SAW HER, BUT I COULD FEEL HER, OILY FILTH IN THE PSYCHIC OZONE.

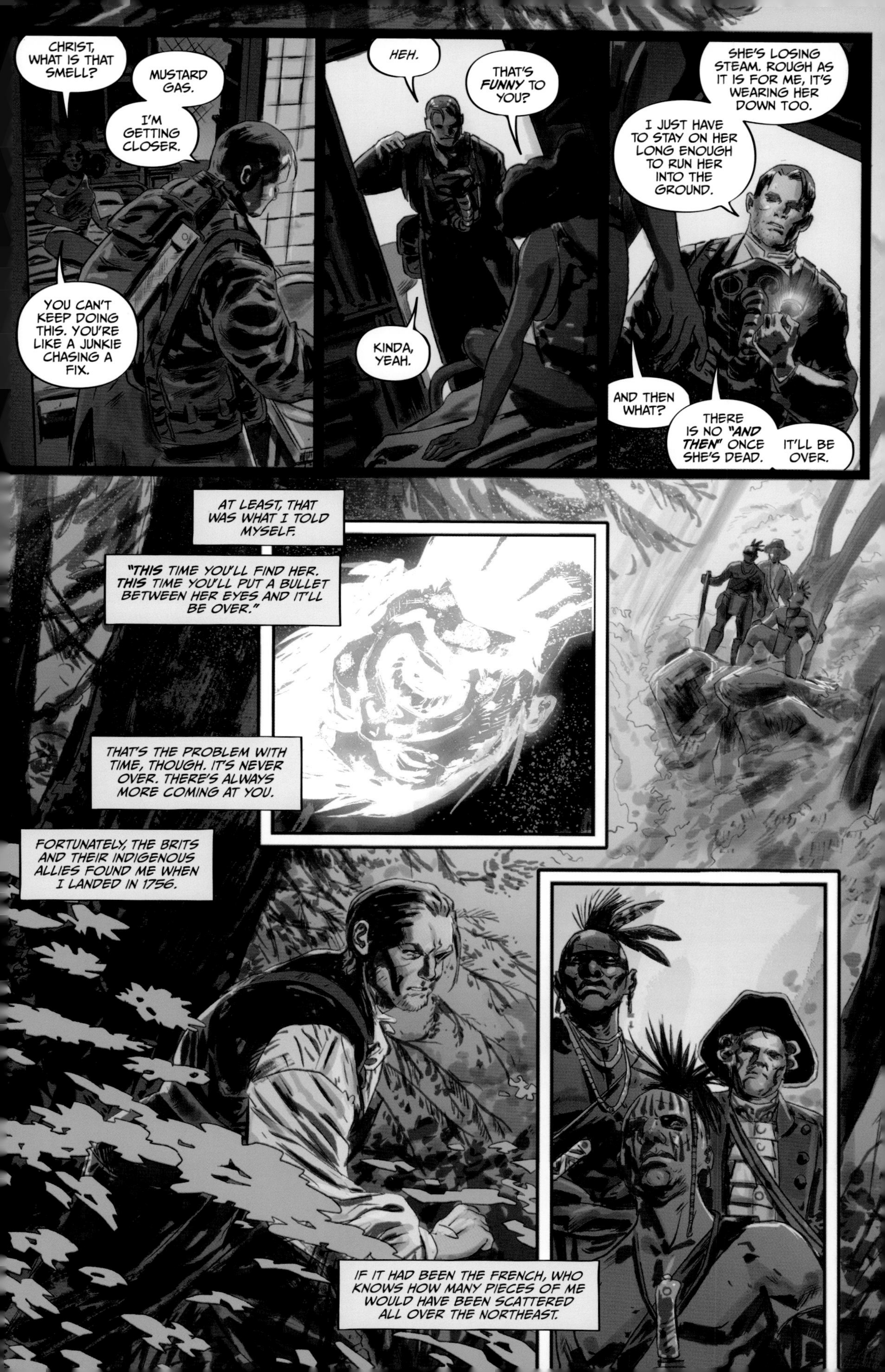
CHRIST, WHAT IS THAT SMELL?
MUSTARD GAS.
I'M GETTING CLOSER.
YOU CAN'T KEEP DOING THIS. YOU'RE LIKE A JUNKIE CHASING A FIX.
HEH.
THAT'S FUNNY TO YOU?
KINDA, YEAH.
SHE'S LOSING STEAM. ROUGH AS IT IS FOR ME, IT'S WEARING HER DOWN TOO.
I JUST HAVE TO STAY ON HER LONG ENOUGH TO RUN HER INTO THE GROUND.
AND THEN WHAT?
THERE IS NO "AND THEN" ONCE SHE'S DEAD.
IT'LL BE OVER.
AT LEAST, THAT WAS WHAT I TOLD MYSELF.
"THIS TIME YOU'LL FIND HER. THIS TIME YOU'LL PUT A BULLET BETWEEN HER EYES AND IT'LL BE OVER."
THAT'S THE PROBLEM WITH TIME, THOUGH. IT'S NEVER OVER. THERE'S ALWAYS MORE COMING AT YOU.
FORTUNATELY, THE BRITS AND THEIR INDIGENOUS ALLIES FOUND ME WHEN I LANDED IN 1756.
IF IT HAD BEEN THE FRENCH, WHO KNOWS HOW MANY PIECES OF ME WOULD HAVE BEEN SCATTERED ALL OVER THE NORTHEAST.

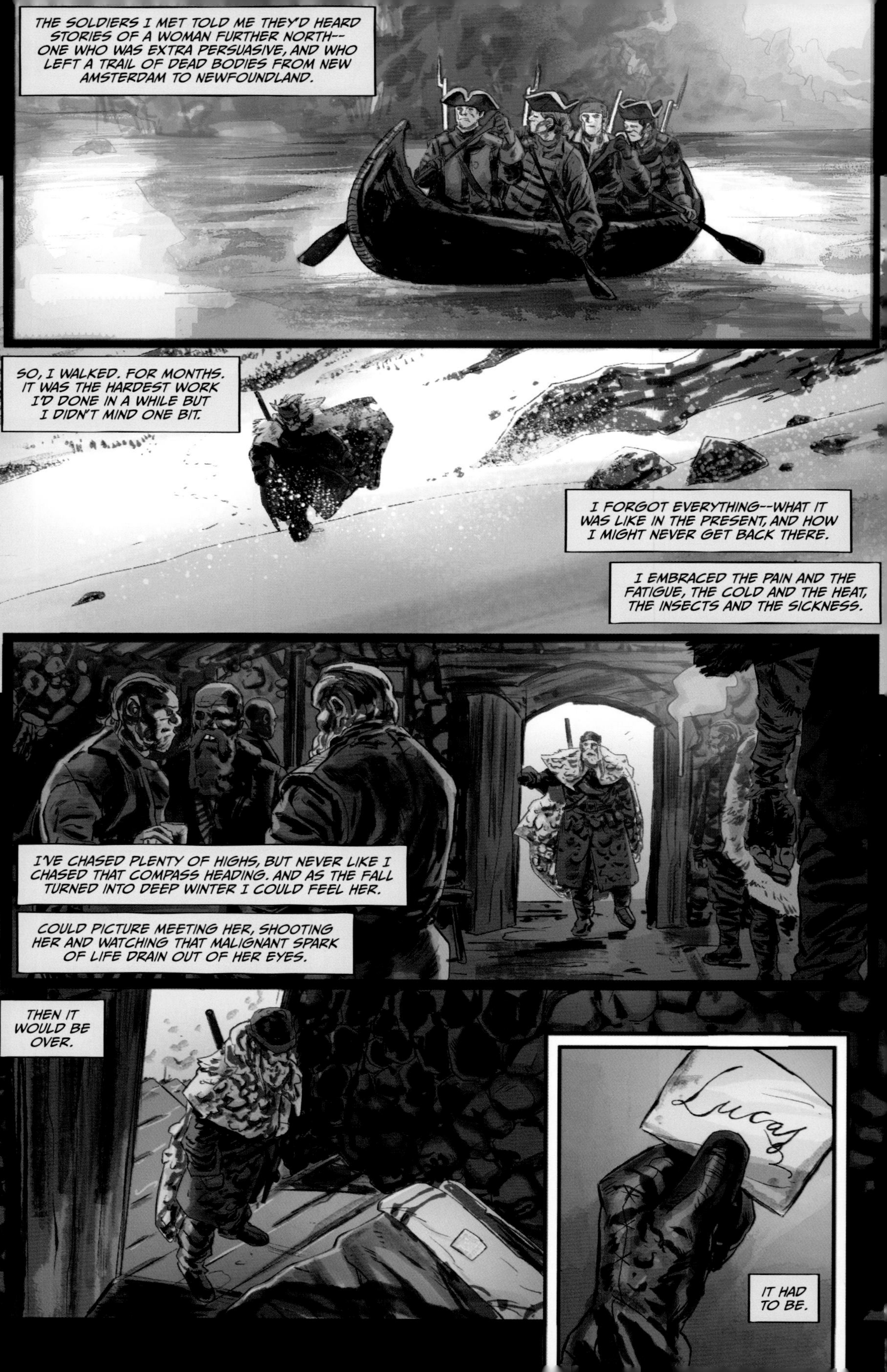
THE SOLDIERS I MET TOLD ME THEY'D HEARD STORIES OF A WOMAN FURTHER NORTH--ONE WHO WAS EXTRA PERSUASIVE, AND WHO LEFT A TRAIL OF DEAD BODIES FROM NEW AMSTERDAM TO NEWFOUNDLAND.
SO, I WALKED. FOR MONTHS. IT WAS THE HARDEST WORK I'D DONE IN A WHILE BUT I DIDN'T MIND ONE BIT.
I FORGOT EVERYTHING--WHAT IT WAS LIKE IN THE PRESENT, AND HOW I MIGHT NEVER GET BACK THERE.
I EMBRACED THE PAIN AND THE FATIGUE, THE COLD AND THE HEAT, THE INSECTS AND THE SICKNESS.
I'VE CHASED PLENTY OF HIGHS, BUT NEVER LIKE I CHASED THAT COMPASS HEADING. AND AS THE FALL TURNED INTO DEEP WINTER I COULD FEEL HER.
COULD PICTURE MEETING HER, SHOOTING HER AND WATCHING THAT MALIGNANT SPARK OF LIFE DRAIN OUT OF HER EYES.
THEN IT WOULD BE OVER.
Lucas
IT HAD TO BE.

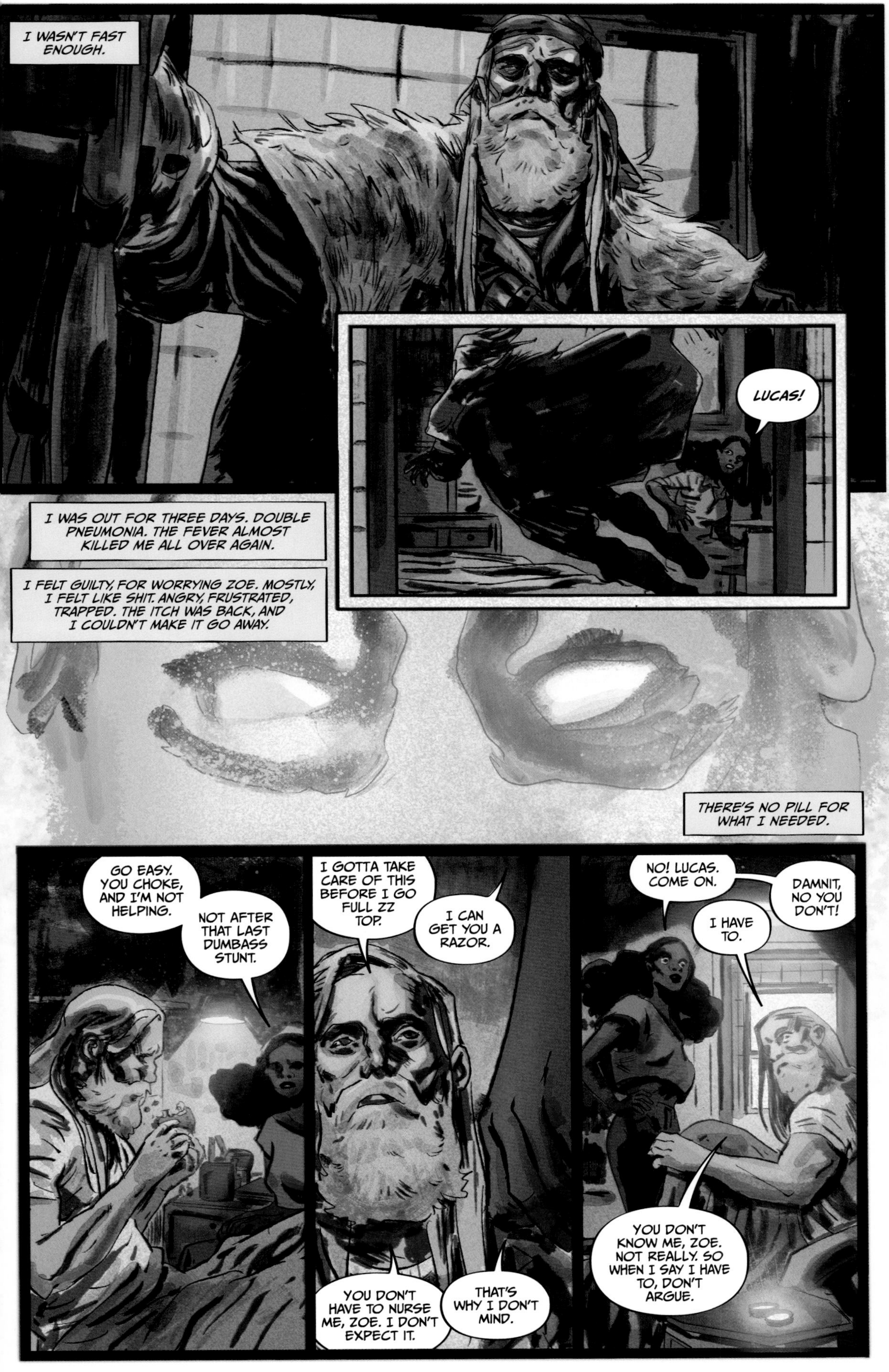
I WASN'T FAST ENOUGH.
LUCAS!
I WAS OUT FOR THREE DAYS. DOUBLE PNEUMONIA. THE FEVER ALMOST KILLED ME ALL OVER AGAIN.
I FELT GUILTY, FOR WORRYING ZOE. MOSTLY, I FELT LIKE SHIT. ANGRY, FRUSTRATED, TRAPPED. THE ITCH WAS BACK, AND I COULDN'T MAKE IT GO AWAY.
THERE'S NO PILL FOR WHAT I NEEDED.
GO EASY. YOU CHOKE, AND I'M NOT HELPING.
NOT AFTER THAT LAST DUMBASS STUNT.
I GOTTA TAKE CARE OF THIS BEFORE I GO FULL ZZ TOP.
I CAN GET YOU A RAZOR.
YOU DON'T HAVE TO NURSE ME, ZOE. I DON'T EXPECT IT.
THAT'S WHY I DON'T MIND.
NO! LUCAS. COME ON.
I HAVE TO.
DAMNIT, NO YOU DON'T!
YOU DON'T KNOW ME, ZOE. NOT REALLY. SO WHEN I SAY I HAVE TO, DON'T ARGUE.

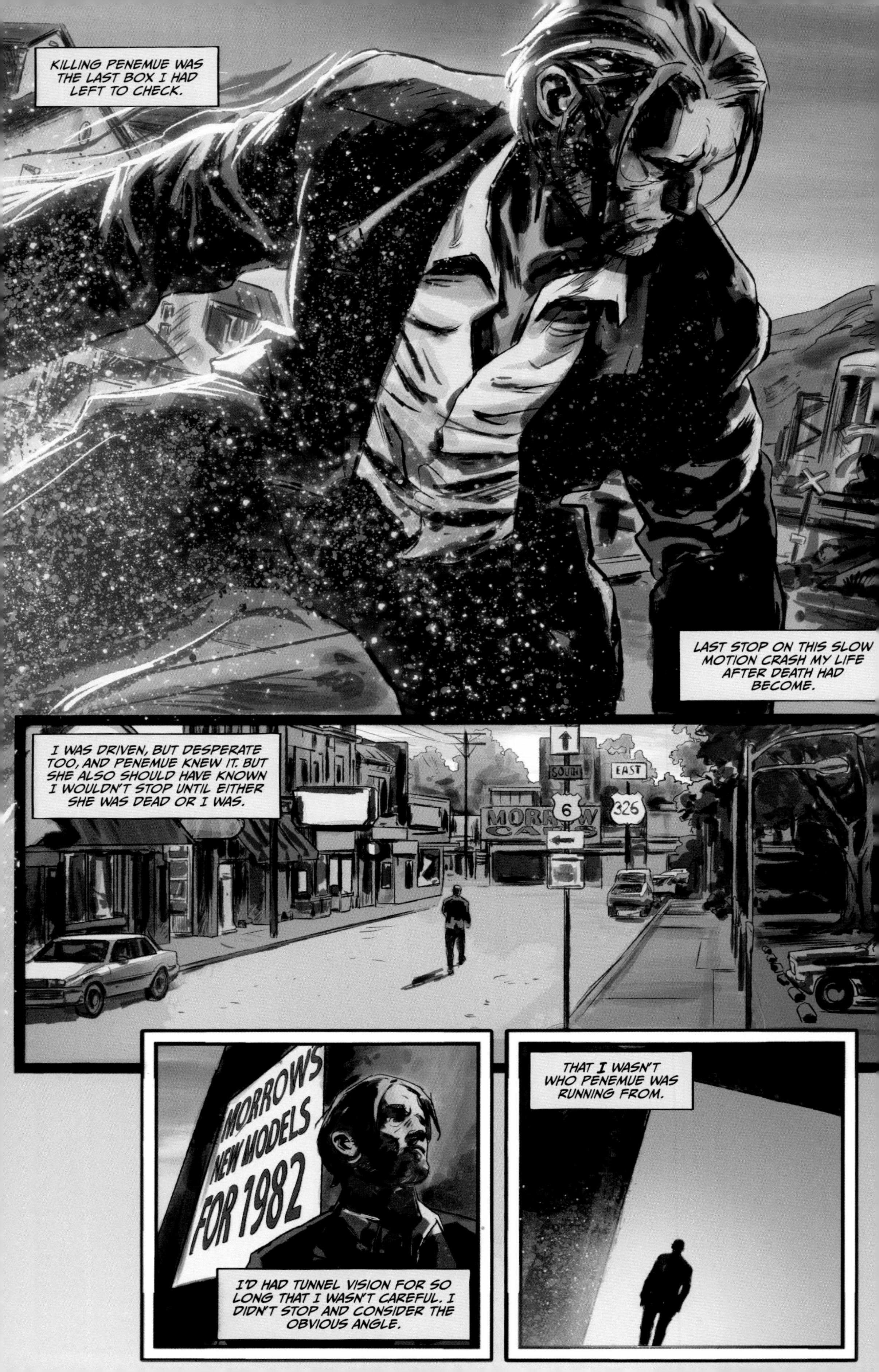
KILLING PENEMUE WAS THE LAST BOX I HAD LEFT TO CHECK.
LAST STOP ON THIS SLOW MOTION CRASH MY LIFE AFTER DEATH HAD BECOME.
I WAS DRIVEN, BUT DESPERATE TOO, AND PENEMUE KNEW IT. BUT SHE ALSO SHOULD HAVE KNOWN I WOULDN'T STOP UNTIL EITHER SHE WAS DEAD OR I WAS.
SOUTH
EAST
6
326
MORROW CARS
MORROWS NEW MODELS FOR 1982
I'D HAD TUNNEL VISION FOR SO LONG THAT I WASN'T CAREFUL. I DIDN'T STOP AND CONSIDER THE OBVIOUS ANGLE.
THAT I WASN'T WHO PENEMUE WAS RUNNING FROM.

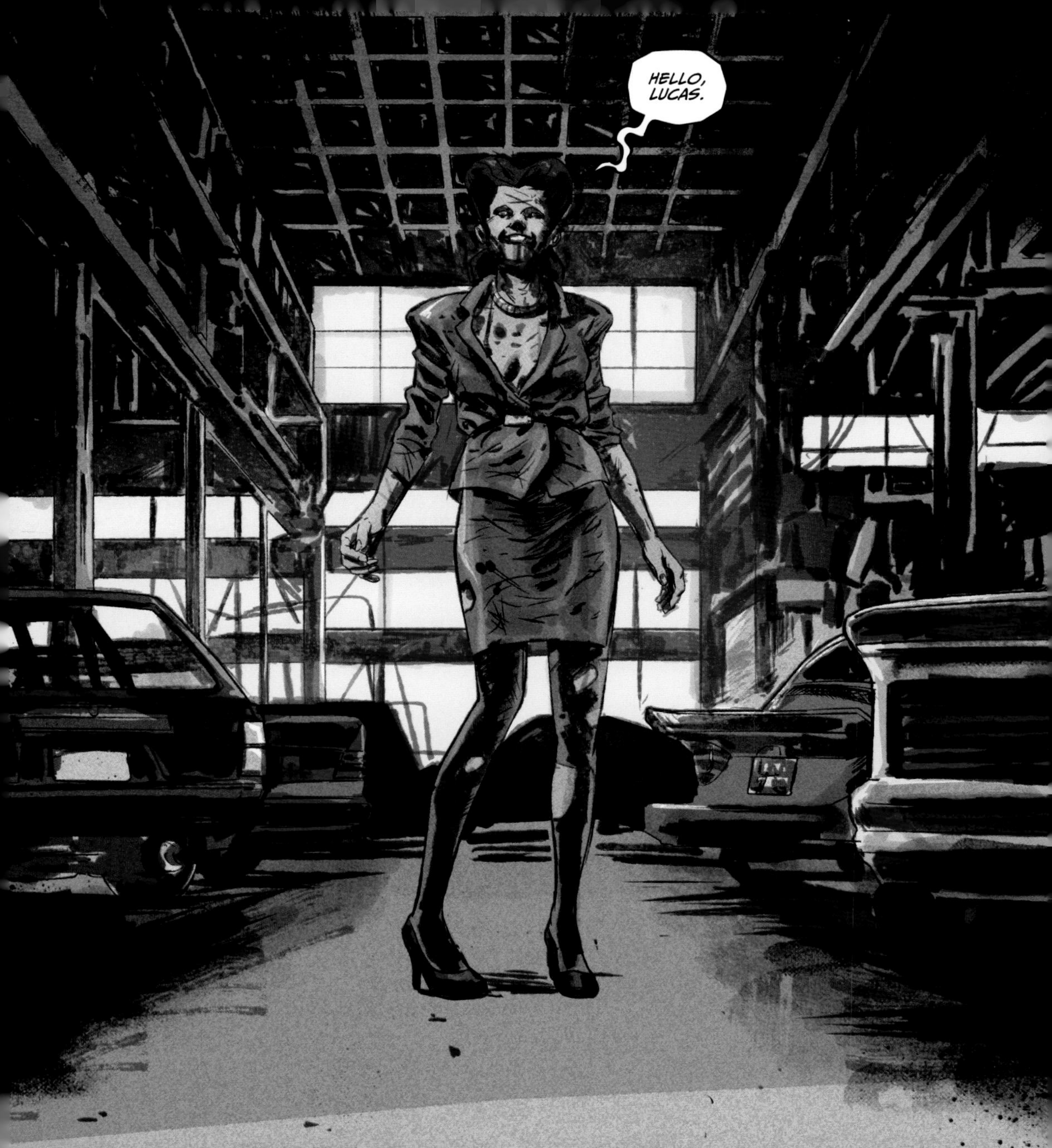
HELLO, LUCAS.

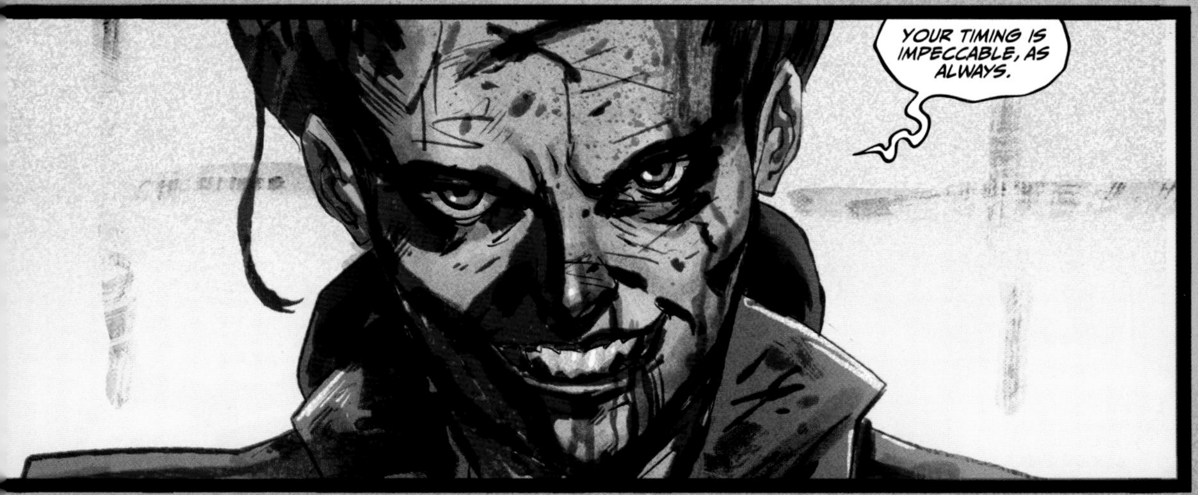
YOUR TIMING IS IMPECCABLE, AS ALWAYS.

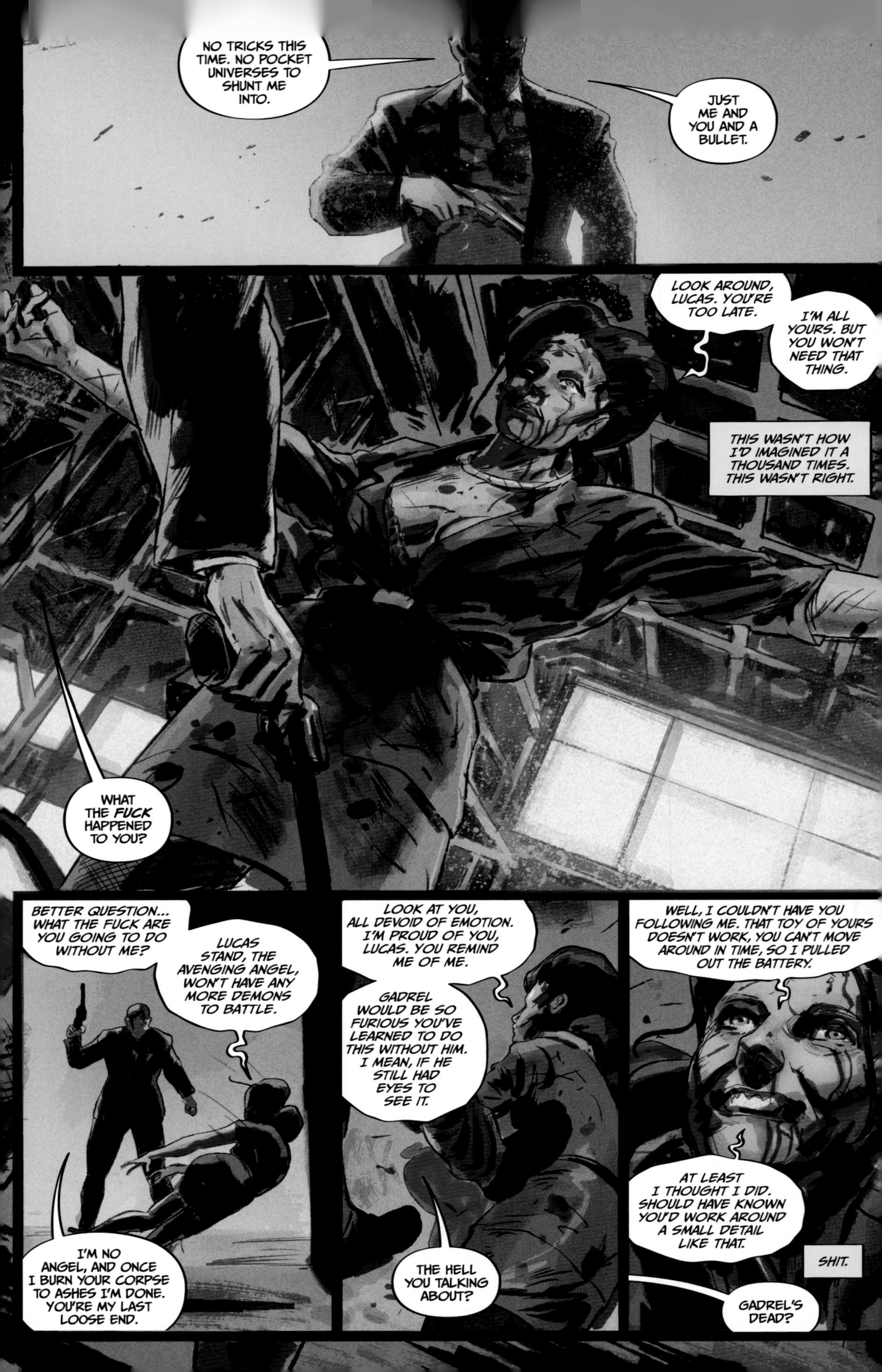

NO TRICKS THIS TIME. NO POCKET UNIVERSES TO SHUNT ME INTO.
JUST ME AND YOU AND A BULLET.
LOOK AROUND, LUCAS. YOU'RE TOO LATE.
I'M ALL YOURS. BUT YOU WON'T NEED THAT THING.
THIS WASN'T HOW I'D IMAGINED IT A THOUSAND TIMES. THIS WASN'T RIGHT.
WHAT THE FUCK HAPPENED TO YOU?
BETTER QUESTION... WHAT THE FUCK ARE YOU GOING TO DO WITHOUT ME?
LUCAS STAND, THE AVENGING ANGEL, WON'T HAVE ANY MORE DEMONS TO BATTLE.
I'M NO ANGEL, AND ONCE I BURN YOUR CORPSE TO ASHES I'M DONE. YOU'RE MY LAST LOOSE END.
LOOK AT YOU, ALL DEVOID OF EMOTION. I'M PROUD OF YOU, LUCAS. YOU REMIND ME OF ME.
GADREL WOULD BE SO FURIOUS YOU'VE LEARNED TO DO THIS WITHOUT HIM. I MEAN, IF HE STILL HAD EYES TO SEE IT.
THE HELL YOU TALKING ABOUT?
WELL, I COULDN'T HAVE YOU FOLLOWING ME. THAT TOY OF YOURS DOESN'T WORK, YOU CAN'T MOVE AROUND IN TIME, SO I PULLED OUT THE BATTERY.
AT LEAST I THOUGHT I DID. SHOULD HAVE KNOWN YOU'D WORK AROUND A SMALL DETAIL LIKE THAT.
SHIT.
GADREL'S DEAD?

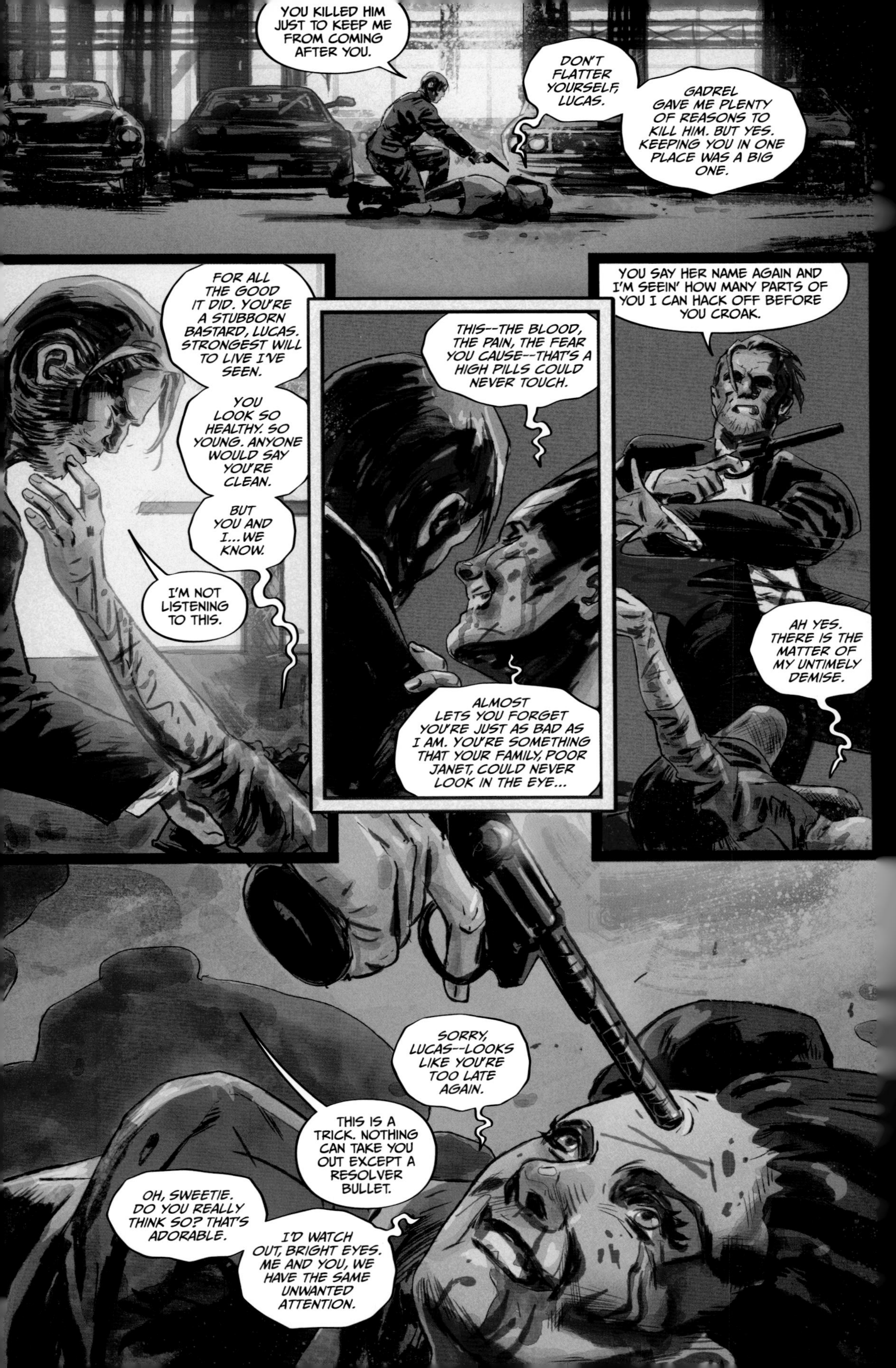
YOU KILLED HIM JUST TO KEEP ME FROM COMING AFTER YOU.
DON'T FLATTER YOURSELF, LUCAS.
GADREL GAVE ME PLENTY OF REASONS TO KILL HIM. BUT YES. KEEPING YOU IN ONE PLACE WAS A BIG ONE.
FOR ALL THE GOOD IT DID. YOU'RE A STUBBORN BASTARD, LUCAS. STRONGEST WILL TO LIVE I'VE SEEN.
YOU LOOK SO HEALTHY. SO YOUNG. ANYONE WOULD SAY YOU'RE CLEAN.
BUT YOU AND I...WE KNOW.
I'M NOT LISTENING TO THIS.
THIS--THE BLOOD, THE PAIN, THE FEAR YOU CAUSE--THAT'S A HIGH PILLS COULD NEVER TOUCH.
ALMOST LETS YOU FORGET YOU'RE JUST AS BAD AS I AM. YOU'RE SOMETHING THAT YOUR FAMILY, POOR JANET, COULD NEVER LOOK IN THE EYE...
YOU SAY HER NAME AGAIN AND I'M SEEIN' HOW MANY PARTS OF YOU I CAN HACK OFF BEFORE YOU CROAK.
AH YES. THERE IS THE MATTER OF MY UNTIMELY DEMISE.
SORRY, LUCAS--LOOKS LIKE YOU'RE TOO LATE AGAIN.
THIS IS A TRICK. NOTHING CAN TAKE YOU OUT EXCEPT A RESOLVER BULLET.
OH, SWEETIE. DO YOU REALLY THINK SO? THAT'S ADORABLE.
I'D WATCH OUT, BRIGHT EYES. ME AND YOU, WE HAVE THE SAME UNWANTED ATTENTION.

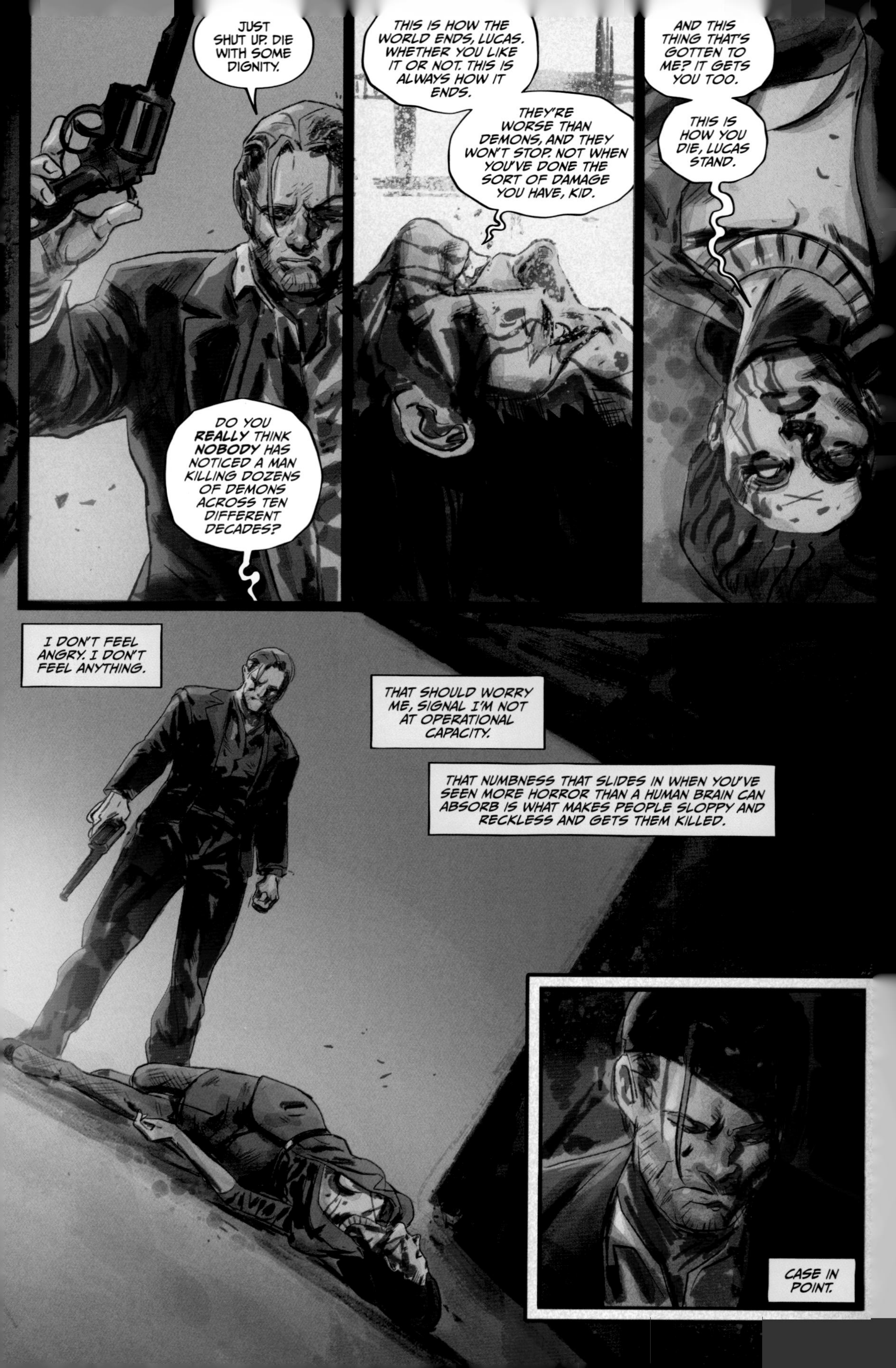
JUST SHUT UP. DIE WITH SOME DIGNITY.
DO YOU REALLY THINK NOBODY HAS NOTICED A MAN KILLING DOZENS OF DEMONS ACROSS TEN DIFFERENT DECADES?
THIS IS HOW THE WORLD ENDS, LUCAS. WHETHER YOU LIKE IT OR NOT. THIS IS ALWAYS HOW IT ENDS.
THEY'RE WORSE THAN DEMONS, AND THEY WON'T STOP. NOT WHEN YOU'VE DONE THE SORT OF DAMAGE YOU HAVE, KID.
AND THIS THING THAT'S GOTTEN TO ME? IT GETS YOU TOO.
THIS IS HOW YOU DIE, LUCAS STAND.
I DON'T FEEL ANGRY. I DON'T FEEL ANYTHING.
THAT SHOULD WORRY ME, SIGNAL I'M NOT AT OPERATIONAL CAPACITY.
THAT NUMBNESS THAT SLIDES IN WHEN YOU'VE SEEN MORE HORROR THAN A HUMAN BRAIN CAN ABSORB IS WHAT MAKES PEOPLE SLOPPY AND RECKLESS AND GETS THEM KILLED.
CASE IN POINT.

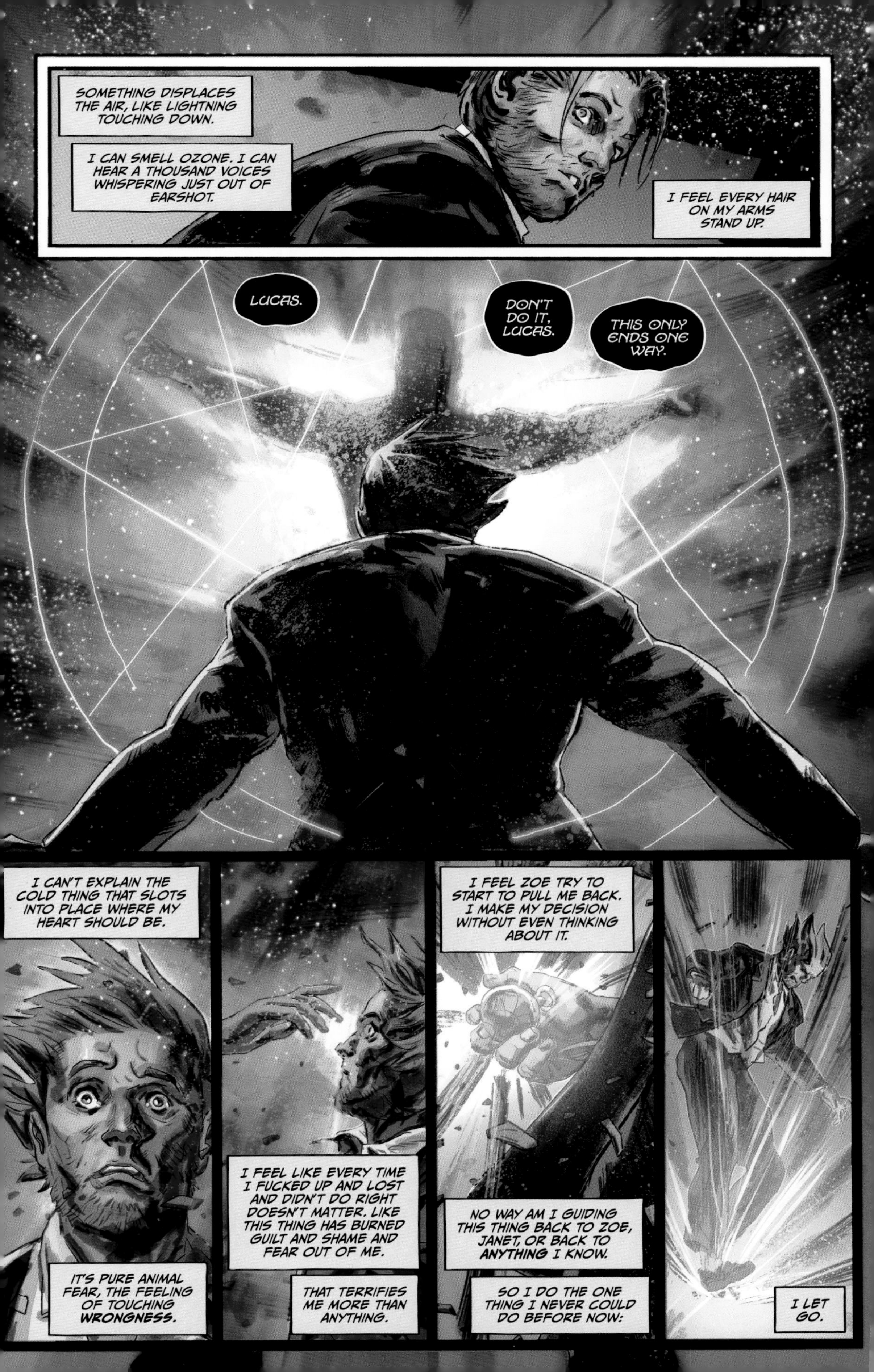
SOMETHING DISPLACES THE AIR, LIKE LIGHTNING TOUCHING DOWN.
I CAN SMELL OZONE. I CAN HEAR A THOUSAND VOICES WHISPERING JUST OUT OF EARSHOT.
I FEEL EVERY HAIR ON MY ARMS STAND UP.
LUCAS.
DON'T DO IT, LUCAS.
THIS ONLY ENDS ONE WAY.
I CAN'T EXPLAIN THE COLD THING THAT SLOTS INTO PLACE WHERE MY HEART SHOULD BE.
IT'S PURE ANIMAL FEAR, THE FEELING OF TOUCHING **WRONGNESS**.
I FEEL LIKE EVERY TIME I FUCKED UP AND LOST AND DIDN'T DO RIGHT DOESN'T MATTER. LIKE THIS THING HAS BURNED GUILT AND SHAME AND FEAR OUT OF ME.
THAT TERRIFIES ME MORE THAN ANYTHING.
I FEEL ZOE TRY TO START TO PULL ME BACK. I MAKE MY DECISION WITHOUT EVEN THINKING ABOUT IT.
NO WAY AM I GUIDING THIS THING BACK TO ZOE, JANET, OR BACK TO **ANYTHING** I KNOW.
SO I DO THE ONE THING I NEVER COULD DO BEFORE NOW:
I LET GO.

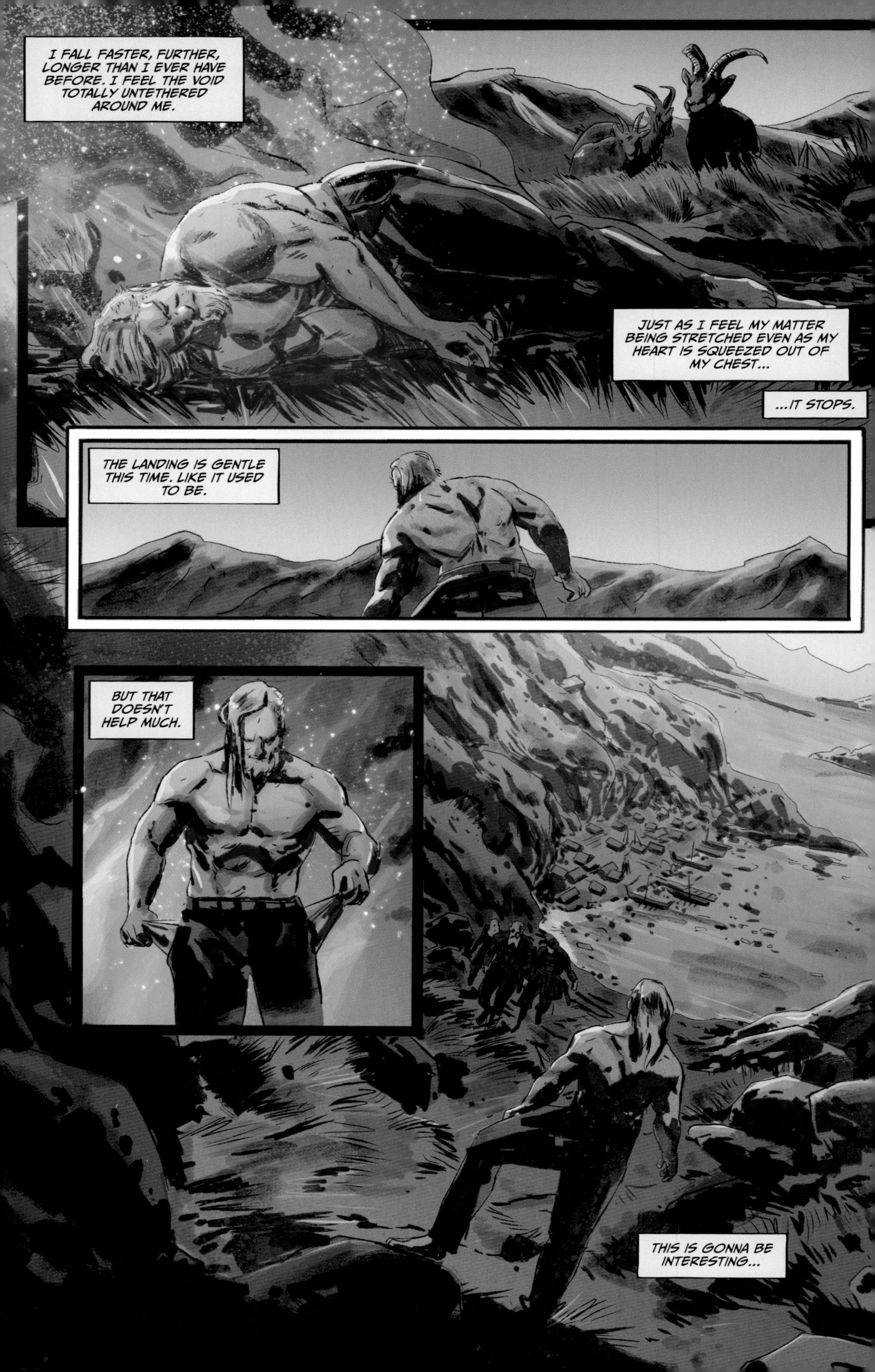
I FALL FASTER, FURTHER, LONGER THAN I EVER HAVE BEFORE. I FEEL THE VOID TOTALLY UNTETHERED AROUND ME.
JUST AS I FEEL MY MATTER BEING STRETCHED EVEN AS MY HEART IS SQUEEZED OUT OF MY CHEST...
...IT STOPS.
THE LANDING IS GENTLE THIS TIME. LIKE IT USED TO BE.
BUT THAT DOESN'T HELP MUCH.
THIS IS GONNA BE INTERESTING...

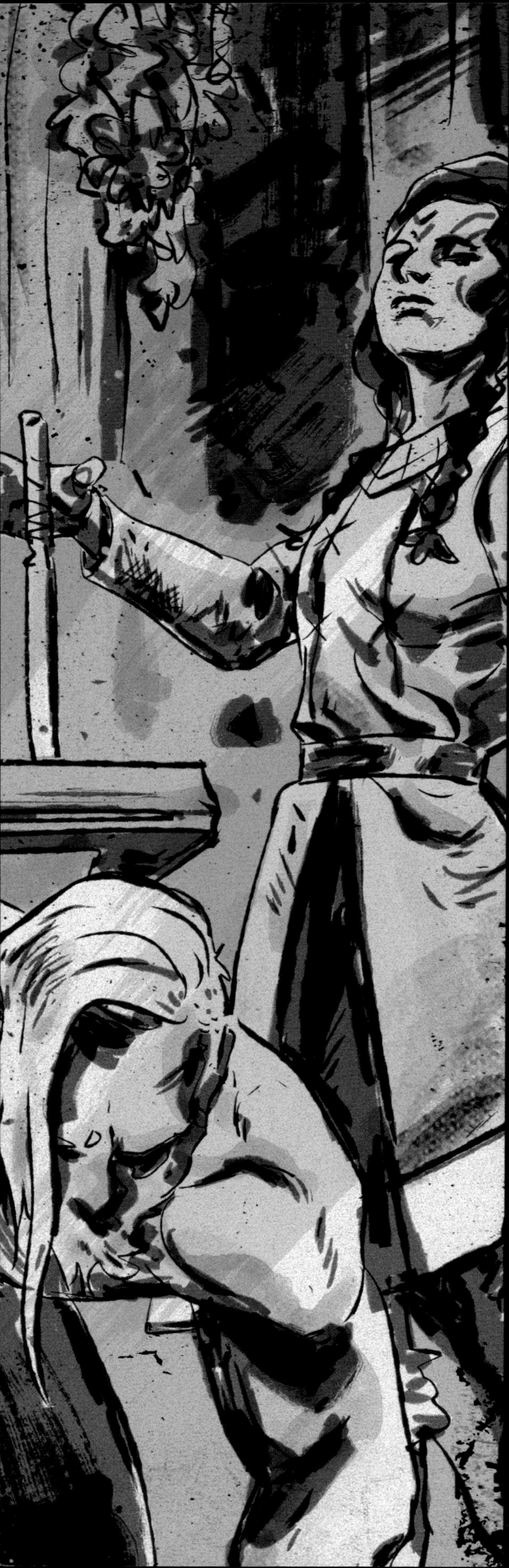

TWO

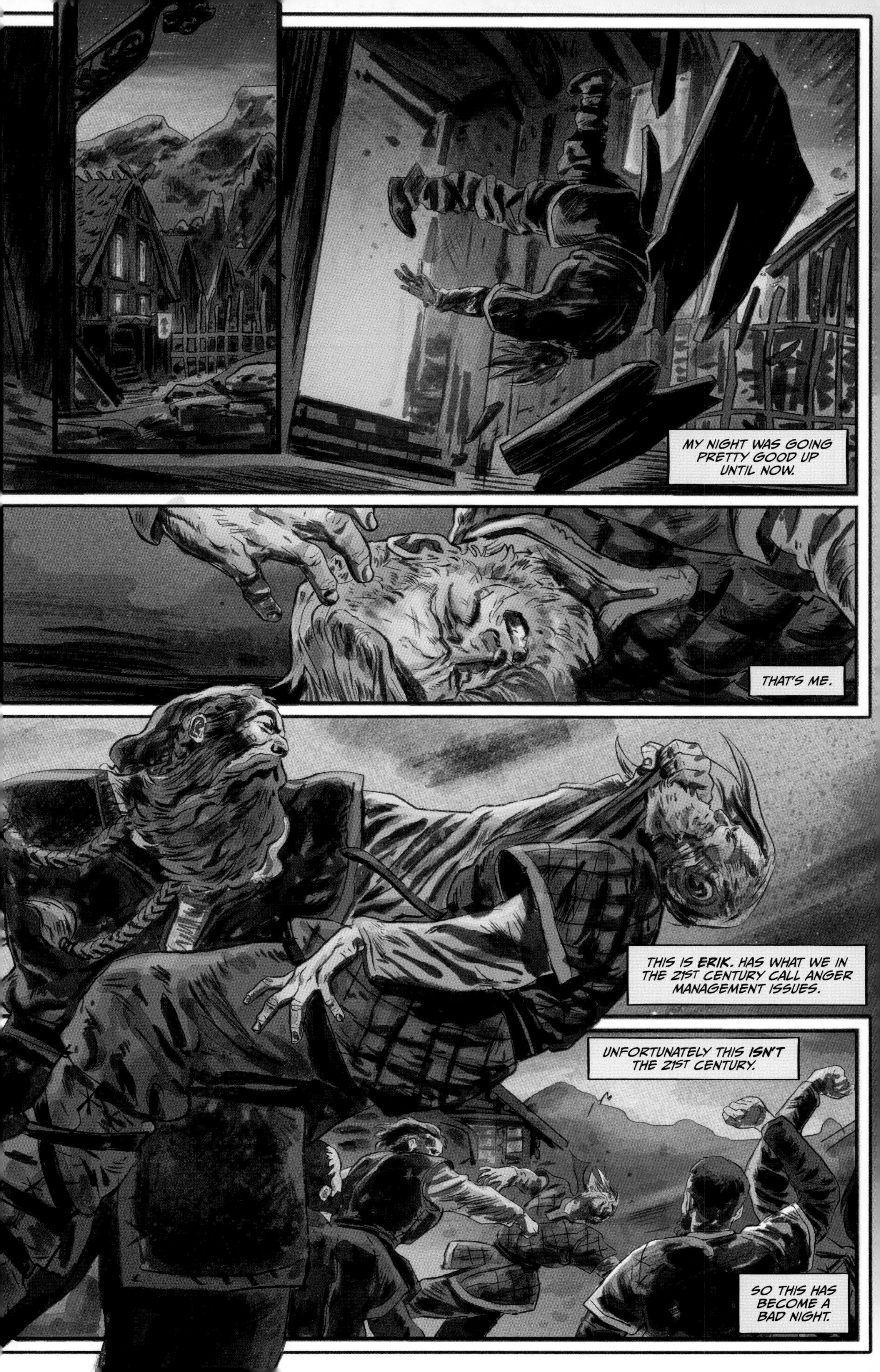
MY NIGHT WAS GOING PRETTY GOOD UP UNTIL NOW.
THAT'S ME.
THIS IS **ERIK.** HAS WHAT WE IN THE 21ST CENTURY CALL ANGER MANAGEMENT ISSUES.
UNFORTUNATELY THIS **ISN'T** THE 21ST CENTURY.
SO THIS HAS BECOME A BAD NIGHT.

ONE DAY EARLIER.

I'VE BEEN TO A LOT OF TIMES AND PLACES. THE SECOND WORLD WAR, AND THE FIRST. THE FRONTIER, HOLLYWOOD'S GOLDEN AGE.

I'VE EVEN BEEN TO MY OWN FUTURE.

BUT NEVER THIS FAR BACK.

AND NEVER WITHOUT A WAY TO GET BACK TO MY OWN TIME.

ᛟᚩᚺᚾᚱᛏᛃᛈ ᚾ ᛘᚾᚤᛈᛟᚾᚦᚺ.

OH, FOR FUCK'S SAKE...

ᛒᛚᛖᚺ ᚾᚺᚱᚱᛏᛃᛈ ᚦᛚᛃᛏ!

NOT HAPPENING, PAL. NOT REMOTELY ON THE SAME PAGE LANGUAGE-WISE.

HEY! NOT MY FAULT!

STAND DOWN!

SHNNK

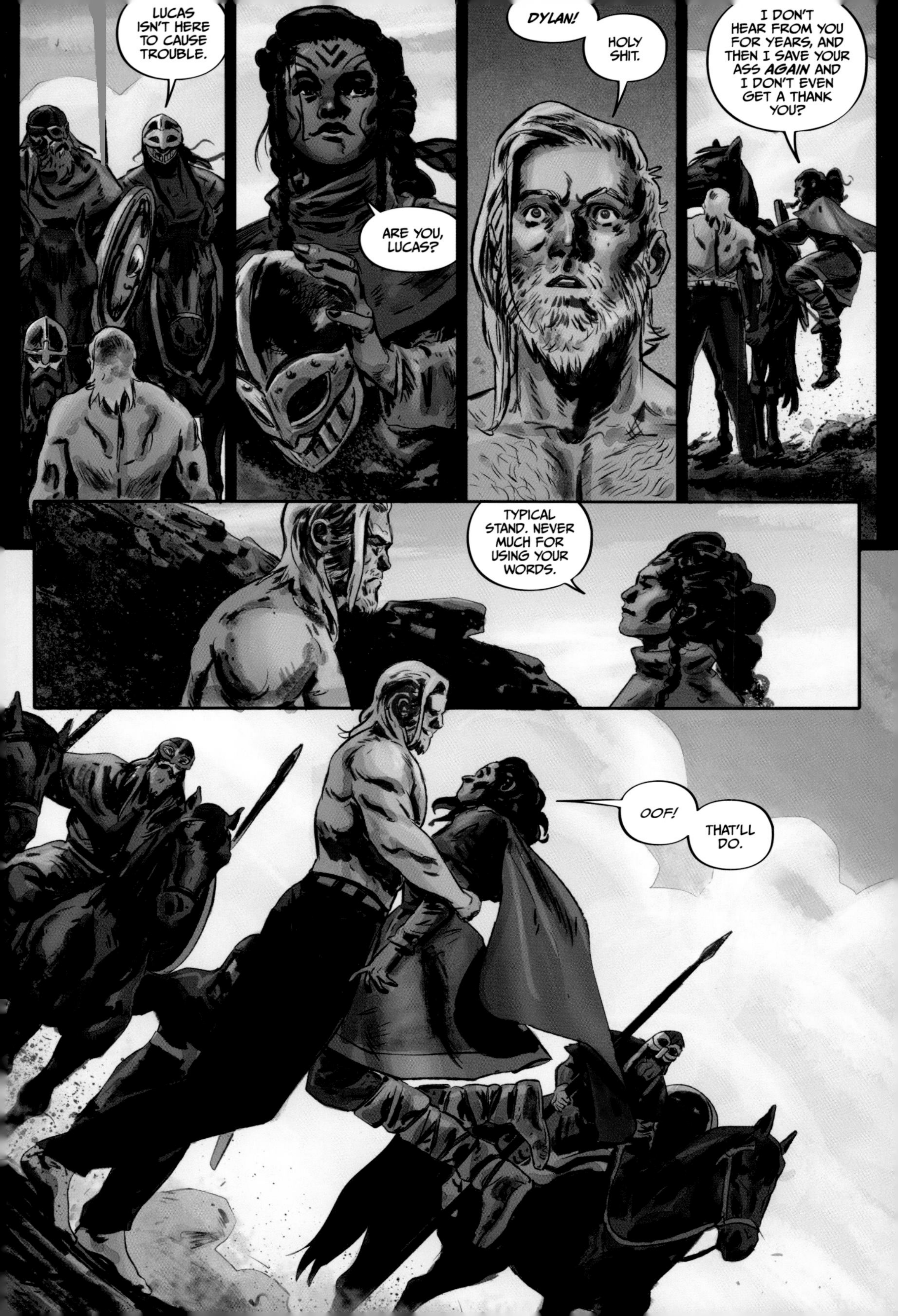
LUCAS ISN'T HERE TO CAUSE TROUBLE.
ARE YOU, LUCAS?
DYLAN!
HOLY SHIT.
I DON'T HEAR FROM YOU FOR YEARS, AND THEN I SAVE YOUR ASS *AGAIN* AND I DON'T EVEN GET A THANK YOU?
TYPICAL STAND. NEVER MUCH FOR USING YOUR WORDS.
OOF!
THAT'LL DO.

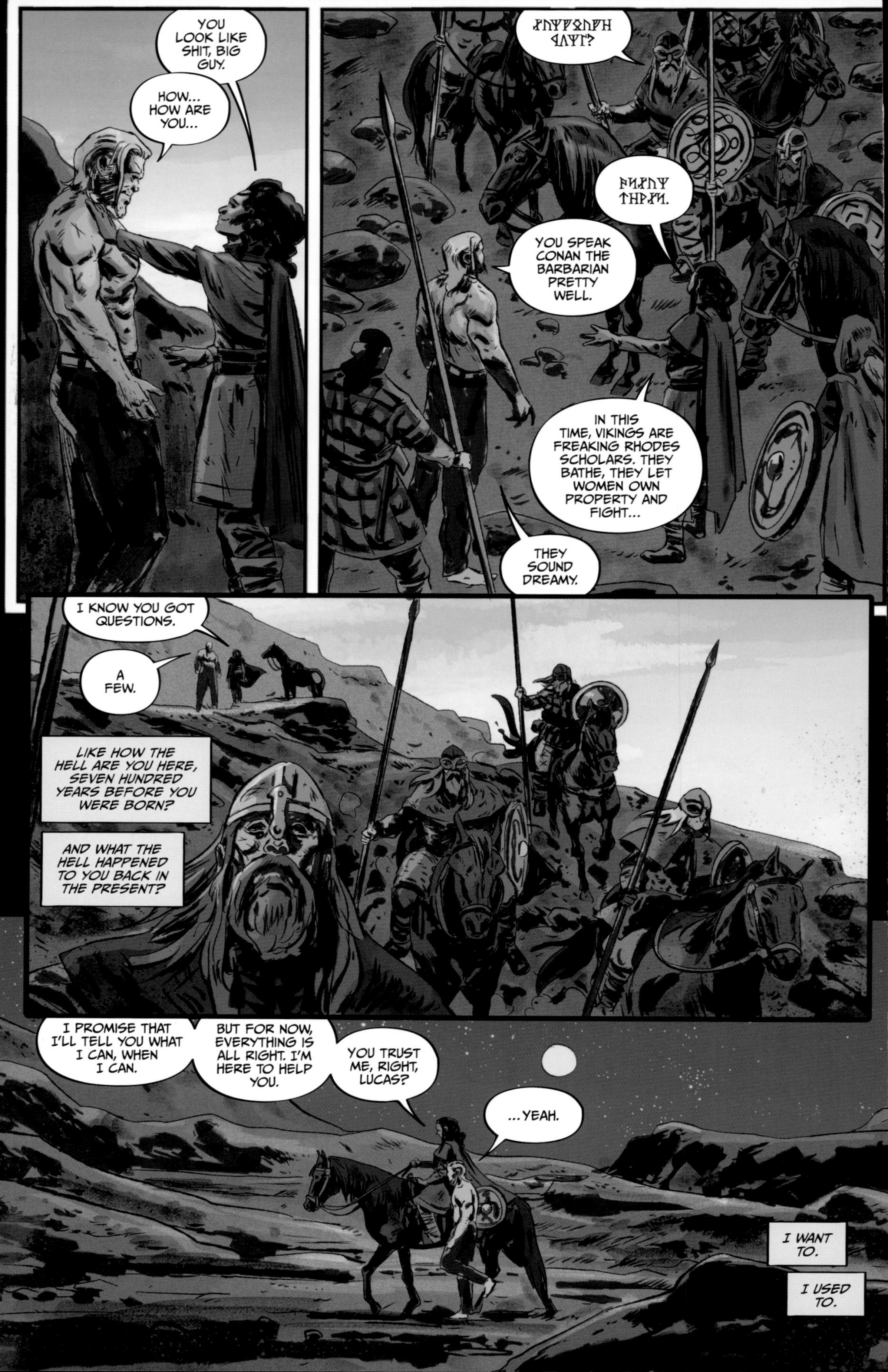
YOU LOOK LIKE SHIT, BIG GUY.
HOW... HOW ARE YOU...
YOU SPEAK CONAN THE BARBARIAN PRETTY WELL.
IN THIS TIME, VIKINGS ARE FREAKING RHODES SCHOLARS. THEY BATHE, THEY LET WOMEN OWN PROPERTY AND FIGHT...
THEY SOUND DREAMY.
I KNOW YOU GOT QUESTIONS.
A FEW.
LIKE HOW THE HELL ARE YOU HERE, SEVEN HUNDRED YEARS BEFORE YOU WERE BORN?
AND WHAT THE HELL HAPPENED TO YOU BACK IN THE PRESENT?
I PROMISE THAT I'LL TELL YOU WHAT I CAN, WHEN I CAN.
BUT FOR NOW, EVERYTHING IS ALL RIGHT. I'M HERE TO HELP YOU.
YOU TRUST ME, RIGHT, LUCAS?
...YEAH.
I WANT TO.
I USED TO.

AFGHANISTAN.

‹I KNOW YOUR FAMILY IS NO FRIEND TO THE TALIBAN.›

I'LL TELL YOU RIGHT NOW, ALL THOSE BULLSHIT 'CONCERNS' ABOUT WOMEN IN YOUR UNIT ARE JUST THAT: SHIT.

WHAT WE WAITING FOR? THEY'RE TALKIN' ABOUT WHO KNOWS WHAT SHIT AND WE COULD BE OUT KICKING DOWN DOORS.

‹IF YOU HELP US, WE'LL MAKE SURE NO HARM COMES TO YOU OR YOUR CHILDREN.›

BASICALLY, IT BOILS DOWN TO A FEW ASSHOLES WHO ARE SCARED OF GIRLS.

ANYONE ELSE, IT DOESN'T MATTER WHAT YOU'RE PACKING IN YOUR PANTS--IF YOU CAN WATCH MY ASS, I AIN'T GOT A PROBLEM WITH YOU.

BESIDES, I LIKED HER. SHE WAS SMART AND SPOKE THE LOCAL LANGUAGE AND COULD PICK A PEBBLE OFF A GOAT'S HEAD FROM FIVE HUNDRED YARDS WITH A RIFLE.

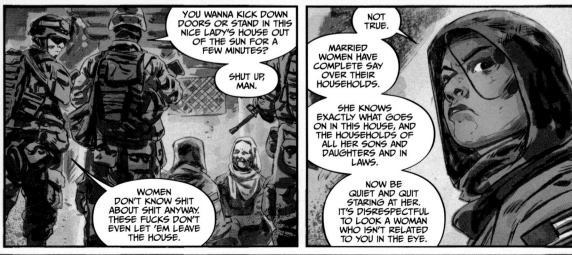

YOU WANNA KICK DOWN DOORS OR STAND IN THIS NICE LADY'S HOUSE OUT OF THE SUN FOR A FEW MINUTES?

SHUT UP, MAN.

WOMEN DON'T KNOW SHIT ABOUT SHIT ANYWAY. THESE FUCKS DON'T EVEN LET 'EM LEAVE THE HOUSE.

NOT TRUE.

MARRIED WOMEN HAVE COMPLETE SAY OVER THEIR HOUSEHOLDS.

SHE KNOWS EXACTLY WHAT GOES ON IN THIS HOUSE, AND THE HOUSEHOLDS OF ALL HER SONS AND DAUGHTERS AND IN LAWS.

NOW BE QUIET AND QUIT STARING AT HER. IT'S DISRESPECTFUL TO LOOK A WOMAN WHO ISN'T RELATED TO YOU IN THE EYE.

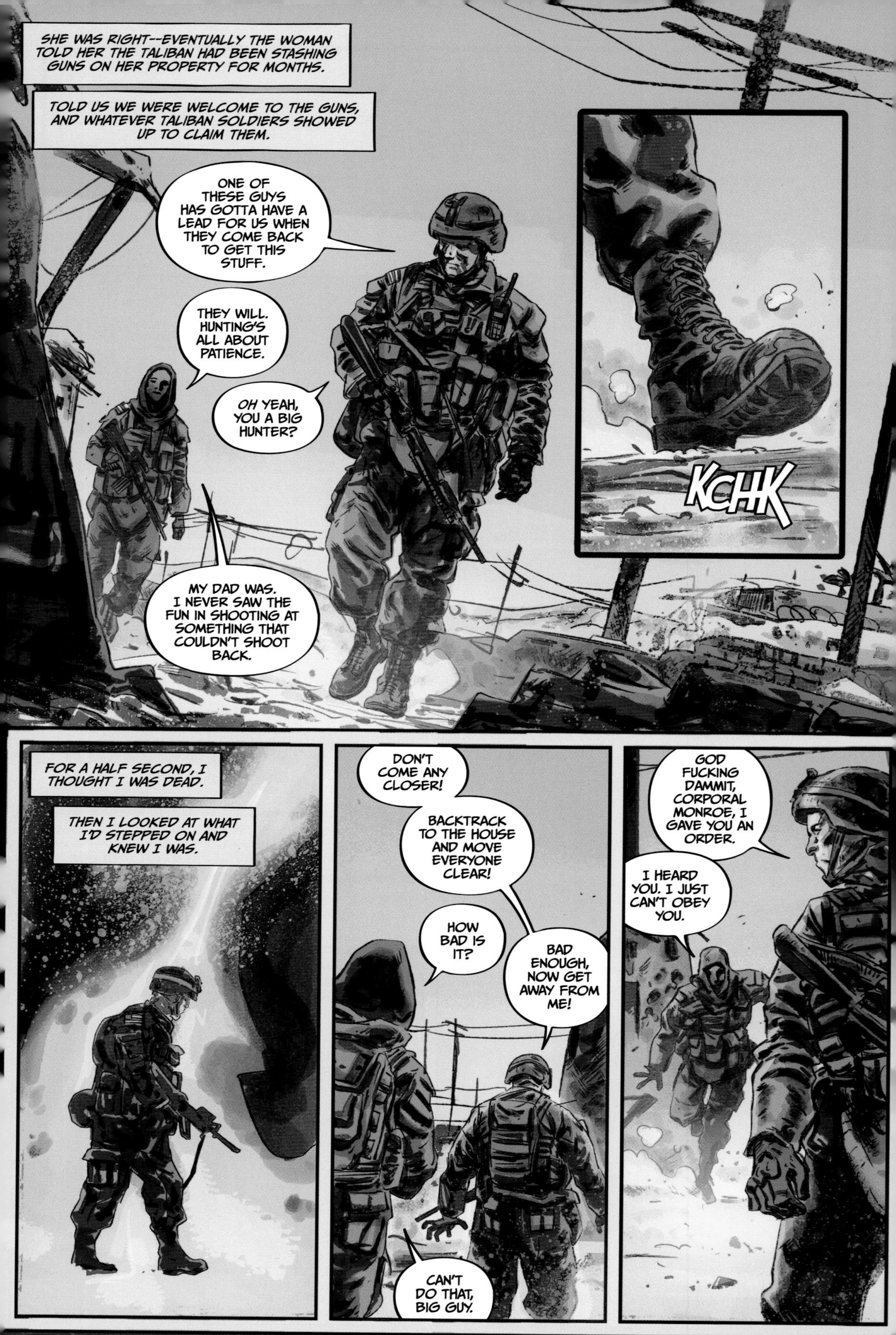
SHE WAS RIGHT--EVENTUALLY THE WOMAN TOLD HER THE TALIBAN HAD BEEN STASHING GUNS ON HER PROPERTY FOR MONTHS.
TOLD US WE WERE WELCOME TO THE GUNS, AND WHATEVER TALIBAN SOLDIERS SHOWED UP TO CLAIM THEM.
ONE OF THESE GUYS HAS GOTTA HAVE A LEAD FOR US WHEN THEY COME BACK TO GET THIS STUFF.
THEY WILL. HUNTING'S ALL ABOUT PATIENCE.
OH YEAH, YOU A BIG HUNTER?
MY DAD WAS. I NEVER SAW THE FUN IN SHOOTING AT SOMETHING THAT COULDN'T SHOOT BACK.
KCHK
FOR A HALF SECOND, I THOUGHT I WAS DEAD.
THEN I LOOKED AT WHAT I'D STEPPED ON AND KNEW I WAS.
DON'T COME ANY CLOSER!
BACKTRACK TO THE HOUSE AND MOVE EVERYONE CLEAR!
HOW BAD IS IT?
BAD ENOUGH, NOW GET AWAY FROM ME!
CAN'T DO THAT, BIG GUY.
GOD FUCKING DAMMIT, CORPORAL MONROE, I GAVE YOU AN ORDER.
I HEARD YOU. I JUST CAN'T OBEY YOU.

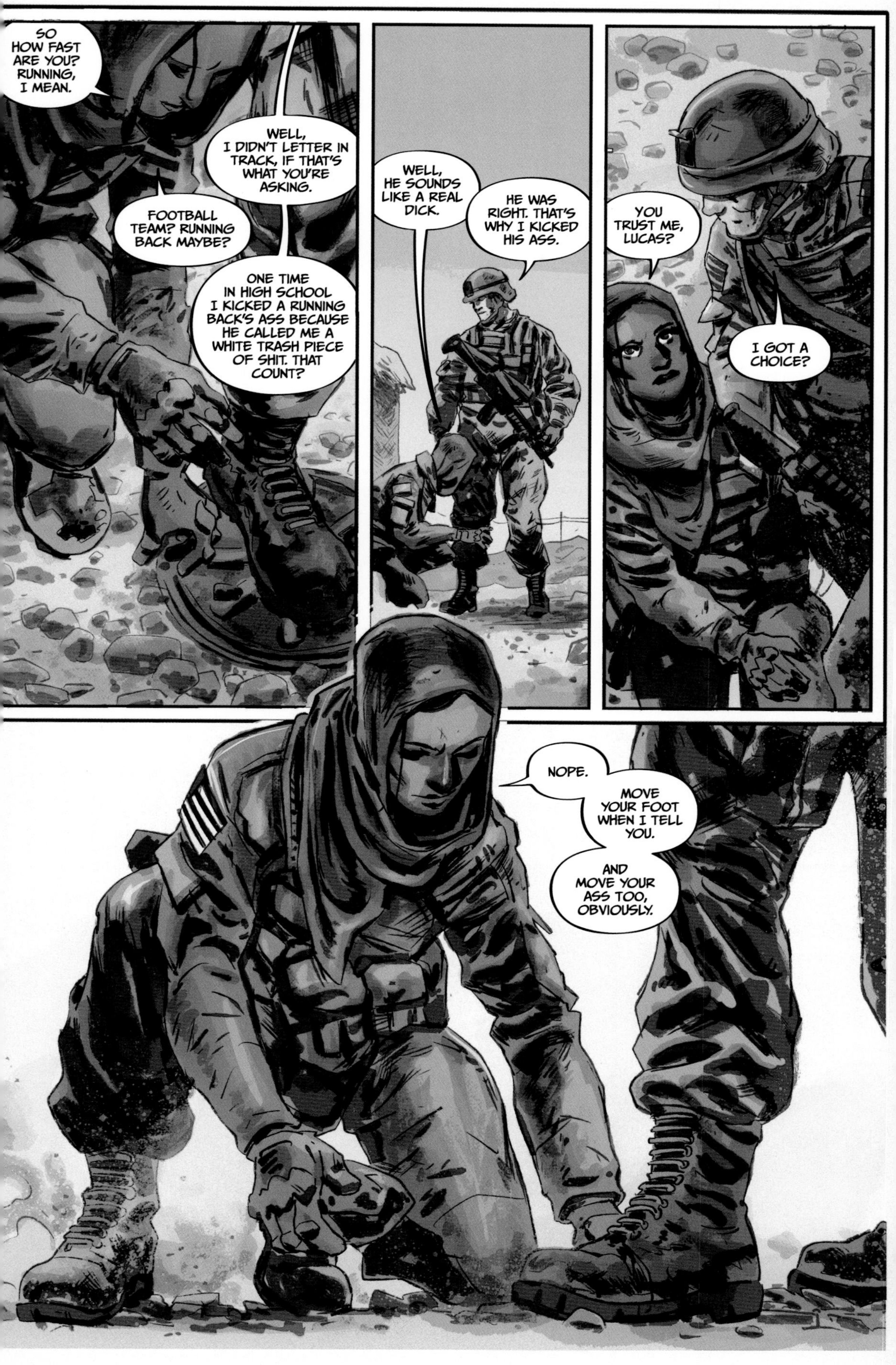
SO HOW FAST ARE YOU? RUNNING, I MEAN.
WELL, I DIDN'T LETTER IN TRACK, IF THAT'S WHAT YOU'RE ASKING.
FOOTBALL TEAM? RUNNING BACK MAYBE?
ONE TIME IN HIGH SCHOOL I KICKED A RUNNING BACK'S ASS BECAUSE HE CALLED ME A WHITE TRASH PIECE OF SHIT. THAT COUNT?
WELL, HE SOUNDS LIKE A REAL DICK.
HE WAS RIGHT. THAT'S WHY I KICKED HIS ASS.
YOU TRUST ME, LUCAS?
I GOT A CHOICE?
NOPE.
MOVE YOUR FOOT WHEN I TELL YOU.
AND MOVE YOUR ASS TOO, OBVIOUSLY.

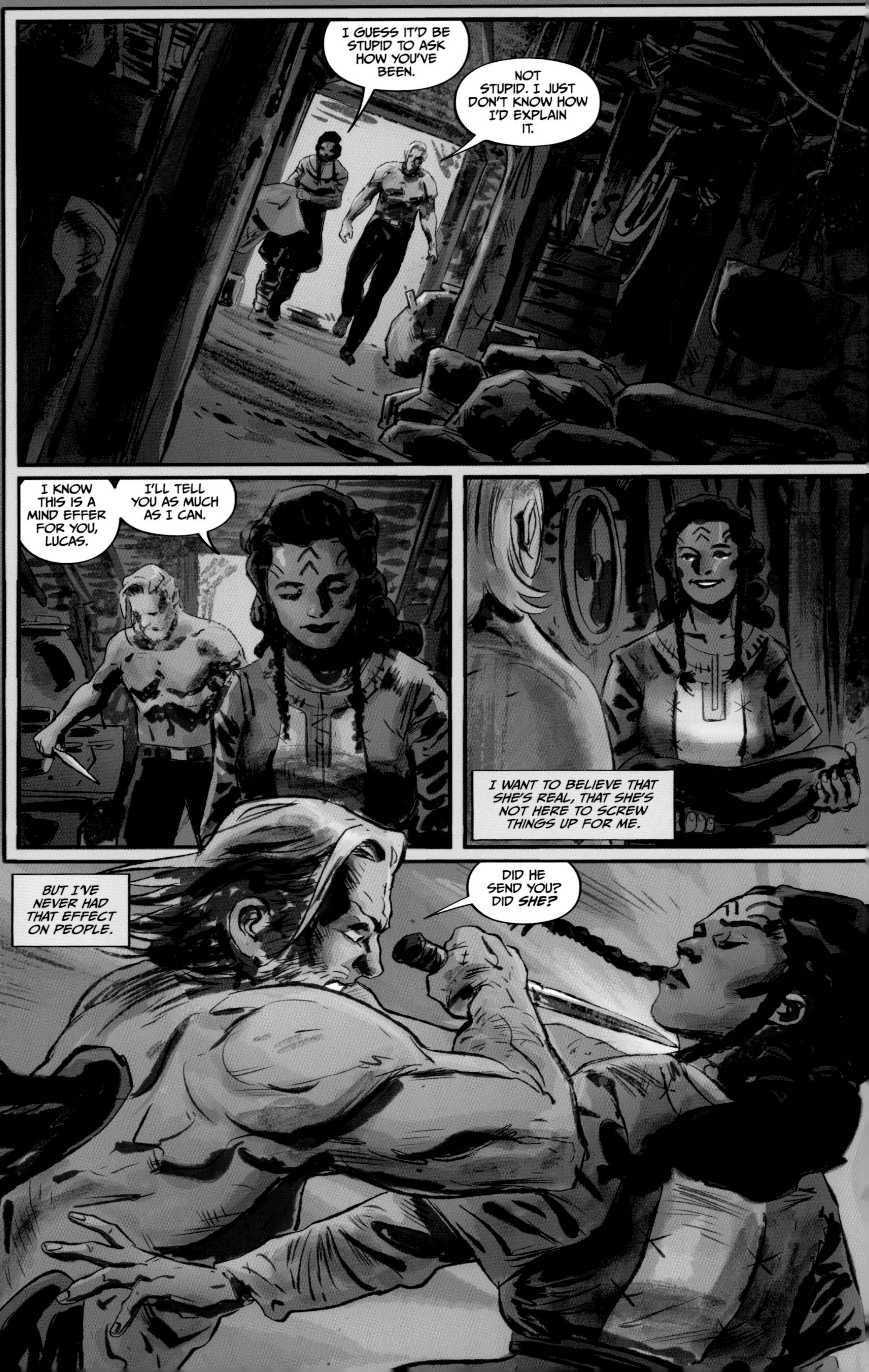
I GUESS IT'D BE STUPID TO ASK HOW YOU'VE BEEN.
NOT STUPID. I JUST DON'T KNOW HOW I'D EXPLAIN IT.
I KNOW THIS IS A MIND EFFER FOR YOU, LUCAS.
I'LL TELL YOU AS MUCH AS I CAN.
I WANT TO BELIEVE THAT SHE'S REAL, THAT SHE'S NOT HERE TO SCREW THINGS UP FOR ME.
BUT I'VE NEVER HAD THAT EFFECT ON PEOPLE.
DID HE SEND YOU? DID *SHE?*

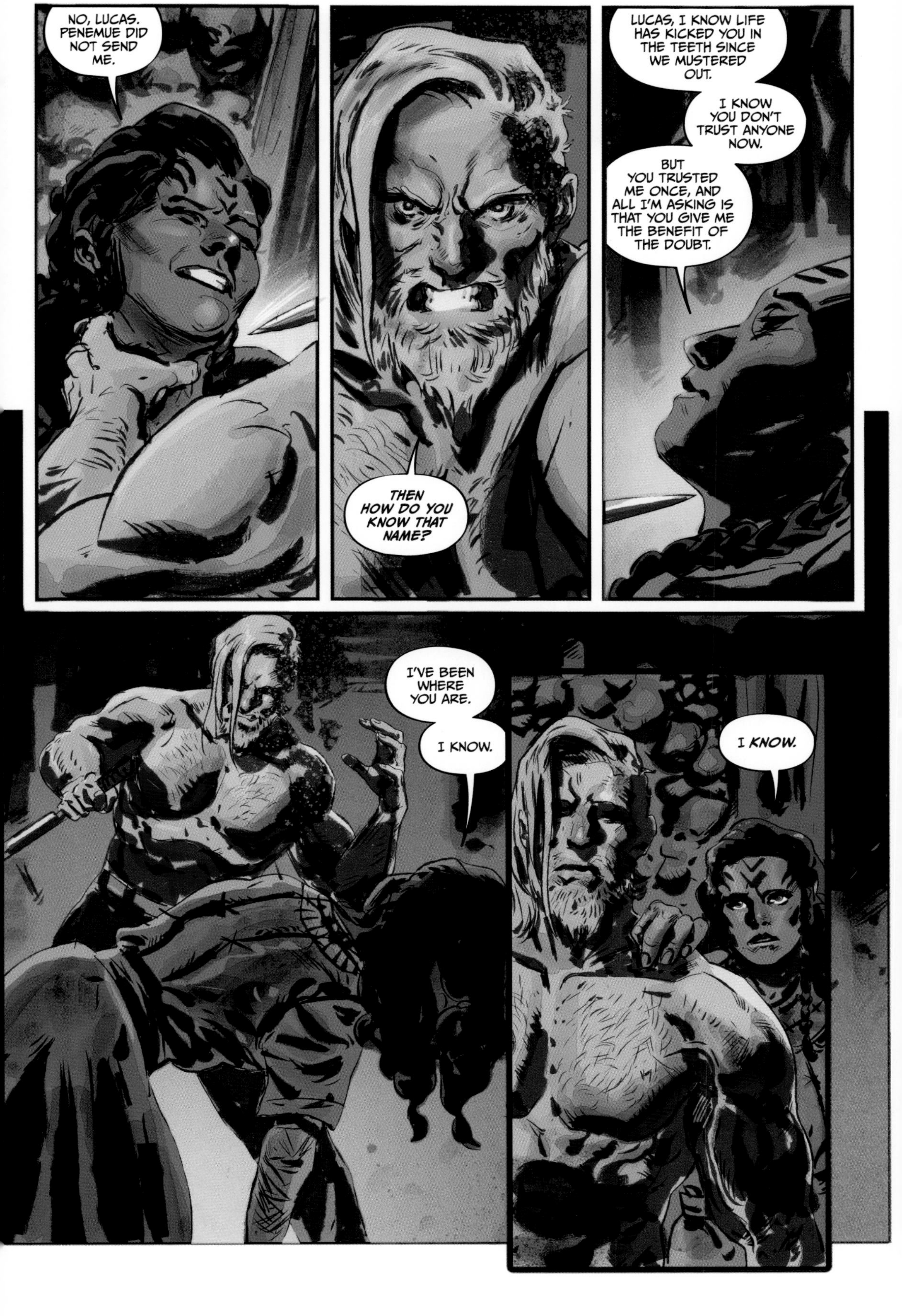NO, LUCAS. PENEMUE DID NOT SEND ME.
THEN HOW DO YOU KNOW THAT NAME?
LUCAS, I KNOW LIFE HAS KICKED YOU IN THE TEETH SINCE WE MUSTERED OUT.
I KNOW YOU DON'T TRUST ANYONE NOW.
BUT YOU TRUSTED ME ONCE, AND ALL I'M ASKING IS THAT YOU GIVE ME THE BENEFIT OF THE DOUBT.
I'VE BEEN WHERE YOU ARE.
I KNOW.
I KNOW.

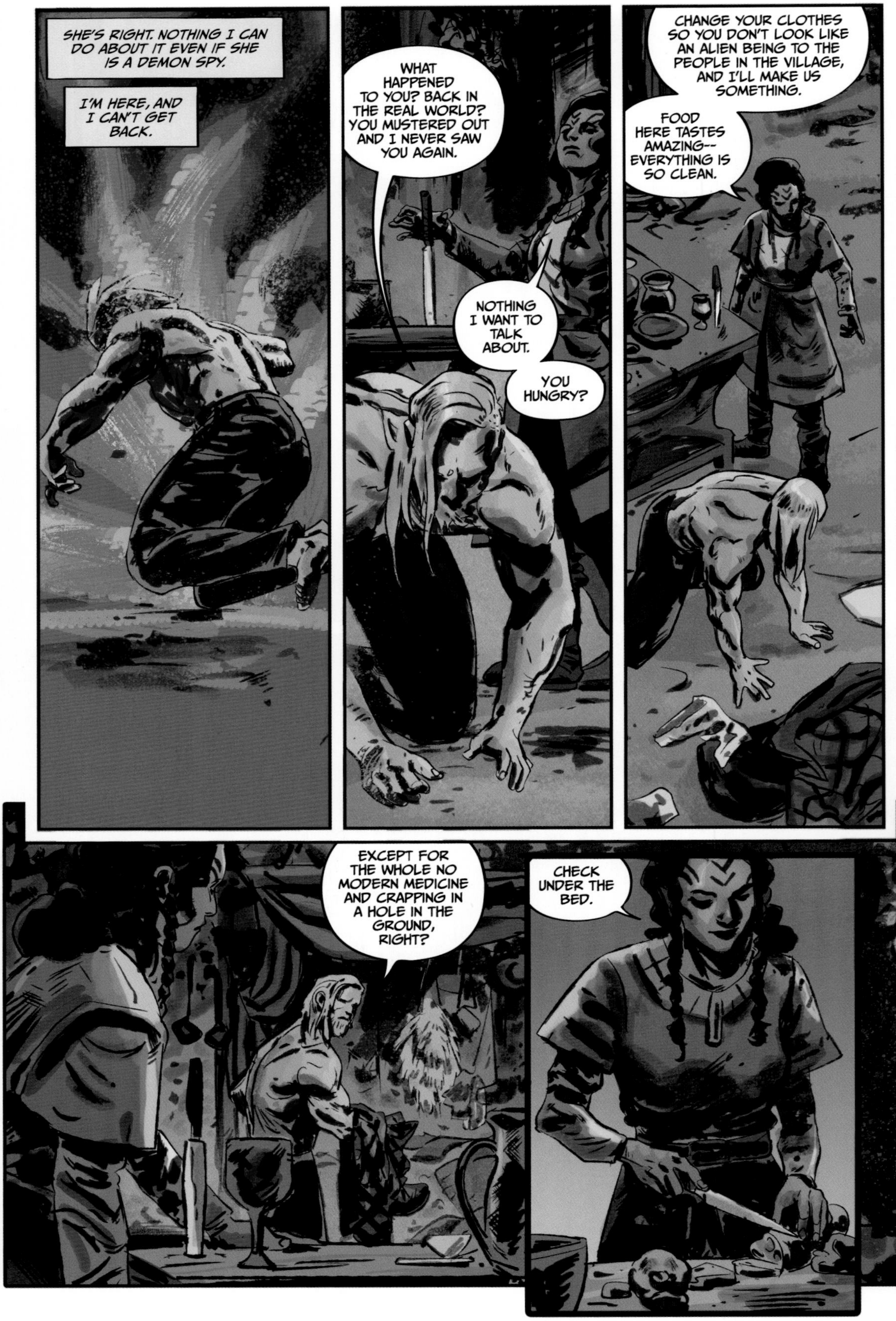

SHE'S RIGHT. NOTHING I CAN DO ABOUT IT EVEN IF SHE IS A DEMON SPY.
I'M HERE, AND I CAN'T GET BACK.
WHAT HAPPENED TO YOU? BACK IN THE REAL WORLD? YOU MUSTERED OUT AND I NEVER SAW YOU AGAIN.
NOTHING I WANT TO TALK ABOUT.
YOU HUNGRY?
CHANGE YOUR CLOTHES SO YOU DON'T LOOK LIKE AN ALIEN BEING TO THE PEOPLE IN THE VILLAGE, AND I'LL MAKE US SOMETHING.
FOOD HERE TASTES AMAZING-- EVERYTHING IS SO CLEAN.
EXCEPT FOR THE WHOLE NO MODERN MEDICINE AND CRAPPING IN A HOLE IN THE GROUND, RIGHT?
CHECK UNDER THE BED.

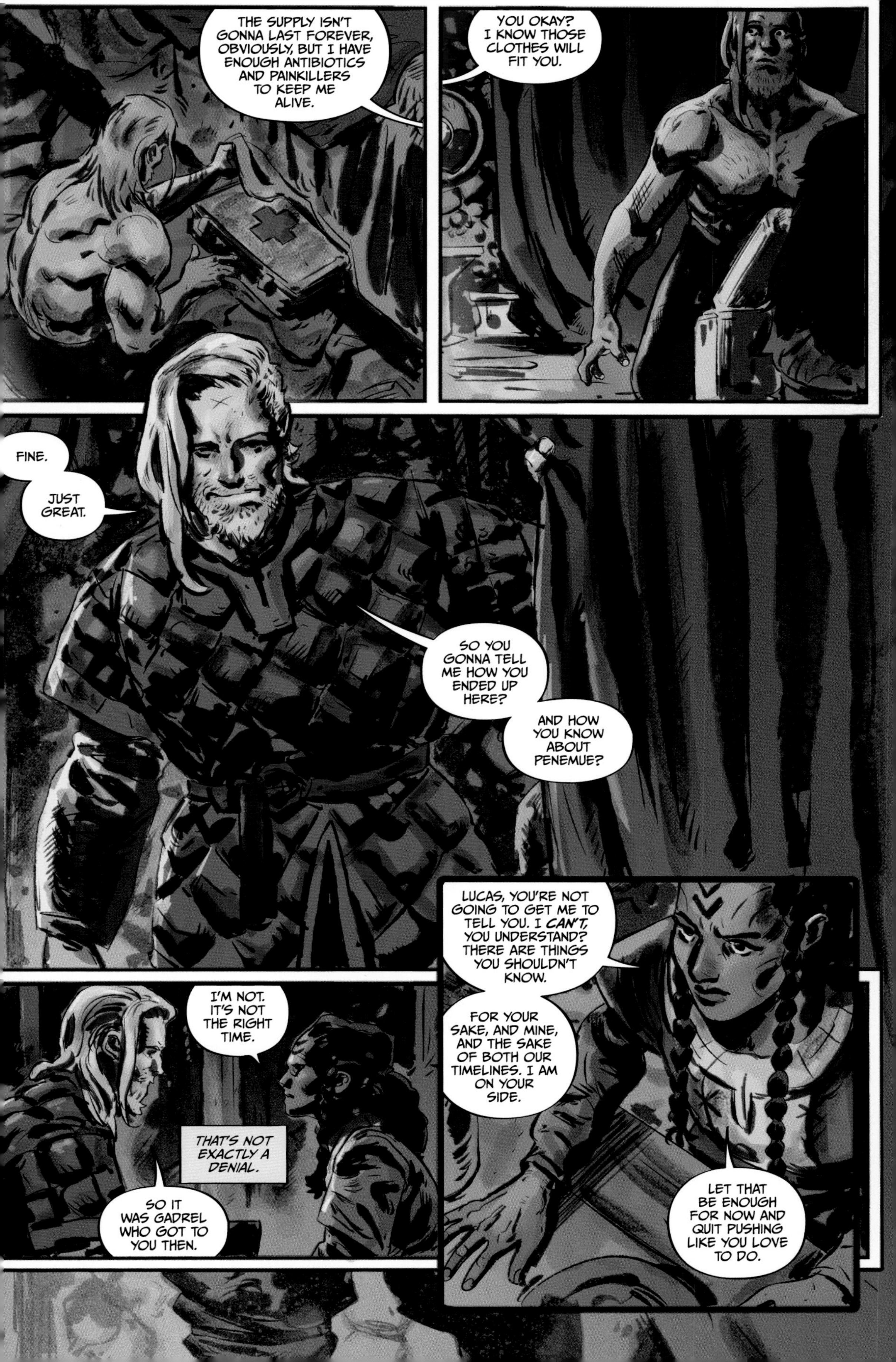
THE SUPPLY ISN'T GONNA LAST FOREVER, OBVIOUSLY, BUT I HAVE ENOUGH ANTIBIOTICS AND PAINKILLERS TO KEEP ME ALIVE.
YOU OKAY? I KNOW THOSE CLOTHES WILL FIT YOU.
FINE.
JUST GREAT.
SO YOU GONNA TELL ME HOW YOU ENDED UP HERE?
AND HOW YOU KNOW ABOUT PENEMUE?
I'M NOT. IT'S NOT THE RIGHT TIME.
THAT'S NOT EXACTLY A DENIAL.
SO IT WAS GADREL WHO GOT TO YOU THEN.
LUCAS, YOU'RE NOT GOING TO GET ME TO TELL YOU. I CAN'T, YOU UNDERSTAND? THERE ARE THINGS YOU SHOULDN'T KNOW.
FOR YOUR SAKE, AND MINE, AND THE SAKE OF BOTH OUR TIMELINES. I AM ON YOUR SIDE.
LET THAT BE ENOUGH FOR NOW AND QUIT PUSHING LIKE YOU LOVE TO DO.

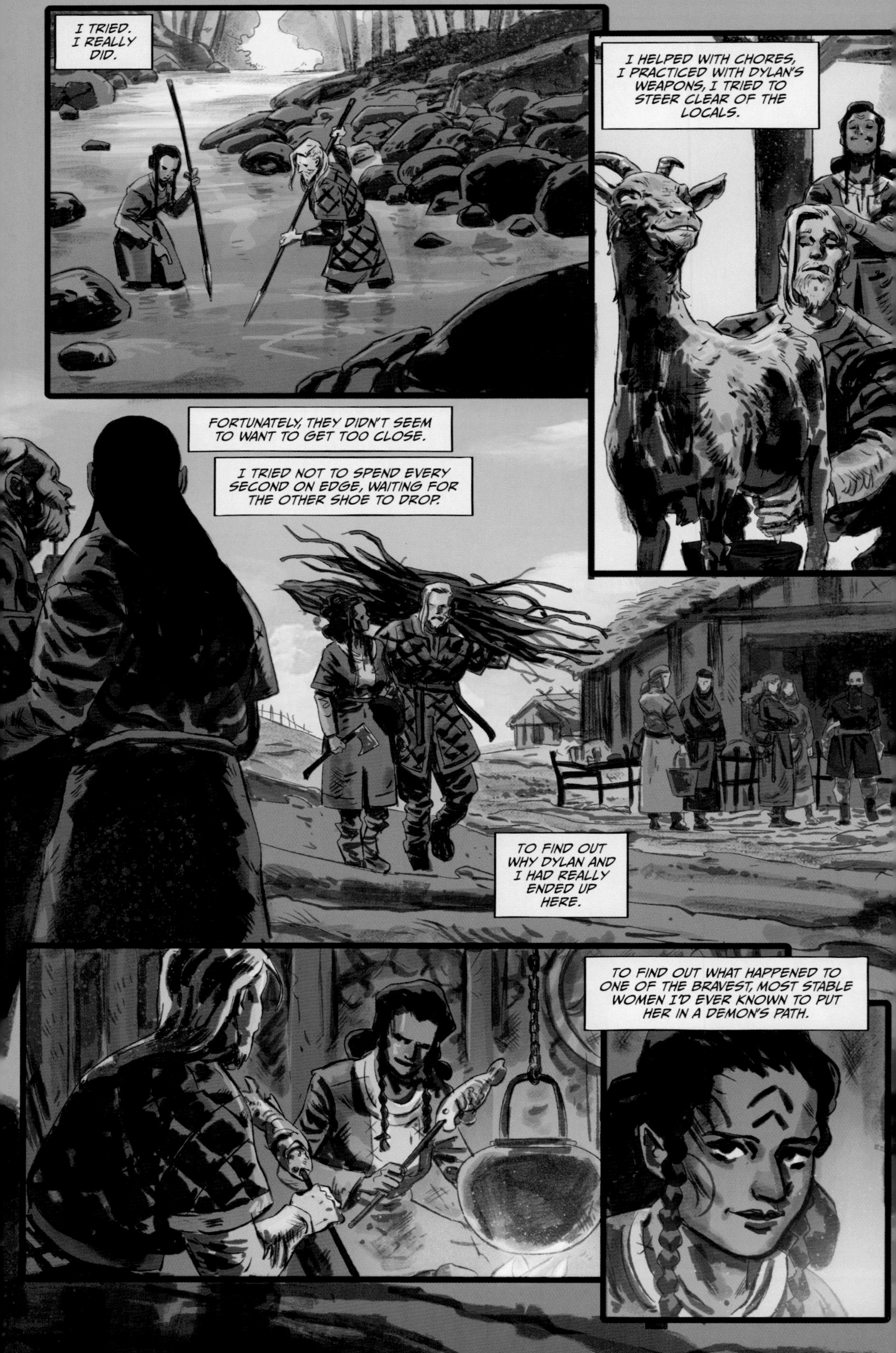
I TRIED. I REALLY DID.
I HELPED WITH CHORES, I PRACTICED WITH DYLAN'S WEAPONS, I TRIED TO STEER CLEAR OF THE LOCALS.
FORTUNATELY, THEY DIDN'T SEEM TO WANT TO GET TOO CLOSE.
I TRIED NOT TO SPEND EVERY SECOND ON EDGE, WAITING FOR THE OTHER SHOE TO DROP.
TO FIND OUT WHY DYLAN AND I HAD REALLY ENDED UP HERE.
TO FIND OUT WHAT HAPPENED TO ONE OF THE BRAVEST, MOST STABLE WOMEN I'D EVER KNOWN TO PUT HER IN A DEMON'S PATH.

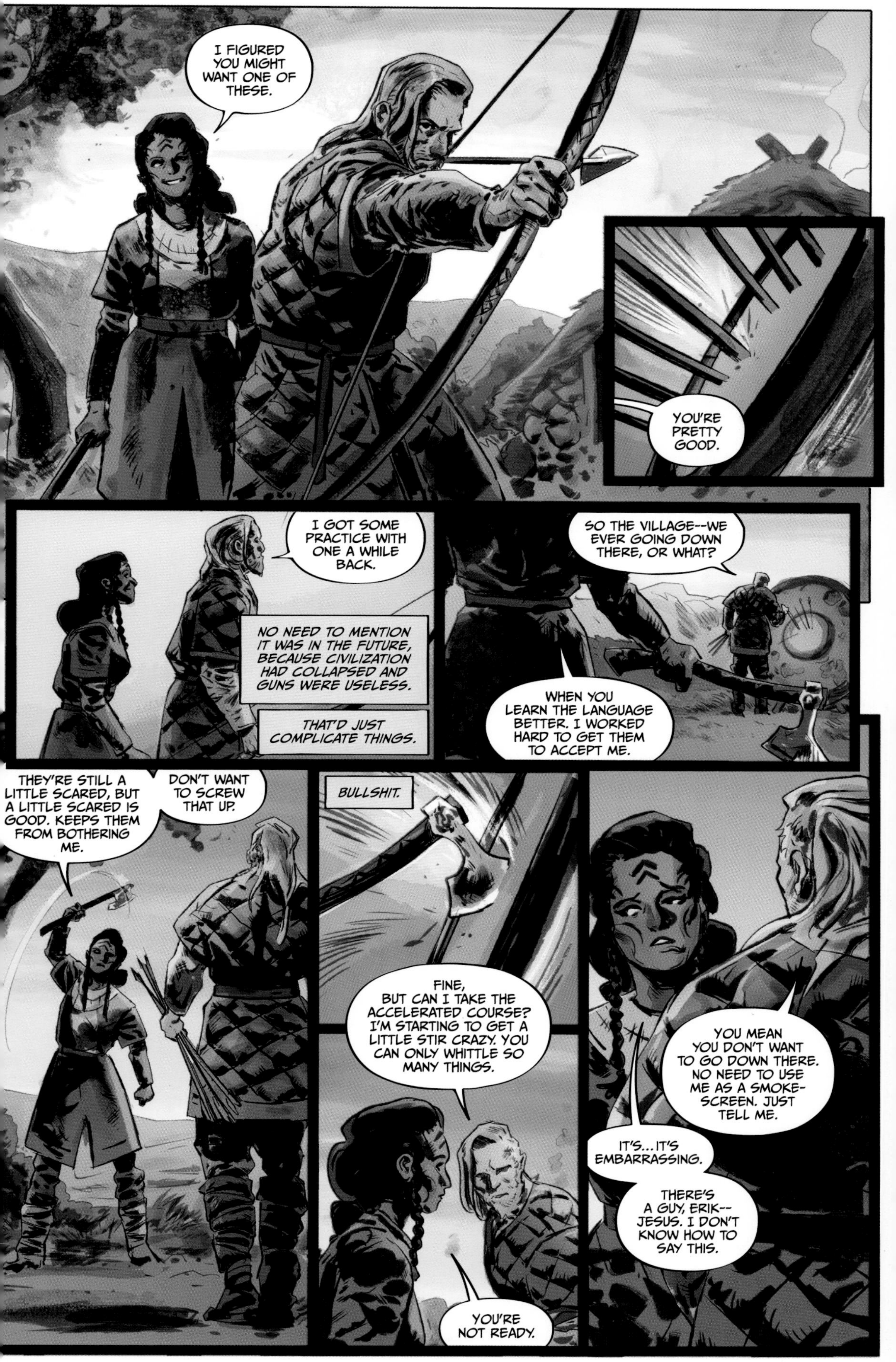
I FIGURED YOU MIGHT WANT ONE OF THESE.
YOU'RE PRETTY GOOD.
I GOT SOME PRACTICE WITH ONE A WHILE BACK.
NO NEED TO MENTION IT WAS IN THE FUTURE, BECAUSE CIVILIZATION HAD COLLAPSED AND GUNS WERE USELESS.
THAT'D JUST COMPLICATE THINGS.
SO THE VILLAGE--WE EVER GOING DOWN THERE, OR WHAT?
WHEN YOU LEARN THE LANGUAGE BETTER. I WORKED HARD TO GET THEM TO ACCEPT ME.
THEY'RE STILL A LITTLE SCARED, BUT A LITTLE SCARED IS GOOD. KEEPS THEM FROM BOTHERING ME.
DON'T WANT TO SCREW THAT UP.
BULLSHIT.
FINE, BUT CAN I TAKE THE ACCELERATED COURSE? I'M STARTING TO GET A LITTLE STIR CRAZY. YOU CAN ONLY WHITTLE SO MANY THINGS.
YOU'RE NOT READY.
YOU MEAN YOU DON'T WANT TO GO DOWN THERE. NO NEED TO USE ME AS A SMOKE-SCREEN. JUST TELL ME.
IT'S... IT'S EMBARRASSING.
THERE'S A GUY, ERIK-- JESUS. I DON'T KNOW HOW TO SAY THIS.

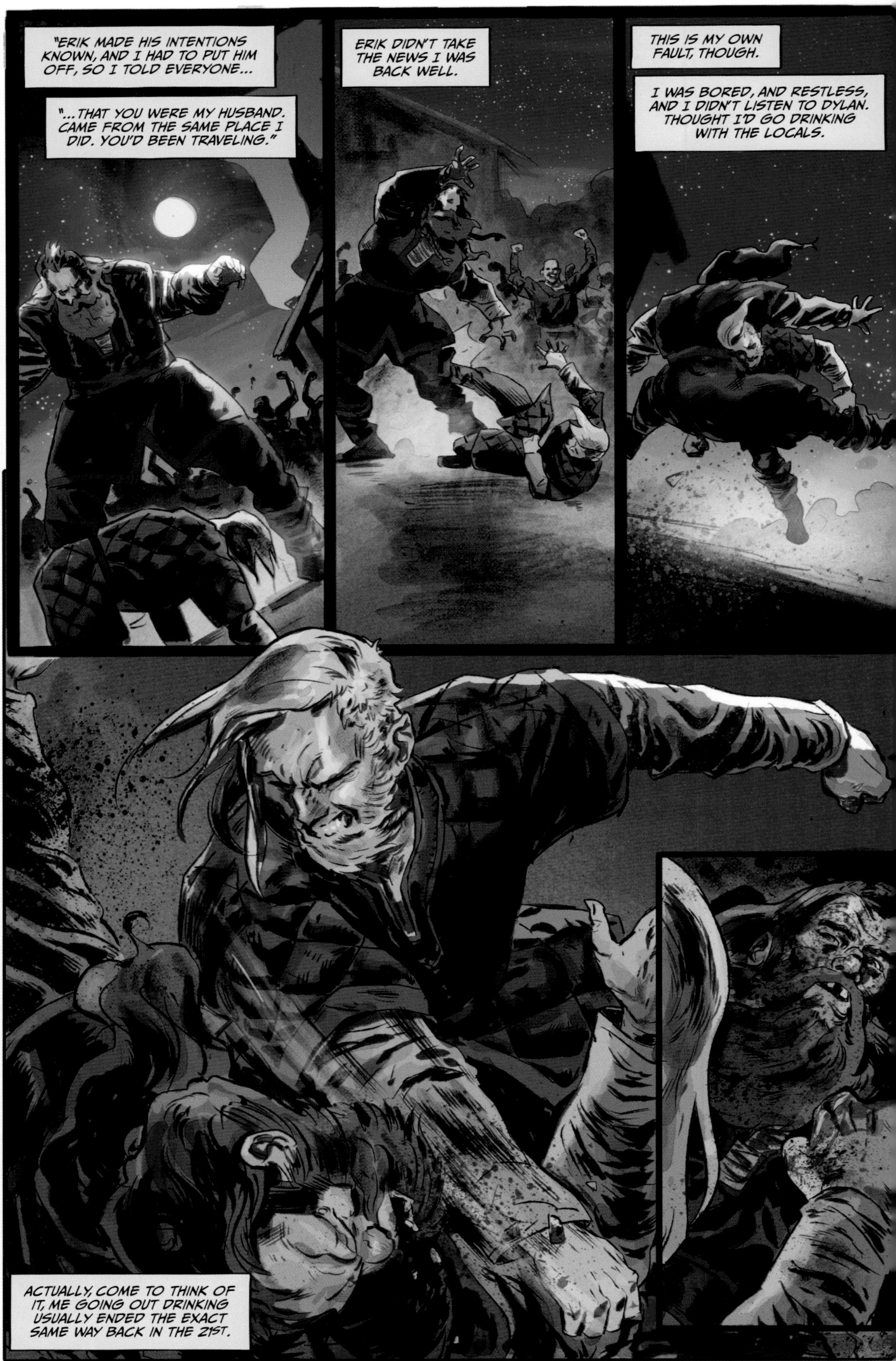
"ERIK MADE HIS INTENTIONS KNOWN, AND I HAD TO PUT HIM OFF, SO I TOLD EVERYONE...
"...THAT YOU WERE MY HUSBAND. CAME FROM THE SAME PLACE I DID. YOU'D BEEN TRAVELING."
ERIK DIDN'T TAKE THE NEWS I WAS BACK WELL.
THIS IS MY OWN FAULT, THOUGH.
I WAS BORED, AND RESTLESS, AND I DIDN'T LISTEN TO DYLAN. THOUGHT I'D GO DRINKING WITH THE LOCALS.
ACTUALLY, COME TO THINK OF IT, ME GOING OUT DRINKING USUALLY ENDED THE EXACT SAME WAY BACK IN THE 21ST.

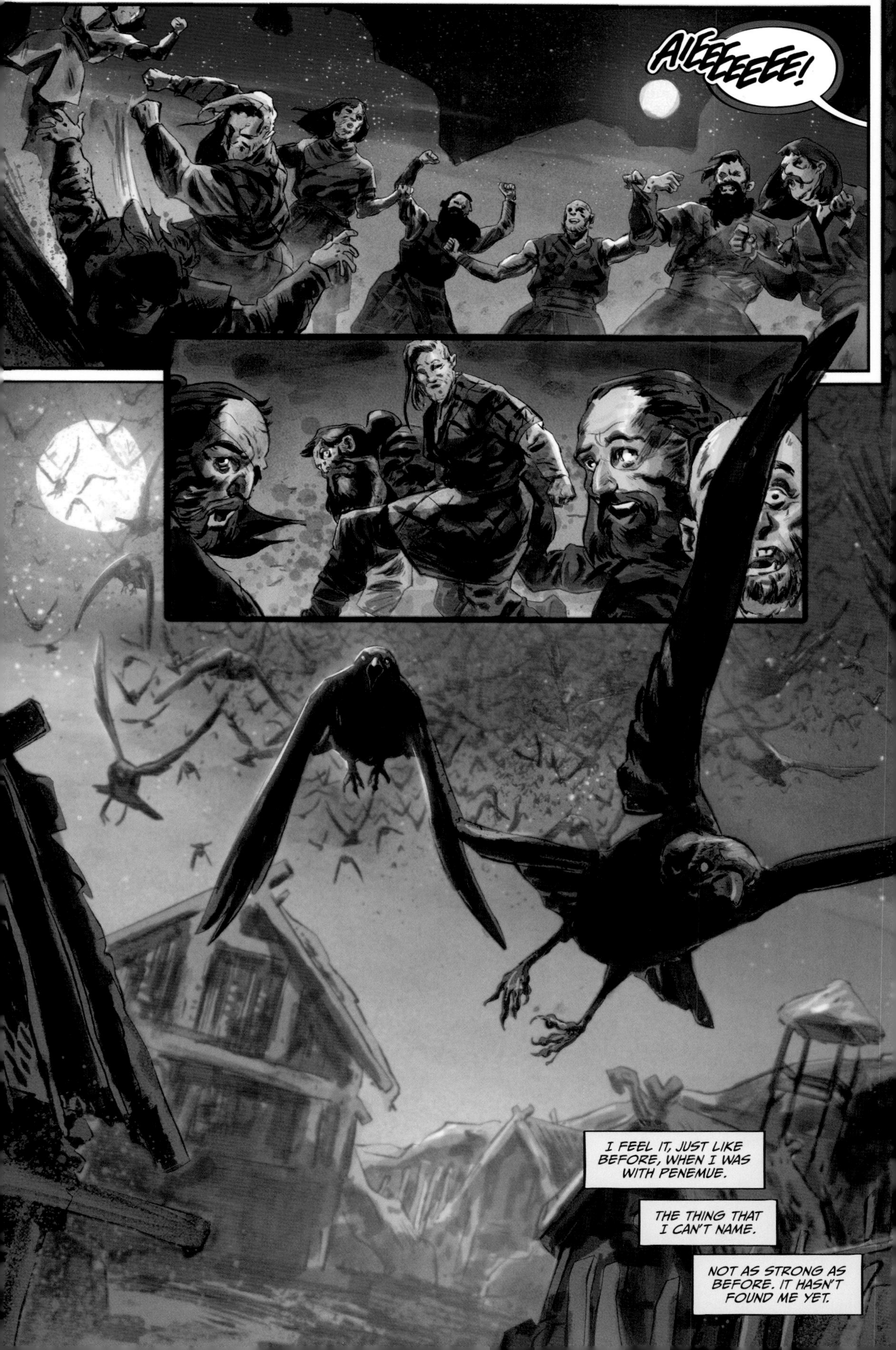
AIEEEEEEEEE!
I FEEL IT, JUST LIKE BEFORE, WHEN I WAS WITH PENEMUE.
THE THING THAT I CAN'T NAME.
NOT AS STRONG AS BEFORE. IT HASN'T FOUND ME YET.

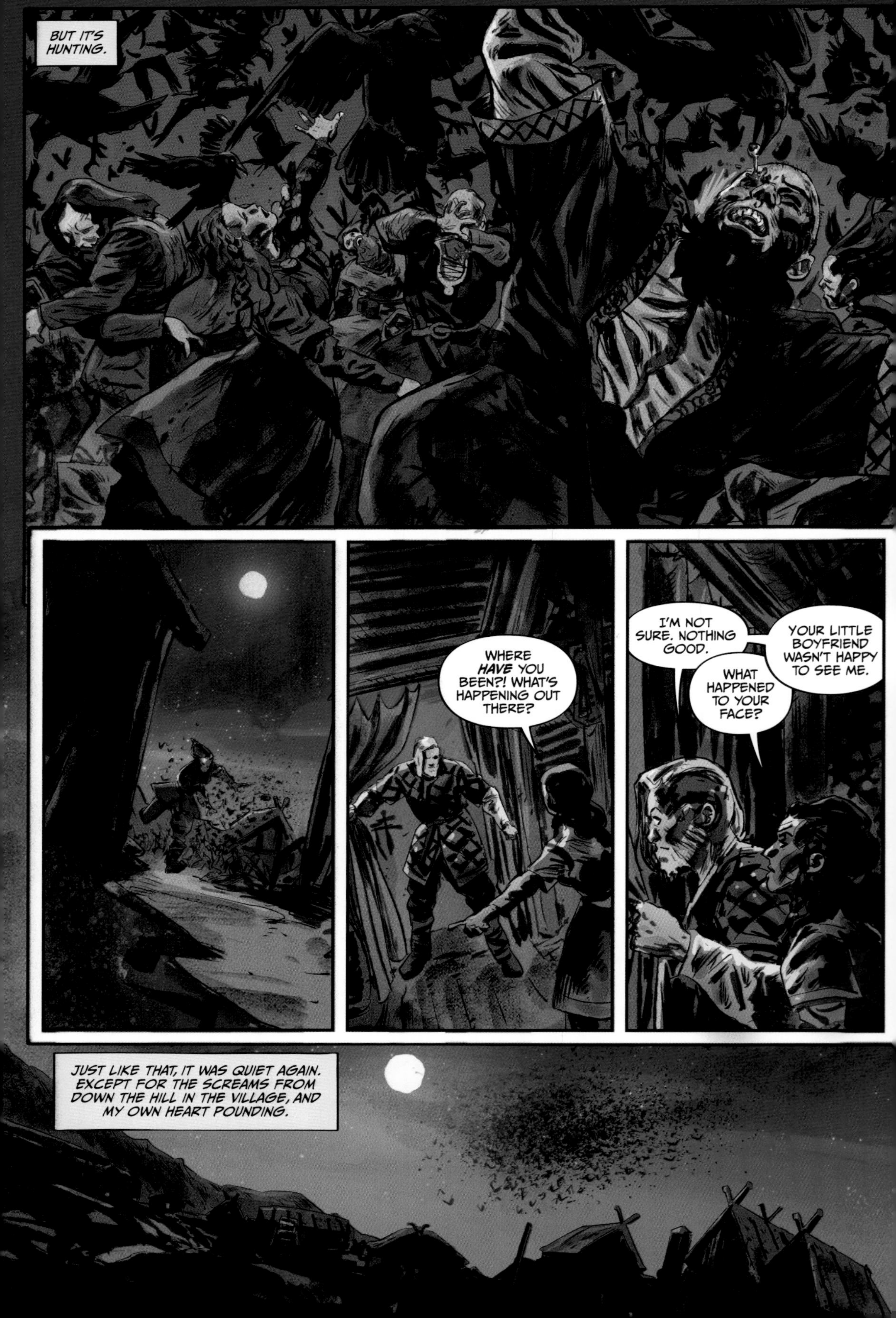
BUT IT'S HUNTING.
WHERE HAVE YOU BEEN?! WHAT'S HAPPENING OUT THERE?
I'M NOT SURE. NOTHING GOOD.
WHAT HAPPENED TO YOUR FACE?
YOUR LITTLE BOYFRIEND WASN'T HAPPY TO SEE ME.
JUST LIKE THAT, IT WAS QUIET AGAIN. EXCEPT FOR THE SCREAMS FROM DOWN THE HILL IN THE VILLAGE, AND MY OWN HEART POUNDING.

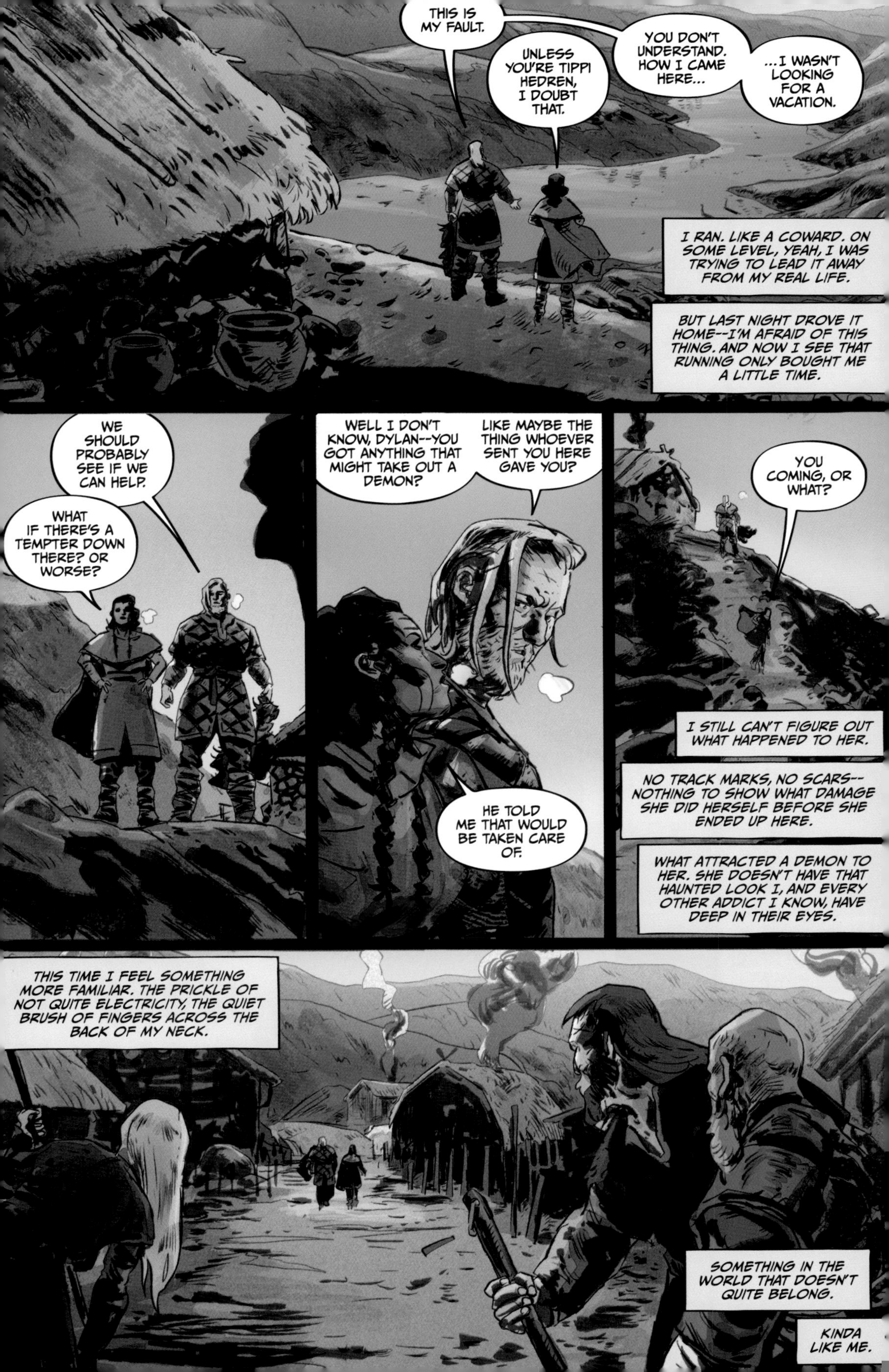
THIS IS MY FAULT.
UNLESS YOU'RE TIPPI HEDREN, I DOUBT THAT.
YOU DON'T UNDERSTAND. HOW I CAME HERE...
...I WASN'T LOOKING FOR A VACATION.
I RAN. LIKE A COWARD. ON SOME LEVEL, YEAH, I WAS TRYING TO LEAD IT AWAY FROM MY REAL LIFE.
BUT LAST NIGHT DROVE IT HOME--I'M AFRAID OF THIS THING. AND NOW I SEE THAT RUNNING ONLY BOUGHT ME A LITTLE TIME.
WE SHOULD PROBABLY SEE IF WE CAN HELP.
WHAT IF THERE'S A TEMPTER DOWN THERE? OR WORSE?
WELL I DON'T KNOW, DYLAN--YOU GOT ANYTHING THAT MIGHT TAKE OUT A DEMON?
LIKE MAYBE THE THING WHOEVER SENT YOU HERE GAVE YOU?
HE TOLD ME THAT WOULD BE TAKEN CARE OF.
YOU COMING, OR WHAT?
I STILL CAN'T FIGURE OUT WHAT HAPPENED TO HER.
NO TRACK MARKS, NO SCARS--NOTHING TO SHOW WHAT DAMAGE SHE DID HERSELF BEFORE SHE ENDED UP HERE.
WHAT ATTRACTED A DEMON TO HER. SHE DOESN'T HAVE THAT HAUNTED LOOK I, AND EVERY OTHER ADDICT I KNOW, HAVE DEEP IN THEIR EYES.
THIS TIME I FEEL SOMETHING MORE FAMILIAR. THE PRICKLE OF NOT QUITE ELECTRICITY, THE QUIET BRUSH OF FINGERS ACROSS THE BACK OF MY NECK.
SOMETHING IN THE WORLD THAT DOESN'T QUITE BELONG.
KINDA LIKE ME.

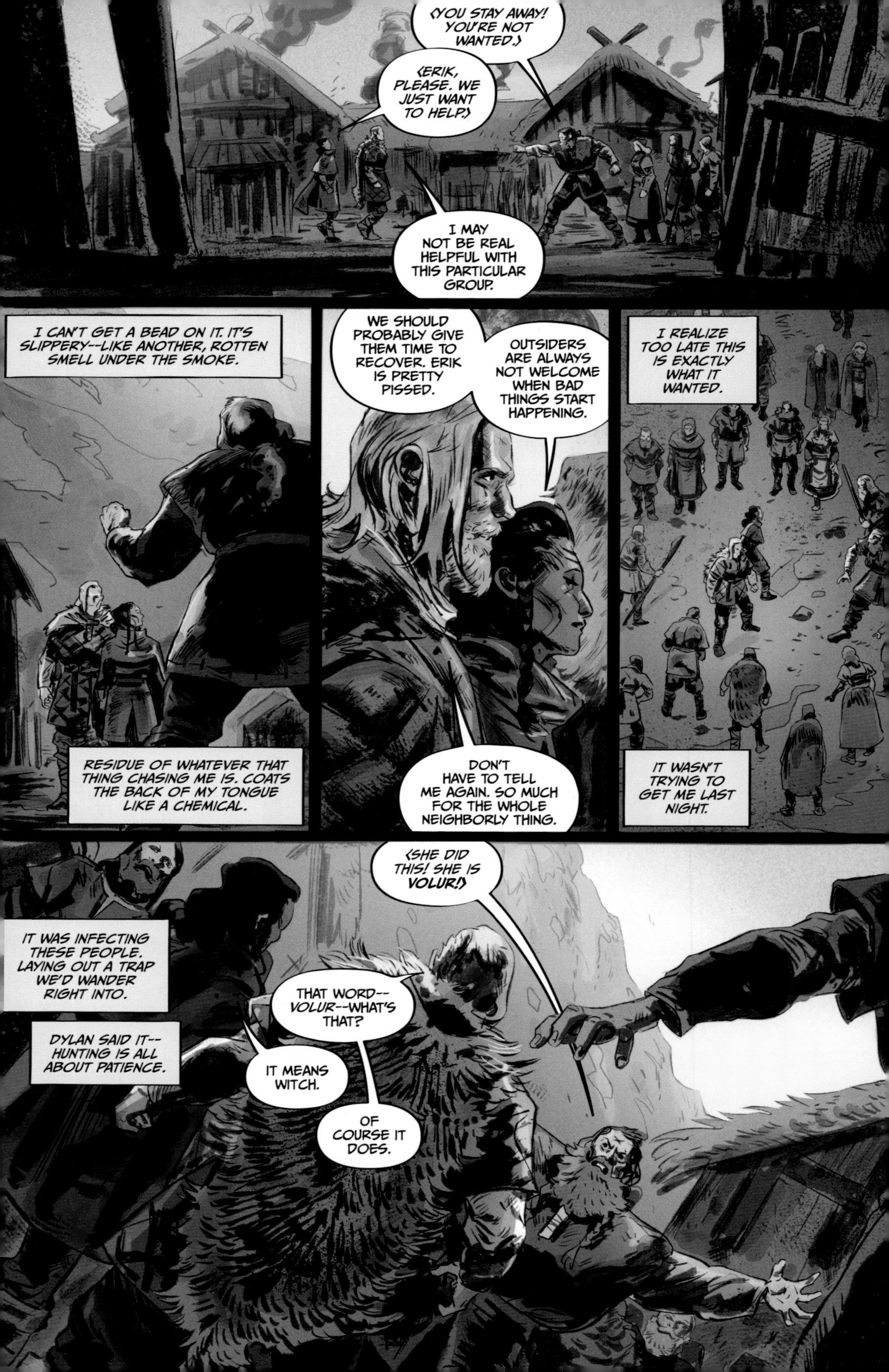
‹YOU STAY AWAY! YOU'RE NOT WANTED.›
‹ERIK, PLEASE. WE JUST WANT TO HELP.›
I MAY NOT BE REAL HELPFUL WITH THIS PARTICULAR GROUP.
I CAN'T GET A BEAD ON IT. IT'S SLIPPERY--LIKE ANOTHER, ROTTEN SMELL UNDER THE SMOKE.
RESIDUE OF WHATEVER THAT THING CHASING ME IS. COATS THE BACK OF MY TONGUE LIKE A CHEMICAL.
WE SHOULD PROBABLY GIVE THEM TIME TO RECOVER. ERIK IS PRETTY PISSED.
OUTSIDERS ARE ALWAYS NOT WELCOME WHEN BAD THINGS START HAPPENING.
DON'T HAVE TO TELL ME AGAIN. SO MUCH FOR THE WHOLE NEIGHBORLY THING.
I REALIZE TOO LATE THIS IS EXACTLY WHAT IT WANTED.
IT WASN'T TRYING TO GET ME LAST NIGHT.
‹SHE DID THIS! SHE IS VOLUR!›
IT WAS INFECTING THESE PEOPLE. LAYING OUT A TRAP WE'D WANDER RIGHT INTO.
DYLAN SAID IT-- HUNTING IS ALL ABOUT PATIENCE.
THAT WORD-- VOLUR--WHAT'S THAT?
IT MEANS WITCH.
OF COURSE IT DOES.

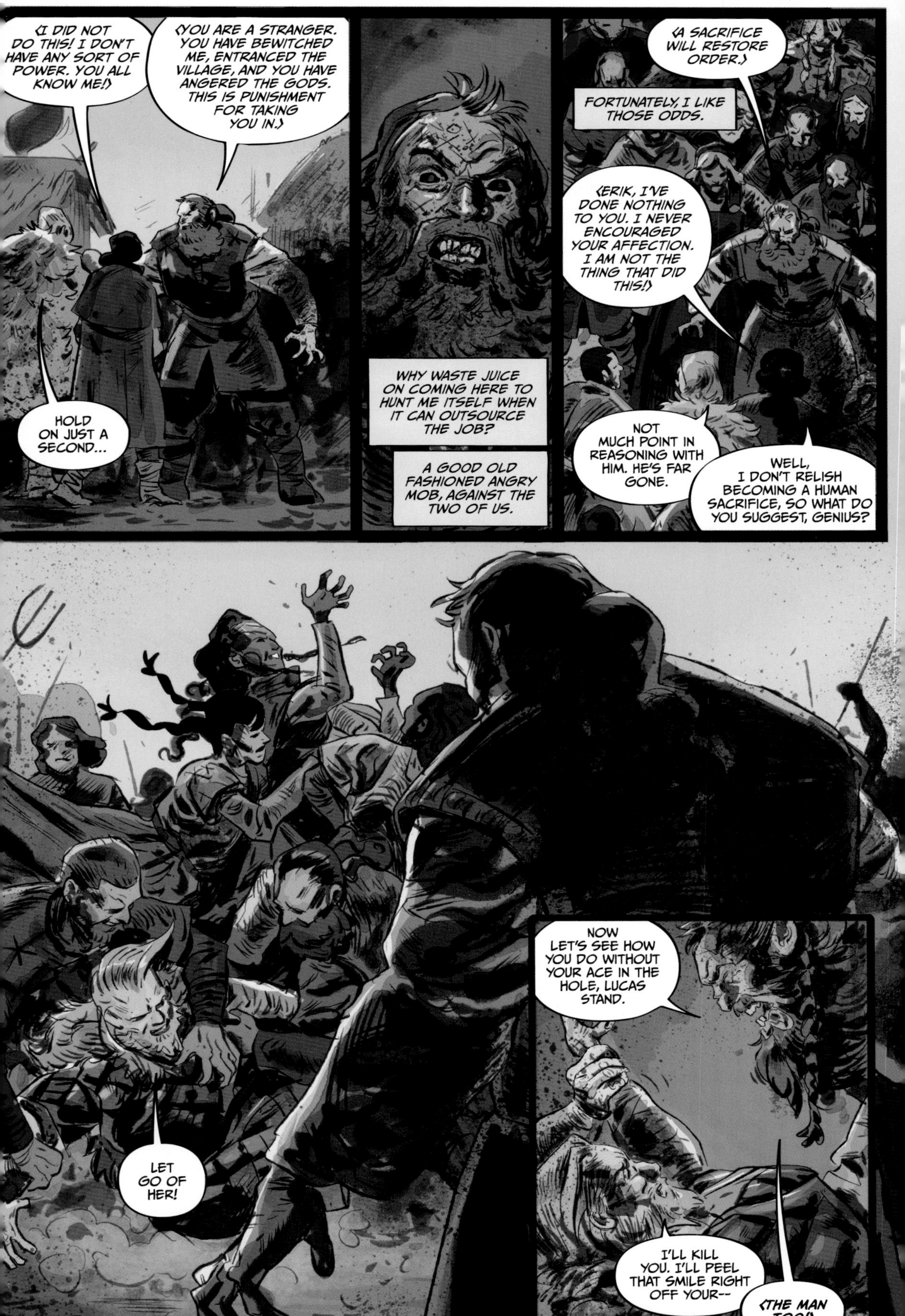

‹I DID NOT DO THIS! I DON'T HAVE ANY SORT OF POWER. YOU ALL KNOW ME!›
‹YOU ARE A STRANGER. YOU HAVE BEWITCHED ME, ENTRANCED THE VILLAGE, AND YOU HAVE ANGERED THE GODS. THIS IS PUNISHMENT FOR TAKING YOU IN.›
HOLD ON JUST A SECOND...
WHY WASTE JUICE ON COMING HERE TO HUNT ME ITSELF WHEN IT CAN OUTSOURCE THE JOB?
A GOOD OLD FASHIONED ANGRY MOB, AGAINST THE TWO OF US.
‹A SACRIFICE WILL RESTORE ORDER.›
FORTUNATELY, I LIKE THOSE ODDS.
‹ERIK, I'VE DONE NOTHING TO YOU. I NEVER ENCOURAGED YOUR AFFECTION. I AM NOT THE THING THAT DID THIS!›
NOT MUCH POINT IN REASONING WITH HIM. HE'S FAR GONE.
WELL, I DON'T RELISH BECOMING A HUMAN SACRIFICE, SO WHAT DO YOU SUGGEST, GENIUS?
LET GO OF HER!
NOW LET'S SEE HOW YOU DO WITHOUT YOUR ACE IN THE HOLE, LUCAS STAND.
I'LL KILL YOU. I'LL PEEL THAT SMILE RIGHT OFF YOUR--
‹THE MAN TOO!›

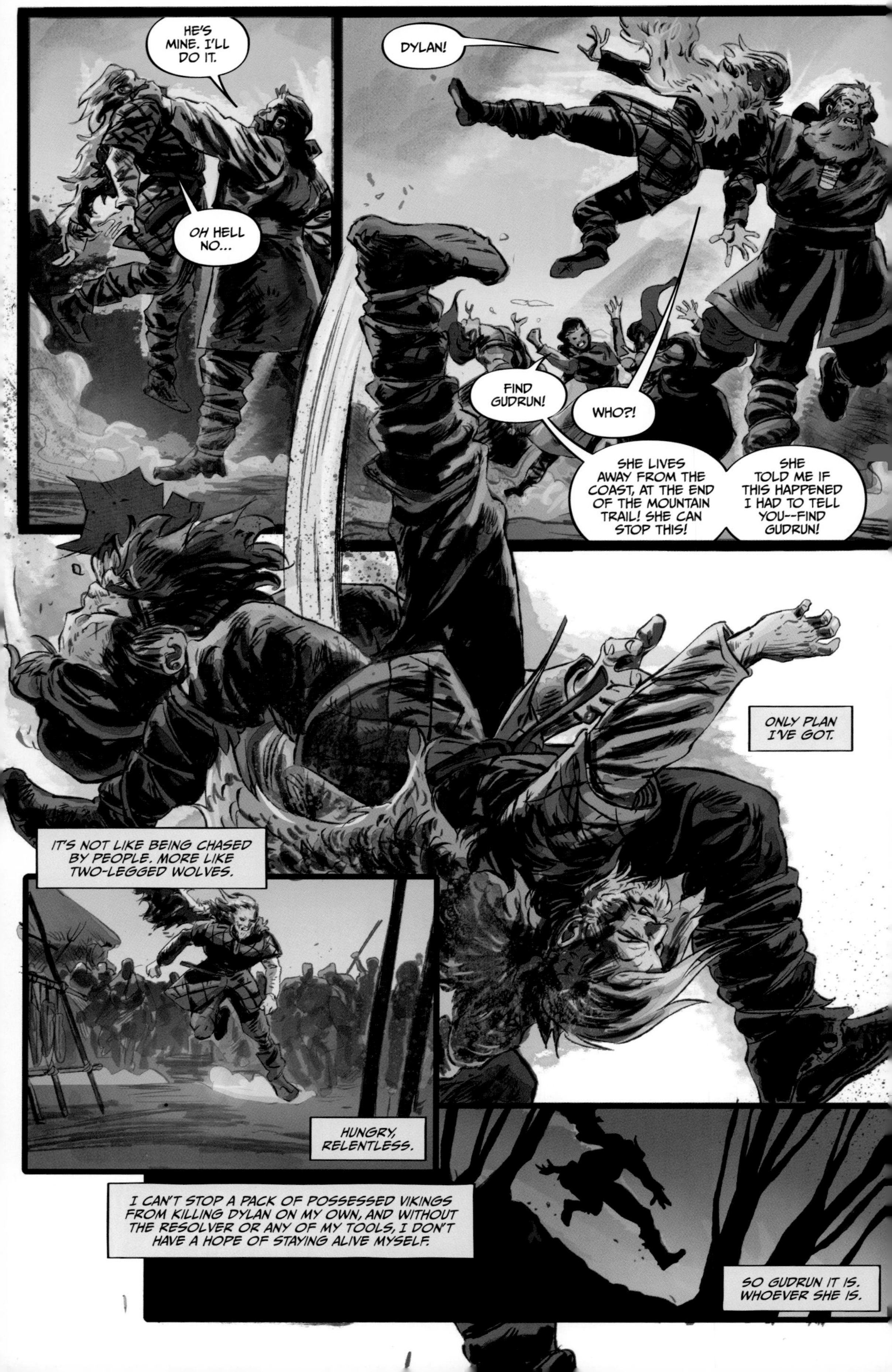
HE'S MINE. I'LL DO IT.
OH HELL NO...
DYLAN!
FIND GUDRUN!
WHO?!
SHE LIVES AWAY FROM THE COAST, AT THE END OF THE MOUNTAIN TRAIL! SHE CAN STOP THIS!
SHE TOLD ME IF THIS HAPPENED I HAD TO TELL YOU--FIND GUDRUN!
ONLY PLAN I'VE GOT.
IT'S NOT LIKE BEING CHASED BY PEOPLE. MORE LIKE TWO-LEGGED WOLVES.
HUNGRY, RELENTLESS.
I CAN'T STOP A PACK OF POSSESSED VIKINGS FROM KILLING DYLAN ON MY OWN, AND WITHOUT THE RESOLVER OR ANY OF MY TOOLS, I DON'T HAVE A HOPE OF STAYING ALIVE MYSELF.
SO GUDRUN IT IS. WHOEVER SHE IS.

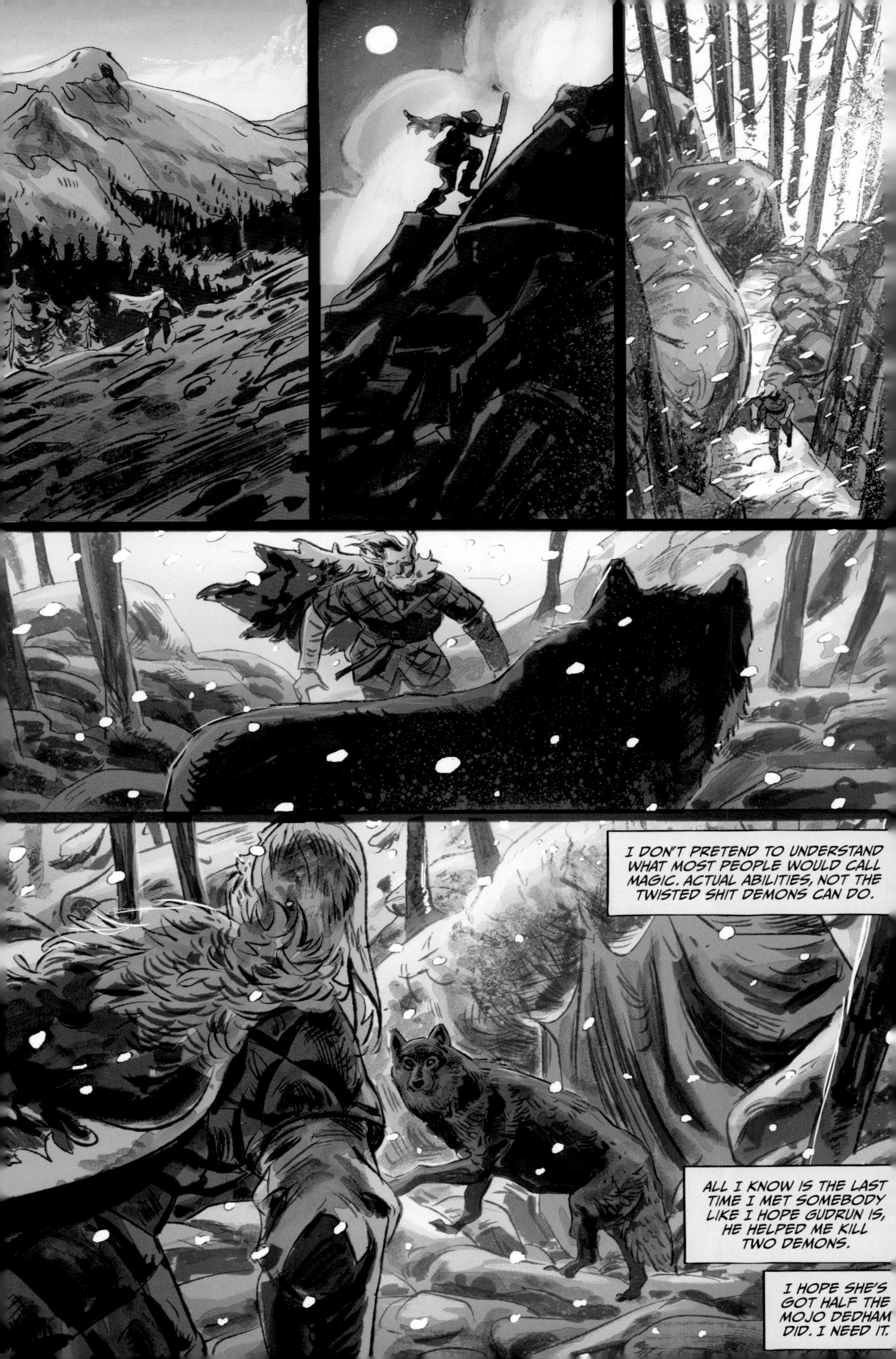
I DON'T PRETEND TO UNDERSTAND WHAT MOST PEOPLE WOULD CALL MAGIC. ACTUAL ABILITIES, NOT THE TWISTED SHIT DEMONS CAN DO.
ALL I KNOW IS THE LAST TIME I MET SOMEBODY LIKE I HOPE GUDRUN IS, HE HELPED ME KILL TWO DEMONS.
I HOPE SHE'S GOT HALF THE MOJO DEDHAM DID. I NEED IT.

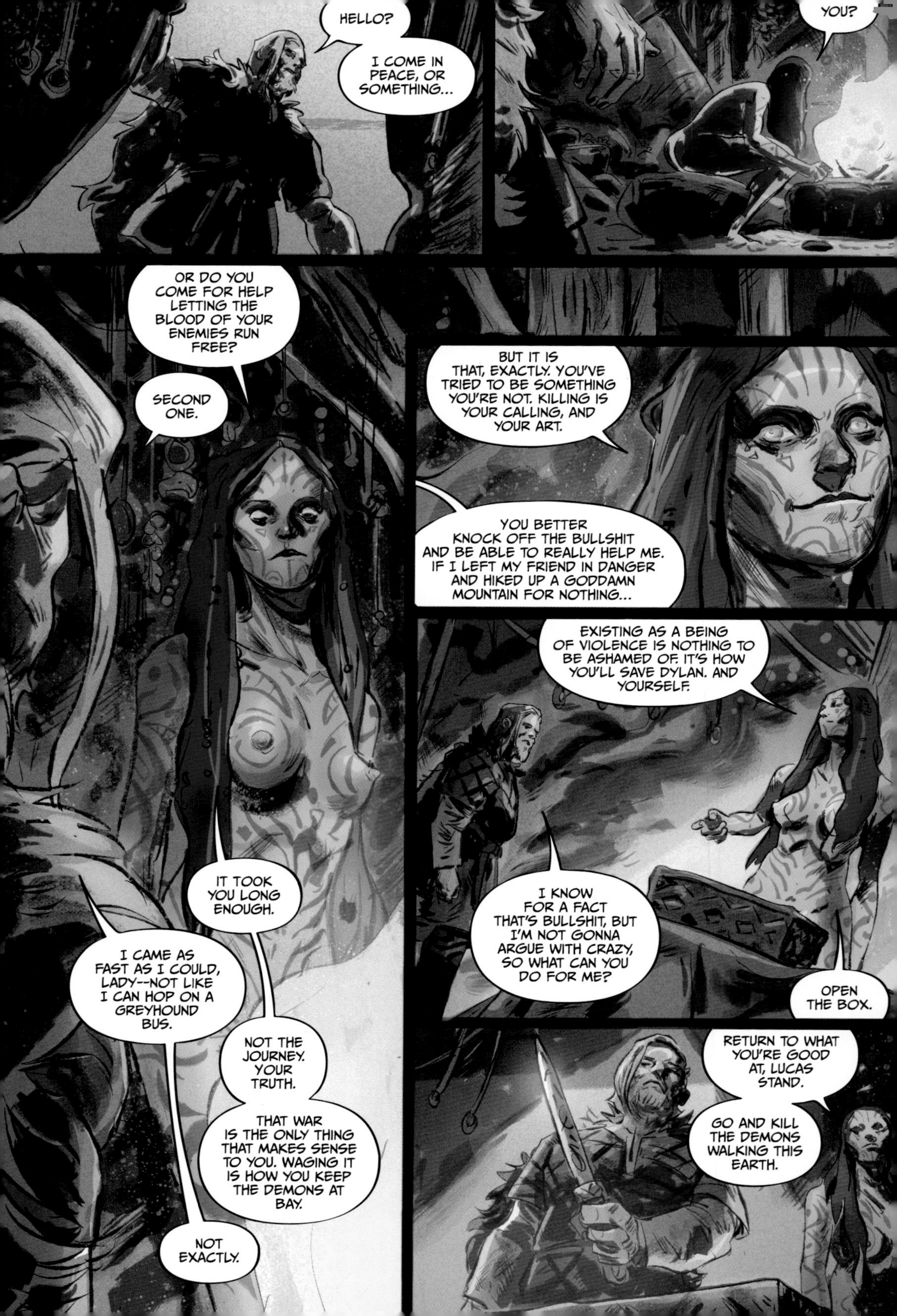
HELLO?
I COME IN PEACE, OR SOMETHING...
YOU?
OR DO YOU COME FOR HELP LETTING THE BLOOD OF YOUR ENEMIES RUN FREE?
SECOND ONE.
IT TOOK YOU LONG ENOUGH.
I CAME AS FAST AS I COULD, LADY--NOT LIKE I CAN HOP ON A GREYHOUND BUS.
NOT THE JOURNEY. YOUR TRUTH.
THAT WAR IS THE ONLY THING THAT MAKES SENSE TO YOU. WAGING IT IS HOW YOU KEEP THE DEMONS AT BAY.
NOT EXACTLY.
BUT IT IS THAT, EXACTLY. YOU'VE TRIED TO BE SOMETHING YOU'RE NOT. KILLING IS YOUR CALLING, AND YOUR ART.
YOU BETTER KNOCK OFF THE BULLSHIT AND BE ABLE TO REALLY HELP ME. IF I LEFT MY FRIEND IN DANGER AND HIKED UP A GODDAMN MOUNTAIN FOR NOTHING...
EXISTING AS A BEING OF VIOLENCE IS NOTHING TO BE ASHAMED OF. IT'S HOW YOU'LL SAVE DYLAN. AND YOURSELF.
I KNOW FOR A FACT THAT'S BULLSHIT, BUT I'M NOT GONNA ARGUE WITH CRAZY, SO WHAT CAN YOU DO FOR ME?
OPEN THE BOX.
RETURN TO WHAT YOU'RE GOOD AT, LUCAS STAND.
GO AND KILL THE DEMONS WALKING THIS EARTH.

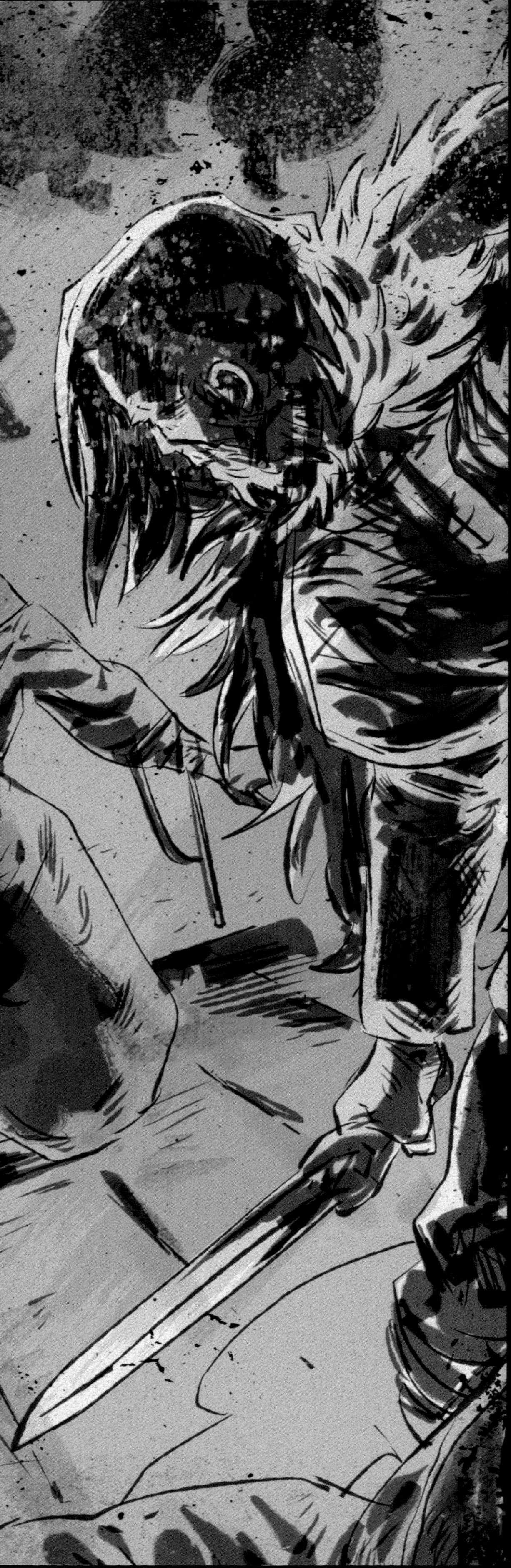

THREE

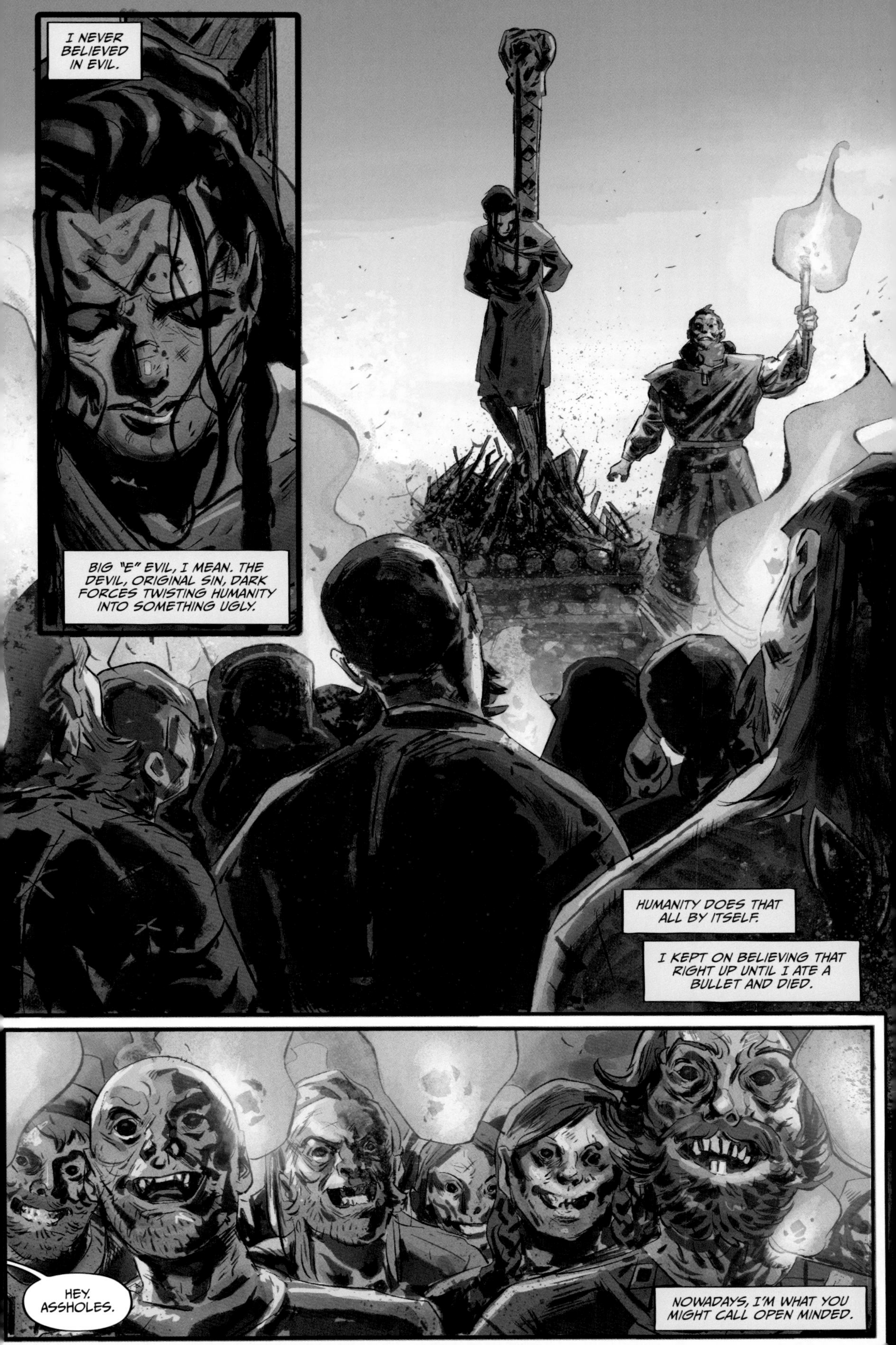
I NEVER BELIEVED IN EVIL.
BIG "E" EVIL, I MEAN. THE DEVIL, ORIGINAL SIN, DARK FORCES TWISTING HUMANITY INTO SOMETHING UGLY.
HUMANITY DOES THAT ALL BY ITSELF.
I KEPT ON BELIEVING THAT RIGHT UP UNTIL I ATE A BULLET AND DIED.
HEY. ASSHOLES.
NOWADAYS, I'M WHAT YOU MIGHT CALL OPEN MINDED.

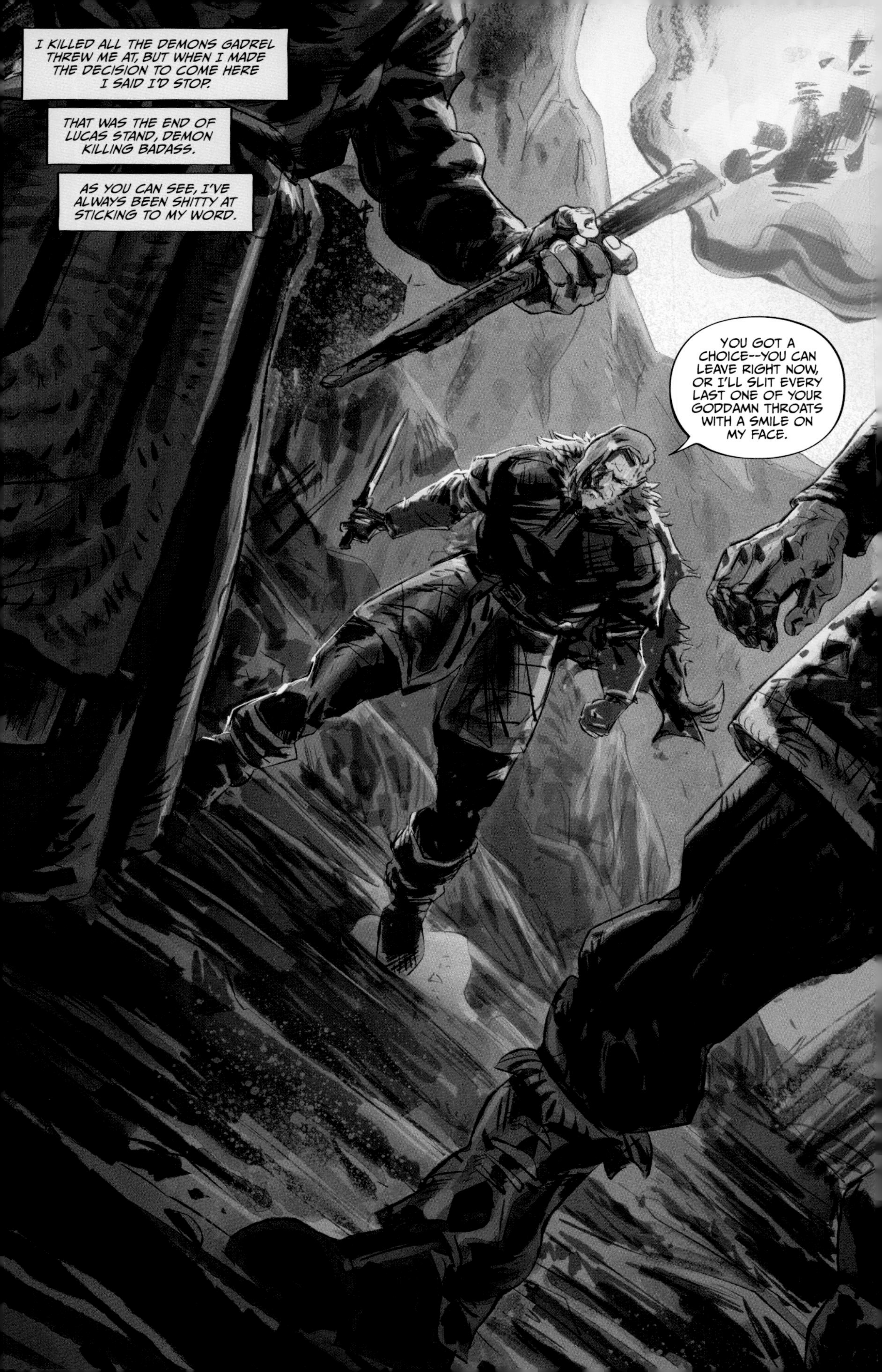
I KILLED ALL THE DEMONS GADREL THREW ME AT, BUT WHEN I MADE THE DECISION TO COME HERE I SAID I'D STOP.
THAT WAS THE END OF LUCAS STAND, DEMON KILLING BADASS.
AS YOU CAN SEE, I'VE ALWAYS BEEN SHITTY AT STICKING TO MY WORD.
YOU GOT A CHOICE--YOU CAN LEAVE RIGHT NOW, OR I'LL SLIT EVERY LAST ONE OF YOUR GODDAMN THROATS WITH A SMILE ON MY FACE.

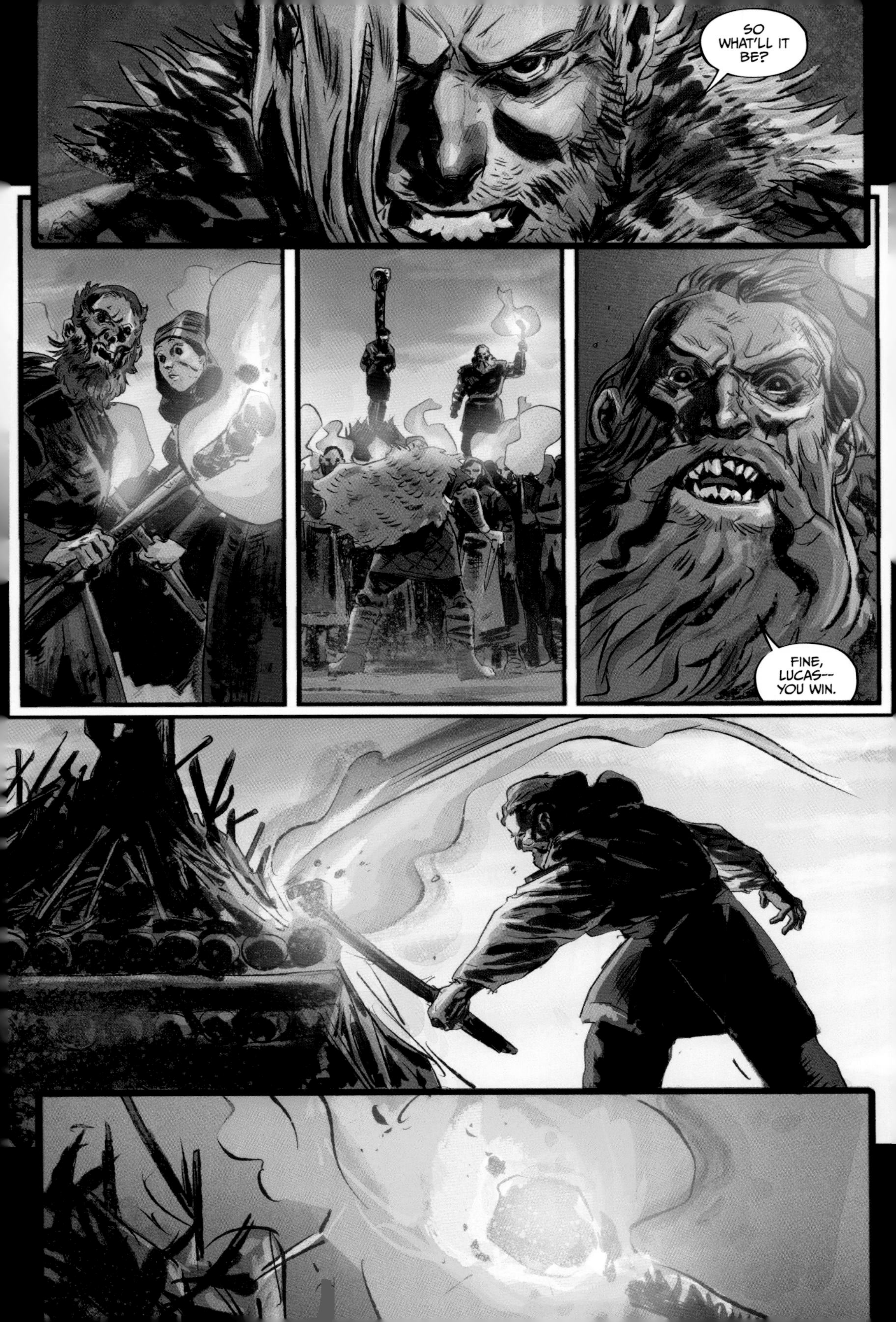
SO WHAT'LL IT BE?
FINE, LUCAS-- YOU WIN.

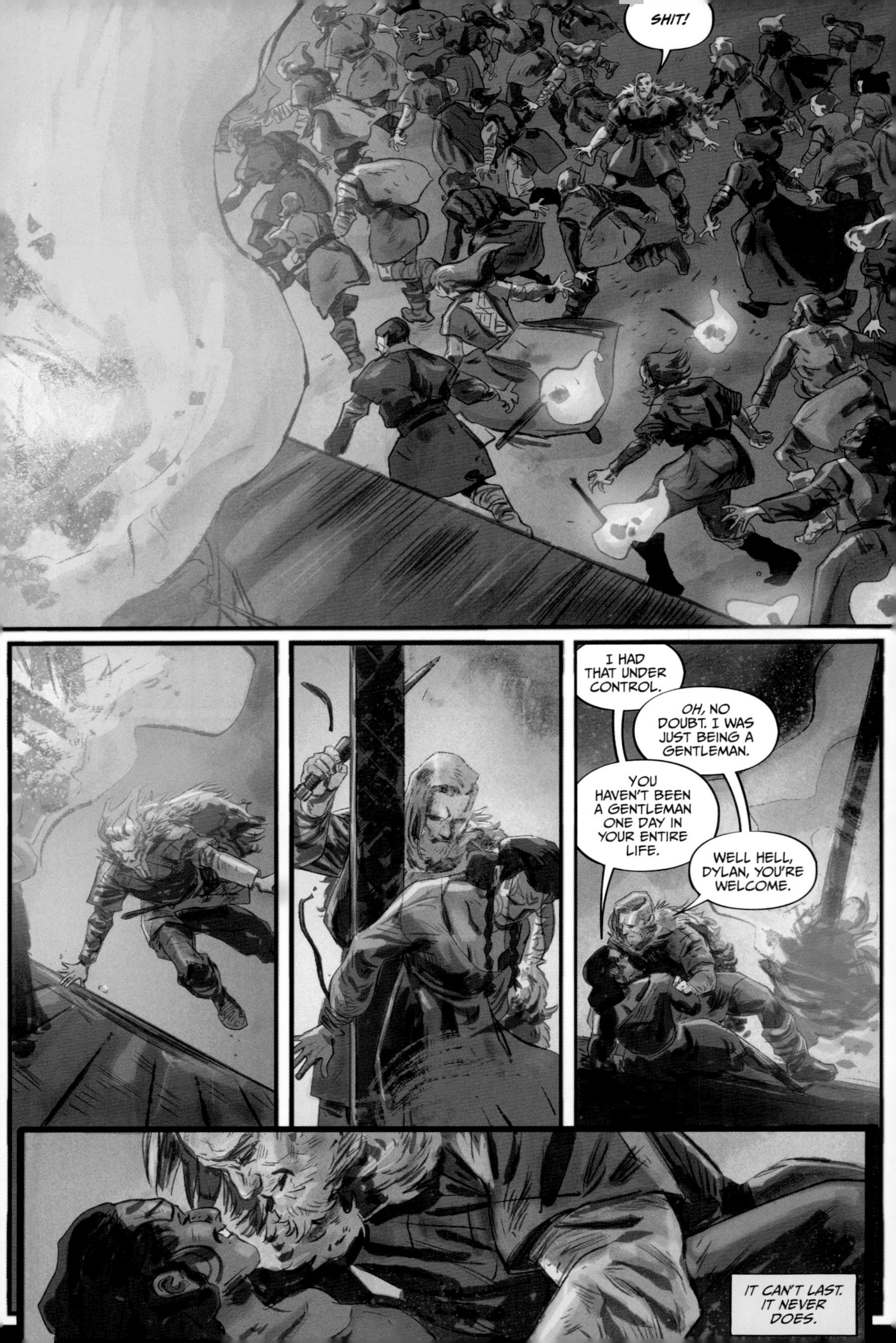
SHIT!
I HAD THAT UNDER CONTROL.
OH, NO DOUBT. I WAS JUST BEING A GENTLEMAN.
YOU HAVEN'T BEEN A GENTLEMAN ONE DAY IN YOUR ENTIRE LIFE.
WELL HELL, DYLAN, YOU'RE WELCOME.
IT CAN'T LAST. IT NEVER DOES.

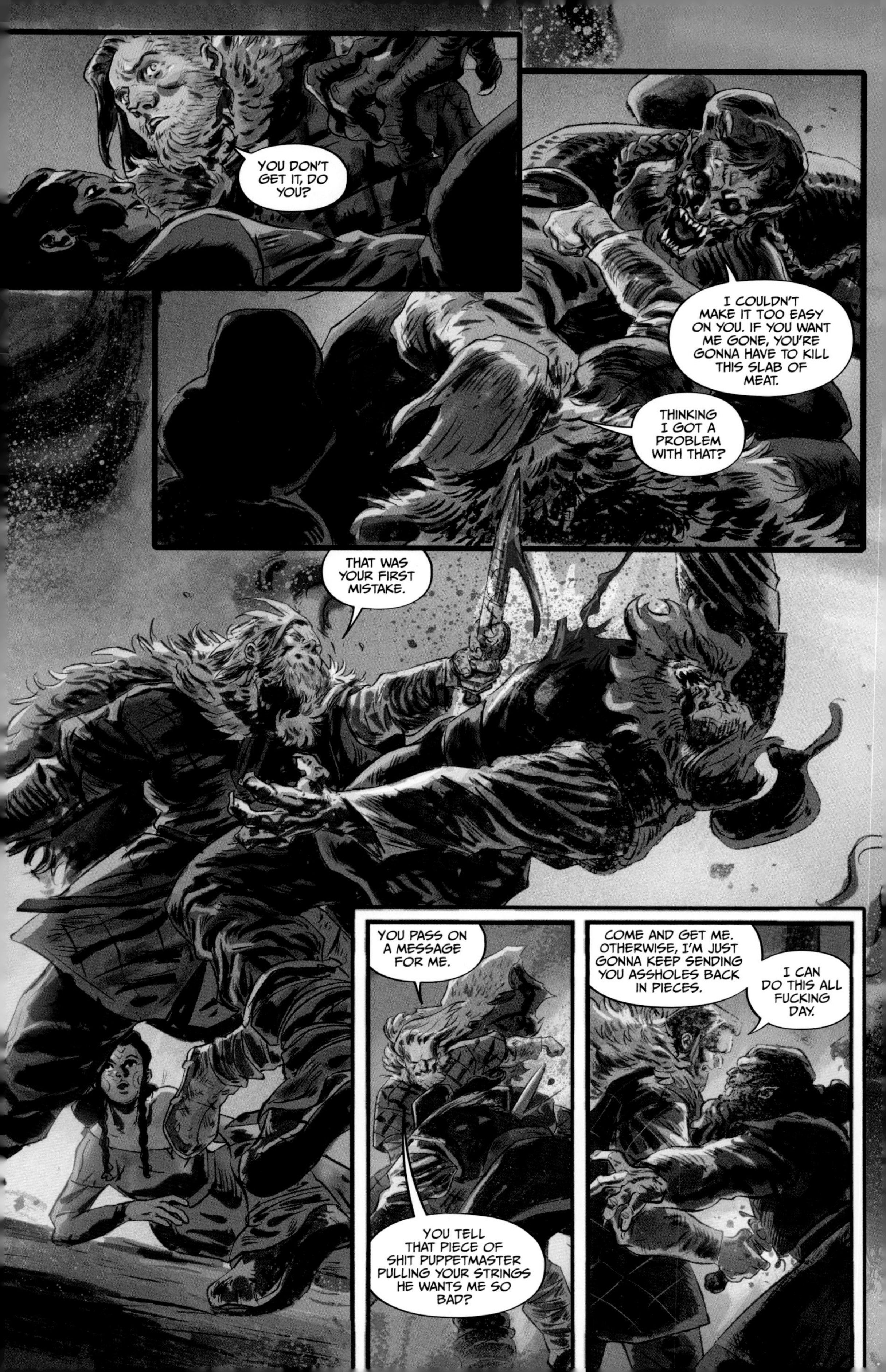
YOU DON'T GET IT, DO YOU?
I COULDN'T MAKE IT TOO EASY ON YOU. IF YOU WANT ME GONE, YOU'RE GONNA HAVE TO KILL THIS SLAB OF MEAT.
THINKING I GOT A PROBLEM WITH THAT?
THAT WAS YOUR FIRST MISTAKE.
YOU PASS ON A MESSAGE FOR ME.
YOU TELL THAT PIECE OF SHIT PUPPETMASTER PULLING YOUR STRINGS HE WANTS ME SO BAD?
COME AND GET ME. OTHERWISE, I'M JUST GONNA KEEP SENDING YOU ASSHOLES BACK IN PIECES.
I CAN DO THIS ALL FUCKING DAY.

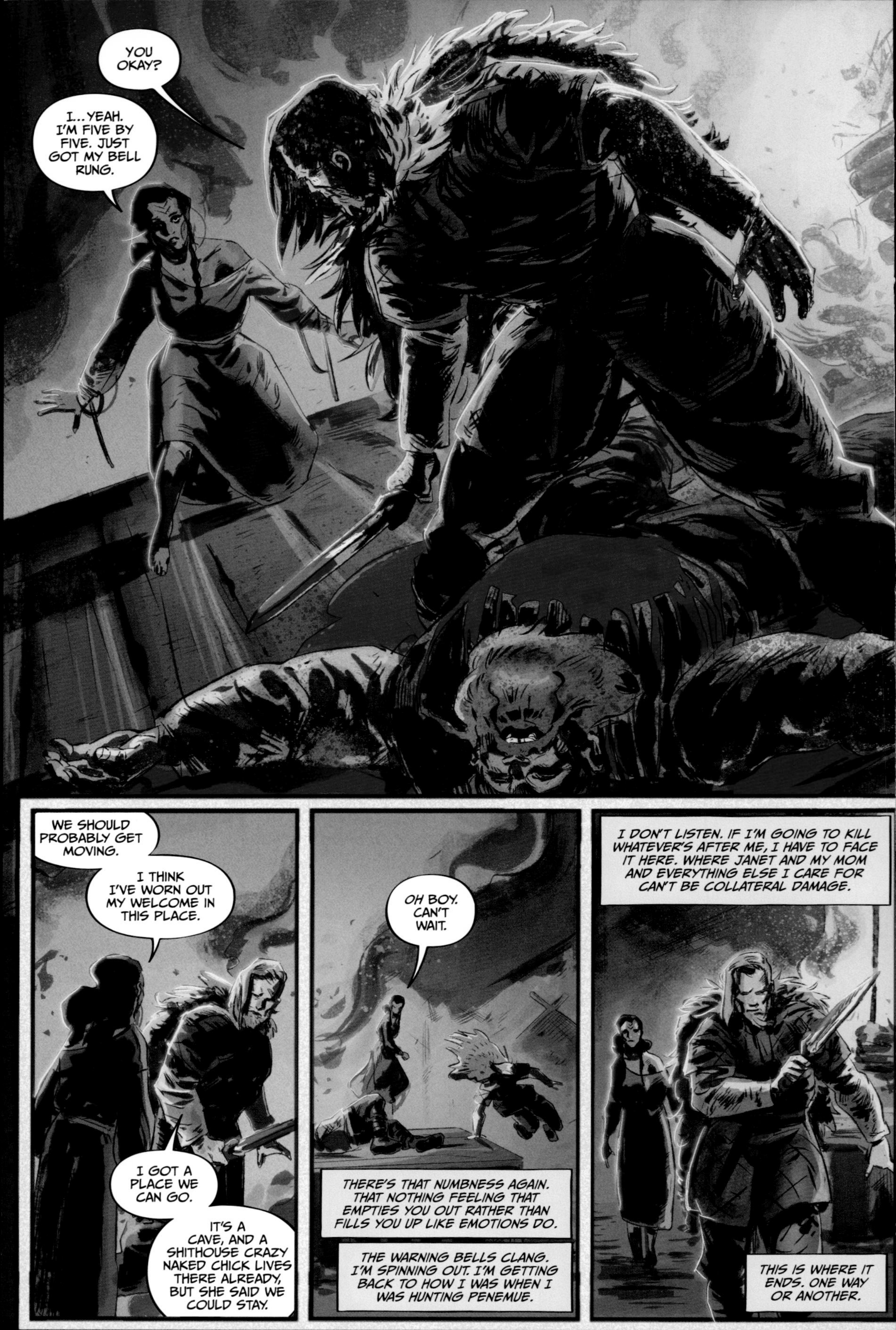

YOU OKAY?
I...YEAH. I'M FIVE BY FIVE. JUST GOT MY BELL RUNG.
WE SHOULD PROBABLY GET MOVING.
I THINK I'VE WORN OUT MY WELCOME IN THIS PLACE.
I GOT A PLACE WE CAN GO.
IT'S A CAVE, AND A SHITHOUSE CRAZY NAKED CHICK LIVES THERE ALREADY, BUT SHE SAID WE COULD STAY.
OH BOY. CAN'T WAIT.
THERE'S THAT NUMBNESS AGAIN. THAT NOTHING FEELING THAT EMPTIES YOU OUT RATHER THAN FILLS YOU UP LIKE EMOTIONS DO.
THE WARNING BELLS CLANG. I'M SPINNING OUT. I'M GETTING BACK TO HOW I WAS WHEN I WAS HUNTING PENEMUE.
I DON'T LISTEN. IF I'M GOING TO KILL WHATEVER'S AFTER ME, I HAVE TO FACE IT HERE. WHERE JANET AND MY MOM AND EVERYTHING ELSE I CARE FOR CAN'T BE COLLATERAL DAMAGE.
THIS IS WHERE IT ENDS. ONE WAY OR ANOTHER.

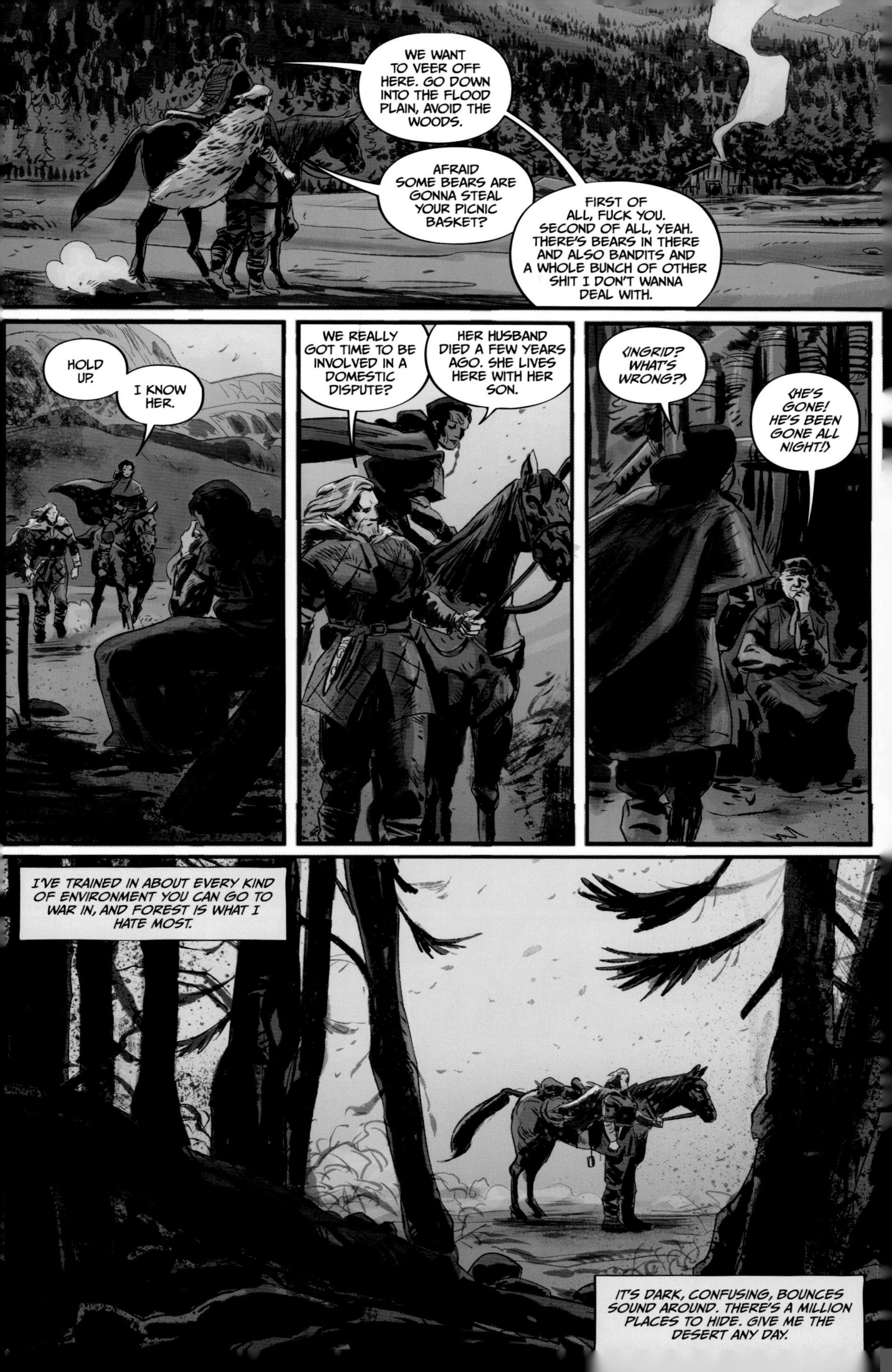
WE WANT TO VEER OFF HERE. GO DOWN INTO THE FLOOD PLAIN, AVOID THE WOODS.
AFRAID SOME BEARS ARE GONNA STEAL YOUR PICNIC BASKET?
FIRST OF ALL, FUCK YOU. SECOND OF ALL, YEAH. THERE'S BEARS IN THERE AND ALSO BANDITS AND A WHOLE BUNCH OF OTHER SHIT I DON'T WANNA DEAL WITH.
HOLD UP.
I KNOW HER.
WE REALLY GOT TIME TO BE INVOLVED IN A DOMESTIC DISPUTE?
HER HUSBAND DIED A FEW YEARS AGO. SHE LIVES HERE WITH HER SON.
‹INGRID? WHAT'S WRONG?›
‹HE'S GONE! HE'S BEEN GONE ALL NIGHT!›
I'VE TRAINED IN ABOUT EVERY KIND OF ENVIRONMENT YOU CAN GO TO WAR IN, AND FOREST IS WHAT I HATE MOST.
IT'S DARK, CONFUSING, BOUNCES SOUND AROUND. THERE'S A MILLION PLACES TO HIDE. GIVE ME THE DESERT ANY DAY.

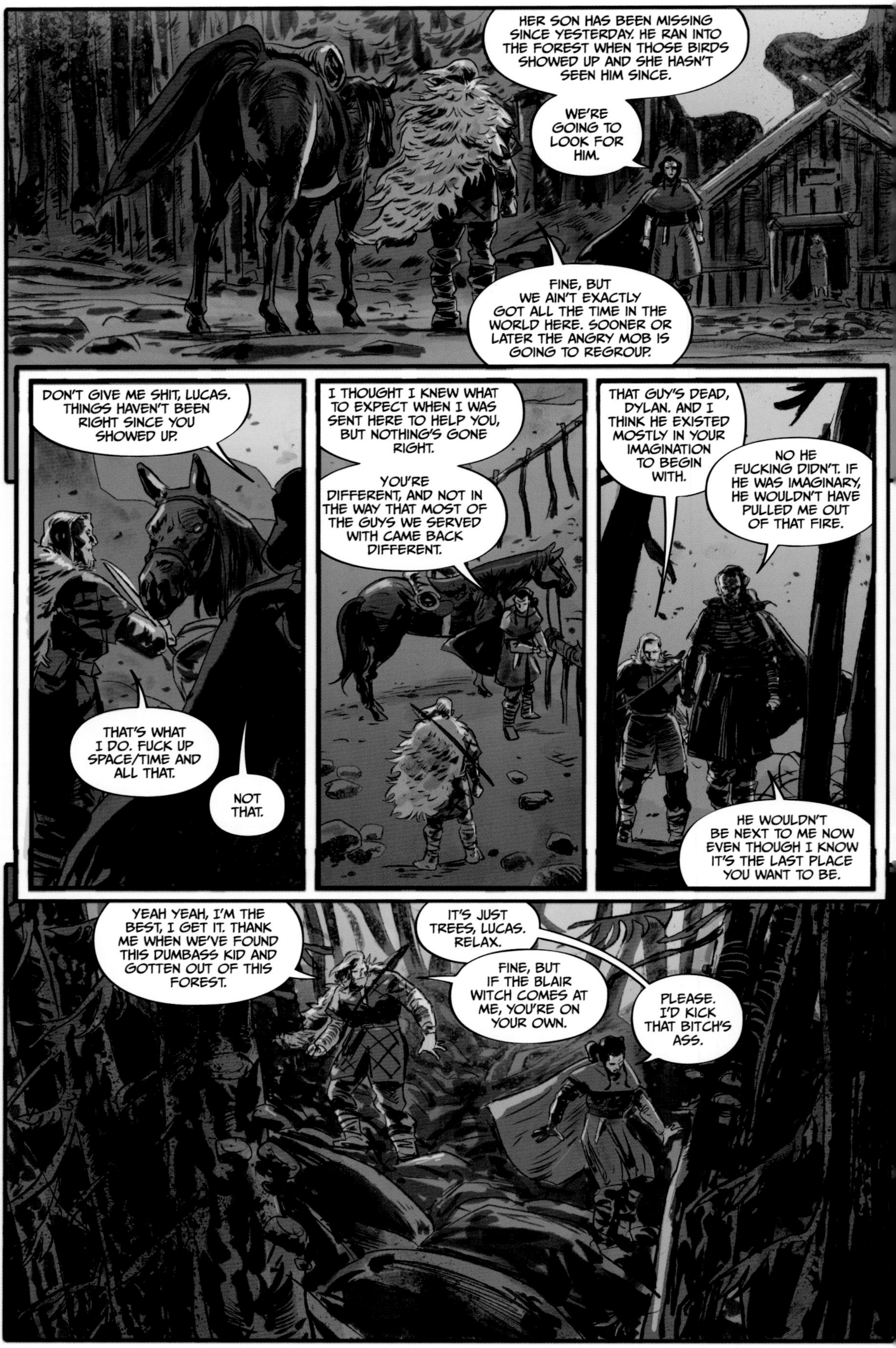
HER SON HAS BEEN MISSING SINCE YESTERDAY. HE RAN INTO THE FOREST WHEN THOSE BIRDS SHOWED UP AND SHE HASN'T SEEN HIM SINCE.
WE'RE GOING TO LOOK FOR HIM.
FINE, BUT WE AIN'T EXACTLY GOT ALL THE TIME IN THE WORLD HERE. SOONER OR LATER THE ANGRY MOB IS GOING TO REGROUP.
DON'T GIVE ME SHIT, LUCAS. THINGS HAVEN'T BEEN RIGHT SINCE YOU SHOWED UP.
THAT'S WHAT I DO. FUCK UP SPACE/TIME AND ALL THAT.
NOT THAT.
I THOUGHT I KNEW WHAT TO EXPECT WHEN I WAS SENT HERE TO HELP YOU, BUT NOTHING'S GONE RIGHT.
YOU'RE DIFFERENT, AND NOT IN THE WAY THAT MOST OF THE GUYS WE SERVED WITH CAME BACK DIFFERENT.
THAT GUY'S DEAD, DYLAN. AND I THINK HE EXISTED MOSTLY IN YOUR IMAGINATION TO BEGIN WITH.
NO HE FUCKING DIDN'T. IF HE WAS IMAGINARY, HE WOULDN'T HAVE PULLED ME OUT OF THAT FIRE.
HE WOULDN'T BE NEXT TO ME NOW EVEN THOUGH I KNOW IT'S THE LAST PLACE YOU WANT TO BE.
YEAH YEAH, I'M THE BEST, I GET IT. THANK ME WHEN WE'VE FOUND THIS DUMBASS KID AND GOTTEN OUT OF THIS FOREST.
IT'S JUST TREES, LUCAS. RELAX.
FINE, BUT IF THE BLAIR WITCH COMES AT ME, YOU'RE ON YOUR OWN.
PLEASE. I'D KICK THAT BITCH'S ASS.

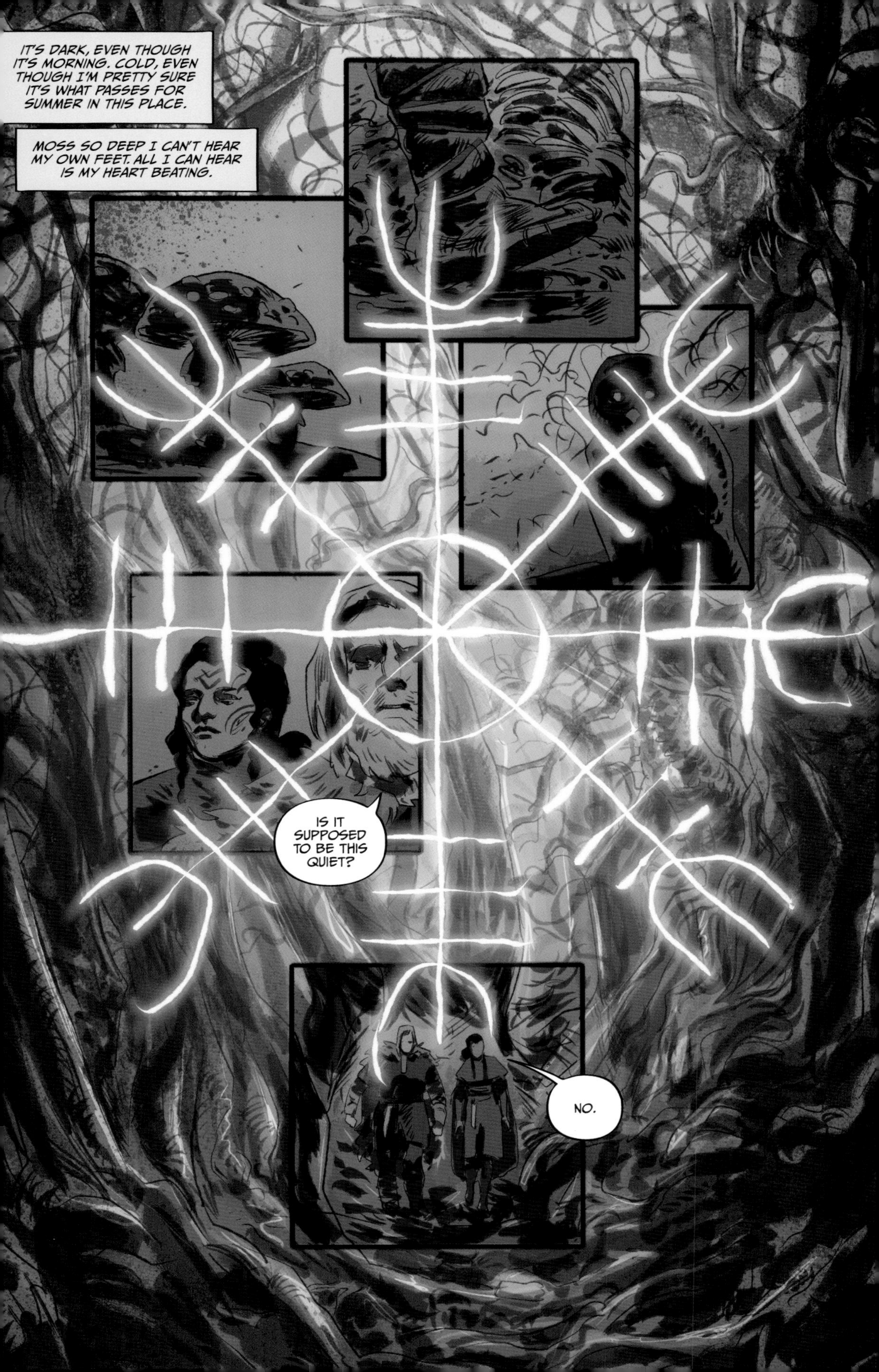
IT'S DARK, EVEN THOUGH IT'S MORNING. COLD, EVEN THOUGH I'M PRETTY SURE IT'S WHAT PASSES FOR SUMMER IN THIS PLACE.
MOSS SO DEEP I CAN'T HEAR MY OWN FEET. ALL I CAN HEAR IS MY HEART BEATING.
IS IT SUPPOSED TO BE THIS QUIET?
NO.

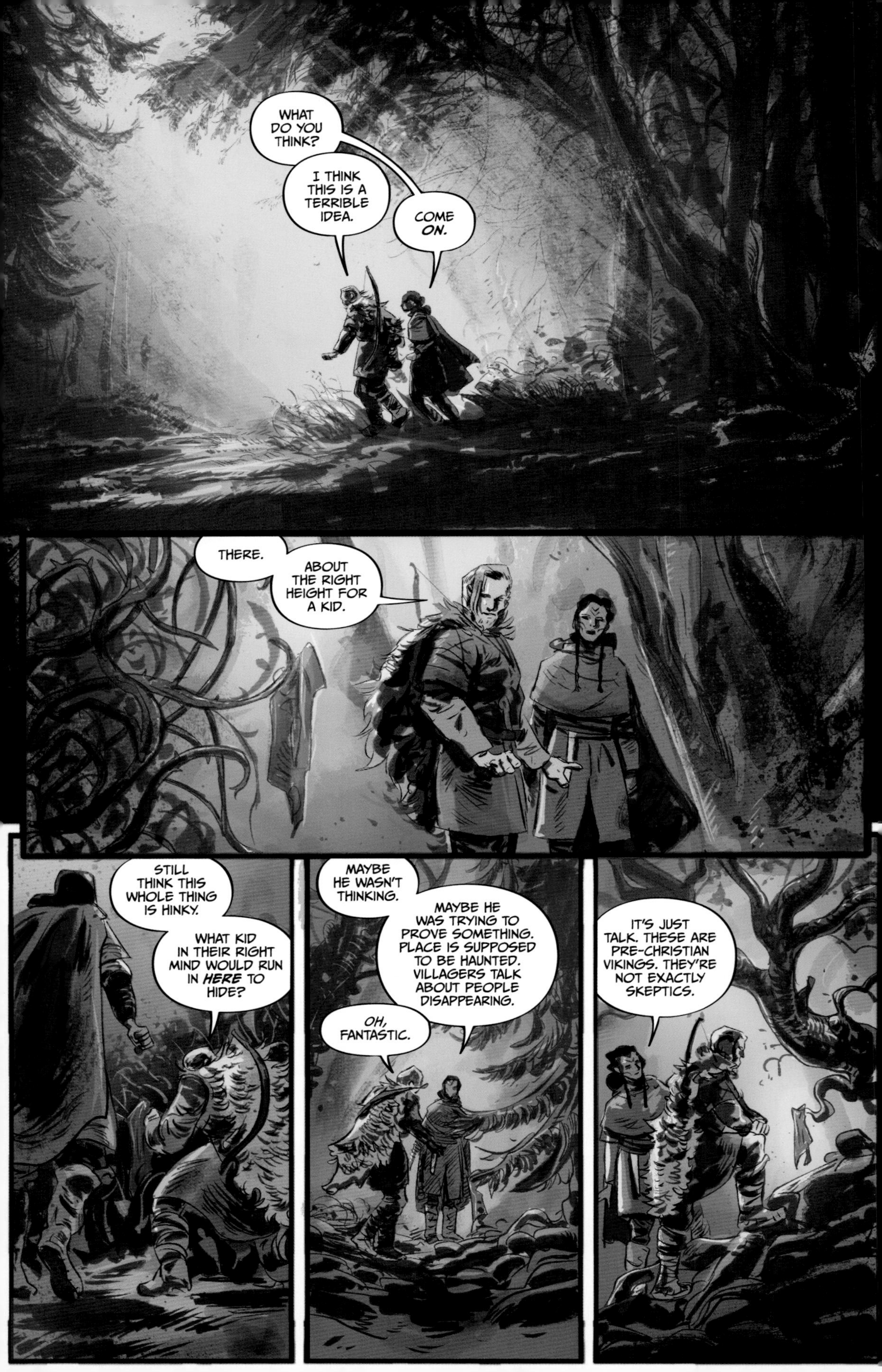
WHAT DO YOU THINK?
I THINK THIS IS A TERRIBLE IDEA.
COME *ON.*
THERE.
ABOUT THE RIGHT HEIGHT FOR A KID.
STILL THINK THIS WHOLE THING IS HINKY.
WHAT KID IN THEIR RIGHT MIND WOULD RUN IN *HERE* TO HIDE?
MAYBE HE WASN'T THINKING.
MAYBE HE WAS TRYING TO PROVE SOMETHING. PLACE IS SUPPOSED TO BE HAUNTED. VILLAGERS TALK ABOUT PEOPLE DISAPPEARING.
OH, FANTASTIC.
IT'S JUST TALK. THESE ARE PRE-CHRISTIAN VIKINGS. THEY'RE NOT EXACTLY SKEPTICS.

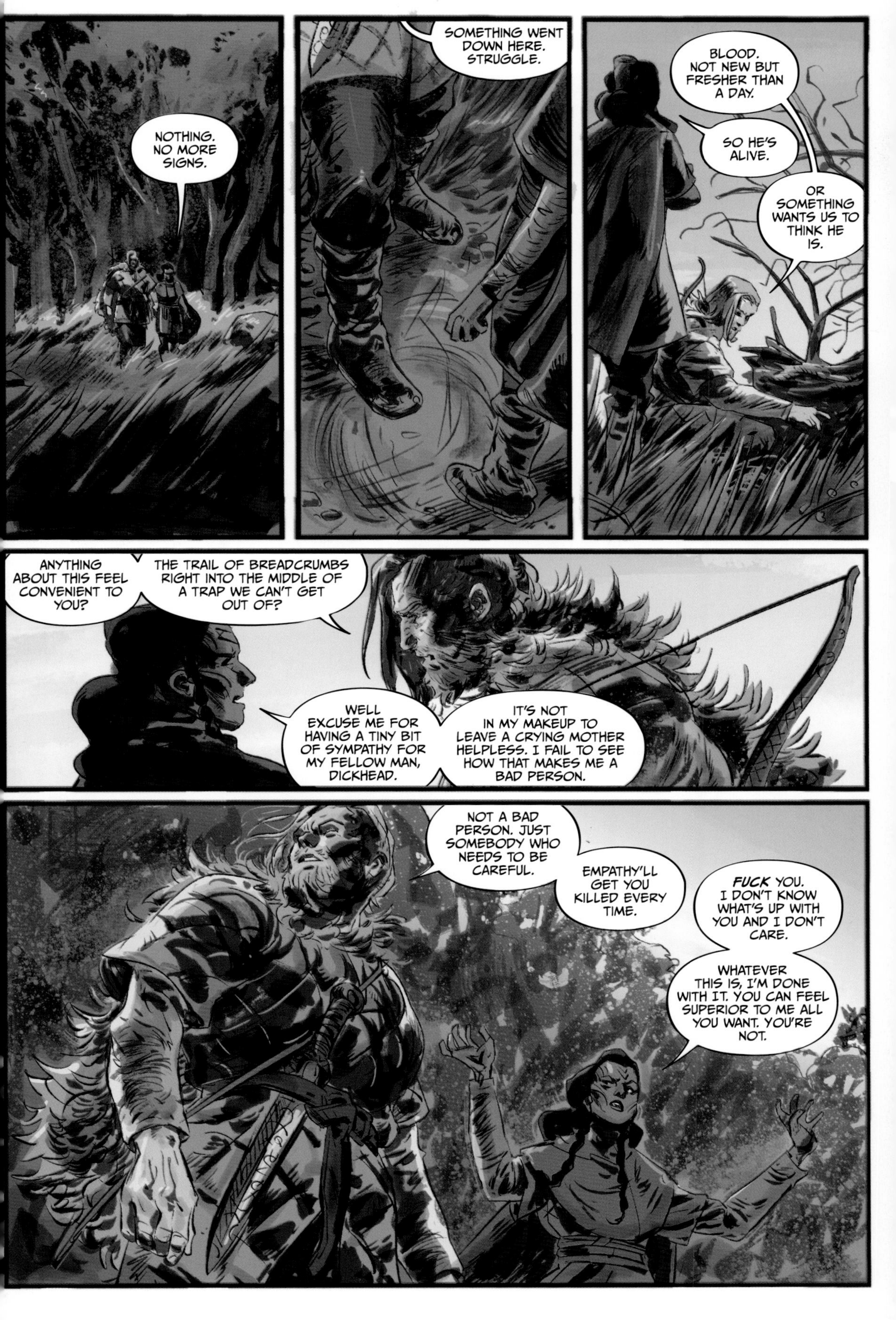
NOTHING. NO MORE SIGNS.
SOMETHING WENT DOWN HERE. STRUGGLE.
BLOOD. NOT NEW BUT FRESHER THAN A DAY.
SO HE'S ALIVE.
OR SOMETHING WANTS US TO THINK HE IS.
ANYTHING ABOUT THIS FEEL CONVENIENT TO YOU?
THE TRAIL OF BREADCRUMBS RIGHT INTO THE MIDDLE OF A TRAP WE CAN'T GET OUT OF?
WELL EXCUSE ME FOR HAVING A TINY BIT OF SYMPATHY FOR MY FELLOW MAN, DICKHEAD.
IT'S NOT IN MY MAKEUP TO LEAVE A CRYING MOTHER HELPLESS. I FAIL TO SEE HOW THAT MAKES ME A BAD PERSON.
NOT A BAD PERSON. JUST SOMEBODY WHO NEEDS TO BE CAREFUL.
EMPATHY'LL GET YOU KILLED EVERY TIME.
FUCK YOU. I DON'T KNOW WHAT'S UP WITH YOU AND I DON'T CARE.
WHATEVER THIS IS, I'M DONE WITH IT. YOU CAN FEEL SUPERIOR TO ME ALL YOU WANT. YOU'RE NOT.

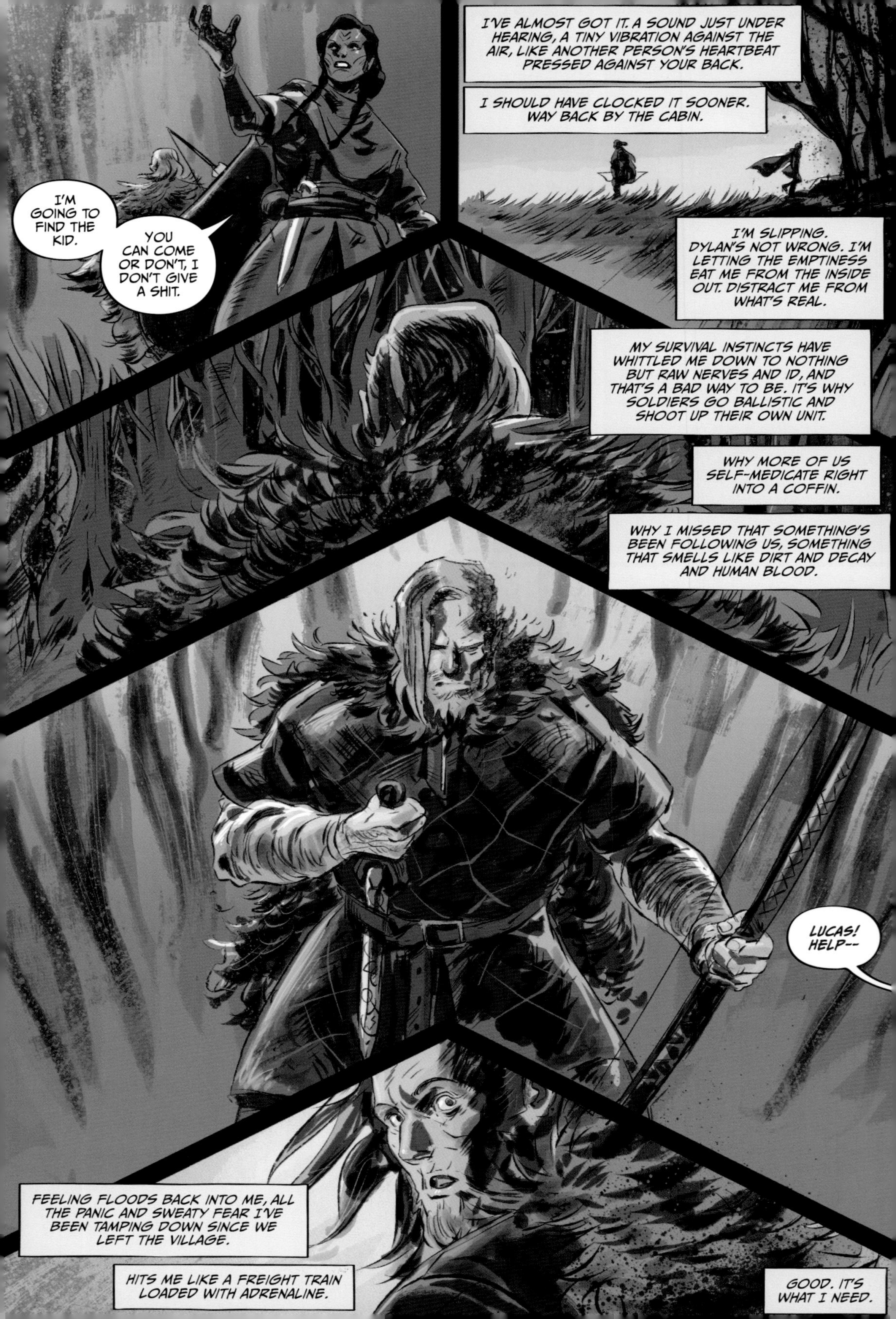
I'M GOING TO FIND THE KID.
YOU CAN COME OR DON'T, I DON'T GIVE A SHIT.
I'VE ALMOST GOT IT. A SOUND JUST UNDER HEARING, A TINY VIBRATION AGAINST THE AIR, LIKE ANOTHER PERSON'S HEARTBEAT PRESSED AGAINST YOUR BACK.
I SHOULD HAVE CLOCKED IT SOONER. WAY BACK BY THE CABIN.
I'M SLIPPING. DYLAN'S NOT WRONG. I'M LETTING THE EMPTINESS EAT ME FROM THE INSIDE OUT. DISTRACT ME FROM WHAT'S REAL.
MY SURVIVAL INSTINCTS HAVE WHITTLED ME DOWN TO NOTHING BUT RAW NERVES AND ID, AND THAT'S A BAD WAY TO BE. IT'S WHY SOLDIERS GO BALLISTIC AND SHOOT UP THEIR OWN UNIT.
WHY MORE OF US SELF-MEDICATE RIGHT INTO A COFFIN.
WHY I MISSED THAT SOMETHING'S BEEN FOLLOWING US, SOMETHING THAT SMELLS LIKE DIRT AND DECAY AND HUMAN BLOOD.
LUCAS! HELP--
FEELING FLOODS BACK INTO ME, ALL THE PANIC AND SWEATY FEAR I'VE BEEN TAMPING DOWN SINCE WE LEFT THE VILLAGE.
HITS ME LIKE A FREIGHT TRAIN LOADED WITH ADRENALINE.
GOOD. IT'S WHAT I NEED.

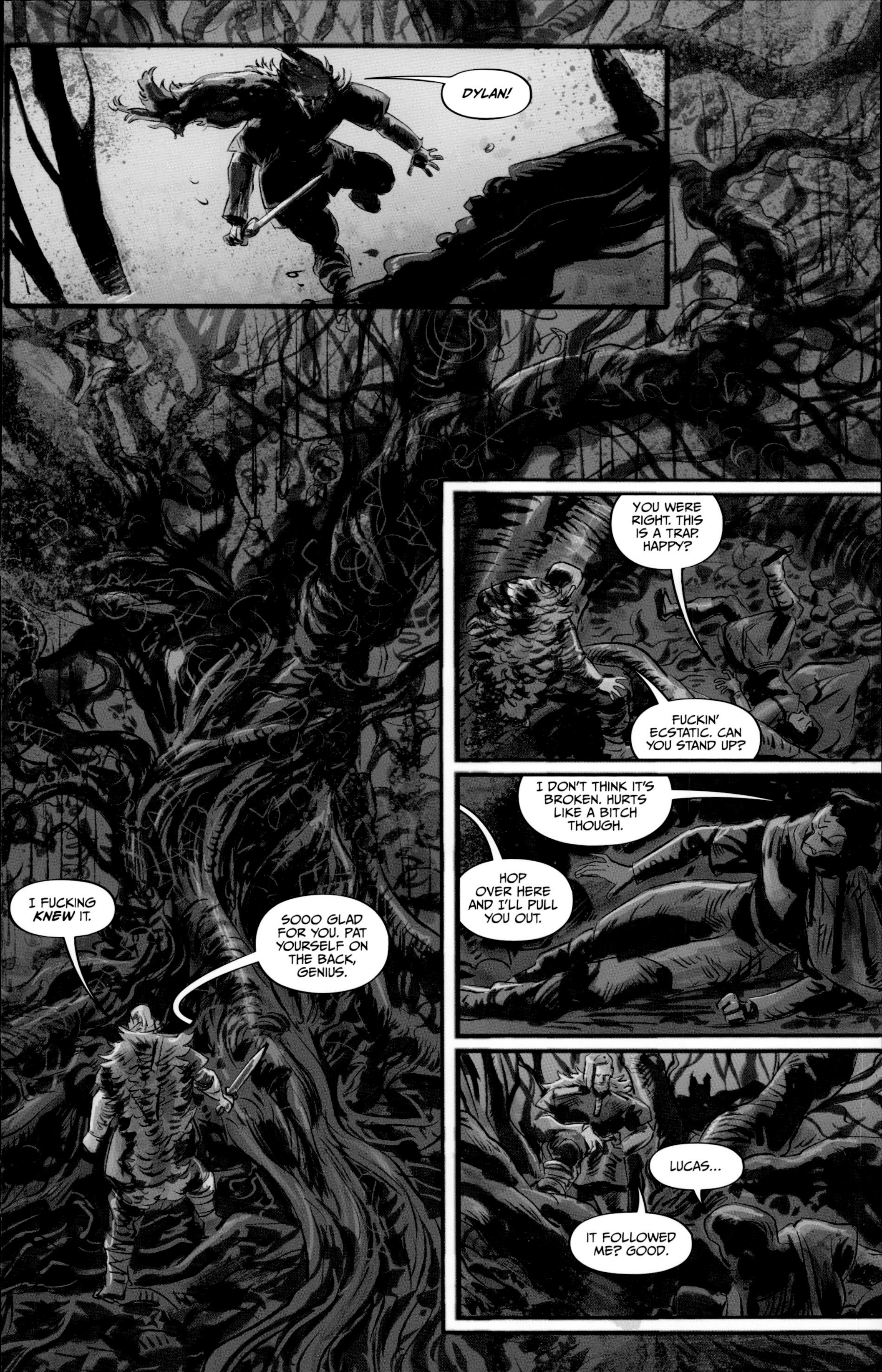
DYLAN!
YOU WERE RIGHT. THIS IS A TRAP. HAPPY?
FUCKIN' ECSTATIC. CAN YOU STAND UP?
I DON'T THINK IT'S BROKEN. HURTS LIKE A BITCH THOUGH.
HOP OVER HERE AND I'LL PULL YOU OUT.
I FUCKING KNEW IT.
SOOO GLAD FOR YOU. PAT YOURSELF ON THE BACK, GENIUS.
LUCAS...
IT FOLLOWED ME? GOOD.

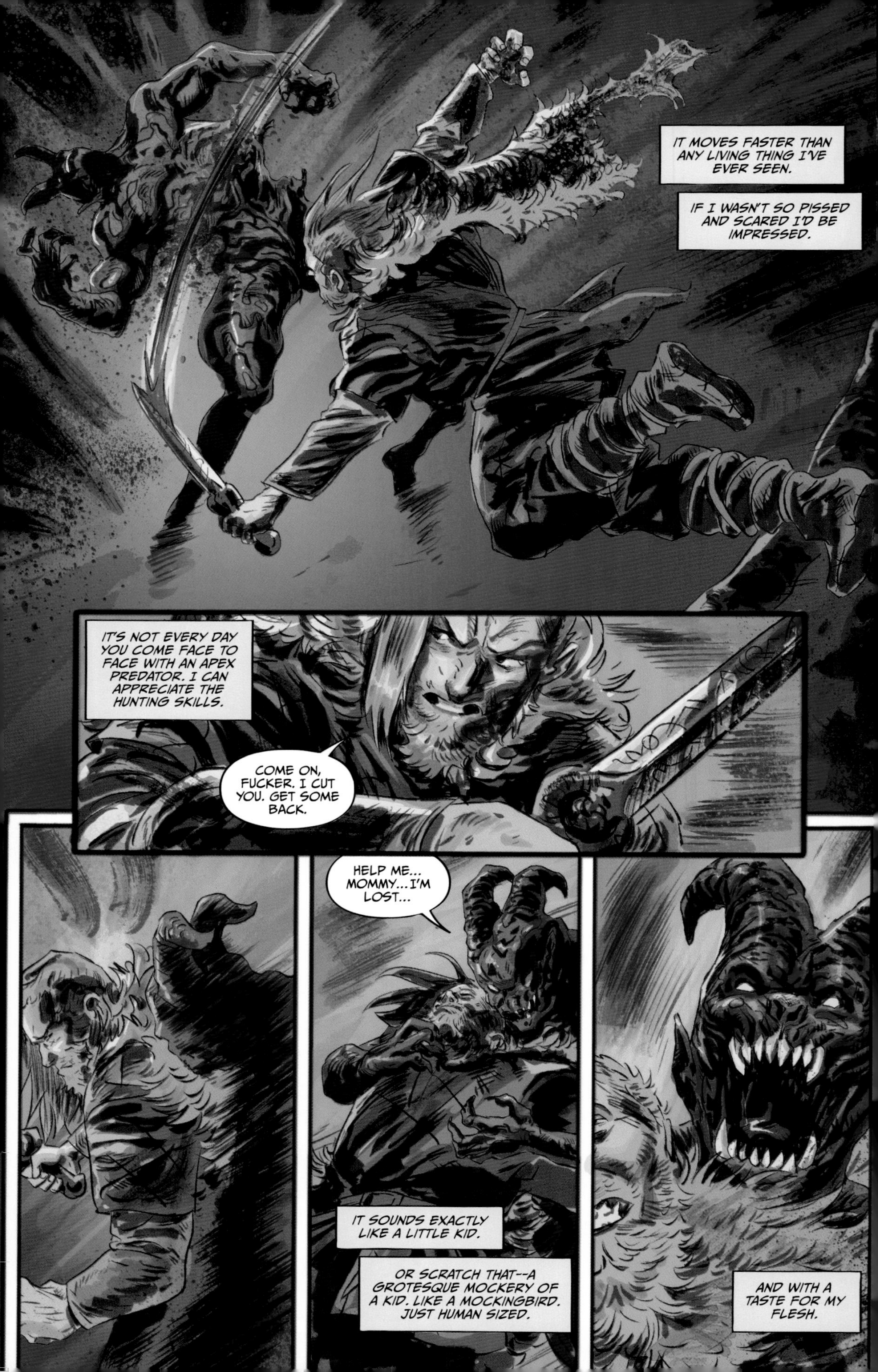
IT MOVES FASTER THAN ANY LIVING THING I'VE EVER SEEN.
IF I WASN'T SO PISSED AND SCARED I'D BE IMPRESSED.
IT'S NOT EVERY DAY YOU COME FACE TO FACE WITH AN APEX PREDATOR. I CAN APPRECIATE THE HUNTING SKILLS.
COME ON, FUCKER. I CUT YOU. GET SOME BACK.
HELP ME... MOMMY...I'M LOST...
IT SOUNDS EXACTLY LIKE A LITTLE KID.
OR SCRATCH THAT--A GROTESQUE MOCKERY OF A KID. LIKE A MOCKINGBIRD. JUST HUMAN SIZED.
AND WITH A TASTE FOR MY FLESH.

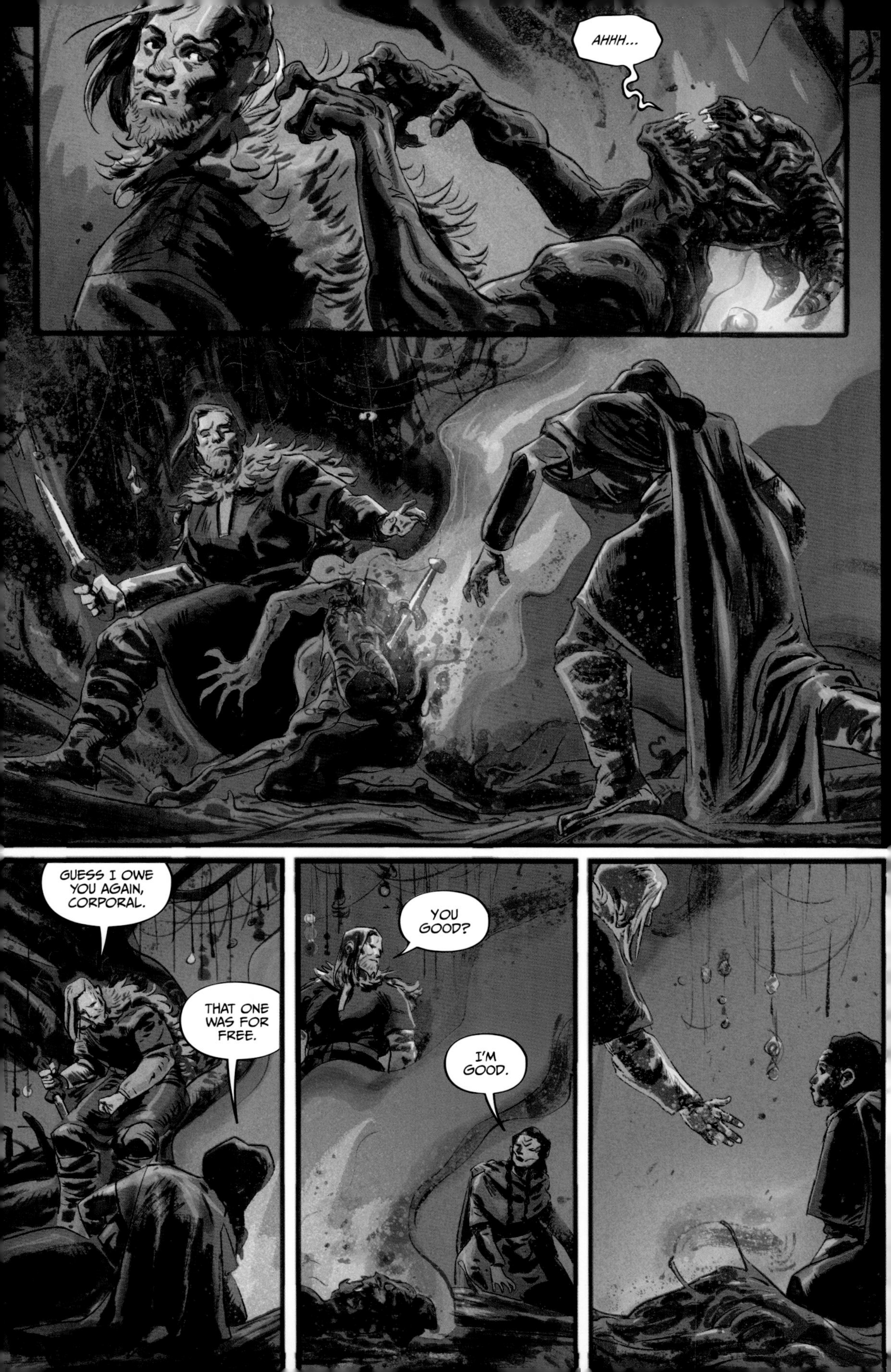
AHHH...
GUESS I OWE YOU AGAIN, CORPORAL.
THAT ONE WAS FOR FREE.
YOU GOOD?
I'M GOOD.

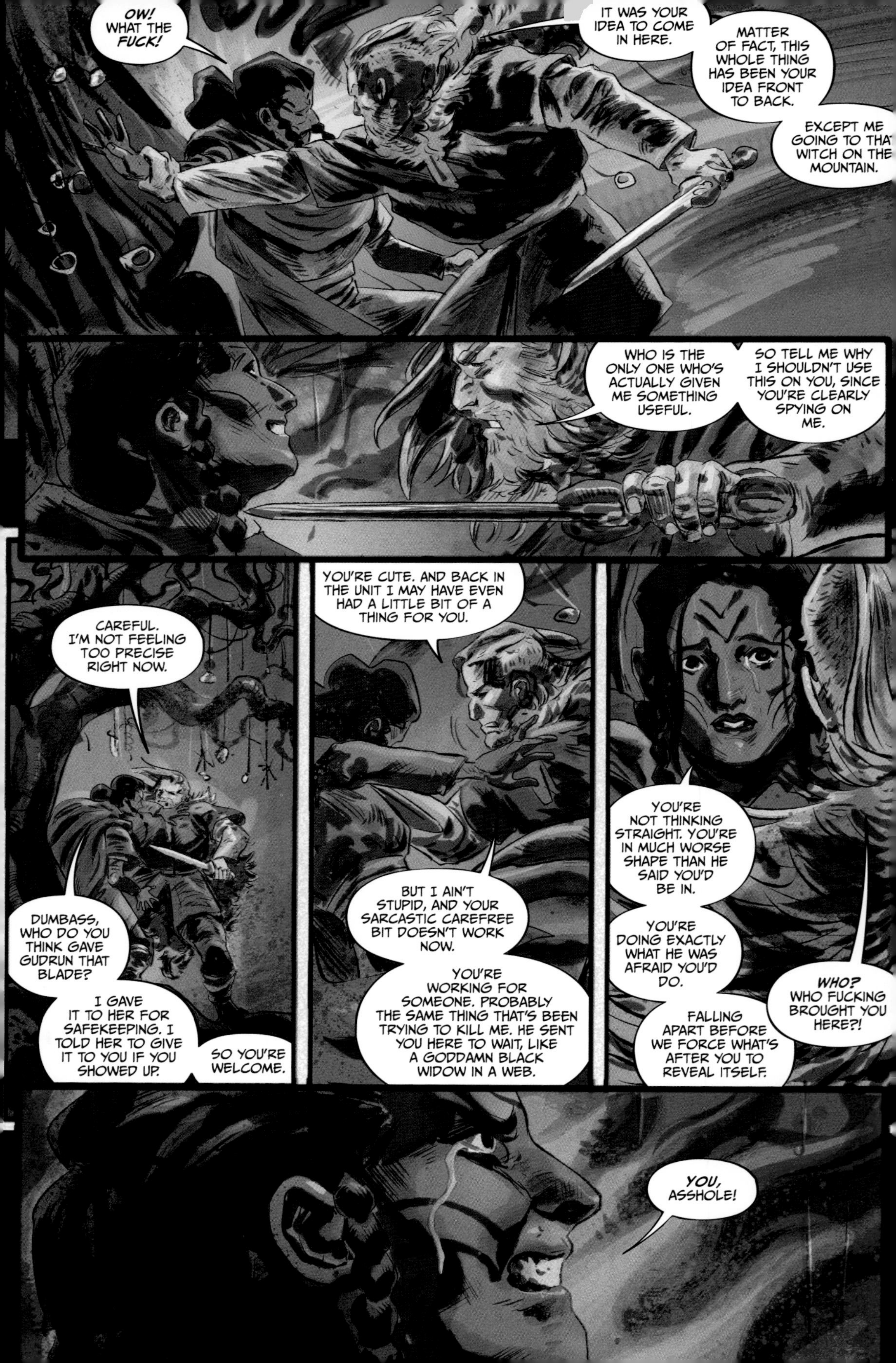
OW! WHAT THE FUCK!
IT WAS YOUR IDEA TO COME IN HERE.
MATTER OF FACT, THIS WHOLE THING HAS BEEN YOUR IDEA FRONT TO BACK.
EXCEPT ME GOING TO THAT WITCH ON THE MOUNTAIN.
WHO IS THE ONLY ONE WHO'S ACTUALLY GIVEN ME SOMETHING USEFUL.
SO TELL ME WHY I SHOULDN'T USE THIS ON YOU, SINCE YOU'RE CLEARLY SPYING ON ME.
CAREFUL. I'M NOT FEELING TOO PRECISE RIGHT NOW.
DUMBASS, WHO DO YOU THINK GAVE GUDRUN THAT BLADE?
I GAVE IT TO HER FOR SAFEKEEPING. I TOLD HER TO GIVE IT TO YOU IF YOU SHOWED UP.
SO YOU'RE WELCOME.
YOU'RE CUTE. AND BACK IN THE UNIT I MAY HAVE EVEN HAD A LITTLE BIT OF A THING FOR YOU.
BUT I AIN'T STUPID, AND YOUR SARCASTIC CAREFREE BIT DOESN'T WORK NOW.
YOU'RE WORKING FOR SOMEONE. PROBABLY THE SAME THING THAT'S BEEN TRYING TO KILL ME. HE SENT YOU HERE TO WAIT, LIKE A GODDAMN BLACK WIDOW IN A WEB.
YOU'RE NOT THINKING STRAIGHT. YOU'RE IN MUCH WORSE SHAPE THAN HE SAID YOU'D BE IN.
YOU'RE DOING EXACTLY WHAT HE WAS AFRAID YOU'D DO.
FALLING APART BEFORE WE FORCE WHAT'S AFTER YOU TO REVEAL ITSELF.
WHO? WHO FUCKING BROUGHT YOU HERE?!
YOU, ASSHOLE!

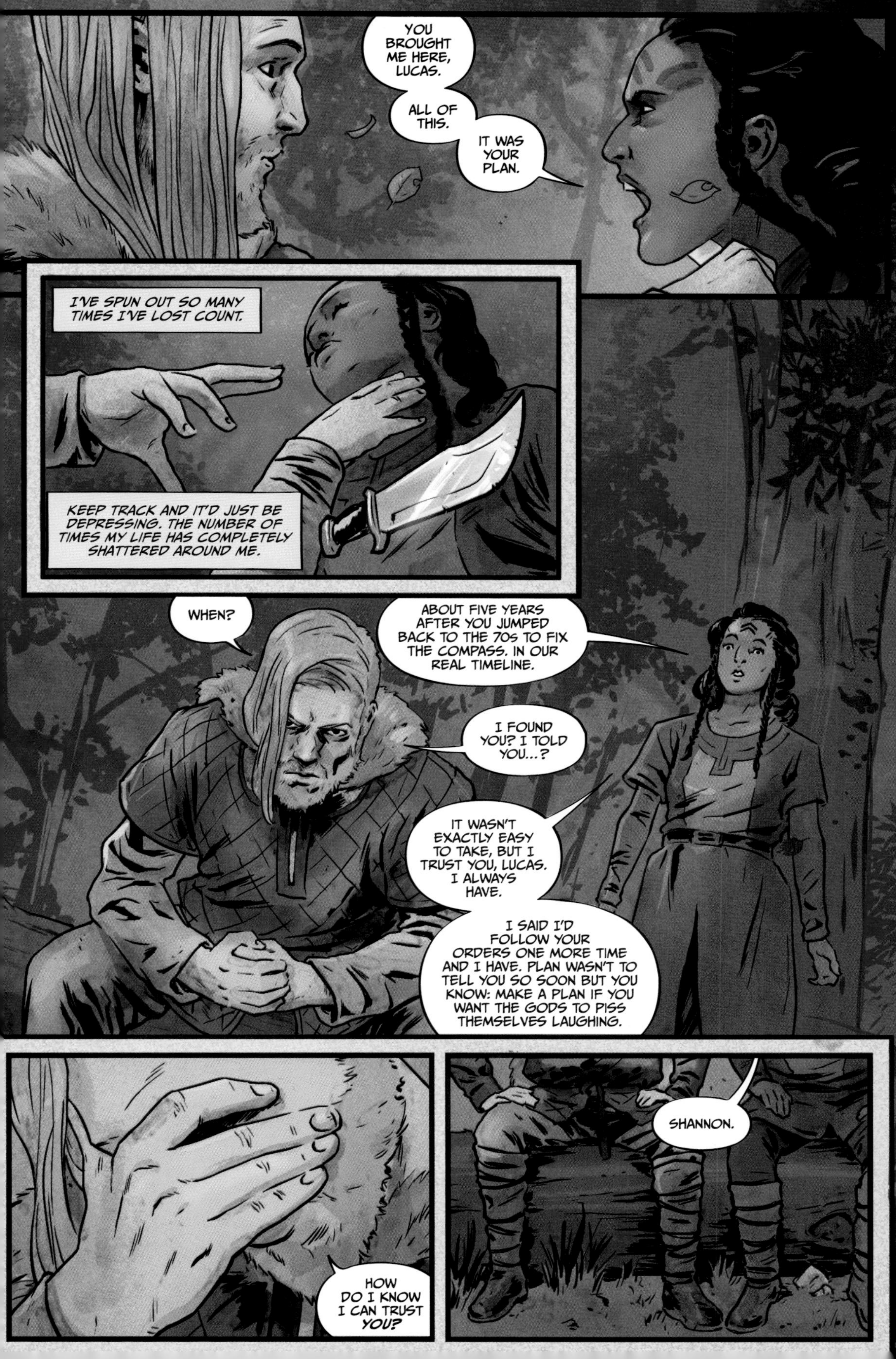
YOU BROUGHT ME HERE, LUCAS.
ALL OF THIS.
IT WAS YOUR PLAN.
I'VE SPUN OUT SO MANY TIMES I'VE LOST COUNT.
KEEP TRACK AND IT'D JUST BE DEPRESSING. THE NUMBER OF TIMES MY LIFE HAS COMPLETELY SHATTERED AROUND ME.
WHEN?
ABOUT FIVE YEARS AFTER YOU JUMPED BACK TO THE 70s TO FIX THE COMPASS. IN OUR REAL TIMELINE.
I FOUND YOU? I TOLD YOU...?
IT WASN'T EXACTLY EASY TO TAKE, BUT I TRUST YOU, LUCAS. I ALWAYS HAVE.
I SAID I'D FOLLOW YOUR ORDERS ONE MORE TIME AND I HAVE. PLAN WASN'T TO TELL YOU SO SOON BUT YOU KNOW: MAKE A PLAN IF YOU WANT THE GODS TO PISS THEMSELVES LAUGHING.
HOW DO I KNOW I CAN TRUST YOU?
SHANNON.

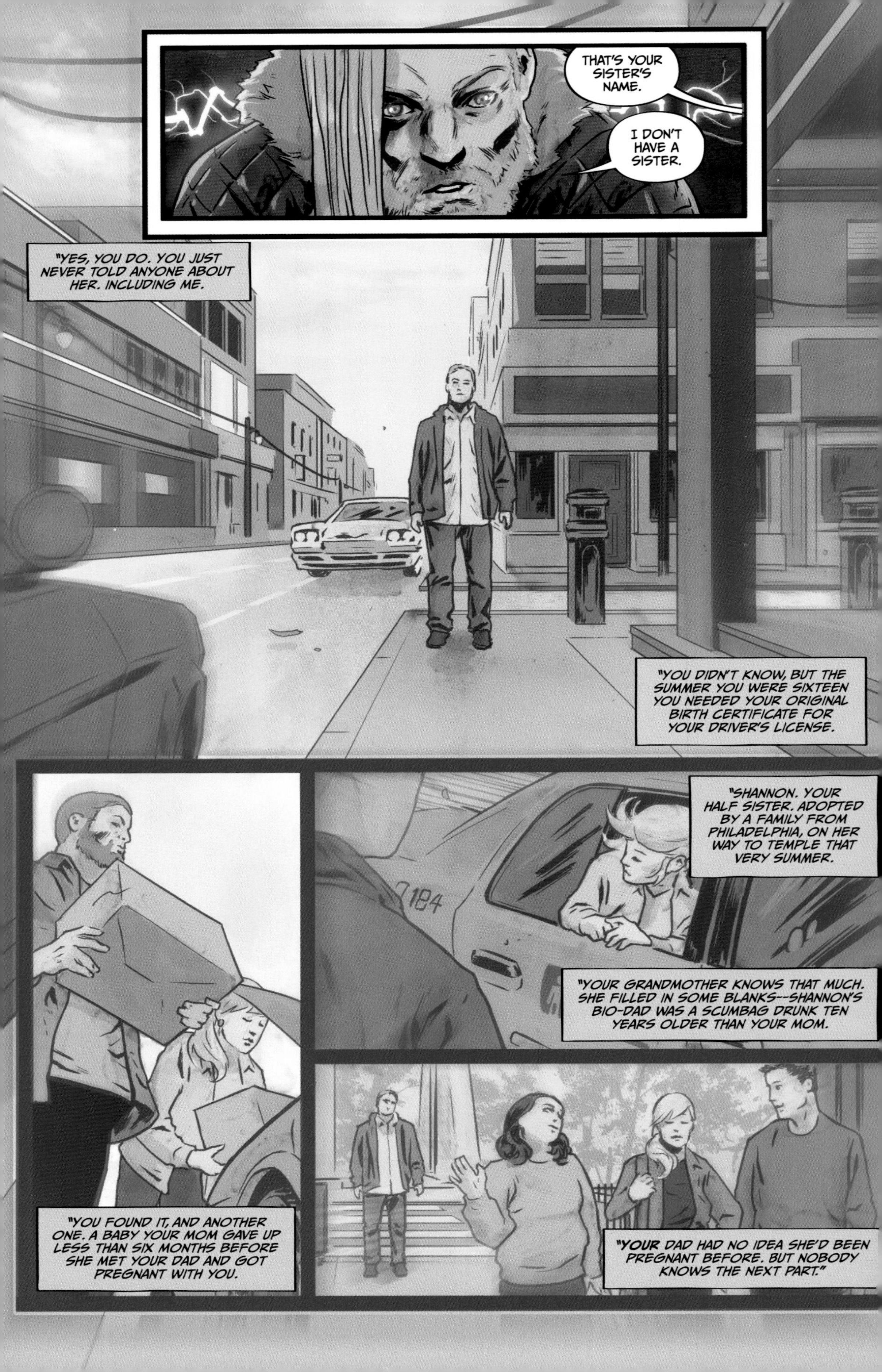
THAT'S YOUR SISTER'S NAME.
I DON'T HAVE A SISTER.
"YES, YOU DO. YOU JUST NEVER TOLD ANYONE ABOUT HER. INCLUDING ME.
"YOU DIDN'T KNOW, BUT THE SUMMER YOU WERE SIXTEEN YOU NEEDED YOUR ORIGINAL BIRTH CERTIFICATE FOR YOUR DRIVER'S LICENSE.
"YOU FOUND IT, AND ANOTHER ONE. A BABY YOUR MOM GAVE UP LESS THAN SIX MONTHS BEFORE SHE MET YOUR DAD AND GOT PREGNANT WITH YOU.
"SHANNON. YOUR HALF SISTER. ADOPTED BY A FAMILY FROM PHILADELPHIA, ON HER WAY TO TEMPLE THAT VERY SUMMER.
"YOUR GRANDMOTHER KNOWS THAT MUCH. SHE FILLED IN SOME BLANKS--SHANNON'S BIO-DAD WAS A SCUMBAG DRUNK TEN YEARS OLDER THAN YOUR MOM.
"YOUR DAD HAD NO IDEA SHE'D BEEN PREGNANT BEFORE. BUT NOBODY KNOWS THE NEXT PART."

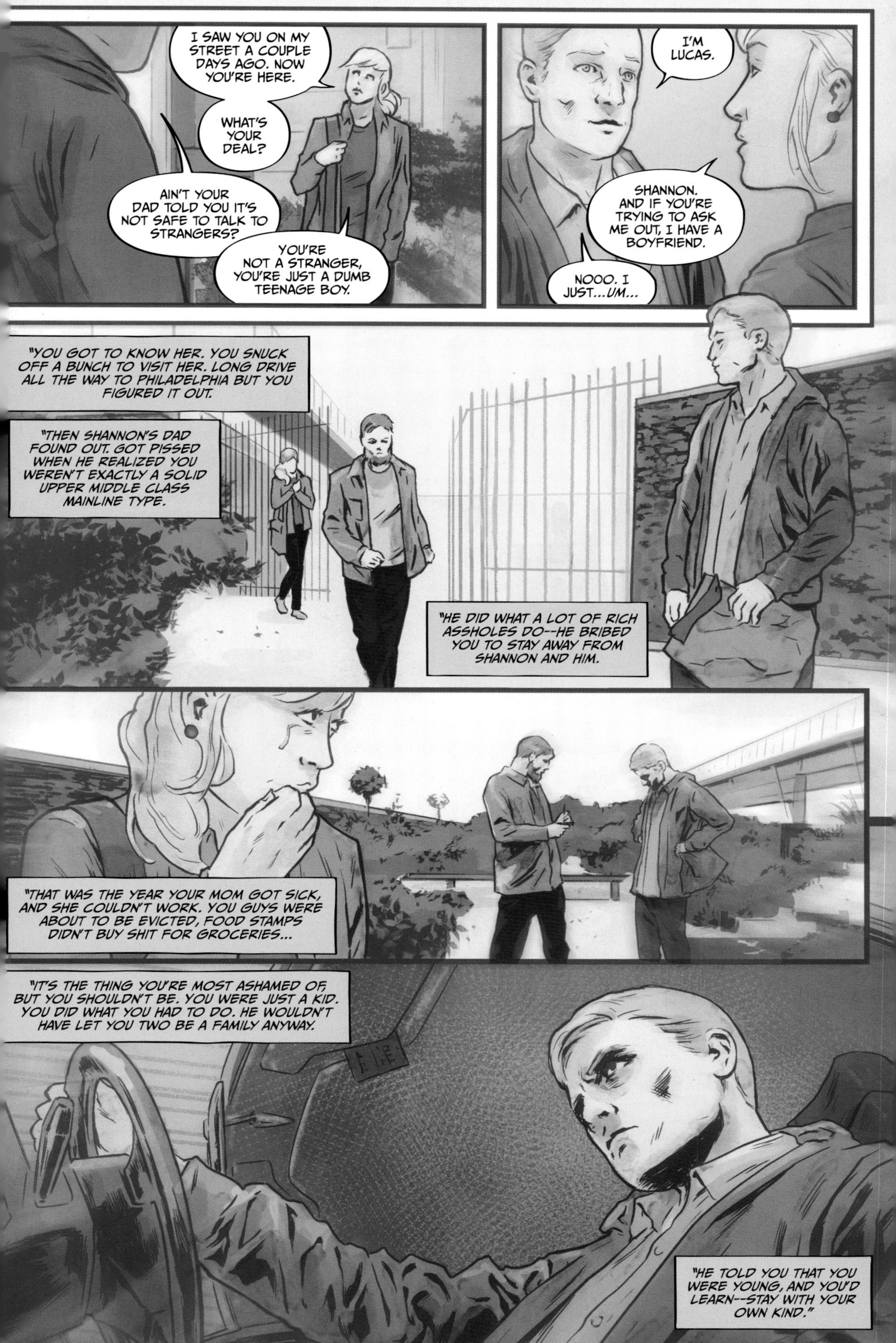
I SAW YOU ON MY STREET A COUPLE DAYS AGO. NOW YOU'RE HERE.
WHAT'S YOUR DEAL?
AIN'T YOUR DAD TOLD YOU IT'S NOT SAFE TO TALK TO STRANGERS?
YOU'RE NOT A STRANGER, YOU'RE JUST A DUMB TEENAGE BOY.
I'M LUCAS.
SHANNON. AND IF YOU'RE TRYING TO ASK ME OUT, I HAVE A BOYFRIEND.
NOOO. I JUST...UM...
"YOU GOT TO KNOW HER. YOU SNUCK OFF A BUNCH TO VISIT HER. LONG DRIVE ALL THE WAY TO PHILADELPHIA BUT YOU FIGURED IT OUT.
"THEN SHANNON'S DAD FOUND OUT. GOT PISSED WHEN HE REALIZED YOU WEREN'T EXACTLY A SOLID UPPER MIDDLE CLASS MAINLINE TYPE.
"HE DID WHAT A LOT OF RICH ASSHOLES DO--HE BRIBED YOU TO STAY AWAY FROM SHANNON AND HIM.
"THAT WAS THE YEAR YOUR MOM GOT SICK, AND SHE COULDN'T WORK. YOU GUYS WERE ABOUT TO BE EVICTED, FOOD STAMPS DIDN'T BUY SHIT FOR GROCERIES...
"IT'S THE THING YOU'RE MOST ASHAMED OF, BUT YOU SHOULDN'T BE. YOU WERE JUST A KID. YOU DID WHAT YOU HAD TO DO. HE WOULDN'T HAVE LET YOU TWO BE A FAMILY ANYWAY.
"HE TOLD YOU THAT YOU WERE YOUNG, AND YOU'D LEARN--STAY WITH YOUR OWN KIND."

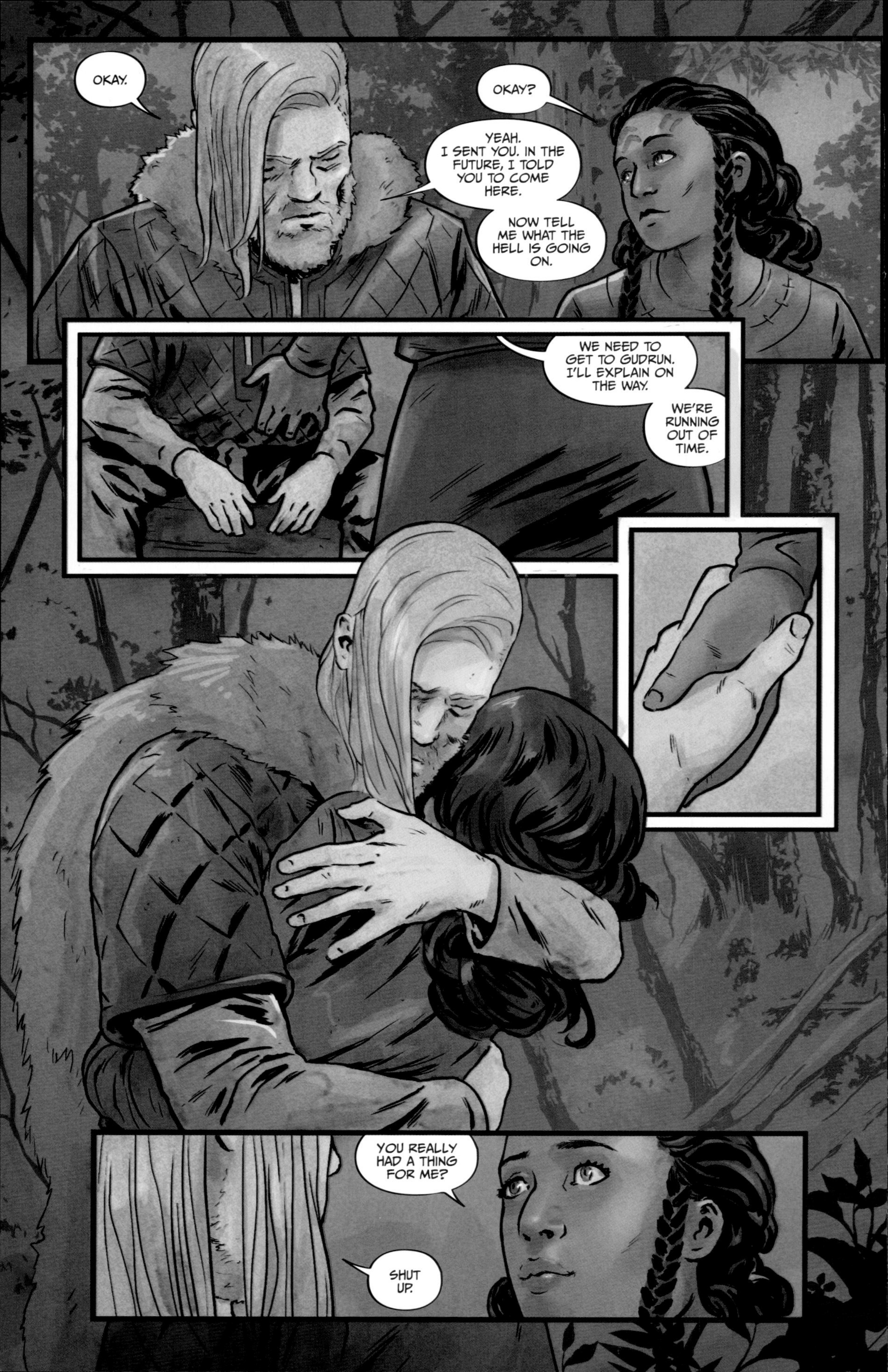
OKAY.
OKAY?
YEAH. I SENT YOU. IN THE FUTURE, I TOLD YOU TO COME HERE.
NOW TELL ME WHAT THE HELL IS GOING ON.
WE NEED TO GET TO GUDRUN. I'LL EXPLAIN ON THE WAY.
WE'RE RUNNING OUT OF TIME.
YOU REALLY HAD A THING FOR ME?
SHUT UP.

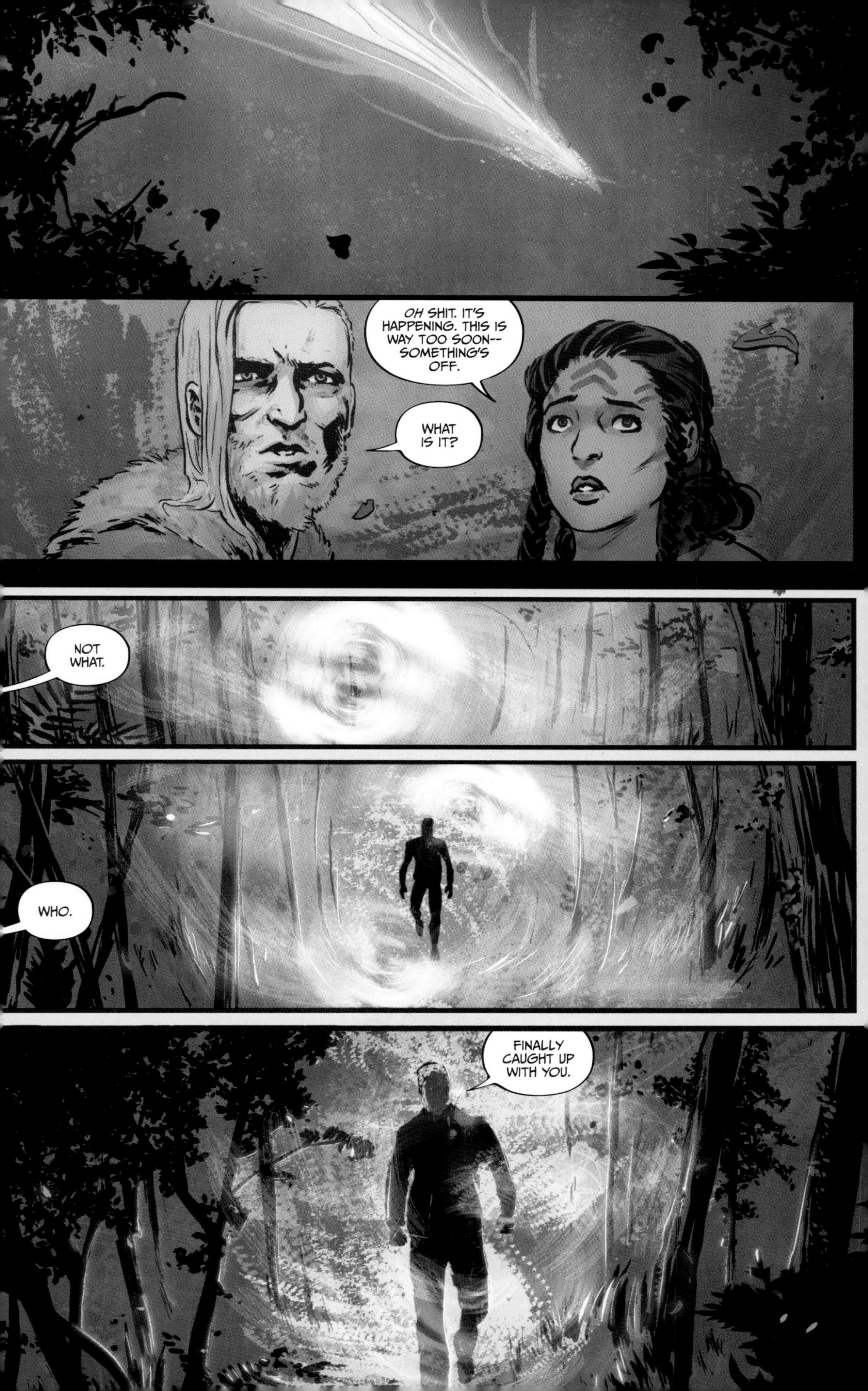
OH SHIT. IT'S HAPPENING. THIS IS WAY TOO SOON-- SOMETHING'S OFF.
WHAT IS IT?
NOT WHAT.
WHO.
FINALLY CAUGHT UP WITH YOU.

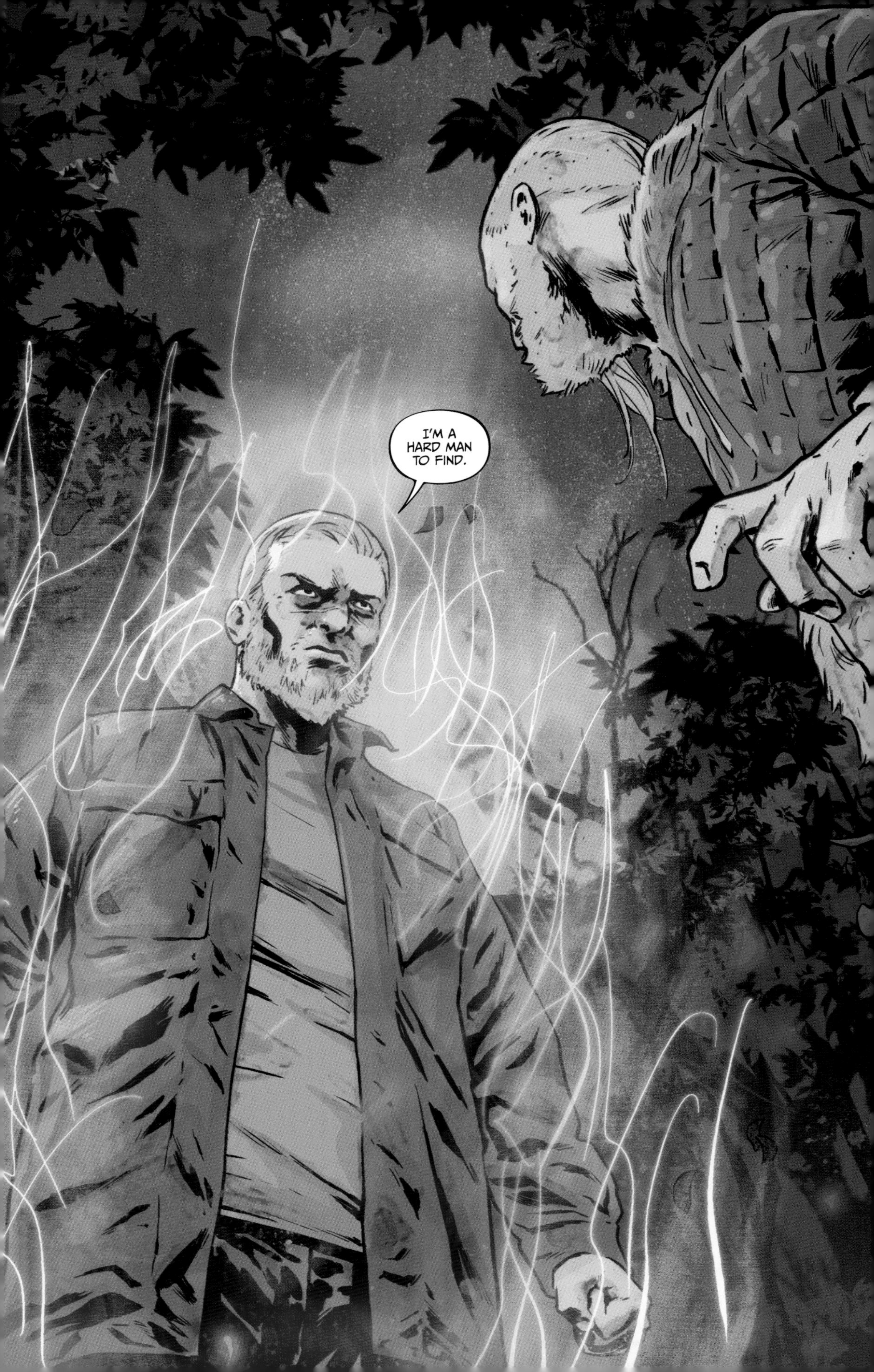
I'M A HARD MAN TO FIND.

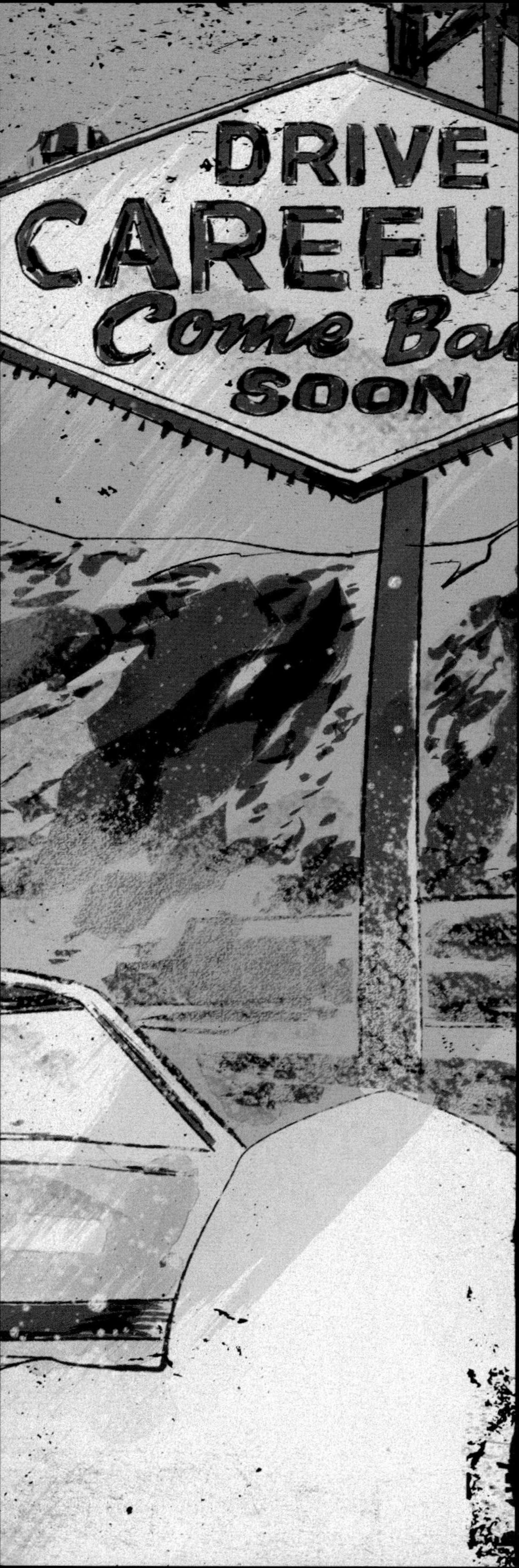
DRIVE
CAREFU
Come Ba
SOON

FOUR

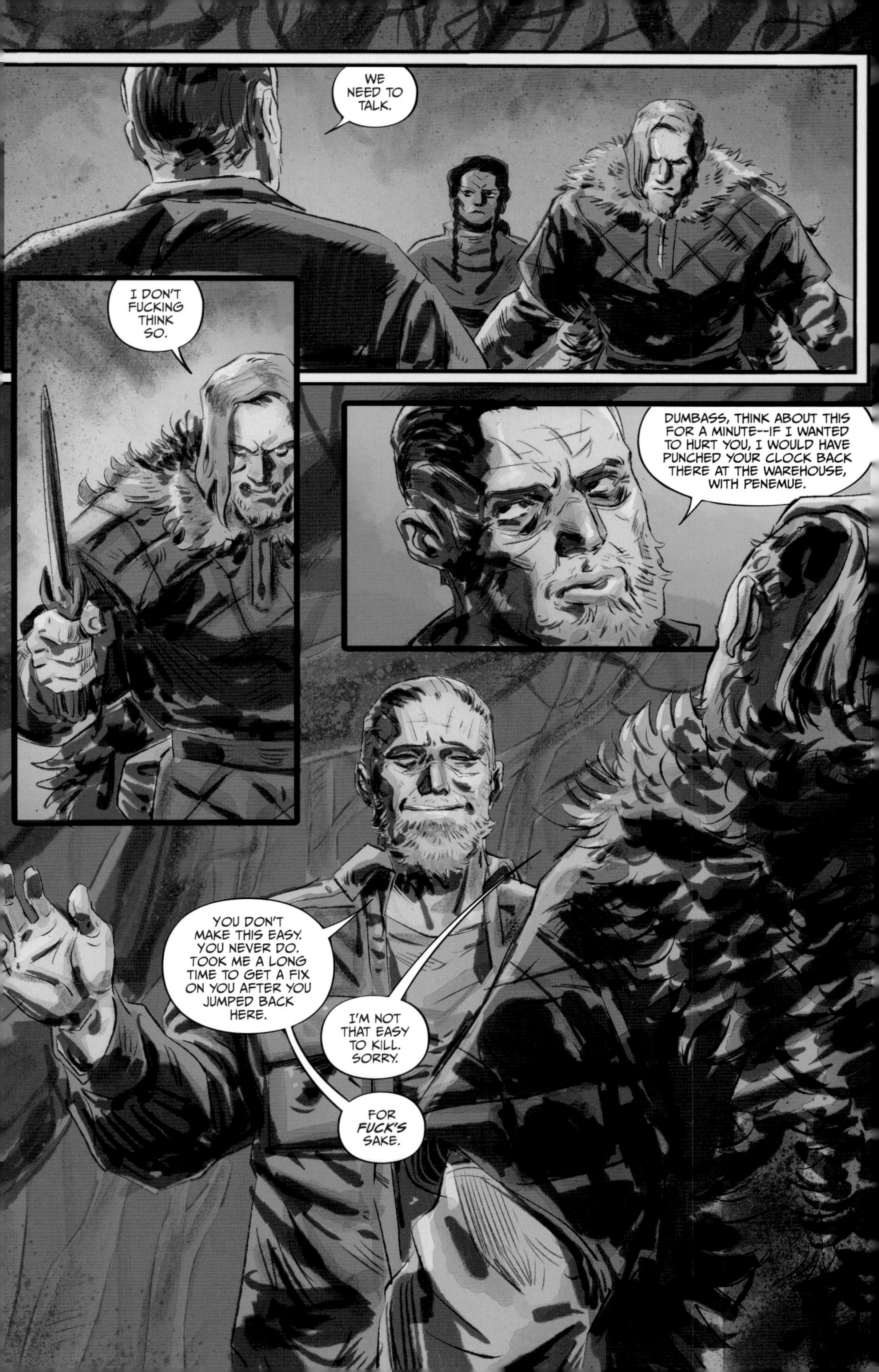
WE NEED TO TALK.
I DON'T FUCKING THINK SO.
DUMBASS, THINK ABOUT THIS FOR A MINUTE--IF I WANTED TO HURT YOU, I WOULD HAVE PUNCHED YOUR CLOCK BACK THERE AT THE WAREHOUSE, WITH PENEMUE.
YOU DON'T MAKE THIS EASY. YOU NEVER DO. TOOK ME A LONG TIME TO GET A FIX ON YOU AFTER YOU JUMPED BACK HERE.
I'M NOT THAT EASY TO KILL. SORRY.
FOR *FUCK'S* SAKE.

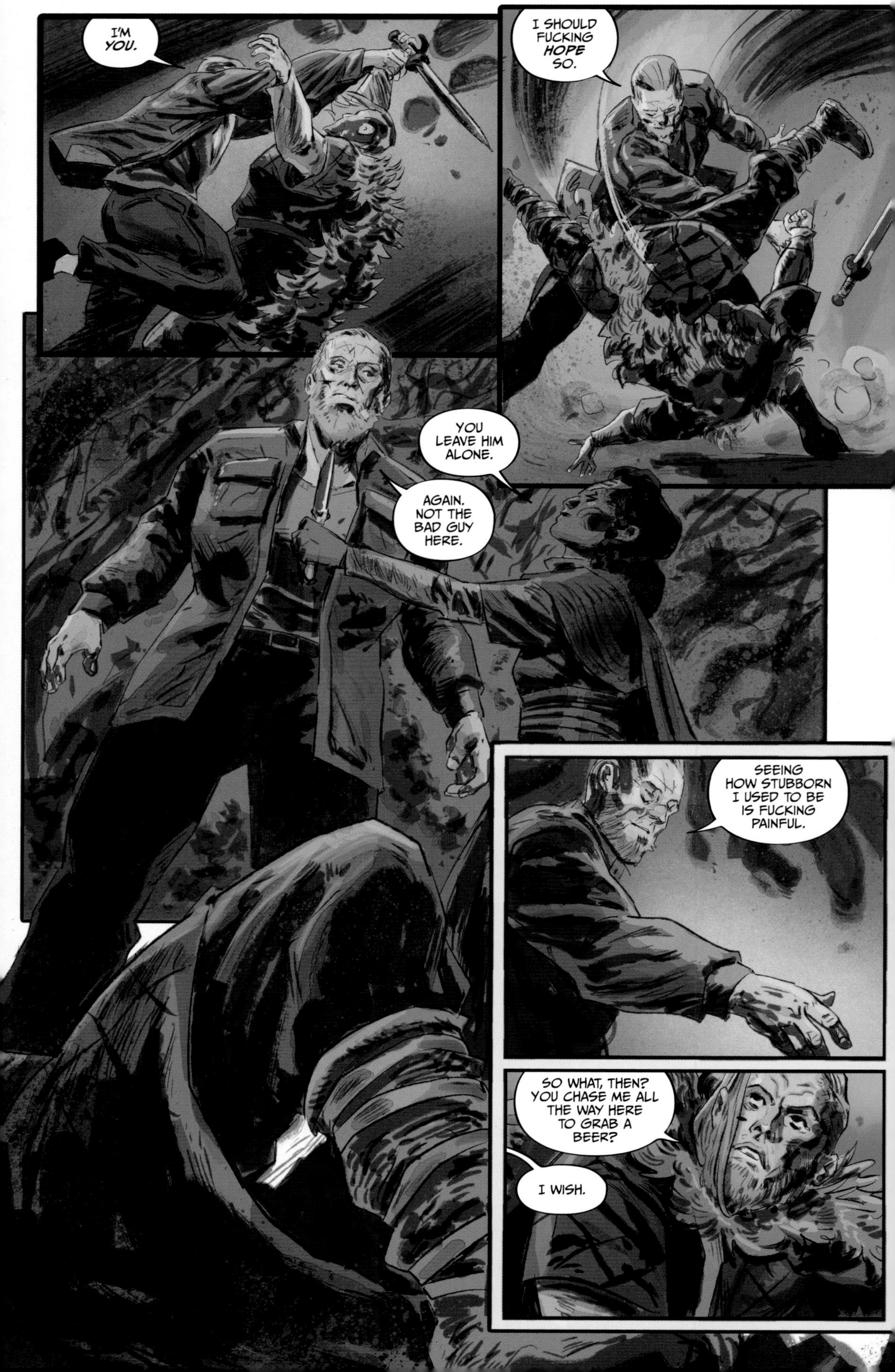
I'M *YOU.*
I SHOULD FUCKING ***HOPE*** SO.
YOU LEAVE HIM ALONE.
AGAIN. NOT THE BAD GUY HERE.
SEEING HOW STUBBORN I USED TO BE IS FUCKING PAINFUL.
SO WHAT, THEN? YOU CHASE ME ALL THE WAY HERE TO GRAB A BEER?
I WISH.

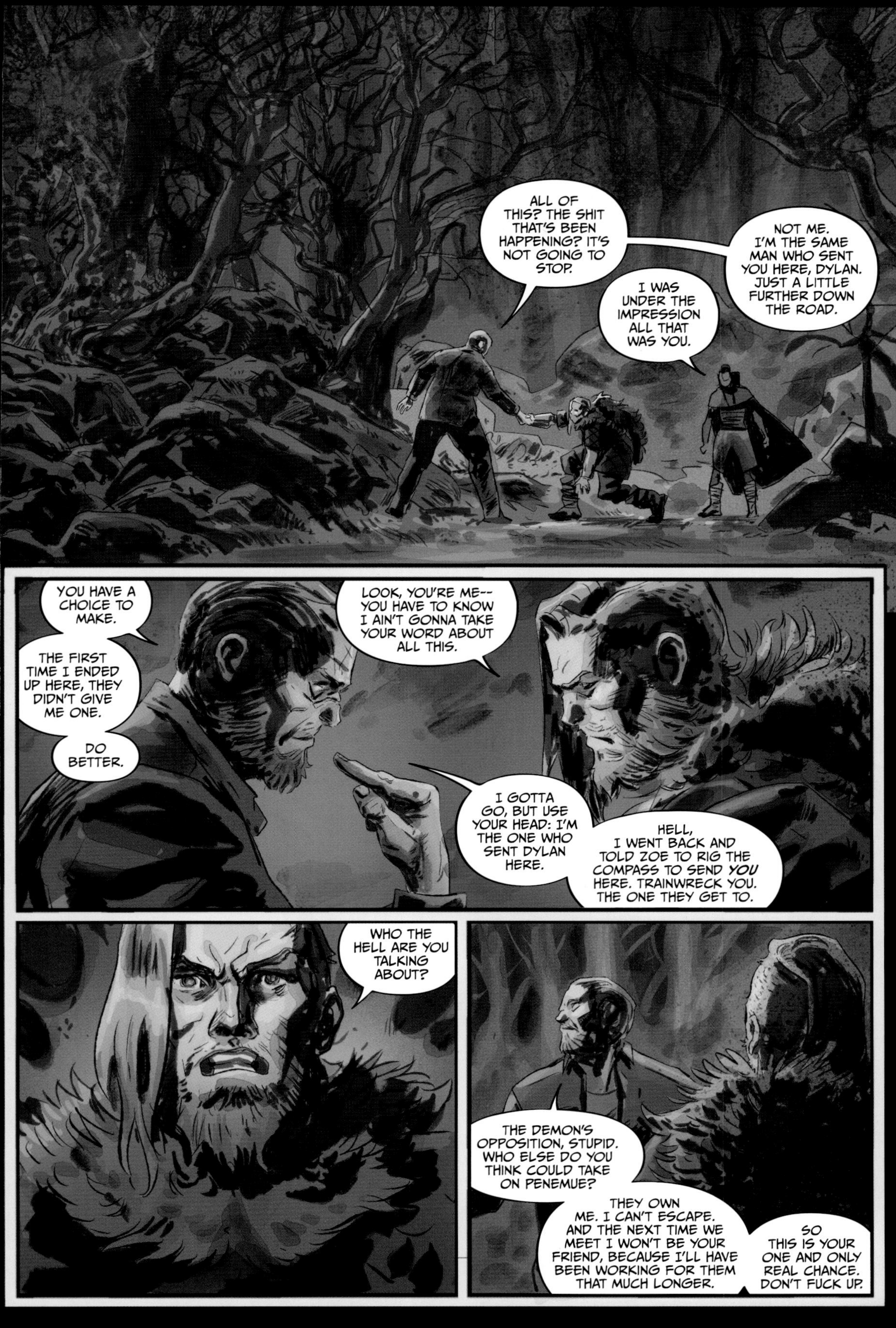
ALL OF THIS? THE SHIT THAT'S BEEN HAPPENING? IT'S NOT GOING TO STOP.
I WAS UNDER THE IMPRESSION ALL THAT WAS YOU.
NOT ME. I'M THE SAME MAN WHO SENT YOU HERE, DYLAN. JUST A LITTLE FURTHER DOWN THE ROAD.
YOU HAVE A CHOICE TO MAKE.
THE FIRST TIME I ENDED UP HERE, THEY DIDN'T GIVE ME ONE.
DO BETTER.
LOOK, YOU'RE ME-- YOU HAVE TO KNOW I AIN'T GONNA TAKE YOUR WORD ABOUT ALL THIS.
I GOTTA GO, BUT USE YOUR HEAD: I'M THE ONE WHO SENT DYLAN HERE.
HELL, I WENT BACK AND TOLD ZOE TO RIG THE COMPASS TO SEND *YOU* HERE. TRAINWRECK YOU. THE ONE THEY GET TO.
WHO THE HELL ARE YOU TALKING ABOUT?
THE DEMON'S OPPOSITION, STUPID. WHO ELSE DO YOU THINK COULD TAKE ON PENEMUE?
THEY OWN ME. I CAN'T ESCAPE. AND THE NEXT TIME WE MEET I WON'T BE YOUR FRIEND, BECAUSE I'LL HAVE BEEN WORKING FOR THEM THAT MUCH LONGER.
SO THIS IS YOUR ONE AND ONLY REAL CHANCE. DON'T FUCK UP.

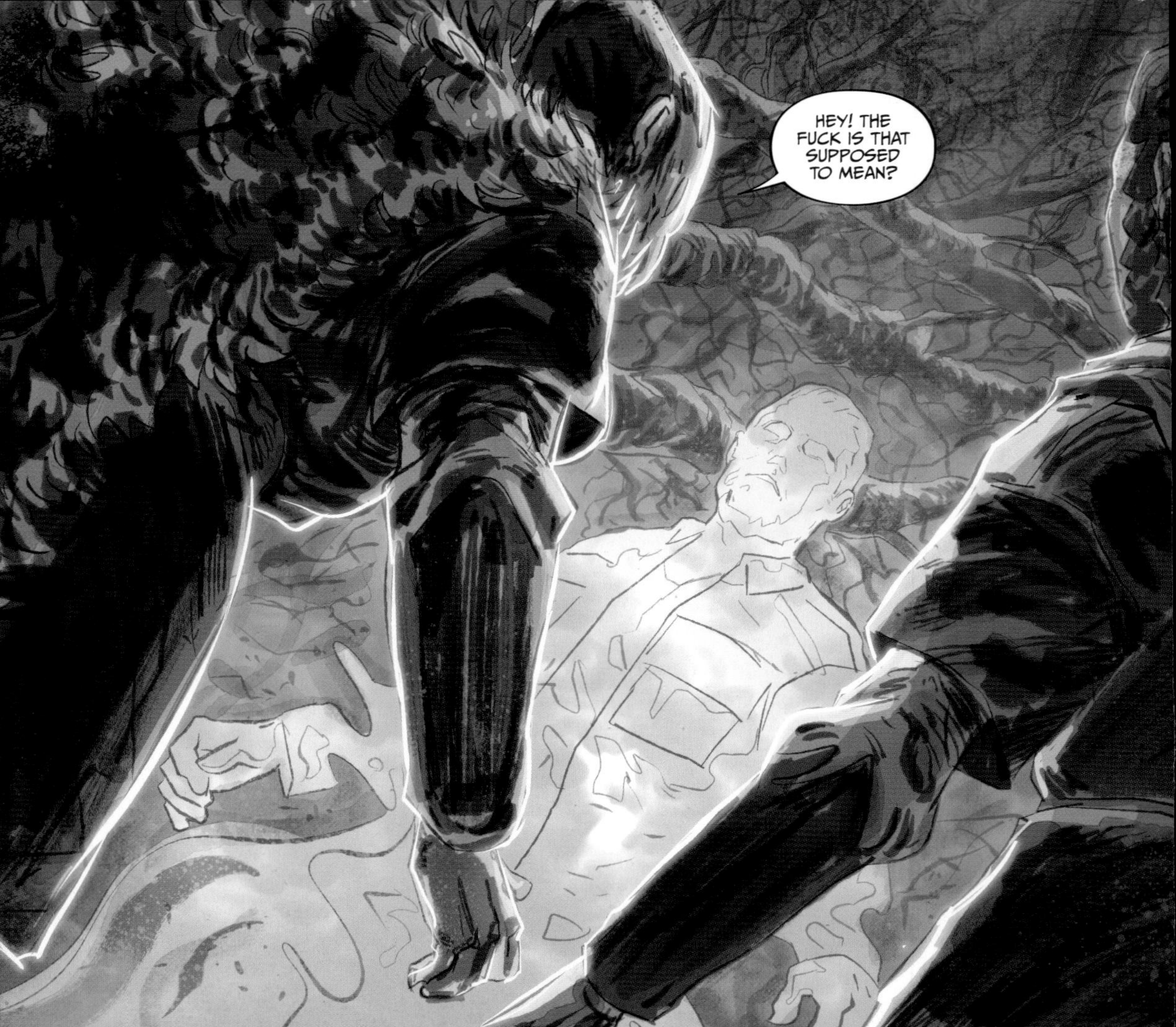
HEY! THE FUCK IS THAT SUPPOSED TO MEAN?

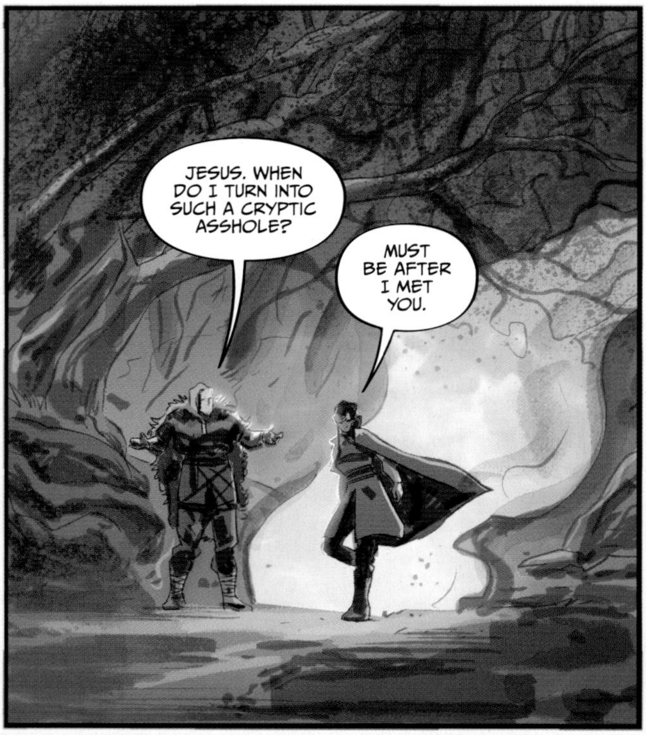
JESUS. WHEN DO I TURN INTO SUCH A CRYPTIC ASSHOLE?
MUST BE AFTER I MET YOU.

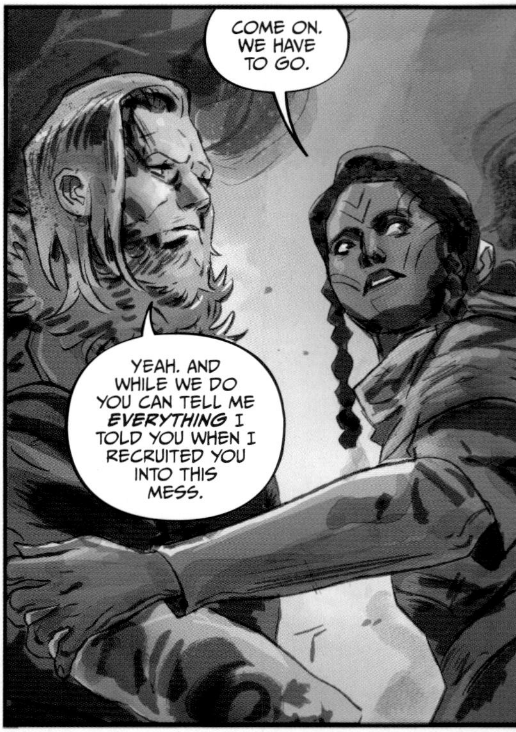
COME ON. WE HAVE TO GO.
YEAH. AND WHILE WE DO YOU CAN TELL ME *EVERYTHING* I TOLD YOU WHEN I RECRUITED YOU INTO THIS MESS.

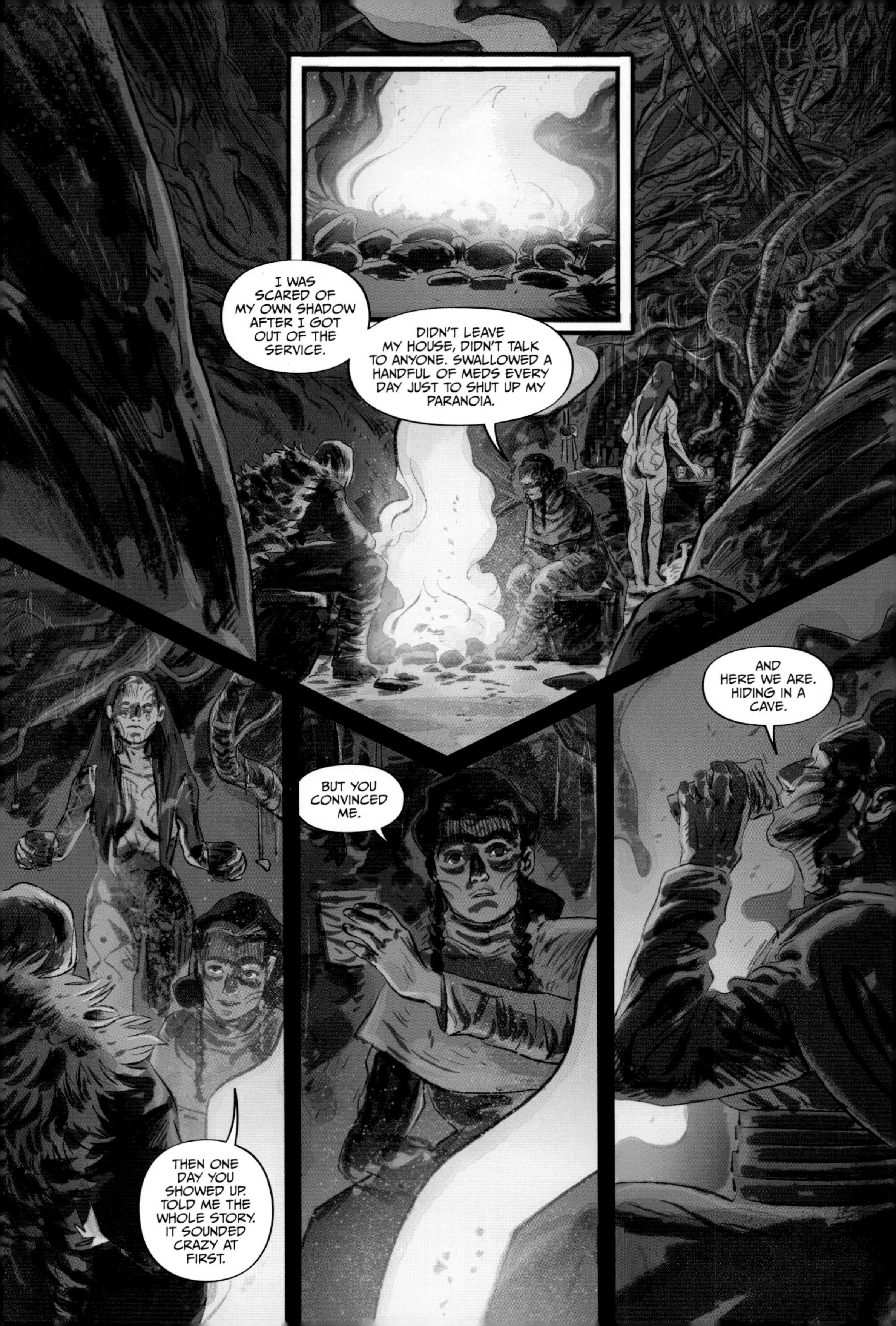
I WAS SCARED OF MY OWN SHADOW AFTER I GOT OUT OF THE SERVICE.
DIDN'T LEAVE MY HOUSE, DIDN'T TALK TO ANYONE. SWALLOWED A HANDFUL OF MEDS EVERY DAY JUST TO SHUT UP MY PARANOIA.
THEN ONE DAY YOU SHOWED UP. TOLD ME THE WHOLE STORY. IT SOUNDED CRAZY AT FIRST.
BUT YOU CONVINCED ME.
AND HERE WE ARE. HIDING IN A CAVE.

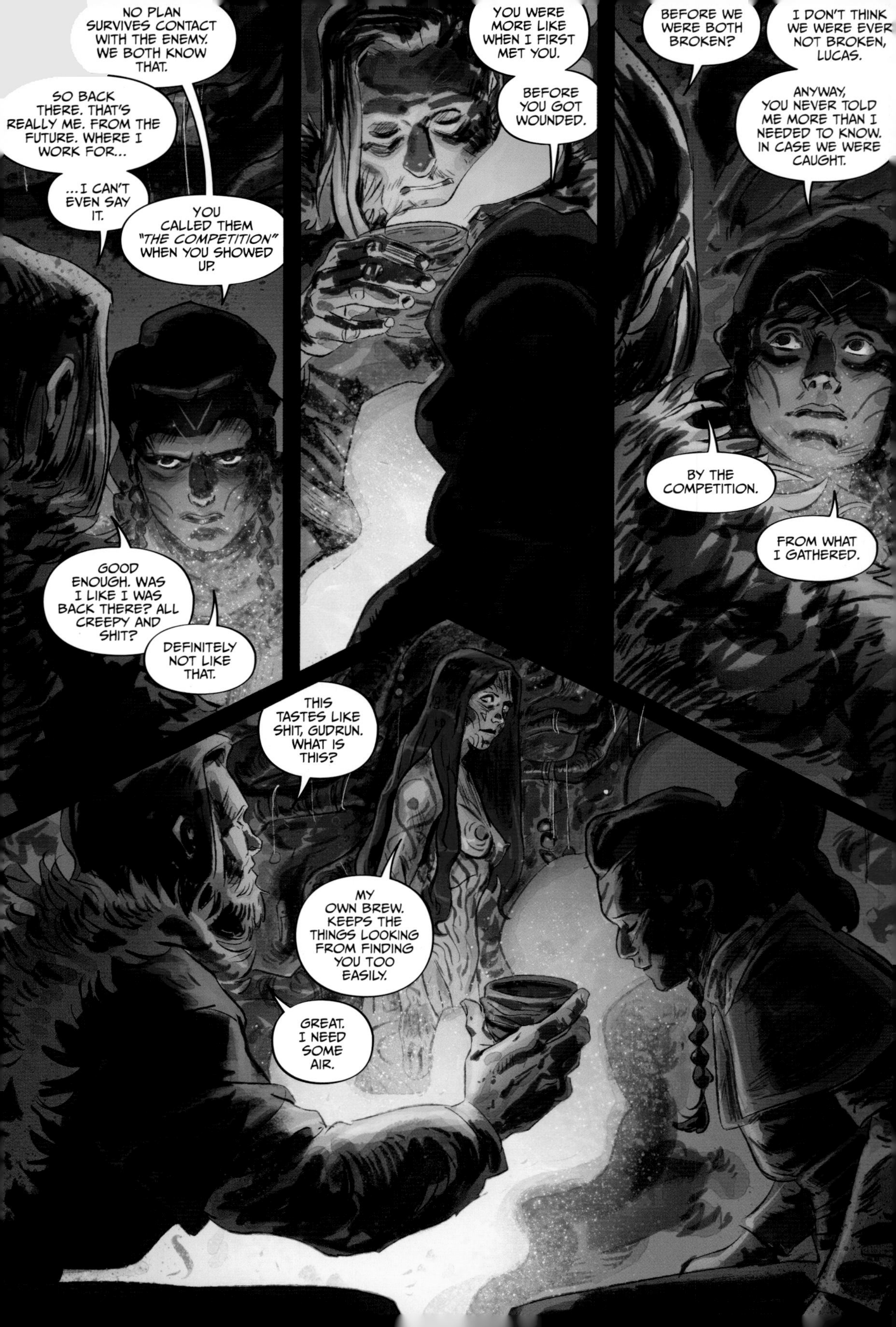
NO PLAN SURVIVES CONTACT WITH THE ENEMY. WE BOTH KNOW THAT.
SO BACK THERE. THAT'S REALLY ME. FROM THE FUTURE. WHERE I WORK FOR...
...I CAN'T EVEN SAY IT.
YOU CALLED THEM "THE COMPETITION" WHEN YOU SHOWED UP.
GOOD ENOUGH. WAS I LIKE I WAS BACK THERE? ALL CREEPY AND SHIT?
DEFINITELY NOT LIKE THAT.
YOU WERE MORE LIKE WHEN I FIRST MET YOU.
BEFORE YOU GOT WOUNDED.
BEFORE WE WERE BOTH BROKEN?
I DON'T THINK WE WERE EVER NOT BROKEN, LUCAS.
ANYWAY, YOU NEVER TOLD ME MORE THAN I NEEDED TO KNOW. IN CASE WE WERE CAUGHT.
BY THE COMPETITION.
FROM WHAT I GATHERED.
THIS TASTES LIKE SHIT, GUDRUN. WHAT IS THIS?
MY OWN BREW. KEEPS THE THINGS LOOKING FROM FINDING YOU TOO EASILY.
GREAT. I NEED SOME AIR.

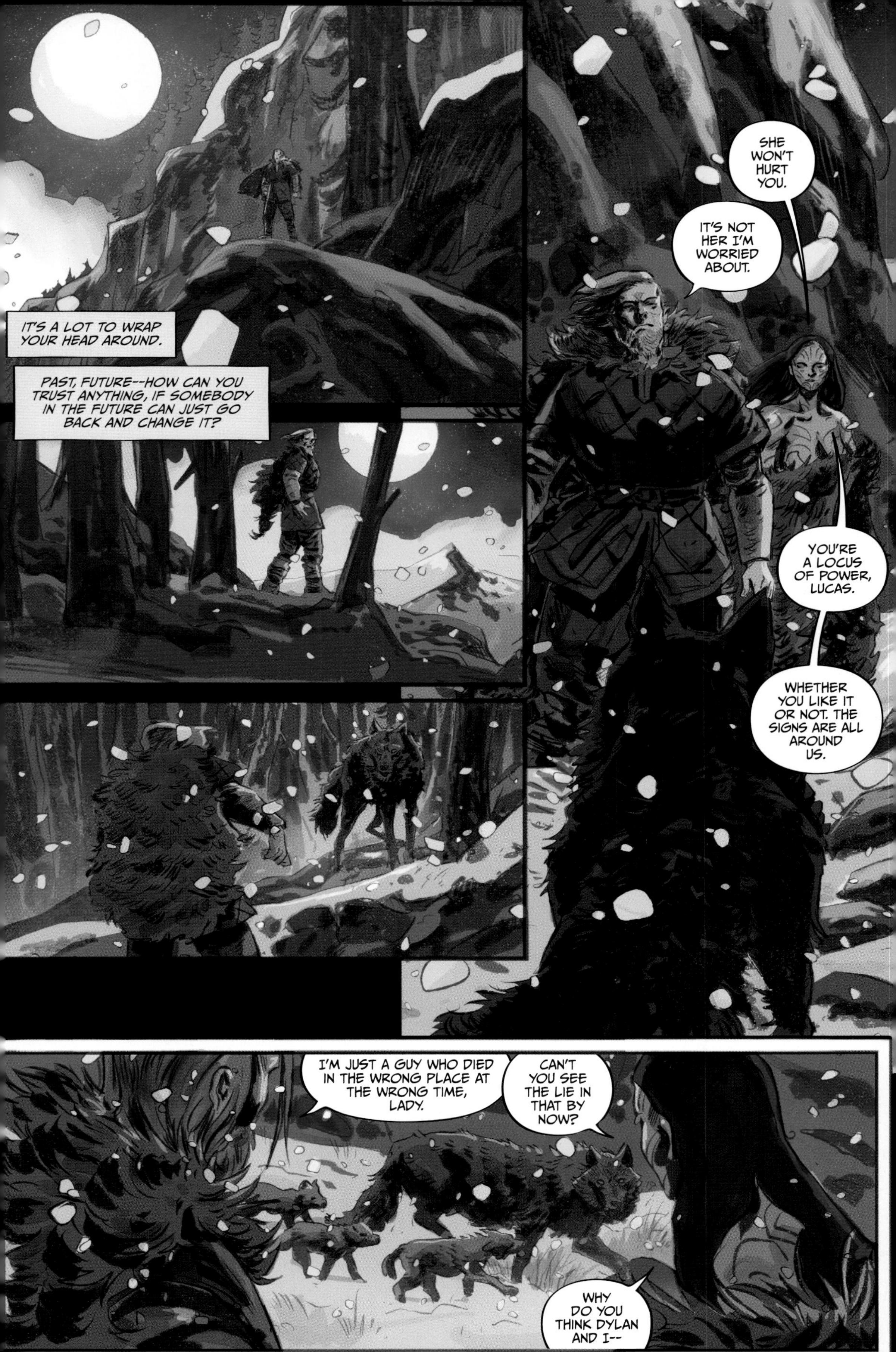
IT'S A LOT TO WRAP YOUR HEAD AROUND.
PAST, FUTURE--HOW CAN YOU TRUST ANYTHING, IF SOMEBODY IN THE FUTURE CAN JUST GO BACK AND CHANGE IT?
SHE WON'T HURT YOU.
IT'S NOT HER I'M WORRIED ABOUT.
YOU'RE A LOCUS OF POWER, LUCAS.
WHETHER YOU LIKE IT OR NOT. THE SIGNS ARE ALL AROUND US.
I'M JUST A GUY WHO DIED IN THE WRONG PLACE AT THE WRONG TIME, LADY.
CAN'T YOU SEE THE LIE IN THAT BY NOW?
WHY DO YOU THINK DYLAN AND I--

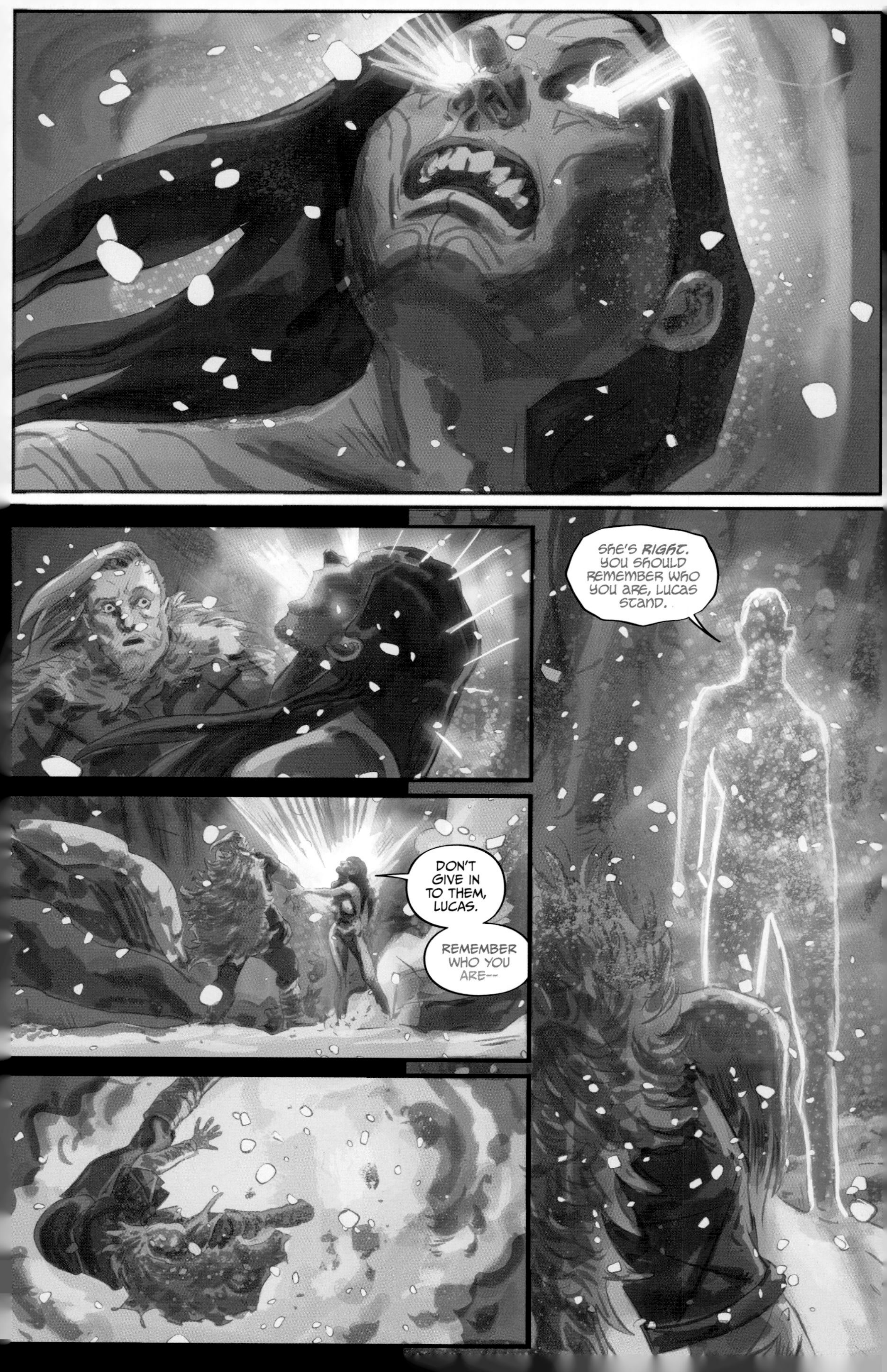
DON'T GIVE IN TO THEM, LUCAS.
REMEMBER WHO YOU ARE--
SHE'S RIGHT. YOU SHOULD REMEMBER WHO YOU ARE, LUCAS STAND.

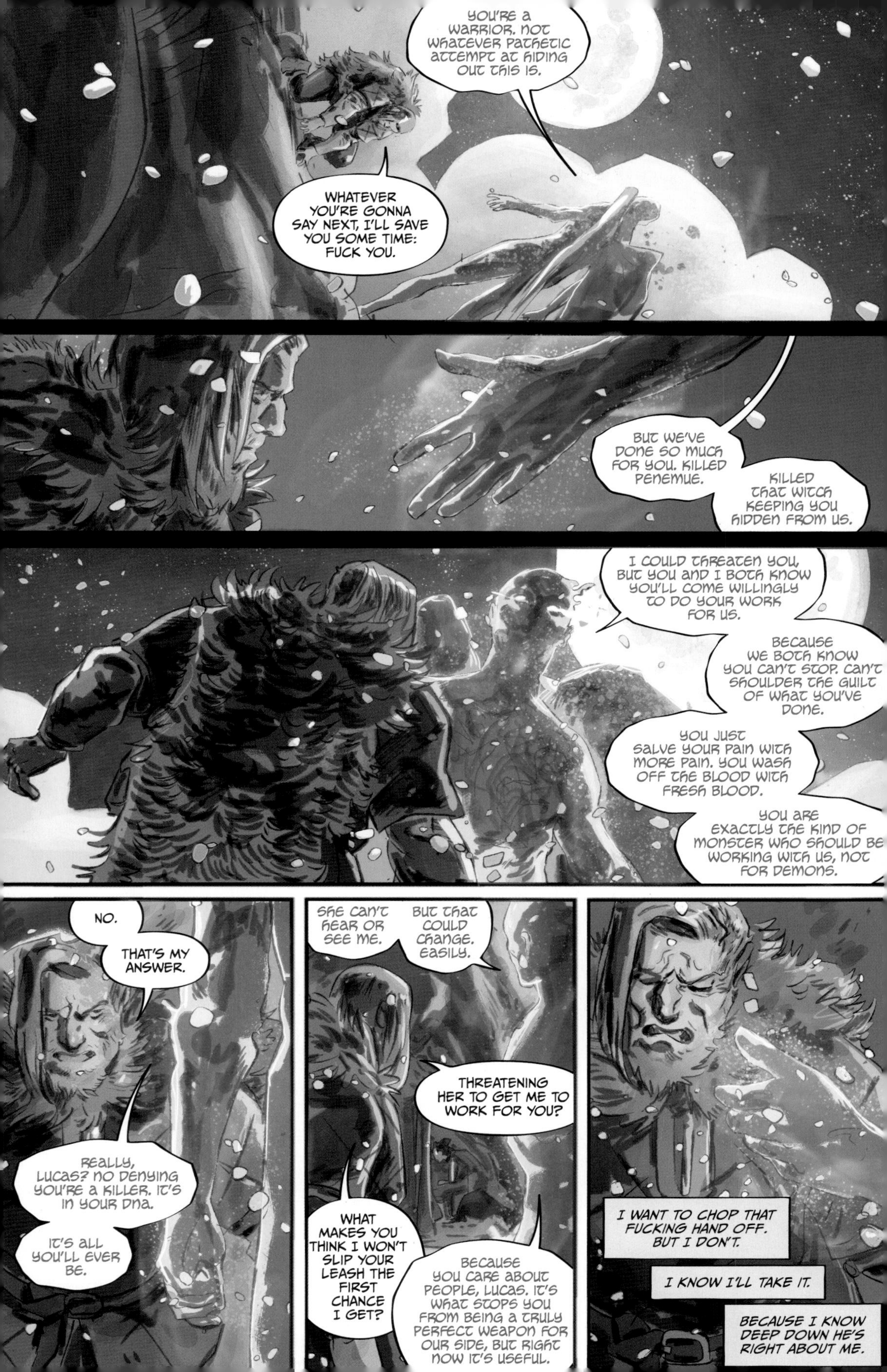
YOU'RE A WARRIOR. NOT WHATEVER PATHETIC ATTEMPT AT HIDING OUT THIS IS.
WHATEVER YOU'RE GONNA SAY NEXT, I'LL SAVE YOU SOME TIME: FUCK YOU.
BUT WE'VE DONE SO MUCH FOR YOU. KILLED PENEMUE.
KILLED THAT WITCH KEEPING YOU HIDDEN FROM US.
I COULD THREATEN YOU, BUT YOU AND I BOTH KNOW YOU'LL COME WILLINGLY TO DO YOUR WORK FOR US.
BECAUSE WE BOTH KNOW YOU CAN'T STOP. CAN'T SHOULDER THE GUILT OF WHAT YOU'VE DONE.
YOU JUST SALVE YOUR PAIN WITH MORE PAIN. YOU WASH OFF THE BLOOD WITH FRESH BLOOD.
YOU ARE EXACTLY THE KIND OF MONSTER WHO SHOULD BE WORKING WITH US, NOT FOR DEMONS.
NO.
THAT'S MY ANSWER.
REALLY, LUCAS? NO DENYING YOU'RE A KILLER. IT'S IN YOUR DNA.
IT'S ALL YOU'LL EVER BE.
SHE CAN'T HEAR OR SEE ME.
BUT THAT COULD CHANGE. EASILY.
THREATENING HER TO GET ME TO WORK FOR YOU?
WHAT MAKES YOU THINK I WON'T SLIP YOUR LEASH THE FIRST CHANCE I GET?
BECAUSE YOU CARE ABOUT PEOPLE, LUCAS. IT'S WHAT STOPS YOU FROM BEING A TRULY PERFECT WEAPON FOR OUR SIDE, BUT RIGHT NOW IT'S USEFUL.
I WANT TO CHOP THAT FUCKING HAND OFF. BUT I DON'T.
I KNOW I'LL TAKE IT.
BECAUSE I KNOW DEEP DOWN HE'S RIGHT ABOUT ME.

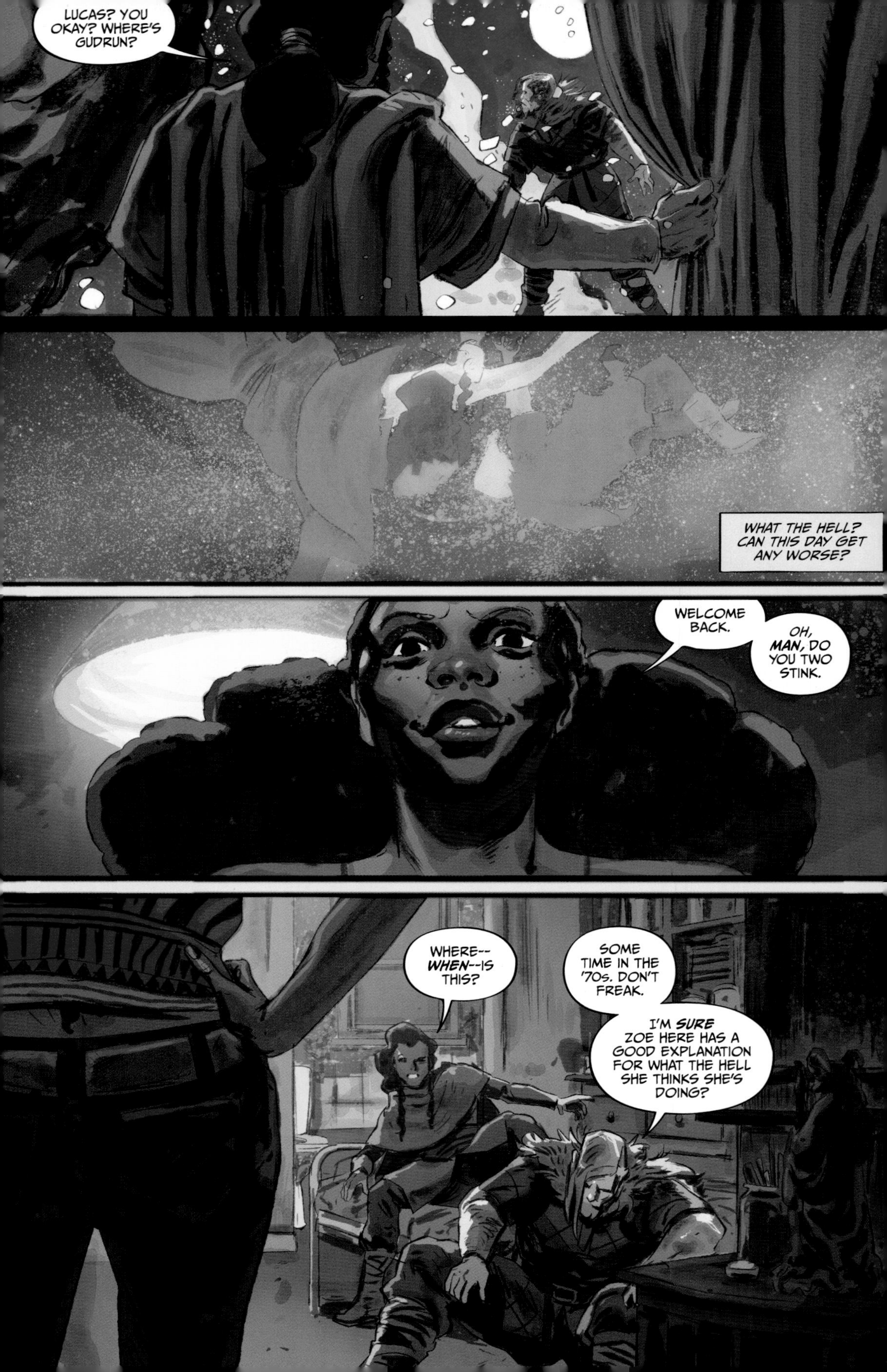
LUCAS? YOU OKAY? WHERE'S GUDRUN?
WHAT THE HELL? CAN THIS DAY GET ANY WORSE?
WELCOME BACK.
OH, MAN, DO YOU TWO STINK.
WHERE-- WHEN--IS THIS?
SOME TIME IN THE '70s. DON'T FREAK.
I'M SURE ZOE HERE HAS A GOOD EXPLANATION FOR WHAT THE HELL SHE THINKS SHE'S DOING?

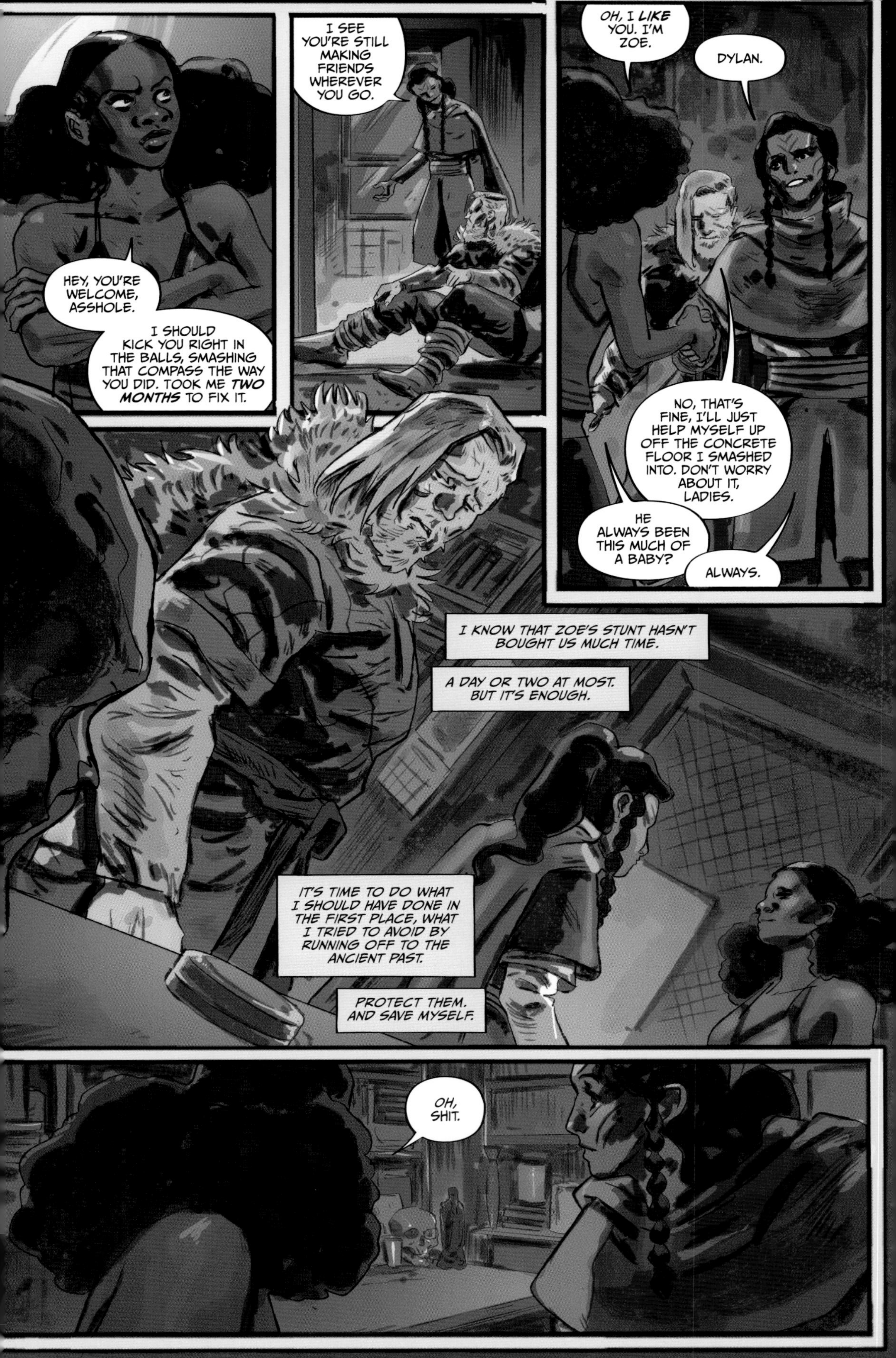
HEY, YOU'RE WELCOME, ASSHOLE.
I SHOULD KICK YOU RIGHT IN THE BALLS, SMASHING THAT COMPASS THE WAY YOU DID. TOOK ME TWO MONTHS TO FIX IT.
I SEE YOU'RE STILL MAKING FRIENDS WHEREVER YOU GO.
OH, I LIKE YOU. I'M ZOE.
DYLAN.
NO, THAT'S FINE, I'LL JUST HELP MYSELF UP OFF THE CONCRETE FLOOR I SMASHED INTO. DON'T WORRY ABOUT IT, LADIES.
HE ALWAYS BEEN THIS MUCH OF A BABY?
ALWAYS.
I KNOW THAT ZOE'S STUNT HASN'T BOUGHT US MUCH TIME.
A DAY OR TWO AT MOST. BUT IT'S ENOUGH.
IT'S TIME TO DO WHAT I SHOULD HAVE DONE IN THE FIRST PLACE, WHAT I TRIED TO AVOID BY RUNNING OFF TO THE ANCIENT PAST.
PROTECT THEM. AND SAVE MYSELF.
OH, SHIT.

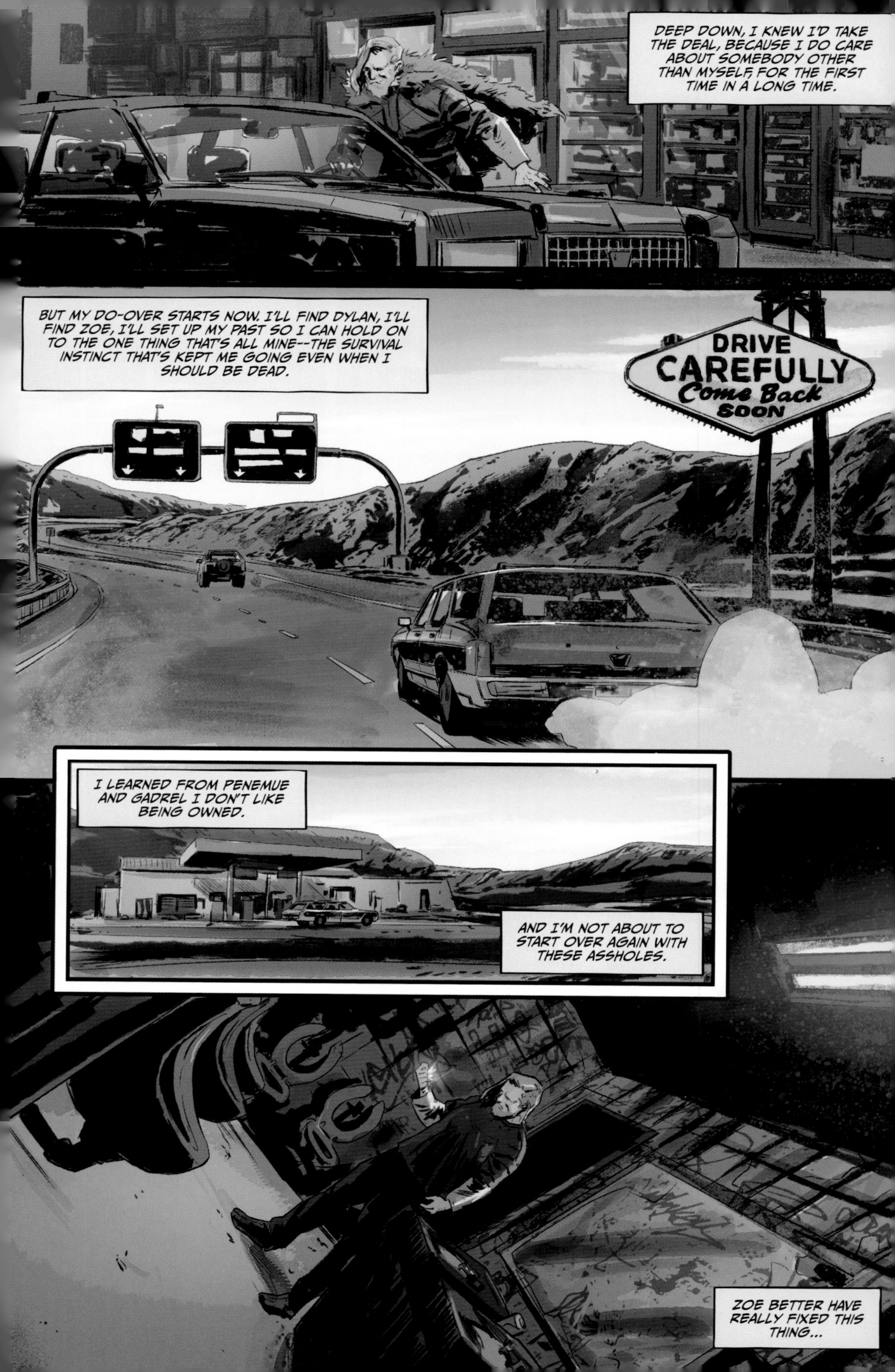
DEEP DOWN, I KNEW I'D TAKE THE DEAL, BECAUSE I DO CARE ABOUT SOMEBODY OTHER THAN MYSELF, FOR THE FIRST TIME IN A LONG TIME.
BUT MY DO-OVER STARTS NOW. I'LL FIND DYLAN, I'LL FIND ZOE, I'LL SET UP MY PAST SO I CAN HOLD ON TO THE ONE THING THAT'S ALL MINE--THE SURVIVAL INSTINCT THAT'S KEPT ME GOING EVEN WHEN I SHOULD BE DEAD.
DRIVE CAREFULLY Come Back SOON
I LEARNED FROM PENEMUE AND GADREL I DON'T LIKE BEING OWNED.
AND I'M NOT ABOUT TO START OVER AGAIN WITH THESE ASSHOLES.
ZOE BETTER HAVE REALLY FIXED THIS THING...

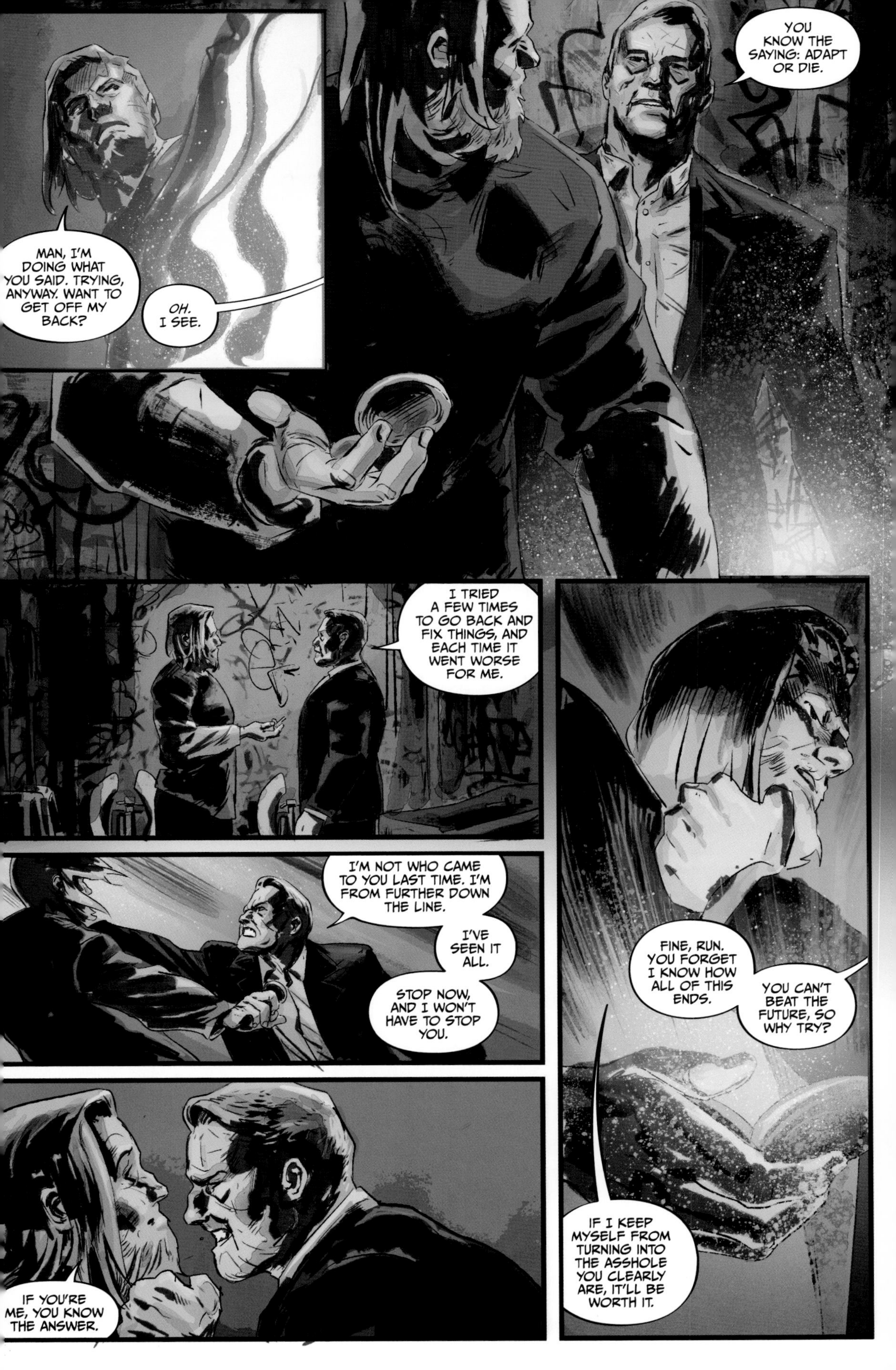
YOU KNOW THE SAYING: ADAPT OR DIE.
MAN, I'M DOING WHAT YOU SAID. TRYING, ANYWAY. WANT TO GET OFF MY BACK?
OH. I SEE.
I TRIED A FEW TIMES TO GO BACK AND FIX THINGS, AND EACH TIME IT WENT WORSE FOR ME.
I'M NOT WHO CAME TO YOU LAST TIME. I'M FROM FURTHER DOWN THE LINE.
I'VE SEEN IT ALL.
STOP NOW, AND I WON'T HAVE TO STOP YOU.
IF YOU'RE ME, YOU KNOW THE ANSWER.
FINE, RUN. YOU FORGET I KNOW HOW ALL OF THIS ENDS.
YOU CAN'T BEAT THE FUTURE, SO WHY TRY?
IF I KEEP MYSELF FROM TURNING INTO THE ASSHOLE YOU CLEARLY ARE, IT'LL BE WORTH IT.

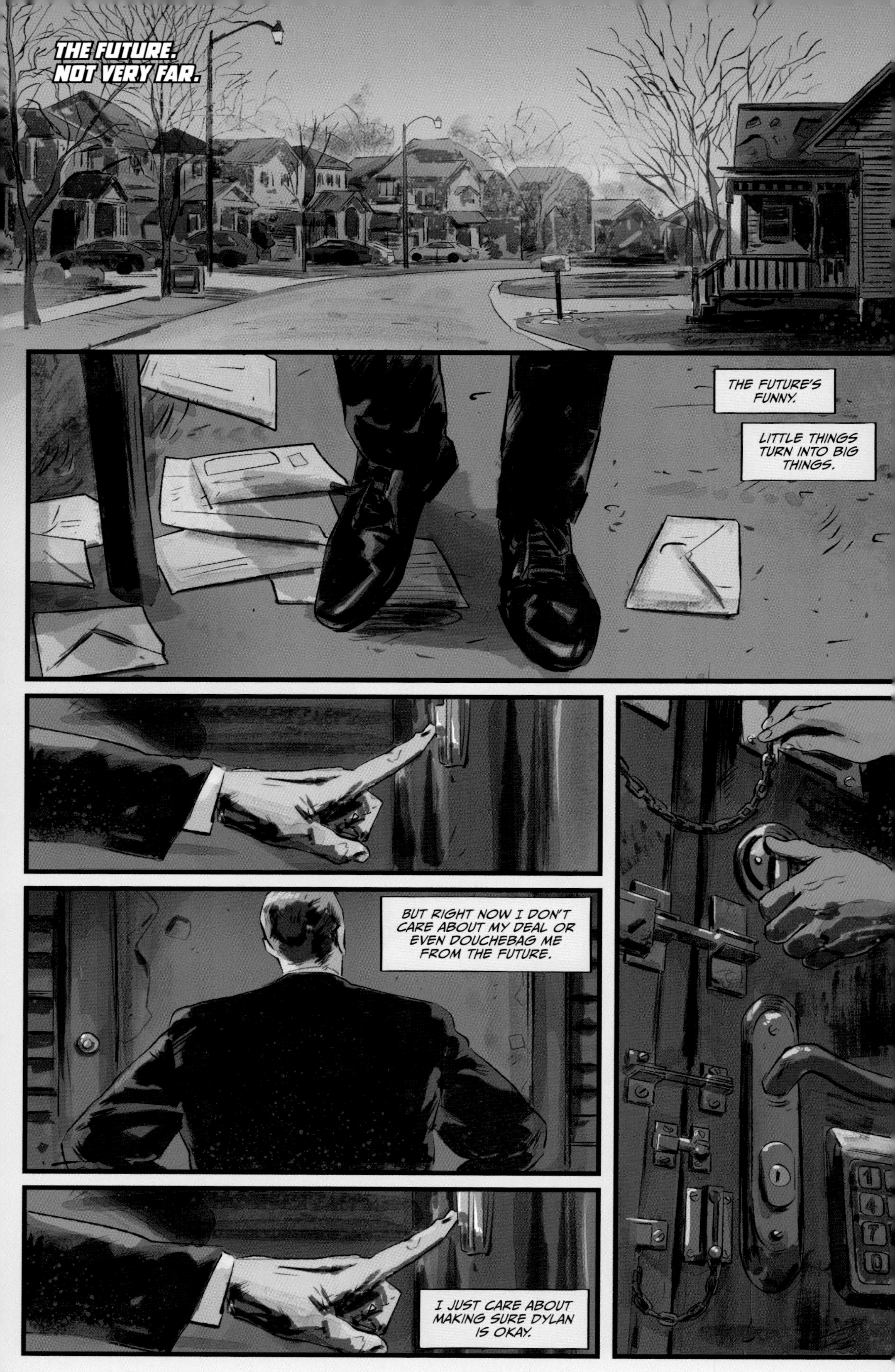
THE FUTURE. NOT VERY FAR.
THE FUTURE'S FUNNY.
LITTLE THINGS TURN INTO BIG THINGS.
BUT RIGHT NOW I DON'T CARE ABOUT MY DEAL OR EVEN DOUCHEBAG ME FROM THE FUTURE.
I JUST CARE ABOUT MAKING SURE DYLAN IS OKAY.

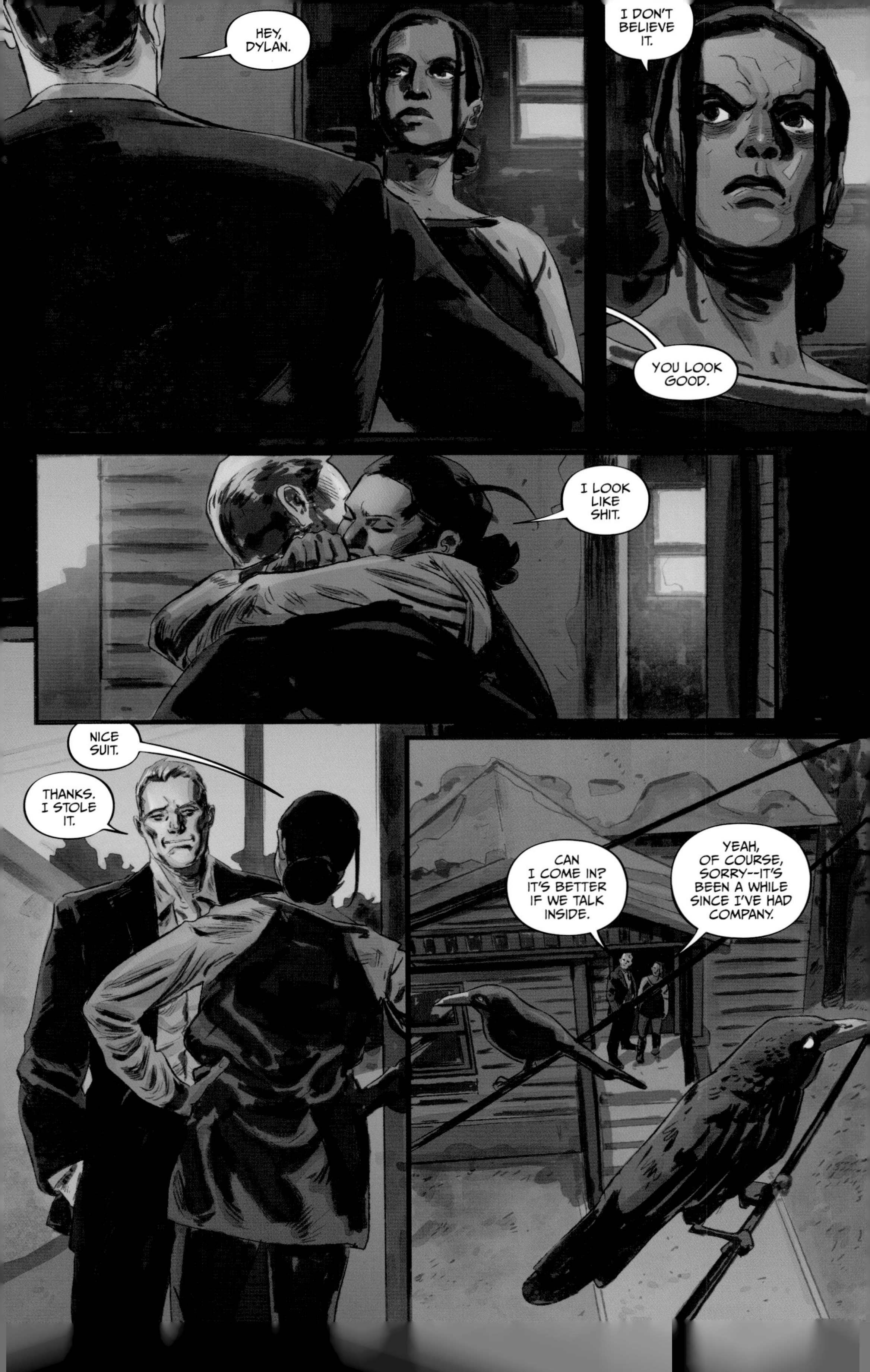
HEY, DYLAN.
I DON'T BELIEVE IT.
YOU LOOK GOOD.
I LOOK LIKE SHIT.
NICE SUIT.
THANKS. I STOLE IT.
CAN I COME IN? IT'S BETTER IF WE TALK INSIDE.
YEAH, OF COURSE, SORRY--IT'S BEEN A WHILE SINCE I'VE HAD COMPANY.

YOU WANT SOME COFFEE? BOOZE? COFFEE WITH BOOZE IN IT?

SHIT. I WAS HOPING TO MAKE THIS A CALM THING. EXPLAIN IT TO HER SO SHE DOESN'T THINK I BELONG IN A LOCKED WARD.

ACTUALLY, I NEED YOU TO COME WITH ME.

NOW.

WHAT IS GOING ON... THOSE ARE JUST BIRDS.

THAT'S THE *COMPETITION*.

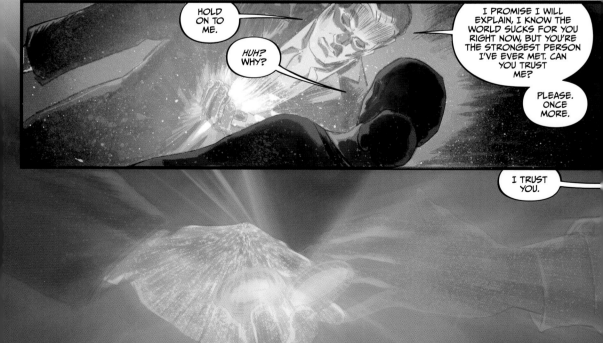

HOLD ON TO ME.

HUH? WHY?

I PROMISE I WILL EXPLAIN, I KNOW THE WORLD SUCKS FOR YOU RIGHT NOW, BUT YOU'RE THE STRONGEST PERSON I'VE EVER MET. CAN YOU TRUST ME?

PLEASE. ONCE MORE.

I TRUST YOU.

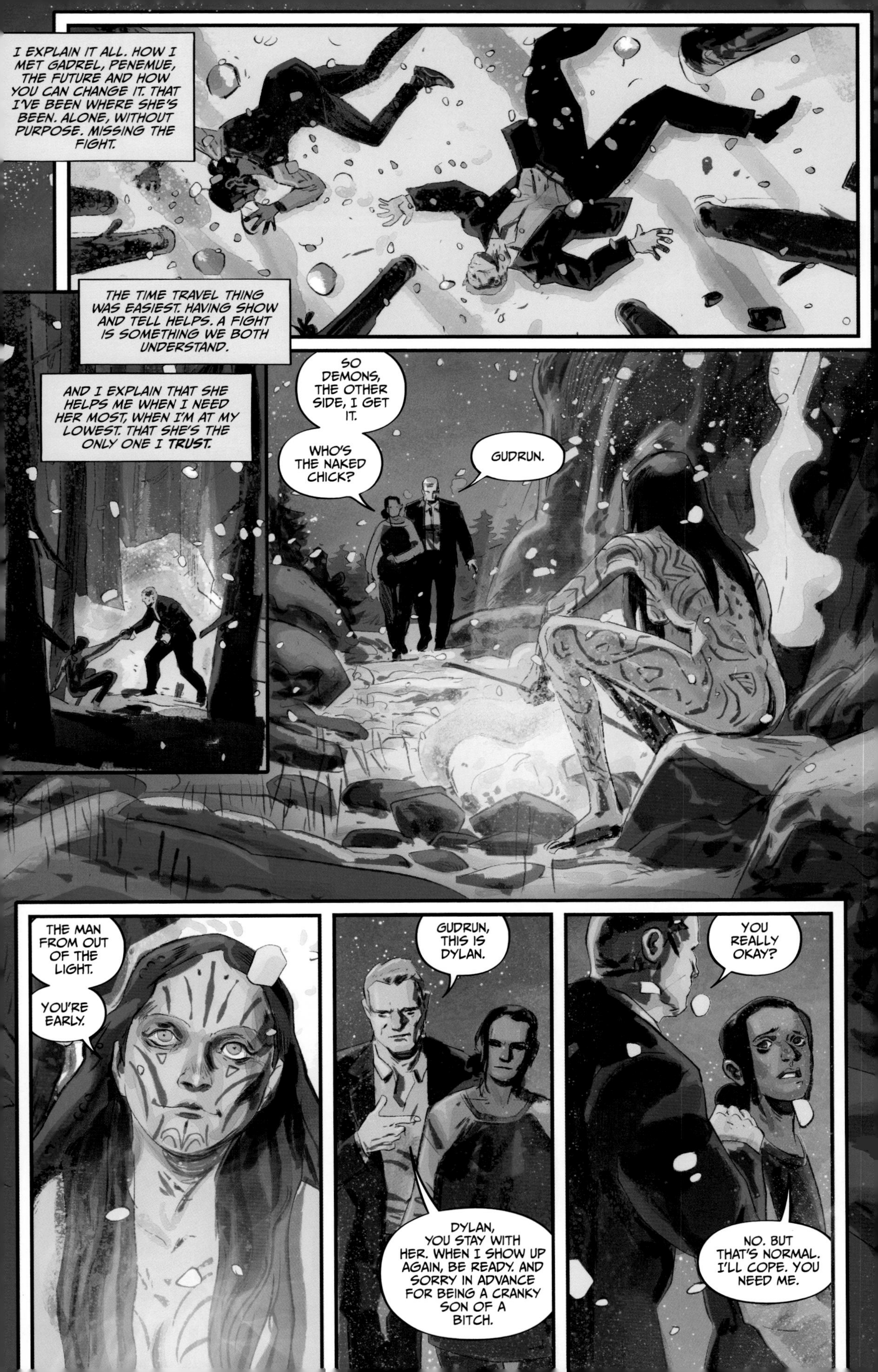
I EXPLAIN IT ALL. HOW I MET GADREL, PENEMUE, THE FUTURE AND HOW YOU CAN CHANGE IT. THAT I'VE BEEN WHERE SHE'S BEEN. ALONE, WITHOUT PURPOSE. MISSING THE FIGHT.
THE TIME TRAVEL THING WAS EASIEST. HAVING SHOW AND TELL HELPS. A FIGHT IS SOMETHING WE BOTH UNDERSTAND.
AND I EXPLAIN THAT SHE HELPS ME WHEN I NEED HER MOST, WHEN I'M AT MY LOWEST. THAT SHE'S THE ONLY ONE I TRUST.
SO DEMONS, THE OTHER SIDE, I GET IT.
WHO'S THE NAKED CHICK?
GUDRUN.
THE MAN FROM OUT OF THE LIGHT.
YOU'RE EARLY.
GUDRUN, THIS IS DYLAN.
DYLAN, YOU STAY WITH HER. WHEN I SHOW UP AGAIN, BE READY. AND SORRY IN ADVANCE FOR BEING A CRANKY SON OF A BITCH.
YOU REALLY OKAY?
NO. BUT THAT'S NORMAL. I'LL COPE. YOU NEED ME.

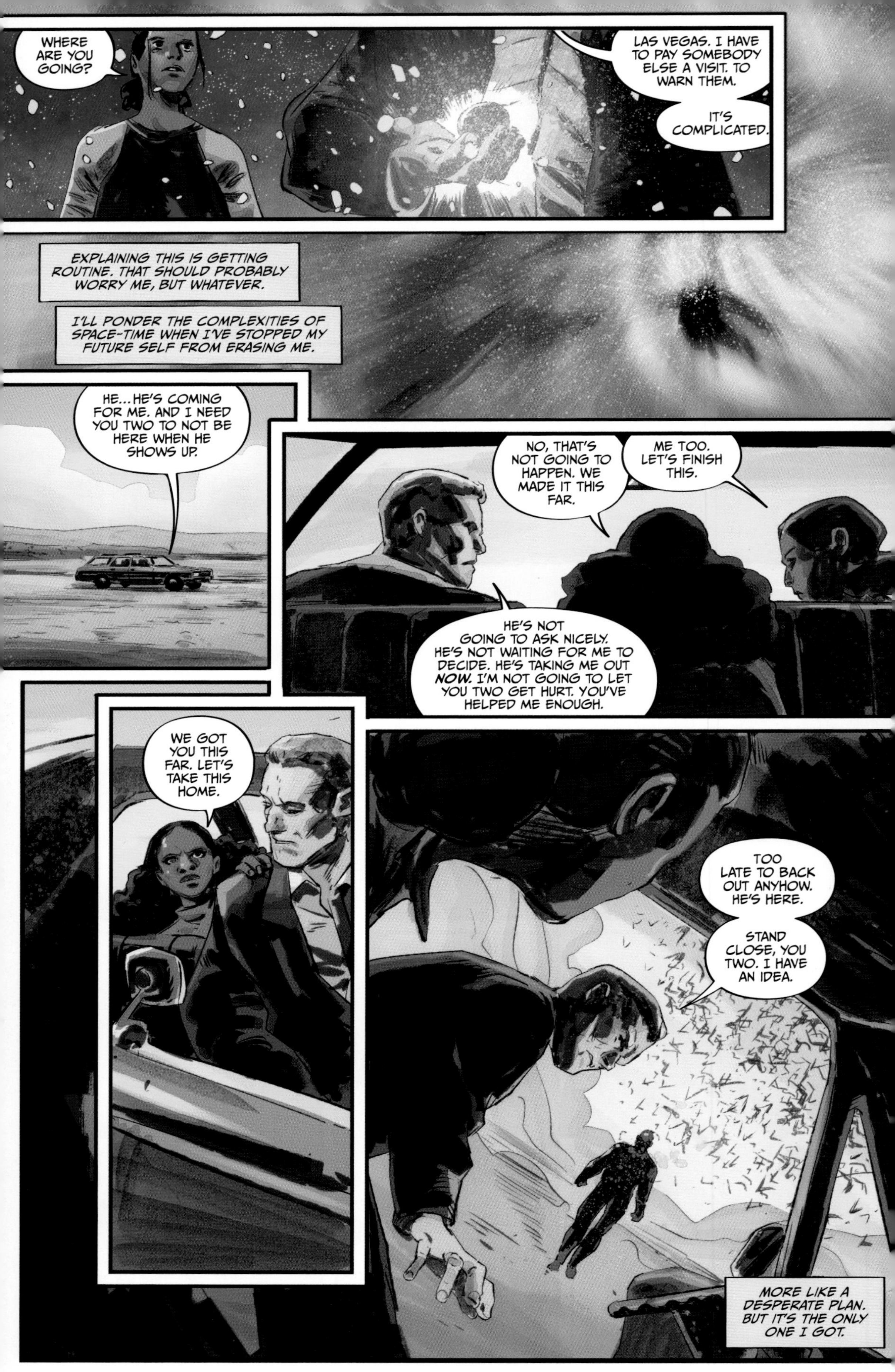
WHERE ARE YOU GOING?
LAS VEGAS. I HAVE TO PAY SOMEBODY ELSE A VISIT. TO WARN THEM.
IT'S COMPLICATED.
EXPLAINING THIS IS GETTING ROUTINE. THAT SHOULD PROBABLY WORRY ME, BUT WHATEVER.
I'LL PONDER THE COMPLEXITIES OF SPACE-TIME WHEN I'VE STOPPED MY FUTURE SELF FROM ERASING ME.
HE...HE'S COMING FOR ME. AND I NEED YOU TWO TO NOT BE HERE WHEN HE SHOWS UP.
NO, THAT'S NOT GOING TO HAPPEN. WE MADE IT THIS FAR.
ME TOO. LET'S FINISH THIS.
HE'S NOT GOING TO ASK NICELY. HE'S NOT WAITING FOR ME TO DECIDE. HE'S TAKING ME OUT *NOW*. I'M NOT GOING TO LET YOU TWO GET HURT. YOU'VE HELPED ME ENOUGH.
WE GOT YOU THIS FAR. LET'S TAKE THIS HOME.
TOO LATE TO BACK OUT ANYHOW. HE'S HERE.
STAND CLOSE, YOU TWO. I HAVE AN IDEA.
MORE LIKE A DESPERATE PLAN. BUT IT'S THE ONLY ONE I GOT.

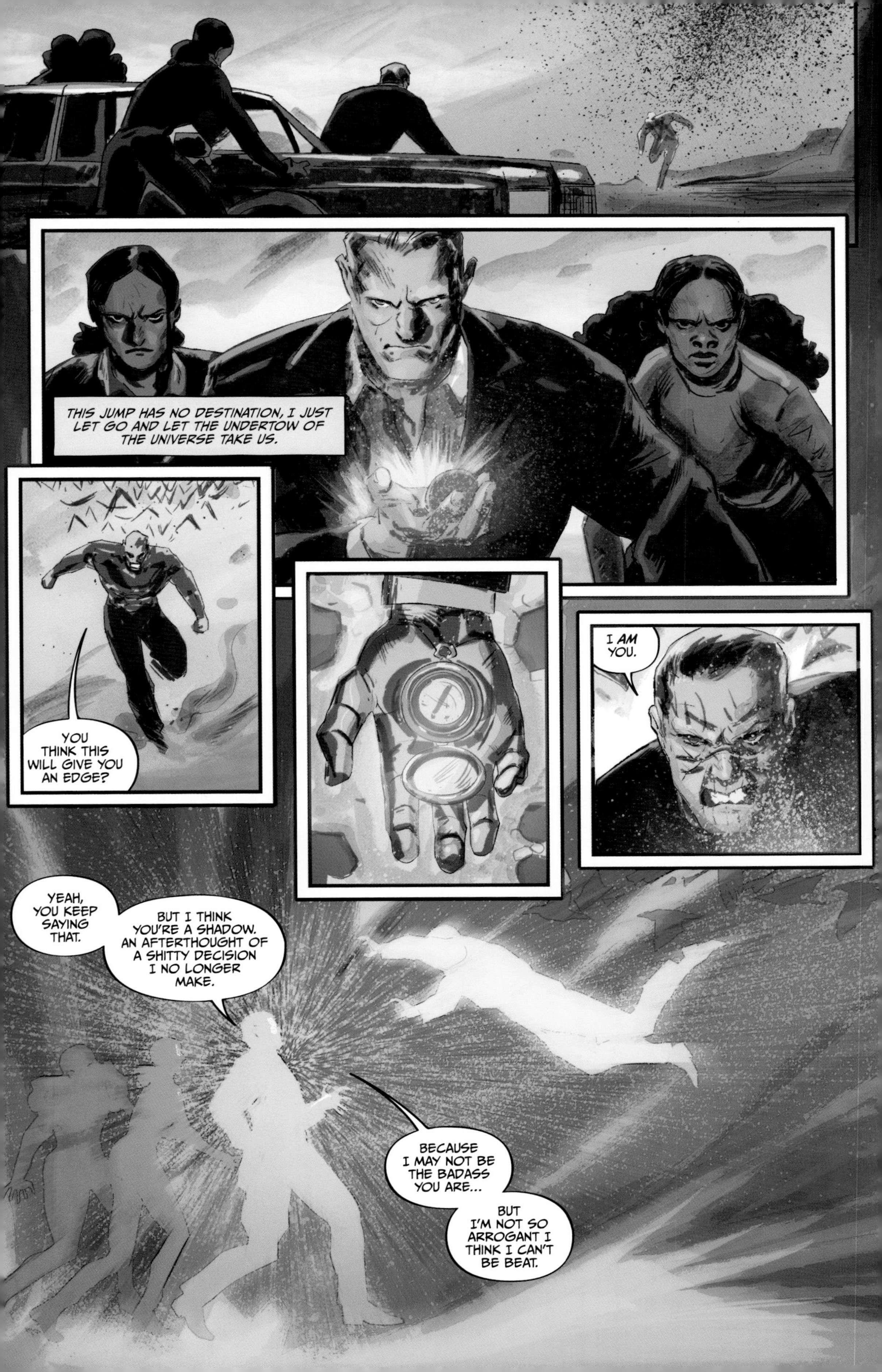
THIS JUMP HAS NO DESTINATION, I JUST LET GO AND LET THE UNDERTOW OF THE UNIVERSE TAKE US.
YOU THINK THIS WILL GIVE YOU AN EDGE?
I AM YOU.
YEAH, YOU KEEP SAYING THAT.
BUT I THINK YOU'RE A SHADOW. AN AFTERTHOUGHT OF A SHITTY DECISION I NO LONGER MAKE.
BECAUSE I MAY NOT BE THE BADASS YOU ARE...
BUT I'M NOT SO ARROGANT I THINK I CAN'T BE BEAT.

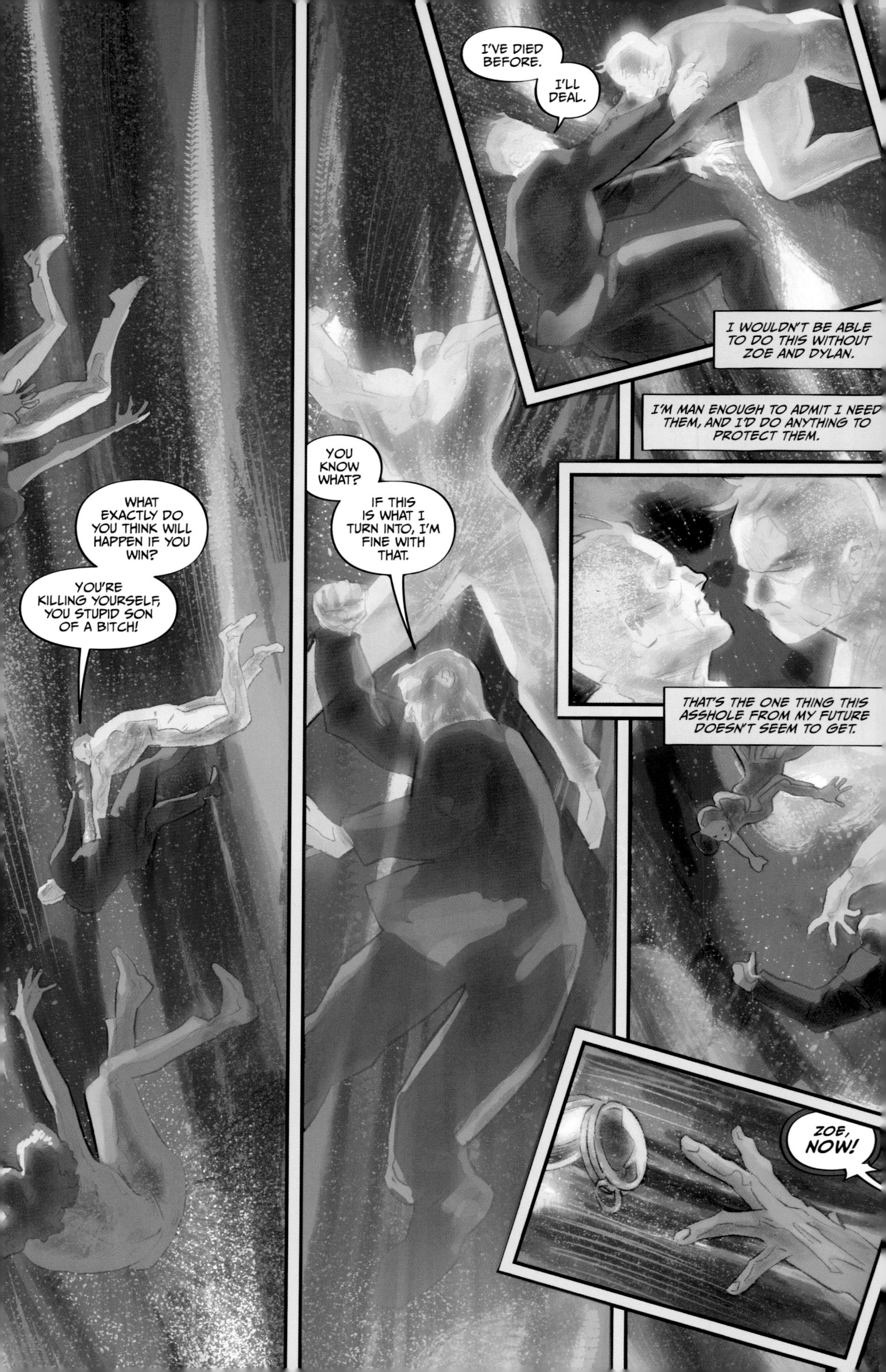

WHAT EXACTLY DO YOU THINK WILL HAPPEN IF YOU WIN?
YOU'RE KILLING YOURSELF, YOU STUPID SON OF A BITCH!
YOU KNOW WHAT?
IF THIS IS WHAT I TURN INTO, I'M FINE WITH THAT.
I'VE DIED BEFORE.
I'LL DEAL.
I WOULDN'T BE ABLE TO DO THIS WITHOUT ZOE AND DYLAN.
I'M MAN ENOUGH TO ADMIT I NEED THEM, AND I'D DO ANYTHING TO PROTECT THEM.
THAT'S THE ONE THING THIS ASSHOLE FROM MY FUTURE DOESN'T SEEM TO GET.
ZOE, NOW!

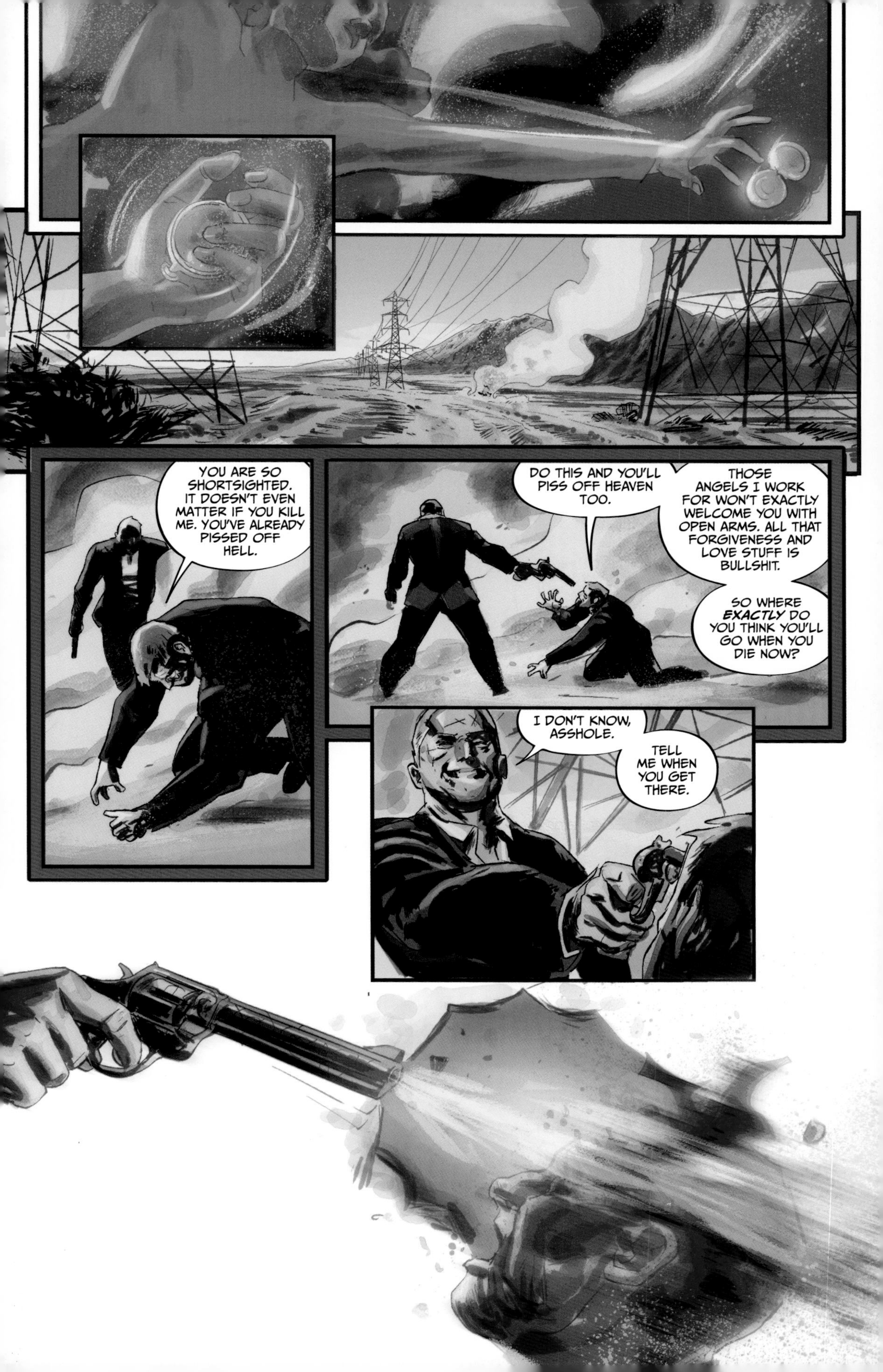
YOU ARE SO SHORTSIGHTED. IT DOESN'T EVEN MATTER IF YOU KILL ME. YOU'VE ALREADY PISSED OFF HELL.
DO THIS AND YOU'LL PISS OFF HEAVEN TOO.
THOSE ANGELS I WORK FOR WON'T EXACTLY WELCOME YOU WITH OPEN ARMS. ALL THAT FORGIVENESS AND LOVE STUFF IS BULLSHIT.
SO WHERE EXACTLY DO YOU THINK YOU'LL GO WHEN YOU DIE NOW?
I DON'T KNOW, ASSHOLE.
TELL ME WHEN YOU GET THERE.

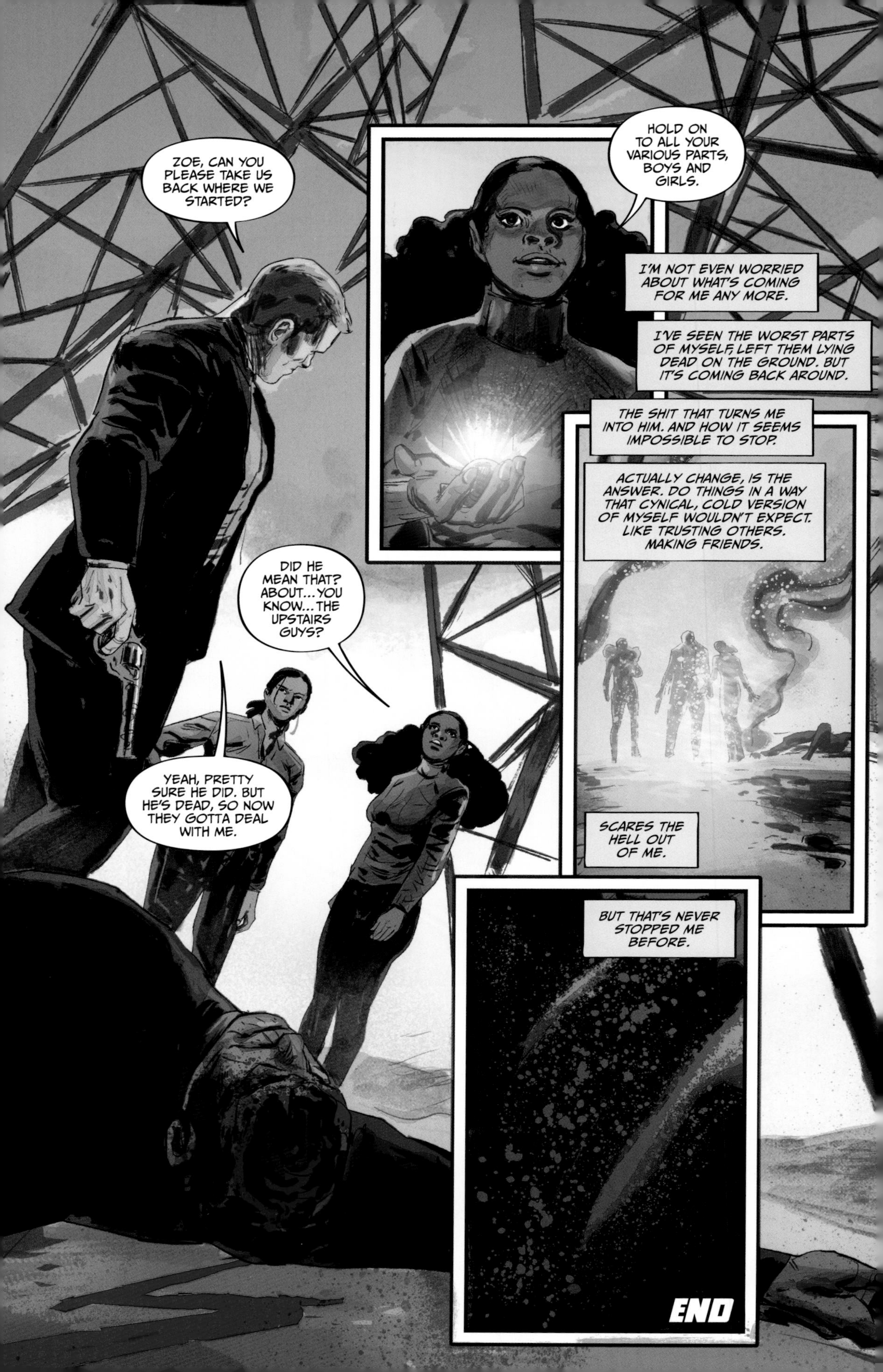
ZOE, CAN YOU PLEASE TAKE US BACK WHERE WE STARTED?
HOLD ON TO ALL YOUR VARIOUS PARTS, BOYS AND GIRLS.
I'M NOT EVEN WORRIED ABOUT WHAT'S COMING FOR ME ANY MORE.
I'VE SEEN THE WORST PARTS OF MYSELF, LEFT THEM LYING DEAD ON THE GROUND. BUT IT'S COMING BACK AROUND.
THE SHIT THAT TURNS ME INTO HIM. AND HOW IT SEEMS IMPOSSIBLE TO STOP.
ACTUALLY CHANGE, IS THE ANSWER. DO THINGS IN A WAY THAT CYNICAL, COLD VERSION OF MYSELF WOULDN'T EXPECT. LIKE TRUSTING OTHERS. MAKING FRIENDS.
DID HE MEAN THAT? ABOUT... YOU KNOW... THE UPSTAIRS GUYS?
YEAH, PRETTY SURE HE DID. BUT HE'S DEAD, SO NOW THEY GOTTA DEAL WITH ME.
SCARES THE HELL OUT OF ME.
BUT THAT'S NEVER STOPPED ME BEFORE.
END

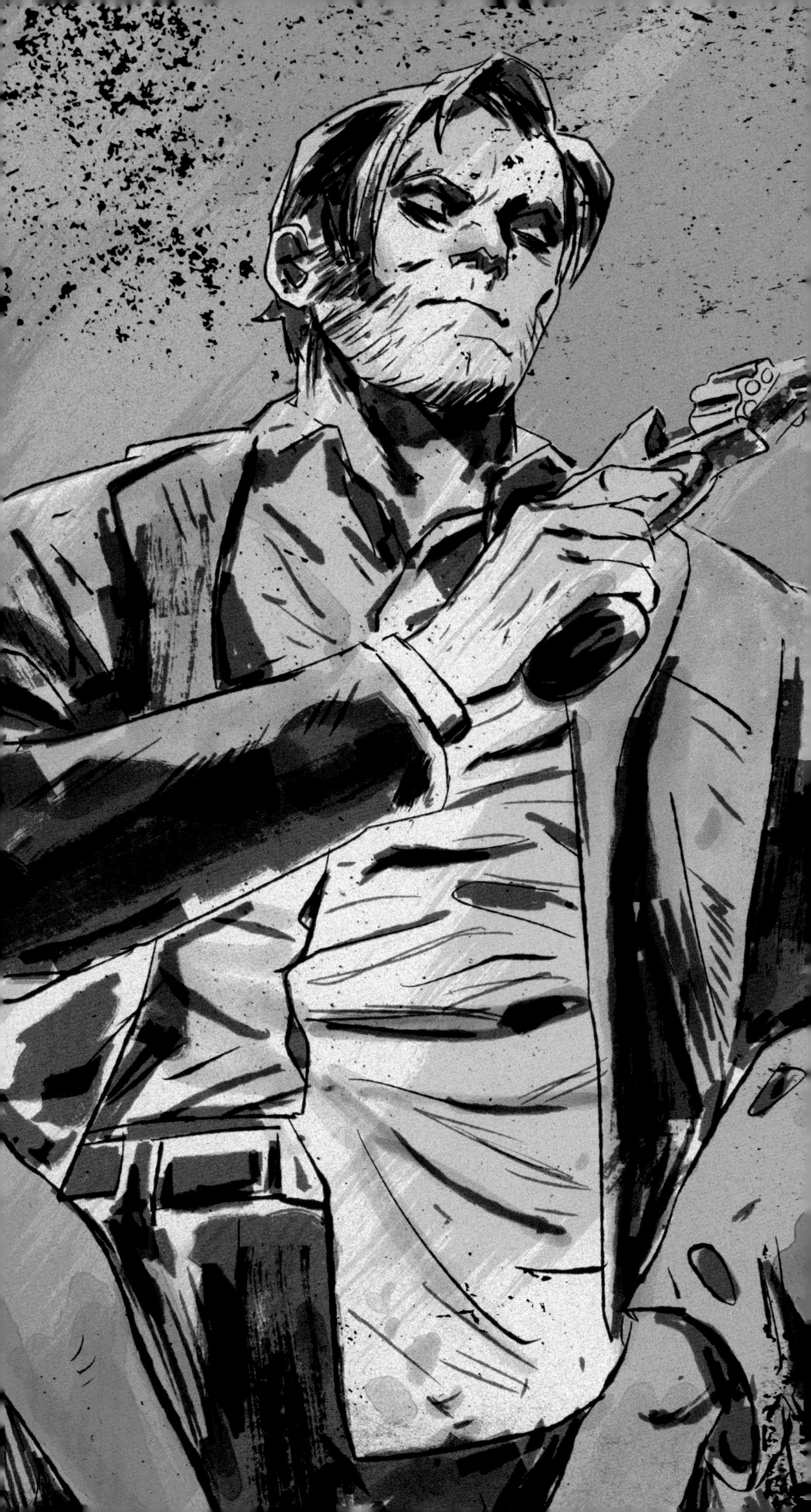

COVER GALLERY

ISSUE ONE COVER
ADAM GORHAM
COLORS BY MICHAEL SPICER

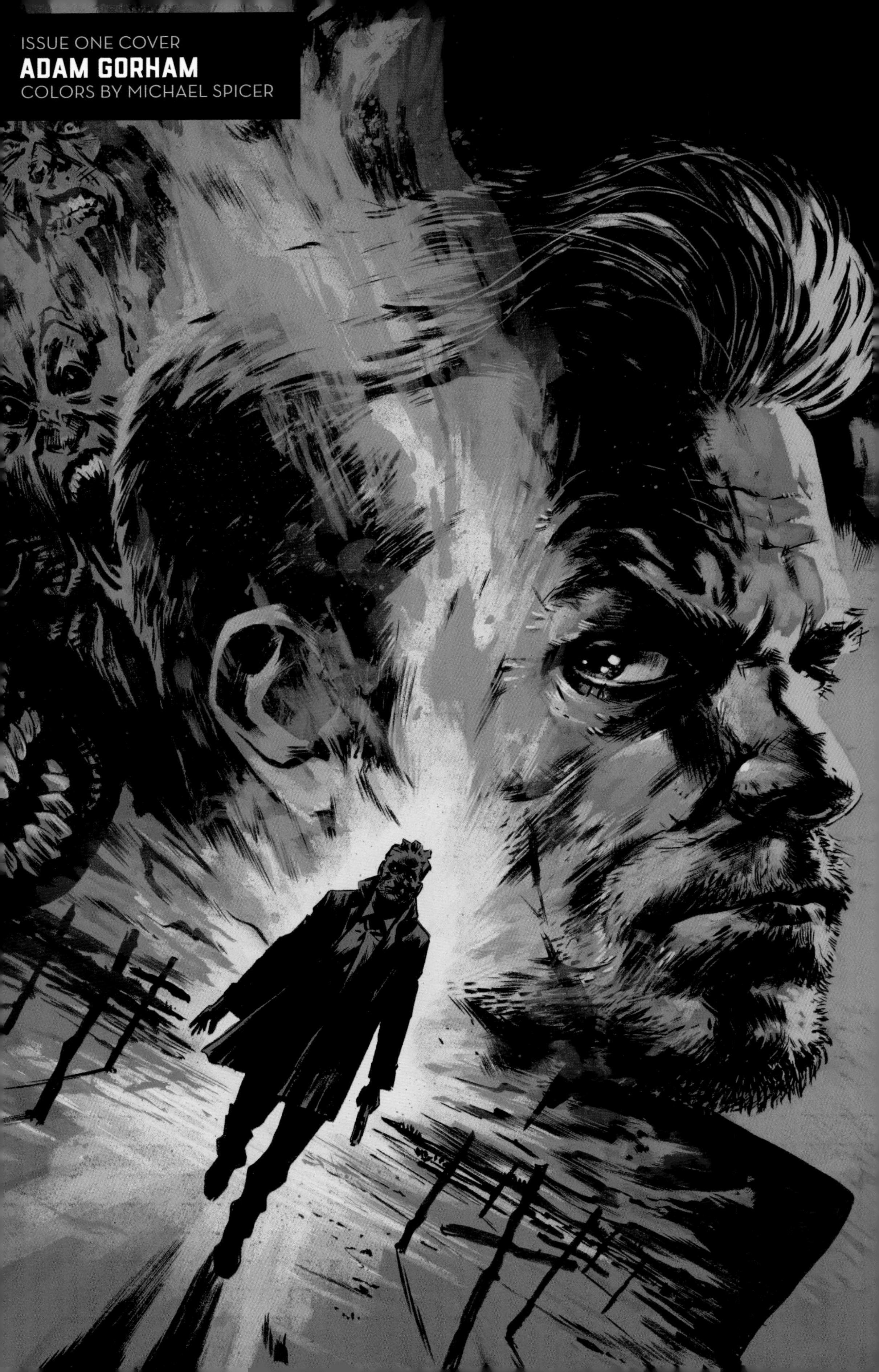

ISSUE TWO COVER
ADAM GORHAM
COLORS BY MICHAEL SPICER

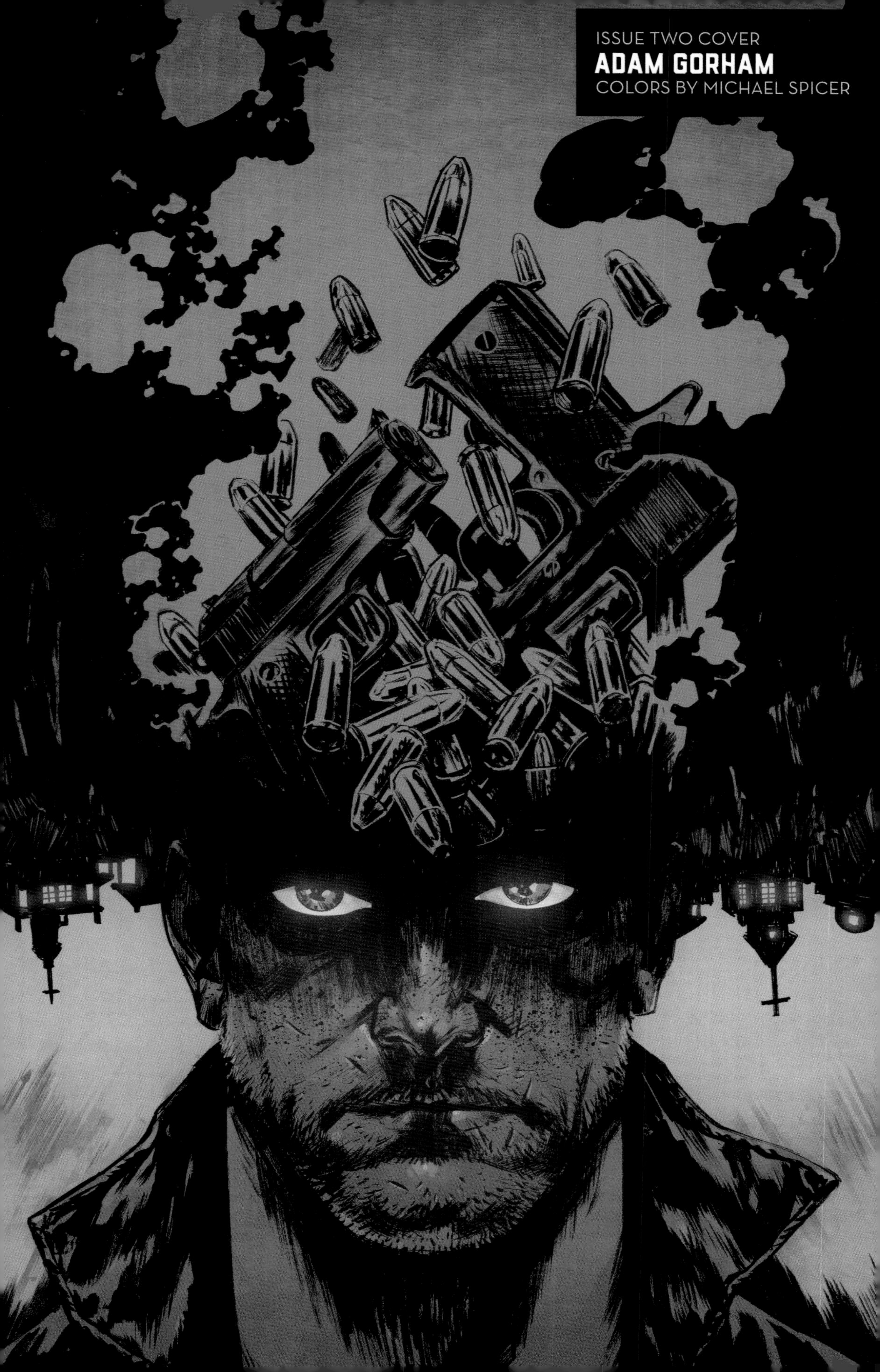

ISSUE THREE COVER
ADAM GORHAM
COLORS BY MICHAEL SPICER

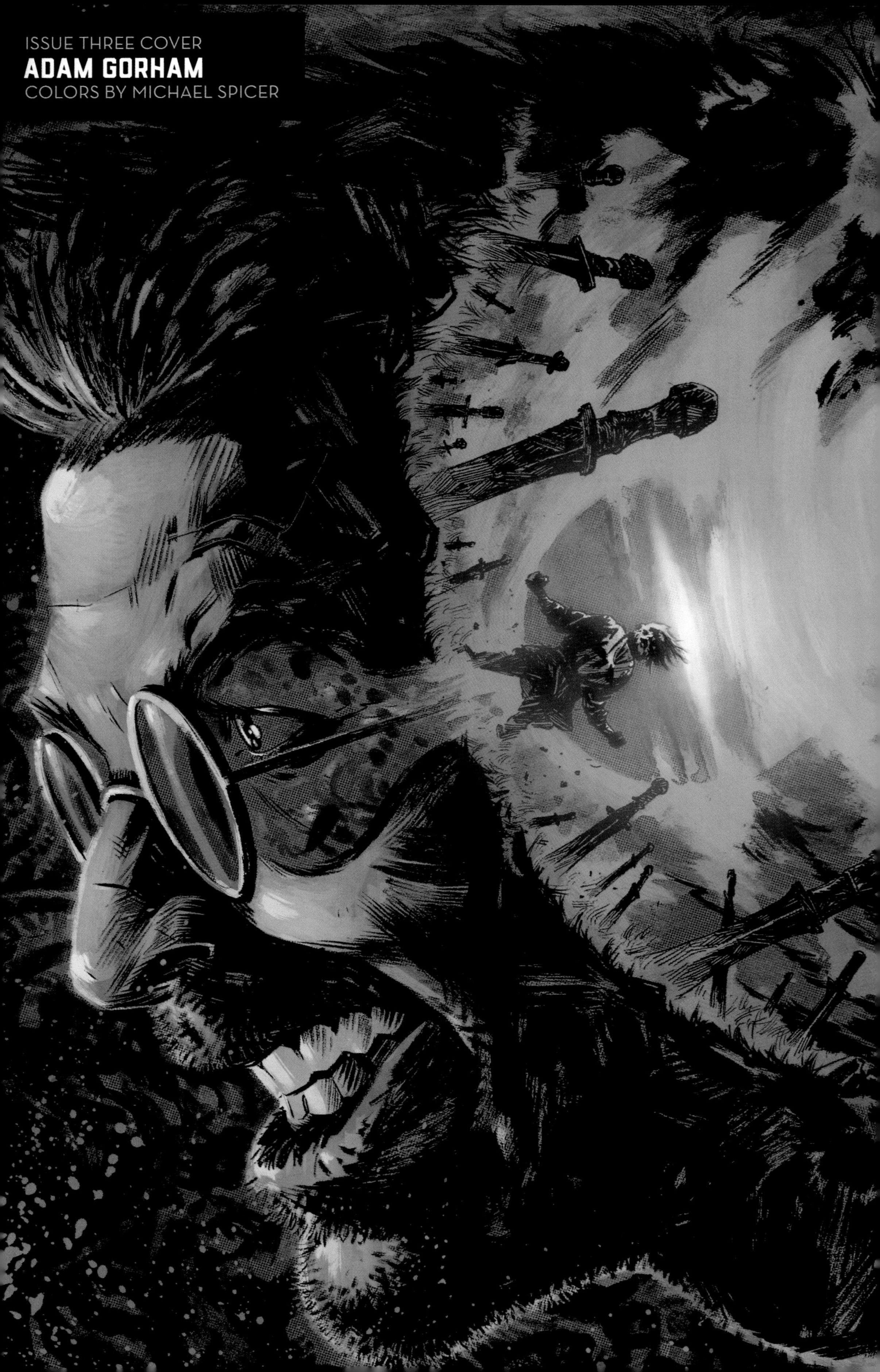

ISSUE FOUR COVER
ADAM GORHAM
COLORS BY MICHAEL SPICER

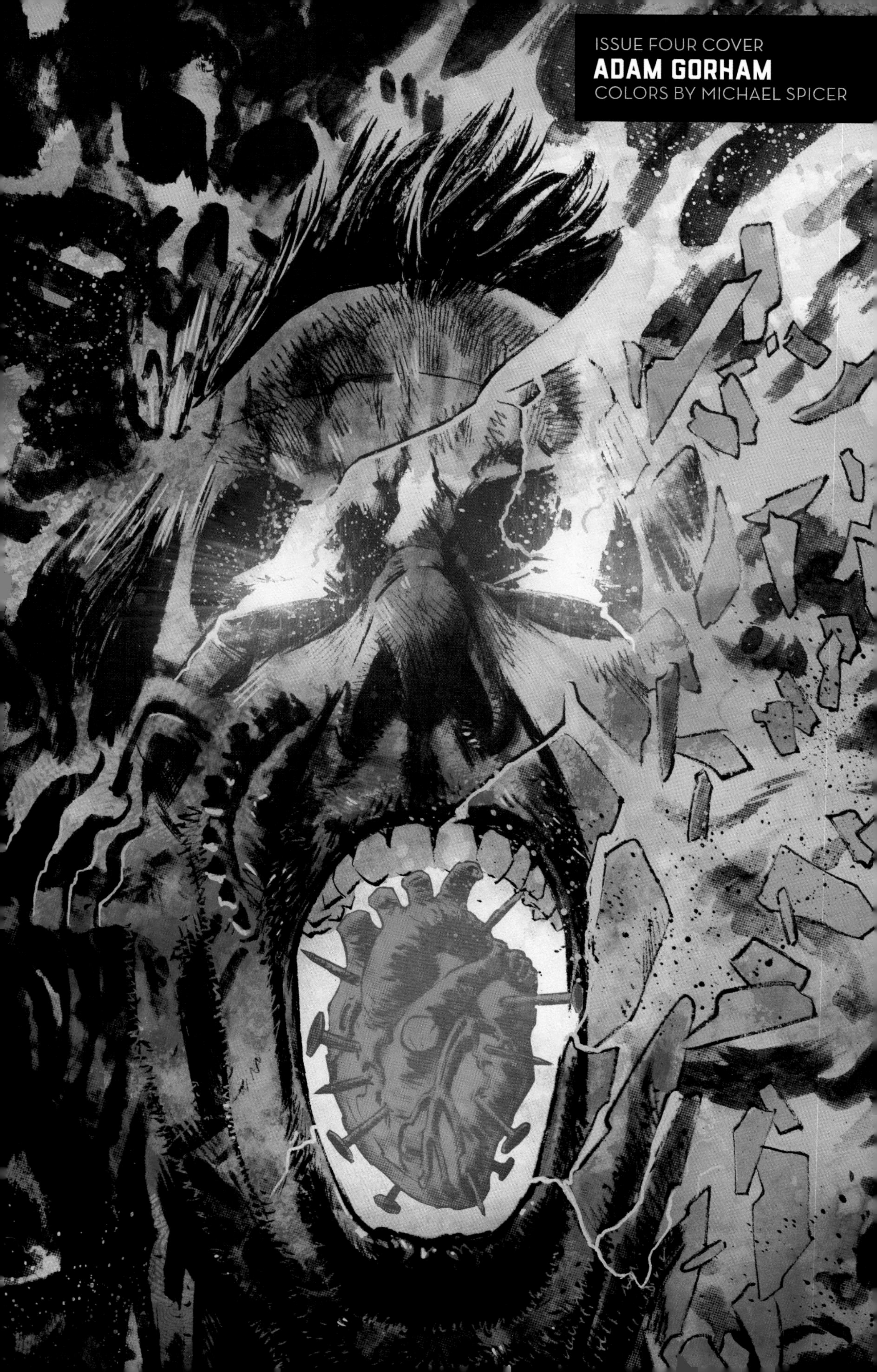

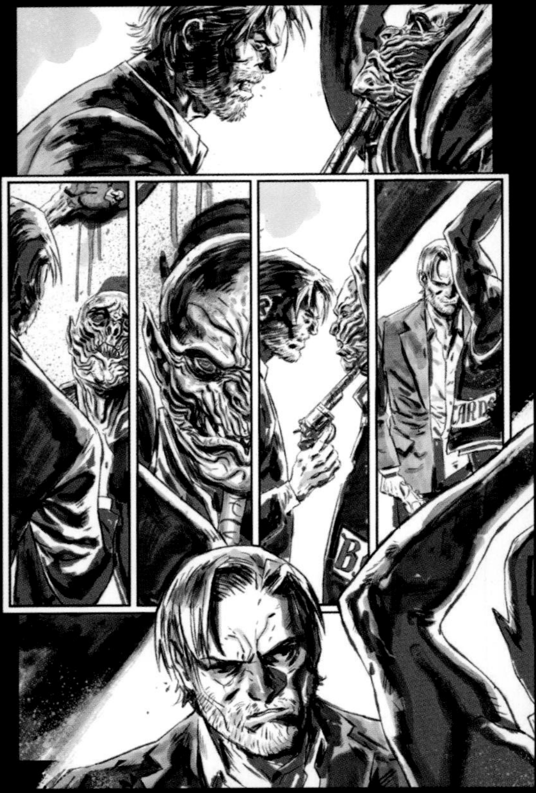
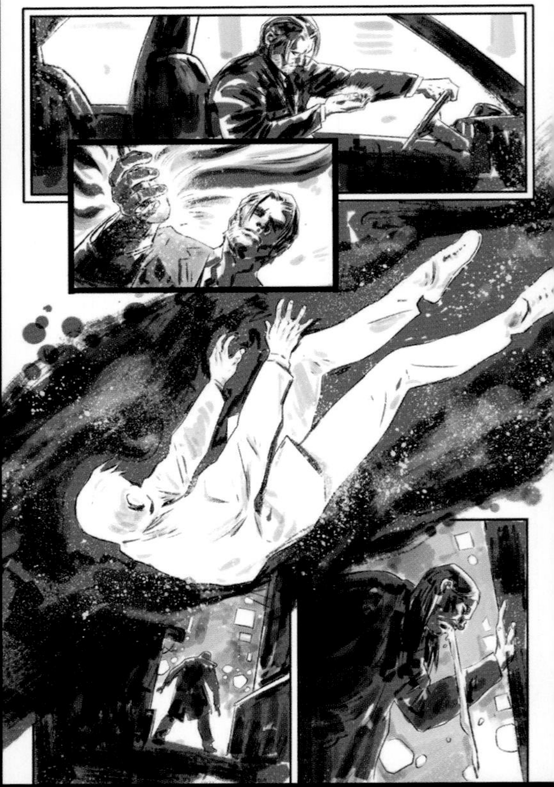
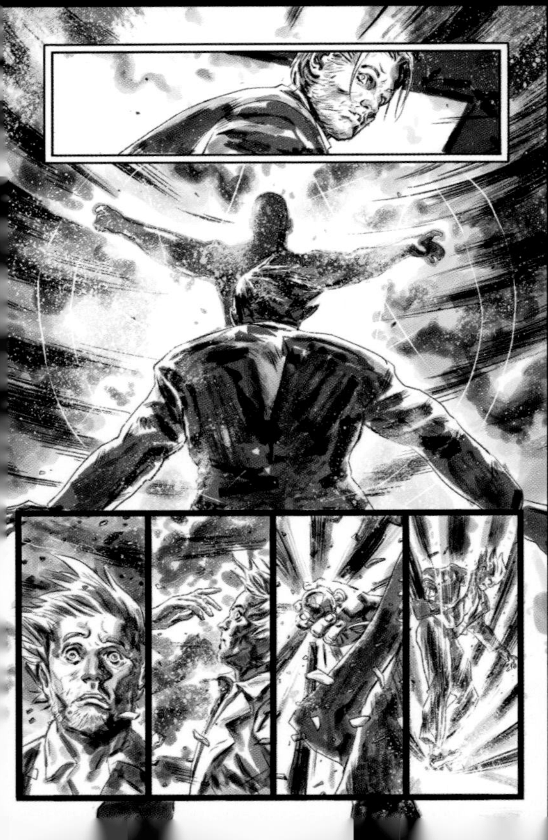
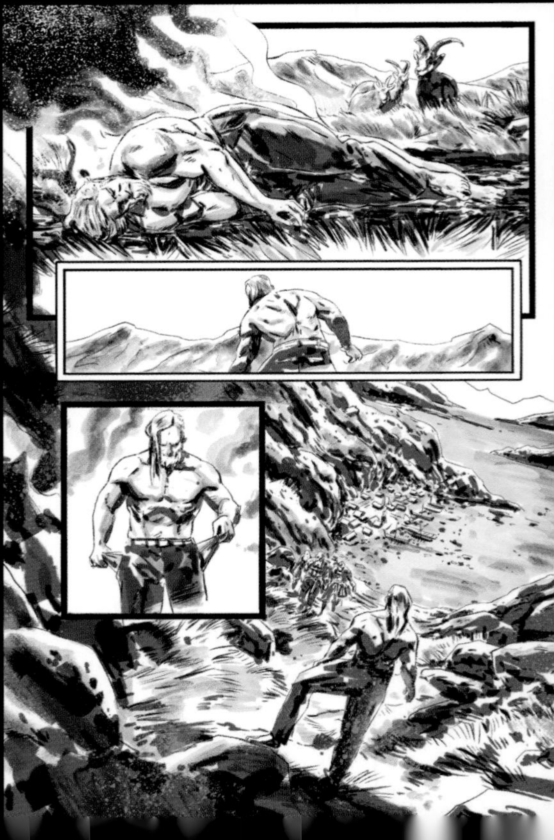

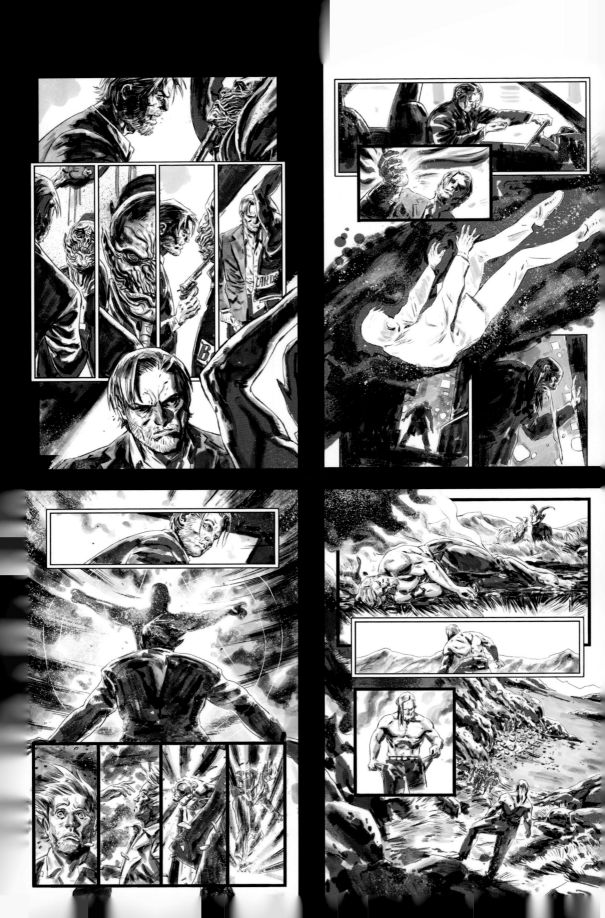

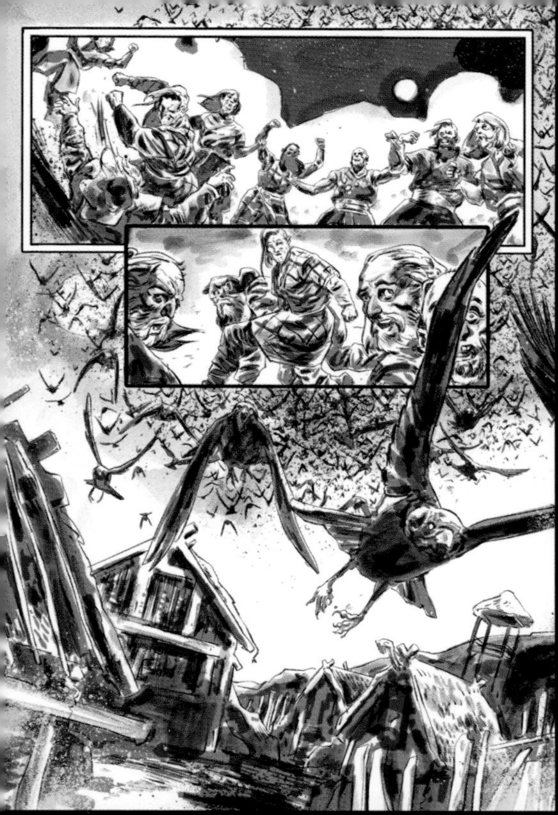
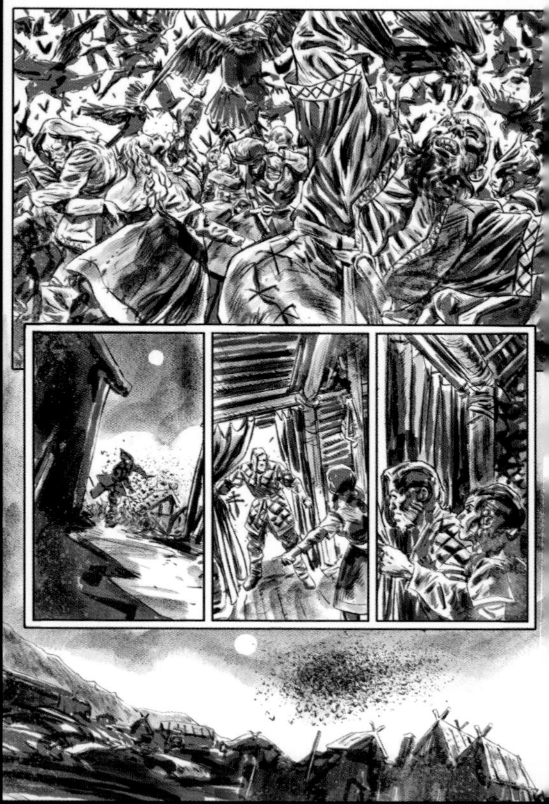
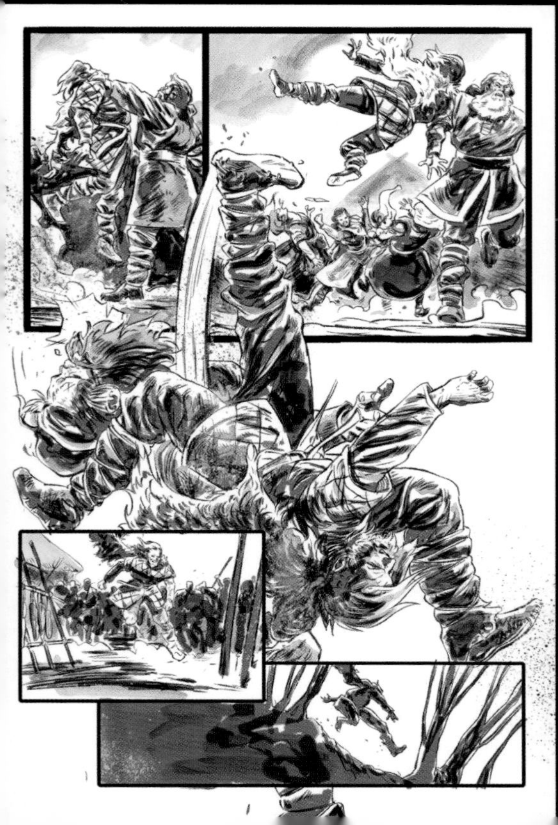
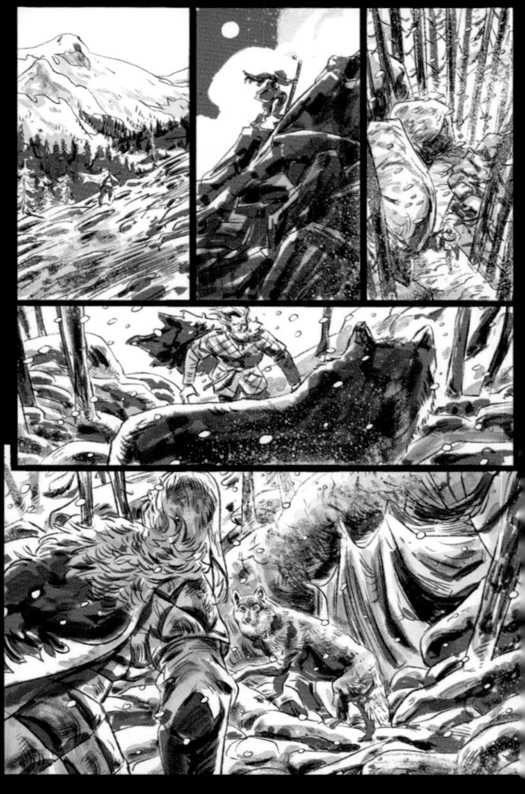

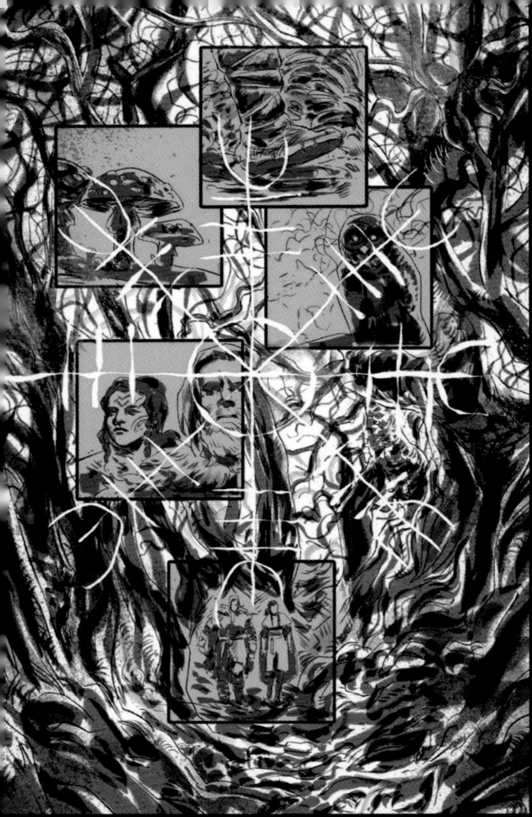
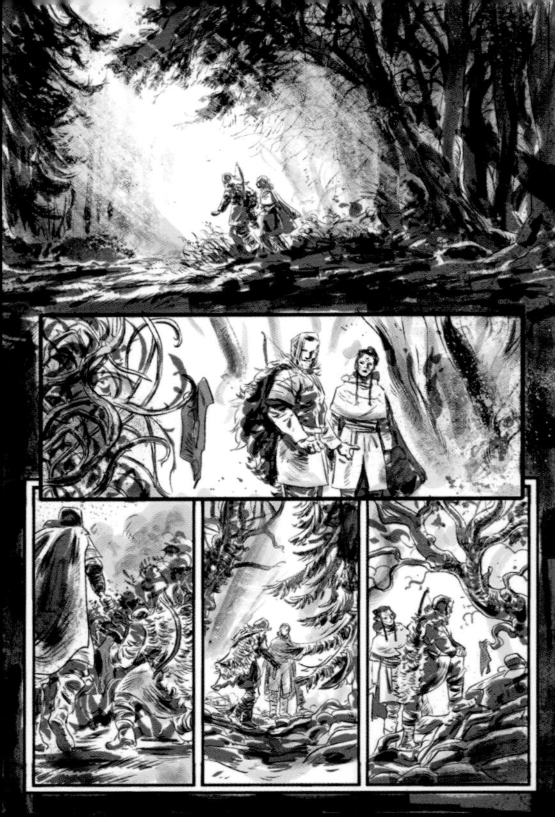
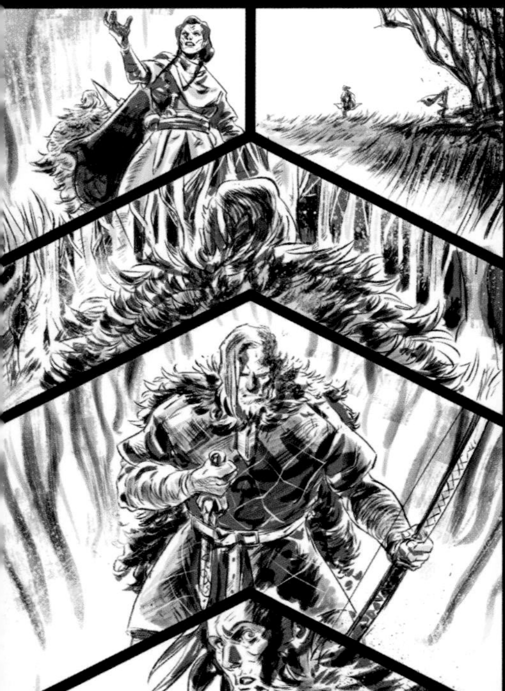
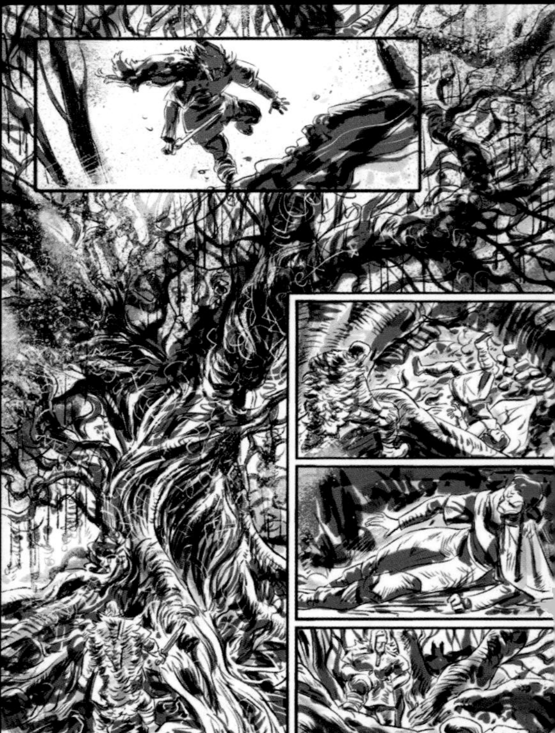

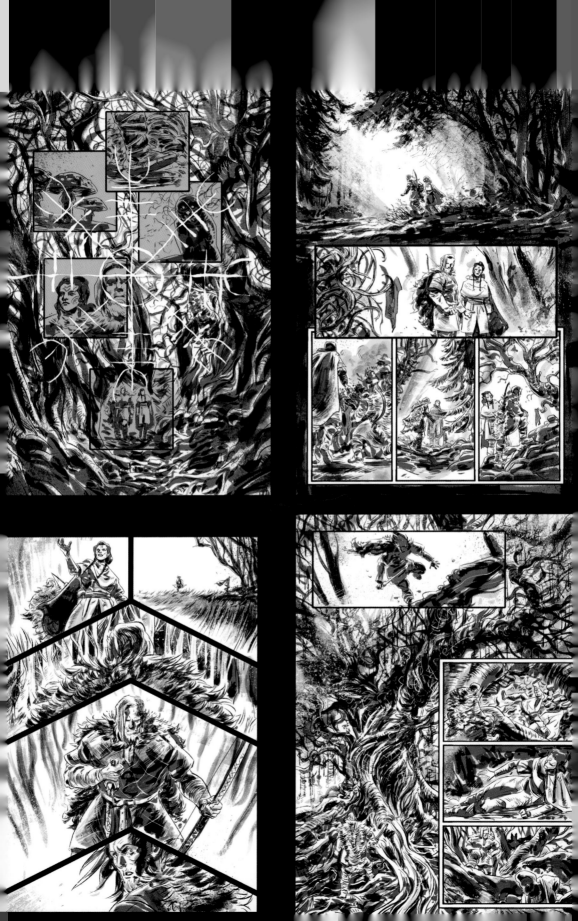

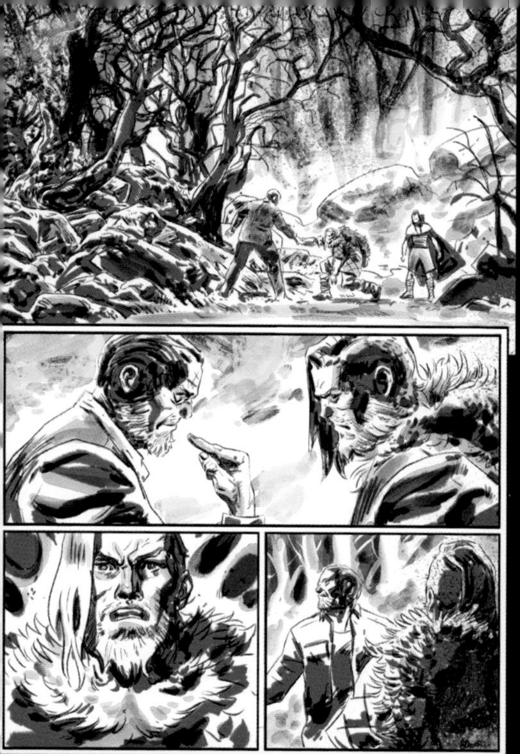
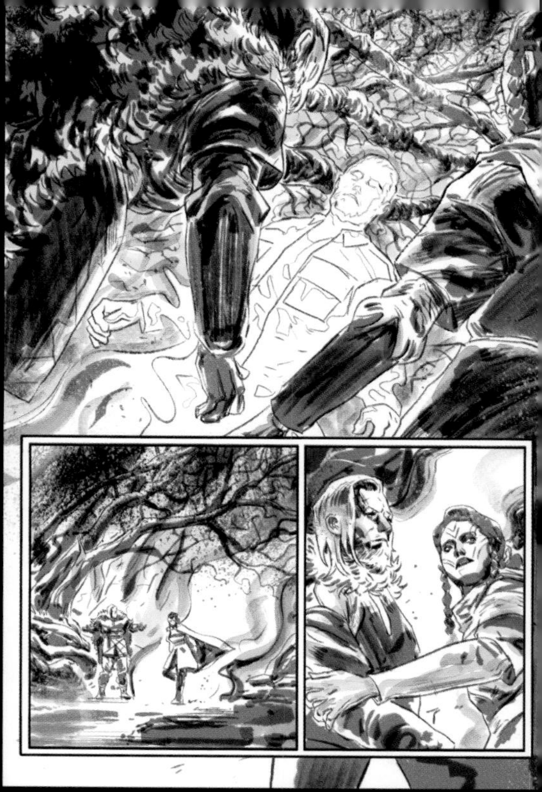
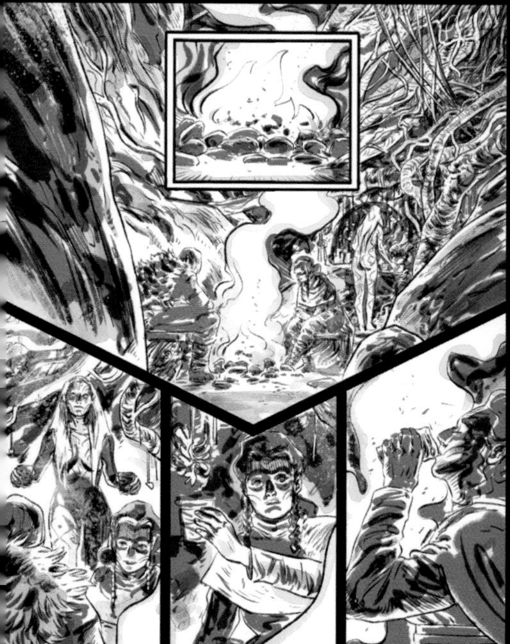
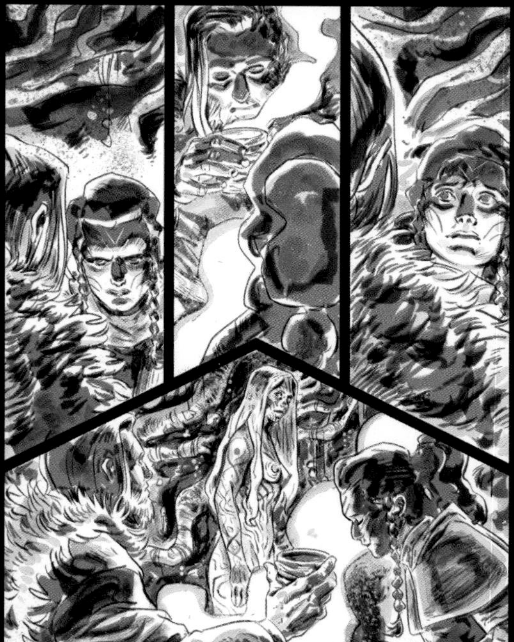

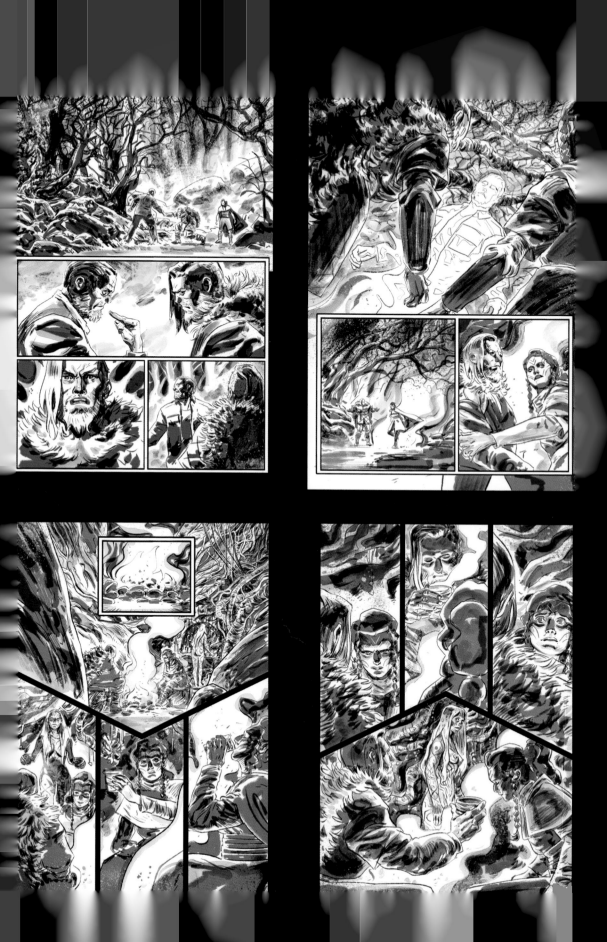

DISCOVER
VISIONARY CREATORS

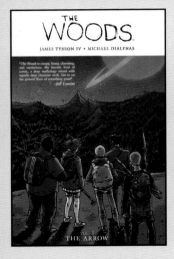

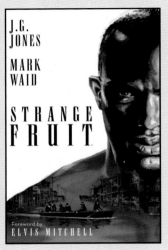

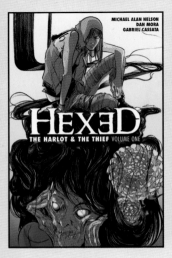

THE WOODS
JAMES TYNION IV • MICHAEL DIALYNAS
VOL. 1
THE ARROW

"The Spire is fantastic! My kind of genre free-for-all."
—BRIAN K. VAUGHAN (Saga)
THE SPIRE
SIMON SPURRIER
JEFF STOKELY
ANDRÉ MAY

MARK WAID • PETER KRAUSE
IRREDEEMABLE
AFTERWORD BY GRANT MORRISON

J.G. JONES
MARK WAID
STRANGE FRUIT
Foreword by
ELVIS MITCHELL

MICHAEL ALAN NELSON
DAN MORA
GABRIEL CASSATA
HEXED
THE HARLOT & THE THIEF VOLUME ONE

ABNETT & CULBARD
WILD'S END
FIRST LIGHT
"IT'S REALLY GREAT!"
JEFF LEMIRE

James Tynion IV
The Woods
Volume 1
ISBN: 978-1-60886-454-6 | $9.99 US
Volume 2
ISBN: 978-1-60886-495-9 | $14.99 US
Volume 3
ISBN: 978-1-60886-773-8 | $14.99 US

The Backstagers
Volume 1
ISBN: 978-1-60886-993-0 | $14.99 US

Simon Spurrier
Six-Gun Gorilla
ISBN: 978-1-60886-390-7 | $19.99 US

The Spire
ISBN: 978-1-60886-913-8 | $29.99 US

Weavers
ISBN: 978-1-60886-963-3 | $19.99 US

Mark Waid
Irredeemable
Volume 1
ISBN: 978-1-93450-690-5 | $16.99 US
Volume 2
ISBN: 978-1-60886-000-5 | $16.99 US

Incorruptible
Volume 1
ISBN: 978-1-60886-015-9 | $16.99 US
Volume 2
ISBN: 978-1-60886-028-9 | $16.99 US

Strange Fruit
ISBN: 978-1-60886-872-8 | $24.99 US

Michael Alan Nelson
Hexed The Harlot & The Thief
Volume 1
ISBN: 978-1-60886-718-9 | $14.99 US
Volume 2
ISBN: 978-1-60886-816-2 | $14.99 US

Day Men
Volume 1
ISBN: 978-1-60886-393-8 | $9.99 US
Volume 2
ISBN: 978-1-60886-852-0 | $9.99 US

Dan Abnett
Wild's End
Volume 1: First Light
ISBN: 978-1-60886-735-6 | $19.99 US
Volume 2: The Enemy Within
ISBN: 978-1-60886-877-3 | $19.99 US

Hypernaturals
Volume 1
ISBN: 978-1-60886-298-6 | $16.99 US
Volume 2
ISBN: 978-1-60886-319-8 | $19.99 US